Major Voices:
The Drama of Slavery

Major Voices
The Drama of Slavery

SELECTED WITH INTRODUCTIONS BY

Dr. Eric Gardner

The Toby Press

The Toby Press
The Drama of Slavery
Toby Press Edition 2005

The Toby Press LLC
POB 8531, New Milford, CT. 06776–8531, USA
& POB 2455, London WIA 5WY, England
www.tobypress.com

Introductions copyright © Eric Gardner 2005

ISBN 1 59264 118 0, *paperback*
ISBN 1 59264 117 2, *hardcover*

A CIP catalogue record for this title is available
from the British Library

Typeset in Garamond by Jerusalem Typesetting

Printed and bound in the United States by
Thomson-Shore Inc., Michigan

As always, for my family

Contents

Introduction, ix

Bibliography, xxxiii

A Note on the Texts, xxxvii

SLAVES IN ALGIERS; OR A STRUGGLE FOR FREEDOM

Introduction, 3

A Note on the Text, 9

Preface, 13

Slaves In Algiers, *15*

EARLY ABOLITIONIST DRAMA

Introduction, 67

The Kidnapped Clergyman; or, Experience the Best

Teacher, *75*

The Fugitives, *109*

EARLY MINSTREL MATERIAL

Introduction, 135

A Note on the Texts, 139

Minstrel Song Lyrics, 141

Oh, Hush! or, the Virginny Cupids, *149*

UNCLE TOM'S CABIN

Introduction, 165

A Note on the Text, 169

Uncle Tom's Cabin, *171*

THE CHRISTIAN SLAVE

Introduction, 259

A Note on the Text, 265

The Christian Slave, *267*

THE ESCAPE; OR, A LEAP FOR FREEDOM

Introduction, 365

A Note on the Text, 369

The Escape; or, A Leap for Freedom, *371*

Author's Preface, 373

Opinions Of The Press, 433

THE STARS AND STRIPES; A MELO-DRAMA

Introduction, 437

viii

A Note on the Text, 441

The Stars and Stripes, 443

THE OCTOROON; OR, LIFE IN LOUISIANA

Introduction, 479

A Note on the Text, 483

The Octoroon, 485

LATER MINSTREL MATERIAL

Introduction, 557

A Note on the Texts, 561

Bones Finds Himself Famous, 565

Brudder Bones as a Carpet-Bagger, 569

Presidency on the Brain, 573

Bones on de War Path, 575

The Colored Senators, 579

PECULIAR SAM; OR, THE UNDERGROUND RAILROAD

Introduction, 589

A Note on the Text, 593

Peculiar Sam; or The Underground Railroad, 595

Acknowledgments, 625

About the Editor, 627

ix

Introduction

Of Black Tragedians and Opossums

I magine this:

It is early 1823. You're a white man of some means, and you're in New York City. You're fascinated with the theater—so fascinated that you've managed to wrangle an invitation to dinner with the noted British actor Charles Mathews, who is already internationally known for his skill at humorous monologues. Mathews has been touring for several months, and he seems almost obsessed with the United States and especially with African Americans.

He tells the dinner guests a story. He's recently attended a production of *Hamlet* by an all-Black theater company. In a racist caricature of African American dialect, he recounts how the title character, played by one of the "black tragedians" was interrupted in the infamous "To be, or not to be" speech: "To be or not to be, dat is him question, whether him nobler in de mind to suffer or lift up him arms against a sea of hubble bubble and by opossum end 'em." Most in the room know or pretend to know their Shakespeare—and recognize the malapropism in Mathews' rendition: Shakespeare's "opposing" comes out "opossum."

After the initial laughter around the dinner table, Mathews goes on. The whole audience, he says, began chanting "Opossum, Opossum, Opossum" and would not stop until the Black actor stepped forward on the stage and informed the audience that he would, indeed, sing the popular song "Opossum up a Gum-Tree."

At this, Mathews jumps up from the dinner table and begins his own rendition of the popular dialect song about how a "poor possum" is stalked by both a raccoon and a hungry "cunning Nigger." He delivers it with gusto, playing to the group's stereotypical sense of enslaved Southern Blacks—even though everyone knows that the Black company must be composed of Northern freemen. He lets the pause at the end of the song sit. Then, he delivers the final punch line: he says that after the song was over, the Black actor stepped forward and "bellowed" out a revised line from *Richard* iii: "Now is de winter of our discontent made de glorious summer by de sun of New York."

It is a fascinating night. You've always been an inquisitive sort; tomorrow, you vow, you will go and see the African American company. You're a bit frightened, but your curiosity is overwhelming—and you know that Mathews makes his living telling lies….

Such an exercise in imagination is difficult—and perhaps even a bit dangerous. In some ways, such is a centerpiece of drama (an actor "playing" at something he or she is not) and in the reading of plays (imagining how they were or will be "played"). Still, doing the above asks you to step back in time, perhaps change place. It may also ask you to take (and think for a moment of the implications of that word "take") on a different gender and/or race—to take positions that you can never experience yourself. Doing so might allow you a revolutionary consideration of the lives of other folks; just as likely, doing so might encourage or even force you to engage in stereotypes and assumptions. Either way, if you presented your imaginings with enough talent and to the right audience, you might have tremendous power to shape the ways in which that audience considered a range of issues—like, for example, the issues surrounding Mathews' appropriation of what supposedly happened to the early Black tragedian.

Given these difficulties, this "general introduction" hopes to aid you as you imagine not only the plays included in this anthology, but also the complex worlds that surrounded them. Key in this, it offers some handholds centered on what we know of the histories of some of these worlds.

Take the story above about Mathews. Here's some of what we do know. Charles Mathews did tour the United States in late 1822 and 1823, and one of his primary goals was to look for new material. In March of 1825, Mathews offered his show *A Trip to America* to excited audiences at the English Opera House; soon after, a pamphlet titled *Sketches of Mr. Mathews' Celebrated Trip to America* appeared. Both featured roughly the account given above.

And there was, indeed, an all-Black theater company active in New York City in the early 1820s. Under the management of William Brown and featuring actors James Hewlett and Ira Aldridge, the company performed a range of plays—from Shakespearean texts like *Othello* to William Moncrieff's *Tom and Jerry; or Life in London*, a musical that featured two dancing Africans. Only in the last decade or so have scholars begun to recognize and study the company's complex negotiation of racial politics and theatrical conventions in antebellum New York. We know much less about the company's actual performances than we would like—including their performance of a play written *by* Brown about Black struggles for freedom in the Caribbean. No text of that play, *The Drama of King Shotaway*, has been found—in the language of historians, the play is no longer "extant"—a great loss, given, among other things, that it may have been the first play written by an African American.

The history and character of race relations in the world—and specifically the New York City—of Brown's African American theater have also only become clearer in recent years. American popular culture still assumes slavery to be purely a Southern phenomena. In fact, though New York State had passed a gradual emancipation law, its effects would not be final until 1827. In addition to a notable slave community—some of whose roots have been examined by the African Burial Ground archaeological project—New York also had a strong, if small, free Black community. There was consistent tension—often race-based, but also sometimes class-based—between Blacks and whites in the city; in perhaps the most notable example, in 1741, several enslaved African Americans were publicly executed for their roles in a supposed conspiracy against white New York. More immediate for our consideration of the Black tragedians, on August 10, 1822, Brown's theater had been the site of a small riot: over a dozen whites destroyed much of the company's property and beat Brown savagely. Some reports suggest that Stephen Price, manager of the rival (white) Park Theater, was involved. In what may be an apocryphal story, Brown supposedly defiantly posted a placard outside of his theater on reopening that read: "White people do not know how to behave at entertainments designed for ladies and gentlemen of colour."

Whether, in this charged atmosphere, Mathews' account is anywhere close to true is much more debatable. Marvin McAllister's groundbreaking study of Brown and his theater asserts, for example, that "there is ample evidence that Mathews never attended Brown's theater or witnessed" an African American actor on his trip—evidence that includes the hesitation of Brown's company to perform songs like "Opossum," Mathews' relative elitism, and Mathews' considerable borrowing from white New York playwright Mordecai Noah—which includes the story's *Richard III* punchline (159–160). Further, in a complex attempt to both capitalize on Mathews' popularity and to distance themselves from Mathews' portrayal, both Hewlett and Aldridge issued public denials that they were the "Black Tragedian" of Mathews' account. To complicate matters further, Aldridge, who moved to England and finally found the recognition as an actor that the American stage had denied him, *did*, for reasons not fully known, incorporate "Opossum up a Gum-Tree" into some of his performances. (He might have done it to play to audiences familiar with Mathews; he might have been forced into a racist conception he hated; both statements might be true....)

In addition to setting the stage for the mixing of white and Black in the anthology's plays and exemplifying the ways that the popular American stage often reduced all Black characters to stereotypical Southern slaves (who sang about possums and gum trees), the Mathews story suggests the difficulty of writing a concise history of the American theater—and, more generally, the difficulty in writing any history. Indeed, as a reflection about the complexities of one artifact—Mathews' racist sketch of the "Black tragedian"—it reminds us that the practice of providing "historical context" (so common in literature texts and classes) is sometimes even more problematic. In the rush to set out a few facts that help us understand texts in certain ways, we often forget that such "facts" may be in conflict, may be based on complex (and even troubling) assumptions, and may even ignore key issues or material. Indeed, they may engage in some of the same kind of imagining marked out above. Prior to 1980, for example, if the subject of the Brown's African American company was broached at all, Mathews would be one of the few sources cited—and, in most cases, trusted.

The story of Mathews, the Black tragedian, and the opossum also reminds us of how large a topic the Black presence in American drama is. Mathews' popular portrayal, for example, would shape later representations on both sides of the Atlantic. And while several historians and cultural critics have noted how minstrelsy served as one ancestor to cultural artifacts ranging from jazz to Broadway, and from D.W. Griffith's *The Birth of a Nation* (1915) to Spike Lee's *Bamboozled* (2000), minstrelsy is often presented as if it, in Harriet Beecher Stowe's words, "grew like Topsy" without any ancestry or context. More importantly, though, even suggesting that the Black presence on the early American stage was *solely* made up of and by white minstrel performers playing out cultural stereotypes is a tragic error, albeit one that many theater historians prior to 1970 made.

With these caveats in mind, this introduction attempts to offer a provisional sense of a set of key events in political and social history during the rough century covered by this anthology. Like Mathews' story, though, it should be sifted, tested, and questioned, even as it is used to aid in gaining certain understanding from the texts. For readers who want a fuller sense of its bases and issues, the texts in the bibliography provided below, as well as the introductions to the individual plays and suggestions for further reading, offer more detail. It also begins to sketch out the rationale for the selection of texts. In this, it foregrounds that fact that this anthology is only a small—albeit hopefully both an exciting and instructive—sampling of one area (American-authored plays that focus on slavery) of the much larger set of dramatic texts that include, invoke, or evoke a Black presence.

A General Introduction to the Period

This anthology takes an approach to periodization more commonly used with British literature; that is, it looks at an elongated version of the nineteenth century rather than stopping, as many American literature texts and surveys do, at 1865. Its goal in this is simple: to demonstrate that the drama of slavery certainly did not stop with the close of the Civil War.

That said, most readers are probably familiar with a skeletal outline of major political events during this "long" nineteenth century in the United States. When Susanna Rowson's play *Slaves in Algiers* opened in Philadelphia in 1794, the American Revolution (1773–1783) was still fresh in the minds of both players and audience members—as were the sentiments of the *Declaration of Independence* (1776) and the *U.S. Constitution* (1787), which began to place the new nation on a road to federalism (that is, a centralized, national government that trumped the rights of individual states on some questions). The early national period is most remembered in the popular mind as a time of national definition and initial expansion (especially through the Louisiana Purchase of 1803)—and of a continuing struggle for independence from the British empire, as embodied in the War of 1812.

Depending on how nationalist or critical the history is, the next few decades are seen as a time of pioneering and rapid expansion, perhaps culminating in the California Gold Rush of 1849, or a period where racist and classist expansionism (centered on the idea that the United States' "Manifest Destiny" was to reach from coast to coast) led to the massive "removal" of Native Americans from much of the East, as well as to the opportunistic Mexican War (1846–1848), which yielded much new territory to the young nation. Within either framework, as well as within several middle versions, the 1850s are generally seen as a prelude to the imminent Civil War (1861–1865).

That war, which still fascinates many contemporary Americans (consider developments ranging from Ken Burns's massive PBS documentary to the activities of Civil War "re-enactors" across the nation), also maintains a complex place in American history and historiography. Most recognize it as, ultimately, the war that ended slavery, though several historians—and several politicians of the times on both sides—have argued for a range of other causes, including a new struggle over the old question of individual states' rights. Further, both the arguably-central figure of the Civil War—Abraham Lincoln—and the central anti-slavery government document of the War—the *Emancipation Proclamation* (1863)—were decidedly lukewarm about fully abolishing slavery. Lincoln, at one point, considered colonization—that is, removing all freed slaves from the United States and permanently relocating them to Africa, Canada, or the Caribbean—and the famed proclamation freed only the slaves in areas in open rebellion to the federal government (some of the document actually lists areas that are exempt).

Nonetheless, for a variety of complex reasons—Lincoln's assassination, the rise of a version of radical Republicanism that wanted to box the Old South out of governmental power, the growing voices of African Americans throughout the nation, etc.—the period immediately following the Civil War, known as the Reconstruction (1865–1877), saw unprecedented leaps from the slave system. The passage of the Thirteenth, Fourteenth, and Fifteenth Amendments to the *Constitution* not only permanently destroyed legalized American chattel slavery, but also granted suffrage to all Black men—leading to the first Black members of the U.S. Congress as well as other Black elected officials in several state governments. And though the freed slaves never received the "40 acres and a mule" that some in the Union army hoped to give through repatriating planter land (thus setting up the current debates over reparations for slavery), the Federal government did set up both aid groups like the Freedmen's Bureau and protection for some African Americans through keeping a large federal military presence in the South.

These years also saw an explosion of modern technology—ranging from the first transcontinental railroad in 1869 to the electric light bulb in 1879—as well as unprecedented immigration to the United States (Ellis Island was opened in 1890). As citizens fought to make sense of the new world around them—sometimes through virulent xenophobia—they also dealt with strides toward women's rights, including the complex events surrounding the withholding of suffrage for women even as Black men were enfranchised, which led some prominent feminists like Susan B. Anthony to lapse into racism. And in 1890, the U.S. Census Bureau declared the American frontier closed, capping the decimation of Native American peoples across the nation. But the United States's further imperial designs would nonetheless lead, in 1898, to the annexation of Hawaii and the Spanish-American War.

But while the Civil Rights Act of 1875, which granted a range of rights for Blacks in public settings, marked one culmination of the gains of African Americans during Reconstruction, the 1883 declaration by the Supreme Court that the Act was unconstitutional, the 1865 founding of the Ku Klux Klan, the 1877 removal of Federal troops from the South, and increasing restrictions on Black voters across the South started a quick slide into a South ruled by Jim Crow—a South of forced segregation. The North was little better—and, in some places, worse. Most of the gains of the Reconstruction had been lost by the time the Supreme Court rendered its decision in *Plessy v. Ferguson* in 1896, which codified the idea of "separate but equal" and the practice of "separate and unequal."

Within this skeletal outline of American history, though, three areas especially need further discussion in reference to the anthology's subject: slavery and free African Americans, the abolitionist movement, and the development of the American theater.

Slavery in the Developing Nation

Slavery began well before the United States existed as an entity: Spaniards brought African slaves to the Americas in the early 1500s, and twenty Africans were brought to the English colony at Jamestown, Virginia, in 1619 as "indentured servants." As the colonies grew—and especially as Southern agriculture evolved into a massive and labor-intensive system—chattel slavery became codified as well as firmly tied to ideologies of race (specifically ideologies that said that lifetime servitude was the proper and ordained position for Black Africans and their descendents). Within these ties, though, a strand developed that allowed white men extreme power: the condition of the child followed that of the mother—and so sexual violence committed against slave women could increase a white master's slave holdings. Thus, while North American chattel slavery was clearly tied to specific notions of racial genealogy, it was not as neatly tied to skin color.

The conditions of slavery varied widely across the nation—dependent on region, dominant crop, class of the slave owner, size and character of the owner's holdings (whether rural or urban, plantation or small industry), as well as, of course, personalities of individual slave owners. Still, historians have documented the ways in which violence (physical, sexual, and psychological), as well as the consistent potential for sale (and separation from family and friends) and the Southern legal system, gave slave owners power over literally every aspect of slaves' lives. Given this, historians have carefully documented that resistance—in a range of forms—was often present, even though there was never a massive revolution. (This is not to suggest, though, that there was not violent, organized resistance at times. Attempts at slave revolt happened long before the well-known Nat Turner rebellion in 1831: Denmark Vesey's in 1822 and Gabriel Prosser's in 1800 are perhaps most notable, but we need also remember, for example, the 1739 Stono Rebellion that led to South Carolina's legal restriction of slave literacy and even the 1712 rebellion in that bastion of the South, New York City....)

And slavery *did* reach into the North. Though it was never a massive presence there, only after the American Revolution did most Northern states move toward abolition; even then, many states, like New York, put in place gradual emancipation laws that ensured, among other things, that slave owners were guaranteed extensive work from slaves before "losing" their "investments." Even in Illinois, correctly remembered as both a free state and as the proving ground for the young Lincoln, early nineteenth-century laws noted that slaveholders moving to the state had to register their slaves within sixty days and that slaveholders and their slaves, nominally "freed" with extended residence in Illinois, could enter into indentures—contracts that guaranteed work in exchange for basic support for multi-year periods. Slaves who did not agree to indentures could, within the allotted window, be returned and/or sold South....

While the United States outlawed participation in the international slave trade beginning on January 1, 1808, such legislation reflected more the sheer fact of numbers of slaves—i.e., that slave reproduction would fill future labor needs—than any great moral outrage.

Numbers begin to tell one of the myriad stories of slavery. The 1790 Federal Census tallied almost 700,000 slaves in the new nation—including just over 40,000 in the North. Many of these were Africans; many others had been born enslaved in North America and were the children and grandchildren of Africans. By 1810, the enslaved population was close to 1.2 million; slavers had rushed to beat the 1808 deadline and meet the demands caused by, among other developments, the invention of the cotton gin (which was probably done by a mix of white and Black individuals, but is usually credited to the white Eli Whitney in 1793). Still, as massive a number as 1.2 million slaves seems, these enslaved people were only a portion of the Africans kidnapped into slavery and brought to the Americas; some scholars estimate that over 12 million Africans survived the "Middle Passage" and formed the roots not only of African American culture, but also of large African populations in the Caribbean and Brazil.

By 1860, the Census counted almost four million slaves in the United States and seven Southern states with slave populations of higher than 300,000. In addition to demonstrating how essential slave labor was to the South, these counts had a much more pragmatic value to the white Southerners of the time: the Constitution's infamous "three-fifths clause" allowed states to count a slave as three-fifths of a person when figuring population for Congressional representation.

Thus, though the slaves could, obviously, never vote, their numbers allowed the South to maintain notable power in the House of Representatives. Paired with the Missouri Compromise of 1820, which, in essence, forced the U.S. to wait for a new slave state to enter the Union with any new free state (thus keeping the balance of seats in the U.S. Senate even), such measures gave the slaveholding South some real national power—power enough in 1836, for example, to institute a "gag rule" that stopped anti-slavery legislation from even being *introduced* in Congress.

Still, such numbers perhaps make it too easy to forget that each of those enslaved people had a family, had stories, had dreams—the memory of much of which has often, simply, been lost, even though historians and archeologists have begun to piece together the remnants. American popular culture has also conveniently forgotten that during the first years of the Civil War, enslaved people were called and treated as "contraband" and as "stolen property" by the Union: not until 1864 were the United States' fugitive slave laws repealed, and not until the passage of the Thirteenth Amendment in 1865 were all slaves freed.

Almost as forgotten—especially until the late 1960s—was the fairly large population of free African Americans—almost 500,000 by 1860, mainly living in the North and upper South. A group perhaps as diverse as their enslaved brethren, they had almost as long a history: the 1790 Census counted almost 60,000 free Blacks, and the first records of free Blacks in Massachusetts date to the 1640s. In the South and in much of the North, they faced oppressive "Black codes"—laws that not only allowed discrimination, but practiced it, and sometimes even forced free Blacks out of specific localities and even whole states. Schools in Boston, a hotbed of abolitionist activity and Transcendental thought, remained legally segregated until well into the 1850s—and segregated in practice for much longer. A few free African Americans flourished: Philadelphia's James Forten, for example, not only became wealthy, but also became a powerful voice for equal rights, an important worker for the anti-slavery cause, and an early supporter and financial backer of Garrison. Many lived in an obscurity and poverty only a few steps removed from slavery. Still, some of the most important abolitionists came from the free African American population. Some members of the community mobilized early—as witnessed by the series of "National Negro Conventions" beginning in 1830, and free African Americans were long a source of aid to enslaved people, culminating in their active service in the Civil War.

Abolition

Anti-slavery thought in North America also began before the United States existed as an entity: Rhode Island outlawed slavery as early as 1652; select Pennsylvania Quakers were arguing for abolition in the 1680s; and the first anti-slavery tract, Samuel Sewall's *The Selling of Joseph*, was published in 1700. Still, major organized abolitionist efforts did not fully begin until the era of the Revolution, and even then, until the 1820s, many white efforts focused on colonization. Of these, the American Colonization Society, founded in 1816 and centering on sending freed Blacks to Liberia, was the most notable venture—and the one that produced the most ire from both Black activists and liberal white abolitionists.

One of the standard narratives of the history of abolitionism is that its rise in the early 1830s was tied to the remnants of religious revivalist movements and to firebrand William Lloyd Garrison, who began publishing *The Liberator*, a radical newspaper that advocated immediate abolition, in 1831. In some ways, this story oversimplifies: Garrison had worked with Benjamin Lundy, a Quaker abolitionist who considered colonization and who pioneered the abolitionist press with his *Genius of Universal Emancipation*. But Garrison was also influenced by David Walker's fiery *Appeal to the Colored Citizens of the World* (1829). Written by a Black Bostonian, this tract, in essence, threatened violent revolution to ensure abolition and equality. And, of course, Walker was influenced by other free Blacks, including colleagues who started the first African American newspaper, *Freedom's Journal*, in 1827.

Regardless of his roots, though, Garrison quickly became a major force in making abolitionism a national movement—especially through the American Anti-Slavery Society (founded in 1833). This organization, as well as a growing number of state and local societies, employed lecturers across the North, published tracts, raised money for the cause, and carried a message centered on immediate abolition, even though the flavor of that message changed over time. By the late 1830s, there were also several female anti-slavery societies—given that many male abolitionists at least initially favored separating the sexes (and limiting women's public roles severely) and that many women felt it was their moral duty to oppose slavery.

Garrison was a notable exception among male abolitionists, and, throughout the 1830s, his ethos became more clearly and radically defined: immediate abolition, opposition to colonization, opposition to political participation (he saw the *Constitution* as a pro-slavery document), and support for participation in the movement (and the culture) by African Americans and women. Garrison also, early on, left organized religion—arguing that church bodies often countenanced slavery and rarely, as he felt they should, saw abolition as ordained by God—and he argued consistently for a range of social reforms: pacifism, temperance, etc.

Though all of these issues certainly shaped growing splits in the movement, the "woman question" and the "political question" proved most divisive in this early period, and, in a fierce struggle, Garrisonians took full control of the American Anti-Slavery Society in 1840 when anti-Garrisonians split to form the American and Foreign Anti-Slavery Society (a more conservative version of abolitionism active in the organized church) and the Liberty Party (a political party that fielded candidates in the early 1840s).

Factionalism and individual conflicts continued throughout the movement's existence: a key Garrison lieutenant, lecturer John A. Collins (who was Frederick Douglass's first lecturing partner) left the movement to found a utopian socialist commune; Frederick Douglass, initially a disciple of Garrison and an incredibly popular lecturer, chafed under Garrisonian paternalism and the limitations the movement placed on African Americans, and finally broke with

Garrison; the Liberty Party eventually lost much of its strong abolitionist focus and moved into the much more diffuse ideology of the
Free Soil party; a handful of radical Black leaders speculated on plans
ranging from nationalistic emigration to Haiti to violent revolution
against the slave system.

Still, for all of this, the various pieces of the movement maintained constant pressure for the immediate abolition of slavery, in part
buoyed by abolitionist successes in the British West Indies. But much
of the energy for that pressure came from a steady stream of evidence
of the atrocities of the slave system—ranging from the murder of
white newspaperman Elijah Lovejoy for taking an abolitionist stance
in 1839, to the unnumbered acts of slaveholder brutality described in
the classic *American Slavery as It Is* (1839), to the events described in a
bookshelf-full of slave narratives published in the 1840s and 1850s.

While the factionalism never stopped, the Compromise of
1850 further intensified the movement's fervor—especially given the
provisions of a new, much tougher Fugitive Slave Law that not only
stiffened penalties for aiding escaping slaves, but forced Northern
citizens (and especially lawmen) to aid in recapturing fugitives. The
Fugitive Slave Law pushed many abolitionists to produce their most
compelling work ever. Still, it was from the pen of a writer who had
never been active in the movement (and whose father had been a
notable adversary to immediatists) that the most popular anti-slavery
message came. Harriet Beecher Stowe's *Uncle Tom's Cabin*, published
in book form in 1852, ran roughshod over all previous best-seller
records and quickly spawned a mass of copycat novels, protest texts
(including yet more novels), songs, plays, and memorabilia ranging
from dolls to playing cards. The novel's implicit messages—that
most slaves, like Uncle Tom, were docile, childlike, and imminently
Christian; that slavery was an affront to families because it separated
such and encouraged slaveholder adultery; and that freed slaves (like
her characters George and Eliza) would be best off in Canada—were
quite palatable to much of the white public, especially when wrapped
in a sentimental framework. While most in Garrison's camp were
lukewarm about Stowe's ideas and while several Black activists were
deeply troubled by her representations of African Americans, Stowe

nonetheless was courted by a range of abolitionists, all hoping to use her popularity to further the cause. For all of the novel's popularity, though—and for all of Stowe's activism after the novel—the national government was not swayed and continued to push for full enforcement of the Fugitive Slave Law.

Groups like Boston's Vigilance Committee—a mixed race group dedicated to helping fugitive slaves—sprang up at key points across the nation, promising active and even violent resistance if the law was invoked, and this led to a number of public spectacles, including actions surrounding fugitives like Anthony Burns and Shadrach Minkins. The growing recognition that violence might be necessary to resolve the slavery question served as one of the roots of both "bleeding Kansas"—a sort of mini-Civil War between forces who wanted Kansas to enter the Union as a slave state and those (among them, John Brown) who wanted Kansas to be free—and Brown's own failed raid on Harper's Ferry in 1859. Black abolitionists—especially in the wake of the Supreme Court's 1857 *Dred Scott* decision, which essentially marked Blacks as non-persons—grew even more intense in their struggles against slavery.

As the Civil War began, organized abolitionists fought and lobbied for anti-slavery action—as well as for Black equality and especially for the chance for African Americans to serve in the Union army, a chance granted only fairly late in the war. Still, in what some historians mark as an important factor in the Union's victory, over 186,000 African Americans served, and over 38,000 were killed in the line of duty. The movement finally fragmented for good after the war—with some activists retiring from public life, some moving on to other reform causes, and only a handful focusing on the continuing struggle against the remnants of the slave system.

The Early American Theater

While the history of the early American theater begins at least as early as the histories of slavery and abolition—scholars note a pair of comedies performed at a Spanish mission near Miami, Florida, in 1567—drama did not become a vital force in American culture until the Revolution. Part of this delay was due to the Puritan resistance to plays—and to many forms of entertainment—which even led to anti-theater laws in some colonies and cities. Still, a theater was built as early as 1716 in Williamsburg, Virginia, and by the Revolution, several playhouses graced larger cities. The 1790s, though, saw not only an increase in available stages, but also an influx of English actors, some simply touring and some, like Susanna Rowson, deciding to stay in the new nation. Americans, including notable authors of the period like Royall Tyler and Mercy Otis Warren, also began writing plays. And while theaters still retained a questionable reputation, they attracted larger audiences—including, on several occasions, figures like George Washington. While New York City and Philadelphia became centers for drama, by 1810, there were playhouses and troupes (including amateur troupes) in frontier cities in Tennessee, Kentucky, and Ohio—far from the settled coast.

Early on, the theater became a place not only for entertainment—though there was certainly plenty, given that companies sometimes shared space and cards with magicians, circuses, and musicians—but also a place for patriotic sentiment. But theaters were far from the only places where drama found purchase. More and more readers were able to obtain print copies of plays and read them like novels; the genre of the "closet drama"—plays never meant to be performed—found readers, too. Perhaps most importantly, "amateur theatricals" entered a range of educational and social settings across gender, race, and even sometimes class.

This growing popularity meant that the theater could support—and rely on—what theater historians have called a "star system," a pool of major actors like Edwin Forrest and Junius Booth who had name recognition and drawing power. (Indeed, Forrest especially encouraged American playwrights by offering a series of prizes for star vehicles.) This "star system" was mainly male, and women in the theater (like women in any public speaking role) were often accused of being promiscuous simply by virtue of putting themselves on display. Still, from Susanna Rowson on, actresses made some notable inroads:

Anna Mowatt, for example, made the construction of a "virtuous actress" image a focus of her stage career.

Black Americans, too, were a part of this expansion of the theater, even though they were consciously marginalized. Rare figures like Brown and Philadelphia musician Francis Johnson carved out niches in the Northern entertainment industry, and, across the South, planters called on their slaves for a range of entertainment. Of course, Black participation in audiences was severely limited by race, but some theaters managed to create occasional accommodations with "appropriate" separation in both the North and even in a few areas of the South. Beyond the formal theater, though, slaves and free Blacks both engaged in their own performative practices, some drawn from various African traditions and some born of American experiences.

Within these contexts, by the 1830s and 1840s, the American theater offered a diverse slate to an audience that varied significantly in class and background if not race. Theater seating in several of the newer, larger, big-city theaters like the rebuilt Park Theater in New York, the Bowery Theater in New York, the Arch Street Theater in Philadelphia, the National Theater in New York, and the National Theater in Washington, D.C., reflected this class differential, with cheap gallery seats priced around a quarter and better box seats sometimes fetching more than a dollar. While some theaters and some productions attained an air of respectability, many remained notorious for encouraging prostitution, and working-class theaters—the Bowery was often the embodiment—gained fame for raucousness, especially with the rise of minstrelsy.

As a central piece of antebellum American theater, minstrelsy has held both deep embarrassment and deep fascination for theater and cultural historians—in part because it so directly and malevolently addressed central issues of the day (race, slavery, class, etc.) and in part because it shaped much American performance to come (from vaudeville to film). Some historians mark 1828 as the beginning of minstrelsy, as this is the year when Thomas Dartmouth Rice supposedly first "jumped Jim Crow"—that is, when he began performing music and dance material supposedly based on the slave practices of African Americans in the South. Others date the beginning to 1832, when Rice performed at the Bowery in blackface; and still others point to dates later in the 1830s and 1840s, when full minstrel troupes were established. Minstrelsy's history is actually much more complex—and a full study would incorporate roots as diverse as early stage Africans in British drama, "Election Day" celebrations among Northern Blacks, and the forced singing and dancing on the decks of slave ships during the Middle Passage (a practice nominally tied to exercising and "airing out" the slaves that dates back to at least the mid-seventeenth century). But regardless of—or perhaps because of—its complex origins, minstrelsy became one of the most popular components of the American stage for decades. Needless to say, much that went on in minstrel shows had little to do with giving a true representation of Blackness or of the harsh realities of slavery.

That white actors in blackface became such a centerpiece of the theater—and that, much more broadly, American drama was seen as a popular phenomenon rather than an artistic one—perhaps explains some of drama's absence from much literary study. Indeed, only in the last two decades have anthologies of early American drama become readily available for use in classrooms. Part of the reentry of drama into a sense of early American literature is based specifically on historians' concurrent realization that the "popular" and the "literary" (to say nothing of the political) may inform each other deeply. Like many of their fellow writers, for example, American playwrights worked to find a unique national voice and deal with American subjects. Further, major figures of the American literary canon like Walt Whitman, Edgar Allan Poe, and Herman Melville were all fascinated by the theater—and Frederick Douglass spent significant energy in both speeches and his newspapers attacking minstrelsy. And, of course, writers like Susanna Rowson, William Wells Brown, Harriet Beecher Stowe, and Lydia Maria Child are included in the pages of this anthology.

The quick rise of minstrelsy and the longer rise of melodrama as the central form for many of the American stage's new plays meant that the theater was ripe for consideration of a range of issues of the day—especially social issues—and such can be seen in the spate of plays focusing on Native Americans beginning in the 1820s, on temperance (including the immensely popular 1844 play *The Drunkard*), and, ultimately, on slavery and race, especially as theater managers, actors, and playwrights recognized both the power and the money-making potential of Harriet Beecher Stowe's *Uncle Tom's Cabin*.

Still, like those who capitalized on *Uncle Tom's Cabin*'s popularity, many in the theater recognized that the American stage had become not only part of popular culture, but also a business. The 1850s saw more and more sensation—in staging, but also in acting and in writing. While the Civil War perhaps slowed the progress of the theater, it certainly did not stop it (and it was, of course, a theater—notably showing a play that mingled American-ness with British-ness, *Our American Cousin*—that was the setting for the assassination of Abraham Lincoln). By the 1870s, the theater was clearly a national phenomenon—with world-class theaters on both coasts, traveling troupes throughout the country (including among them both white minstrel troupes and a handful of African American groups), and smaller theaters as well as amateur companies nationwide.

The Texts

This anthology presents only a sampling of the great number of plays and other performative texts that addressed slavery on the American stage before 1900. Given this, a word on what *isn't* included is appropriate while we consider what *is* included—and why.

First, the text focuses on plays written by Americans. Thus, key texts by William Shakespeare like *Othello* and *The Tempest* that were regularly performed in American theaters throughout the period and that shaped (and were shaped by) American thinking about the representations of Blackness and slavery are absent, as are early British texts including various versions of Aphra Behn's fascinating *Oroonoko* (1688) and Thomas Bellamy's play *The Benevolent Planter* (1789). Later British texts, including a great deal of minstrelsy as well as plays based (sometimes as loosely as their American cousins) on *Uncle Tom's Cabin*—like *Uncle Tom in England; or, a Proof that Black's*

White (1852), Mark Lemon and Tom Taylor's *Slave Life; or, Uncle Tom's Cabin* (1852), and George Pitt's *Uncle Tom's Cabin: A Nigger Drama in Three Acts* (1852)—are also absent, though they, too, sometimes saw time on the American stage.

Two sets of texts from the early national period have a limited presence here: plays focused on the Barbary pirates' enslavement of white Americans, and plays by the earliest African American playwrights. Susanna Haswell Rowson's *Slaves in Algiers* represents the first group, which centers on the American outcry against (white) U.S. citizens being taken captive on the high seas, forced into slavery, and held until exorbitant ransom was paid—an outcry that led to the little-remembered U.S. Tripolitan War and that is described in more depth in the introduction to the play. *Slaves in Algiers* is, frankly, more readable than most—but Rowson's inclusion here is also tied to the fact that she is becoming recognized as an important voice in the early literature of the nation, that the play was one of the earliest of the type, and that it was fairly popular. Still, advanced students interested in such texts will—in addition to seeking out the fine anthology of Barbary captive narratives, *White Slaves, African Masters: An Anthology of American Barbary Captivity Narratives* (1999)—want to consider plays like Maria Pinckney's *The Young Carolinians; or, Americans in Algiers* (1818).

Unfortunately, as noted above, though we know of the potential existence of a handful of plays in the second group—those by early nineteenth century African Americans—including the well-documented *King Shotaway*, none of these texts have been found.

The largest cluster of texts in this anthology centers on plays written between 1830 and 1861, the era of the flowering of organized abolitionism as well as minstrelsy, of the blockbuster *Uncle Tom's Cabin*, and of the massive literary and performative production allowed by bigger cities, better presses, better theaters, and large-scale public debate over slavery and race. Thus, in addition to representing early abolitionist drama through presenting excepts from *The Kidnapped Clergyman* (1839) and the full text of *The Fugitives* (1841)—which have not been published since their original editions—the anthology includes a selection of early minstrel material, two "Uncle Tom" plays

(George Aiken's 1852 minstrel-influenced version of *Uncle Tom's Cabin* and Harriet Beecher Stowe's own rare 1855 dramatization of her novel, *The Christian Slave*), two later plays by abolitionists (Lydia Maria Child's 1858 *The Stars and Stripes* and the first published play by an African American, William Wells Brown's 1858 *The Escape*), and an opportunistic play performed in the immediate wake of John Brown's execution in late 1859, Dion Boucicault's *The Octoroon*.

Again, though, there are other texts that the advanced student of the period and subject would want to consider to gain a fuller sense of the drama of slavery. Greco-Roman slavery, for example, often came to the American stage—most famously, in Robert Montgomery Bird's *The Gladiator* (1831), which some audiences considered anti-slavery—but also in lesser known texts like pro-slavery polemicist Louisa S. McCord's turgid *Caius Gracchus* (1851). Minstrelsy could take—and recently has taken—full anthologies in and of itself; two of the most notable collections are *This Grotesque Essence* (1978) and *Jump Jim Crow* (2003). But even these fine anthologies only scratch the surface of what was a massive site of multimedia cultural production. Minstrelsy also shaped popular plays; students interested in such might do well to begin with Anna Mowatt's immensely popular comedy *Fashion* (1845), which features a minstrel-like Black "servant." Outside of minstrelsy, extant plays that take an explicitly pro-slavery agenda *and* focus on slavery are fairly rare. Often, such sentiments filtered into more mainstream attempts like William Gilmore Simms's cumbersome *Norman Maurice; or, The Man of the People* (1853)—or even Mowatt's *Fashion*. Additional anti-slavery dramatic texts are also extant—ranging from dramatizations of Stowe's later anti-slavery novel *Dred* (1856), which was never as popular as its predecessor *Uncle Tom's Cabin*, to Sophia L. Little's "dramatic sketch" in verse, *The Branded Hand* (1845), which, while fascinating, is at times quite difficult to read.

Finally, there were other popular melodramas in the mold of *The Octoroon*—most notably, a play somewhat similar in subject matter, J.T. Trowbridge's popular dramatization of his novel *Neighbor Jackwood* (1857). And there were plays that were just as opportunistic. Even though it shows neither slavery nor developed African American characters, Mrs. J.C. Swayze's dramatization of the life of anti-slavery radical John Brown, *Ossawattomie Brown* (1859), is an example of a play created specifically to capitalize on current events surrounding the slavery controversy. Interested readers should also note that some of these approaches, sentiments, and subjects would be carried into plays now referred to as "Civil War drama," some of which are collected in the useful anthology *Fateful Lightning: America's Civil War Plays* (2000).

Even such additional reading, though, would still miss some key texts and issues because some important plays are, simply, lost. These include all of the pro-slavery dramatic answers to *Uncle Tom's Cabin* that scholars have found mention of (including one simply called *Rebuke to Uncle Tom's Cabin*)—as well as William Wells Brown's first play, *Experience*, which he read as a sort of one-man show at lecture events in 1856 and which seems to have had similarities to *The Kidnapped Clergyman*. Further, as Henry Louis Gates's recent discovery of Hannah Crafts's manuscript novel *The Bondwoman's Narrative* (2002) demonstrates, texts by and about African Americans that we do not even yet know about may well be found as we plunge deeper into the archive.

Indeed, it is the archive—specifically the Special Collections at Fisk University—from whence one of the post-Civil War texts in this anthology comes: *Peculiar Sam; or, the Underground Rail Road* (1879), which a young Pauline Hopkins wrote for prominent African American minstrel Sam Lucas (the first African American to play Uncle Tom on the stage). While the play has been occasionally anthologized elsewhere, the text here returns to Hopkins's handwritten version. In addition to being written by an important figure in Black literature and being one of only a handful of nineteenth-century Black-authored plays found to date, *Peculiar Sam* is also illustrative of some of the ways in which Black entertainers had to struggle with and against the much more dominant approach to depicting slavery on the American stage in the late nineteenth-century: the post-Civil War minstrel show. Such later minstrelsy is summarized here with a selection of late-nineteenth century texts. Like earlier plays in the anthology, these selections could be further complemented by additional reading: Bartley Campbell's 1882 play *The White Slave*, which has echoes of *The Octoroon*, and the fourteen-minute Thomas Edison / Edwin S. Porter film version of *Uncle Tom's Cabin* (1903) might be among the most interesting comparisons, as might M.C. Browne's *The Landlord's Revenge; or, Uncle Tom's Up to Date* (1894), a short minstrel text that takes the Tom-show as its subject.

The work collected here, then, should be seen as a primer to a massive subject. Given this, each play is accompanied by a brief introduction that offers contextual information specific to that play's performance and publication, as well as (when known) biographical information on the author, a brief discussion of key textual issues (which includes information like that generally given in footnotes), and a short list of supplemental readings.

The opening of this introduction asked you to consider an image that became central to the drama of slavery in pre-twentieth century America: the minstrel caricature of an African American. It also, though, set out an image that was never allowed such prominence, the image of an independent African American company of players putting on plays by a white man recognized as one of the central figures of the Western dramatic canon: Shakespeare.

To conclude, I ask you to consider an image perhaps almost as loaded—and one that went through many variations during the latter half of the nineteenth and the early twentieth centuries, one of which can be found on the anthology's cover. The image of Little Eva and her slave Uncle Tom reading the *Bible* together was a centerpiece not only of Stowe's novel, but of several dramatizations—and so of several theater posters. On the surface, it is a simple image, one that attests to the deep care the characters seem to have not only for each other, but for the text they are sharing. But the image is more complex than that. Uncle Tom here is much older than he is in Stowe's novel: most theater companies and illustrators were unwilling to put a virile Black man so close to a young white girl, so they aged him. Tom is illiterate; Eva is reading to him. While this is true in the novel—and in most of the dramatizations—in the novel, *Tom* usually explains the concepts behind the words Eva shares, often in a homey, simple

Christian theology. And Uncle Tom himself became—appropriately or not—the symbol for many later African Americans of a non-resistance that sank into non-action, so much so that "tomming" became synonymous with kow-towing to whites and that an "Uncle Tom" became synonymous with selling out…

Explore that image, even as you explore the plays and their contexts—sifting, challenging, questioning, and reading further.

Bibliography

Brown's African American Theater Company and Charles Mathews

Klepac, Richard L. *Mr. Mathews at Home*. London: Society for Theatre Research, 1979.

Mathews, Mrs. *A Continuation of the Memoirs of Charles Mathews*. Philadelphia: Lea and Blanchard, 1839.

McAllister, Marvin. *White People Do Not Know How to Behave at Entertainments Designed for Ladies & Gentlemen of Colour: William Brown's African & American Theater*. Chapel Hill: University of North Carolina Press, 2003.

Sketches of Mr. Mathews' Celebrated Trip to America. London: J. Limbird, nd.

White, Shane. *Stories of Freedom in Black New York*. Cambridge: Harvard University Press, 2002.

Drama Anthologies

Engle, Gary D., ed. *This Grotesque Essence: Plays from the Minstrel Stage*. Baton Rouge: Louisiana State University Press, 1978.

Hatch, James v., ed. *Black Theater, U.S.A.: Forty-five Plays by Black Americans, 1847–1974*. New York: Free Press, 1974.

Kritzer, Amelia Howe, ed. *Plays by Early American Women, 1775–1850*. Ann Arbor: University of Michigan Press, 1995.

Lhamon, W.T., Jr., ed. *Jump Jim Crow: Lost Plays, Lyrics, and Street Prose of the First Atlantic Popular Culture.* Cambridge: Harvard University Press, 2003.

Richards, Jeffrey H., ed. *Early American Drama.* New York: Penguin, 1997.

Wilmeth, Don B., ed. *Staging the Nation: Plays from the American Theater, 1787–1909.* New York: Bedford/St. Martin's, 1997.

Slavery, Free Blacks, and Abolition

Berlin, Ira. *Many Thousands Gone: The First Two Centuries of Slavery in North America.* Cambridge: Harvard University Press, 1998.

Blassingame, John. *The Slave Community: Plantation Life in the Antebellum South.* New York: Oxford, 1979.

Foner, Eric. *Reconstruction: America's Unfinished Revolution, 1863–1877.* New York: Harper and Row, 1988.

——. *Slavery and Freedom in Nineteenth Century America.* New York: Oxford University Press, 1994.

Franklin, John Hope and Alfred A. Moss, Jr. *From Slavery to Freedom: A History of African Americans.* Seventh Edition. New York: Knopf, 1994.

Genovese, Eugene. *Roll, Jordan, Roll: The World the Slaves Made.* New York: Pantheon, 1974.

Hoffer, Peter Charles. *The Great New York Conspiracy of 1741: Slavery, Crime, and Criminal Law.* Lawrence: University of Kansas Press, 2003.

Horton, James Oliver. *Free People of Color: Inside the African-American Community.* Washington, D.C.: Smithsonian Institution Press, 1993.

Horton, James Oliver and Lois Horton. *In Hope of Liberty: Culture, Community and Protest among Northern Free Blacks.* New York: Oxford University Press, 1997.

Kolchin, Peter. *American Slavery, 1619–1877.* New York: Hill and Wang, 1993.

Levine, Lawrence. *Black Culture and Black Consciousness: Afro-American Folk Thought from Slavery to Freedom.* New York: Oxford University Press, 1977.

Litwack, Leon and August Meier, eds. *Black Leaders of the Nineteenth Century.* Urbana: University of Illinois Press, 1988.

Mayer, Henry. *All on Fire: William Lloyd Garrison and the Abolition of Slavery.* New York: St. Martin's Griffin, 1998.

Parris, Peter. *Slavery: History and Historians.* New York: Harper and Row, 1989.

Pease, William and Jane Pease. *They Who Would Be Free: Blacks' Struggle for Freedom, 1830–1861.* New York: Athenaeum 1974.

Stuckey, Sterling. *Slave Culture: Nationalist Thought and the Foundations of Black America.* New York: Oxford University Press, 1987.

White, Deborah Gray. *Ar'n't I a Woman: Female Slaves in the Plantation South.* Revised Edition. New York: W.W. Norton, 1999.

Yee, Shirley J. *Black Women Abolitionists: A Study in Activism, 1828–1860.* Knoxville: University of Tennessee Press, 1992.

Yellin, Jean Fagan. *Women and Sisters: The Antislavery Feminists in American Culture.* New Haven: Yale University Press, 1989.

Yellin, Jean Fagan and John C. Van Horne, eds. *The Abolitionist Sisterhood: Women's Political Culture in Antebellum America.* Ithaca: Cornell University Press, 1994.

Theater History and Minstrelsy History

Bank, Rosemary K. *Theatre Culture in America, 1825–1860.* Cambridge: Cambridge University Press, 1997.

Bean, Annemarie, James v. Hatch, and Brooks McNamara, eds. *Inside the Minstrel Mask: Readings in Nineteenth-Century Blackface Minstrelsy.* Hanover: Wesleyan University Press, 1996.

Birdoff, Harry. *The World's Greatest Hit: Uncle Tom's Cabin.* New York: Vanni, 1947.

Booth, Michael R. *Theatre in Victorian America.* Cambridge: Cambridge University Press, 1991.

Dormon, James H., Jr. *Theater in the Antebellum South, 1815–1860.* Chapel Hill: University of North Carolina Press, 1967.

Elam, Harry J., Jr., and David Krasner, eds. *African American Performance and Theater History.* New York: Oxford University Press, 2001.

Engle, Ron and Tice L. Miller, eds. *The American Stage: Social and Economic Issues from the Colonial Period to the Present.* Cambridge: Cambridge University Press, 1993.

Gossett, Thomas. *Uncle Tom's Cabin and American Culture.* Dallas: Southern Methodist University Press, 1986.

Hill, Errol G. and James v. Hatch, eds. *A History of African American Theatre.* Cambridge: Cambridge University Press, 2003.

Hixon, Don L. and Don A. Hennesse. *Nineteenth-Century American Drama: A Finding Guide.* Metuchen, N.J.: Scarecrow, 1977.

Levine, Lawrence. *Highbrow/Lowbrow: The Emergence of Cultural Hierarchy in America.* Cambridge: Harvard University Press, 1988.

Lott, Eric. *Love and Theft: Blackface Minstrelsy and the American Working Class.* New York: Oxford University Press, 1993.

McConachie, Bruce A. *Melodramatic Formations: American Theatre and Society,* Iowa City: University of Iowa Press, 1992.

Roppolo, Joseph R. "Uncle Tom in New Orleans: Three Lost Plays." *The New England Quarterly* 27.2 (June 1954): 213–226.

Toll, Robert C. *Blacking Up: The Minstrel Show in Nineteenth-Century America.* New York: Oxford University Press, 1974.

A Note on the Texts

The reader may notice that spelling and punctuation vary from text to text. We have intentionally preserved the spelling and punctuation of the original editions of the plays to give the modern reader an authentic sense of these historic works.

Slaves in Algiers; or a Struggle for Freedom

Introduction

Several of the major slave characters in Susanna Haswell Rowson's *Slaves in Algiers* (1794)—including the protagonists—are white Americans.

This statement alone may give several contemporary readers pause, and it hints at the complex contexts surrounding Rowson's play, which was first performed in Philadelphia. The city was already becoming known as the "Cradle of Liberty," given its hosting of the creation of the *Declaration of Independence* and the initial drafts of the *U.S. Constitution*. But, in addition to the pro-slavery victories in the writing of both documents—the removal of references to slavery in the former and the codification of chattel slavery in the latter—Philadelphia was already beginning to struggle with the racism that would flare into riots in the early nineteenth century, and several in Rowson's audience were only beginning to come to terms with Pennsylvania's gradual emancipation and abolition law passed in 1780.

Rowson was actually born Susanna Haswell in Portsmouth, England, in 1762. Her mother died during the birth, and Haswell was raised by relatives because her father, army officer William Haswell, had been posted to Massachusetts. Four years later, the elder

Haswell brought his daughter to the American colonies. During the Revolution, the family—now including Haswell's new wife and two sons—were detained by American troops and eventually returned to England as part of a prisoner exchange. There, Rowson began writing while working as a governess; her first novel, the sentimental *Victoria*, was published in 1786.

That same year, she married a merchant, William Rowson. When Rowson lost his business, though, the two turned to the stage: in addition to acting, Susanna Rowson wrote a range of texts—most notably, her novel *Charlotte, A Tale of Truth* (1791). *Charlotte* was published in the U.S. in 1794, and—retitled *Charlotte Temple*—it went through literally hundreds of editions during the nineteenth and early twentieth centuries. Rowson had returned to the United States in 1793 with a touring theater company. Setting aside her father's loyalism—probably for a combination of personal and pecuniary reasons—Rowson's work for the American theater (like *Slaves in Algiers*, her only extant play) became fervently patriotic. Though she was only on the stage until 1797 and saw little money from American sales of *Charlotte Temple* (given incredibly loose copyright laws), she did parlay her fame and talents—which ended up being ideally suited for teaching—into a successful school for young women in Boston, a regular column in the *Boston Weekly Magazine*, and a number of textbooks. When she died in 1824, she was known throughout the North.

Rowson understood the need to connect the stage to the everyday, and *Slaves in Algiers* thus speaks directly to a phenomenon that obsessed Americans at the end of the eighteenth century and the beginning of the nineteenth century, though that phenomenon was not, as one might expect, the enslavement of African Americans. Rather, *Slaves in Algiers* focuses on American citizens who have been kidnapped into slavery by pirates off of the Barbary Coast of North Africa.

Barbary pirates had taken captives and turned them into slaves for over two centuries; indeed, Miguel De Cervantes, from whose *Don Quixote* Rowson's *Slave in Algiers* borrows heavily, was held between 1575 and 1580. American Joshua Gee would become one of the earliest

American captives when he was taken in 1680; he was enslaved until he was ransomed by a group led by prominent jurist Samuel Sewall. This pattern—enslavement, but also the chance for freedom if ransom monies were forthcoming—shaped much of the Barbary captives' lives, and this pattern governs much of the play's action.

British protection—through both treaties and an impressive navy—had limited such captures for much of the eighteenth century, but, after the American Revolution, such protections were lost. (Some have even suggested that the angry and beaten British actively encouraged the pirates.) Throughout the 1780s and 1790s, American newspapers reported the taking of American ships like the *Betsey*, the *Maria*, and the *Dauphin*, and by 1793, the number of Americans held in Algiers was estimated to be over a hundred. Later, this ongoing conflict would lead to both attempts to ransom prisoners and buy a peace—and then, ultimately, the Tripolitan War between 1801 and 1805, which ended with victories by American naval heroes Stephen Decatur and William Eaton. But when *Slaves in Algiers* was first performed in Philadelphia's Chestnut Street Theatre in June of 1794—and then later in Baltimore, Boston, and, probably, New York City—the American public was waiting anxiously, sometimes angrily, for their country to figure out how to stand against the pirates.

Slaves in Algiers, which was subtitled "A Struggle for Freedom" and sometimes went by the titles *Americans in Algiers* and *Slaves Released from Algiers*, was probably just what many American audiences wanted: a text that idealized Americans and demonized at least some of the Barbary Coast inhabitants—and did it in an entertaining fashion. Indeed, when William Cobbett, under the pseudonym "Peter Porcupine," criticized the play's treatment of gender (including what can be read as a call for more equality between the sexes), no less than a congressman, John Swanick, stepped forward to defend Rowson's play. Further, the same year the play was produced, Congress passed the Navy Act, which would begin to build American resistance to the pirates. Throughout the first part of the nineteenth century, bookshops would see several narratives written by Barbary captives who had been ransomed or rescued, all calling for patriotism and victory over the "heathen" Barbary natives.

5

But in addition to being a patriotic text, *Slaves in Algiers* had other attractions. As a comedy first and foremost, it picks up a number of devices—cross-dressing, mistaken identity, sexual puns, etc.—common in Shakespearean comedy. (Rowson's company actually performed both *As You Like It* and a version of *The Taming of the Shrew* at the Chestnut.) And, though a comedy, the play danced on the edge of issues of sex and power—and violence. At the play's opening, both the mature Rebecca and the young Olivia—who was sometimes played by Rowson herself—have been enslaved. Both are at risk of sexual violence. Rebecca is held by Ben Hassan, a stereotypical Jew reminiscent of Shylock, and Olivia is held by the Dey (supreme ruler) of Algiers, the demonically named Muley Moloc. Both men desire the women and attempt to threaten and cajole them into sexual relationships. Only their American-ness—read: the fact that they are full of virtue, smart, Christian, etc.—and the efforts of four male American captives offer the potential to hold off Hassan and the Dey.

Within this framework—a comedy with Shakespearean undertones that was designed to speak directly to the furor over the Barbary pirates—the obvious question becomes: did Rowson's audience draw connections between these white slaves and the African American slaves held throughout the nation? Did the audiences that saw Rebecca claim that "By Christian law, no man should be a slave"—and teach the slave Fetnah to believe the same sentiments—apply these ideals to slavery in the United States?

Perhaps. Samuel Sewall had already drawn connections between Americans' outrage at the Barbary pirates and the simultaneous tolerance of American slavery in his landmark *The Selling of Joseph* (1700). Closer to Rowson's time, in 1790, Benjamin Franklin, briefly rumored to have been captured by pirates himself, wrote an editorial in a direct critique of a Southern congressmen's defense of slavery under the name "Historicus" and claimed that he was an Algerian leader. Later, in a scathing tract, abolitionist Senator Charles Sumner would draw a direct connection between Barbary slavery and American slavery in *White Slavery in the Barbary States* (1853).

Still, even if Rowson was anti-slavery—and there is no documentation that this was, in fact, the case—she did a range of things to separate Barbary slavery from American slavery. She repeatedly emphasized the whiteness of her protagonists—and linked whiteness, American-ness, and Christianity tightly. The Algerian slaveholders are Other—because they are brown, yes, but mainly because they are Muslim or Jewish. While the play treats a serious subject, it is a comedy—and the slapstick elements and reliance on stereotypes (which it fully endorses) limit its power of critique. And, of course, the play contains no mention of African American chattel slavery.... All this may explain why critics since have focused much more on the play's sometimes radical gender politics—and the ways in which women like Rebecca and Olivia use and invert the time's stereotypical views of women to defend themselves.

A Note on the Text

The text, reproduced here with only a handful of cosmetic changes from the 1794 edition printed for the author by Wrigley and Berriman of Philadelphia, is still relatively readable in the twenty-first century. Readers will want to note the interchangeability of the terms "Moriscan," "Moor," and "Moorish," as well as the use of an early American slang term "Pil-garlick," a perversion of "peeled garlic," which means "poor me." Ben Hassan's language is marked by an uneven attempt to give him a stereotypical Jewish/Yiddish accent, though reading his lines aloud generally clarifies his meaning. And much is made of the Dey's "huge seymetar"—a scimitar he carries, full of phallic innuendo—as well as the "bastinado," a form of Algerian torture where the victim was tied, upside down, and then beaten on the soles of the feet.

For Further Reading

Baepler, Paul, ed. *White Slaves, African Masters: An Anthology of*

American Barbary Captivity Narratives. Chicago: University of Chicago Press, 1999.

Franklin, Benjamin. *Benjamin Franklin, Writings.* New York: Library of America, 1987.

Gee, Joshua. *Narrative of Joshua Gee of Boston, Mass.* Hartford: Wadsworth Athenaeum, 1943.

Margulis, Jennifer and Karen E. Poremski. "Introduction" to Susanna Haswell Rowson's *Slaves in Algiers.* Acton, Massachusetts: Copley, 2000.

Parker, Patricia L. *Susanna Rowson.* Boston: G.K. Hall, 1986.

Porcupine, Peter [Corbett, William]. *A Kick for a Bite; or, Review Upon Review with a Critical Essay on the Works of Mrs. S. Rowson.* Second edition. Philadelphia: Thomas Bradford, 1796.

Rowson, Susanna Haswell. *Charlotte Temple.* Ed. Cathy N. Davidson. New York: Oxford University Press, 1987.

Sewall, Samuel. *The Selling of Joseph.* Ed. Sidney Kaplan. Amherst: University of Massachusetts Press, 1969.

Sumner, Charles. *White Slavery in the Barbary States.* Boston: John P. Jewett, 1853.

Swanick, John. *A Rub from Snub; of a Cursory Analytical Epistle, Addressed to Peter Porcupine.* Philadelphia, np: 1795.

Tucker, Glen. *Dawn like Thunder: The Barbary Wars and the Birth of the U.S. Navy.* Indianapolis: Bobbs-Merril, 1963.

To The Citizens of the United States of North-America. This First Dramatic Effort is Inscribed, By Their Obliged Friend, and Humble Servant, S. Rowson.

Preface

In offering the following pages to the public, I feel myself necessitated to apologize for the errors which I am fearful will be evident to the severe eye of criticism.

The thought of writing a Dramatic Piece was hastily conceived, and as hastily executed; it being not more than two months, from the first starting of the idea, to the time of its being performed.

I feel myself extremely happy, in having an opportunity, thus publicly to acknowledge my obligation to Mr. Reinagle, for the attention he manifested, and the taste and genius he displayed in the composition of the music. I must also return my thanks to the performers, who so readily accepted, and so ably supported their several characters: Since it was chiefly owing to their exertions, that the play was received with such unbounded marks of approbation.

Since the first performance, I have made some alterations; and flatter myself those alterations have improved it: But that, as well as of its merits in general, I am content to abide the decision of a candid and indulgent Public.

Some part of the plot is taken from the Story of the Captive, related by Cervantes, in his inimitable Romance of the Don Quixote, the rest is entirely the offspring of fancy.

I am fully sensible of the many disadvantages under which I consequently labour from a confined education: nor do I expect my style will be thought equal in elegance or energy, to the productions of those who, fortunately, from their sex, or situation in life, have been influenced in the Classics, and have reaped both pleasure and improvement by studying the Ancients in their original purity.

My chief aim has been, to offer to the Public a Dramatic Entertainment, which, while it might excite a smile, or call forth the tear of sensibility, might contain no one sentiment, in the least prejudicial, to the moral or political principles of the government under which I live. On the contrary, it has been my endeavour, to place the social virtues in the fairest point of view, and hold up, to merited contempt and ridicule, their opposite vices. If, in this attempt, I have been the least successful, I shall reap the reward to which I aspire, in the smiles and approbation of a Liberal Public.

Slaves In Algiers

DRAMATIS PERSONAE

Men

MULLEY MOLOC, (*Dey of Algiers*)	Mr. Green
MUSTAPHA,	Mr. Darley, jun.
BEN HASSAN, (*a Renegado*)	Mr. Francis
SEBASTIAN, (*a Spanish Slave*)	Mr. Bates

(AMERICAN CAPTIVES)

AUGUSTUS,	Master T. Warrell
FREDERIC,	Mr. Moreton
HENRY,	Mr. Cleveland

CONSTANT,	Mr. Whitlock
SADI,	Master Warrel
SELIM,	Mr. Bliffett

Women
(MORISCAN WOMEN)

ZORIANA,	Mrs. Warrell
FETNAH,	Mrs. Marshall
SELIMA,	Mrs. Cleveland

(AMERICAN WOMEN)

REBECCA,	Mrs. Whitlock
OLIVIA,	Mrs. Rowson

ACT I, SCENE I

[Apartment at the Dey's. FETNAH *and* SELIMA.]

FETNAH: Well, it's all vastly pretty, the gardens, the house and these fine cloaths; I like them very well, but I don't like to be confined.

SELIMA: Yes, surely you have no reason to complain, chosen favourite of the Dey, what can you wish for more.

FETNAH: O, a great many things. In the first place, I wish for liberty. Why do you talk of my being a favourite; is the poor bird that is confined in a cage (because a favourite with its enslaver) consoled for the loss of freedom. No! tho' its prison is of golden wire, its food delicious, and it is overwhelm'd with caresses, its little heart still pants for liberty: gladly would it seek the fields of air, and even perched upon a naked bough, exulting, carrol forth its song, nor once regret the splendid house of bondage.

SELIMA: Ah! But then our master loves you.

FETNAH: What of that, I don't love him.

SELIMA: Not love him?

FETNAH: No—he is old and ugly, then he wears such tremendous whiskers; and when he makes love, he looks so grave and stately, that I declare, if it was not for fear of his huge seymetar, I shou'd burst out a laughing in his face.

SELIMA: Take care you don't provoke him too far.

FETNAH: I don't care how I provoke him, if I can but make him keep his distance. You know I was brought here only a few days since—well, yesterday, as I was amusing myself, looking at the fine things I saw every where about me, who should bolt into the room, but that great ugly thing Mustapha. What do you want, said I?—Most beautiful Fetnah, said he, bowing till the tip of his long, hooked nose almost touched the toe of his slipper—most beautiful Fetnah, our powerful and gracious master, Muley Moloc, sends me, the humblest of his slaves, to tell you, he will condescend to sup in your apartment to night, and commands you to receive the high honour with proper humility.

SELIMA: Well—and what answer did you return.

FETNAH: Lord, I was too frightened, and so provoked, I hardly know what I said, but finding the horrid looking creature didn't move, at last I told him, that if the Dey was determined to come, I supposed he must, for I could not hinder him.

SELIMA: And did he come?

FETNAH: No—but he made me go to him, and when I went trembling into the room, he twisted his whiskers and knit his great beetle brows. Fetnah said he, you abuse my goodness, I have condescended to request you to love me. And then he gave me such a fierce look, as if he would say, and if you don't love me, I'll cut your head off.

SELIMA: I dare say you are finely frightened.

FETNAH: Frightened! I was provoked beyond all patience, and thinking he would certainly kill me one day or other, I thought I might as well speak my mind, and be dispatched out of the way at once.

SELIMA: You make me tremble.

FETNAH: So, mustering as much courage as I could; great powerful Muley, said I—I am sensible, I am your slave; you took me from an humble state, placed me in this fine palace, and gave me these rich cloaths; you bought my person of my parents, who loved gold better than they did their child; but my affections you could not buy. I can't love you.—How! cried he, starting from his feat; how, can't love me?—and he laid his hand upon his seymetar.

SELIMA: Oh dear! Fetnah.

FETNAH: When I saw the seymetar half drawn, I caught hold of his arm.—Oh! good my lord, said I, pray do not kill a poor little girl like me, send me home again, and bestow your favour on some other, who may think splendor a compensation for their loss of liberty.—Take her away, said he, she is beneath my anger.

SELIMA: But, how is it Fetnah, that you have conceived such an aversion to the manners of a country where you were born.

FETNAH: You are mistaken.—I was not born in Algiers, I drew my first breath in England; my father Ben Hassan, as he is now called, was a Jew. I can scarcely remember our arrival here, and have been educated in the Moorish religion, tho' I always had a natural antipathy to their manners.

SELIMA: Perhaps imbibed from your mother.

FETNAH: No; she has no objection to any of their customs, except that of their having a great many wives at a time. But some few months since, my father, (who sends out many corsairs) brought home a female captive, to whom I became greatly attached; it was she who nourished in my mind the love of liberty, and taught me, woman was never formed to be the abject slave of man. Nature made us equal with them, and gave us the power to render ourselves superior.

SELIMA: Of what nation was she?

FETNAH: She came from that land, where virtue in either sex is the only mark of superiority.—She was an American.

SELIMA: Where is she now?

FETNAH: She is still at my father's, waiting the arrival of her ransom, for she is a woman of fortune. And tho' I can no longer listen to her instructions, her precepts are engraven on my heart, I feel that I was born free, and while I have life, I will struggle to remain so.

SONG

I.

The rose just bursting into bloom,
    Admir'd where'er 'tis seen;
Diffuses round a rich perfume
    The garden's pride and queen.

When gather'd from its native bed,
    No longer charms the eye;
Its vivid tints are quickly fled,
    'Twill wither, droop, and die.

II.

So woman when by nature drest,
    In charms devoid of art;
Can warm the stoic's icy breast,
    Can triumph o'er each heart.
Can bid the soul to virtue rise,
    To glory prompt the brave,
But sinks oppress'd, and drooping dies,
    When once she's made a slave.

[*Exit.*]

SCENE II

[*Ben Hassan's house.*]

REBECCA: [*Discovered reading.*]

The soul, secure in its existence, smiles
At the drawn dagger, and defies its point.
The stars shall fade away, the sun itself
Grow dim with age, and nature sink in years,
Unhurt, amidst the war of elements,
The wreck of matter, or the crush of worlds.

[*Lays down the book.*]

Oh! blessed hope, I feel within myself, that spark of intellectual heavenly fire, that bids me soar above this mortal world, and all its pains or pleasures—its pleasures! Oh!—long—long since I have been dead to all that bear the name.—In early youth—torn from the husband of my heart's election—the first only object of my love—bereft of friends cast on an unfeeling world, with only one poor stay, on which to rest the hope of future joy.—I have a son—my child! my dear Augustus—where are you now?—in slavery.—Grant me patience Heaven! must a boy born in Columbia, claiming liberty as his birth-right, pass all his days in slavery.—How often have I gazed upon his face, and fancied I could trace his father's features; how often have I listen'd to his voice, and thought his father's spirit spoke within him. Oh! my adored boy! must I no more behold his eyes beaming with youthful ardour, when I have told him, how his brave countrymen purchased their freedom with their blood.—Alas! I see him now seldom; and when we meet to think that we are slaves, poor, wretched slaves each serving different masters, my eyes o'erflow with tears.—I have but time to press him to my heart, entreat just Heaven, to protect his life, and at some future day restore his liberty.

[*Enter* BEN HASSAN.]

BEN HASSAN: How do you do, Mrs. Rebecca?

REBECCA: Well, in health, Hassan, but depressed in spirit.

BEN HASSAN: Ah! dat be very bad—come, come cheer up, I wants to talk vid you, you must not be so melancholy, I be your very good friend.

REBECCA: Thank you Hassan, but if you are in reality the friend you profess to be, leave me to indulge my grief in solitude, your intention is kind, but I would rather be alone.

BEN HASSAN: You like mightily to be yourselves, but I must talk to you a little; I vantsh to know ven you think your ransom vil come, 'tis a long time, Mrs. Rebecca, and you knows.—

REBECCA: Oh yes, I know, I am under many obligations to you, but I shall soon be able to repay them

BEN HASSAN: That may be, but 'tis a very long time, since you wrote to your friends, 'tis above eight months; I am afraid you have deceived me.

REBECCA: Alas! Perhaps I have deceived myself.

BEN HASSAN: Vat, den you have no friends—you are not a voman's of fortune?

REBECCA: Yes, yes, I have both friends and ability—but I am afraid my letters have miscarried.

BEN HASSAN: Oh! Dat ish very likely, you may be here dish two or three years longer; perhaps all your life times.

REBECCA: Alas! I am very wretched. [*Weeps.*]

BEN HASSAN: Come, now don't cry so; you must consider I never suffered you to be exposed in the slave market.

REBECCA: But, my son—Oh! Hassan; why did you suffer them to sell my child?

BEN HASSAN: I could not help it, I did all I could—but you knows I would not let you be sent to the Dey, I have kept you in my own house, at mine own expence, [*aside*] for which I have been more than doubly paid.

REBECCA: That is indeed true, but I cannot at present return your kindness.

BEN HASSAN: Ah! You be very sly rogue—you pretend not to know how I loves you.

REBECCA: [*Aside.*] What means the wretch.

BEN HASSAN: You shou'd forget your Christian friends, for I dare say they have forgot you.—I vill make you my vife, I vill give you von, two, tree slaves to vait on you.

REBECCA: Make me your wife! why, are you not already married?

BEN HASSAN: Ish, but our law gives us great many vives,—our law gives liberty in love; you are an American and you must love liberty.

REBECCA: Hold, Hassan; prostitute not the sacred word by applying it to licentiousness; the sons and daughters of liberty, take justice, truth, and mercy, for their leaders, when they list under her glorious banners.

BEN HASSAN: Your friends will never ransom you.

REBECCA: How readily does the sordid mind judge of others by its own contracted feelings; you who much I fear, worship no deity but gold, who could sacrifice friendship, nay, even the ties of nature at the shrine of your idolatry, think other hearts as selfish as your own;—but there are souls to whom the afflicted never cry in vain, who, to dry the widow's tears, or free the captive, would share their last possession.—Blest spirits of philanthropy, who inhabit my native land, never will I doubt your friendship, for sure I am, you never will neglect the wretched.

BEN HASSAN: If you are not ransomed soon, I must send you to the Dey.

REBECCA: E'en as you please, I cannot be more wretched than I am; but of this be assured; however depressed in fortune, however sunk in adversity, the soul secure in its own integrity will rise superior to its enemies, and scorn the venal wretch, who barters truth for gold.

[*Exit.*]

BEN HASSAN [*Solus*]: 'Tis a very strange woman, very strange indeed; she does not know I got her pocket-book, with bills of exchange in it; she thinks I keep her in my house out of charity, and yet she talks about freedom and superiority, as if she was in her own country. 'Tis dev'lish hard indeed, when masters may not do what they please with their slaves. Her ransom arrived yesterday, but den she don't know it—Yesh, here is the letter; ransom for Rebecca Constant, and six other Christian slaves; vell I vill make her write for more, she is my slave, I must get all I can by her. Oh, here comes that wild young Christian, Frederic, who ransom'd himself a few days since.

[*Enter* FREDERIC.]

FREDERIC: Well, my little Israelite, what are you muttering about; have you thought on my proposals, will you purchase the vessel and assist us?

BEN HASSAN: What did you say you wou'd give me?

FREDERIC: We can amongst us, muster up two thousand sequins, 'tis all we have in the world.

BEN HASSAN: You are sure you can get no more?

FREDERIC: Not a farthing more.

BEN HASSAN: Den I vill be satisfied with dat, it will in some measure reward me—[*aside*] for betraying you.

FREDERIC: And you will purchase the vessel.

BEN HASSAN: I will do everything that is necessary—[*aside*] for my own interest.

FREDERIC: You have convey'd provision to the cavern by the sea side, where I am to conceal the captives, to wait the arrival of the vessel.

BEN HASSAN: Most shartingly, I have provided for them as—[*aside*] as secure a prison as any in Algiers.

FREDERIC: But, are you not a most extortionate old rogue, to require so much, before you will assist a parcel of poor devils to obtain their liberty.

BEN HASSAN: Oh! Mr. Frederic, if I vash not your very good friend, I could not do it for so little; the Moors are such uncharitable dogs, they never think they can get enough for their slaves, but I have a vast deal of compassion; I feels very mush for the poor Christians; I should be very glad [*aside*] to have a hundred or two of them my prisoners.

FREDERIC: You would be glad to serve us?

BEN HASSAN: Shartingly. [*Aside.*] Ven I can serve myself at the same time.

FREDERIC: Prithee, honest Hassan, how came you to put on the turban?

BEN HASSAN: I'll tell you.

SONG[1]

Ven I was a mighty little boy,
    Heart-cakes I sold and pepper-mint drops;
Wafers and sweet chalk I used for to cry,
    Alacumpaine and nice lolly-pops,
The next thing I sold vas the rollers for the macs
    To curl dere hair, 'twas very good;
Rosin I painted for sealing wax
    And I forg'd upon it vel brand en vast houd.

1   This song was not written by Mrs. Rowson. (Author's note.)

Next to try my luck in the alley I vent,
  But of dat I soon grew tired and wiser;
Monies I lent out at fifty percent,
  And my name was I.H. in the Public Advertiser.

The next thing I did was a spirited prank,
  Which at one stroke my fortune was made;
I wrote so very like the cashiers of the bank,
  The clerks did not know the difference, and the monies was paid.

So, having cheated the Gentiles, as Moses commanded,
  Oh! I began to tremble at every gibbet that I saw;
But I got on board a ship, and here was safely landed,
  In spite of the judges, counselors, attorneys, and law.

FREDERIC: And so to complete the whole, you turn'd Mahometan.

BEN HASSAN: Oh 'twas the safest way.

FREDERIC: But Hassan, as you are so fond of cheating the Gentiles, perhaps you may cheat us.

BEN HASSAN: Oh no! I swear by Mahomet.

FREDERIC: No swearing, old Trimmer, if you are true to us you will be amply rewarded, should you betray us [*sternly*] by heaven you shall not live an hour after.—Go, look for a vessel, make every necessary preparation; and remember, instant death shall await the least appearance of treachery.

BEN HASSAN: But I have not got monies.

FREDERIC: Go, you are a hypocrite, you are rich enough to purchase an hundred vessels, and if the Dey knew of your wealth—

BEN HASSAN: Oh! Dear Mr. Frederic, indeed I am very poor, but I will do all you desire, and you will pay me afterwards. [*Aside.*]—Oh, I wish I could get you well paid with the bastinado.

[*Exit.*]

FREDERIC: I will trust this fellow no farther, I am afraid he will play us false—but should he, we have yet one resource, we can but die; and to die, in a struggle for freedom, is better far than to live in ignominious bondage.

[*Exit.*]

SCENE III

[*Another Apartment at the Dey's.* ZORIANA and OLIVIA.]

ZORIANA: Alas! It was pitiful, pray proceed.

OLIVIA: My father's ill health obliging him to visit Lisbon we embarked for that place, leaving my betrothed lover to follow us—but e'er we reached our destined port, we were captured by an Algerine corsair, and I was immediately sent to the Dey, your father.

ZORIANA: I was then in the country, but I was told he became enamoured of you.

OLIVIA: Unfortunately he did; but my being a Christian has hitherto preserved me from improper solicitations, tho' I am frequently pressed to abuse my religion.

ZORIANA: Were you not once near making your escape.

OLIVIA: We were; my father, by means of some jewels which he had concealed in his cloaths, bribed one of the guards to procure false keys to the apartments, but on the very night when we meant to put our plan in execution, the Dey, coming suddenly into the room, surprised my father in my arms.

ZORIANA: Was not his anger dreadful?

OLIVIA: Past description; my dear father was torn from me and loaded with chains, thrown into a dungeon, where he still remains, secluded from the cheering light of heaven; no resting place but on the cold, damp ground; the daily portion of his food so poor and scanty, it hardly serves to eke out an existence, lingering as it is forlorn.

ZORIANA: And where are the false keys?

OLIVIA: I have them still, for I was not known to possess them.

ZORIANA: Then banish all your sorrow; if you have still the keys, to-morrow night shall set us all at liberty.

OLIVIA: Madam!

ZORIANA: Be not alarmed sweet Olivia, I am a Christian in my heart, and I love a Christian slave, to whom I have conveyed money and jewels, sufficient to ransom himself and several others; I will appoint him to be in the garden this evening, you shall go with me and speak to him.

OLIVIA: But how can we release my father.

ZORIANA: Every method shall be tried to gain admittance to his prison; the Christian has many friends, and if all other means fail, they can force the door.

OLIVIA: Oh! heavens, could I but see him once more at liberty, how gladly would I sacrifice my own life to secure his.

ZORIANA: The keys you have will let us out of the house when all are lock'd in the embrace of sleep; our Christian friends will be ready to receive us, and before morning we shall be in a place of safety; in the mean time, let hope support your sinking spirits.

SONG

Sweet cherub clad in robes of white,
  Descend celestial Hope;
And on the pinions, soft and light,
  Oh bear thy votary up.
'Tis thou can sooth the troubled breast,
  The tear of furrow dry;
Can'st lull each doubt and fear to rest,
  And check the rising sigh.
Sweet cherub &c.

[*Exeunt.*]

SCENE IV

[A Garden—Outside of a house, with small high lattices. HENRY *and* FREDERIC.]

FREDERIC: Fearing the old fellow would pocket our cash and betray us afterwards, I changed my plan, and have entrusted the money with a Spaniard, who will make the best bargain he can for us; have you tried our friends, will they be staunch?

HENRY: To a man; the hope of liberty, like an electric spark, ran instantly through every heart, kindling a flame of patriotic ardour. Nay, even those whom interest or fear have hitherto kept silent, now openly avowed their hatred of the Dey, and swore to assist our purpose.

FREDERIC: Those whose freedom we have already purchased, have concerted proper measures for liberating many others and by twelve o'clock tomorrow night, we shall have a party large enough to surround the palace of the Dey, and covey from thence in safety the fair Zoriana. [*Window opens and a white handkerchief is waved.*]

HENRY: Soft;—behold the signal of love and peace.

FREDERIC: I'll catch it as it falls. [*He approaches, it is drawn back.*]

HENRY: 'Tis not design'd for you, stand aside. [HENRY *approaching; the handkerchief is let fall, a hand waved, and then the lattice shut.*] 'Tis a wealthy fall, and worth receiving.

FREDERIC: What says the fair Mahometan?

HENRY: Can I believe my eyes; here are English characters; and, but I think 'tis impossible, I should say, this was my Olivia's writing.

FREDERIC: This is always the way with you happy fellows, who are favourites with the women; you slight the willing fair one, and dote on those who are only to be obtained with difficulty.

HENRY: I wish the lovely Moor had fixed her affections on you instead of me.

FREDERIC: I wish she had with all my soul—Moor or Christian, slave or free woman, 'tis no matter; if she was but young, and in love with me, I'd kneel down and worship her. But I'm a poor miserable dog, the women never say civil things to me.

HENRY: But, do you think it can be possible that my adorable Olivia is a captive here?

FREDERIC: Prithee man, don't stand musing and wondering, but remember this is the time for action. If chance has made your Olivia a captive, why, we must make a bold attempt to set her at liberty, and then I suppose you will turn over the fair Moriscan to me. But what says the letter.

HENRY: [*Reads.*] "As you have now the means of freedom in your power, be at the north garden gate at ten o'clock, and when you hear me sing, you will be sure all is safe, and that you may enter without danger; do not fail to come, I have some pleasant intelligence to communicate." Yes, I will go and acquaint her with the real state of my heart.

FREDERIC: And so make her our enemy.

HENRY: It would be barbarous to impose on her generous nature.—What?—avail myself of her liberality to obtain my own freedom; take her from her country and friends, and then sacrifice her a victim to ingratitude, and disappointed love.

FREDERIC: Tush, man, women's hearts are not so easily broken, we may, perhaps give them a slight wound now and then, but they are seldom or never incurable.

HENRY: I see our master coming this way; begone to our friends; encourage them to go through with our enterprise: the moment I am released I will join you.

FREDERIC: 'Till when adieu.

[*Exeunt severally.*]

ACT II, SCENE I

[*Moonlight—A Garden.* ZORIANA *and* OLIVIA.]

ZORIANA: Sweet Olivia, chide me not; for tho' I'm fixed to leave this place, and embrace Christianity, I cannot but weep when I think what my poor father will suffer. Methinks I should stay to console him for the loss of you.

OLIVIA: He will soon forget me; has he not already a number of beautiful slaves, who have been purchased, to banish me from his remembrance.

ZORIANA: True, but he slights them all; you only, are the mistress of his heart.

OLIVIA: Hark, did you not hear a footstep?

ZORIANA: Perhaps it is the young Christian, he waits the appointed signal; I think all is safe, he may approach.

SONG

Wrap't in the evening's soft and pensive shade,
    When passing zephyrs scarce the herbage moves;
Here waits a trembling, fond, and anxious maid,
    Expecting to behold the youth she loves.
Tho' Philomela on a neighbouring tree,
    Melodious warbles forth her nightly strain;
Thy accents would be sweeter far to me,
    Would from my bosom banish doubt and pain.
Then come dear youth, come haste away,
    Haste to this silent grove,
The signal's given, you must obey,
    'Tis liberty and love.

[*Enter* HENRY.]

HENRY: Lovely and benevolent lady, permit me thus humbly to thank you for my freedom.

OLIVIA: Oh Heavens, that voice!

ZORIANA: Gentle Christian, perhaps I have over-stepped the bounds prescribed my sex. I was early taught a love of Christianity, but I must now confess, my actions are impelled by a tenderer passion.

HENRY: That passion which you have so generously avowed, has excited my utmost gratitude, and I only wish for power to convince you, how much you have bound me to your service.

OLIVIA: Oh! [*Faints.*]

ZORIANA: What ails my friend, help me to support her; she is an amiable creature, and will accompany us in our flight.

ZORIANA: She revives; how are you?—Speak, my Olivia.

HENRY: Olivia, did you say?

OLIVIA: Yes; Henry, your forsaken Olivia.

HENRY: Oh my beloved! is it possible that I see you here in bondage; where is your father?

OLIVIA: In bondage too—but, Henry, you had forgot me; you could renounce your vows and wed another.

HENRY: Oh no; never for one moment has my thoughts strayed from my Olivia—I never regretted slavery, but as it deprived me of your sweet converse, nor wished for freedom, but to ratify my vows to you.

ZORIANA: [*Aside.*] How? mutual lovers! My disappointed heart beats high with resentment, but in vain; I wish to be a Christian, and I will, tho' my heart breaks, perform a Christian's duty.

HENRY: Pardon, beauteous lady, an involuntary error. I have long loved this Christian maid; we are betrothed to each other. This evening I obey'd your summons, to inform you, that grateful thanks and fervent prayers, were all the return I could make for the unmerited kindness you have shown me.

OLIVIA: Generous Zoriana, blame not my Henry.

ZORIANA: Think not so meanly of me, as to suppose I live but for myself—that I loved your Henry, I can without a blush avow, but 'twas a love so pure, that to see him happy will gratify my utmost wish; I still rejoice that I've procured his liberty, you shall with him, embrace the opportunity, and be henceforth as blest—[*aside*] as I am wretched.

HENRY: You will go with us.

ZORIANA: Perhaps I may—but let us now separate;—to morrow, from the lattice, you shall receive instructions how to proceed: in the mean time here is more gold and jewels. I never knew the value, till I found they could ransom you from slavery.

33

HENRY: Words are poor.

ZORIANA: Leave us, my heart's oppress'd, I wish to be alone; doubt not the safety of your Olivia; she must be safe with me, for she is dear to you.

[HENRY *kisses her hand, bows and exits.—They stand sometime without speaking.*]

ZORIANA: Olivia!

OLIVIA: Madam!

ZORIANA: Why are you silent, do you doubt my sincerity!

OLIVIA: Oh no—but I was thinking, if we should fail in our attempt; if we should be taken.

ZORIANA: Gracious heaven forbid!

OLIVIA: Who then could deprecate your father's wrath. Yourself, my Henry, and my, dearest father, all, all, would fall a sacrifice.

ZORIANA: These are groundless fears.

OLIVIA: Perhaps they are; but yet, I am resolved to stay behind.

ZORIANA: Do not think of it.

OLIVIA: Forgive me; I am determined, and that so firmly, it will be in vain to oppose me.—If you escape—the Power who protects you, will also give me the means of following; should you be taken, I may perhaps move the Dey to forgive you, and even should my prayers and tears have no effect, my life shall pay the forfeiture of yours.

ZORIANA: I will not go.

OLIVIA: Yes, gentle lady, yes; you must go with them; perhaps you think it will be a painful task to meet your father's anger; but indeed it will not; the thought of standing forth the preserver of the dear author of my being, of the man who loves me next to heaven, of the friend who could sacrifice her own happiness to mine, would fill my soul with such delight, that even death, in its most horrid shape, could not disturb its tranquility.

ZORIANA: But, can you suppose your father, and your lover,

OLIVIA: You must assist my design, you must tell them I am already at liberty, and in a place of safety; when they discover the deception, be it your task, my gentle Zoriana, to wipe the tear of sorrow from their eyes. Be a daughter to my poor father, comfort his age, be kind and tender to him, let him not feel the loss of his Olivia. Be to my Henry, (Oh! my bursting heart) a friend, to sooth in his deep affliction; poor consolation on his wounded mind, and love him if you can, as I have done.

[*Exeunt.*]

SCENE II

[*Dawn of day—another part of the garden—with an alcove.*]

[*Enter* FREDERIC.]

FREDERIC: What a poor unfortunate dog I am; last night I slipped into the garden behind Henry, in hopes I should find some distressed damsel, who wanted a knight-errant, to deliver her from captivity; and here have I wandered through windings, turnings, alleys and labyrinths, till the Devil himself could not find the way out again: some one approaches—by all that's lovely 'tis a woman—young, and handsome too, health glows upon her cheek, and good humour sparkles in her eye;—I'll conceal myself that I may not alarm her.

[*Exit into the alcove.*]

[*Enter* FETNAH.]

SONG

Aurora, lovely blooming fair,
    Unbarr'd the eaten skies;
While many a soft pellucid tear,
    Ran trickling from her eyes.
Onward she came, with heart-felt glee,

> Leading the dancing hours;
> For tho' she wept, she smil'd to see,
> Her tears refresh the flowers.
> Phoebus, who long, her charms admir'd,
> With bright refulgent ray;
> Came forth, and as the maid retir'd,
> He kiss'd her tears away.

What a sweet morning, I could not sleep, so the moment the doors were open, I came out to try and amuse myself.—'Tis a delightful garden, but I believe I should hate the finest place in the world, if I was obliged to stay in it, whether I would or no. If I am forced to remain here much longer, I shall fret myself as old and as ugly as Mustapha. That's no matter, there's nobody here to look at one, but great, black, goggle-ey'd creatures, that are posted here and there to watch us. And when one speaks to them, they shake their frightful heads, and make such a horrid noise—lord, I wish I could run away, but that's impossible; there is no getting over these nasty high walls. I do wish, some dear, sweet, Christian man, would fall in love with me, break open the garden gates, and carry me off.

FREDERIC: [*Stealing out.*] Say you so my charmer, then I'm your man.

FETNAH: And take me to that charming place, where there are no bolts and bars; no mutes and guards; no bowstrings and seymetars.—Oh! It must be a dear delightful country, where women do just what they please.

FREDERIC: I'm sure you are a dear, delightful creature.

FETNAH: [*Turning, sees him and shrieks.*]

FREDERIC: Hush, my sweet little infidel, or we shall be discovered.

FETNAH: Why, who are you; and how came you here?

FREDERIC: I am a poor forlorn fellow, beautiful creature, over head and ears in love with you, and I came here, to tell you how much I adore you.

FETNAH: [*Aside.*] Oh dear! What a charming man. I do wish he would run away with me.

FREDERIC: Perhaps this is the lady who wrote to Henry, she looks like a woman of quality, if I may judge from her dress. I'll ask her.—You wish to leave this country, lovely Moor?

FETNAH: Lord, I'm not a Moriscan; I hate 'em all, there is nothing I wish so much as to get away from them.

FEDERIC: Your letters said so.

FETNAH: Letters!

FEDERIC: Yes, the letters you dropped from the window upon the terrace.

FETNAH: [*Aside.*] He takes me for some other. I'll not undeceive him, and may be, he'll carry off.—Yes, sir; yes, I did write to you.

FEDERIC: To me!

FETNAH: To be sure; did you think it was to any body else?

FEDERIC: Why, there has been a small mistake.

FETNAH: [*Aside.*] And there's like to be a greater if you knew all.

FEDERIC: And, do you indeed love me?

FETNAH: Yes, I do, better than anybody I ever saw in my life.

FEDERIC: And if I can get you out of the palace, you will go away with me?

FETNAH: To be sure I will, that's the very thing I wish.

FEDERIC: Oh! Thou sweet, bewitching, little—[*Catching her in his arms.*]

MULEY MOLOC: [*Without.*] Tell him, Fetnah shall be sent home to him immediately.

FETNAH: Oh lord! what will become of us? That's my lord the Dey—you'll certainly be taken.

FEDERIC: Yes, I feel the bowstring round my neck already; what shall I do—where shall I hide.

FETNAH: Stay, don't be frightened—I'll bring you off; catch me in your arms again.

[*She throws herself in his arms as tho' fainting.*]

[*Enter* MULEY *and* MUSTAPHA.]

37

MULEY: I tell thee, Mustapha, I cannot banish the beautiful Christian one moment from my thoughts. The women seem all determined to perplex me; I was pleased with the beauty of Fetnah, but her childish caprice.—

MUSTAPHA: Behold, my lord, the fair slave you mention, in the arms of a stranger.

FEDERIC: [*Aside.*] Now, goodbye to poor Pil-garlick.

FETNAH: [*Pretending to recover.*] Are they gone, and am I safe.—Oh! courteous stranger, when the Dey my master knows—

MULEY: What's the matter Fetnah; who is this slave?

FETNAH: [*Kneeling.*] Oh mighty prince, this stranger has preserved me from the greatest outrage.

MULEY: What outrage?

FETNAH: Now, do not look angry at your poor little slave, who knowing she had offended you, could not rest, and came early into the garden, to lament her folly.

FEDERIC: [*Aside.*] Well said, woman.

MULEY: Rise, Fetnah; we have forgot your rashness—proceed.

FETNAH: So, I was sitting, melancholy and sad, in the alcove, I heard a great noise, and presently, four or five Turks leap'd over the wall, and began to plunder the garden; I screamed; did not you hear me Mustapha?

FEDERIC: [*Aside.*] Well said, again.

FETNAH: But, the moment they saw me, they seized me, and would have forced me away, had not this gallant stranger run to my assistance—they, thinking they were pursued by many, relinquished their hold, and left me fainting in the stranger's arms.

MULEY: 'Tis well.

MUSTAPHA: But, gracious Sir, how came the stranger here?

FEDERIC: [*Aside.*] Oh! Confound your inquisitive tongue.

MULEY: Aye, Christian; how came you in this garden?

FETNAH: He came from my father. Did not you say my father sent you here?

FEDERIC:—[*Aside.*] [*Bows.*]—Now, who the devil is her father?

FETNAH: He came to beg leave to gather some herbs for a salad, while they were still fresh with morning dew.

FREDERIC: [*Aside.*] Heaven bless her invention!

MULEY: Go to your apartment.

FETNAH: Oh dear! if he should ask him any questions when I am gone, what will become of him.

[*Exit.*]

MULEY: Christian, gather the herbs you came for, and depart in peace.—Mustapha, go to my daughter Zoriana; tell her I'll visit her some two hours hence, 'till when, I'll walk in the refreshing morning air.

[*Exit* MULEY *and* MUSTAPHA.]

FREDERIC: [*Solus.*] Thanks to dear little infidel's ready wit; I breath again—Good Mr. Whiskers I am obliged by your dismission of me—I will depart as fast as I can; and yet I cannot but regret leaving my lovely little Moor behind—who comes here—the apostate Hassan.—Now could I swear some mischief was a foot.—I'll keep out of sight and try to learn his business.

[*Retires.*]

[*Enter* BEN HASSAN *and* MUSTAPHA.]

BEN HASSAN: Indeed, I am vashtly sorry that my daughter has offended my good lord the Dey; but if he will admit me to his sublime presence, I can give him intelligence of so important a nature, as I makes no doubt, will incline him to pardon her, for my sake.

MUSTAPHA: I will tell him you wait his leisure.

[*Exit.*]

FREDERIC: The traitor is on the point of betraying us.—I must if possible prevent his seeing the Dey. [*Runs to* BEN HASSAN *with all the appearance of violent terror.*] Oh! my dear friend Hassan, for heaven's sake what brought you here; don't you know the Dey is so highly offended with you, that he vows to have you impaled alive.

BEN HASSAN: Oh dear! Mr. Frederic, how did you know.

FREDERIC: It was by the luckiest chance in the world; I happened to be in this garden, when I overheard a slave of yours informing the Dey, that you had not only amassed immense riches, which you intended to carry out of his territories; but, that you had many valuable slaves, which you kept concealed from him, that you might reap the benefit of their ransom.

BEN HASSAN: Oh, what will become of me!—but, come, come; Mr. Frederic, you only say this to frighten me.

FREDERIC: Well, you'll see that; for I heard him command his guards to be ready to seize you, when he gave the signal, as he expected you here every moment.

BEN HASSAN: Oh! What shall I do?

FEDERIC: If you stay here, you will certainly be bastinadoed—impaled—burnt.

BEN HASSAN: Oh dear! Oh dear!

FEDERIC: Make haste my dear friend; run home as fast as possible; hide your treasure, and keep out of the way.

BEN HASSAN: Oh dear! I wish I was safe in Dukes place. [*Exit.*]

FEDERIC: Let me but get you once safe into your house, and I'll prevent your betraying us I'll warrant. [*Exit.*]

[*Fetnah's Apartment.*]

[FETNAH *and* SELIMA.]

FETNAH: Now will you pretend to say, you are happy here, and that you love the Dey.

SELIMA: I have been here many years; the Dey has been very good to me, and my chief employment has been to wait on his daughter, Zoriana, till I was appointed to attend you, to you perhaps, he may be an object of disgust; but looking up to him, as a kind and generous master, to me he appears amiable.

FETNAH: Oh! To be sure, he is a most amiable creature; I think I see him now, seated on his cushion, a bowl of sherbet by his side, and a long pipe in his mouth. Oh! how charmingly the tobacco must perfume his whiskers—here, Mustapha, says he,

"Go bid the slave Selima come to me"—well it does not signify, that word slave does so stick in my throat—I wonder how any woman of spirit can gulp it down.

SELIMA: We are accustomed to it.

FETNAH: The more's the pity: for how sadly depressed must the soul be, to whom custom has rendered bondage supportable.

SELIMA: Then, if opportunity offered, you would leave Algiers.

FETNAH: That I would, most cheerfully.

SELIMA: And perhaps, bestow your affections on some young Christian.

FETNAH: That you may be sure of; for say what you will, I am sure the woman must be blind and stupid, who would not prefer a young, handsome, good humoured Christian, to an old, ugly, ill natured Turk.

[*Enter* SADI—*with robe, turban, etc.*]

FETNAH: Well, what's your business?

SADI: I—I—I—I'm afraid I'm wrong.

SELIMA: Who sent you here?

SADI: I was told to take these to our master's son, young Soliman. But some how, in the turnings and windings in this great house, I believe I have lost myself.

SELIMA: You have mistaken—

FETNAH: Mistaken—no, he is very right; here give me the cloaths, I'll take care of them, [*takes them*] there, there, go about your business, it's all very well.—[*Exit* SADI.] Now, Selima, I'll tell you what I'll do; I'll put these on—go to the Dey, and see if he will know me.

SELIMA: He'll be angry.

FETNAH: Pshaw! you're so fearful of his anger, if you let the men see you are afraid of them, they'll hector and domineer finely, no, no, let them think you don't care whether they are pleased or no, and then they'll be as condescending and humble.—Go, go—take the cloaths into the next apartment. [*Exit* SELIMA.] Now. If by means of these cloaths, I can get out of the palace, I'll seek the charming young Christian I saw this morning, we'll get my dear instructress from my fathers, and fly together, from this land of captivity to the regions of Peace and Liberty.

End of the Second Act

ACT III, SCENE I

[*A kind of Grotto.* FREDERIC, HENRY, SEBASTIAN, *and* SLAVES.]

SEBASTIAN: Now, if you had trusted me, at first, I'll answer for it, I had got you all safe out; aye, and that dear sweet creature, madam Zoriana too—what a pity it is she's Mahometan, your true bred Mahometans never drink any wine—now, for my part, I like a drop of good liquor, it makes a body feel so comfortable, so—so, I don't know howish, as if they were friends with all the world—I always keep a friend or two hid here, [*takes out some bottles*] mum, don't be afraid, they are no tell tales—only when they are trusted too far.

FREDERIC: Well, Sebastian, don't be too unguarded in trusting these very good friends to night.

SEBASTIAN: Never fear me; did not I tell you I'd show you a place of safety;—well, havn't I perform'd my promise:—When I first discovered this cave, or cavern, or grotto, or cell, or whatever your fine spoken folks may call it; this, said I, would be a good place to hide people in;—so I never told my master.

HENRY: This fellow will do some mischief, with his nonsensical prate.

FREDERIC: I don't fear him, he has an honest heart, hid under appearance of ignorance, it grows duskish, Sebastian, have we good centinals placed at the entrance of this cell?

SEBASTIAN: Good centinals! Why do you suppose I would trust any with that post but those I could depend on?

HENRY: Two hours past midnight we must invest the garden of the Dey; I have here a letter from Zoriana, which says, she will, at that time be ready to join us—and lead us to the prison of my Olivia's father; Olivia is by some means already at liberty.

CENTINEL: [*Without.*] You must not not pass.

FETNAH: No—but I must, I have business.

SEBASTIAN: What, what, what's all this?

[*Exit.*]

FETNAH: Nay, for pity's sake, don't kill me. [*Re-enter* SEBASTIAN, *forcing in* FETNAH *habited like a boy.*]

SEBASTIAN: No, no, we wont kill you, we'll only make you a slave, and you know that's nothing.

FETNAH: [*Aside.*] There is my dear Christian, but I won't discover myself, till I try if he will know me.

HENRY: Who are you, young man, and for what purpose were you loitering about this place.

FETNAH: I am Soliman, son to the Dey, and I heard by chance that a band of slaves had laid a plot to invest the palace, and so I traced some of them to this cell, and was just going—

FIRST SLAVE: To betray us.

SECOND SLAVE: Let us dispatch him, and instantly disperse till the appointed hour.

SEVERAL SLAVES: Aye, let us kill him.

HENRY: Hold; why should we harm this innocent youth.

FIRST SLAVES: He would be the means of our suffering most cruel tortures.

HENRY: True, but he is now in our power; young, innocent, and unprotected. Oh my friends! let us not, on this auspicious night, when we hope to emancipate ourselves from slavery, tinge the bright standard of liberty with blood.

SLAVES: 'Tis necessary; our safety demands it.

[*They rush on* FETNAH, *in her struggle her turban falls off—she breaks from them, and runs to* FREDERIC.]

FETNAH: Save me, dear Christian! its only poor little Fetnah.

FREDERIC: Save you my sweet little Infidel—why, I'll impale the wretch, who should move but a finger against you.

43

SEBASTIAN: Oh! Oh! A mighty pretty boy to be sure.

FREDERIC: But tell me—how got you out of the palace, and how did you discover us.

FETNAH: I have not time now, but this I will assure you, I came with a full intention to go with you, if you will take me, the whole world over.

FREDERIC: Can you doubt—

FETNAH: Doubt, not to be sure I don't, but you must comply with one request, before we depart.

FREDERIC: Name it.

FETNAH: I have a dear friend, who is a captive at my father's; she must be released, or Fetnah cannot be happy, even with the man she loves. [*Draws aside, and confers with* HENRY.]

SEBASTIAN: Well, here am I, Sebastian; who have been a slave, two years, six months, a fortnight and three days and have, all that time worked in the garden of the Alcaide, who has twelve wives, thirty concubinus, and two pretty daughters; and yet not one of the insensible husseys ever took a fancy to me.—'Tis dev'lish hard—that when I go home, I can't say to my honoured father, the barber, and to my reverend mother, the laundress—this is the beautiful princess, who fell in love with me; jumped over the garden wall of his serene holiness her father, and ran away with your dutiful son, Sebastian—then, falling on my knees—thus.

HENRY: What's the matter, Sebastian? There is no danger, don't be afraid, man.

FREDRIC: Sebastian, you must take a party of our friends, go to the house of Ben Hassan, and bring from thence an American lady. I have good reason to think you will meet with no opposition; she may be at first unwilling to come, but tell her—friends and countrymen await her here.

FETNAH: Tell her, her own Fetnah expects her.

FREDERIC: Treat her with all imaginable respect:—Go, my good Sebastian; be diligent, silent, and expeditious. You, my dear Fetnah, I will place in an inner part of the grotto, where you will be safe, while we effect the escape of Olivia's father.

FETNAH: What, shut me up!—Do you take me for a coward?

HENRY: We respect you as a woman, and would shield you from danger.

FETNAH: A woman!—Why, so I am; but in the cause of love or friendship, a woman can face danger with as much spirit, and as little fear, as the bravest man amongst you.—Do you lead the way, I'll follow to the end. [*Exit* FETNAH, FREDERIC, HENRY, *etc.*]

SEBASTIAN: [*Solus.*] Bravo! Excellent! Bravissimo!—Why, 'tis a little body; but ecod, she's a devil of a spirit.—It's a fine thing to meet with a woman that has a little fire in her composition. I never much liked your milk-and-water ladies; to be sure, they are easily managed—but your spirited lasses require taming; they make a man look about him—dear, sweet, angry creature, here's their health. This is the summum-bonum of all good:—If they are kind, this, this, makes them appear angels and goddesses:—If they are fancy, why then, here, here, in this we'll drown the remembrance of the bewitching, froward, little devils—in all kind of difficulties and vexations, nothing helps the invention, or cheers the courage, like a drop from the jorum.

SONG

When I was a poor, little innocent boy,
    About sixteen or eighteen years old;
At Susan and Marian I cast a sheep's eye,
    But Susan was saucy and Marian was shy;
So I flirted with Flora, with Cecily and Di,
    But they too, were frumpish and cold.
Says Diego, one day, what ails you I pray?
    I fetch'd a deep sigh—Diego, says I,
Women hate me.—Oh! how I adore 'em.
    Pho; nonsense, said he, never mind it my lad.
Hate you, then hate them boy, come, never be sad,
    Here, take a good sup of the jorum.

If they're foolish and mulish, refuse you, abuse you,
    No longer pursue,
They'll soon buckle too
    When they find they're neglected,
Old maids, unprotected,
    Ah! then 'tis their turn to woo;
But bid them defiance, and form an alliance,
    With the mirth-giving, care-killing jorum.

I took his advice, but was sent to the war,
    And soon I was call'd out to battle;
I heard the drums beat, Oh! How great was my fear,
    I wish'd myself sticking, aye, up to each ear
In a horse-pond—and skulk'd away into the rear.
    When the cannon and bombs 'gan to rattle,
Said I to myself, you're damn'd foolish elf,
    Sebastian keep up, then I took a good sup.
Turkish villains, shall we fly before 'em;
    What, give it up tamely and yield ourselves slaves,
To a pack of rabscallions, vile infidel knaves,
    Then I kiss'd the sweet lips of my jorum.

No, hang 'em, we'll bang 'em, and rout 'em, and scout 'em.
    If we but persue,
They must buckle too;
    Ah! Then without wonder,
I heard the loud thunder,
    Of cannon and musquetry too.
But bid them defiance, being firm in alliance,
    With the courage-inspiring jorum.

[*Exit.*]

SCENE II

[*Ben Hassan's House.* REBECCA *and* AUGUSTUS.]

AUGUSTUS: Dear mother, don't look so sorrowful; my master is not very hard with me. Do pray be happy.

REBECCA: Alas! My dear Augustus, can I be happy while you are a slave? My own bondage is nothing—but you, my child.

AUGUSTUS: Nay, mother, don't mind it; I am but a boy you know.—If I was a man—

REBECCA: What would you do my love?

AUGUSTUS: I'd stamp beneath my feet, the wretch that would enslave my mother.

REBECCA: There burst forth the scared flame which heaven itself fixed in the human mind; Oh! my brave boy, [*embracing him*] ever may you preserve that independent spirit, that dares assert the rights of the oppressed, by power unawed, unchecked by servile fear.

AUGUSTUS: Fear, mother, what should I be afraid of? an't I an American, and I am sure you have often told me, in a right cause, the Americans did not fear any thing.

[*Enter* HASSAN.]

HASSAN: So, here's a piece of vork; I'se be like to have fine deal of troubles on your account. Oh! that ever I should run the risque of my life by keeping you concealed from the Dey.

REBECCA: If I am a trouble to you, if my being here endangers your life, why do you not send me away?

BEN HASSAN: There be no ships here, for you to go in; besides, who will pay me?

REBEECCA: Indeed, if you send me to my native land, I will faithfully remit to you my ransom; aye, double what you have required.

BEN HASSAN: If I thought I could depend—

[*Enter* SERVANT.]

SERVANT: Sir, your house is is surrounded by arm'd men.

BEN HASSAN: What, Turks?

SERVANT: Slaves, Sir; many of whom I have seen in the train of the Dey.

BEN HASSAN: Vhat do they vant?

SERVANT: One of my companions asked them, and received for answer, they would shew us presently.

SEBASTIAN: [*Without*] Stand away, fellow; I will search the house.

REBECCA: Oh heavens! what will become of me?

BEN HASSAN: What will become of me? Oh! I shall be impaled, burnt, bastinadoed, murdered, where shall I hide, how shall I escape them.—[*Runs thro' a door, as tho' into another apartment.*]

SEBASTIAN—[*without*] This way, friends; this way.

REBECCA: Oh, my child, we are lost!

AUGUSTUS: Don't be frightened, mother, thro' this door is a way into the garden; If I had but a sword, boy as I am, I'd fight for you till I died.

[*Exit with* REBECCA.]

[*Enter* SEBASTIAN *&* Co.]

SEBASTIAN: I thought I heard voices this way; now my friends, the lady we seek, is a most lovely, amiable creature, whom we must accost with respect, and convey hence in safety—she is a woman of family and fortune, and is highly pleased with my person and abilities; let us therefore, search every cranny of the house till we find her; she may not recollect me directly, but never mind, we will carry her away first, and assure her of her safety afterwards; go search the rooms in that wing, I will myself, investigate the apartments on this side. [*Exit* SLAVES.] Well I have made these comrades of mine, believe I am a favoured lover, in pursuit of a kind mistress, that's something for them to talk of; and I believe many a fine gentleman is talked of for love affairs, that has a little foundation; and so one is but talked of, as a brave or gallant man, what signifies whether there is any foundation for it or no;—and yet, hang it, who knows but I may prove it a reality, if I release this lady from captivity, she may cast an eye of affection,—may—why I dare say she will.—I am but poor Sebastian, the barber of Cordova's son, 'tis true; but I am well made, very well made; my leg is not amiss,—then I can make a graceful bow; and as to polite compliments, let me but find her, and I'll shew them what it is to have a pretty person, a graceful air, and a smooth tongue.—But I must search this apartment.

[*Exit.*]

SCENE III

[*Another apartment.*]

[*Enter* BEN HASSAN, *with a petticoat and robe on, a bonnet, and deep veil in his hand.*]

BEN HASSAN: I think now, they will hardly know me, in my vife's cloaths: I could not find a turban, but this head dress of Rebecca's will do better, because it vill hide may face—but, how shall I hide my monies: I've got a vast deal, in bills of exchange and all kind of paper; if I can but get safe off with this book in my pocket. I shall have enough to keep me easy as long as I live. [*Puts it in his pocket and drops it.*] Oh! this is a judgment fallen upon me for betraying the Christians. [*Noise without.*] Oh lord! Here they come. [*Ties on the bonnet, and retires into one corner of the apartment.*]

[*Enter* SEBASTIAN *& Co.*]

SEBASTIAN: There she is, I thought I traced the sweep of her train this way, don't mind her struggles or entreaties, but bring her away.—Don't be alarmed, madam, you will meet with every attention, you will be treated with the greatest respect, and let me whisper to you there is more happiness in store for you, than you can possibly imagine. Friends convey her gently to the appointed place. [*They take up* HASSAN *and carry him off.*]

BEN HASSAN: Oh!—o—o—o!

[*Exit.*]

[*Enter* AUGUSTUS *and* REBECCA.]

AUGUSTUS: See, my dear mother, there is no one here, they are all gone; it was not you, they came to take away.

REBECCA: It is for you, I fear, more than for myself, I do not think you are safe with me, go, my beloved, return to your master.—

AUGUSTUS: What, go and leave my mother, without a protector?

REBECCA: Alas? my love, you are not able to protect yourself—and your staying here, only adds to my distress; leave me for the present; I hope the period is not far off, when we shall never be separated.

AUGUSTUS: Mother! dear mother!—my heart is so big it almost choaks me.—Oh! How I wish I was a man.

[*Exit* AUG.]

REBECCA: [*Solus.*] Heaven guard my precious child—I cannot think him quite safe any where—but with me, his danger would be imminent; the emotions of his heart hang on his tongue; and the least outrage, offered to his mother, he would resent at peril of his life.—My spirits are oppressed—I have a thousand fears for him, and for myself—the house appears deserted—all is silent—what's this [*takes up the pocket-book*] Oh! Heaven! is it possible! bills, to the amount of my own ransom and many others—transporting thought—my son—my darling boy, this would soon emancipate you—here's a letter address'd to me—the money is my own—Oh joy beyond expression! my child will soon be free. I have also the means of cheering many children of affliction, with the blest found of liberty. Hassan, you have dealt unjustly by me, but I forgive you—for, while my own heart o'erflows with gratitude for this unexpected blessing, I will wish every human being as happy as I am this moment.

[*Exit.*]

SCENE IV

[*Dey's Garden.*]

ZORIANA: [*Solus.*] How vain are the resolves, how treacherous the heart of a woman in love; but a few hours since, I thought I could have cheerfully relinquished the hope of having my tenderness returned; and found a relief from my own sorrow, in reflecting on the happiness of Henry and Olivia.—Then why does this selfish heart beat with transport, at the thought of their separation? Poor Olivia—how deep must be her affliction. Ye silent shades, scenes of content and peace, how sad would you appear to the poor wretch, who wander'd here, the victim of despair—but the fond heart, glowing with all the joys of mutual love, delighted views the beauties scattered round, thinks every flower is sweet, and every prospect gay.

SONG

In lowly cot or mossy cell,
    With harmless nymphs and rural swains;
'Tis there contentment loves to dwell,
    'Tis there soft peace and pleasure resigns;
But even there, the heart may prove,
    The pangs of disappointed love.

But softly, hope persuading,
    Forbids me long to mourn;
My tender heart pervading,
    Portends my love's return.

51

> Ah! then how bright and gay,
> > Appears the rural scene,
> More radiant breaks the day,
> > The night is more serene.

[*Enter* HENRY.]

HENRY: Be not alarmed madam. I have ventured here earlier than I intended, to enquire how my Olivia effected her escape.

ZORIANA: This letter will inform you—but early as it is, the palace is wrapped in silence, my father is retired to rest—follow me, and I will conduct you to the old man's prison.

HENRY: Have you the keys?

ZORIANA: I have;—follow in silence, the least alarm would be fatal to our purpose.

[*Exeunt.*]

SCENE V

[*The Grotto again.*]

[SEBASTIAN, *leading in* BEN HASSAN.]

SEBASTIAN: Beautiful creature, don't be uneasy, I have risked my life to procure your liberty, and will at the utmost hazard, convey you to your desired home: but, Oh! most amiable—most divine—most delicate lady, suffer me thus humbly on my knees to confess my adoration of you; to solicit your pity, and—

BEN HASSAN: [*In a feign'd tone.*] I pray tell me why you brought me from the house of the good Ben Hassan, and where you design to take me.

SEBASTIAN: Oh! thou adorable, be not offended at my presumption, but having an opportunity of leaving this place of captivity, I was determined to take you with me, and prevent your falling into the power of the Dey, who would no doubt, be in raptures, should he behold your exquisite beauty.—Sweet innocent

52

charmer permit your slave to remove the envious curtain that shades your enchanting visage.

BEN HASSAN: Oh no! not for the world; I have in consideration of many past offences, resolved to take the veil and hide myself from mankind for ever.

SEBASTIAN: That my dear, sweet creature, would be the highest offence you could commit.—Women were never made, with all their prettiness and softness, and bewitching ways, to be hid from us men, who came into the world for no other purpose, than to see, admire, love and protect them.—Come, I must have a peep under that curtain; I long to see your dear little sparkling eyes, your lovely blooming cheeks—and I am resolved to taste your cherry lips. [*In struggling to kiss him, the bonnet falls off.*] Why, what in the devil's name, have we here?

BEN HASSAN: Only a poor old woman—who has been in captivity—

SEBASTIAN: These fifty years at least, by length of your beard.

FEDERIC: [*without*] Sebastian—bring the lady to the water side, and wait till we join you.

BEN HASSAN: I wish I was in any safe place.

SEBASTIAN: Oh ma'am you are in no danger any where—come make haste.

BEN HASSAN: But give me my veil again, if any one saw my face it would shock me.

SEBASTIAN: And damme, but I think it would shock them—here, take your curtain, tho' I think to be perfectly safe, you had best go barefaced.

BEN HASSAN: If you hurry me I shall faint, consider the delicacy of my nerves.

SEBASTIAN: Come along, there's no time for fainting now.

BEN HASSAN: The respect due—

SEBASTIAN: To old age—I consider it all—you are very respectable— Oh! Sebastian what as cursed ninny you were to make so much fuss about a woman old enough to be your grand-mother.

[*Exeunt.*]

53

SCENE VI

[Inside the Palace. MULEY *and* MUSTAPHA.]

MULEY: Fetnah gone, Zoriana gone, and the fair slave Olivia?

MUSTAPHA: All, dread Sir.

MULEY: Send instantly to the prison of the slave Constant, 'tis he who has again plotted to rob me of Olivia, [*exit* MUSTAPHA.] my daughter too he has seduced from her duty; but he shall not escape my vengeance.

[*Re-enter* MUSTAPHA.]

MUSTAPHA: Some of the fugitives are overtaken, and wait in chains without.

MULEY: Is Zoriana taken?

MUSTAPHA: Your daughter is safe; the old man too is taken; but Fetnah and Olivia have escaped.

MULEY: Bring in the wretches—[HENRY, CONSTANT *and several* SLAVES *brought in chained.*]—Rash old man—how have you dared to tempt your fate again; do you not know the torments that await the Christians, who attempts to rob the haram of a Musselman?

CONSTANT: I know you have the power to end my being—but that's a period I more wish than fear.

MULEY: Where is Olivia?

CONSTANT: Safe I hope, beyond your power. Oh! gracious heaven, protect my darling from this tyrant; and let my life pay the dear purchase of her freedom.

MULEY: Bear them to the torture: who and what am I, that a vile slave dares brave me to my face?

HENRY: Hold off—we know that we must die, and we are prepared to meet our fate, like men: impotent vain boaster, call us not slaves;—you are a slave indeed, to rude ungoverned passion; to pride, to avarice and lawless love;—exhaust your cruelty in finding tortures for us, and we will smiling tell you, the blow that ends our chains, and sets our souls at liberty.

MULEY: Hence take them from my sight;—[*Captives taken off.*]—

devise each means of torture; let them linger—months, years, ages, in their misery.

[*Enter* OLIVIA.]

OLIVIA: Stay, Muley, stay—recall your cruel sentence.

MULEY: Olivia here; is it possible?

OLIVIA: I have never left the palace; those men are innocent, so is your daughter. It is I alone deserve your anger—then on me only let it fall; it was I procured false keys to the apartments, it was I seduced your daughter to our interest; I brib'd the guards, and with entreaty won the young Christian to attempt to free my father; then since I was the cause of their offences, it is fit my life should pay the forfeiture of theirs.

MULEY: Why did you not accompany them?

OLIVIA: Fearing what has happened, I remained, in hopes, by tears and supplications to move you to forgive my father, Oh! Muley, save his life, save all his friends; and if you must have blood, to appease your vengeance, let me alone be the sacrifice.

MULEY: [*Aside.*]—How her softness melts me.—Rise Olivia—you may on easier terms give them both life and freedom.

OLIVIA: No—here I kneel till you recall your order; haste, or it may be too late.

MULEY: Mustapha, go bid them delay the execution.

[*Exit* MUSTAPHA.]

OLIVIA: Now teach me to secure their lives and freedom, and my last breath shall bless you.

MULEY: Renounce your faith—consent to be my wife.—Nay, if you hesitate—

OLIVIA: I do not—give me but an hour to think.

MULEY: Not a moment, determine instantly; your answer gives them liberty or death.

OLIVIA: Then I am resolved. Swear to me, by Mahomet, an oath I know you Musselmen never violate—that the moment I become your wife, my father and his friends are free.

MULEY: By Mahomet I swear, not only to give them life and freedom, but safe conveyance to their desired home.

OLIVIA: I am satisfied;—now leave me to myself a few short moments, that I my calm my agitated spirits, and prepare to meet you in the mosque.

MULEY: Henceforth I live, but to obey you.

[*Exit.*]

OLIVIA: On what a fearful precipice I stand; to go forward is ruin, shame and infamy; to recede is to pronounce sentence of death upon my father, and my adored Henry. Oh insupportable!—there is one way, and only one, by which I can fulfill my promise to the Dey, preserve my friends and not abjure my faith—Source of my being, thou can'st read the heart which thou hast been pleased to try in the school of adversity, pardon the weakness of an erring mortal—if rather than behold a father perish; if rather than devote his friends to death, I cut the thread of my existence, and rush unbidden to thy presence.—Yes, I will to the mosque, perform my promise, preserve the valued lives of those I love; then sink at once into the silent grave, and bury all my sorrows in oblivion.

[*Exit.*]

SCENE VII

[*Another apartment.*]

[*Enter* OLIVIA *with* MULEY MOLOC.]

MULEY: Yes on my life they are free, in a few moments they will be here.

OLIVIA: Spare me the trial; for the whole world I would not see them now, nor would I have them know at what price I have secured their freedom.

[*Enter* HENRY *and* CONSTANT.]

CONSTANT: My child.—

HENRY: My love—

OLIVIA: My Henry—O my dear father?—pray excuse these tears.

[*Enter* MUSTAPHA.]

MUSTAPHA: Great sir, the mosque is prepared, and the priest waits your pleasure.

MULEY: Come, my Olivia.

HENRY: The mosque—the priest—what dreadful sacrifice is then intended.

OLIVIA: Be not alarmed—I must needs attend a solemn rite which gratitude requires—go my dear father—dearest Henry leave me; and be assured, when next you see Olivia, she will be wholly free.

[*Enter* REBECCA.]

REBECCA: Hold for a moment.

MULEY: What means this bold intrusion?

REBECCA: Muley, you see before you a woman unused to forms of state, despising titles: I come to offer ransom for six Christian slaves. Waiting your leisure, I was informed a Christian maid, to save her father's life, meant to devote herself a sacrifice to your embraces. I have the means—make your demand to ransom, and set the maid, with those she loves, at liberty.

MULEY: Her friends are free already;—but for herself she voluntarily remains with me.

REBECCA: Can you unmoved, behold her anguish;—release her Muley—name the sum that will pay her ransom, 'tis yours.

MULEY: Woman, the wealth of Golconda could not pay her ransom; can you imagine that I, whose slave she is; I, who could force her obedience to my will, and yet gave life and freedom to those Christians, to purchase her compliance, would now relinquish her to paltry gold; contemptible idea.—Olivia, I spare you some few moments to your father; take leave of him, and as you part remember his life and liberty depends on you.

[*Exit.*]

REBECCA: Poor girl—what can I do to mitigate your sufferings?

OLIVIA: Nothing—my fate alas! is fixed; but, generous lady—by what name shall we remember you—what nation are you of?

REBECCA: I am an American—but while I only claim kindred with the afflicted, it is of little consequence where I first drew my breath.

CONSTANT: An American—from what state?

REBECCA: New York is my native place; there did I spend the dear delightful days of childhood, and there alas, I drain'd the cup of deep affliction, to the very dregs.

CONSTANT: My heart is strangely interested—dearest lady will you impart to us your tale of sorrow, that we may mourn with one who feels so much for us.

REBECCA: Early in life, while my brave countrymen were struggling for their freedom, it was my fate, to love and be beloved by a young British officer, to whom, tho' strictly forbid by my father, I was privately married.

CONSTANT: Married! say you?

REBECCA: My father soon discovered our union; enraged, he spurned me from him, discarded, cursed me, and for four years I followed my husband's fortune; at length my father relented; on a sick bed he sent for me to attend him; I went taking with me an infant son, leaving my husband, and a lovely girl, then scarcely three years old.—Oh heavens! what sorrows have I known from that unhappy hour. During my absence the armies met—my husband fell—my daughter was torn from me; what then avail'd the wealth my dying father had bequeathed me;—long—long did I lose all sense of my misery, and returning reason shewed me the world only one universal blank. The voice of my darling boy first call'd me to myself, for him I strove to mitigate my sorrow; for his dear sake I have endured life.

CONSTANT: Pray proceed.

REBECCA: About a year since I heard a rumour that my husband was still alive; full of the fond hope of again beholding him, I, with my son embarked for England; but before we reached the coast we were captured by an Algerine.

CONSTANT: Do you think you should recollect your husband.

REBECCA: I think I should—but fourteen years of deep affliction has impaired my memory and may have changed his features.

CONSTANT: What was his name?—Oh! speak it quickly.

REBECCA: His name was Constant—but wherefore—

CONSTANT: It was—it was—Rebecca, don't you know me?

REBECCA: Alas—how you are altered.—Oh! Constant, why have you forsaken me so long?

CONSTANT: In the battle you mention, I was indeed severely wounded, nay, left for dead in the field; there, my faithful servant found me, when some remaining signs of life encourag'd him to attempt my recover, and by his unremitting care I was at length restored; my first returning thought was fixed of my Rebecca, but after repeated enquiries all I could hear was that your father was dead and yourself and child removed farther from the seat of war. Soon after, I was told you had fallen a martyr to grief for my supposed loss.—But see my love, our daughter, our dear Olivia; heaven preserved her to be my comforter.

OLIVIA: [*Kneeling and kissing* REBECCA.] My mother, blessed word; Oh! do I live to say I have a mother.

REBECCA: Bless you my child, my charming duteous girl; but tell me, by what sad chance you became captives?

CONSTANT: After peace was proclaimed with America, my duty called me to India, from whence I returned with a ruined constitution. Being advised to try the air of Lisbon, we sailed for that place, but Heaven ordained that here in the land of captivity, I should recover a blessing which will amply repay me for all my past sufferings.

[*Enter* MULEY.]

MULEY: Christians you trifle with me—accept your freedom go in peace, and leave Olivia to perform her promise—for should she waver or draw back—on you I will wreak my vengeance.

REBECCA: Then let your vengeance fall—we will die together; for never shall Olivia, a daughter of Columbia, and a Christian, tarnish her name by apostacy, or live the slave of a despotic tyrant.

MULEY: Then take your wish—who's there?

[*Enter* MUSTAPHA—(*hastily*)]

MUSTAPHA: Arm, mighty sir—the slaves throughout Algiers have mutinied—they bear down all before them—this way they come—they say, if all the Christian slaves are not immediately released, they'll raze the city.

REBECCA: Now! bounteous heaven, protect my darling boy, and aid the cause of freedom.

MULEY: Bear them to instant death.

MUSTAPHA: Dread sir—consider.

MULEY: Vile abject slave obey me and be silent—what have I power over these Christian dogs, and shall I not exert it. Dispatch I say—[*Huzza and clash of swords without.*]—Why am I not obeyed?—[*Clash again—confused noise—several Hazza's,—*]

AUGUSTUS: [*without.*] Where is my mother? save, Oh! save, my mother.

FREDERIC: [*Speaking.*] Shut up the palace gates, secure the guards, and at your peril suffer none to pass.

AUGUSTUS: [*Entering.*] Oh! mother are you safe.

CONSTANT: Bounteous heaven! and am I then restored to more— much more than life—my Rebecca! my children!—Oh! this joy is more than I can bear.

[*Enter* FREDERIC, FETNAH, SEBASTIAN, BEN HASSAN, SLAVES, &c.]

SEBASTIAN: Great and mighty Ottoman, suffer my friends to shew you what pretty bracelets these are.—Oh, you old dog, we'll give you the bastinado presently.

FREDERIC: Forbear Sebastian.—Muley Moloc, though your power

over us is at end, we neither mean to enslave your person, or put a period to your existence—we are freemen, and while we assert the rights of men, we dare not infringe the privileges of a fellow-creature.

SEBASTIAN: By the law of retaliation, he should be a slave.

REBECCA: By the Christian law, no man should be a slave; it is a word so abject, that, but to speak it dyes the cheek with crimson. Let us assert our own prerogative, be free ourselves, but let us not throw on another's neck, the chains we scorn to wear.

SEBASTIAN: But what must we do with this old gentlewoman?

BEN HASSAN: Oh, pray send me home to Duke's place.

FREDERIC: Ben Hassan, your avarice, treachery and cruelty should be severely punished; for, if any one deserves slavery, it is he who could raise his own fortune on the miseries of others.

BEN HASSAN: Oh! that I was but crying old cloaths, in the dirtiest alley in London.

FETNAH: So, you'll leave that poor old man behind?

FREDERIC: Yes, we leave that poor old man behind?

FETNAH: [*Going to* BEN HASSAN.] Very well, good bye Frederic— good bye dear Rebecca; while my father was rich and had friends, I did not much think about my duty; but now he is poor and forsaken, I know it too well to leave him alone in his affliction.

MULEY: Stay,—Fetnah—Hassan stay.—I fear from following the steps of my ancestors, I have greatly erred: teach me then, you who so well know how to practice what is right, how to amend my faults.

CONSTANT: Open your prison doors; give freedom to your people; sink the name of subject in the endearing epithet of fellow-citizen;—then you will be loved and reverenced—then will you find, in promoting the happiness of others, you have secured your own.

MULEY: Henceforward, then, I will reject all power but such as my united friends shall think me incapable of abusing. Hassan, you are free—to you my generous conquerors what can I say?

HENRY: Nothing, but let your future conduct prove how much you value the welfare of your fellow-creatures—to-morrow, we shall leave your capital, and return to our native land, where liberty has established her court—where the warlike Eagle extends his glittering pinions in the sunshine of prosperity.

OLIVIA: Long, long, may that prosperity continue—may Freedom spread her benign influence thro' every nation, till the bright Eagle, united with the dove and olive-branch, waves high, the acknowledged standard of the world.

The End

EPILOGUE

Written and spoken by MRS. ROWSON.

PROMPTER: [*behind.*] Come—Mrs. Rowson! Come!—Why don't
you hurry?
MRS. R: [*behind.*] Sir I am here—but I'm in such a flurry,
Do let me stop a moment! just for breath,

[*Enter.*]

Bless me! I'm almost terrify'd to death.
Yet sure, I had no real cause for fear,
Since none but liberal—generous friends are here.
Say—will you kindly overlook my errors?
You smile.—Then to the winds I give my terrors.
Well, Ladies tell me—how d'ye like my play?
"The creature has some sense," methinks you say;
"She says that we should have supreme dominion,
"And in good truth, we're all of her opinion.
"Women were born for universal sway.
"Men to adore, be silent, and obey."

True, Ladies—bounteous nature made us fair.
To strew sweet ropes round the bed of care.
A parent's heart, of sorrow to beguile,
Cheer an afflicted husband by a smile.
To bind the truant, that's inclined to roam,
Good humour makes a paradise at home.
This is our noblest, best prerogative.
By these, pursuing nature's gentle plan,
We hold in silken chains—the lordly tyrant man.

But pray, forgive this flippancy—indeed.
Of all your clemency I stand in need.
To own the truth, the scenes this night display'd,
Are only fictions—drawn by fancy's aid.

'Tis what I wish—But we have cause to fear,
No ray of comfort, the sad bosoms cheer,
Of many a Christian, shut from light and day,
In bondage, languishing their lives away.

Say!—You who feel humanity's soft glow,
What rapt'rous joy must the poor captive know;
Who, free'd from slavery's ignominious chain,
Views his dear native land, and friends again?

If there's a sense, more exquisitely fine,
A joy more elevated, more divine;
'Tis felt by those, whose liberal minds conceiv'd,
The generous plan, by which he reliev'd.

When first this glorious universe began,
And heaven to punish disobedient man;
Sent to attend him, through life's dreary shade,
Affliction—poor dejected, weeping maid.
Then came Benevolence, by all rever'd,
He dry'd the mourner's tears, her heart he cheer'd;
He woo'd her to his breast—made her his own,
And Gratitude appear'd, their first-born son.
Since when, the father and the son has join'd,
To shed their influence o'er the human mind:
And in the heart, where either deign to rest,
Rife transports, difficult to be express'd.
Such, as within your generous bosoms glow,
Who feel return'd, the blessings you bestow.
Oh! ever may you taste, those joys divine,
While Gratitude—sweet Gratitude is mine.

Early Abolitionist Drama

Introduction

S o rare were abolitionist plays before 1850 that few scholars
expect to hear the words "early," "abolitionist," and "drama" together.
Of course, much of the public face of organized Northern abolitionism in the 1830s and 1840s was certainly dramatic—as this was the
period when abolitionists (including fugitive slaves who spoke in
great detail about the violence of slavery) took the lectern across the
North. Abolitionists' attempts to move to the early American stage,
though rare, were often inspired by fugitives' stories. Two such texts
are represented here: the long 1839 play *The Kidnapped Clergyman*
is excerpted, and the shorter 1841 *The Fugitives* is included in its
entirety. Both texts alert us to some of the complex questions abolitionists faced not only in "staging" their political beliefs, but also in
answering the already-dominant minstrel-like stage representations
of African Americans.

The Kidnapped Clergyman has remained something of a mys-
tery—even though some elements will be quite familiar to modern
readers. Though the play predates Charles Dickens's *The Christmas
Carol* (1843), for example, some of its plot has the feel of that classic. After giving a "great" sermon on how the Bible supports slavery

and then eating a cake with too much lard in it, the title character, the Reverend David Dorsey, falls into a troubled sleep. He is visited by three strangers. The first turns out to be a famous but long-dead clergyman; the second, a bookseller who promises to make Dorsey rich by publishing his sermon; and the third, a doctor, also famous and dead, who assures him that he has indigestion. Then Dorsey and all of his family are kidnapped by a slave trader and forced into slavery. What follows calls to mind texts very different from Dickens'. In recounting what "the kidnapped clergyman" and his family go through once enslaved, the play sounds much like some of the earliest slave narratives and other abolitionist texts. (Theodore Weld's *American Slavery as It Is* was published in the same year.)

The play's authorship remains undetermined, and there is little trace of its reception. Nonetheless, we can guess that the author knew a fair amount about the law—at least enough to cite cases and wade into the thicket of intersections between U.S. constitutional law and various state laws—and may have been a resident of Massachusetts. The author was also familiar with the roots and practices of New England clergy and with various Biblical arguments about slavery. Most obviously, the author was an abolitionist, as was the press that the author chose: Dow and Jackson of Boston had published one of William Lloyd Garrison's lectures and would later publish the 1841 Annual Report of the Massachusetts Anti-Slavery Society as well as an edition of African American Nancy Prince's *The West Indies* (1842). *The Kidnapped Clergyman*—like these texts—seems to conclude that the *Constitution* was fundamentally flawed in its treatment of slavery, consciously considers the humanity of African Americans, and sees slavery as an international national issue—one that specifically threatens the fabric of our nation.

Still, the play does not seem to have received the circulation of Dow and Jackson's other texts. As yet, scholars have found no detailed discussion of it, and it is unlikely that it was ever staged. The play may have been specifically written as a "closet drama," and the author may have expected it to be read as a sort of novel in dialogue. Most theaters would have rejected it out of hand, given its subject matter. Three factors may have limited even its specific appeal to abolitionists. First, in the era before *Uncle Tom's Cabin*, the watchword of many in the abolitionist movement was veracity: fiction (and drama based on fiction) simply had little place. Second, the African American character Dinah is incredibly direct about the horrors of the slave system—arguably, at times, more direct than even some slave narratives—and at some times bluntly sarcastic about the failings of white people. Among conservative abolitionists in the late 1830s, such testimony as Dinah's might not have been welcome; outside of abolitionist circles, it would have been dismissed outright. Finally, while the play's opening and closing scenes are often fascinating, some of the middle sections of the play (which are not included here)—especially those in courtroom settings which focus on legal arguments on slavery—are, simply, often quite turgid.

While some of the play's value is historical—it seems to be one of the earliest texts of its type—*The Kidnapped Clergyman* is also an interesting window into how some abolitionists saw slaves, how they questioned the organized church and government, and how they sometimes held Northerners just as accountable for slavery as Southerners. It also offers an early template for a literary argument against slavery. (In examining extant reports of William Wells Brown's 1856 play *Experience*, for example, W. Edward Farrison has suggested that Brown either read or knew about *The Kidnapped Clergyman*, given similarities between the plots and characters.)

The Fugitives offers an interesting counterpoint to *The Kidnapped Clergyman*—not in the least because its enslaved characters sound like they have had classical educations. The first and only appearance to date of this short play was in *The Star of Emancipation* (1841), a miscellany produced by the Massachusetts Female Emancipation Society. Most likely, this volume was created in part for one of their bazaars, which they, like many anti-slavery organizations (especially women's groups), held to raise money for the cause. As such, like later abolitionist miscellanies like *Autographs for Freedom* and *The Liberty Bell*, it was probably sold alongside textile items and food, as well as various tracts.

This means that the unnamed author of *The Fugitives* was likely female and a member of the Society. As such, she was probably a resident of Boston, a woman who had received some significant schooling, and the child of a father in one of the professions. She was an active Christian and was probably involved in other reform efforts. She probably speculated on just what roles women could take in public, but she might have leaned more toward a relative conservatism. Indeed, by her very membership in the Society, she was eschewing the calls of more radical abolitionists like Garrison: the Society had been founded only a year before the publication of *The Star of Emancipation* as part of one of several bitter factional splits in the late 1830s and early 1840s among abolitionists. Some of the members of the Society, including its founding president, Mary S. Parker, had been involved in the Boston Female Anti-Slavery Society. This early women's group worked—albeit often uneasily—across racial lines to further the cause of enslaved African Americans. In this, the Boston Female Anti-Slavery Society was rarer than twenty-first century readers might like to think. Racism was rampant in some parts of the abolitionist movement; the Female Anti-Slavery Society in Fall River, Massachusetts, for example, almost dissolved in a bitter fight over whether to grant three free Black women membership. If the author of *The Fugitives* had been involved with the cause for a long time, she might well have worked with African American women like Susan Paul in the Boston Female Anti-Slavery Society and would have known about the tensions like those experienced at Fall River.

As the larger abolitionist movement moved toward splits centered on Garrisonian politics (whether to engage in politics or not, for example) and on the potential of women and men to participate together in the same groups (rather than women being, in essence, forced into separate female societies), the ruptures hit the Boston Female Anti-Slavery Society especially hard. In a series of conflicts in late 1839 and early 1840 between Garrisonians (led by, among others, Maria Weston Chapman) and anti-Garrisonians (led by Parker), Parker was elected president of the Boston Female Anti-Slavery Society—under the protest of the Garrisonians, which included most of the Black women members. Parker quickly severed ties with Garrison and dissolved the group. Again, the Garrisonians protested. This time, Parker and her followers founded the Massachusetts Female

Emancipation Society. *The Star of Emancipation* was both one of the Society's first and last major efforts: its pages contain a prose eulogy and a verse elegy to Parker, who died in either late 1840 or early 1841. The collection emphasizes a combination of Christian moral suasion and growing hints that organized religion and government could shape an end to slavery; in this, it draws several connections to Great Britain's abolition of slavery—which happened in 1833, at the end of a long political process. It is also fairly suggestive about a semi-Colonizationist ethos: several pieces, including *The Fugitives*, mark Canada as the goal for African Americans (rather than any location in the U.S.). In short, it marks the Society's moves away from Garrison and toward more conservative abolitionism.

Within this framework—women writing for a mainly female audience, with hopes of swaying male opinion and political action—representing slaves in language that hearkens back to Greco-Roman tragedy seems somewhat understandable, especially if the author wanted to distance such characters from the minstrel types that dominated the popular stage. The plot and characters of *The Fugitives* echo types common in both anti-slavery lectures and accounts of the slave system like Weld's *American Slavery As It Is*. Fearing that her daughter Iola will become the victim of sexual violence at the hands of their evil master Bandaloz, the elderly slave Malie (the leader of "the fugitives") escapes from Bandaloz's Carolina plantation with the aid of her two sons, Ghestler and Zongola. With Canada—to be found by the North Star, the "Star of Emancipation"—as their goal, during their journey, the title fugitives debate the role Christianity must play in their lives and escape; they wonder if Carlos, a field slave who Iola loves, will betray them; and they worry that the aged Malie will not withstand the trip.

The play was almost certainly not designed for the theater. It might, perhaps like *The Kidnapped Clergyman*, have been designed to be read like a novel. But it may have had another purpose. Nineteenth-century literature and history are rife with examples of family and friends doing small, social theatricals in their parlors. *The Fugitives* could certainly have been "played" by members of the Massachusetts Female Emancipation Society after a meeting, by other female abolitionist groups, by families and friends with abolitionist leanings, etc.

And this gives rise to some fascinating possibilities. While the play certainly represents fugitive slaves in ways that might be more comfortable for white women to identify with, in "playing" the various parts, these white women would have been attempting to place themselves in the roles of African Americans—including the young, potential victim of sexual violence, Iola, and the struggling mother, Malie. Such work would be key to the sentimental strategies of identification central to novels like *Uncle Tom's Cabin* (1852), to women's slave narratives, and to later drama—ranging from Stowe's *The Christian Slave* (1855) to Lydia Maria Child's *Stars and Stripes* (1858).

A Note on the Texts

The excerpts from *The Kidnapped Clergyman* provided here are drawn from the beginning and ending of the play's first (and perhaps only) edition. While the language in the excerpts is generally understandable—Dinah's dialect is actually much more readable than several minstrel corruptions of African American speech—contemporary readers may have questions about a handful of allusions in the play. British bishop Francis Atterbury (1662–1732), to whom Dorsey pompously compares himself, and Archbishop of Canterbury John Tillotson (1630–1691), who praises Dorsey near the beginning of his dream, are not nearly as commonly known now as they were in early nineteenth-century New England; the same is true of Dr. John Abernathy (1764–1831), a digestive specialist who also makes an appearance. The references late in the play to "the mulatto who they burned" are direct allusions to the case of Francis McIntosh, a free Black boatman who, after a fracas involving St. Louis lawmen, was arrested. Probably fearing for his life (and knowing that he could easily be taken into slavery), McIntosh killed the two arresting officers and escaped before being recaptured and lynched—burned in such a horrendous display of mob violence that it outraged abolitionists across the nation.

The text of *The Fugitives* has been reproduced from *The Star of Emancipation*. Generally, the language remains understandable to modern readers. Readers may note the rather curious names of some of the slave characters; scholars have not yet been able to determine their significance. Of special interest, Iola's name reappears in an important post-Reconstruction novel, Frances Ellen Watkins Harper's *Iola Leroy* (1892), and as the psydeuonym of Ida B. Wells.

For Further Reading

Bacon, Jacqueline. *The Humblest May Stand Forth: Rhetoric, Empowerment, and Abolition*. Columbia: University of South Carolina Press, 2002.

Farrison, W. Edward. "*The Kidnapped Clergyman* and Brown's *Experience*." *College Language Association Journal* 18 (1975): 507–515.

Finkelman, Paul. *An Imperfect Union: Slavery, Federalism, and Comity*. Chapel Hill: University of North Carolina Press, 1981.

Hansen, Debra Gold. *Strained Sisterhood: Gender and Class in the Boston Female Anti-Slavery Society*. Amherst: University of Massachusetts Press, 1993.

Jeffrey, Julie Roy. *The Great Silent Army of Abolitionism: Ordinary Women in the Antislavery Movement*. Chapel Hill: University of North Carolina Press, 1998.

Mayer, Henry. *All on Fire: William Lloyd Garrison and the Abolition of Slavery*. New York: St. Martin's Griffin, 1998.

Prince, Nancy. *The West Indies, Being a Description of the Islands, Progress of Christianity, Education, and Liberty among the Colored Population Generally*. Boston: Dow and Jackson, 1842.

*The Kidnapped Clergyman; or,
Experience the Best Teacher*

FROM THE OPENING OF THE PLAY

[*A Clergyman's Library, handsomely furnished. A warm afternoon in Summer. Enter a* CLERGYMAN, *apparently fatigued and heated.*]

CLERGYMAN: [*Taking off his hat and seating himself in an arm-chair.*] Soh! [*Puffs and blows.*] My business is over for to-day. My people seemed uncommonly well pleased, as *I* think. [*Puffs and blows.*] Pretty warm afternoon's work. It was a good sermon, though—Atterbury himself never delivered a better.—Let me see what good thing have I done to-day.—Hum.—Sent the poor woman, down Ann Street, with the sick child, five dollars. It was not much, but all I can afford.—I wish I had a greater salary. I would do more in the way of charity. My salary, however, is pretty good. In fact, I have no reason to complain. My wife is in good health, and my three little darlings, playful as kittens, and as good as they can be. My grown up daughter Clara, a perfect beauty; and the most amiable and accomplished young lady I know of—I think she will soon be well settled. I think Mr. Bluff's son has taken a fancy to her—a young man of immense expectations. My two eldest sons, Jack and Bill, just entering College.—[*Puffs and blows.*] Nothing to trouble me. I have no anxiety at all, but to keep up the good feelings of the parish toward me.—Very good parish—very good parish. [*Puffs and blows.*] A wedding last week.—Fifteen dollars.—My wife had a new silk gown yesterday; the day before, ten dollars were subscribed to make me a life-member of some fiddle-faddle society.—Never mind; it shows that I am popular. In fact, I do preach beautiful discourses; beautiful discourses;—[*Puffs and blows.*] I have no cause to complain, on the contrary, every reason to be thankful. As I keep myself entirely within

Christian bounds, the burthen of Christianity sits light upon me indeed. I discharge all my duties to my parish, as well—as well as I can.—But I find it will not do to take the bull by the horns.—Some of my parish, I am ashamed of; but it is of no use to preach to them, or at them, respecting their failings. They will say I am personal, and it will only make a difficulty. No—it will not do—it will not do. Milk for babes—milk for babes—[*Puffs and blows.*] I believe I will get neighbor Rough to exchange with me, and give him a hint what vice to lash, and he will do it, and it will not be supposed to be intended for any one in particular. Yes—yes—that will do—[*Puffs and blows.*] Confounded warm! Rather uncanonical to say so—it is a fact, but I cannot help it.—[*Pauses and is lost in a reverie.*]—Upon my word, that was a beautiful passage in my discourse.—Fine topics, benevolence, decency of behaviour, quiet and orderly conduct, submission to superiors; and the duty to carefully avoid every thing that will disturb the tranquillity and happiness of society; beautiful passage—beautiful passage.—Think I must print that discourse. [*Puffs and blows.*] Yes, it will do a great deal of good. It will put a complete stop to fanaticism and nonsense. Rather about upon the abolitionists: almost uncanonical—Must not be too severe, though. Burk's letter to a noble lord, is in fact not to be named with it, nor—Junius himself, if I had not suppressed some things, for fear of being satirical. No—no—no—that wont do—that wont do—The abolitionists deserve it, though, and more too. [*Puffs and blows. Pauses in a reverie.*] Negroes, a degraded, incorrigible race, it is to be feared, different from white people, altogether inferior. Stories of cruelty exaggerated, made up; I dislike Slavery in the abstract, but it does not appear to be forbidden in the New Testament, and seems to be consistent with Christianity. No hardship to the blacks to be kept at work.—[*Puffs and blows.*] Why should the planters give up their property, Mr. Abolitionist?—tell me that—tell me that. The Constitution recognizes slavery, and I have nothing to do with the institutions of the people at the South.—Must not go too far, though. My parishioners go too far: don't like to offend them, after all; but I mean to do my duty as far—as far as I think it will do any good—hum—[*reverie again—Puffs and blows.*] Confound it, how oppressed I am with Mrs. Marjoram's pound-cake; I am sure she must have put lard in it. The next time I come home, I will come through another street. Mrs. Marjoram always waylays me, and compels me to go home with her, and then she stuffs me and my wife with her cake, till I can hardly breathe. [*Puffs and blows.—Reverie.*] Beautiful passages, those in my discourse against the abolitionists. "Scintillating corruscations of fertilizing fancy." Let me see, where did I get that expression.—The North American Review, was it?—Let me see—let me see—no, no, no. The North American indeed!—A solemn, magisterial piece of pomp enough—well printed, to be sure, very fair-seeming and grave; but shallow, quite shallow, and prodigiously dull; I would not read a page in it this hot afternoon, to be made Chaplain of Congress. I would have dropped it long ago, but the work is called the first American periodical, and I am obliged to have it, or compromise my literary taste. Fudge, fudge, all fudge; money thrown away.—Let me see, where was it—"scintillating corruscations of fertilizing fancy." Beautiful, beautiful; however, this I think is superior still, "extacising glimpses of terrene, aye, superterrene beatitude." I must be careful how I pronounce the last words, however, or the people in the gallery will be apt to mistake it for "soup tureen," and the least thought of crockery would spoil the most elevated and resplendent expressions in the world.—[*Puffs and blows.*] Bless me, how heavy I am! I believe I had better compose myself and take a nap; but I am almost afraid I should have a touch of the night-mare. Too often plagued with that horrid affection. The Dr. says it arises from indigestion, and that I must be abstemious in my food. He says some of the Clergy are apt to eat a little too much, for perfect health. If my wife was at home, I would have a cup of strong hyson tea, which would relieve me, but it always makes a difficulty if I order tea before she comes, and when she is one gossipping

79

with Mrs. Lobster, that used to live in Marblehead, she never knows how the time flies. I wish I had not read those horrid slave stories. Negroes must feel, some of them at least. They are certainly true; my friend was in Richmond, when the slave killed his wife at the auction, after he found she was sold away from him to a southern dealer, and then he cut his own hand off with a hatchet. Jealous, I suppose. And the other, that lately took place in the District of Columbia. The woman must have been out of her senses, to have tried to kill her children.—One she killed; and she put out the eye of another, trying to kill it; and she broke the arm of another. Shocking—shocking. I am sure I shall dream of some such thing to-night. Yes, I dislike slavery in the abstract, but there is nothing against it in the Bible.—[*Reverie.*] I wonder how kidnapping is done? The abolitionists are very much to blame, to endeavor to protect runaways; they must be put down. I think my discourse will do it. I wish Tillotson could have seen that discourse, it is so methodical and profound, like himself. It is a little against my conscience to be so severe upon the abolitionist, to be sure, but it will please my parish very much; I shall be complimented by the Clergy of the South and perhaps by some of the more influential planters. I intend to print it and send some copies on. [*Puffs and blows.*] Bless me, how my wife stays—Well, I can stand it no longer. [*Composes himself to sleep.*]

[*Enter a grave person in an old-fashioned dress, with a mitre on his head, and bows with respect.*]

STRANGER: Sir, I am rejoiced to see you.

CLERGYMAN: Pray sir, who are you?

STRANGER: I am Archbishop Tillotson, at your service.

CLERGYMAN: Is it possible? I had thought Archbishop Tilloston had been dead many years; but pray, sir, what procures me the honor of this delightful visit?

TILLOTSON: Sir, the pleasure I have received from your most beautiful and interesting discourse against the Abolitionists, has induced me to wait on you.

CLERGYMAN: Sir, it would be a most foolish affectation, on my part, to pretend, that I was not aware, that my discourse possessed considerable merit, as an American discourse; but I must confess, I never before had so high an opinion of it. Words cannot express my delight, when I hear you state that it receives your decided approbation.

TILLOTSON: Say, my unqualified applause, my dear Sir. The influence which such judicious writings have upon the public mind, furnishes a source of congratulation to all philanthropists, both in the Old world and the New.

CLERGYMAN: Perhaps there was some particular passage, Sir, that pleased you very much; would you have the goodness to point it out, in order that I may have the benefit of your critical taste and judgment?

TILLOTSON: My dear Sir, the whole was fine, admirable, beautiful, superlative. But there were two passages of such exquisite delicacy,—

CLERGYMAN: Allow me to anticipate you, my dear Sir. I am sure I know which you mean. "The scintillating corruscations of fertilizing fancy," and "the extracising glimpses of terrene, aye, super-terrene beatitude."

TILLOTSON: You are right, my dear Sir, there is no man of taste, but must at once perceive and relish the beauty of such composition. Allow me to present you, my dear Sir, with 1000 pounds sterling, sent by the learned Clergy of England, as a small token of respect for the "scintillating corruscations of your fertilizing fancy." [*Presents the money.*]

CLERGYMAN: Sir, I receive this testimonial rather as an offering of friendship, than as a testimonial of my talents, which have been successfully employed in the discovery of new ethical truth. [*Puts the note in his pocket-book.*]

TILLOTSON: I must now withdraw. But allow me to ask, my dear Sir, if you are in perfect health. Pray take care of a life so valuable to the Christian world. The anxiety I feel for your sake, and the oppression, under which you seem to labor, makes me ask you, if your stomach, weakened by the prodigious efforts of your mind, has not become incapable of a suitable digestion of its proper aliments? Let me recommend, my dear Sir, great moderation in this respect. Though repletion may not be a sin, it is far from being a virtue; abstinence in a Clergyman, is much more graceful. Sir, I take my leave. [*Withdraws.*]

[*Enter another stranger.*]

STRANGER: [*Bowing.*] Sir, your most obedient. I believe I have not the honor of being known to you. I am Mr. Lackington, of London, bookseller: having heard of your famous sermon against the abolitionists, I have crossed the Atlantic as speedily as possible, in order to anticipate the enterprising American booksellers, and request you to give me the pre-emption of the copy-right. I give you a carte blanche as to terms.

CLERGYMAN: How many copies, do you think, will be wanted, Mr. Lackington?

STRANGER: I think one hundred thousand copies for America; and three hundred thousand for Great Britain, will do to begin with.

CLERGYMAN: Well Sir, I wish to be reasonable with you. Probably we shall deal again. I will take twenty thousand dollars for the copy-right.

STRANGER: I am very well satisfied, if you are; and will give you a draft for the amount on the Commonwealth Bank, in Boston.

CLERGYMAN: I should prefer a different Bank, if you please.

STRANGER: Sir, I will give you a bill of Exchange on London; that, I am sure, will satisfy you. [*Handing him the bill.*] But, my dear Sir, if I may take the liberty, you seem to be unwell; you seem oppressed, and short-breathed; perhaps, however, you have not been exact in your diet, a little too much pudding, perhaps. Farewell, Sir, business calls. [*Retires.*]

[*Enter another* STRANGER.]

STRANGER: Not being personally acquainted with anyone here, I am under the necessity of announcing myself;—Dr. Abernethy, of London. I come by order of her majesty, Queen Victoria, to inquire after your health. Allow me to feel your pulse. [*Feels his pulse.*]—Life of such a man invaluable to all nations. Celebrated and wonderful discourse.—Hum: Not feverish, a case of dyspepsy, merely temporary indigestion; dumplings, perhaps.

CLERGYMAN: No, Dr. Abernethy, an excess of pound-cake.

DR. ABERNETHY: No cause of serious alarm: [*feels in his pocket.*]—beg pardon,—left prescription behind. No matter—a better at hand.—Your discourse every way salutary and highly medicinal; you must have a little physic. Read a page at the beginning of your discourse: produces nausea, the pages, excellent emetic,—three, a purge; a sentence at the end, an anodyne. Excuse haste.—Another patient. [*Retires.*]

[*Enter five* STRANGERS. (*two of them bearing an enormous silver spoon.*)]

FIRST STRANGER: Sir, I have the honor to be chairman of a Committee of the House of Representatives of the State of Ohio, appointed to wait on you, and present you with their thanks for you most excellent, learned, deep, sublime, interesting, and important discourse against the abolitionists, who have so long been the pest of a country, a nation, a people, and a race of men, the wisest, the most warlike, the most ingenious, and the most growing in the world. Sir, I know your benevolent and philanthropic heart will be ready to expand with delight, when you hear, that abolitionism is henceforth dead, totally dead, expired, departed, henceforth and forever. The Legislature, on the application of certain Commissioners of Kentucky, principally however through the influence of your discourse, have seen fit to pass a law, which is an extinguisher on the plans of that lawless race. And, respected Sir, as an offering and testimonial of their gratitude, they beg your acceptance of this spoon, which I assure you, is of solid silver, and well adapted not only for your own use, in the common way, but may well serve as a type or emblem of the effectual mode which you adopt to fill the greedy mental gapings of your parish, with the intellectual dainties of your imagination.

CLERGYMAN: Sir, I accept, with much gratitude, the handsome and almost undeserved offering of friendship, so delicately and gracefully presented by the Chairman of the Honorable Committee of the House of Representatives of the independent, magnanimous and respectable state of Ohio. Their perspicacity to perceive merit, is only equaled by the desire they always show, to reward it. I shall most carefully treasure it up with my most valuable deposits, to stimulate my children to follow their father's steps, by the exhibition of the reward of wisdom and virtue. Having performed your very grateful mission to me, I beg you will not permit any fastidious regard for etiquette, to detain you longer from your beloved State, which must be longing for the return of such distinguished talents, to grace its councils and bless its people. [*Bows and waves his hand, and the five gentlemen bow and retire.*]

[*Enter a* KIDNAPPER, *armed with pistols, and three ruffians armed with cudgels, whips, gags, and hand-cuffs.*]

KIDNAPPER: Seize him. [*They assault the Clergyman, knock him down, and handcuff him.*]

CLERGYMAN: Help! Murder! Help!

KIDNAPPER: Gag the noisy rascal. Choke him. [*They seize him by the throat.*] Mr. Gouge, strip him and give him twenty lashes, well laid on.

[GOUGE *whips him.*]

CLERGYMAN: Oh! Oh! Oh!

KIDNAPPER: Knock him down with the butt end, if he is not still. [GOUGE *whips him.*]

CLERGYMAN: [*Groans.*]

GOUGE: [*Whispers to him.*] Say, Dont master, dont; O God Almighty, master, dont: Say it, or else I will cut you to pieces.

CLERGYMAN: Dont, master, dont; O God Almighty master, dont!

KIDNAPPER: You need not whip him any more now; he submits. I dont wish to be cruel. He knows now he is my slave. Take the woman and the three children down to that boat to Mr.

Gormon. Dont separate the mother from the children. That would be cruel, I have sold them all together.

CLERGYMAN: Good Heaven; what do you mean? Am I to be kidnapped? Is my poor wife and my children to be carried off thus? Help! murder! neighbors, help! Murder! Murder! Murder!

KIDNAPPER: Gouge, knock him down. [*To the* CLERGYMAN.] You scoundrel, if you are not quiet, I will shoot you. Gouge give him a dozen more lashes well laid on. [GOUGE *whips him.*] You must break him in, as you do a colt.

CLERGYMAN: [*Groans.*]

GOUGE: [*Whispers.*] Say what I told you, or I will cut you to pieces.

CLERGYMAN: Dont, master, dont; O God Almighty, master, dont!

KIDNAPPER: My lads, have you carried the woman and children down to the boat?

ATTENDANTS: Yes, Sir! The woman struggled, and fought, and screamed; and we knocked her down, and one of the children fell into the water.

CLERGYMAN: Oh! Oh! Oh! Murder! Help! Murder! Murder!

KIDNAPPER: Give it to him with the butt end. [GOUGE *knocks him down.*] Give him a dozen more. [GOUGE *whips him.*]

CLERGYMAN: [*Groans.*]

GOUGE: Say what I told you, or I will cut you to pieces.

CLERGYMAN: Dont, master, dont; Oh! mercy master, mercy.

KIDNAPPER: Dont whip him any more Gouge. He submits. I am afraid I shall have to salt him; the weather is so hot. What is your name?

CLERGYMAN: [*Sullen, will not answer.*]

KIDNAPPER: Answer, or I will cut you to pieces. [*Kicks him.*]

CLERGYMAN: [*Sulkily.*] David: curse you.

KIDNAPPER: Give it to him, Gouge. [GOUGE *whips him.*]

CLERGYMAN: [*Groans.*]

GOUGE: I will cut you to pieces now, sure enough. [*Whips him.*]

CLERGYMAN: Oh, mercy, master; mercy; show some pity. I did not mean what I said: mercy, master, mercy.

KIDNAPPER: Let him alone, Gouge. He submits. David, I have sold you to a respectable planter, who will soon be here after you.

Take care what you say, for, if he refuses to take you, look out. Gouge, what was done with David's two sons?

GOUGE: They were sent off to the Cotton Plantation. Bill fought desperately, and was very much cut up; but the other submitted.

CLERGYMAN: Oh, my poor boys! my poor boys! Oh! Oh!

KIDNAPPER: David, will you behave yourself?

CLERGYMAN: Yes, master, I will.

KIDNAPPER: Gouge, where is Clara?

GOUGE: Down in the kitchen with the mulatto woman.

CLERGYMAN: [*Groans.*]

KIDNAPPER: Send her up stairs to me.

CLERGYMAN: Oh, Sir! Oh, Sir! Spare my poor innocent child. [*Falls on his knees.*] O, as you hope for mercy, yourself; spare my poor child! Oh! Oh!

KIDNAPPER: What does the fool mean? I have sold her to go to St. Louis; to a Missouri gentleman, Mr. Lawkins Mawgridge; he said she was a fine girl; and he would give me two thousand dollars for her. She will be very kindly treated.

CLERGYMAN: Oh! Oh! Oh! I shall go distracted! Spare my poor innocent child; spare her! Save her! Save her!

KIDNAPPER: David, will you behave? I don't want to whip you again.

CLERGYMAN: Help! murder! help! Oh, mercy, master, spare her! save her!

KIDNAPPER: [*Calls out.*] Gouge! Peter Gouge! Peter! O Peter! O Peter! You damned son of a bitch, Peter! Bring the whip.

CLERGYMAN: Kill me, if you please, but spare my poor child! my poor child!

KIDNAPPER: Will you behave yourself, David?

CLERGYMAN: I cant help it, master. Oh, my poor child! my poor child!

KIDNAPPER: Well, David, I will see what can be done, if you behave yourself. If you dont, mind me, off she goes to Alabama.

CLERGYMAN: [*Weeps and wrings his hands.*] Oh! oh my poor wife, and my dear little children; my two brave boys sent away, and then my dear daughter, so beautiful and innocent, to be carried off by vile ruffians! Oh! Oh! Oh!

KIDNAPPER: Peter: O Peter! O Peter! Bring me the whip. Will you be still now, or must I whip you myself? I shall strip you and tie you up to the ladder. Be quiet, I say. I don't want to whip you. But I see I must.

CLERGYMAN: Kill me, if you please; but I cannot help it. Are you a man, and can you treat people so?

KIDNAPPER: Villain! You are my slave. Would you rebel against your master? Do you dare to disobey my orders?

CLERGYMAN: I am not your slave, if you kill me for saying so. What right have you to treat me so?

KIDNAPPER: You impudent scoundrel! when Peter brings the whip, I will let you see what right I have. The law gives me the right, to correct my slave, till he submits to my authority. I have answered your question, you rebel. Will you submit? My humanity is all that saves you now.

[*Enter* GOUGE *with the whip.*]

KIDNAPPER: Mr. Gouge, you must contrive to be a little quicker, when I call you, or you don't remain in my employ long. You need not whip him now: I see he submits. If he is sulky again, I will make him feel. Stop, here comes Mr. Hurdle, for David.

[*Enter* PLANTER, *with his* OVERSEER.]

PLANTER: Well, Mr. Gormon, I have come for my new servant. What is his name?

KIDNAPPER: David.—Here is a receipt for the money. I leave the runaway with you. He is a fine strong fellow, and has no other fault except running away; if it was not for that, I would not take double the money for him. I am in great haste, and must be off. [*Goes away with* GOUGE, *and the other attendants.*]

PLANTER: David, what work can you do?

CLERGYMAN: I am not used to any kind of work. I am a scholar.

PLANTER: A scholar indeed! what kind of a scholar? Are you a doctor?

87

CLERGYMAN: No, master. I am a preacher.

PLANTER: Oh ho! A nigger preacher, eh? what did you preach last? Tell me that, if you are a preacher.

CLERGYMAN: I preached against the abolitionists.

PLANTER: What did you say, David?

CLERGYMAN: I said there was nothing in the Scriptures against holding slaves.

PLANTER: Did you? David, you are a good boy; I will use you well. Have you that discourse with you, David?

CLERGYMAN: I have it in my pocket, master. Here it is. [*Shows him the discourse.*]

PLANTER: I could not have believed that you could read and write. You shall preach that to my slaves to-night. That will do very well, indeed. Overseer, send Dinah up to me. [OVERSEER *goes out.*]

[*Enter* DINAH.]

DINAH: [*After going towards the* CLERGYMAN *and looking at him very inquisitively.*] O, master, dis is white man. Dis no colored man, at all.

PLANTER: What do you mean, Dinah? I say he is a colored man.

DINAH: No, master: no coloured man. He very dark, but he white man. I know um directly. He got no freckles on his nose. Look at him, master. White man, full of himself, proud, cross, great eater. He crammed now so full of hoe-cake, he cant breathe. [PLANTER *goes out.*]

DINAH: White man, where you come from?

CLERGYMAN: I was kidnapped and brought here and I don't know where I am myself. I am distracted. What shall I do? Oh my poor wife, my poor children. [*Weeps and wrings his hands.*]

DINAH: Don't cry and take on so, white man. Master very good man. He be very good to you, if you behave yourself. When you speak to him, always say, "Master." And when he calls you always say, "what Master please to have?" He will give you a peck of corn a week to make homminy. He very kind to his slaves. When my brother Tom was sick, he called de Doctor to him, and when he found Tom did not get better he told Tom, if he only would get well, he should not work so hard again. Tom was never whipped, and he worked very hard, cause he fraid he might be whipped. But poor Tom, he died, and master said he very sorry, very sorry indeed, for Tom. Tom was his best servant: he said when Tom died it was a thousand dollars right out of his pocket. O dear! O dear! Master very kind man. I had three little children. Master lost money at a horse race, and then he sold my husband, and they chained him, and carried him to 'Bama State. But he run away to get back here, and they chase him with dogs and rifles, and they shoot him and took him and carried him off and wedder he dead or wedder he live now, I don't know. I nebber see him again. And then master wanted more money, and he sold my three little children, and I screamed and fit with the men, that took em away, till they knocked me down; and I was out of my head a fortnight, crying for my children; till de Doctor tell massa I should die, if he did not get back my youngest child. And massa, he say, it was too bad, and he sent after my youngest child, and got it back. Massa very tender heart. My dear little child was a colored child; my two others, black, they were my husband's children; my little child, overseer's child. Overseer very cruel, wicked bad man. He beat me, he kick me, he choak me, he abuse me very bad.

CLERGYMAN: Oh! oh! what will become of my poor child, oh! oh! Why did you not complain to your master?

DINAH: No use. Overseer say, it master's child; master say, it overseer's child.

CLERGYMAN: Why did you not complain to a magistrate?

DINAH: No use, white man. Law made for white man, do what he please. Black man's word never taken against a white man. Master comical man when he pleased. He told the overseer, he would shoot him, if he ever ill treated me.

CLERGYMAN: Dinah, will he let me speak to him?

DINAH: O yes. White man, if any occasion, mind dat.

CLERGYMAN: Dinah, will you ask him to let me say a few words to him?

DINAH: Deliver you own message, if you please. You no better dan me, as I know of. You servant, well as me.

CLERGYMAN: I know it, Dinah. Another time, I will ask for you, Dinah.

DINAH: Now you speak like gemman, I ask him. [*Opens the door and speaks.*] Massa, David wish to speak wid you, but he fraid to offend you.

PLANTER: [*Comes in.*] Well, David, what do you want?

CLERGYMAN: Master, if I might be permitted without offence, I should like to speak to you.

PLANTER: If it is nothing unreasonable or saucy, I am very willing to hear it; what do you want?

CLERGYMAN: Sir, whether you know it or not, I am a white man, and have been kidnapped.

PLANTER: Whether you was kidnapped or not, I do not know, but I bought you fairly of a slave dealer and gave nine hundred dollars for you, which I am afraid is more than you are worth—I have the bill of sale in my pocket, given me by Jonas Ruffle. He told me you could read and write, and had often tried to pass for a white man. You saw him give me the receipt, but you said nothing.

CLERGYMAN: Jonas Ruffle, if that is his name, is a kidnapping villain. I am as much entitled to my liberty as any man, but I was afraid to speak, and wanted to get out of his hands.

PLANTER: It may be so; but you see you are entirely in my power, or to use your own phrase in your discourse, "Providence, for some inscrutable purposes, which it does not become us to pry into," has delivered you into my hands. And, as you have proved in your discourse, which you preached, that the institution of slavery is not inconsistent with Christianity, I shall have no scruple to keep you in my service. If you were kidnapped, I know nothing of it; I bought you fairly and paid nine hundred dollars for you. Still, as I profess to be a just man, if you can show any sufficient reasons why you should be emancipated, that will not apply to all my servants, I will emancipate you, though it has cost so much; and I will not be very hard with you, for I will leave Dinah to speak for herself. Ask me no questions, but stick to your text, and be respectful, and abide by the result.

DINAH: Massa, if you go for let white man go, let Dinah go too.

PLANTER: Hold your tongue, Dinah. Let David speak, and then you may answer.

CLERGYMAN: I am a free man: I was kidnapped. I was born free.

DINAH: All men born free. I was kidnapped as soon as I was born. Master buy me. Master buy David. David say slavery not wrong; den not wrong to make David slave. If slavery lawful, den kidnapping lawful. If massa let David go, den massa let Dinah go; my children, dat massa sold, more than pay for Dinah.

CLERGYMAN: I am a gentleman; a minister of the Gospel. My wife is a lady like yours; my little tender children, would you have them brought up as poor, ignorant, degraded beings? Think of your own children, if you have any. My two sons just entering college, would you have them taken away and sent to work in the cotton-fields, exposed to the broiling sun, and fed on a peck of corn a week, and liable to be whipped on the naked back, whenever they were unable to complete their stint. My beautiful daughter:—oh sir!—oh sir!—[*weeps and wrings his hands;*] we are not of such a degraded race. The negroes are a degraded race, but I am not: O spare us, sir, spare us.

DINAH: Massa, great changes in dis world. De great king in de Bible was sent to eat grass in old time. De great French king in our time, sent into the wilderness, where he died all alone. Dey offended God. White man preach in de pulpit, slavery right; now, he feel de change too; he made a slave himself. He say de negro degraded race. White man a little degraded himself, now. Let him and his woman and children be slaves a few years, dey will be more degraded dan de negroes, and if his beautiful darter he is so proud on, is made a breeding wench, as dey made me be, her children will be of all de colors of de rainbow. Massa's grandfather, as massa knows, was a Virginia convict; my grandfather was an African King. Master great man now; my grandfather kidnapped, and I a poor negro slave; white minister preach, slavery right, and now he and all his folks are made slaves. White man very proud; when he free; very mean when he slave; very cruel when he master; when he slave, no trust him at all. Negro, self first, friend next. White man, all self. Massa, I serve you long; I bear all; when you whip me, I bear it: what you bid, dat I do. If I have enough to eat, I glad; if I have not, I go hungry. Massa, if you let white man go, let me go. Great change in de world massa.—

PLANTER: Stop, Dinah; don't run on forever; and be more respectful. Speak, David.

CLERGYMAN: My indignation chokes me. Is it not enough, that I am obliged to humble myself, and entreat for my release, for the sake of my poor wife and children, when I am as much entitled to freedom as yourself; but I must be obliged to speak alternately with this—? for shame, sir, for shame.

PLANTER: If your indignation chokes you, I am glad of it, as it will save me the trouble. You impudent scoundrel, if you speak to me in that way again, I will have you tied up and whipped. Remember that is not the way to get any thing of me; now speak, if you have any thing reasonable to say, or I shall say at once, I will not grant your request.

CLERGYMAN: Pardon me, master, I forgot myself.—yet, I must say, though I am a Clergyman, and a man of peace, by nature and education, if we were in the wilderness, alone.

PLANTER: You scoundrel; do you mean to challenge your master?

CLERGYMAN: Pardon me, Sir, it is the weakness of human nature. Your have me in your power, and I must submit; but, if it were not for my poor wife and children's sake, I feel as if I could be cut to pieces, sooner than say one word more; but as it is, Sir, hear me patiently. Do you suppose you can keep me here a slave?

PLANTER: I told you to ask me no questions, and to behave respectfully; you have disobeyed me: but I will overlook it this once. If you are very turbulent, I will not trouble myself with you, but will sell you to a more humane master than myself, at the horse market, tomorrow, and then you may settle the question with him. Do you mind me, now?

DINAH: Please, Massa, let me speak. You no understand de white man like me. White man's justice no use de scales and weights, he use the steelyards; one white man weigh down one hundred black men. White man say, slavery right; but he mean, for de black. He say dat, cause he white himself. If he black man, den he say slavery bad for black man, good for white man. But de poor negro, he say slavery bad for all; for de white, for de black, for de colored. White man tell black man to submit and obey master; but when de white man be slave, he no submit himself, tho' he be preacher. David say, wrong to fight master, yet he want to fight master himself. White man despise de negro, because he black, and not shaped so well as de white man. Black preacher say, nebber mind, wedder you be black or wedder you be white; nebber be ashamed of dat, God made you as he please; and he say if you are a slave, obey massa, and never run away, submit to God's will, we be raised again, de black as well as white. Den, if de black be good, he be changed, and become beautiful, just as de crawling cater-pillar be changed to beautiful butterfly; so de poor, whipped, branded and despised negro become changed to beautiful smiling creature. Den cruel, wicked, handsome white man, be changed too. Den his white face be changed to suit his cruel, wicked heart. Den de Judge come, and brand de cruel white man on de face, wid de thumb screw, de whip and de ladder; den de mark of Cain be on him forever; and den dese wicked white men keep company together, and no need of any oder hell, or any oder devil.

PLANTER: Don't be impudent, Dinah; if you are, look out.

DINAH: No, massa, no. Dinah not be impudent. Den massa, if Dinah get to heaven, if you kind to Dinah, den Dinah kind to you, massa. But de white preacher, who say it right to keep slaves—O massa—massa! what do you think come of him? Will not de priests of Baal and Moloch and Jumbo rise in judgment against him? What harm did de priests of Baal and Moloch and Jumbo do? De priests of Baal honor Baal instead of God! de priests of Moloch honor Moloch instead of God; and de new negro honor Jumbo, and tink he honor de true God; but de white Christian minister, when he say, slavery right, den he dishonor God; den what will become of de white minister, who do so when he know better? De white minister, he put on de fine clothes, and he go into pulpit, and he have de white handkerchief in his hand, and de shining ring on his little finger, and he read something dat he has written in a book, and he spreads out his hand, and he turn his face to de right and to de left, and he speak pretty words, and he tink he preach de Gospel, and he call himself ambassador of Christ. But Christ preached to de poor man; de white man preach, for please de rich man. Very pleasant to preach sermon, when he get quarter dollar a piece, for dem all; but poor black have work hard all day for nothing. De white minister take de quarter dollar in his pocket, and he say, right to keep slaves who get nothing for what dey do, but a minister is well paid for what he does. White minister very tender of his own daughter; he cares nothing for de black man's daughter. He very tender of his own sons, he cares nothing for black man's sons. He hate to have his son work, so he make de poor negro work for him. Den he calls de negro lazy rascal, cause he cant work all de time. He do nothing himself, but he call negro lazy; O massa, massa. Where all de tobacco, and de wheat, and de rice, and de cotton come from? De poor, lazy, 'graded negro raise um all. White man no work; but he call de negro lazy, and he whip de poor negro; de poor black man, de poor black woman, and de boys, and de gals, cause dey cant work *all* de time. Den massa give some of his corn to de horse, and some to de cow, and some to de hogs, and some to de poor negro. Den massa take all de money his poor negroes get for him by de cotton, de rice, de wheat, and de tobacco, and he go to de cock fight, and he lose money dare; and he go to de horse race, and he lose his money dare; and he play cards all day and all night, a week at a time, and he lose his money dare, till all de money his poor negroes got him, all gone, and den he 'bliged to sell one of de poor negroes to raise money. Den he sell de husband away from de black woman, and he sell de children away from dare moder, and he berry cross wid his poor slaves, and he whip em, and sometimes he get drunk, and den he berry bad indeed. But my master berry good for white man. When he sell my husband away from me, master said he berry sorry to part wid him, but he must have de money. And when he sell my three young children from me, and I was 'stracted, he sent and got back my youngest child, but de poor child took sick and died, but I never forgot master so good, and den massa berry good to broder Tom, when he died, and I never forgot dat neder. White people and black people bery different, massa. Do good to de white people all de days of your life, and de white man tank you bery much; den you 'fend de white man in a berry little matter, den he angry and he forget all de good you have done him all your life, and he hate you for dat little ting. But de black man, spoze you 'buse him every day, starve him, kick him, whip him, den afterwards speak one kind word to de poor black man, and you laugh and do little ting for him, or for his fader or for his moder, or his child, den he forget all de 'buse you gave him. You take de handsome white man, you send him College, where he learn to spell, to read, and to write and cypher, and every ting, and he read de good Book, and you give him money, and you try every way to make him good, but you cant make him good. White man always fight and quarrel, and he stab wid de knife and he fight de duel, and he kill his friend, and he berry cruel; always cruel and proud; and he tink he berry brave, but de white man not very brave; he always have de pistol or de knife in his pocket; he 'fraid, when he has no knife, no pistol. White man not bery brave; white man 'shamed to lie, but he deceive always, and he cheat; white man no like to steal, but he rob; he no like to rob white man,

95

dat 'gainst de law; but he cheat de Indian, he rob de Indian; he 'fraid of de Indian: white man not berry brave; he practise wid de pistol, and he practise wid de rifle, den he go into de bush, and he shoot de Indian, den berry proud; white man 'fraid of de Indian: why white man always practice wid de pistol; why wid de rifle? cause he 'fraid. Gib de white man every ting, you cant make him good; always greedy, never satisfied. White man tink he preach de gospel; he no preach de gospel. He tell a poor negro, "obey your massa." He never tell massa, go to de horse race, or de cock fight, or play cards. He tell poor negro, not to steal. He never tell massa, give your servants 'nuff to eat. He tell de negro, not to run away; he never tell masters not be cruel and make poor negro run away. Yet de gospel say, massa, don't treaten your slave: why dont de white minister say, white man, don't beat your slave, dont curse him, don't abuse em; white minister 'fraid to say dat. But de poor negro, he not allowed to read, he kept to work *all* de time; he hab but little to eat—not allowed to go from the plantation,—not allowed to have a gun, de white man so 'fraid; how can poor negro learn any ting? And de white man say, de poor negro 'graded. Tis de cruel law 'grade de poor negro. Yet de planter 'fraid of de poor negro for all dat. Massa no 'casion to fear de negro; de yellow man,—massa de yellow man,—your own son, massa, he part white man, look out for him, massa. He cunning like de white man, he strong like de negro, he brave like de negro; look out for de yellow man. He know, he white man's son, he proud too. When de yellow man whispers in de black man's ear, den master be 'fraid, den you have 'casion.

PLANTER: Hold you tongue, Dinah. How dare you say such a thing?

DINAH: Please, master, let Dinah say one word, and den I done.

PLANTER: Say on, Dinah, but dont be impudent.

DINAH: Massa, when your moder sick, I 'tended her night and day till she died: when mistress sick, I 'tended her night and day till she died; now massa, what has dis white man done, dat you make him free, and keep poor Dinah slave?

PLANTER: Well, Dinah, upon the whole, I have concluded to give you your freedom; and now you may leave me when you please.

DINAH: I tank you very much, massa. Now I free woman, I hope I shall not be 'bused by de overseer any more. But massa, Dinah never leave you. Where I go? My husband if he alive, is a slave; and wedder slave or no, he never see Dinah more. If I go to him, he say "Go away, you had yellow child; go away." No massa, I stay wid you and work for you just de same as before I made free. O massa, white people tink dey very wise, but dey very foolish. Why dey do wrong for nothing? Why not make good laws, and set all de negros free? Give dem nuff to eat; make dem strong, den dey work harder for you den dey do now. Let every black man have his wife to himself: no more sell de children from de moder. Den de black people live without fear, dey work hard again for you. Only gib dem a little share, very little share of what de black man raise for you, only a little share of de wheat and de corn, dey raise for you, and a little share of de tobacco to smoke de pipe, and let dem have it for dare own, to do what dey please wid, den dey have heart to work, and no need to pay overseer to whip de poor negro. Den what do negro raise over dare own share, be more dan all you get now, and all be honest and fair; no cheat, no wrong. Den no starve negro, no whip, no 'buse poor negro woman; den no more colored child any more. Den no need of de pistol or de knife in de pocket, for fear of de negro; den no need of dogs to hunt de runaways or rifles to shoot dem. O massa, massa, only treat de black well, dey make your bravest soldiers. Dey not brag and curse and swear like de white man, nor hide behind de cotton bags, nor creep away in de bush, nor take de scalp; but dey stand out bold in de open field, and no run away. O massa, why you take so much trouble to do wrong, when, only do right, it cost you no trouble at all? You 'fraid of de negro now cause he slave: make de negro free, he fight all your enemies for you, and drive dem away.

Massa, you 'member de battle of Bladensburgh, when de white men brag so?

97

Massa, you 'member de dunghill cock you bought for five dollars, dat you tout was a game-cock, how he crowed and clapped his wings, and looked so bold, till he saw the henhawk come, and den he run and hid in a hole; yet de dunghill cock taut he was very brave, till he saw de hen-hawk. So de white soldiers brag, till bimby dey see de English come, and den dey all flung down de guns and run away. And den all de bravest officers tried to get before de white soldiers to stop dem: den Major Bluster, and Col. Bombast, and Capt. Buttermilk tried which could run fastest *to stop de soldiers*, but Capt. Buttermilk won de race, but he could not stop de soldiers. Massa, white soldiers like de dunghill cock, dey crow very loud. Massa, black man not crow very loud; he no like to fight, he love peace. But, for all dat, he fight when he 'bliged to. Massa, you 'member Col. Bully? [PLANTER *in a reverie, pay no attention.*] Col. Bully use to come play all fours wid master and he bridge de cards, and he turn up Jack so often dat massa lose one hundred dollars. Den massa called Colonel Bully "damn cheat—damn rascal." Den Colonel Bully sent Mr. Thomas Fool wid de challenge to fight de duel, and master 'greed to fight him wid rifles, and Mr. Thomas Fool was Colonel Bully's second, and Mr. Likewise, de great member or Congress, was massa's second; and master practiced wid de rifle for a week, till de day 'pinted come. Den dey all went out in de field together, Master and Colonel Bully, and Mr. Thomas Fool and Mr. Likewise. Den broder Tom told me master look very pale, wid de taut of killing his old friend, Colonel Bully; and his hand trembled very much when he took de rifle, and Colonel Bully's trembled very much too; I spose he hate to kill massa, his old friend. And when de seconds, Mr. Thomas Fool, and Mr. Likewise, told em to take dare ground, Col. Bully told master he did not wish to take his life, and master very glad, cause he did not wish to kill his old friend Colonel Bully, and den master say dat when he called Colonel Bully "damn cheat, damn rascal," perhaps he was wrong, perhaps he was right; and broder Tom told me it was de handsomest 'pology he ever heard in his life. And Colonel

Bully said master was a brave man and a man of honor, and he was satisfied; and den dey shook hands. But Mr. Thomas Fool said he smelt a rat, and he always hated de smell of a rat, and he would not stop a moment longer. And Mr. Likewise said he'd be damn'd, if it was not a skunk, that he smelt, and he'd be off. So dey both of dem went away. Den Master and Colonel Bully had a bowl of hot toddy togeder, and afterward dey marched round de yard, arm in arm, and all de servants made a procession after dem, and master told Jack de fiddler to play "see de conquering hero come;" but Jack, he make mistake and play de rogue's march; but de Colonel and master so agitated, dey never find em out till next day; den massa was going to whip Jack, but Jack begged master not to whip him, 'cause he very old; and he said he was so tosticated with joy, cause master come back alive, when he was so desperate bold, dat he never mind what he did. Den master give Jack half pint of rum. Den broder Tom say Mr. Thomas Fool was like a drum, he made a great noise, but he got nothing in him for all dat. And broder Tom say Mr. Likewise was de bravest, de most venturesome, de most daring, de most 'dacious man he eber saw in all his life, *to be second in a duel.* He was de noblest specimen he ever seed of de shovelry of de soud.

PLANTER: Hold you tongue, Dinah. Are you going to run on forever. I have not heard a word, that you have said, this half hour. What have you been saying, Dinah?

DINAH: Nothing at all, massa, I only say, when I see a bold young man, wid a knife or a dirk under his jacket, I always tink of de dung-hill cock, he no match for de game cock, unless he have de gaffs on, he know dat berry well.

PLANTER: Hold your tongue, Dinah. Now, what have you to say, David?

CLERGYMAN: When you have done with the black woman, I will speak.

PLANTER: You speak in a saucy manner, as if you were better than she is; but I tell you I will not bear half so much from you.

CLERGYMAN: Will you be so good as to tell me, if you know, what

99

are to become of my wife and little children, where my two sons are gone, and what is to become of my daughter; as to myself I will speak afterwards.

PLANTER: Your wife and children are sent to Kentucky, your two boys are gone to Alabama, your daughter is gone with the Louisiana young man, to Natchez.

CLERGYMAN: [*Wrings his hands a moment and weeps.*]—Sir, you must know, whatever you pretend, that I am really a free white citizen of the United States.

PLANTER: Whatever you may pretend, I have slaves whiter than you, much. If I take the word of every light-complexioned slave that I buy, that he is a free man, I should be very simple indeed. I gave nine hundred dollars for you and have the bill of sale in my drawer: your wife and three children were sold for one thousand dollars: your two sons were sold for five hundred a piece: your daughter was sold for two thousand dollars, but she would have brought a great deal more, if she had been set up at auction in Washington, where there are so many rich southern planters. You preach pretty well, but I have a colored boy, who can read and write as well as you, and the former black preacher preached much better sense than you, but he spoke out too plain, and your doctrine is much more agreeable to my interest as well as my conscience and I think I shall keep you at that business. But, I will hear what you have to say. But, either you have ate too much hoe-cake, or you do not like your text, for you seem incapable of saving any thing for yourself.

CLERGYMAN: Sir, I am now satisfied, that I have nothing to expect either from your justice or humanity. I shall therefore appeal to the justice and law of my country for protection. I have given you sufficient notice and warning, that I am a white man, and that I am a free man, and all my family are free. I shall condescend to no further intreaties or representations, but shall take measures as I see fit to obtain and secure my liberty. That I shall recover heavy, perhaps ruinous damages, from some tribunal of justice, if I can but obtain a hearing, I will not suffer myself to doubt; in the mean time, I caution you, for your own sake, not to proceed too far.

PLANTER: [*Calling.*] Peter, bring the whip. [PETER *comes in with a whip.*] Now tie this impudent scoundrel up, and give him thirty-nine lashes. [PETER *ties him up and whips him.*]

PLANTER: Now run over to the tavern, to the slave-dealer from Georgia, and tell him he can have David for eight hundred dollars, as he offered.

CLERGYMAN: Infernal villain! but you will meet your reward for this.

[CLERGYMAN *in deep wood. A sound of rifles firing at a distance, and dogs barking. He climbs up into a high tree with very thick foliage, and conceals himself. Enter an* OVERSEER *with ten* ASSISTANTS, *armed with muskets and rifles, and a large number of dogs. After smelling round some time, the dogs stop at the large tree, and begin to bark.*]

OVERSEER: The villain must be here. Look up and see if you can discover him. [*The* ASSISTANTS *step backwards and forwards, looking up, at different distances from the tree.*]

ASSISTANT: Yes, there he is; I see him plainly. Come down, you villain, or I will shoot. Let me fire first, I will bring him down. [*Fires.*]

CLERGYMAN: Don't fire again; I will come down. [*He descends. The ball has cut off half of one ear. They beat him with their whips, and knock him down; then tie and carry him off.*]

FROM THE PLAY'S CONCLUSION

[*St. Louis, in Missouri. Enter* COLONEL FUSTIAN, *followed by the* CLERGYMAN, *handcuffed.*]

COL. FUSTIAN: David, here you are now, at home, at St. Louis. Stay here, and I will send one of the wenches to you in a moment. You must learn to be active and handy, and you will have enough to eat. We dont starve our servants here. But, you must not be sulky. You shall have kind treatment, if you behave well; but, if you are saucy and disorderly, look out; for I will shoot you as quick as I would an Indian. [*Goes out.*]

[*Enter* CLARA, *dressed in dirty, shabby clothes.*]

CLERGYMAN: Clara! O Clara, my dear child! can it be you? Come to me my dear child.

CLARA: My dear, dear father, [*She runs towards him, then suddenly turns away, puts her hands before her face, and sobs and weeps.*] O my father, my father, I can never come near you any more. I am a poor degraded, worthless creature, not fit to come into your presence. I have been abused; as if I had been one of the Mormon girls.

CLERGYMAN: Is it so—my poor child? [*Weeps and groans, then gnashes his teeth with rage.*] This trial is too much for me. None but the humble negro can bear this. Clara, my child, unfasten my hands, if you can. [*She assists to unfasten his hands.*] Do you know where your poor mother is, my dear child?

CLARA: [*Sobbing violently.*] I do not, indeed, Sir. I have never seen her since the night when we were kidnapped. I can never look my mother in the face again. I wish I was dead.

CLERGYMAN: Where are your little brothers? Do you know, Clara?

CLARA: I dont know whether they are alive or dead. But brother Bill is dead.

COL. FUSTIAN'S VOICE IS HEARD: Clara! Clara!

CLARA: O my father; what shall I do? what shall I do?

COL. FUSTIAN'S VOICE AGAIN: Clara! Clara! where are you?

CLARA: I will come in a moment. [*Sobs violently, while she releases her father's hands.*]

[*Enter* COLONEL FUSTIAN.]

COL. FUSTIAN: Why did you not come, the moment you heard me call, you worthless hussey? [*Strikes her with the cow-hide, and kicks her.*]

CLERGYMAN: [*Interposing.*] What do you mean, vile ruffian? [CLARA *runs out.*]

COL. FUSTIAN: O, you rise against your master, do you? [*Strikes the* CLERGYMAN *over the head and face with the cow-hide, till the* CLERGYMAN *wrests it out of his hands.*]

COL. FUSTIAN: [*Drawing out a pistol.*] So you will have it, will you? [*Fires and wounds the* CLERGYMAN, *who immediately knocks him down, and tramples on him.*]

COL. FUSTIAN: Murder! murder! help! O I am killed. Oh! oh! oh!

[*Enter* SLAVES.]

SLAVES: O, David has killed Massa! David has killed Massa! Get away as fast as you can, or we shall all be killed. [*They all run out, leaving* DAVID *alone.*]

CLERGYMAN: [*Turning over the body.*] I have killed him, sure enough, I am afraid. God forgive me.

MOB: [*Heard without.*] Where is the murdering villain? Shoot him! shoot him! hang him! hang him! drown him! drown him! Cut him to pieces! No, no! burn him alive! burn him alive, over a slow fire, like the mulatto fellow!

[*Last.* CLERGYMAN'S *study.* MR. DORSEY *fast asleep. Enter* MRS. DORSEY *and* CLARA.]

MRS. DORSEY: [*Taking off her things.*] Bless me! Clara, how late we have staid. It is almost eight o'clock, and here is your poor father, fast asleep. I suppose, he was tired of waiting for his tea. I have been too negligent. He ought to have had it by five o'clock. [*Goes to the top of the stairs, and speaks.*] Elsavena, get tea ready immediately, and call us down. [*Returns.*] Clara, did you observe how strangely Mrs. Cranberry had herself rigged out, this afternoon? 'Tis strange; how some people love to make themselves conspicuous, even by absurdities, and at church.

CLARA: You know, mother, she is called very handsome, and is much celebrated among the men. Dr. Jalap is said to admire her very much. Do you think it will be a match?

MRS. DORSEY: No, you little fool; no. He is an old bachelor, and is too much filled with a false notion of his own beauty, to think of hers. She is a coquet, and, like all coquets, must have somebody or other to flirt with. She is pretty well known, and has nobody else, and he flirts with her, to keep up some appearance of importance. Did you mind, Clara, what a strange looking thing Mrs. Cawdle had on her head?—something between a cap and a bonnet.

CLARA: Yes, mother; but she is so pretty, she looks well in any thing; any body else would look like a fright in it. Did you observe Mr. Popinjay? What beautiful whiskers he has? How very genteel and graceful!

MRS. DORSEY: Pooh! you silly fool: he is only fit to stand behind a counter, to attract customers, and help young misses to tape and bobbin.

CLARA: That is not his business—

MRS. DORSEY: I know that very well; but he is nothing but a handsome calf. He perfumes himself, and wears rings on his fingers. I don't know, but I am told he belongs to a foppish uniform company, has made a caucus speech; and when he is fifty years old, if he lives so long, will be a colonel in the Militia. Did you mind the middle-sized man, next to him, dressed quite plain, with a very cheerful composed look; he is worth a dozen of that large, tall handsome fellow. There is a lion in him; the big fellow has no more heart than a mouse.

CLARA: Why mother? How can you say so?

CLERGYMAN: [*Groans and starts in his sleep.*] Oh! oh! oh!

MRS. DORSEY: Your father is dreaming, Clara; wake him up. Mr. Dorsey! Mr. Dorsey!

CLARA: [*Kisses her father, then shakes him, but cannot rouse him.*] Mother, shall I bring up a pitcher of cold water, and throw over him?

MRS. DORSEY: Oh no; that is not necessary; he will wake, presently. It is a touch of the night-mare; or what the Doctors call catalepsy. Your father ate too much of Mrs. Thingumbob's pound cake. I kept winking to him, not to do it, but he would.

CLARA: I suppose catalepsy is Hebrew for cat sleep; but I thought cat-sleep was the next thing to being wide awake. But father is sound asleep, very sound indeed.

CLERGYMAN: [*Groans and mutters in his sleep.*] O, dear! O dear! O dear!

MRS. DORSEY: [*Alarmed.*] Run and fetch the smelling-bottle immediately, Clara, and bring up the camphorated spirits. [*She takes* MR. DORSEY's *hand and claps it very hard a number of times.*] Wake up, Mr. Dorsey, wake up! [CLARA *runs out and returns with the bottles.*]

MRS. DORSEY: [*Puts the smelling-bottle to his nose, then pours a few drops of the camphorated spirits in his mouth.*] Wake up, Mr. Dorsey; wake up—Oh, he is coming to—I see.

CLERGYMAN: [*Opens his eyes, stares wildly round a few seconds, looks at* MRS. DORSEY, *and* CLARA *by turns.*] Can I believe my eyes? Are you safe, my dear wife! My dear Clara! [*starts up suddenly, and kisses them with great joy.*]

CLARA: Why, what is the matter, father?

CLERGYMAN: [*Goes to the looking-glass, and examines his ear.*] No, my ear is safe and sound. Glad enough of that, am I. [*Opens his mouth, and examines his front teeth.*] No, my teeth are all in their places. Glad of that too! wonderful! wonderful! Am I not all over dirt and blood, Clara?

CLARA: No, father, not at all. [*Whispers her mother.*] Father must be out of his head, to talk so, mother.

CLERGYMAN: [*Looks in his pocket-book.*] Dear me, dear me, where is the thousand pound note? Gone, I am afraid. Sorry for that;—very sorry indeed. [*Looks in his secretary.*] What, the silver spoon gone? very sorry for that, too. My dear, have you taken away a great silver spoon, that I put in here?

MRS. DORSEY: What silver spoon do you mean? I have seen none, Mr. Dorsey.

CLERGYMAN: I mean the great spoon, that was sent me by the Honorable Committee of the State of Ohio; long enough *to sup with the evil one*, and twice as valuable as the Webster Vase.

MRS. DORSEY: You are dreaming still, with your eyes wide open. Wake up! wake up!

CLERGYMAN: My dear, have you heard how long Archbishop Tillotson has been in town?

MRS. DORSEY: For shame, Mr. Dorsey, for shame: Bishop Tillotson has been dead this hundred years.

CLERGYMAN: Strange! strange! Have you see Dr. Abernethy, from London; sent here by Queen Victoria, to inquire after my health?

MRS. DORSEY: Nonsense! You are dreaming still: wake up, wake up!—Pull your father's hair, Clara.

CLARA: Why, mother! How can you talk so? I would not pull a hair out of father's head, unless it was a gray one, for the handsomest tortoise-shell comb in Boston.

CLERGYMAN: Why, Mrs. Dorsey, it must be you that are dreaming. Have you not seen the great London bookseller, Mr. Lackington?

MRS. DORSEY: My patience is entirely gone, Mr. Dorsey. [*She fetches him a rousing box in the ear.*]

CLERGYMAN: Why, woman, what do you mean? I have not received such a blow since I was a boy, when I fell down chimney.

MRS. DORSEY: I struck harder than I intended; but you have told me a great many times, that if I could not wake you, when you had the night-mare, not to stand upon any ceremony, but to give you a good cuff. You said your good mother always did so. You said the pain of the blow was nothing to the distress you felt in your sleep.

CLERGYMAN: Well, well; this is by way of homoeopathic practice. This blow that has brought back, my senses, I am sure, would have taken them away, if I had been in possession of them.—Yes, yes; I see plainly enough now, how it is. I have been dreaming; and now I am awake, I find the course of the world is always the same. By waking, I have saved my ear, it is true; but I have lost the great silver spoon; and if I have saved my front teeth, have lost the thousand pounds sterling; but I and my dear Clara safe, and that to me is worth a thousand such notes.

CLARA: [*Beginning to weep.*] Don't talk so, father, don't; you frighten me to death, and distress mother, very much.

CLERGYMAN: Never mind, Clara. I am well enough now, and entirely awake. But I have had the most strange, frightful, horrible dream;—it is incredible, almost impossible;—but, whether awake or asleep, whether dreaming or burning alive, as I thought I was, Clara, in St. Louis, for protecting you, when Mrs. Dorsey awaked me, hand me that manuscript sermon, you see on the shelf yonder, tied with a blue ribbon. [*She hands him the sermon, and he tears it to atoms.*]

MRS. DORSEY: Why, Mr. Dorsey, what are you doing? You will want a straight-jacket soon. That sermon, all your parishioners said, was the best you ever delivered.

CLERGYMAN: Best or worst; this hand shall be consumed like Bishop Cranmer's, before it shall ever write such another. Next Sunday, my dear, I deliver my solemn recantation, and, as I presume, take leave of my parish forever. My conscience, that worldly prosperity has long deadened, is now roused to life and activity, and, with the blessing of God, ever again shall a regard for the applause of men, the hope of riches and honors, or the fear of poverty and approach, so dull my moral sense, as to induce me to speak complacently of a system of shocking cruelty and injustice, or quiet the caustic but healthful action of penitence and remorse, by crying "*peace, peace, when there is no peace.*" But this may require some sacrifices on your part, Mrs. Dorsey, which, possibly, you may think too great for me to ask of you. Will you leave your husband, Nancy?

MRS. DORSEY: Never; I am fully satisfied that you are in your right senses, now. I have long thought you were wrong in relation to the subject you refer to; but I have said nothing, because I thought you knew best; and I was partly persuaded by your arguments and the opinions of others. But I am ready to make any sacrifice, you think necessary, and to bear my lot in the path of duty, be it what it may; relying cheerfully upon that Providence, which never forsakes those who trust in it. But, Bill and Jack are just come in with the three little ones, and Elsavena calls us to tea.

The End

107

The Fugitives

CHARACTERS

A GROUP OF SLAVES

MALIE,	*an aged woman*
GHESTLER AND ZONGOLA,	*her sons*
IOLA,	*a daughter*
CARLOS,	*a field slave*
BANDALOZ,	*the master*

SCENE I

[A Carolinian Plantation.]

GHESTLER: Come, come dear mother, look ye, the joyous
    Moon is up, and the old house clock, heedless
    Of our march, shows that the old sentinel
    Who watches vigilantly when night comes
    With its lone weary hours, will tell the tale
    Of our departure,—then, then dear mother,
    All is up with us and, and Iola—
    O God protect her! Iola, she will fall
    A prey to that hyena—Bandaloz.
MALIE: Speak yet more gently, Ghestler; for I fear
    Your words may fall upon some listening
    Ear, and then we may find our miserable
    Forms upon yon trees, where others like us
    Seeking heaven's boon to enjoy, have been
    The gaze of many passers by. O Ghestler,
    Much my heart fails me; but to-night I watched
    Yon star, and oft it seemed to talk with me
    And bid me hope that in that land where dwells
    No vile Bandaloz, I may rest myself
    And die in peace.
GHESTLER: *[Looking wildly and listening.]*
    Depart!—haste, quick, for lo,
    Bandaloz comes! *[Exit* GHESTLER.*]*

    *[*MALIE *enters a low cottage where lies* IOLA *just waked from sleep.]*

IOLA: Mother, I've had sweet dreams
    To-night,—methought that we were in that happy

Land of which Ghestler so often tells us, yes,
The land where wakes no Bandaloz to fright
Us evermore. But mother, shall we haste
To-night, or shines the moon too brilliant now?
Zongola told me yesternight that ere
The midnight hour should come, we'd gather up
Ourselves, and guided by that star in yon
Fair sky, speed us to the northern regions,
Where smiles all that is glorious, aye, all
That is beautiful.
MALIE: Yes, yes my daughter,
Ghestler has been here and bids us wait for him
Ere twelve shall strike; for he says Bandaloz
Will be passing from the revel and you
May then fall a prey to his foul passions,—
And my child, thou knows't I'd rather lay thee
In thy grave quickly, and mourn, aye mourn till
All my heart were gone, than cast thee forth to lead
A life of infamy, howe'er thy beauty
May attract the gaze of those around his board
Who throng, and quaff the wine that turns to fierce
Madness his every thought and look.
Iola, darling child! it is for thee
That I will brave the dangers that attend
A flight from this vile land of servitude.
'Twould not be long ere my poor weary limbs
Would find a grave beneath the sighing palm,
Should I remain; but O for thee my heart
Is wakeful ever, and the midnight hour
Finds me upon my knees, beseeching heaven
To compass thee around, to shield thy frail
And delicate form from the touch of night
That would contaminate, or bid depart
The Holy Spirit from thy trembling soul.
Iola, child,—fear not, you tremble,—strong
Is heaven in the defence of innocence,

Place there thy trust, and guardian angels
Shall encompass thee. But 'tis eleven;
Soon Ghestler and Zongola will be here,
And we must not detain them, lest a worse
Cup far than death should be dealt to us—Hark!
They come; take now that parcel on the shelf
And place it close in thy bosom; O keep
It near thy heart, for it contains a token
Fair of thy own father's love, who sweetly
Sleeps in yon lowly vale, and knows no more
These griefs that throng around.

[*Enter* GHESTLER *and* ZONGOLA.]

ZONGOLA: Come, mother, come,
And dear Iola you will go with me;
You, mother, with good Ghestler; for he knows
All the wild woods around us, and his arm
Is strong for you to lean upon. The star shines
Bright which is to guide us to the northern
Skies, and the moon begins to hasten down
Behind the hills. [IOLA *weeps*.] Now, now Iola, shame;
Why do you weep? You promised yesternight
That you'd be strong and mind me all the way,
And then you know I promised sacredly,
To help you every hour, to carry
You when weary. Come now, and do not fear.

IOLA: Well, Zongola, I do know I promised
You 'neath the shade of the old palm which rears
Its lofty head close by the clustering
Vines that I've so often tended, that fear
Should not be found within my heart so long
As God should strengthen me; but mother tells
Me of the dreadful doom that may await
Us should we be discovered, and my heart
Does shake most fearfully! Yet I forbear
'Tis not that for a moment I would dwell

Longer beneath this cot, but then the tears
Will come gushing from my eyes, unhidden,
When I think of—[*She pauses.*]

ZONGOLA: Yes, yes, I see, I know,
When you remember Carlos; but I saw
Him ere the sun was low, and he bade me
Say farewell for him, and that soon he'd meet
You by those northern streams whither we hasten.

IOLA: [*Eagerly.*] O, Zongola, did he say thus?
Surely I had not thought that he were free from those
Huge chains that clanked about his heel when last
I gazed upon him from the door as he pass'd
By. I did not dare to cast one farewell
Glance, although my heart were nigh to breaking;
For Bandaloz was near, and though he spoke
No words concerning Carlos, yet methought
He looked searchingly, as if he'd know why
I pressed my side so fearfully, for much
I trembled, lest he'd bear my heart's throbbings!
I feigned a smile, though I had well nigh fainted—
But now I go,—I will be strong, brother,
I will be strong.

ZONGOLA: Do, do, Iola dear.

GHESTLER: [*Coming towards them.*] Hush,
children—haste, it is no time to talk
Of tears: soon the revel will be ended,
And then Bandaloz, like a mad demon,
Will be here to snatch from us Iola!
This is the night he swore he'd make her his;
And then no more shall we behold her form
Gliding among us; and her voice, sweeter
Than music from the rich harp that's played
Within the hall, be lost to us forever.
But never shall he snatch that lamb away
From the embrace of Ghestler. No, never;
For I vowed when last I saw his cursed

Hand smoothing her flowing hair, that never
Should he see her more, save we were lying
In one common grave. Come, dear mother, come;
On Let us pass, and bid adieu, a last
Adieu to this vile sod.

[*They all pass out.*]

SCENE II

[*The Woods—Morning.*]

ZONGOLA: Look, mother, look, Iola sleeps; gladly
I look upon those lids so gently closed;
For well I know her tender feet
Are even now full weary of the way;
But when again we journey, I shall take
Her in my arms, and I know that Ghestler
Will be kind to you and ease you onward.
How I love to look upon her as she
Breathes so gently:—now she sighs, poor thing!
No doubt her womanish heart is shaken
By sad dreams, the fear that we may never
Reach that stream which, crossed, will give us Freedom.
MALIE: No doubt, my boy, 'tis so, or else she fears
The touch of Bandaloz; for daily did
She weep, lest he might come perchance by night,
While sleep dwelt heavy on me, and command
Her to depart and dwell with him. Often
When midnight frowned around us, hath she cried
In dreamy agony, O save me, mother,
For he comes, he comes! but heaven protect
Her now, nor e'er permit her innocence
To pass away.
GHESTLER: You must be faint, my mother,

A weary way we've come since twelve tolled
On the air;—let us break our fast; see, here
Is bread and a few berries that I've gathered
While you slept for a short hour after our
Journey. [GHESTLER *waiting.*] You do not speak,
my mother; are You sick?

MALIE: No, no, my son, but heaven hath
Dealt most kindly with us. Shall we not give
Thanks ere we partake its bounties?

GHESTLER: [*Looking thoughtful.*] Give thanks
Then, mother, if you will; but truly when
I've stood beside my master's board—[*he stops*]—no, not
My master's, but Bandaloz's board, and heard
Mutter'd those words of grace, I've wondered much
If there were any God, or, if a God, where
Dwelt he, or, if he lived, were he aware
Of the affairs of men? Is he righteous,
Mother? If so, how reconcile you all
Of deep, dark, damning sin that hath been witnessed
By the gazing heavens upon that curs'd
Plantation we have left? If God be just
And merciful, as you have often told,
Methinks Bandaloz would less often crave
His supervision!

MALIE: Ghestler, not all who cry
Lord, Lord, shall enter heaven; many will
Claim affinity with him, to whom he'll
Say, Depart, I know you not. That goodness
Is his nature; that his mercy and his love
Unbounded flow, my heart attests. Ghestler,
Cast off that vile suspicion of his justice.
I know thy path hath been with perils rife,
I know the bitter draughts, the scourgings vile,
And all the woes strewed thick within thy path;
Yet hath he not been merciful to thee?
Forgettest thou the hour they sold thy brother

To a Georgian lord, and thou, my boy,
Wast left by my entreaty? Then thou did'st thank
Heaven, and bore witness to the kindness
Of his heart who heard my deep lamenting,
And granted thee to sojourn near my shed!
O Ghestler, he *is merciful*, and much
It pains my heart when my boy dares question
His o'erflowing love.

GHESTLER: I would not pain thee,
That thou knowest well, my mother; I would
To heaven that I could even now, shake
Off each vestige of that unbelief clinging
To my torn heart. But let us eat, only
Give us the blessing, mother. Zongola
Come, and let Iola rest. Now we are
Ready. [*They give thanks and eat.*]

IOLA: [*Waking and looking round.*] Ghestler,
Shall we not hasten? how the sun
Pours down its rays,—the birds are out again,
And o, I long to be fast hastening
To that land where the sun of Freedom shines
With mild, sweet beams,—Come, Ghestler, may we now
Proceed?

GHESTLER: We may not travel by the light of day.

IOLA: What, are we to remain till night
Fall on us with its dim and sable hue?

GHESTLER: Yes, we must venture forth only when night
Shall cover us, and our guide appear.

IOLA: But, brother, much I fear we may not reach
Where all is free, if we thus linger here.

ZONGOLA: Iola, Ghestler sure can tell when best
It suits our safety; besides, Carlos hath
Told us 'twere best to wait the guidance
Of the star in the night heavens, than trust
To the poor knowledge of which we are masters.

IOLA: Yes, now I do remember what he said;

But yet my eye so longs to view that land;
My heart so leaps, e'en at the thought of rest,
(That other name for Freedom) that I would
Hasten night and day, nor tire till touching
That good shore. Now I bethink me, surely
Carlos said he had not been detected
In his flight had he but waited night-fall.
We must, then, now take warning, lest perchance
Our wanderings be discovered. I'm sure
I'd rather die here in these lonely woods,
Where the cool winds sighing their endless tale,
Might tell that poor Iola fled, and laid
Her 'neath their kindly shade. Yes, sooner would
I die, than fall again into the hands
Of Bandaloz; for though he often said
That you, dear mother, should not want for bread,
Nor e'er be sold to labor for another,
(Because of me), I did not much believe;
For well I knew he loved the cursed gold
That's found in Georgian hands, and waited
Only for a timely hour to cast you
Forth, to die in lonesome wretchedness!

MALIE: 'Tis true, Iola, true, my darling child;
He only waited for a favored hour
To part us. Then no more should I hear those
Words of cheer from the bless'd book, which oft hath
Been my only solace. You, Iola,
He permitted to gain knowledge—knowledge,
Which to me, and to your brother, he denied;—
You have read from out these holy leaves, words
That have wiped the gathering tears away—
And given such comfort to my stricken soul,
As I believe none but the Holy One
Could grant. Had'st thou departed, gone then were
Every hope from this poor heart. But yet thou
Liv'st to bless me, child; and though thy beauty

May attract the gaze of some, to me thy
Chief attraction is that filial love, that
Deep hatred of whate'er contaminates,
Taught by the blessed lips of him who bore
Our sins on Calvary's hill. 'Tis this, dear
Child, I trust, that hath giv'n strength, purpose
Of soul to thee, and taught thy every thought
To rise to Him who watches o'er my path,
Who though unseen, will guide thee to that shore
Where Freedom smiles. Keep thou this
book, [*Giving her the Bible*], 'twill teach
Thee more of heaven than yet thou know'st.
Could I but read its sacred lines, how blest
My soul. But soon I trust I shall behold
All that is there revealed of those bright walls
And mansions, fitted up for the abode
Of souls who trust in Christ.

IOLA: Mother, I trust
You will live many years, to eat the bread
And drink the cup of Freedom. Others who
Left the sultry South, with more of hoary
Age upon them, have sought and found with joy
That goodly land.

GHESTLER: [*Rising suddenly and listening.*]
Iola, hush! hark!
Sure amid the brush I hear strange trampling.
Save us, O God! they come! Crouch, Zongola.
Iola, breathe not, lest we die.—Heaven,
High heaven be praised, they've passed and we
Have not been seen. I saw Bandaloz foremost
In the chase, and Carlos too was there.

IOLA: What!
Carlos with him? How this? You do amaze
Me,—Ghestler, it could not be!

GHESTLER: 'Tis even thus, Iola.
Others too were there. Perchance

> They took him, hoping to obtain some track
> Of the wild haunts through which he journeyed
> When he sought to fly from their oppressions.

IOLA: But Ghestler, think you he would betray us,
> Should he chance to pass us?

GHESTLER: I know not, dear Iola.
> But do not fear, for they will
> Not pass this way as they return. Three moons
> Ago, poor Carlos fled, and when the hounds were
> With us, they lost track of him; and, passing
> O'er the river, we returned again.
> So will they do, if I judge rightly, now.
> But let us further go into the woods,
> Where we may lie concealed till the dark night
> O'ertake us—then will we hasten onward.

MALIE: Do, do, dear Ghestler; for my heart well nigh
> Had ceased its throbbings, when your words of praise
> Came to my low crouched ear. Sure it was meet,
> My first-born, that your lips should pour forth
> Praise to Him whose hand hath been a darkening
> Cloud before the eyes of our pursuers.
> What think you now, my Ghestler, of his
> Mercy? Dare you farther question his kind
> Hand, displayed for our deliverance?

GHESTLER: Enough,
> My mother, 'twas his love, his kindness all,
> That turned their feet from this our resting place;
> And never shall my lips forget their song,
> Or my heart fail to offer unto Him,
> Its homage reverent. But we must haste,
> And seek a shelter in the forest woods.

SCENE III

[*A cave in a dense forest.*]

GHESTLER: [*Aside to* ZONGOLA.] Zongola, very much I fear that
      this
  Our toilsome way will fatal prove to our
  Good mother. Her hands are fevered, and her
  Brow is throbbing far too quick, for aught save
  Raging fever. She hardly spake the night
  Past; and the way to me seemed far more drear,
  Because she breathed no prayer—audible,
  I mean; for though I think not much of prayer,
  A kind of feeling cometh over me
  When the name of Jesus is pronounced, which,
  To be honest now, I feel no other time.
ZONGOLA: Ah, yes, I too have watched her for three days
  More closely than before; and though I sought
  To hide it from Iola, yes, and e'en
  Myself, I could but think that she were fast
  Weakening. When I spoke to her, she answered
  But in feeble tones, and in her words
  There seemed less of that ardor than was wont
  To bless our ears. Oh, should she not survive,
  Ghestler, how should we comfort Iola?
  Sure she would wither like a tender plant
  Snapped from the stem that gave it nourishment.
  But, Ghestler, it may be only weariness;
  Can we not rest awhile and nourish her?
  A stream is near at hand. I'll haste and bring
  Fresh water to bathe her limbs, and to refresh
  Her spirit.
GHESTLER: Do it; but much I fear 'twill
  All be vain. This is the seventh night the stars
  Have seen us wandering forth in silence.
  When I carried her within these willing arms
  The night that's fled, she wept, but spoke no words;

I feared to ask the cause, lest she should say
What my heart dreaded. She clasped her wither'd
Arms around my neck, and wept profusely.
Bitter and dreary were the hours that passed.
But yet she lives; and O, heaven grant she
May not die, but live to be our comfort in that
Longed for land to which we haste.

[*Exit* ZONGOLA.]

IOLA: Mother, are
You awake? [*Answering herself.*] No, no, she sleeps.
Ghestler, look!
How parched and fevered are her lips; I fear
She is too weary with the tedious paths
Through which we've traversed, though full well I know
You've carried her quite oft, and bore her through
The tangled swamps, and tarried oftentimes
That she might gain a little rest. But—peace
Upon her rest! Perhaps sleep will refresh
Her spirit, and bring back her strength.
GHESTLER: [*To himself.*] Poor thing, her
hopes, I fear, are idle dreams.

[ZONGOLA *enters.*]

ZONGOLA: How is our mother? has she not waked?
I feared she would be thirsty ere I found
This shell in which to bring her drink. Here are
Some berries, which perchance may strengthen her;
For sparingly hath food been given since
Yesternight.
IOLA: Dear mother, wake; for Zongola
Hath brought you cooling drink, and berries fresh
From the trees.
MALIE: I see, my daughter. Ghestler,
Raise me up, for I feel but poorly. Why!
Is it morning? or what time? I surely

Have been sleeping far too long—shall we haste?
I see the moon,—Ghestler, is it time?
GHESTLER: No,
    Mother, morn will soon be here; but we'll rest
    Ourselves till night shall find us. You were ill;
    And much we feared for you, lest overcome
    With weariness and the cold, chill night damps,
    You might find a grave within this dark
    And lonely forest.
MALIE: Thank you, kind Ghestler;
    For I now remember that my poor heart
    Had the same fear, as sorrowful I laid
    Myself to rest upon these gathered leaves.
    Again hath heaven been kind, to guide our
    Footsteps to this shelter.
IOLA: Yes, mother, true—
    Heaven hath been kind to us; but now, eat
    I pray you, and refresh yourself.
ZONGOLA: [*Aside.*] She looks
    Much better, Ghestler, and I hope she will
    Recover, so that we may soon pursue
    Our route. Iola will do well, for she
    Hath traveled far, though she could scarce forbear
    To weep, as her feet bled profusely. Poor
    Child, how my *heart* bled for her, as she wiped
    The tears from her bright sparkling eyes,
    And tried to smile. I kissed her, but my heart
    Forbade the utterance of a word, lest
    I should weaken the strong purpose displayed
    In her more than earthly face, as she threw
    Back her long dark hair, and called upon high
    Heaven for further strength. O, Ghestler, much
    I wish we had the faith treasured within
    Her breast. It surely does support the soul
    Amid severest trial.
GHESTLER: Yes, perhaps,

'Tis heaven supports her—for far too frail
Were she, to brave the storm we've passed, and those
Chill night winds. But let us go and see
If mother will not come and breathe the fresh
Sweet air, beneath this tree; perhaps it were
Not well, that she should longer lie within
The cave.

SCENE IV

[MALIE *and* IOLA, *seated beneath the shade of a tree near the entrance to the cave.*]

IOLA: How gloriously the sun shines over
　　　The hills. Mother, does not the gentle breeze
　　　Refresh you. O 'tis pleasant here, and were
　　　We but escaped quite out of this vile land,
　　　How would I sing. How long before our feet
　　　Shall tread that fair green spot where Freedom lives,
　　　Sweet mother?
MALIE: I know not, daughter, but trust
　　　In heaven 'twill not be long. Ghestler can
　　　Tell perhaps how near we are to that bright
　　　Shore. I trust that I shall reach it; though oft
　　　My heart has failed since we left the dwelling
　　　Where my poor heart hath felt so much of ill,
　　　And bitter grief.
IOLA: O yes, dear mother, heaven
　　　Will hear our prayers; and though kind Ghestler
　　　Says he does not much believe in Him whom
　　　Our hearts love, yet when we are delivered,
　　　I know he can but feel that God is good,
　　　And that his care hath brought us to that shore.
MALIE: Yes, yes, I trust he may be taught, though late,
　　　That love divine appointed e'en his lot.
　　　True, sorrow hath been his, as well as mine.

He would not be subdued,—'twas this that caused
Bandaloz to deal thus roughly with him:
If he but learn of Christ, my heart will cease
Its throbbings with sweet peace.

[GHESTLER *and* ZONGOLA *come to the cave, bringing* CARLOS *with them.*]

IOLA: O, Carlos! What!
    Oh! mother, do we dream? Say, say, and can
    It be?—tell us, O tell us, how came you
    Thus to find our resting place?
ZONGOLA: Yes, 'tis Carlos, Iola, he hath come
    Ere we have reached the spot whither the star
    That guides us, rests itself. We found him 'neath
    A tree, as we sought to gather something
    For yourself and mother to partake. Look,
    Iola, 'tis he himself!
MALIE: Heaven hath sent him hither; but how changed.
GHESTLER: Yes, he is changed, but he shall tell us, how he hath
    escaped.
CARLOS: Yes, Iola, I'm here,
    Here to go with you to that happy spot
    Which we've so often longed for; and for which
    Our nights are turned to day, our day to night.
    But I must tell you how at last I 'scaped.
GHESTLER: Yes, do, we wait to hear, for oft we spoke
    Of you. Did you not pass us ere that fearful
    Storm o'ertook us in those woods where we lay
    Concealed?
CARLOS: Yes, and I saw you; but I goaded
    On my beast, and passed you, trembling lest those
    Who hunted with me should discover you.
IOLA: How took they you to seek us?
CARLOS: 'Tis not strange
    You wonder at their course. But I will tell
    You all. They charged upon me your departure;

> They bade me pass forest and glade,
> O'er which I traversed, when I ventured forth
> To seek that shore to which we now, all haste.
> High hopes were theirs, that they would overtake
> You in the woods; but ha! they failed. Joyous
> Then, I turned my steps to the poor rice swamp;
> Thanking kind heaven that you were safe; resolved
> To gird me once again, and strike for freedom.

ZONGOLA: How, then, are you thus far?

CARLOS: Aye! truly, will
> I tell you the escape. That very night
> I fled and journeyed; but alas! three days
> Had not elapsed, ere I was captured, bound,
> And cast bleeding with wounds, within the walls
> Of the old prison house. Again I called
> On heaven. My heart kept hoping ever;
> Though I saw no power could help, save His
> Whose hand, wondrous in working, evermore
> Succor affords, to those who pour their souls
> In prayer.

IOLA: How wonderful that you are here!
> Is it not thrice that you have been detected?

CARLOS: Yes, thrice, ere last they cast my weary limbs
> Into that loathsome den.

IOLA: Yes; now then, tell
> Us how deliverance came to your sad heart.

CARLOS: Well, as I told you; bleeding, torn, oppressed
> As with a millstone on my aching heart,
> I sank upon the floor. Lifting my soul
> To heav'n, I prayed for help; nor was that prayer
> In vain. A storm arose,—the heavens were
> Red with lightnings. Thunders uttered loud their
> Awful voice; as though the earth and arching
> Sky would meet in dire commotion. Casting
> My eyes around the dismal cell, they fell
> Upon this weapon. [*Holding up an axe.*]

Quick as the lightning,
Visions of freedom passed before my mind!
Fair fields regained and forests dark traversed,
No more to be recrossed. Forward I sprang,
Loosing my fretted heel from the vile chain;
And watching where to strike, as the
Lightning played around. Then, when deep thunder,
Poured its notes upon the air, I struck! once!—
Twice!—again!—and lo! the door unclosed.
I sallied forth, all breathless, tremblingly
Feeble, through excess of joy. The clouds poured
Forth their stores in floods, and the forked lightnings
Were my guide; till, all o'ercome, I cast myself
Beneath a sheltering tree, and knew not aught
Of joy, or grief, till the sun rose high o'er
Each vale and hill. Forward I've hasted since;
And now how good to look upon you once
Again, and hope that we may soon be found
Upon that shore, for love of which we've periled all.
GHESTLER: How my heart leaps at thought of your escape,
And at the loss of Bandaloz. Methinks
He'll sleep, less easily now we have fled.
He thought to prey upon Iola.
CARLOS: Bless you, for all your love and care for her,
My Ghestler. Heaven will due recompense
Afford thee; and thy heart, I trust, will soon
Pour out its thanks to heaven, beside
Those streams, in which we long to bathe ourselves.
GHESTLER: Mother, if all is well, we'll hasten forth
To-night, for Carlos now will give us aid,
And you will not be weary. With his help,
We soon shall reach where liberty is known;
Where Bandaloz no more, with angry glance,
Calls us to labor, and to unpaid toil.
MALIE: The sight of Carlos, and this freshing breeze,
Hath much refreshed me; and unwaveringly

My heart is fixed in confidence, that heaven
Will bring us to our rest. Ghestler, I wait
Only the word. Iola's heart is glad;
And well she may rejoice at sight of him
Whom she had left behind, whom she had mourned
As one who might no more be seen on earth.
Oh heaven be praised for all its love to these
My children.

SCENE V

[A cottage on the bank of a river in Canada.]

IOLA: Oh! mother, are we here? Here, where we breathe
The blessed air of Liberty, so sweet,
So passing sweet to our torn hearts? I gaze
Upon this sparkling tide, hour after hour,—
Till my eyes fail me, all o'ercharged with tears.
I cast them upward to the smiling heaven,
All radiant with beauty, and I read,
Nothing but Freedom, Liberty, yes, Life!
Is it not worth the toilsome way we've trod,
To breathe this air? to feel this rest of soul?
And know that ne'er again shall we behold
The scourge, or chain, or hear the fearful voice
Of Bandaloz?

MALIE: Yes, daughter, it is sweet
To feel no terror creeping o'er our souls;
To know that we have nought of ill to fear,
From those who late oppressed us; to cherish
The bless'd hope of dying free; of laying
Our poor weary limbs upon the spot where
Dwells no base oppressor; this is worth all
Of toil and want encountered in the woods,
And dreary forests. I shall die happy

Now, knowing that He who guided our frail
Steps to this glad shore, will watch and bless you
With a Father's tenderness.

[*Enter* GHESTLER, ZONGOLA, *and* CARLOS.]

ZONGOLA: Well, mother,
And Iola, how like you this our land?
CARLOS: So you count this *your* land, Zongola, ha!
How think you this would fall upon the ear
Of Bandaloz! Would he not curse heaven
That e'er the star in the night sky, should point
To this bright spot of earth, and guide our feet
To Freedom's soil?
ZONGOLA: [*Laughing.*] Yes, yes, no doubt he would;
But now, 'tis all in vain! Methinks howe'er
His memory may fail, he will not *soon*
Forget the night that gave *you* liberty.
IOLA: Nor shall we, Zongola.
ZONGOLA: Well said, Iola.
Doubtless 'tis treasured in your heart with more
Of grateful love, than aught beside.
GHESTLER: But come,
Good mother, and Iola, let us know
How you have passed the hours, since morn arose?
MALIE: All happy, Ghestler. God hath filled our cup
With choicest gifts. We have been praising heaven
For all its love to us while journeying
Through the wilderness; and oft we breathe
The prayer that you, my son, may yet believe
In Him who comforteth the sorrowing
Of earth, and bids them joy in hope of heavenly
Rest.
IOLA: Yes, Ghestler will, I know, remember
All his love, and pour his soul an offering
Unto heaven!

CARLOS: So it shall be, Iola.

ZONGOLA: Amen! Then shall we be that family
    Which nought may sever.

MALIE: Nought, my sweet children.
    Already do I feel, that he who gave
    Me all of love and pleasure I possess,
    Will guide us to one home,—one joyous, bright,
    Yes, everlasting rest.

End

Early Minstrel Material

Introduction

The minstrel show has both fascinated and repelled modern critics and historians. Built on racist stereotypes of African Americans, it was perhaps the most popular and certainly one of the most important phenomena in the nineteenth-century American theater; in part because of this, it says a great deal about the ways in which audiences considered questions of power, class, gender, and, of course, race—and so is worthy of close and careful study.

Nostalgic early histories of minstrelsy tell this story of its beginnings: entertainer Thomas Dartmouth Rice (1808–1860) was touring with a theater troupe in 1828 and witnessed an amazing dance by a disabled, elderly African American man, during which the man sang a song that consistently returned to the line "Eb'ry time I weel about, I jump Jim Crow." Rice supposedly revised and expanded the song, adapted the dance, costumed himself like the African American and "jumped Jim Crow" for the first time to an amazed and excited white audience.

More recent historians have recognized that, by the 1820s, several theater companies featured "Negro singers"—whites in blackface who sang and danced, supposedly as African Americans did—between acts to keep audiences entertained. And, of course, this approach sprang from, among other phenomenon, folk clowns, early blackface festival performers, and a host of stereotypical African characters in English and early American drama. (Actor Lewis Hallam's supposedly drunken portrayal of an African American slave in a 1769 New York City performance of Isaac Bickerstaff's *The Padlock* has been pointed to as a key early example of the last).

Still, Rice was clearly an early force in popularizing minstrelsy to a point where it left the intermission and became the show: Rice gave his "Ethiopian operas" off and on throughout the 1830s and beyond, first in the United States—especially in New York City, where he offered a popular show at the Bowery in 1832—and then in England. But while Rice's version of the character of Jim Crow—the rural, enslaved, but happy African American who sings, dances, spews malapropisms, and cracks jokes—propelled much of the tenor of minstrelsy, later groups further shaped the content and form of the minstrel show.

Led by Dan Emmett, one of the most noted early minstrel troupes, the Virginia Minstrels (Emmett along with Billy Whitlock, Frank Pelham, and Frank Brower) performed at the Bowery in 1843. They wore blackface, and, as their name implied, promised to share the "peculiar" music and manners of Southern slaves. In what would become a key piece of the structure of the minstrel show, the Virginia Minstrels sat in a semi-circle, with Pelham, who played the tambourine, and Brower, who played the "bones" (in essence, castanets) sitting on the ends—thus marking the "end-men" famous throughout minstrelsy, "Tambo" and "Bones." Immensely popular, they soon left the States for a tour of England; in their wake, several other groups quickly expanded and formalized the minstrel show; by 1844, a group called "the Ethiopian Serenaders" became the first of many minstrel troupes to perform at the White House.

The most famous minstrel troupe, though, was easily Christy's Minstrels, led by Edwin Pearce Christy (1815–1862) who came to New York City with six other performers after finding some success in Buffalo and Northern New York. Immensely popular, they not only drew large New York City audiences steadily between 1846 and 1854, but also helped launch the career of songwriter Stephen Foster. (Early versions of Foster's classic "Old Folks at Home" were attributed to Christy because Foster penned the song specifically for him.) Christy himself built a small empire—with a number "Christy's Opera Houses" across the North and a succession of songsters that featured his name prominently—before ultimately committing suicide in 1862.

Beyond their immense popularity—which reached into the twentieth century with the naming of the popular singers "The New Christy Minstrels"—though, Christy's troupe formalized a three-part organization for their shows which was widely adopted. Initially, performers would march in, sit in a semicircle like the Virginia Minstrels, and mix music and quick comic routines that focused on exchanges between the somewhat stuffy and proper "Interlocutor" (seated in the middle of the semicircle) and the end-men, who played Jim Crow (and, later, other stereotyped African Americans: the city dandy Zip Coon, the foolish slave Sambo, etc.). Next, in what became called the "olio," acts that played to company members' special strengths (often including dances—"plantation breakdowns") followed, still interspersed with comic exchanges. Finally, in the "afterpiece," the full company—often with sets—would do a scene or full one-act play.

Traditionally, performances were somewhat interactive, and audiences, boisterous. This was especially true at theaters like the Bowery, where white people of lower socio-economic classes (often including immigrants) made up the bulk of the spectators. Tamer audiences might call for encores and for numbers to be repeated—or even throw small change; when they were unhappy, they threw much worse, often driving unpopular performers from the theater in what could border on mob action. As the minstrel show aged—and especially as it began to attract wealthier audiences—this, too, shifted, and some minstrels paired pictures of themselves in blackface costume with pictures showing them as "dignified" white men to help "genteel" audiences reconcile attending such a show. Still, the rowdy audience remains intimately paired with the historical conception of the minstrel show.

The content of the shows—and especially the afterpieces—varied considerably. Recent critics like William J. Mahar, based on an exhaustive survey of extant texts, have argued that most sketches did not focus on Southern plantation life but instead burlesqued Shakespeare (as well as popular plays and opera), considered domestic and courtship issues, etc. Still, even though these texts may not have focused on slave life *per se*, minstrels—from the Virginia Minstrels on—were costumed in the garb audiences associated with Southern slavery and, of course, always wore blackface. Further, much of the music (including the dancing) did directly attempt to invoke a pro-slavery picture of happy slaves; by the time the audience got to the afterpieces, the minstrel players were assuredly marked as impersonating Southern slaves. And, of course, the afterpieces relied on the same kinds of racist humor (especially dialect-centered malapropisms) that the early parts of the show foregrounded.

As this discussion demonstrates, recent critics have had a range of arguments about just what to "do" with minstrel texts. After more than a century of glorifying the practice, in the late 1950s, critics—arguably led by Ralph Ellison's powerful work—reminded Americans of the destructive effects such racial stereotyping could cause. Later critics like Eric Lott have attempted to remember Ellison's lessons even as they consider the ways in which minstrelsy also spoke to questions of class and gender, given minstrel audiences and program content.

The selections here address all of these issues and are designed not only to give a very basic sense of the large mass of antebellum minstrel material produced, but also to consider the ways in which minstrelsy speaks specifically to the drama of slavery—as these were the character types and approaches that shaped representations ranging from the various Topsys (both the redeemed figure in Stowe's novel and the unrepentant female Jim Crow in various Tom-shows) as well as figures like the revisionary Cato in William Wells Brown's 1858 *The Escape.*

A Note on the Texts

The three song lyrics offered here, "Blue-Tailed Fly," "Ole Wurginny," and "Old Folks at Home," were all part of the Christy Minstrels' repertoire by the early 1850s. They popularized the first two in the 1840s; many readers will recognize the last as Stephen Foster's famous composition—though they may not recognize the original, race-centered lyrics. The first two are included in *Christy's Nigga Songster, As Sung by Christy's, Pierce's, White's, and Dumbleton's Minstrels* (New York: T.W. Strong, 1850); Foster's composition, under Christy's name, was published separately in 1851 (New York: Firth, Pond, & Co.).

The one-act play, "Oh, Hush! or, the Virginny Cupids," though subtitled an "olio," was probably actually often performed as an afterpiece. Contemporary critics generally ascribe authorship to Thomas Dartmouth "Daddy" Rice and date it to fairly early in minstrelsy. The text included here is an adaptation—more contemporary with the versions of the songs—done by another important minstrel author, Charles White.

Readers may find the dialect here more pronounced than in most other texts; still, reading aloud will generally aid in comprehension. Allusions in the songs, which focus on representing happy slaves, are also generally comprehensible, too—"Washy" and "General George," for example, speak to George Washington; "Cornwalle" is General Cornwallis, the defeated British commander. Though the title characters of "Oh, Hush! or, the Virginny Cupids" are clearly free African Americans in New York City (one even carries his free papers), they are all, equally clearly, former slaves and designed to evoke enslaved "Virginny girls" and "Carolina boys"—one of whom, the reader will note, is accused of "jumping Jim Crow." Finally, the reference to "Day and Martin" plays on both a famous maker of "blacking" and the minstrel implications of such.

For Further Reading

Bean, Annemarie, James V. Hatch, and Brooks McNamara, eds. *Inside the Minstrel Mask: Readings in Nineteenth-Century Blackface Minstrelsy*. Hanover: Wesleyan University Press, 1996.

Dormon, James H., Jr. *Theater in the Antebellum South, 1815–1860*. Chapel Hill: University of North Carolina Press, 1967.

Elam, Harry J., Jr., and David Krasner, eds. *African American Performance and Theater History*. New York: Oxford University Press, 2001.

Hill, Errol G. and James V. Hatch. *A History of African American Theatre*. Cambridge: Cambridge University Press, 2003.

Levine, Lawrence. *Highbrow/Lowbrow: The Emergence of Cultural Hierarchy in America*. Cambridge: Harvard University Press, 1988.

Lott, Eric. *Love and Theft: Blackface Minstrelsy and the American Working Class*. New York: Oxford University Press, 1993.

Maher, William J. "Ethiopian Skits and Sketches: Contents and Contexts of Blackface Minstrelsy, 1840–1890." *Inside the Minstrel Mask: Readings in Nineteenth-Century Blackface Minstrelsy*. Eds. Annemarie Bean, James V. Hatch, and Brooks McNamara. Hanover: Wesleyan University Press, 1996. 179–220.

Toll, Robert C. *Blacking Up: The Minstrel Show in Nineteenth-Century America*. New York: Oxford University Press, 1974.

Minstrel Song Lyrics

BLUE-TAILED FLY

If you should go, in summer time,
To South Carolinar's sultry clime,
An' in de shade you chance to lie,
You'll soon find out de blue tail fly.
An' scratch 'um wid a briar too.

Dar's many kind ob curious tings,
From different sort ob inseck springs;
Some hatch in June an' some July,
But Augus fotches de blue tail fly.
An' scratch 'um wid a briar too.

When I was young I used to wait
On massa table and hand de plate
I'd pass de bottle when he dry,
Den brush away de blue tail fly.
An' scratch 'um wid a briar too.

Den arter dinner massa sleeps,
He bid dis nigga vigils keeps;
An' when he gwine to shut his eye,
He tell me watch de blue tail fly.
An' scratch 'um wid a briar too.

When he ride in de arternoon,
I foller wid a hickory brom;
De pony being berry shy,
When bitten by de blue tail fly.
An' scratch 'um wid a briar too.

One day he rode aroun de farm,
De flies so numerous did swarm,
One chance to bite 'im on de thigh,
De debil take de blue tail fly.
An' scratch 'um wid a briar too.

De pony run he jump an' pitch,
An' tumbl'd massa in de ditch;
He died and de jury wondered why—
De verdic was de blue tail fly.
An' scratch 'um wid a briar too.

Dey laid him under a 'simmon tree,
His epitaph am dere to see
'Beneath this stone I'm forced to lie,
All by de means ob de blue tail fly.
An' scratch 'um wid a briar too.

Ole massa's gone, now let 'im rest,
Dey say all tings am for de best;
I neber shall forget till de day I die,
Ole massa an' dat blue tail fly.
An' scratch 'um wid a briar too.

De hornet gets in your eyes and nose,
De skeeter bite you troo your clothes;
De yalla nipper sweeten high,
But wusser yet de blue tail fly.
An' scratch 'um wid a briar too.

OLE WURGINNY

In a little log house in ole Wurginny
Some niggas lib dat cum from Guinny,
Dere massa flog 'em berry little—

But gib 'em plenty work and wittle
Ole massa Jim real cleber body,
Ebery day he gib dem toddy,
And wen de sun fall in de riber,
Dey stop de work—an rest de liber.

Chah! chah! dat de way,
De niggas spend de nite an day.

At nite dey gadder round de fire,
To take ob tings wot hab perspire—
De ashes on der tater toss'em,
Parch de corn, and roast de possum,
An ater dat de niggas splutter,
An hop an dance de chicken flutter;
Dey happy den an hab no bodder,
Dey snug as rat in a stack a fodder.

Chah! chah! etc.

'Twas on de nineteenth ob October,
When de Juba dance was ober,
Dey heard a great noise dat sound like tunder,
Which made de niggas stare an wonder!
Now, Caesar says he lay a dolla,
De debil in the corn, for he heard him holler.
But Cuffee say now come see,
I bliebe it's notin but a possum up a gum tree.

Chah! chah! etc.

Den one nigga run an open de winda
De moon rush in like fire on tinda
De nois sound plainer, de niggas got friten,
Dey tink 'twas a mixture of tunder an litenen,

Some great brack mob cum cross de medder,
Dey kind a roll themselves togedder,
But soon dey journ dis exhalation
Was notin more dan de niggas from anoder plantation.

Chah! chah! etc.

Dese noisy blacks surround the dwellin,
While de news one nigga got a tellin
De rest ob 'em grin to hear ole Quashy,
Menshun de name ob General Washy.
He says dat day in York Holler,
Massa George catch ole Cornwalle;
An seben thousand corn off shell him
Leff him notin more dan a cob for to tell him.

Chah! chah! etc.

He say den arter all dis fusion,
Dat was de end ob de rebolushun;
Dey gwanin for to keep him as dey ort to,
And dat dere massas specially say den
De niggas mout hab rum all day to be quaffin,
All de niggas den buss right out—a laffin.

Chah! chah! etc.

OLD FOLKS AT HOME
an Ethiopian Melody

Way down upon de Swanee ribber,
Far, far away,
Dere's wha my heart is turning ebber,
Dere's wha de old folks stay.

All up and down de whole creation,
Sadly I roam,
Still longing for de old plantation,
And for de old folks at home.

All de world am sad and dreary,
Ebry where I roam,
Oh! darkeys how my heart grows weary,
Far from de old folks at home.

All round de little farm I wander'd
When I was young,
Den many happy days I squander'd,
Many de songs I sung.

When I was playing wid my brudder,
Happy was I,
Oh! take me to my kind old mudder,
Dere let me live and die.

All de world am sad and dreary,
Ebry where I roam,
Oh! darkeys how my heart grows weary,
Far from de old folks at home.

One little hut among de bushes,
One dat I love,
Still sadly to my mem'ry rushes,
No matter where I rove.

When will I see de bees a humming,
All round de comb?
When will I hear de banjo tumming,
Down in my good ole home?

All de world am sad and dreary,
Ebry where I roam,
Oh! darkeys how my heart grows weary,
Far from de old folks at home.

Oh, Hush! or, the Virginny Cupids

An Operatic Olio, in One Act, and Three Scenes, Arranged by Charles White

CHARACTERS

SAMBO JOHNSON   *a retired bootblack*
CUFF   *a boss bootblack*
PETE WILLIAMS   *Cuff's foreman*
MISS DINAH ROSE   *a fascinating wench*
WATCHMAN
KNIGHTS OF THE BRUSH

SCENE I

[*Exterior, street. The characters discovered blacking boots, some sitting down.* SAM JOHNSON *sits on a chair, right, his feet resting on a barrel. He is reading a newspaper which he holds upside down. All laugh and begin to get up as the curtain rises.*]

CUFF: Pete, I hab been round to all the hotels to-day, an' I got so many boots to black by four o'clock dat I don't tink I can do it. Now, den, boys, if you polish dem by dat time, I'll gib you all a holiday dis ebenin'.

PETE: Ah! dat's right, Cuff, we'll gib 'em de shine ob de best Day and Martin—but, Cuff, gib us a song.

CUFF: [*Sings.*] Come all you Virginny gals, and listen to my noise,
Neber do you wed wid de Carolina boys;
For if dat you do, your portion will be,
Cowheel and sugar cane, wid shangolango tea.

[*Full Chorus.*]
Mamzel ze marrel—ze bunkum sa?
    Mamzel ze marrel—ze bunkum sa?

When you go a courting, de pretty gals to see,
You kiss 'em and you hug 'em like de double rule ob free.
De fust ting dey ax you when you are sitting down, is,
"Fetch along de Johnny cake—it's gitting radder brown."

[*Chorus.*]—Mamzel ze marrel, etc.

Before you are married, potatoes dey am cheap,
But money am so plenty dat you find it in the street.
But arter you git married, I tell you how it is—
Potatoes dey am berry high, and sassengers is riz.

[*Chorus.*]—Mamzel ze marrel, etc.

CUFF: [*Turning round after the song discovers Johnson.*] I say, Pete, who is dat consumquencial darkey ober dar, dat is puttin' on so many airs?

PETE: I don't know, Cuff. He stopped here a few minutes arter you went away, an' he's been reading dar eber since. Speak to him.

CUFF: [*Approaching* JOHNSON, *scrutinizes his person.*] Why, it am Sam Johnson!

ALL: Sam Johnson!

CUFF: Yes, to be sure it am.

JOHNSON: [*Looking through his eyeglass.*] Gemblem, is you distressing your conversation to me?

CUFF: Yes, sar, I is distressing my observation to you inderwidually, collectively, skientifically and alone. [*Seats himself on the barrel.*]

JOHNSON: [*Rising.*] Well, sar, den I would hab you to know dat my name, sar, is Mr. Samuel Johnson, Exquire, an' I don't wish to be addressed by such—[*Pointing to crowd.*] low, common, vulgar trash! You had better mind your business and brack your filthy boots. [*He sits down again.*]

CUFF: [*Gets off the barrel.*] I say, Pete, I'll tell you whar I seed dat darkey. He used to work in de same shop wid me for old Jake Simmons, but he drawed a high prize in de lottery, and retired from de 'spectable perfession of bracking boots. De last time I seed him he was down in old Virginny on a coon hunt. I'll tell you suffin' 'bout it. [*He sings.*]

'Way down in old Virginny, 'twas in de arternoon,
Oh! Roley, boley!
Wid de gun dat maswsa gib me, I went to shoot the coon.

[*Chorus.*]
Wid my hiddy-co-dink-er—mi! who dar?
Good-mornin', ladies fair.
Wid my hiddy-co-dink-er—mi! who call?
Good-mornin' ladies all.

He sat on a pine branch, whistlin' a tune,
Oh! Roley, boley!
I up wid my gun, and brought down Mr. Coon.

[*Chorus.*] Wid my hiddy-co-dink-er, etc.

PETE: I tell you what, Cuff; speak to him in a more eliphant manner.

CUFF: Yes, I will. [*Goes over to Johnson in his best style.*] Johnson! [*No answer.*] Mr. Johnson! [*No answer.*] I'll fetch him dis time, Pete. Mr. Samuel Johnson, Exquire!

JOHNSON: [*Rises and bows politely.*] Sar, I am at your sarbice.

CUFF: Excuse my interrupting you for I see you am busy readin' de paper. Would you be so kind as to enlighten us upon de principal topicks ob de day?

JOHNSON: Well, Mr. Cuff, I hab no objection, 'kase I see dat you common unsophisticated gemmen hab not got edgemcation yourself, and you am 'bliged to come to me who has. So spread around, you unintellumgent bracks, hear de news ob de day discoursed in de most fluid manner. [*He reads out some local items.*] Dar has been a great storm at sea and de ships hab been turned upside down.

CUFF: [*Looks at the paper.*] Why, Mr. Johnson, you've got the paper upside down. [*All laugh heartily.*]

JOHNSON: Well, yes, so I is. Golly! I didn't take notice ob dat. [*He starts with amazement.*] Oh, what do I see? has de perfession come to dis degraded persition?

ALL: [*Shout.*] What is it?

JOHNSON: Does my eyes deceibe me! Bracking boots on de Canal street plan for free cents a pair!

ALL: [*Grab at the paper, which is torn in pieces, and cry.*] Whar? wharabouts?

CUFF: I say, Pete, I can't see nuffin' like dat here. [*To JOHNSON.*] Mr. Johnson, show me dat? [*Holds the torn piece to him.*]

JOHNSON: Oh, I can't show you now—it's torn out.

CUFF: It won't do, Mr. Johnson. Say, darkeys, don't you tink dat nigger am in lub?

ALL: Yes, yes! [JOHNSON *paces the stage in anger.*]

CUFF: [*Sings.*] Sam Johnson, why so solitacious?
　　　Hah, hah, hah, hah, hah?
　　　'Tis lub dat makes you so vexatious,
　　　Sam Johnson ho!
　　　Does your lub lib in Philumdelphy?
　　　Hah, hah, hah, hah, hah?
　　　Oh! is she poor, or am she wealthy?
　　　Sam Johnson, ho!
　　　Now, gib him boots and make him travel,
　　　Hah, hah, hah, hah, hah!
　　　Oh, chuck dem at him widout cavil,
　　　Sam Johnson, ho!

　　　[JOHNSON *exits. All throw a perfect shower of boots at Johnson as soon as he leaves, and begin laughing.*]

CUFF: Dar he goes, Pete. I radder guess Mr. Samuel Johnson, Exquire, won't trouble dis crowd any more wid his presence. [*He sings.*]
　　　De greatest man dat eber libed was Day and Martin,
　　　Johnny, my lango la!
　　　For he was de fust ob de boot black startin'.

　　　[*Chorus.*]
　　　Johnny, my lango la!
　　　Did you eber see a ginsling made out of brandy?
　　　Johnny, my lango la!
　　　Did you eber see a pretty gal lickin' lasses candy?

　　　[*Chorus.*]
　　　Johnny, my lango la!

　　　[*Full Chorus.*]
　　　Johnny, my lango la!

　　　[*Full Chorus.*]
　　　Ah, oh—ah! ah, oh—ah! oh—oo—o—o—o!
　　　Ah, oh—ah! ah, oh—ah! oh—oo—o—o—o!

WATCHMAN: [*Crosses in front, or he may sing outside.*]
　　Past twelve o'clock and a cloudy mornin',
　　Johnny, my lango la!
　　Past twelve o'clock and de daylight dawning,
　　Johnny, my lango la!
CUFF: [*Resumes singing.*]
　　Dat's de old watchman, we're going to fool him,
　　Johnny, my lango la!
　　If he stays outside, de weder will cool him,

　　[*Chorus.*]
　　Johnny, my lango la!

　　Now, cut your sticks, niggers, de daylight's dawning,
　　Johnny, my lango la!
　　We'll meet right here quite early in de mornin'.

　　[*Chorus.*]
　　Johnny, my lango la!

　　[*All exit, right and left, singing very piano.*]

SCENE II

[*Exterior of* ROSE's *house. Dark stage. Stacato music.* JOHNSON *enters with banjo or guitar to serenade.*]

JOHNSON: Tank heaben! I hab got clar ob dem ruffian darkeys at last. I neber was so grossly insulted in all my life. Dey nearly spiled my best clothes, and—but let's see, I promised to gib my lubly Rosa a serenade dis ebenin', and if I can only find de house. [*Goes up to house.*] Yes, here is de house—I know it from a tack in de door. [*Sings.*]
　　Oh! lubly Rosa, Sambo has cum
　　To salute his lub wid his tum, tum, tum.
　　So open de door, Rose, and luff me in,
　　For de way I lub you am a sin.

ROSE: [*Appears at window and sings.*] Ah, who's dat knocking at my
        door,
    Making such a noise wid his saucy jaw?
    Ise looking down upon de stoop,
    Like a henhawk on a chicken-coop.
    So clar de kitchen.
JOHNSON: 'Tis Sambo Johnson, dearest dove,
    Come like Bacchus, God of Love;
    To tell his lubly Rosa how
    He's quit his old perfesion now.
    So clar de kitchen.
ROSE: Oh, hold yer hat and cotch de key,
    Come into de little back room wid me;
    Sit by de fire and warm your shin,
    And on de shelf you'll find some gin.
    So clar de kitchen.

[*She drops the key.* JOHNSON *catches it in his hat and exits in
house.*]

SCENE III

[*Interior of Rose's house. Table set—cups and saucers for two—two
chairs.*]

CUFF: [*Enters, right, and sings.*] I wonder whar de debil my lubly
    Rosa's gone,
    She's luff me half an hour sittin' all alone.
    If she don't come back an' tell me why she didn't stay wid
        me,
    I'll drink all de sassengers and eat up al de tea.

[*Chorus.*]
Oh, Rose! you coal-black Rose!
I neber lub a gal like I lub dat Rose.

ROSE: [*Enters, right, and sings.*] Now, get up you Cuffy, and gib up
  dat chair,
  Mr. Johnson'll pay de dickens if he cotch you sitting dar.
CUFF: I doesn't fear de devil, Rose, luff alone dat Sam.
  If dat nigger fool his time wid me, I'll hit him
  I'll be—[*Breaks a plate.*]

  [*Chorus.*]
  —Oh, Rose, etc.

ROSE: Now, get you in de cupboard, Cuff, a little while to stay, I'll
  give you plenty applejack when Sambo's gone away.
CUFF: I'll keep my eye upon him—if he 'tempts to kiss or hug, I'll
  be down upon him like a duck upon a bug.

  [ROSE *conducts* CUFF *to the closet, puts him in, and closes the
  door.*]

JOHNSON: [*Heard singing without.*] Oh, make haste, Rose, for sure
  as I am born,
  I'm trembling like a sweep-oh on a frosty morn.
ROSE: Walk in, Sambo, and don't stand dar a-shakin',
  De fire am a-burnin' and de hoe-cake am a-bakin'.
JOHNSON: [*Enters, left, looks around the room, and converses ad libitum;
  he then discovers the table, starts with surprise and sings.*] From
  de chairs around de table and de two cups of tea,
  I see you been to supper and had some company.
ROSE: 'Twas de missionary preacher, dey call him Dr. Birch,
  He come to raise a 'scription to build hisself a church.
  Come sit you down, Sambo, an' tell me how you've bin.

  [JOHNSON *laughs.*]

  Why, la bress you, honey, what does make you grin?
JOHNSON: I'd laugh to tink if you was mine, my dear, my lub, my
  Rose,
  I'd gib you eberyting dat's nice, de Lord above knows,
  Dar's possum fat an' hominy, and sometimes—

CUFF: [*Signs out from closet.*] Rice!

JOHNSON: Cowheel an' sugar cane, an' eberyting dat's—

CUFF: [*Sings out from closet.*] Nice!

JOHNSON: [*Gets up, comes front and sings.*] I thought I heard a noise,
　　　　Rose, it come from ober dar,

ROSE: It was de plaster fallin' down upon de chair.

JOHNSON: But it hollered out rice! as sure as I'm Sambo.

ROSE: It was dat nigger Cuffy upstairs, dat jumps Jim Crow.

JOHNSON: I wish I was a glove, Rose upon dat lubly hand,
　　　　I'd be de happiest nigger ob all in dis land.
　　　　My bosom am so full ob lub—'twould soon find some
　　　　　　relief,
　　　　When you took de glove to wipe your nose instead ob a
　　　　　　handkerchief.

　　　　[*Chorus.*]
　　　　Oh, Rose, etc.

ROSE: My love is strong, and of it's strength dar's none but you can
　　　　tell.

CUFF: Half past twelve o'clock and all's not well.

JOHNSON: Dat's de old watchman took me up de udder night.

CUFF: Half past twelve o'clock, dar's going to be a fight.

　　　　[*Chorus.*]
　　　　Oh, Rose, etc.

ROSE: Johnson, now you'd better go, for you see it's getting late,
　　　　An' missus will be coming home from de freminate.

JOHNSON: Well, gib me one kiss, Rose—[*Tries to kiss her.*]

ROSE: Why, Sam, what is you at?

JOHNSON: Why, I'll hug you like a grizzly—what de debil noise am
　　　　dat? [CUFF *is trying to get down the gun from shelf, falls down and
　　　　spills the flour over him. Johnson gets up stage, brings* CUFF *down
　　　　front and sings.*] Who is you, and from whar did you cum?

ROSE: Oh, it am dat nigger Cuff—foreber I'm undone.

CUFF: Ise been out whitewashin' an' feelin' a little tire,
　　　　I merely cum to ax Miss Rose for a shobelful ob fire.

JOHNSON: Tell me, you saucy nigger, how you do on dat shelf?

CUFF: I was pretty well, I thank you, pray, how do you find yourself?

JOHNSON: Come, no prevarication, or I'll smash dat calabash.

ROSE: Oh, Johnson, be advised by me—he's noffin's else but trash.

JOHNSON: Is dis your constancy, Miss Rose, you tell me ob all day!

CUFF: Why, de wench she am dumbfounded, and don't know what to say.

ROSE: I never saw his face before—his berry sight I hates—
I believe he am a runaway from de nullifying States.

CUFF: Say, tell me, Mr. Johnson, what dat nigger 'jaculates?

JOHNSON: Why, she says you am a runaway from de nullifyin' States.

CUFF: Dat's enuff to make a jaybird split his shin in two,
For here's my free papers dat I carry in my shoe.

[*Shows his papers.*]

[*Chorus.*]
Oh, Rose, etc.

By dat darkey's peroration and his sarcarmastus grin,
I'll bet he gets a lickin' afore he does begin.

JOHNSON: Be off, you common nigger!

CUFF: Not until we hab a fight.
And, Rose, don't you interfere, I'll show dis moke a sight.

[*Clinches* JOHNSON, *and they fight.*]

ROSE: [*Screams, siezes frying pan, and strikes* CUFF *over his head, breaking the bottom.*] Fire! help! murder, suicide, all sorts ob death!

JOHNSON: Stand off, you common nigger, gib me time to draw a breff.

[PETE *and others enter, down front.*]

PETE: What's de matter, Rose, dat you gib dat Injun yelp?

ROSE: Why, it's Cuffy killin' Sambo, and I was cryin' out for help.

PETE: [*raises and supports* CUFF, *while someone does the same to* JOHNSON.] Cuffy, is you much hurt?

CUFF: Oh, no, I'm only drawing my last breff. You'd better take me to the hosspistol.

PETE: Why, Cuff?

CUFF: Oh, I don't know; but I hardly tink I shall live more dan twenty-five years longer: [CUFF *and* JOHNSON *have now regained their feet.*]

JOHNSON: [*starts.*] Why Cuff!

CUFF: Why Johnson!

JOHNSON: Rose, my love, pray tell me how this cum so?

ROSE: Well dear, I will, since you really want to know:
You see, he sweeps de street, and blacks de gemmen's shoes,
But when he gets de liquor in, he don't know what he does.

CUFF: [*sings to* ROSE.] If I'd married you, Miss Rose, I'd surely had a curse,
I offered for to take you for better or for worse;
But I was blind wid lub, your faults I couldn't see.
You is a deal sight worser dan I took you for to be.

[*Chorus.*]
Oh, Rose, etc.

JOHNSON: [*crosses over to* CUFF.] Mr. Cuff, I ax your pardon.

CUFF: Mr. Johnson, dar's my hand. An Rose, I'm glad to find my head was harder dan your pan. But dar's no use to keep up grievances, since love am all by chance. So jest hand down de fiddle, Pete, and let us hab a dance. Come, darks, take your places and I'll saw the catgut.

[*Curtain.*]

Uncle Tom's Cabin

Introduction

Harriet Beecher Stowe's anti-slavery novel *Uncle Tom's Cabin* (1852) was a phenomenon like no other. Within a year of its release, publishers were thinking of sales in hundreds of thousands of copies—instead tens of thousands generally associated with bestsellers of the time; when one recognizes that most nineteenth-century books went through several hands, it is easy to suggest a readership that surpassed most twentieth-century bestsellers.

But weak copyright laws allowed unscrupulous copycats to take characters, plot devices, and even the novel's title and use them in a range of ways. Before long, consumers could buy everything from *Uncle Tom's Cabin* commemorative plates to sheet music. Such free adaptation rarely addressed the social concerns of Stowe's novel. Pro-slavery novels "answering" *Uncle Tom's Cabin* shamelessly stole plot and character elements, and, most notably, theaters across the nation began putting on "Tom shows." From Chicago to Boston, and from Baltimore to New Orleans, by late 1853, theater-goers could see a production that featured a version of Uncle Tom, though the productions rarely had more than a cursory connection to the novel.

In the case of most Southern productions, Uncle Tom was invoked only so that he and Stowe could be mocked.

Many of these plays, especially the pro-slavery burlesques of Stowe's novel (including one claiming to be by "Harriet Screecher Blow") are no longer extant. But some of the most prominent Northern versions were performed well into the twentieth century: H.J. Conway's version began a two hundred-night run in Boston in November of 1852; showman P.T. Barnum offered a long-running version at his "museum," where it competed with a fascinating range of freakish exhibits; and Clifton Tayleure opened a popular version in Detroit.

Of all of these, though, George Aiken's was easily the most popular. While there has been comparatively little in-depth biographical study of Aiken, we do know that the runaway success of his dramatization of Stowe's novel must have been a surprise. Born in Boston on December 19, 1830, Aiken was forced to stop his education as a youth to go to work for a carpet warehouse. He had always been interested in the theater, though—an interest that came, in part, from his cousins, the Fox family (George, James, Henry, Charles, and Caroline) who toured as the "Little Foxes" in the late 1830s and 1840s. Aiken began acting himself in 1849 in Providence, Rhode Island, and had a string of minor roles—mostly with small companies—until his cousin Caroline, now married to actor and entrepreneur George C. Howard, contacted him.

Howard was looking for a vehicle for his family, especially his talented four-year-old daughter, Cordelia. *Uncle Tom's Cabin*, with its angelic little Eva, seemed perfect—especially given the sensation surrounding the novel and the melodramatic potential of several of its scenes. Aiken initially wrote a four-act version that covered only up to Eva's death scene, and it began playing to packed houses in Troy, New York, in September of 1852, with George Howard as St. Clare, Caroline Howard as Topsy, Cordelia Howard as Little Eva, and Aikens as both George Shelby and George Harris. Later, he wrote a second four-act version that moved from Eva's death to the novel's end—and, still later, the six-act version that combined the two plays and that is presented here.

After over a hundred performances, the Howards and Aiken were engaged by the National Theatre in New York City, and there began an unparalleled run until mid-1854. The Howards stayed with the play at a variety of theaters until 1857, and consistently came back to it—and to a handful of spin-offs, including *The Death of Little Eva.*

No longer just a bit-player, Aiken had other successes in the theater—especially his version of Ann S. Stephens's *Old Homestead*—and continued acting throughout the North, including work for Barnum's Museum and Philadelphia's Arch Street Theatre. He took over as the Troy Theatre's manager in 1861 and finally retired from the stage ten years later. Throughout, he continued to write—branching off into dime novels and serialized stories for a range of penny papers before his death in Jersey City, New Jersey, on April 27, 1876. He never, though, saw the kind of success he had with *Uncle Tom's Cabin* again.

Part of the success of Aiken's *Uncle Tom's Cabin* can undoubtedly be attributed to the Howard family's savvy sense of the Uncle Tom mania sweeping the nation; readers will note full scenes devoted to tableaux of key "picture" moments like Eliza crossing the icy Ohio as she escapes with her child and, of course, the death of Little Eva. Part, too, resulted from some very good and very clearly stolen writing: Aiken lifted some passages—in addition to most of the characters and plot—directly from Stowe's work.

Still, it would be a serious mistake to suggest that Aiken's play looks much like Stowe's novel, and critics who have asserted that Aiken's version is the closest "match" to the novel are simply incorrect. First, Aiken was highly selective in what he included—reducing Ophelia to a cardboard spinster (who says the word "shiftless" too many times to count), cutting several scenes from the novel which show interaction between slaves, and removing wholesale key moments like the aid Mrs. Bird (a Senator's wife) gives runaway Eliza in the face of the Fugitive Slave Law. Second, he adds new characters—the "teetotally" Quaker Phineas Fletcher, Deacon Perry, and the hapless vagabond Gumption Cute—and a new plotline, in which Perry and Cute compete for Ophelia's affections. All of these additions work to add comic relief to an already watered-down version of Stowe's anti-slavery text. Third, the character of Topsy is greatly foregrounded and expanded, and it is no mistake that Cute accuses her of being "a juvenile specimen of Day and Martin," a well-known blacking company mentioned by several minstrel troupes of the day. These additions, written with the skills of an experienced minor actor who knew the minstrel show well, radically undermine Stowe's anti-slavery message. This sense, though, more than Stowe's sentimental, Christ-like figure, seems to have been the Tom that more and more theater-going Americans wanted to see, especially as sectional tensions increased and the nation moved to civil war. And this was the Tom that again became popular when Jim Crow took over the South.

Still, for all of this, Aiken's version did receive some positive notice in a selection of anti-slavery papers, and young Cordelia Howard—who lived until 1941—steadfastly maintained that her father and her father's company—including Aiken—were anti-slavery, even though records show that Howard adapted the play to tone down the evils of the slaveholding characters when playing in border areas like Baltimore.

A Note on the Text

The text of Aiken's play presented here is the six-act version, reproduced from the "acting edition" published by Samuel French of New York in 1858. While contemporary readers might benefit from comparing the play directly to both the text of Stowe's novel and Stowe's own dramatization of *Uncle Tom's Cabin*, *The Christian Slave* (included in this anthology), the play stands fairly well on its own.

Still, understanding a handful of references will aid reading. The reference to "spiritual rappings" as Gumption Cute's past occupation mocks many nineteenth-century Americans' fascination with Spiritualism and specifically with contacting the "spirit world" through séance-like events. Similarly, his claim late in the play that he is a "Fillibusterow" refers to select Southerners' failed attempt to invade Cuba in the early 1850s with the hopes of making it a new (and slaveholding) possession of the United States. Both "occupations," like his brief speculation that he might engage Topsy and start a minstrel show, are comic markers of his foolishness. Readers will also note the reference to Barnum—initially a shot at his competing version of *Uncle Tom's Cabin* and, later, when Aiken teamed with Barnum, a sort of inside joke.

For Further Reading

Birdoff, Harry. *The World's Greatest Hit: Uncle Tom's Cabin*. New York: Vanni, 1947.

Hedrick, Joan. *Harriet Beecher Stowe: A Life*. New York: Oxford University Press, 1994.

Gossett, Thomas. *Uncle Tom's Cabin and American Culture*. Dallas: Southern Methodist University Press, 1986.

McConachie, Bruce. "Out of the Kitchen and into the Marketplace: Normalizing *Uncle Tom's Cabin* for the Antebellum Stage." *Journal of American Drama and Theatre* 3 (1991): 5–28.

Reiss, Benjamin. *The Showman and the Slave: Race, Death, and Memory in Barnum's America*. Cambridge: Harvard University Press, 2001.

Roppolo, Joseph R. "Uncle Tom in New Orleans: Three Lost Plays." *The New England Quarterly* 27.2 (June 1954): 213–226.

Senelick, Laurence. *The Age and Stage of George L. Fox*. Hanover, NH: University Press of New England, 1988.

Winslow, Ola Elizabeth. "Cordelia Howard." In *Notable American Women, 1607–1950*. Ed. Edward T. James. Cambridge: Harvard University Press, 1971.

Uncle Tom's Cabin

THE CAST

UNCLE TOM

GEORGE HARRIS

GEORGE SHELBY

ST. CLARE

PHINEAS FLETCHER

GUMPTION CUTE

MR. WILSON

DEACON PERRY

SHELBY

HALEY

LEGREE

TOM LOKER

MARKS

SAMBO

QUIMBO

DOCTOR

WAITER

HARRY

EVA

ELIZA

CASSY

MARIE

OPHELIA

CHLOE

TOPSY

ACT I, SCENE I

[*Plain Chamber. Enter* ELIZA, *meeting* GEORGE.]

ELIZA: Ah! George, is it you? Well, I am so glad you've come. [GEORGE *regards her mournfully.*] Why don't you smile, and ask after Harry?

GEORGE: [*Bitterly.*] I wish he'd never been born! I wish I'd never been born myself!

ELIZA: [*Sinking her head upon his breast and weeping.*] Oh George!

GEORGE: There now, Eliza, it's too bad for me to make you feel so. Oh! how I wish you had never seen me—you might have been happy!

ELIZA: George! George! how can you talk so? What dreadful thing has happened, or is going to happen? I'm sure we've been very happy till lately.

GEORGE: So we have, dear. But oh! I wish I'd never seen you, nor you me.

ELIZA: Oh, George! how can you?

GEORGE: Yes, Eliza, it's all misery! misery! The very life is burning out of me! I'm a poor, miserable, forlorn drudge! I shall only drag you down with me, that's all! What's the use of our trying to do anything—trying to know anything—trying to be anything? I wish I was dead!

ELIZA: Oh! now, dear George, that is really wicked. I know how you feel about losing your place in the factory, and you have a hard master; but pray be patient—

GEORGE: Patient! Haven't I been patient? Did I say a word when he came and took me away—for no earthly reason—from the place where everybody was kind to me? I'd paid him truly every cent of my earnings, and they all say I worked well.

ELIZA: Well, it *is* dreadful; but, after all, he is your master, you know.

GEORGE: My master! And who made him my master? That's what I think of. What right has he to me? I'm as much a man as he is. What right has he to make a dray-horse of me?—to take me from things I can do better than he can, and put me to work that any horse can do? He tries to do it; he says he'll bring me down and humble me, and he puts me to just the hardest, meanest and dirtiest work, on purpose.

ELIZA: Oh, George! George! you frighten me. Why, I never heard you talk so. I'm afraid you'll do something dreadful. I don't wonder at your feelings at all; but oh! do be careful—for my sake, for Harry's.

GEORGE: I have been careful, and I have been patient, but it's growing worse and worse—flesh and blood can't bear it any longer. Every chance he can get to insult and torment me he takes. He says that though I don't say anything, he sees that I've got the devil in me, and he means to bring it out; and one of these days it will come out, in a way that he won't like, or I'm mistaken.

ELIZA: Well, I always thought that I must obey my master and mistress, or I couldn't be a Christian.

GEORGE: There is some sense in it in your case. They have brought you up like a child—fed you, clothed you and taught you, so that you have a good education—that is some reason why they should claim you. But I have been kicked and cuffed and sworn at, and what do I owe? I've paid for all my keeping a hundred times over. I won't bear it!—no, I *won't!* Master will find out that I'm one whipping won't tame. My day will come yet, if he don't look out!

ELIZA: What are you going to do? Oh! George, don't do anything wicked; if you only trust in heaven and try to do right, it will deliver you.

GEORGE: Eliza, my heart's full of bitterness. I can't trust in heaven. Why does it let things be so?

ELIZA: Oh, George! we must all have faith. Mistress says that when all things go wrong to us, we must believe that heaven is doing the very best.

GEORGE: That's easy for people to say who are sitting on their sofas and riding in their carriages; but let them be where I am—I guess it would come some harder. I wish I could be good; but my heart burns and can't be reconciled. You couldn't, in my place, you can't now, if I tell you all I've got to say; you don't know the whole yet.

ELIZA: What do you mean?

GEORGE: Well, lately my master has been saying that he was a fool to let me marry off the place—that he hates Mr. Shelby and all his tribe—and he says he won't let me come here any more, and that I shall take a wife and settle down on his place.

ELIZA: But you were married to *me* by the minister, as much as if you had been a white man.

GEORGE: Don't you know I can't hold you for my wife if he chooses to part us? That is why I wish I'd never seen you—it would have been better for us both—it would have been better for our poor child if he had never been born.

ELIZA: Oh! but my master is so kind.

GEORGE: Yes, but who knows?—he may die, and then Harry may be sold to nobody knows who. What pleasure is it that he is handsome and smart and bright? I tell you, Eliza, that a sword will pierce through your soul for every good and pleasant thing your child is or has. It will make him worth too much for you to keep.

ELIZA: Heaven forbid!

GEORGE: So, Eliza, my girl, bear up now, and good by, for I'm going.

ELIZA: Going, George! Going where?

GEORGE: To Canada; and when I'm there I'll buy you—that's all the hope that's left us. You have a kind master, that won't refuse to sell you. I'll buy you and the boy—heaven helping me, I will!

ELIZA: Oh, dreadful! If you should be taken?

GEORGE: I won't be taken, Eliza—I'll *die* first! I'll be free, or I'll die.

ELIZA: You will not kill yourself?

GEORGE: No need of that; they will kill me, fast enough. I will never go down the river alive.

ELIZA: Oh, George! for my sake, do be careful. Don't lay hands on yourself, or anybody else. You are tempted too much, but don't. Go, if you must, but go carefully, prudently, and pray heaven to help you!

GEORGE: Well, then Eliza, hear my plan. I'm going home quite resigned, you understand, as if all was over. I've got some preparations made, and there are those that will help me; and in the course of a few days I shall be among the missing. Well, now, good by.

ELIZA: A moment—our boy.

GEORGE: [*Choked with emotion.*] True, I had forgotten him; one last look, and then farewell!

ELIZA: And heaven grant it be not forever! [*Exeunt.*]

SCENE II

[*A dining room. Table and chairs. Dessert, wine, etc., on table.* SHELBY *and* HALEY *discovered at table.*]

SHELBY: That is the way I should arrange the matter.

HALEY: I can't make trade that way—I positively can't, Mr. Shelby. [*Drinks.*]

SHELBY: Why, the fact is, Haley, Tom is an uncommon fellow! He is certainly worth that sum anywhere—steady, honest, capable, manages my whole farm like a clock!

HALEY: You mean honest, as niggers go. [*Fills glass.*]

SHELBY: No; I mean, really, Tom is a good, steady, sensible, pious fellow. He got religion at a camp-meeting, four years ago, and I believe he really *did* get it. I've trusted him since then, with everything I have—money, house, horses, and let him come and go round the country, and I always found him true and square in everything.

HALEY: Some folks don't believe there is pious niggers, Shelby, but *I do.* I had a fellow, now, in this yer last lot I took to Orleans—'twas as good as a meetin' now, really, to hear that critter pray; and he was quite gentle and quiet like. He fetched me a good sum, too, for I bought him cheap of a man that was 'bliged to sell out, so I realized six hundred on him. Yes, I consider religion a valeyable thing in a nigger, when it's the genuine article and no mistake.

SHELBY: Well, Tom's got the real article, if ever a fellow had. Why last fall I let him go to Cincinnati alone, to do business for me and bring home five hundred dollars. "Tom," says I to him, "I trust you, because I think you are a Christian—I know you wouldn't cheat." Tom comes back sure enough, I knew he would. Some low fellows, they say, said to him—"Tom, why don't you make tracks for Canada?" "Ah, master trusted me, and I couldn't," was his answer. They told me all about it. I am sorry to part with Tom, I must say. You ought to let him cover the whole balance of the debt and you would, Haley, if you had any conscience.

HALEY: Well, I've got just as much conscience as any man in business can afford to keep, just a little, you know, to swear by, as twere; and then I'm ready to do anything in reason to 'blige friends, but this yer, you see, is a leetle too hard on a fellow—a leetle too hard! [*Fills glass again.*]

SHELBY: Well, then, Haley, how will you trade?

HALEY: Well, haven't you a boy or a girl that you could throw in with Tom?

SHELBY: Hum! none that I could well spare; to tell the truth, it's only hard necessity makes me willing to sell at all. I don't like parting with any of my hands, that's a fact. [HARRY *runs in.*] Hulloa! Jim Crow! [*Throws a bunch of raisins towards him.*] Pick that up now! [HARRY *does so.*]

HALEY: Bravo, little 'un! [*Throws an orange, which* HARRY *catches. He sings and dances around the stage.*] Hurrah! Bravo! What a young 'un! That chap's a case, I'll promise. Tell you what, Shelby, fling in that chap, and I'll settle the business. Come, now, if that ain't doing the thing up about the rightest!

[ELIZA *enters. Starts on beholding* HALEY, *and gazes fearfully* at HARRY, *who runs and clings to her dress, showing the orange, etc.*]

SHELBY: Well, Eliza?

ELIZA: I was looking for Harry, please, sir.

SHELBY: Well, take him away, then.

[ELIZA *grasps the child eagerly in her arms, and casting another glance of apprehension at* HALEY, *exits hastily.*]

HALEY: By Jupiter! there's an article, now. You might make your fortune on that ar gal in Orleans any day. I've seen over a thousand in my day, paid down for gals not a bit handsomer.

SHELBY: I don't want to make my fortune on her. Another glass of wine. [*Fills the glasses.*]

HALEY: [*Drinks and smacks his lips.*] Capital wine—first chop. Come, how will you trade about the gal? What shall I say for her? What'll you take?

SHELBY: Mr. Haley, she is not to be sold. My wife wouldn't part with her for her weight in gold.

HALEY: Ay, ay! women always say such things, 'cause they hain't no sort of calculation. Just show 'em how many watches, feathers and trinkets one's weight in gold would buy, and that alters the case, I reckon.

SHELBY: I tell you, Haley, this must not be spoken of—I say no, and I mean no.

HALEY: Well, you'll let me have the boy tho'; you must own that I have come down pretty handsomely for him.

SHELBY: What on earth can you want with the child?

HALEY: Why, I've got a friend that's going into this yer branch of the business—wants to buy up handsome boys to raise for the market. Well, what do you say?

SHELBY: I'll think the matter over and talk with my wife.

HALEY: Oh, certainly, by all means; but I'm in a devil of a hurry and shall want to know as soon as possible, what I may depend on.

[*Rises and puts on his overcoat, which hangs on a chair. Takes hat and whip.*]

SHELBY: Well, call up this evening, between six and seven, and you shall have my answer.

HALEY: All right. Take care of yourself, old boy! [*Exit.*]

SHELBY: If anybody had ever told me that I should sell Tom to those rascally traders, I should never have believed it. Now it must come for aught I see, and Eliza's child too. So much for being in debt, heigho! The fellow sees his advantage and means to push it. [*Exit.*]

SCENE III

[*Snowy landscape. Uncle Tom's Cabin. Snow on roof. Practicable door and window. Dark stage. Music.*]

[*Enter* ELIZA *hastily, with* HARRY *in her arms.*]

ELIZA: My poor boy! they have sold you, but your mother will save you yet! [*Goes to Cabin and taps on window.* AUNT CHLOE *appears at window with a large white night-cap on.*]

CHLOE: Good Lord! what's that? My sakes alive if it ain't Lizy! Get on your clothes, old man, quick! I'm gwine to open the door.

[*The door opens and* CHLOE *enters followed by* UNCLE TOM *in his shirt sleeves holding a tallow candle.*]

TOM: [*Holding the light towards* ELIZA.] Lord bless you! I'm skeered to look at ye, Lizy! Are ye tuck sick, or what's come over ye?

ELIZA: I'm running away, Uncle Tom and Aunt Chloe, carrying off my child! Master sold him!

TOM & CHLOE: Sold him!

ELIZA: Yes, sold him! I crept into the closet by mistress' door tonight and heard master tell mistress that he had sold my Harry and you, Uncle Tom, both, to a trader, and that the man was to take possession to-morrow.

CHLOE: The good lord have pity on us! Oh! it don't seem as if it was true. What has he done that master should sell *him?*

ELIZA: He hasn't done anything—it isn't for that. Master don't want to sell, and mistress—she's always good. I heard her plead and beg for us, but he told her 'twas no use—that he was in this man's debt, and he had got the power over him, and that if he did not pay him off clear, it would end in his having to sell the place and all the people and move off.

CHLOE: Well, old man, why don't you run away, too? Will you wait to be toted down the river, where they kill niggers with hard work and starving? I'd a heap rather die than go there, any day! There's time for ye, be off with Lizy—you've got a pass to come and go any time. Come, bustle up, and I'll get your things together.

TOM: No, no—I ain't going. Let Eliza go—it's her right. I wouldn't be the one to say no—'tain't in natur' for her to stay; but you heard what she said? If I must be sold, or all the people on the place, and everything go to rack, why, let me be sold. I s'pose I can bar it as well as any one. Mas'r always found me on the spot—he always will. I never have broken trust, nor used my pass no ways contrary to my word, and I never will. It's better for me to go alone, than to break up the place and sell all. Mas'r ain't to blame, and he'll take care of you and the poor little 'uns! [*Overcome.*]

CHLOE: Now, old man, what is you gwine to cry for? Does you want to break this old woman's heart? [*Crying.*]

ELIZA: I saw my husband only this afternoon, and I little knew then what was to come. He told me he was going to run away. Do try, if you can, to get word to him. Tell him how I went and why I went, and tell him I'm going to try and find Canada. You must give my love to him, and tell him if I never see him again on earth, I trust we shall meet in heaven!

TOM: Dat is right, Lizy, trust in the Lord—he is our best friend—our only comforter.

ELIZA: You won't go with me, Uncle Tom?

TOM: No; time was when I would, but the Lord's given me a work among these yer poor souls, and I'll stay with 'em and bear my cross with 'em till the end. It's different with you—it's more'n you could stand, and you'd better go if you can.

ELIZA: Uncle Tom, I'll try it!

TOM: Amen! The lord help ye!

[*Exit* ELIZA *and* HARRY.]

CHLOE: What is you gwine to do, old man! What's to become of you?

TOM: [*Solemnly.*] Him that saved Daniel in the den of lions—that saved the children in the fiery furnace—Him that walked on the sea and bade the winds be still—He's alive yet! and I've faith to believe he can deliver me.

CHLOE: You is right, old man.

TOM: The Lord is good unto all that trust him, Chloe. [*Exeunt into cabin.*]

SCENE IV

[*Room in Tavern by the river side. A large window in flat, through which the river is seen, filled wth floating ice. Moon light. Table and chairs brought on.*]

[*Enter* PHINEAS.]

PHINEAS: Chaw me up into tobaccy ends! how in the name of all that's onpossible am I to get across that yer pesky river? It's a reg'lar blockade of ice! I promised Ruth to meet her to-night, and she'll be into my har if I don't come. [*Goes to window.*] Thar's a conglomerated prospect for a loveyer! What in creation's to be done? That thar river looks like a permiscuous ice-cream shop come to an awful state of friz. If I war on the adjacent bank, I wouldn't care a teetotal atom. Rile up, you old varmit, and shake the ice off your back!

[*Enter* ELIZA *and* HARRY.]

ELIZA: Courage, my boy—we have reached the river. Let it but roll between us and our pursuers, and we are safe! [*Goes to window.*] Gracious powers! the river is choked with cakes of ice!

PHINEAS: Holloa, gal!—what's the matter? You look kind of streaked.

ELIZA: Is there any ferry or boat that takes people over now?

PHINEAS: Well, I guess not; the boats have stopped running.

ELIZA: [*In dismay.*] Stopped running?

PHINEAS: Maybe you're wanting to get over—anybody sick? Ye seem mighty anxious.

ELIZA: I—I—I've got a child that's very dangerous. I never heard of it till last night, and I've walked quite a distance to-day, in hopes to get to the ferry.

PHINEAS: Well, now, that's onlucky; I'm re'lly consarned for ye. Thar's a man, a piece down here, that's going over with some truck this evening, if he duss to; he'll be in here to supper to-night, so you'd better set down and wait. That's a smart little chap. Say, young'un, have a chaw tobaccy? [*Takes out a large plug and a bowie-knife.*]

ELIZA: No, no! not any for him.

PHINEAS: Oh! he don't use it, eh? Hain't come to it yet? Well, I have. [*Cuts off a large piece, and returns the plug and knife to pocket.*] What's the matter with the young 'un? He looks kind of white in the gills!

ELIZA: Poor fellow! he is not used to walking, and I've hurried him on so.

PHINEAS: Tuckered, eh? Well, there's a little room there, with a fire in it. Take the baby in there, make yourself comfortable till that thar ferryman shows his countenance—I'll stand the damage.

ELIZA: How shall I thank you for such kindness to a stranger?

PHINEAS: Well, if you don't know how, why, don't try; that's the teetotal. Come, vamose! [*Exit,* ELIZA *and* HARRY.] Chaw me into sassage meat, if that ain't a perpendicular fine gal! she's a reg'lar A No. 1 sort of female! How'n thunder am I to get across this refrigerated stream of water? I can't wait for that ferryman.

[*Enter* MARKS.] Halloa! what sort of a critter's this? [*Advances.*] Say, stranger, will you have something to drink?

MARKS: You are excessively kind: I don't care if I do.

PHINEAS: Ah! he's a human. Holloa, thar! bring us a jug of whisky instantaneously, or expect to be teetotally chawed up! Squat yourself, stranger, and go in for enjoyment. [*They sit at table.*] Who are you, and what's your name?

MARKS: I am a lawyer, and my name is Marks.

PHINEAS: A land shark, eh? Well, I dont' think no worse on you for that. The law is a kind of necessary evil; and it breeds lawyers just as an old stump does fungus. Ah! here's the whisky. [*Enter* WAITER, *with jug and tumblers. Places them on table.*] Here, you—take that shin-plaster. [*Gives bill.*] I don't want any change—thar's a gal stopping in that room—the balance will pay for her—d'ye hear?—vamose! [*Exit* WAITER. *Fills glass.*] Take hold, neighbor Marks—don't shirk the critter. Here's hoping your path of true love may never have an ice-choked river to cross! [*They drink.*]

MARKS: Want to cross the river, eh?

PHINEAS: Well, I do, stranger. Fact is, I'm in love with the teetotalist pretty girl, over on the Ohio side, that ever wore a Quaker bonnet. Take another swig, neighbor. [*Fills glasses, and they drink.*]

MARKS: A Quaker, eh?

PHINEAS: Yes—kind of strange, ain't it? The way of it was this:—I used to own a grist of niggers—had 'em to work on my planta-tion, just below here. Well, stranger, do you know I fell in with that gal—of course I was considerably smashed—knocked into a pretty conglomerated heap—and I told her so. She said she wouldn't hear a word from me so long as I owned a nigger!

MARKS: You sold them, I suppose?

PHINEAS: You're teetotally wrong, neighbor. I gave them all their freedom, and told 'em to vamose!

MARKS: Ah! yes—very noble, I dare say, but rather expensive. This act won you your lady-love, eh?

PHINEAS: You're off the track again, neighbor. She felt kind of pleased about it, and smiled, and all that; but she said she could never be mine unless I turned Quaker! Thunder and earth! what do you think of that? You're a lawyer—come, now, what's your opinion? Don't you call it a knotty point?

MARKS: Most decidedly. Of course you refused.

PHINEAS: Teetotally; but she told me to think better of it, and come to-night and give her my final conclusion. Chaw me into mince meat, if I haven't made up my mind to do it!

MARKS: You astonish me!

PHINEAS: Well, you see, I can't get along without that gal;—she's sort of fixed my flint, and I'm sure to hang fire without her. I know I shall make a queer sort of Quaker, because you see, neighbor, I ain't precisely the kind of material to make a Quaker out of.

MARKS: No, not exactly.

PHINEAS: Well, I can't stop no longer. I must try to get across that candaverous river some way. It's getting late—take care of yourself, neighbor lawyer. I'm a teetotal victim to a pair of black eyes. Chaw me up to feed hogs, if I'm not in a ruinatious state! [*Exit.*]

MARKS: Queer genius, that, very! [*Enter* TOM LOKER.] So you've come at last.

LOKER: Yes. [*Looks into jug.*] Empty! Waiter! more whisky!

[WAITER *enters, with jug, and removes the empty one. Enter* HALEY.]

HALEY: By the land! if this yer ain't the nearest, now, to what I've heard people call Providence! Why, Loker, how are ye?

LOKER: The devil! What brought you here, Haley?

HALEY: [*Sitting at table.*] I say, Tom, this yer's the luckiest thing in the world. I'm in a devil of a hobble, and you must help me out!

LOKER: Ugh! aw! like enough. A body may be pretty sure of that when you're glad to see 'em, or can make something off of 'em. What's the blow now?

HALEY: You've got a friend here—partner, perhaps?

LOKER: Yes, I have. Here, Marks—here's that ar fellow that I was with in Natchez.

MARKS: [*Grasping* HALEY's *hand.*] Shall be pleased with his acquaintance. Mr. Haley, I believe?

HALEY: The same, sir. The fact is, gentlemen, this morning I bought a young 'un of Shelby up above here. His mother got wind of it, and what does she do but cut her lucky with him; and I'm afraid by this time that she has crossed the river, for I tracked her to this very place.

MARKS: So, then, ye're fairly sewed up, ain't ye? He! he! he! it's neatly done, too.

HALEY: This young 'un business makes lots of trouble in the trade.

MARKS: Now, Mr. Haley, what is it? Do you want us to undertake to catch this gal?

HALEY: The gal's no matter of mine—she's Shelby's—it's only the boy. I was a fool for buying the monkey.

LOKER: You're generally a fool!

MARKS: Come now, Loker, none of your huffs; you see, Mr. Haley's a-puttin' us in a way of a good job. I reckon: just hold still—these yer arrangements are my forte. This yer gal, Mr. Haley—how is she? what is she?

[ELIZA *appears, with* HARRY, *listening.*]

HALEY: Well, white and handsome—well brought up. I'd have given Shelby eight hundred or a thousand, and then made well on her.

MARKS: White and handsome—well brought up! Look here now, Loker, a beautiful opening. We'll do a business here on our own account. We does the catchin'; the boy, of course, goes to Mr. Haley—we takes the gal to Orleans to speculate on. Ain't it beautiful? [*They confer together.*]

ELIZA: Powers of mercy, protect me! How shall I escape these human bloodhounds? Ah! the window—the river of ice! That dark stream lies between me and liberty! Surely the ice will bear my trifling weight. It is my only chance of escape—better sink beneath the cold waters, with my child locked in my arms, than have him torn from me and sold into bondage. He sleeps upon my breast—Heaven, I put my trust in thee! [*Gets out of window.*]

MARKS: Well, Tom Loker, what do you say?

LOKER: It'll do! [*Strikes his hand violently on the table.* ELIZA *screams. They all start to their feet.* ELIZA *disappears. Music, chord.*]

HALEY: By the land, there she is now! [*They all rush to the window.*]

MARKS: She's making for the river!

LOKER: Let's after her!

[*Music. They all leap through the window. Change.*]

SCENE V

[*Snow. Landscape. Music.*]

[*Enter* ELIZA, *with* HARRY, *hurriedly.*]

ELIZA: They press upon my footsteps—the river is my only hope. Heaven grant me strength to reach it, ere they overtake me! Courage, my child!—we will be free—or perish! [*Rushes off. Music continued.*]

[*Enter* LOKER, HALEY *and* MARKS.]

HALEY: We'll catch her yet; the river will stop her!

MARKS: No, it won't, for look! she has jumped upon the ice! She's brave gal, anyhow!

LOKER: She'll be drowned!

HALEY: Curse that young 'un! I shall lose him, after all.

LOKER: Come on, Marks, to the ferry!

HALEY: Aye, to the ferry!—a hundred dollars for a boat!

[*Music. They rush off.*]

SCENE VI

[*The entire depth of stage, representing the Ohio River filled with Floating Ice. Set bank on right and in front.* ELIZA *appears, with* HARRY, *on a cake of ice, and floats slowly across to left.* HALEY, LOKER, *and* MARKS, *on bank right, observing.* PHINEAS *on opposite shore.*]

End of Act I

ACT II, SCENE I

[*A Handsome Parlor.* MARIE *discovered reclining on a sofa.*]

MARIE: [*Looking at a note.*] What can possibly detain St. Clare? According to this note he should have been here a fortnight ago. [*Noise of carriage without.*] I do believe he has come at last.

[EVA *runs in.*]

EVA: Mamma! [*Throws her arms around Marie's neck, and kisses her.*]
MARIE: That will do—take care, child—don't you make my head ache! [*Kisses her languidly.*]

[*Enter* ST. CLARE, OPHELIA, *and* TOM, *nicely dressed.*]

ST. CLARE: Well, my dear Marie, here we are at last. The wanderers have arrived, you see. Allow me to present my cousin, Miss Ophelia, who is about to undertake the office of our housekeeper.
MARIE: [*Rising to a sitting posture.*] I am delighted to see you. How do you like the appearance of our city?
EVA: [*Running to* OPHELIA.] Oh! is it not beautiful? My own darling home!—is it not beautiful?
OPHELIA: Yes, it is a pretty place, though it looks rather old and heathenish to me.
ST. CLARE: Tom, my boy, this seems to suit you?

TOM: Yes, mas'r, it looks about the right thing.

ST. CLARE: See here, Marie, I've brought you a coachman, at last, to order. I tell you, he is a regular hearse for blackness and sobriety, and will drive you like a funeral, if you wish. Open your eyes, now, and look at him. Now, don't say I never think about you when I'm gone.

MARIE: I know he'll get drunk.

ST. CLARE: Oh! no he won't. He's warranted a pious and sober article.

MARIE: Well, I hope he may turn out well; it's more than I expect, though.

ST. CLARE: Have you no curiosity to learn how and where I picked up Tom?

EVA: *Uncle* Tom papa; that's his name.

ST. CLARE: Right, my little sunbeam!

TOM: Please, mas'r, that ain't no 'casion to say nothing bout me.

ST. CLARE: You are too modest, my modern Hannibal. Do you know, Marie, that our little Eva took a fancy to Uncle Tom—whom we met on board the steamboat—and persuaded me to buy him.

MARIE: Ah! she is so odd.

ST. CLARE: As we approached the landing, a sudden rush of the passengers precipitated Eva into the water—

MARIE: Gracious heavens!

ST. CLARE: A man leaped into the river, and, as she rose to the surface of the water, grasped her in his arms, and held her up until she could be drawn on the boat again. Who was that man, Eva?

EVA: Uncle, Tom! [*Runs to him. He lifts her in his arms. She kisses him.*]

TOM: The dear soul!

OPHELIA: [*Astonished.*] How shiftless!

ST. CLARE: [*Overhearing her.*] What's the matter now, pray?

OPHELIA: Well, I want to be kind to everybody, and I wouldn't have anything hurt, but as to kissing—

ST. CLARE: Niggers! that you're not up to, hey?

OPHELIA: Yes, that's it—how can she?

ST. CLARE: Oh! bless you, it's nothing when you are used to it!

OPHELIA: I could never be so shiftless!

EVA: Come with me, Uncle Tom, and I will show you about the house. [*Crosses with* TOM.]

TOM: Can I go mas'r?

ST. CLARE: Yes, Tom; she is your little mistress—your only duty will be to attend to her! [TOM *bows and exits.*]

MARIE: Eva, my dear!

EVA: Well, mamma?

MARIE: Do not exert yourself too much!

EVA: No, mamma! [*Runs out.*]

OPHELIA: [*Lifting up her hands.*] How shiftless!

[ST. CLARE *sits next to* MARIE *on sofa.* OPHELIA *next to* ST. CLARE.]

ST. CLARE: Well, what do you think of Uncle Tom, Marie?

MARIE: He is a perfect behemoth!

ST. CLARE: Come, now, Marie, be gracious, and say something pretty to a fellow!

MARIE: You've been gone a fortnight beyond the time!

ST. CLARE: Well, you know I wrote you the reason.

MARIE: Such a short, cold letter!

ST. CLARE: Dear me! the mail was just going, and it had to be that or nothing.

MARIE: That's just the way; always something to make your journeys long and letters short!

ST. CLARE: Look at this. [*Takes an elegant velvet case from his pocket.*] Here's a present I got for you in New York—a Daguerreotype of Eva and myself.

MARIE: [*Looks at it with a dissatisfied air.*] What made you sit in such an awkward position?

ST. CLARE: Well, the position may be a matter of opinion, but what do you think of the likeness?

MARIE: [*Closing the case snappishly.*] If you don't think anything of my opinion in one case, I suppose you wouldn't in another.

OPHELIA: [*Senteniously, aside.*] How shiftless!

ST. CLARE: Hang the woman! Come, Marie, what do you think of the likeness? Don't be nonsensical now.

MARIE: It's very inconsiderate of you, St. Clare, to insist on my talking and looking at things. You know I've been lying all day with the sick headache, and there's been such a tumult made ever since you came. I'm half dead!

OPHELIA: You're subject to the sick headache, ma'am?

MARIE: Yes, I'm a perfect martyr to it!

OPHELIA: Juniper-berry tea is good for sick head-ache; at least, Molly, Deacon Abraham Perry's wife, used to say so; and she was a great nurse.

ST. CLARE: I'll have the first juniper-berries that get ripe in our garden by the lake brought in for that especial purpose. Come, cousin, let us take a stroll in the garden. Will you join us, Marie?

MARIE: I wonder how you can ask such a question, when you know how fragile I am. I shall retire to my chamber, and repose till dinner time. [*Exit.*]

OPHELIA: [*Looking after her.*] How shiftless!

ST. CLARE: Come, cousin! [*As he goes out.*] Look out for the babies! If I step upon anybody, let them mention it.

OPHELIA: Babies under foot! How shiftless! [*Exeunt.*]

SCENE II

[*A Garden.* TOM *discovered, seated on a bank, with* EVA *on his knee—his button holes are filled with flowers, and* EVA *is hanging a wreath around his neck. Music at opening of scene.*]

[*Enter* ST. CLARE *and* OPHELIA, *observing.*]

EVA: Oh, Tom! you look so funny.

TOM: [*Sees* ST. CLARE *and puts* EVA *down.*] I begs pardon, mas'r, but the young missis would do it. Look yer, I'm like the ox, mentioned in the good book, dressed for the sacrifice.

ST. CLARE: I say, what do you think, Pussy? Which do you like the best—to live as they do at your uncle's, up in Vermont, or to have a house-full of servants, as we do?

EVA: Oh! of course our way is the pleasantest.

ST. CLARE: [*Patting her head.*] Why so?

EVA: Because it makes so many more round you to love, you know.

OPHELIA: Now, that's just like Eva—just one of her odd speeches.

EVA: Is it an odd speech, papa?

ST. CLARE: Rather, as this world goes, Pussy. But where has my little Eva been?

EVA: Oh! I've been up in Tom's room, hearing him sing.

ST. CLARE: Hearing Tom sing, hey?

EVA: Oh, yes! he sings such beautiful things, about the new Jerusalem, and bright angels, and the land of Canaan.

ST. CLARE: I dare say; it's better than the opera, isn't it?

EVA: Yes; and he's going to teach them to me.

ST. CLARE: Singing lessons, hey? You are coming on.

EVA: Yes, he sings for me, and I read to him in my Bible, and he explains what it means. Come, Tom. [*She takes his hand and they exit.*]

ST. CLARE: [*Aside.*] Oh, Evangeline! Rightly named; hath not heaven made thee an evangel to me?

OPHELIA: How shiftless! How can you let her?

ST. CLARE: Why not?

OPHELIA: Why, I don't know; it seems so dreadful.

ST. CLARE: You would think no harm in a child's caressing a large dog even if he was black; but a creature that can think, reason and feel, and is immortal, you shudder at. Confess it, cousin. I know the feeling among some of you Northerners well enough. Not that there is a particle of virtue in our not having it, but custom with us does what Christianity ought to do: obliterates the feelings of personal prejudice. You loathe them as you would a snake or a toad, yet you are indignant at their wrongs. You would not have them abused but you don't want to have anything to do with them yourselves. Isn't that it?

OPHELIA: Well, cousin, there may be some truth in this.

ST. CLARE: What would the poor and lowly do without children? Your little child is your only true democrat. Tom, now, is a hero to Eva; his stories are wonders in her eyes; his songs and Methodist hymns are better than an opera, and the traps and little bits of trash in his pockets a mine of jewels, and he the most wonderful Tom that ever wore a black skin. This is one of the roses of Eden that the Lord has dropped down expressly for the poor and lowly, who get few enough of any other kind.

OPHELIA: It's strange, cousin; one might almost think you was a *professor,* to hear you talk.

ST. CLARE: A professor?

OPHELIA: Yes, a professor of religion.

ST. CLARE: Not at all; not a professor as you town folks have it, and, what is worse, I'm afraid, not a *practicer,* either.

OPHELIA: What makes you talk so, then?

ST. CLARE: Nothing is easier than talking. My forte lies in talking, and yours, cousin, lies in doing. And speaking of that puts me in mind that I have made a purchase for your department. There's the article now. Here, Topsy! [*Whistles.*]

[TOPSY *runs on.*]

OPHELIA: Good gracious! what a heathenish, shiftless looking object! St. Clare, what in the world have you brought that thing here for?

ST. CLARE: For you to educate, to be sure, and train in the way she should go. I thought she was rather a funny specimen in the Jim Crow line. Here, Topsy, give us a song, and show us some of your dancing. [TOPSY *sings a verse and dances a breakdown.*]

OPHELIA: [*Paralyzed.*] Well, of all things! If I ever saw the like!

ST. CLARE: [*Smothering a laugh.*] Topsy, this is your new mistress—I'm going to give you up to her. See now that you behave yourself.

TOPSY: Yes, mas'r.

ST. CLARE: You're going to be good, Topsy, you understand?

TOPSY: Oh, yes, mas'r.

OPHELIA: Now, St. Clare, what upon earth is this for? Your house is so full of these plagues now, that a body can't set down their foot without treading on 'em. I get up in the morning and find one asleep behind the door, and see one black head poking out from under the table—one lying on the door mat, and they are moping and mowing and grinning between all the railings, and tumbling over the kitchen floor! What on earth did you want to bring this one for?

ST. CLARE: For you to educate—didn't I tell you? You're always preaching about educating, I thought I would make you a present of a fresh caught specimen, and let you try your hand on her and bring her up in the way she should go.

OPHELIA: I don't want her, I am sure; I have more to do with 'em now than I want to.

ST. CLARE: That's you Christians, all over. You'll get up a society, and get some poor missionary to spend all his days among just such heathen; but let me see one of you that would take one into your house with you, and take the labor of their conversion upon yourselves.

OPHELIA: Well, I didn't think of it in that light. It might be a real missionary work. Well, I'll do what I can. [*Advances to* TOPSY.] She's dreadful dirty and shiftless! How old are you, Topsy?

TOPSY: Dunno, missis.

OPHELIA: How shiftless! Don't know how old you are? Didn't anybody ever tell you? Who was your mother?

TOPSY: [*Grinning.*] Never had none.

OPHELIA: Never had any mother? What do you mean? Where was you born?

TOPSY: Never was born.

OPHELIA: You musn't answer me in that way. I'm not playing with you. Tell me where you was born, and who your father and mother were?

TOPSY: Never was born, tell you; never had no father, nor mother, nor nothin'. I war raised by a speculator, with lots of others. Old Aunt Sue used to take car on us.

st. clare: She speaks the truth, cousin. Speculators buy them up cheap, when they are little, and get them raised for the market.

ophelia: How long have you lived with your master and mistress?

topsy: Dunno, missis.

ophelia: How shiftless! Is it a year, or more, or less?

topsy: Dunno, missis.

st. clare: She does not know what a year is; she don't even know her own age.

ophelia: Have you ever heard anything about heaven, Topsy? [topsy *looks bewildered and grins.*] Do you know who made you?

topsy: Nobody, as I knows on, he, he, he! I spect I growed. Don't think nobody never made me.

ophelia: The shiftless heathen! What can you do? What did you do for your master and mistress?

topsy: Fetch water—and wash dishes—and rub knives—and wait on folks—and dance breakdowns.

ophelia: I shall break down, I'm afraid, in trying to make anything of you, you shiftless mortal!

st. clare: You find virgin soil there, cousin; put in your own ideas—you won't find many to pull up. [*Exit, laughing.*]

ophelia: [*Takes out her handkerchief. A pair of gloves falls.* topsy *picks them up slyly and puts them in her sleeve.*] Follow me, you benighted innocent!

topsy: Yes, missis. [*As* ophelia *turns her back to her, she seizes the end of the ribbon she wears around her waist, and twitches it off.* ophelia *turns and sees her as she is putting it in her other sleeve.* ophelia *takes ribbon from her.*]

ophelia: What's this? You naughty, wicked girl, you've been stealing this?

topsy: Laws! why, that ar's missis' ribbon, a'nt it? How could it got caught in my sleeve?

ophelia: Topsy, you naughty girl, don't you tell me a lie—you stole that ribbon!

topsy: Missis, I declare for't, I didn't—never seed it till dis yer blessed minnit.

OPHELIA: Topsy, don't you know it's wicked to tell lies?

TOPSY: I never tells no lies, missis; it's just de truth I've been telling now and nothing else.

OPHELIA: Topsy, I shall have to whip you, if you tell lies so.

TOPSY: Laws missis, if you's to whip all day, couldn't say no other way. I never seed dat ar—it must a got caught in my sleeve. [*Blubbers.*]

OPHELIA: [*Seizes her by the shoulders.*] Don't you tell me that again, you barefaced fibber! [*Shakes her. The gloves fall on stage.*] There you, my gloves too—you outrageous young heathen! [*Picks them up.*] Will you tell me, now, you didn't steal the ribbon?

TOPSY: No, missis; stole de gloves, but didn't steal de ribbon. It was permiskus.

OPHELIA: Why, you young reprobate!

TOPSY: Yes—I's knows I's wicked!

OPHELIA: Then you know you ought to be punished. [*Boxes her ears.*] What do you think of that?

TOPSY: He, he, he! De Lord, missus; dat wouldn't kill a 'skeeter. [*Runs off laughing,* OPHELIA *follows indignantly.*]

SCENE III

[*The Tavern by the River. Table and chairs. Jug and glasses on table. On flat is a printed placard, headed: "Four Hundred Dollars Reward—Runaway—George Harris!"* PHINEAS *is discovered, seated at table.*]

PHINEAS: So yer I am; and a pretty business I've undertook to do. Find the husband of the gal that crossed the river on the ice two or three days ago. Ruth said I must do it, and I'll be teetotally chawed up if I don't do it. I see they've offered a reward for him, dead or alive. How in creation am I to find the varmint? He isn't likely to go round looking natural, with a full description of his hide and figure staring him in the face. [*Enter* MR. WILSON.] I say, stranger, how are ye? [*Rises and comes forward.*]

WILSON: Well, I reckon.

PHINEAS: Any news? [*Takes out plug and knife.*]

WILSON: Not that I know of.

PHINEAS: [*Cutting a piece of tobacco and offering it.*] Chaw?

WILSON: No, thank ye—it don't agree with me.

PHINEAS: Don't, eh? [*Putting it in his own mouth.*] I never felt any the worse for it.

WILSON: [*Sees placard.*] What's that?

PHINEAS: Nigger advertised. [*Advances towards it and spits on it.*] There's my mind upon that.

WILSON: Why, now, stranger, what's that for?

PHINEAS: I'd do it all the same to the writer of that ar paper, if he was here. Any man that owns a boy like that, and can't find any better way of treating him, than branding him on the hand with the letter H, as that paper states, *deserves* to lose him. Such papers as this ar' a shame to old Kaintuck! that's my mind right out, if anybody wants to know.

WILSON: Well, now, that's a fact.

PHINEAS: I used to have a gang of boys, sir—that was before I fell in love—and I just told em:— "Boys," says I, "run now! Dig! put! jest when you want to. I never shall come to look after you!" That's the way I kept mine. Let 'em know they are free to run any time, and it jest stops their wanting to. It stands to reason it should. Treat 'em like men, and you'll have men's work.

WILSON: I think you are altogether right, friend, and this man described here is a fine fellow—no mistake about that. He worked for me some half dozen years in my bagging factory, and he was my best hand, sir. He is an ingenious fellow, too; he invented a machine for the cleaning of hemp—a really valuable affair; it's gone into use in several factories. His master holds the patent of it.

PHINEAS: I'll warrant ye; holds it, and makes money out of it, and then turns round and brands the boy in his right hand! If I had a fair chance, I'd mark him, I reckon, so that he'd carry it *one* while!

[*Enter* GEORGE HARRIS, *disguised.*]

GEORGE: [*Speaking as he enters.*] Jim, see to the trunks. [*Sees* WILSON.] Ah! Mr. Wilson here?

WILSON: Bless my soul, can it be?

GEORGE: [*Advances and grasps his hand.*] Mr. Wilson, I see you remember me. Mr. Butler, of Oaklands. Shelby county.

WILSON: Ye—yes—yes—sir.

PHINEAS: Holloa! there's a screw loose here somewhere. That old gentlemen seems to be struck into a pretty considerable heap of astonishment. May I be teetotally chawed up! if I don't believe that's the identical man I'm arter. [*Crosses to* GEORGE.] How are ye, George Harris?

GEORGE: [*Starting back and thrusting his hands into his breast.*] You know me?

PHINEAS: Ha, ha, ha! I rather conclude I do; but don't get riled, I an't a bloodhound in disguise.

GEORGE: How did you discover me?

PHINEAS: By a teetotal smart guess. You're the very man I want to see. Do you know I was sent after you?

GEORGE: Ah! by my master?

PHINEAS: No; by your wife.

GEORGE: My wife! Where is she?

PHINEAS: She's stopping with a Quaker family over on the Ohio side.

GEORGE: Then she is safe?

PHINEAS: Teetotally!

GEORGE: Conduct me to her.

PHINEAS: Just wait a brace of shakes and I'll do it. I've got to go and get the boat ready. 'Twon't take me but a minute—make yourself comfortable till I get back. Chaw me up! but this is what I call doing things in short order. [*Exit.*]

WILSON: George!

GEORGE: Yes, George!

WILSON: I couldn't have thought it!

GEORGE: I am pretty well disguised, I fancy; you see I don't answer to the advertisment at all.

WILSON: George, this is a dangerous game you are playing; I could not have advised you to it.

GEORGE: I can do it on my own responsibility.

WILSON: Well, George, I suppose you're running away—leaving your lawful master, George. I don't wonder at it. At the same time, I'm sorry, George, yes, decidedly. I think I must say that it's my duty to tell you so.

GEORGE: Why are you sorry, sir?

WILSON: Why to see you, as it were, setting yourself in opposition to the laws of your country.

GEORGE: *My* country! What country have *I,* but the grave? And I would to heaven that I was laid there!

WILSON: George, you've got a hard master, in fact he is—well, he conducts himself reprehensibly—I can't pretend to defend him. I'm sorry for you, now; it's a bad case—very bad; but we must all submit to the indications of providence. George, don't you see?

GEORGE: I wonder, Mr. Wilson, if the Indians should come and take you a prisoner away from your wife and children, and want to keep you all your life hoeing corn for them, if you'd think it your duty to abide in the condition in which you were called? I rather imagine that you'd think the first stray horse you could find an indication of providence, shouldn't you?

WILSON: Really, George, putting the case in that somewhat peculiar light—I don't know—under those circumstances—but what I might. But it seems to me you are running an awful risk. You can't hope to carry it out. If you're taken it will be worse with you than ever; they'll only abuse you, and half kill you, and sell you down river.

GEORGE: Mr. Wilson, I know all this. I *do* run a risk, but—[*Throws open coat and shows pistols and knife in his belt.*] There! I'm ready for them. Down South I never *will* go! no, if it comes to that, I can earn myself at least six feet of free soil—the first and last I shall ever own in Kentucky!

WILSON: Why, George, this state of mind is awful—it's getting really desperate. I'm concerned. Going to break the laws of your country?

GEORGE: My country again! Sir, I haven't any country any more than I have any father. I don't want anything of *your* country, except to be left alone—to go peaceably out of it; but if any man tries to stop me, let him take care, for I am desperate. I'll fight for my liberty, to the last breath I breathe! You say your fathers did it, if it was right for them, it is right for me!

WILSON: [*Walking up and down and fanning his face with a large yellow silk handkerchief.*] Blast 'em all! Haven't I always said so—the infernal old cusses! Bless me! I hope I an't swearing now! Well, go ahead, George, go ahead. But be careful, my boy; don't shoot anybody, unless—well, you'd *better* not shoot—at least I wouldn't *hit* anybody, you know.

GEORGE: Only in self-defense.

WILSON: Well, well. [*Fumbling in his pocket.*] I suppose, perhaps, I an't following my judgment—hang it, I won't follow my judgment. So here, George. [*Takes out a pocket-book and offers* GEORGE *a roll of bills.*]

GEORGE: No, my kind, good sir, you've done a great deal for me, and this might get you into trouble. I have money enough, I hope, to take me as far as I need it.

WILSON: No but you must, George. Money is a great help everywhere, can't have too much, if you get it honestly. Take it, *do* take it, *now* do, my boy!

GEORGE: [*Taking the money.*] On condition, sir, that I may repay it at some future time, I will.

WILSON: And now, George, how long are you going to travel in this way? Not long or far I hope? It's well carried on, but too bold.

GEORGE: Mr. Wilson, it is *so bold,* and this tavern is so near, that they will never think of it; they will look for me on ahead, and you yourself wouldn't know me.

WILSON: But the mark on your hand?

GEORGE: [*Draws off his glove and shows scar.*] That is a parting mark of Mr. Harris' regard. Looks interesting, doesn't it? [*Puts on glove again.*]

WILSON: I declare, my very blood runs cold when I think of it—your condition and your risks!

GEORGE: Mine has run cold a good many years; at present, it's about up to the boiling point.

WILSON: George, something has brought you out wonderfully. You hold up your head, and move and speak like another man.

GEORGE: [*Proudly.*] Because I'm a *freeman!* Yes, sir; I've said "master" for the last time to any man. *I'm free!*

WILSON: Take care! You are not sure; you may be taken.

GEORGE: All men are free and equal *in the grave,* if it comes to that, Mr. Wilson.

[*Enter* PHINEAS.]

PHINEAS: Them's my sentiment, to a teetotal atom, and I don't care who knows it! Neighbor, the boat is ready, and the sooner we make tracks the better. I've seen some mysterious strangers lurking about these diggings, so we'd better put.

GEORGE: Farewell, Mr. Wilson, and heaven reward you for the many kindnesses you have shown the poor fugitive!

WILSON: [*Grasping his hand.*] Your're a brave fellow, George. I wish in my heart you were safe through, though—that's what I do.

PHINEAS: And ain't I the man of all creation to put him through, stranger? Chaw me up if I don't take him to his dear little wife, in the smallest possible quantity of time. Come, neighbor, let's vamose.

GEORGE: Farewell, Mr. Wilson.

WILSON: My best wishes go with you, George. [*Exit.*]

PHINEAS: You're a trump, old Slow-and-Easy.

GEORGE: [*Looking off.*] Look! look!

PHINEAS: Consarn their picters, here they come! We can't get out of the house without their seeing us. We're teetotally treed!

GEORGE: Let us fight our way through them!

PHINEAS: No, that won't do; there are too many of them for a fair fight—we should be chawed up in no time. [*Looks round and*

sees trap door.] Holloa! here's a cellar door. Just you step down
here a few minutes, while I parley with them. [*Lifts trap.*]

GEORGE: I am resolved to perish sooner than surrender!

[*Goes down trap.*]

PHINEAS: That's your sort! [*Closes trap and stands on it.*] Here they
are!

[*Enter* HALEY, MARKS, LOKER *and three* MEN.]

HALEY: Say, stranger, you haven't seen a runaway darkey about these
parts, eh?

PHINEAS: What kind of a darkey?

HALEY: A mulatto chap, almost as light-complexioned as a white
man.

PHINEAS: Was he a pretty good-looking chap?

HALEY: Yes.

PHINEAS: Kind of tall?

HALEY: Yes.

PHINEAS: With brown hair?

HALEY: Yes.

PHINEAS: And dark eyes?

HALEY: Yes.

PHINEAS: Pretty well dressed?

HALEY: Yes.

PHINEAS: Scar on his right hand?

HALEY: Yes, yes.

PHINEAS: Well, I ain't seen him.

HALEY: Oh, bother! Come, boys, let's search the house. [*Exeunt.*]

PHINEAS: [*Raises trap.*] Now, then, neighbor George. [GEORGE *enters
up trap.*] Now's the time to cut your lucky.

GEORGE: Follow me, Phineas. [*Exit.*]

PHINEAS: In a brace of shakes. [*Is closing trap as* HALEY, MARKS,
LOKER, *etc., re-enter.*]

HALEY: Ah! he's down in the cellar. Follow me, boys! [*Thrusts* PHINEAS
aside, and rushes down trap, followed by the others. PHINEAS
closes trap and stands on it.]

PHINEAS: Chaw me up! but I've got 'em all in a trap. [*Knocking below.*] Be quiet, you pesky varmints! [*Knocking.*] They're getting mighty oneasy. [*Knocking.*] Will you be quiet, you savagerous critters! [*The trap is forced open.* HALEY *and* MARKS *appear.* PHINEAS *seizes a chair and stands over trap—picture.*] Down with you or I'll smash you into apple-fritters! [*Tableau—closed in.*]

SCENE IV

[*A plain chamber.*]

TOPSY: [*Without.*] You go 'long. No more nigger dan you be! [*Enters, shouts and laughter without—looks off.*] You seem to think yourself white folks. You ain't nerry one—black *nor* white. I'd like to be one or turrer. Law! you niggers, does you know you's all sinners? Well, you is—everybody is. White folks is sinners too—Miss Feely says so—but I 'spects niggers is the biggest ones. But Lor! ye ain't any on ye up to me. I's so awful wicked there can't nobody do nothin' with me. I used to keep old missis a-swarin' at me ha' de time. I 'spects I's de wickedest critter in de world. [*Song and dance introduced. Enter* EVA.]
EVA: Oh, Topsy! Topsy! you have been very wrong again.
TOPSY: Well, I 'spects I have.
EVA: What makes you do so?
TOPSY: I dunno; I 'spects it's cause I's so wicked.
EVA: Why did you spoil Jane's earrings?
TOPSY: 'Cause she's so proud. She called me a little black imp, and turned up her pretty nose at me 'cause she is whiter than I am. I was gwine by her room, and I seed her coral earrings lying on de table, so I threw dem on de floor, and put my foot on 'em, and scrunches 'em all to little bits—he! he! he! I's so wicked.
EVA: Don't you know that was very wrong?
TOPSY: I don't car'! I despises dem what sets up for fine ladies, when dey ain't nothing but cream-colored niggers! Dere's Miss Rosa—she gives me lots of 'pertinent remarks. T'other night

she was gwine to a ball. She put on a beau'ful dress dat missis give her—wid her har curled, all nice and pretty. She hab to go down de back stairs—dem am dark—and I puts a pail of hot water on dem, and she put her foot into it, and den she go tumbling to de bottom of de stairs, and de water go all ober her, and spile her dress, and scald her dreadful bad! He! he! he! I's so wicked!

EVA: Oh! how could you!

TOPSY: Don't dey despise me cause I don't know nothing? Don't dey laugh at me 'cause I'm brack, and dey ain't?

EVA: But you shouldn't mind them.

TOPSY: Well, I don't mind dem; but when dey are passing under my winder, I trows dirty water on'em, and dat spiles der complexions.

EVA: What does make you so bad, Topsy? Why won't you try and be good? Don't you love anybody, Topsy?

TOPSY: Can't recommember.

EVA: But you love your father and mother?

TOPSY: Never had none, ye know, I told ye that, Miss Eva.

EVA: Oh! I know; but hadn't you any brother, or sister, or aunt, or—

TOPSY: No, none on 'em—never had nothing nor nobody. I's brack—no one loves me!

EVA: Oh! Topsy, I love you! [*Laying her hand on* TOPSY's *shoulder.*] I love you because you haven't had any father, or mother, or friends. I love you, I want you to be good. I wish you would try to be good for my sake. [TOPSY *looks astonished for a moment, and then bursts into tears.*] Only think of it, Topsy—*you* can be one of those spirits bright Uncle Tom sings about!

TOPSY: Oh! dear Miss Eva—dear Miss Eva! I will try—I will try. I never did care nothin' about it before.

EVA: If you try, you will succeed. Come with me. [*Crosses and takes Topsy's hand.*]

TOPSY: I will try; but den, I's so wicked! [*Exit* EVA *followed by* TOPSY, *crying.*]

SCENE V

[Chamber. Enter GEORGE, ELIZA *and* HARRY.]

GEORGE: At length, Eliza, after many wanderings, we are united.

ELIZA: Thanks to these generous Quakers, who have so kindly sheltered us.

GEORGE: Not forgetting our friend Phineas.

ELIZA: I do indeed owe him much. 'Twas he I met upon the icy river's bank, after that fearful, but successful attempt, when I fled from the slave-trader with my child in my arms.

GEORGE: It seems almost incredible that you could have crossed the river on the ice.

ELIZA: Yes, I did. Heaven helping me, I crossed on the ice, for they were behind me—right behind—and there was no other way.

GEORGE: But the ice was all in broken-up blocks, swinging and heaving up and down in the water.

ELIZA: I know it was—I know it; I did not think I should get over, but I did not care—I could but die if I did not! I leaped on the ice, but how I got across I don't know; the first I remember, a man was helping me up the bank—that man was Phineas.

GEORGE: My brave girl! you deserve your freedom—you have richly earned it!

ELIZA: And when we get to Canada I can help you to work, and between us we can find something to live on.

GEORGE: Yes, Eliza, so long as we have each other, and our boy. Oh, Eliza, if these people only knew what a blessing it is for a man to feel that his wife and child belong to *him!* I've often wondered to see men that could call their wives and children *their own,* fretting and worrying about anything else. Why, I feel rich and strong, though we have nothing but our bare hands. If they will only let me alone now, I will be satisfied—thankful!

ELIZA: But we are not quite out of danger; we are not yet in Canada.

GEORGE: True, but it seems as if I smelt the free air, and it makes me strong!

[*Enter* PHINEAS, *dressed as a Quaker.*]

PHINEAS: [*With a snuffle.*] Verily, friends, how is it with thee?—hum!

GEORGE: Why, Phineas, what means this metamorphosis?

PHINEAS: I've become a Quaker, that's the meaning on't.

GEORGE: What—you?

PHINEAS: Teetotally! I was driven to it by a strong argument, composed of a pair of sparkling eyes, rosy cheeks, and pouting lips. Them lips would persuade a man to assassinate his grandmother! [*Assumes the Quaker tone again.*] Verily, George, I have discovered something of importance to the interests of thee and thy party, and it were well for thee to hear it.

GEORGE: Keep us not in suspense!

PHINEAS: Well, after I left you on the road, I stopped at a little, lone tavern, just below here. Well, I was tired with hard driving, and after my supper I stretched myself down on a pile of bags in the corner, and pulled a buffalo hide over me—and what does I do but get fast asleep.

GEORGE: With one ear open, Phineas?

PHINEAS: No, I slept ears and all for an hour or two, for I was pretty well tired; but when I came to myself a little, I found that there were some men in the room, sitting round a table, drinking and talking; and I thought, before I made much muster, I'd just see what they were up to, especially as I heard them say something about the Quakers. Then I listened with both ears and found they were talking about you. So I kept quiet, and heard them lay off all their plans. They've got a right notion of the track we are going to-night, and they'll be down after us, six or eight strong. So, now, what's to be done?

ELIZA: What *shall* we do, George?

GEORGE: I know what I shall do! [*Takes out pistols.*]

PHINEAS: Ay-ay, thou seest, Eliza, how it will work—pistols—phitz—poppers!

ELIZA: I see; but I pray it come not to that!

GEORGE: I don't want to involve any one with or for me. If you will lend me your vehicle, and direct me, I will drive alone to the next stand.

PHINEAS: Ah! well, friend, but thee'll need a driver for all that. Thee's quite welcome to do all the fighting thee knows; but I know a thing or two about the road that thee doesn't.

GEORGE: But I don't want to involve you.

PHINEAS: Involve me! Why, chaw me—that is to say—when thee does involve me, please to let me know.

ELIZA: Phineas is a wise and skillful man. You will do well, George, to abide by his judgment. And, oh! George, be not hasty with these—young blood is hot! [*Laying her hand on pistols.*]

GEORGE: I will attack no man. All I ask of this country is to be left alone, and I will go out peaceably. But I'll fight to the last breath before they shall take from me my wife and son! Can you blame me?

PHINEAS: Mortal man cannot blame thee, neighbor George! Flesh and blood could not do otherwise. Woe unto the world because of offenses, but woe unto them through whom the offense cometh! That's gospel, teetotally!

GEORGE: Would not even you, sir, do the same, in my place?

PHINEAS: I pray that I be not tried; the flesh is weak—but I think my flesh would be pretty tolerably strong in such a case; I ain't sure, friend George, that I shouldn't hold a fellow for thee, if thee had any accounts to settle with him.

ELIZA: Heaven grant we be not tempted.

PHINEAS: But if we are tempted too much, why, consarn 'em! let them look out, that's all.

GEORGE: It's quite plain you was not born for a Quaker. The old nature has its way in you pretty strong yet.

PHINEAS: Well, I reckon you are pretty teetotally right.

GEORGE: Had we not better hasten our flight?

PHINEAS: Well, I rather conclude we had; we're full two hours ahead of them, if they start at the time they planned; so let's vamose. [*Exeunt.*]

SCENE VI

[*A rocky pass in the hills. Large set rock and platform.*]

PHINEAS: [*Without.*] Out with you in a twinkling, every one, and up into these rocks with me! run *now,* if you *ever* did run! [*Music.* PHINEAS *enters, with* HARRY *in his arms.* GEORGE *supporting* ELIZA.] Come up here; this is one of our old hunting dens. Come up. [*They ascend the rock.*] Well, here we are. Let 'em get us if they can. Whoever comes here has to walk single file between those two rocks, in fair range of your pistols—d'ye see?

GEORGE: I do see. And now, as this affair is mine, let me take all the risk, and do all the fighting.

PHINEAS: Thee's quite welcome to do the fighting, George; but I may have the fun of looking on, I suppose. But see, these fellows are kind of debating down there, and looking up, like hens when they are going to fly up onto the roost. Hadn't thee better give 'em a word of advice, before they come up, just to tell 'em handsomely they'll be shot if they do.

[*Enter* LOKER, MARKS, *and three* MEN.]

MARKS: Well, Tom, your coons are fairly treed.

LOKER: Yes, I see 'em go up right here; and here's a path—I'm for going right up. They can't jump down in a hurry, and it won't take long to ferret 'em out.

MARKS: But, Tom, they might fire at us from behind the rocks. That would be ugly, you know.

LOKER: Ugh! always for saving your skin, Marks. No danger, niggers are too plaguy scared!

MARKS: I don't know why I shouldn't save my skin, it's the best I've got; and niggers do fight like the devil sometimes.

GEORGE: [*Rising on the rock.*] Gentlemen, who are you down there and what do you want?

LOKER: We want a party of runaway niggers. One George and Eliza Harris, and their son. We've got the officers here, and a warrant to take 'em too. D'ye hear? An't you George Harris, that belonged to Mr. Harris, of Shelby county, Kentucky?

GEORGE: I am George Harris. A Mr. Harris, of Kentucky, did call me his property. But now I'm a freeman, standing on heaven's free soil! My wife and child I claim as mine. We have arms to defend ourselves and we mean to do it. You can come up if you like, but the first one that comes within range of our bullets is a dead man!

MARKS: Oh, come—come, young man, this ar no kind of talk at all for you. You see we're officers of justice. We've got the law on our side, and the power and so forth; so you'd better give up peaceably, you see—for you'll certainly have to give up at last.

GEORGE: I know very well that you've got the law on your side, and the power; but you haven't got us. We are standing here as free as you are, and by the great power that made us, we'll fight for our liberty till we die! [*During this,* MARKS *draws a pistol, and when he concludes fires at him.* ELIZA *screams.*] It's nothing, Eliza; I am unhurt.

PHINEAS: [*Drawing* GEORGE *down.*] Thee'd better keep out of sight with thy speechifying; they're teetotal mean scamps.

LOKER: What did you do that for, Marks?

MARKS: You see, you get jist as much for him dead as alive in Kentucky.

GEORGE: Now, Phineas, the first man that advances I fire at; you take the second and so on. It won't do to waste two shots on one.

PHINEAS: But what if you don't hit?

GEORGE: I'll try my best.

PHINEAS: Creation! chaw me up if there a'nt stuff in you!

MARKS: I think I must have hit some on'em. I heard a squeal.

LOKER: I'm going right up for one. I never was afraid of niggers, and I an't a going to be now. Who goes after me?

[*Music.* LOKER *dashes up the rock.* GEORGE *fires. He staggers for a moment, then springs to the top.* PHINEAS *seizes him. A struggle.*]

PHINEAS: Friend, thee is not wanted here! [*Throws* LOKER *over the rock.*]

MARKS: [*Retreating.*] Lord help us—they're perfect devils!

[*Music.* MARKS *and Party run off.* GEORGE *and* ELIZA *kneel in an attitude of thanksgiving, with the* CHILD *between them.* PHINEAS *stands over them exulting. Tableau.*]

End of Act II

ACT III, SCENE I

[*Chamber.*]

[*Enter* ST. CLARE, *followed by* TOM.]

ST. CLARE: [*Giving money and papers to* TOM.] There, Tom, are the bills, and the money to liquidate them.

TOM: Yes, mas'r.

ST. CLARE: Well, Tom, what are you waiting for? Isn't all right there?

TOM: I'm fraid not, mas'r.

ST. CLARE: Why, Tom, what's the matter? You look as solemn as a judge.

TOM: I feel very bad, mas'r. I allays have thought that mas'r would be good to everybody.

ST. CLARE: Well, Tom, haven't I been? Come, now, what do you want? There's something you haven't got, I suppose, and this is the preface.

TOM: Mas'r allays been good to me. I haven't nothing to complain of on that head; but there is one that mas'r isn't good to.

ST. CLARE: Why, Tom, what's got into you? Speak out—what do you mean?

TOM: Last night, between one and two, I thought so. I studied upon the matter then—mas'r isn't good to *himself.*

ST. CLARE: Ah! now I understand; you allude to the state in which

I came home last night. Well, to tell the truth, I *was* slightly elevated—a little more champagne on board than I could comfortably carry. That's all, isn't it?

TOM: [*Deeply affected—clasping his hands and weeping.*] All! Oh! my dear young mas'r, I'm 'fraid it will be *loss of all—all,* body and soul. The good book says "it biteth like a serpent and stingeth like an adder," my dear mas'r.

ST. CLARE: You poor, silly fool! I'm not worth crying over.

TOM: Oh, mas'r! I implore you to think of it before it gets too late.

ST. CLARE: Well, I won't go to any more of their cursed nonsense, Tom—on my honor, I won't. I don't know why I haven't stopped long ago; I've always despised *it,* and myself for it. So now, Tom, wipe up your eyes and go about your errands.

TOM: Bless you, mas'r. I feel much better now. You have taken a load from poor Tom's heart. Bless you!

ST. CLARE: Come, come, no blessings; I'm not so wonderfully good, now. There, I'll pledge my honor to you, Tom, you don't see me so again. [*Exit* TOM.] I'll keep my faith with him, too.

OPHELIA: [*Without.*] Come along, you shiftless mortal!

ST. CLARE: What new witchcraft has Topsy been brewing? That commotion is of her raising, I'll be bound.

[*Enter* OPHELIA, *dragging in* TOPSY.]

OPHELIA: Come here now; I will tell your master.

ST. CLARE: What's the matter now?

OPHELIA: The matter is that I cannot be plagued with this girl any longer. It's past all bearing; flesh and blood cannot endure it. Here I locked her up and gave her a hymn to study; and what does she do but spy out where I put my key, and has gone to my bureau, and got a bonnet-trimming and cut it all to pieces to make dolls' jackets! I never saw anything like it in my life!

ST. CLARE: What have you done to her?

OPHELIA: What have I done? What haven't I done? Your wife says I ought to have her whipped till she couldn't stand.

ST. CLARE: I don't doubt it. Tell me of the lovely rule of woman. I never saw above a dozen women that wouldn't half kill a horse or servant, either, if they had their own way with them—let alone a man.

OPHELIA: I am sure, St. Clare, I don't know what to do. I've taught and taught—I've talked till I'm tired; I've whipped her, I've punished her in every way I could think of, and still she's just what she was at first.

ST. CLARE: Come here, Tops, you monkey! [TOPSY *crosses to* ST. CLARE, *grinning.*] What makes you behave so?

TOPSY: 'Spects it's my wicked heart—Miss Feely says so.

ST. CLARE: Don't you see how much Miss Ophelia has done for you? She says she has done everything she can think of.

TOPSY: Lord, yes, mas'r! old missis used to say so, too. She whipped me a heap harder, and used to pull my ha'r, and knock my head agin the door; but it didn't do me no good. I 'spects if they's to pull every spear of ha'r out o' my head, it wouldn't do no good neither—I's so wicked! Laws! I's nothin' but a nigger, no ways! [*Goes up.*]

OPHELIA: Well, I shall have to give her up; I can't have that trouble any longer.

ST. CLARE: I'd like to ask you one question.

OPHELIA: What is it?

ST. CLARE: Why, if your doctrine is not strong enough to save one heathen child, that you can have at home here, all to yourself, what's the use of sending one or two poor missionaries off with it among thousands of just such? I suppose this girl is a fair sample of what thousands of your heathen are.

OPHELIA: I'm sure I don't know; I never saw such a girl as this.

ST. CLARE: What makes you so bad, Tops? Why won't you try and be good? Don't you love any one, Topsy?

TOPSY: [*Comes down.*] Dunno nothing 'bout love; I loves candy and sich, that's all.

OPHELIA: But, Topsy, if you'd only try to be good, you might.

TOPSY: Couldn't never be nothing but a nigger, if I was ever so good. If I could be skinned and come white, I'd try then.

ST. CLARE: People can love you, if you are black, Topsy. Miss Ophelia would love you, if you were good. [TOPSY *laughs.*] Don't you think so?

TOPSY: No, she can't b'ar me, 'cause I'm a nigger—she'd's soon have a toad touch her. There can't nobody love niggers, and niggers can't do nothin'! I don't car'! [*Whistles.*]

ST. CLARE: Silence, you incorrigible imp, and begone!

TOPSY: He! he! he! didn't get much out of dis chile! [*Exit.*]

OPHELIA: I've always had a prejudice against negroes, and it's a fact—I never could bear to have that child touch me, but I didn't think she knew it.

ST. CLARE: Trust any child to find that out, there's no keeping it from them. but I believe all the trying in the world to benefit a child, and all the substantial favors you can do them, will never excite one emotion of gratitude, while that feeling of repugnance remains in the heart. It's a queer kind of a fact, but so it is.

OPHELIA: I don't know how I can help it—they are disagreeable to me, this girl in particular. How can I help feeling so?

ST. CLARE: Eva does, it seems.

OPHELIA: Well, she's so loving. I wish I was like her. She might teach me a lesson.

ST. CLARE: It would not be the first time a little child had been used to instruct an old disciple, if it were so. Come, let us seek Eva, in her favorite bower by the lake.

OPHELIA: Why, the dew is falling, she mustn't be out there. She is unwell, I know.

ST. CLARE: Don't be croaking, cousin—I hate it.

OPHELIA: But she has that cough.

ST. CLARE: Oh, nonsense, of that cough—it is not anything. She has taken a little cold, perhaps.

OPHELIA: Well, that was just the way Eliza Jane was taken—and Ellen—

ST. CLARE: Oh, stop these hobgoblin, nurse legends. You old hands get so wise, that a child cannot cough or sneeze, but you see desperation and ruin at hand. Only take care of the child, keep her from the night air, and don't let her play too hard, and she'll do well enough. [*Exeunt.*]

SCENE II

[*The flat represents the lake. The rays of the setting sun tinge the waters with gold. A large tree. Beneath this a grassy bank, on which* EVA *and* TOM *are seated side by side.* EVA *has a Bible open on her lap. Music.*]

TOM: Read dat passage again, please, Miss Eva?

EVA: [*Reading.*] "And I saw a sea of glass, mingled with fire." [*Stopping suddenly and pointing to lake.*] Tom, there it is!

TOM: What, Miss Eva?

EVA: Don't you see there? There's a "sea of glass mingled with fire."

TOM: True enough, Miss Eva. [*Sings.*]

Oh, had I the wings of the morning,
I'd fly away to Canaan's shore;
Bright angels should convey me home,
To the New Jerusalem.

EVA: Where do you suppose New Jerusalem is, Uncle Tom?

TOM: Oh, up in the clouds, Miss Eva.

EVA: Then I think I see it. Look in those clouds, they look like great gates of pearl; and you can see beyond them—far, far off—it's all gold! Tom, sing about 'spirits bright.'

TOM: [*Sings.*]

I see a band of spirits bright,
That taste the glories there;
They are all robed in spotless white,
And conquering palms they bear.

EVA: Uncle Tom, I've seen *them.*

TOM: To be sure you have; you are one of them yourself. You are the brightest spirit I ever saw.

EVA: They come to me sometimes in my sleep—those spirits bright— They are all robed in spotless white. And conquering palms they bear. Uncle Tom, I'm going there.

TOM: Where, Miss Eva?

EVA: [*Pointing to the sky.*] I'm going *there,* to the spirits bright, Tom; I'm going before long.

TOM: It's jest no use tryin' to keep Miss Eva here; I've allays said so. She's got the Lord's mark in her forehead. She wasn't never like a child that's to live—there was always something deep in her eyes. [*Rises and comes forward.* EVA *also comes forward, leaving Bible on bank.*]

[*Enter* ST. CLARE.]

ST. CLARE: Ah! my little pussy, you look as blooming as a rose! You are better now-a-days, are you not?

EVA: Papa, I've had things I wanted to say to you a great while. I want to say them now, before I get weaker.

ST. CLARE: Nay, this is an idle fear, Eva; you know you grow stronger every day.

EVA: It's all no use, papa, to keep it to myself any longer. The time is coming that I am going to leave you, I am going, and never to come back.

ST. CLARE: Oh, now, my dear little Eva! you've got nervous and low spirited; you mustn't indulge such gloomy thoughts.

EVA: No, papa, don't deceive yourself, I am *not* any better; I know it perfectly well, and I am going before long. I am not nervous—I am not low spirited. If it were not for you, papa, and my friends, I should be perfectly happy. I want to go—I long to go!

ST. CLARE: Why, dear child, what has made your poor little heart so sad? You have everything to make you happy that could be given you.

EVA: I had rather be in heaven! There are a great many things here that makes me sad—that seem dreadful to me; I had rather be there; but I don't want to leave you—it almost breaks my heart!

ST. CLARE: What makes you sad, and what seems dreadful, Eva?

EVA: I feel sad for our poor people; they love me dearly, and they are all good and kind to me. I wish, papa, they were all *free!*

ST. CLARE: Why, Eva, child, don't you think they are well enough off now?

EVA: [*Not heeding the question.*] Papa, isn't there a way to have slaves made free? When I am dead, papa, then you will think of me and do it for my sake?

ST. CLARE: When you are dead, Eva? Oh, child, don't talk to me so. You are all I have on earth!

EVA: Papa, these poor creatures love their children as much as you do me. Tom loves his children. Oh, do something for them!

ST. CLARE: There, there, darling; only don't distress yourself, and don't talk of dying, and I will do anything you wish.

EVA: And promise me, dear father, that Tom shall have his freedom as soon as—[*Hesitating.*]—I am gone!

ST. CLARE: Yes, dear, I will do anything in the world—anything you could ask me to. There, Tom, take her to her chamber, this evening air is too chill for her. [*Music. Kisses her.* TOM *takes* EVA *in his arms, and exits. Gazing mournfully after* EVA.] Has there ever been a child like Eva? Yes, there has been; but their names are always on grave-stones, and their sweet smiles, their heavenly eyes, their singular words and ways, are among the buried treasures of yearning hearts. It is as if heaven had an especial band of angels, whose office it is to sojourn for a season here, and endear to them the wayward human heart, that they might bear it upward with them in their homeward flight. When you see that deep, spiritual light in the eye when the little soul reveals itself in words sweeter and wiser than the ordinary words of children, hope not to retain that child; for the seal of heaven is on it, and the light of immortality looks out from its eyes! [*Music. Exit.*]

SCENE III

[*Enter: A corridor. Proscenium doors on. Music. Enter* TOM, *he listens at door and then lies down. Enter* OPHELIA, *with candle.*]

OPHELIA: Uncle Tom, what alive have you taken to sleeping anywhere and everywhere, like a dog, for? I thought you were one of the orderly sort, that liked to lie in bed in a Christian way.

TOM: [*Rises. Mysteriously.*] I do, Miss Feely, I do, but now—

OPHELIA: Well, what now?

TOM: We mustn't speak loud; Mas'r St. Clare won't hear on't; but Miss Feely, you know there must be somebody watchin' for the bridegroom.

OPHELIA: What do you mean, Tom?

TOM: You know it says in Scripture, "At midnight there was a great cry made, behold, the bridegroom cometh!" That's what I'm spectin' now, every night, Miss Feely, and I couldn't sleep out of hearing, noways.

OPHELIA: Why, Uncle Tom, what makes you think so?

TOM: Miss Eva, she talks to me. The Lord, he sends his messenger in the soul. I must be thar, Miss Feely; for when that ar blessed child goes into the kingdom, they'll open the door so wide, we'll all get a look in at the glory!

OPHELIA: Uncle Tom, did Miss Eva say she felt more unwell than usual tonight?

TOM: No; but she told me she was coming nearer—thar's them that tells it to the child, Miss Feely. It's the angels—it's the trumpet sound afore the break o' day!

OPHELIA: Heaven grant your fears be vain! Come in, Tom. [*Exeunt.*]

SCENE IV

[EVA's *Chamber.* EVA *discovered on a couch. A table stands near the couch with a lamp on it. The light shines upon* EVA's *face, which is very pale. Scene half dark.* UNCLE TOM *is kneeling near the foot of the couch,* OPHELIA *stands at the head,* ST. CLARE *at back. Scene opens to plaintive music. After a strain enter* MARIE, *hastily.*]

MARIE: St. Clare! Cousin! Oh! what is the matter now?

ST. CLARE: [*Hoarsely.*] Hush! she is dying!

MARIE: [*Sinking on her knees, beside* TOM.] Dying!

ST. CLARE: Oh! if she would only wake and speak once more. [*Bend-*

ing over EVA.] Eva, darling! [EVA *uncloses her eyes, smiles, raises her head and tries to speak.*] Do you know me, Eva?

EVA: [*Throwing her arms feebly about his neck.*] Dear papa. [*Her arms drop and she sinks back.*]

ST. CLARE: Oh heaven! this is dreadful! Oh! Tom, my boy, it is killing me!

TOM: Look at her, mas'r. [*Points to* EVA.]

ST. CLARE: [*A pause.*] She does not hear. Oh Eva! tell us what you see. What is it?

EVA: [*Feebly smiling.*] Oh! love! joy! peace! [*Dies.*]

TOM: Oh! bless the Lord! it's over, dear mas'r, it's over.

ST. CLARE: [*Sinking on his knees.*] Farewell, beloved child! the bright eternal doors have closed after thee. We shall see thy sweet face no more. Oh! woe for them who watched thy entrance into heaven when they shall wake and find only the cold, gray sky of daily life and thou gone forever. [*Solemn music, slow curtain.*]

End of Act III

ACT IV, SCENE I

[*A street in New Orleans.*]

[*Enter* GUMPTION CUTE, *meeting* MARKS.]

CUTE: How do ye dew?

MARKS: How are you?

CUTE: Well, now, squire, it's a fact that I am dead broke and busted up.

MARKS: You have been speculating, I suppose!

CUTE: That's just it and nothing shorter.

MARKS: You have had poor success, you say?

CUTE: Tarnation bad, now I tell you. You see I came to this part of the country to make my fortune.

MARKS: And you did not do it?

CUTE: Scarcely. The first thing I tried my hand at was keeping school. I opened an academy for the instruction of youth in the various branches of orthography, geography, and other graphies.

MARKS: Did you succeed in getting any pupils?

CUTE: Oh, lots on 'em! and a pretty set of dunces they were too. After the first quarter, I called on the repectable parents of the juveniles, and requested them to fork over. To which they politely answered—don't you wish you may get it?

MARKS: What did you do then?

CUTE: Well, I kind of pulled up stakes and left those diggins. Well then I went into Spiritual Rappings for a living. That paid pretty well for a short time, till I met with an accident.

MARKS: An accident?

CUTE: Yes; a tall Yahoo called on me one day, and wanted me to summon the spirit of his mother—which, of course, I did. He asked me about a dozen questions which I answered to his satisfaction. At last he wanted to know what she died of—I said, Cholera. You never did see a critter so riled as he was. 'Look yere, stranger,' said he, 'it's my opinion that you're a pesky humbug! for my mother was blown up in a *Steamboat!*' with that he left the premises. The next day the people furnished me with a conveyance, and I rode out of town.

MARKS: Rode out of town?

CUTE: Yes; on a rail!

MARKS: I suppose you gave up the spirits, after that?

CUTE: Well, I reckon I did; it had such an effect on my spirits.

MARKS: It's a wonder they didn't tar and feather you.

CUTE: There was some mention made of that, but when they said *feathers,* I felt as if I had wings and flew away.

MARKS: You cut and run?

CUTE: Yes; I didn't like their company and I cut it. Well, after that I let myself out as an overseer on a cotton plantation. I made a pretty good thing of that, though it was dreadful trying to my feelings to flog the darkies; but I got used to it after a while, and then I used to lather 'em like Jehu. Well, the proprietor got the fever and ague and shook himself out of town. The place and all the fixings were sold at auction and I found myself adrift once more.

MARKS: What are you doing at present?

CUTE: I'm in search of a rich relation of mine.

MARKS: A rich relation?

CUTE: Yes, a Miss Ophelia St. Clare. You see, a niece of hers married one of my second cousins—that's how I came to be a relation of hers. She came on here from Vermont to be housekeeper to a cousin of hers, of the same name.

MARKS: I know him well.

CUTE: The deuce you do!—well, that's lucky.

MARKS: Yes, he lives in this city.

CUTE: Say, you just point out the locality, and I'll give him a call.

MARKS: Stop a bit. Suppose you shouldn't be able to raise the wind in that quarter, what have you thought of doing?

CUTE: Well, nothing particular.

MARKS: How should you like to enter into a nice, profitable business—one that pays well?

CUTE: That's just about my measure—it would suit me to a hair. What is it?

MARKS: Nigger catching.

CUTE: Catching niggers! What on airth do you mean?

MARKS: Why, when there's a large reward offered for a runaway darkey, we goes after him, catches him, and gets the reward.

CUTE: Yes, that's all right so far—but s'pose there ain't no reward offered?

MARKS: Why, then we catches the darkey on our own account, sells him, and pockets the proceeds.

CUTE: By chowder, that ain't a bad speculation!

MARKS: What do you say? I want a partner. You see, I lost my partner last year, up in Ohio—he was a powerful fellow.

CUTE: Lost him! How did you lose him?

MARKS: Well, you see, Tom and I—his name was Tom Loker—Tom and I were after a mulatto chap, called George Harris, that run away from Kentucky. We traced him though the greater part of Ohio, and came up with him near the Pennsylvania line. He took refuge among some rocks, and showed fight.

CUTE: Oh! then runaway darkies show fight, do they?

MARKS: Sometimes. Well, Tom—like a headstrong fool as he was—rushed up the rocks, and a Quaker chap, who was helping this George Harris, threw him over the cliff.

CUTE: Was he killed?

MARKS: Well, I didn't stop to find out. Seeing that the darkies were stronger than I thought, I made tracks for a safe place.

CUTE: And what became of this George Harris?

MARKS: Oh! he and his wife and child got away safe into Canada. You see, they will get away sometimes though it isn't very often. Now what do you say? You are just the figure for a fighting partner. Is it a bargain?

CUTE: Well, I rather calculate our teams won't hitch, no how. By chowder, I hain't no idea of setting myself up as a target for darkies to fire at—that's a speculation that don't suit my constitution.

MARKS: You're afraid, then?

CUTE: No, I ain't, it's against my principles.

MARKS: Your principles—how so?

CUTE: Because my principles are to keep a sharp lookout for No. 1. I shouldn't feel wholesome if a darkie was to throw me over that cliff to look after Tom Loker. [*Extent arm-in-arm.*]

SCENE II

[*Gothic Chamber. Slow music.* ST. CLARE *discovered, seated on sofa.* TOM *at left.*]

ST. CLARE: Oh! Tom, my boy, the whole world is as empty as an egg shell.

TOM: I know it, mas'r, I know it. But oh! if mas'r could look up—up where our dear Miss Eva is—

ST. CLARE: Ah, Tom! I do look up; but the trouble is, I don't see anything when I do. I wish I could. It seems to be given to children and poor, honest fellows like you, to see what we cannot. How comes it?

TOM: Thou hast hid from the wise and prudent, and revealed unto babes; even so, Father, for so it seemed good in thy sight.

ST. CLARE: Tom, I don't believe—I've got the habit of doubting—I want to believe and I cannot.

TOM: Dear mas'r, pray to the good Lord: "Lord, I believe; help thou my unbelief."

ST. CLARE: Who knows anything about anything? Was all that beautiful love and faith only one of the ever-shifting phases of human feeling, having nothing real to rest on, passing away with the little breath? And is there no more Eva—nothing?

TOM: Oh! dear mas'r, there is. I know it; I'm sure of it. Do, do, dear mas'r, believe it!

ST. CLARE: How do you know there is, Tom? You never saw the Lord.

TOM: Felt Him in my soul, mas'r—feel Him now! Oh, mas'r! when I was sold away from my old woman and the children, I was jest a'most broken up—I felt as if there warn't nothing left—and then the Lord stood by me, and He says, "Fear not, Tom," and He brings light and joy into a poor fellow's soul—makes all peace; and I's so happy, and loves everybody, and feels willin' to be jest where the Lord wants to put me. I know it couldn't come from me, 'cause I's a poor, complaining creature—it comes from above, and I know He's willin' to do for mas'r.

ST. CLARE: [*Grasping* TOM's *hand.*] Tom, you love me!

TOM: I's willin' to lay down my life this blessed day for you.

ST. CLARE: [*Sadly.*] Poor, foolish fellow! I'm not worth the love of one good, honest heart like yours.

TOM: Oh, mas'r! there's more than me loves you—the blessed Saviour loves you.

ST. CLARE: How do you know that, Tom?

TOM: The love of the Saviour passeth knowledge.

ST. CLARE: [*Turns away.*] Singular! that the story of a man who lived and died eighteen hundred years ago can affect people so yet.

But He was no man. [*Rises.*] No man ever has such long and living power. Oh! that I could believe what my mother taught me, and pray as I did when I was a boy! But, Tom, all this time I have forgotten why I sent for you. I'm going to make a freeman of you so have your trunk packed, and get ready to set out for Kentucky.

TOM: [*Joyfully.*] Bless the Lord!

ST. CLARE: [*Dryly.*] You haven't had such very bad times here, that you need be in such a rapture, Tom.

TOM: No, no, mas'r, 'tain't that; it's being a *freeman*—that's what I'm joyin' for.

ST. CLARE: Why, Tom, don't you think, for your own part, you've been better off than to be free?

TOM: No, *indeed,* Mas'r St. Clare—no, indeed!

ST. CLARE: Why, Tom, you couldn't possibly have earned, by your work, such clothes and such living as I have given you.

TOM: I know all that, Mas'r St. Clare—mas'r's been too good; but I'd rather have poor clothes, poor house, poor everything, and have 'em *mine,* than have the best, if they belong to somebody else. I had *so,* mas'r; I think it's natur', mas'r.

ST. CLARE: I suppose so, Tom; and you'll be going off and leaving me in a month or so—though why you shouldn't no mortal knows.

TOM: Not while mas'r is in trouble. I'll stay with mas'r as long as he wants me, so as I can be any use.

ST. CLARE: [*Sadly.*] Not while I'm in trouble, Tom? And when will my trouble be over?

TOM: When you are a believer.

ST. CLARE: And you really mean to stay by me till that day comes? [*Smiling and laying his hand on Tom's shoulder.*] Ah, Tom! I won't keep you till that day. Go home to your wife and children, and give my love to all.

TOM: I's faith to think that day will come—the Lord has a work for mas'r.

ST. CLARE: A work, hey? Well, now, Tom, give me your views on what sort of a work it is—let's hear.

TOM: Why, even a poor fellow like me has a work; and Mas'r St.

Clare, that has larnin', and riches, and friends, how much he might do for the Lord.

ST. CLARE: Tom, you seem to think the Lord needs a great deal done for him.

TOM: We does for him when we does for his creatures.

ST. CLARE: Good theology, Tom. Thank you, my boy; I like to hear you talk. But go now, Tom, and leave me alone. [*Exit* TOM.] That faithful fellow's words have excited a train of thoughts that almost bear me, on the strong tide of faith and feeling, to the gates of that heaven I so vividly conceive. They seem to bring me nearer to Eva.

OPHELIA: [*Outside.*] What are you doing there, you limb of Satan? You've been stealing something, I'll be bound. [OPHELIA *drags in* TOPSY.]

TOPSY: You go 'long, Miss Feely, 'tain't none o' your business.

ST. CLARE: Heyday! what is all this commotion?

OPHELIA: She's been stealing.

TOPSY: [*Sobbing.*] I hain't neither.

OPHELIA: What have you got in your bosom?

TOPSY: I've got my hand dar.

OPHELIA: But what have you got in your hand?

TOPSY: Nuffin'.

OPHELIA: That's a fib, Topsy.

TOPSY: Well, I 'spects it is.

OPHELIA: Give it to me, whatever it is.

TOPSY: It's mine—I hope I may die this bressed minute, if it don't belong to me.

OPHELIA: Topsy, I order you to give me that article; don't let me have to ask you again. [TOPSY *reluctantly takes the foot of an old stocking from her bosom and hands it to* OPHELIA.] Sakes alive! what is all this? [*Takes from it a lock of hair, and a small book, with a bit of crape twisted around it.*]

TOPSY: Dat's a lock of ha'r dat Miss Eva give me—she cut if from her own beau'ful head herself.

ST. CLARE: [*Takes book.*] Why did you wrap *this* [*Pointing to crape.*] around the book?

TOPSY: 'Cause—'cause—'cause 'twas Miss Eva's. Oh! don't take 'em away, please! [*Sits down on stage, and, putting her apron over her head, begins to sob vehemently.*]

OPHELIA: Come, come, don't cry; you shall have them.

TOPSY: [*Jumps up joyfully and takes them.*] I wants to keep 'em, 'cause dey makes me good; I ain't half so wicked as I used to was. [*Runs off.*]

ST. CLARE: I really think you can make something of that girl. Any mind that is capable of a *real sorrow* is capable of good. You must try and do something with her.

OPHELIA: The child has improved very much; I have great hopes of her.

ST. CLARE: I believe I'll go down the street, a few moments, and hear the news.

OPHELIA: Shall I call Tom to attend you?

ST. CLARE: No, I shall be back in an hour. [*Exit.*]

OPHELIA: He's got an excellent heart, but then he's so dreadful shift-less! [*Exit.*]

SCENE III

[*Front Chamber.*]

[*Enter* TOPSY.]

TOPSY: Dar's somethin' de matter wid me—I isn't a bit like myself. I haven't done anything wrong since poor Miss Eva went up in de skies and left us. When I's gwine to do anything wicked, I tinks of her, and somehow I can't do it. I's getting to be good, dat's a fact. I 'spects when I's dead I shall be turned into a little brack angel.

[*Enter* OPHELIA.]

OPHELIA: Topsy, I've been looking for you; I've got something very particular to say to you.

TOPSY: Does you want me to say the catechism?

OPHELIA: No, not now.

TOPSY: [*Aside.*] Golly! dat's one comfort.

OPHELIA: Now, Topsy, I want you to try and understand what I am going to say to you.

TOPSY: Yes, missis, I'll open my ears drefful wide.

OPHELIA: Mr. St. Clare has given you to me, Topsy.

TOPSY: Den I b'longs to you, don't I? Golly! I thought I always belong to you.

OPHELIA: Not till to-day have I received any authority to call you my property.

TOPSY: I's your property, am I? Well, if you say so, I 'spects I am.

OPHELIA: Topsy, I can give you your liberty.

TOPSY: My liberty?

OPHELIA: Yes, Topsy.

TOPSY: Has you got 'um with you?

OPHELIA: I have, Topsy.

TOPSY: Is it clothes or wittles?

OPHELIA: How shiftless! Don't you know what your liberty is, Topsy?

TOPSY: How should I know when I never seed 'um?

OPHELIA: Topsy, I am going to leave this place; I am going many miles away—to my own home in Vermont.

TOPSY: Den what's to become of dis chile?

OPHELIA: If you wish to go, I will take you with me.

TOPSY: Miss Feely, I doesn't want to leave you no how, I loves you I does.

OPHELIA: Then you shall share my home for the rest of your days. Come, Topsy.

TOPSY: Stop, Miss Feely; does dey hab any oberseers in Varmount?

OPHELIA: No, Topsy.

TOPSY: Nor cotton plantations, nor sugar factories, nor darkies, nor whipping nor nothing?

OPHELIA: No, Topsy.

TOPSY: By Golly! de quicker you is gwine de better den.

[*Enter* TOM, *hastily.*]

TOM: Oh, Miss Feely! Miss Feely!

OPHELIA: Gracious me, Tom! what's the matter?

TOM: Oh, Mas'r St. Clare! Mas'r St. Clare!

OPHELIA: Well, Tom, well?

TOM: They've just brought him home and I do believe he's killed?

OPHELIA: Killed?

TOPSY: Oh dear! what's to become of de poor darkies now?

TOM: He's dreadful weak. It's just as much as he can do to speak. He wanted me to call you.

OPHELIA: My poor cousin! Who would have thought of it? Don't say a word to his wife, Tom; the danger may not be so great as you think; it would only distress her. Come with me; you may be able to afford some assistance.

[*Exeunt.*]

SCENE IV

[*Handsome Chamber.* ST. CLARE *discovered seated on sofa.* OPHELIA, TOM *and* TOPSY *are clustered around him.* DOCTOR *back of sofa feeling his pulse. Scene opens to slow music.*]

ST. CLARE: [*Raising himself feebly.*] Tom—poor fellow!

TOM: Well, mas'r?

ST. CLARE: I have received my death wound.

TOM: Oh, no, no, mas'r!

ST. CLARE: I feel that I am dying—Tom, pray!

TOM: [*Sinking on his knees.*] I do, pray, mas'r! I do pray!

ST. CLARE: [*After a pause.*] Tom, one thing preys upon my mind—I have forgotten to sign your freedom papers. What will become of you when I am gone?

TOM: Don't think of that, mas'r.

ST. CLARE: I was wrong, Tom, very wrong, to neglect it. I may be the cause of much suffering to you hereafter. Marie, my wife—she—oh!—

OPHELIA: His mind is wandering.

228

ST. CLARE: [*Energetically.*] No! it is coming *home* at last! [*Sinks back.*] At last at last! Eva, I come! [*Dies. Music—slow curtain.*]

End of Act IV

ACT V, SCENE I

[*An Auction Mart.* UNCLE TOM *and* EMMELINE *at back.* ADOLF, SKEGGS, MARKS, MANN, *and various spectators discovered.* MARKS *and* MANN *come forward.*]

MARKS: Hulloa, Alf! what brings you here?

MANN: Well, I was wanting a valet, and I heard that St. Clare's valet was going; I thought I'd just look at them.

MARKS: Catch me ever buying any of St. Clare's people. Spoiled niggers every one—impudent as the devil.

MANN: Never fear that; if I get 'em, I'll soon have their airs out of them—they'll soon find that they've another kind of master to deal with than St. Clare. 'Pon my word, I'll buy that fellow—I like the shape of him. [*Pointing to* ADOLF.]

MARKS: You'll find it'll take all you've got to keep him—he's deucedly extravagant.

MANN: Yes, but my lord will find that he *can't* be extravagant with *me.* Just let him be sent to the calaboose a few times, and thoroughly dressed down, I'll tell you if it don't bring him to a sense of his ways. Oh! I'll reform him, up hill and down, you'll see. I'll buy him; that's flat.

[*Enter* LEGREE, *he goes up and looks at* ADOLF, *whose boots are nicely blacked).*]

LEGREE: A nigger with his boots blacked—bah! [*Spits on them.*] Holloa, you! [*To* TOM.] Let's see your teeth. [*Seizes* TOM *by the jaw and opens his mouth.*] Strip up your sleeve and show your muscle. [TOM *does so.*] Where was you raised?

TOM: In Kintuck, mas'r.

LEGREE: What have you done?

TOM: Had care of mas'r's farm.

LEGREE: That's a likely story. [*Turns to* EMMELINE.] You're a nice-looking girl enough. How old are you? [*Grasps her arm.*]

EMMELINE: [*Shrieking.*] Ah! you hurt me.

SKEGGS: Stop that, you minx! No whimpering here. The sale is going to begin. [*Mounts the rostrum.*] Gentlemen, the next article I shall offer you to-day is Adolf, late valet to Mr. St. Clare. How much am I offered? [*Various bids are made.* ADOLF *is knocked down to Mann for eight hundred dollars.*] Gentlemen, I now offer a prime article—the quadroon girl, Emmeline, only fifteen years of age, warranted in every respect. [*Business as before.* EMMELINE *is sold to* LEGREE *for one thousand dollars.*] Now, I shall close to-day's sale by offering you the valuable article known as Uncle Tom, the most useful nigger ever raised. Gentlemen in want of an overseer, now is the time to bid. [*Business as before.* TOM *is sold to* LEGREE *for twelve hundred dollars.*]

LEGREE: Now look here, you two belong to me. [TOM *and* EMMELINE *sink on their knees.*]

TOM: Heaven help us, then!

[*Music.* LEGREE *stands over them exulting. Picture—closed in.*]

SCENE II

[*The Garden of* MISS OPHELIA'S *House in Vermont. Enter* OPHELIA *and* DEACON PERRY.]

DEACON: Miss Ophelia, allow me to offer you my congratulations upon your safe arrival in your native place. I hope it is your intention to pass the remainder of your days with us?

OPHELIA: Well, Deacon, I have come here with that express purpose.

DEACON: I presume you were not over-pleased with the South?

OPHELIA: Well, to tell you the truth, Deacon, I wasn't; I liked the country very well, but the people there are so dreadful shiftless.

DEACON: The result, I presume, of living in a warm climate.

OPHELIA: Well, Deacon, what is the news among you all here?

DEACON: Well, we live on in the same even jog-trot pace. Nothing of any consequence has happened—Oh! I forgot. [*Takes out handkerchief.*] I've lost my wife; my Molly has left me. [*Wipes his eyes.*]

OPHELIA: Poor soul! I pity you, Deacon.

DEACON: Thank you. You perceive I bear my loss with resignation.

OPHELIA: How you must miss her tongue!

DEACON: Molly certainly was fond of talking. She always would have the last word—heigho!

OPHELIA: What was her complaint, Deacon?

DEACON: A mild and soothing one, Miss Ophelia: she had a severe attack of the lockjaw.

OPHELIA: Dreadful!

DEACON: Wasn't it? When she found she couldn't use her tongue, she took it so much to heart that it struck to her stomach and killed her. Poor dear! Excuse my handkerchief; she's been dead only eighteen months.

OPHELIA: Why, Deacon, by this time you ought to be setting your cap for another wife.

DEACON: Do you think so, Miss Ophelia?

OPHELIA: I don't see why you shouldn't—you are still a good-looking man, Deacon.

DEACON: Ah! well, I think I do wear well—in fact, I may say remarkably well. It has been observed to me before.

OPHELIA: And you are not much over fifty?

DEACON: Just turned of forty, I assure you.

OPHELIA: Hale and hearty?

DEACON: Health excellent—look at my eye! Strong as a lion—look at my arm!! A No. 1 constitution—look at my leg!!!

OPHELIA: Have you no thoughts of choosing another partner?

DEACON: Well, to tell you the truth, I have.

OPHELIA: Who is she?

DEACON: She is not far distant. [*Looks at* OPHELIA *in an anguishing manner.*] I have her in my eye at this present moment.

OPHELIA: [*Aside.*] Really, I believe he's going to pop. Why, surely, Deacon, you don't mean to—

DEACON: Yes, Miss Ophelia, I do mean; and believe me, when I say—[*Looking off.*] The Lord be good to us, but I believe there is the devil coming!

[TOPSY *runs on, with bouquet. She is now dressed very neatly.*]

TOPSY: Miss Feely, here is some flowers dat I hab been gathering for you. [*Gives bouquet.*]

OPHELIA: That's a good child.

DEACON: Miss Ophelia, who is this young person?

OPHELIA: She is my daughter.

DEACON: [*Aside.*] Her daughter! Then she must have married a colored man off South. I was not aware that you had been married, Miss Ophelia?

OPHELIA: Married! Sakes alive! what made you think I had been married?

DEACON: Good gracious, I'm getting confused. Didn't I understand you to say that this—somewhat tanned—young lady was your daughter?

OPHELIA: Only by adoption. She is my adopted daughter.

DEACON: O—oh! [*Aside.*] I breathe again.

TOPSY: By Golly! dat old man's eyes stick out of 'um head dre'ful. Guess he never seed anything like me afore.

OPHELIA: Deacon, won't you step into the house and refresh yourself after your walk?

DEACON: I accept your polite invitation. [*Offers his arm.*] Allow me.

OPHELIA: As gallant as ever, Deacon. I declare, you grow younger every day.

DEACON: You can never grow old, madam.

OPHELIA: Ah, you flatterer! [*Exeunt.*]

TOPSY: Dar dey go, like an old goose and gander. Guess dat ole gemblemun feels kind of confectionary—rather sweet on my old missis. By Golly! she's been dre'ful kind to me ever since I come away from de South; and I loves her, I does, 'cause she takes such car' on me and gives me dese fine clothes. I tries to be good too, and I's gettin 'long 'mazin' fast. I's not so wicked as I used to was. [*Looks out.*] Holloa! dar's some one comin' here. I wonder what he wants now. [*Retires, observing.*]

[*Enter* GUMPTION CUTE, *very shabby, a small bundle, on stick, over his shoulder.*]

CUTE: By chowder, here I am again. Phew, it's a pretty considerable tall piece of walking between here and New Orleans, not to mention the wear of shoe-leather. I guess I'm about done up. If this streak of bad luck lasts much longer, I'll borrow sixpence to buy a rope, and hang myself right straight up! When I went to call on Miss Ophelia, I swow if I didn't find out that she had left for Vermont; so I kind of concluded to make tracks in that direction myself and as I didn't have any money left, why I had to foot it, and here I am in old Varmount once more. They told me Miss Ophelia lived up here. I wonder if she will remember the relationship. [*Sees* TOPSY.] By chowder, there's a darkey. Look here, Charcoal!

TOPSY: [*Comes forward.*] My name isn't Charcoal—it's Topsy.

CUTE: Oh! your name is Topsy, is it, you juvenile specimen of Day & Martin?

TOPSY: Tell you I don't know nothin' 'bout Day & Martin. I's Topsy and I belong to Miss Feely St. Clare.

CUTE: I'm much obleeged to you, you small extract of Japan, for your information. So Miss Ophelia lives up there in the white house, does she?

TOPSY: Well, she don't do nothin' else.

CUTE: Well, then, just locomote your pins.

TOPSY: What—what's dat?

CUTE: Walk your chalks!

TOPSY: By Golly! dere ain't no chalk 'bout me.

CUTE: Move your trotters.

TOPSY: How you does spoke! What you mean by trotters?

CUTE: Why, your feet, Stove Polish.

TOPSY: What does you want me to move my feet for?

CUTE: To tell your mistress, you ebony angel, that a gentleman wishes to see her.

TOPSY: Does you call yourself a gentleman! By Golly! you look more like a scar'crow.

CUTE: Now look here, you Charcoal, don't you be sassy. I'm a gentleman in distress; a done-up speculator; one that has seen better days—long time ago—and better clothes too, by chowder! My creditors are like my boots—they've no soles. I'm a victim to circumstances. I've been through much and survived it. I've taken walking exercise for the benefit of my health; but as I was trying to live on air at the same time, it was a losing speculation, 'cause it gave me such a dreadful appetite.

TOPSY: Golly! you look as if you could eat an ox, horns and all.

CUTE: Well, I calculate I could, if he was roasted—it's a speculation I should like to engage in. I have returned like the fellow that run away in Scripture; and if anybody's got a fatted calf they want to kill, all they got to do is to fetch him along. Do you know, Charcoal, that your mistress is a relation of mine?

TOPSY: Is she your uncle?

CUTE: No, no, not quite so near as that. My second cousin married her niece.

TOPSY: And does you want to see Miss Feely?

CUTE: I do. I have come to seek a home beneath her roof, and take care of all the spare change she don't want to use.

TOPSY: Den just you follow me, mas'r.

CUTE: Stop! By chowder, I've got a great idee. Say, you Day *&* Martin, how should you like to enter into a speculation?

TOPSY: Golly! I doesn't know what a spec—spec—cu—what-do-you-call-'um am.

CUTE: Well, now, I calculate I've hit upon about the right thing. Why should I degrade the manly dignity of the Cutes by becoming a beggar—expose myself to the chance of receiving the cold shoulder as a poor relation? By chowder, my blood biles as I think of it! Topsy, you can make my fortune, and your own, too. I've an idee in my head that is worth a million of dollars.

TOPSY: Golly! is your head worth dat? Guess you wouldn't bring dat out South for de whole of you.

CUTE: Don't you be too severe, now, Charcoal; I'm a man of genius. Did you ever hear of Barnum?

TOPSY: Barnum! Barnum! Does he live out South?

CUTE: No, he lives in New York. Do you know how he made his fortin?

TOPSY: What is him fortin, hey? Is it something he wears?

CUTE: Chowder, how green you are!

TOPSY: [*Indignantly.*] Sar, I hab you to know I's not green; I's brack.

CUTE: To be sure you are, Day & Martin. I calculate, when a person says another has a fortune, he means he's got plenty of money, Charcoal.

TOPSY: And did he make the money?

CUTE: Sartin sure, and no mistake.

TOPSY: Golly! now I thought money always growed.

CUTE: Oh, git out! You are too cute—you are cuterer than I am—and I'm Cute by name and cute by nature. Well, as I was saying, Barnum made his money by exhibiting a *woolly* horse; now wouldn't it be an all-fired speculation to show you as the woolly gal?

TOPSY: You want to make a sight of me?

CUTE: I'll give you half the receipts, by chowder!

TOPSY: Should I have to leave Miss Feely?

CUTE: To be sure you would.

TOPSY: Den you hab to get a woolly gal somewhere else, Mas'r Cute. [*Runs off.*]

CUTE: There's another speculation gone to smash, by chowder! [*Exit.*]

SCENE III

[*A rude chamber.* TOM *is discovered, in old clothes, seated on a stool. He holds in his hand a paper containing a curl of* EVA's *hair. The scene opens to the symphony of* "*Old Folks at Home.*"]

TOM: I have come to de dark places; I's going through de vale of shadows. My heart sinks at times and feels just like a big lump of lead. Den it gits up in my throat and chokes me till de tears roll out of my eyes; den I take out dis curl of little Miss Eva's hair, and the sight of it brings calm to my mind and I feels strong again. [*Kisses the curl and puts it in his breast—takes out a silver dollar, which is suspended around his neck by a string.*] Dere's de bright silver dollar dat Mas'r George Shelby gave me the day I was sold away from old Kentuck, and I've kept it ever since. Mas'r George must have grown to be a man by this time. I wonder if I shall ever see him again.

[*Song.* "*Old Folks at Home.*" *Enter* LEGREE, EMMELINE, SAMBO *and* QUIMBO.]

LEGREE: Shut up, you black cuss! Did you think I wanted any of your infernal howling? [*Turns to* EMMELINE.] We're home. [EMMELINE *shrinks from him. He takes hold of her ear.*] You didn't ever wear earrings?

EMMELINE: [*Trembling.*] No, master.

LEGREE: Well, I'll give you a pair, if you're a good girl. You needn't be so frightened; I don't mean to make you work very hard. You'll have fine times with me and live like a lady; only be a good girl.

EMMELINE: My soul sickens as his eyes gaze upon me. His touch makes my very flesh creep.

LEGREE: [*Turns to* TOM, *and points to* SAMBO *and* QUIMBO.] Ye see what ye'd get if ye'd try to run off. These yer boys have been raised to track niggers and they'd just as soon chaw one on ye up as eat their suppers; so mind yourself. [*To* EMMELINE.] Come, mistress, you go in here with me. [*Taking Emmeline's hand, and leading her off.*]

EMMELINE: [*Withdrawing her hand, and shrinking back.*] No, no! let me work in the fields; I don't want to be a lady.

LEGREE: Oh! you're going to be contrary, are you? I'll soon take all that out of you.

EMMELINE: Kill me, if you will.

LEGREE: Oh! you want to be killed, do you? Now come here, you Tom, you see I told you I didn't buy you jest for the common work; I mean to promote you and make a driver of you, and to-night ye may jest as well begin to get yer hand in. Now ye jest take this yer gal, and flog her; ye've seen enough on't to know how.

TOM: I beg mas'r's pardon—hopes mas'r won't set me at that. It's what I a'nt used to—never did, and can't do—no way possible.

LEGREE: Ye'll larn a pretty smart chance of things ye never did know before I've done with ye. [*Strikes* TOM *with whip, three blows. Music chord each blow.*] There! now will ye tell me ye can't do it?

TOM: Yes, mas'r! I'm willing to work night and day, and work while there's life and breath in me; but his yer thing I can't feel it right to do, and, mas'r, I *never* shall do it, *never!*

LEGREE: What! ye black beast! tell *me* ye don't think it right to do what I tell ye! What have any of you cussed cattle to do with thinking what's right? I'll put a stop to it. Why, what do ye think ye are? May be ye think yer a gentleman, master Tom, to be telling your master what's right and what a'nt! So you pretend it's wrong to flog the gal?

TOM: I think so, mas'r; 'twould be downright cruel, and it's what I never will do, mas'r. If you mean to kill me, kill me; but as to raising my hand agin any one here, I never shall—I'll die first!

LEGREE: Well, here's a pious dog at last, let down among us sinners—powerful holy critter he must be. Here, you rascal! you make believe to be so pious, didn't you never read out of your Bible, "Servants, obey your masters"? An't I your master? Didn't I pay twelve hundred dollars, cash, for all there is inside your cussed old black shell? An't you mine, body and soul?

TOM: No, no! My soul a'nt yours, mas'r; you haven't bought it—ye can't buy it; it's been bought and paid for by one that is able to keep it, and you can't harm it!

LEGREE: I can't? we'll see, we'll see! Here, Sambo! Quimbo! give this dog such a breaking in as he won't get over this month!

EMMELINE: Oh, no! you will not be so cruel—have some mercy! [*Clings to* TOM.]

LEGREE: Mercy? you won't find any in this shop! Away with the black cuss! Flog him within an inch of his life!

[*Music.* SAMBO *and* QUIMBO *seize* TOM *and drag him up stage.* LEGREE *seizes* EMMELINE, *and throws her round. She falls on her knees, with her hands lifted in supplication.* LEGREE *raises his whip, as if to strike* TOM. *Picture closed in.*]

SCENE IV

[*Plain Chamber.*]

[*Enter* OPHELIA, *followed by* TOPSY.]

OPHELIA: A person inquiring for me, did you say, Topsy?

TOPSY: Yes, missis.

OPHELIA: What kind of a looking man is he?

TOPSY: By golly! he's very queer looking man, anyway; and den he talks so dre'ful funny. What does you think?—yah! yah! he wanted to 'zibite me as de woolly gal! yah! yah!

OPHELIA: Oh! I understand. Some cute Yankee, who wants to purchase you, to make a show of—the heartless wretch!

TOPSY: Dat's just him, missis; dat's just his name. He tole me dat it was Cute—Mr. Cute Speculashum—dat's him.

OPHELIA: What did you say to him, Topsy?

TOPSY: Well, I didn't say much, it was brief and to the point—I tole him I wouldn't leave you, Miss Feely, no how.

OPHELIA: That's right, Topsy; you know you are very comfortable here—you wouldn't fare quite so well if you went away among strangers.

TOPSY: By golly! I know dat; you takes care on me, and makes me good. I don't steal any now, and I don't swar, and I don't dance breakdowns. Oh! I isn't so wicked as I used to was.

OPHELIA: That's right, Topsy; now show the gentleman, or whatever he is, up.

TOPSY: By golly! I guess he won't make much out of Miss Feely. [*Crosses and exits.*]

OPHELIA: I wonder who this person can be? Perhaps it is some old acquaintance, who has heard of my arrival, and who comes on a social visit.

[*Enter* CUTE.]

CUTE: Aunt, how do ye do? Well, I swan, the sight of you is good for weak eyes. [*Offers his hand.*]

OPHELIA: [*Coldly drawing back.*] Really, sir, I can't say that I ever had the pleasure of seeing you before.

CUTE: Well, it's a fact that you never did. You see I never happened to be in your neighborhood afore now. Of course you've heard of me? I'm one of the Cutes—Gumption Cute, the first and only son of Josiah and Maria Cute, of Oniontown, on the Onion river in the north part of this ere State of Varmount.

OPHELIA: Can't say I ever heard the name before.

CUTE: Well then, I calculate your memory must be a little ricketty. I'm a relation of yours.

OPHELIA: A relation of mine! Why, I never heard of any Cutes in our family.

CUTE: Well, I shouldn't wonder if you never did. Don't you remember your niece, Mary?

OPHELIA: Of course I do. What a shiftless question!

CUTE: Well, you see my second cousin, Abijah Blake, married her. So you see that makes me a relation of yours.

OPHELIA: Rather a distant one, I should say.

CUTE: By chowder! I'm *near* enough, just at present.

OPHELIA: Well, you certainly are a sort of connection of mine.

CUTE: Yes, kind of sort of.

OPHELIA: And of course you are welcome to my house, as long as you wish to make it your home.

CUTE: By chowder! I'm booked for the next six months—this isn't a bad speculation.

OPHELIA: I hope you left all your folks well at home?

CUTE: Well, yes, they're pretty comfortably disposed of. Father and mother's dead, and Uncle Josh has gone to California. I am the only representative of the Cutes left.

OPHELIA: There doesn't seem to be a great deal of *you* left. I declare, you are positively in rags.

CUTE: Well, you see, the fact is, I've been speculating—trying to get bank-notes—specie-rags, as they say—but I calculate I've turned out rags of another sort.

OPHELIA: I'm sorry for your ill luck, but I am afraid you have been shiftless.

CUTE: By chowder! I've done all that a fellow could do. You see, somehow, everything I take hold of kind of bursts up.

OPHELIA: Well, well, perhaps you'll do better for the future; make yourself at home. I have got to see to some house-hold matters, so excuse me for a short time. [*Aside.*] Impudent and shiftless. [*Exit.*]

CUTE: By chowder! I rather guess that this speculation will itch. She's a good-natured old critter; I reckon I'll be a son to her while she lives, and take care of her valuables arter she's a defunct departed. I wonder if they keep the vittles in this ere room? Guess not. I've got extensive accommodations for all sorts of eatables. I'm a regular vacuum, throughout—pockets and all. I'm chuck full of emptiness. [*Looks out.*] Holloa! who's this elderly individual coming up stairs? He looks like a compound essence of starch and dignity. I wonder if he isn't another relation of mine. I should like a rich old fellow now for an uncle.

[*Enter* DEACON PERRY.]

DEACON: Ha! a stranger here!

CUTE: How d'ye do?

DEACON: You are a friend to Miss Ophelia, I presume?

CUTE: Well, I rather calculate that I am a leetle more than a friend.

DEACON: [*Aside.*] Bless me! what can he mean by those mysterious words? Can he be her—no I don't think he can. She said she wasn't—well, at all events, it's very suspicious.

CUTE: The old fellow seems kind of stuck up.

DEACON: You are a particular friend to Miss Ophelia, you say?

CUTE: Well, I calculate I am.

DEACON: Bound to her by any tender tie?

CUTE: It's something more than a tie—it's a regular double-twisted knot.

DEACON: Ah! just as I suspected. [*Aside.*] Might I inquire the nature of that tie?

CUTE: Well, it's the natural tie of relationship.

DEACON: A relation—what relation?

CUTE: Why, you see, my second cousin, Abijah Blake, married her niece, Mary.

DEACON: Oh! is that all?

CUTE: By chowder, ain't that enough?

DEACON: Then you are not her husband?

CUTE: To be sure I ain't. What put that ere idee into your cranium?

DEACON: [*Shaking him vigorously by the hand.*] My dear sir, I'm delighted to see you.

CUTE: Holloa! you ain't going slightly insane, are you?

DEACON: No, no fear of that; I'm only happy, that's all.

CUTE: I wonder if he's been taking a nipper?

DEACON: As you are a relation of Miss Ophelia's, I think it proper that I should make you my confidant; in fact, let you into a little scheme that I have lately conceived.

CUTE: Is it a speculation?

DEACON: Well, it is, just at present; but I trust before many hours to make it a surety.

CUTE: By chowder! I hope it won't serve you the way my speculations have served me. But fire away, old boy, and give us the prospectus.

DEACON: Well, then, my young friend, I have been thinking, ever since Miss Ophelia returned to Vermont, that she was just the person to fill the place of my lamented Molly.

CUTE: Say, you, you couldn't tell us who your lamented Molly was, could you?

DEACON: Why, the late Mrs. Perry, to be sure.

CUTE: Oh! then the lamented Molly was your wife?

DEACON: She was.

CUTE: And now you wish to marry Miss Ophelia?

DEACON: Exactly.

CUTE: [*Aside.*] Consarn this old porpoise! if I let him do that he'll Jew me out of my living. By chowder! I'll put a spoke in his wheel.

DEACON: Well, what do you say? will you intercede for me with your aunt?

CUTE: No! bust me up if I do!

DEACON: No?

CUTE: No, I tell you. I forbid the bans. Now, ain't you a purty individual, to talk about getting married, you old superannuated Methuselah specimen of humanity! Why, you've got one foot in etarnity already, and t'other ain't fit to stand on. Go home and go to bed! have your head shaved, and send for a lawyer to make your will, leave your property to your heirs—if you hain't got any, why leave it to me—I'll take care of it, and charge nothing for the trouble.

DEACON: Really, sir, this language to one of my standing, is highly indecorous—it's more, sir, than I feel willing to endure, sir. I shall expect an explanation, sir.

CUTE: Now, you see, old gouty toes, you're losing your temper.

DEACON: Sir, I'm a deacon; I never lost my temper in all my life, sir.

CUTE: Now, you see, you're getting excited; you had better go; we can't have a disturbance here!

DEACON: No, sir! I shall not go, sir! I shall not go until I have seen

Miss Ophelia. I wish to know if she will countenance this insult.

CUTE: Now keep cool, old stick-in-the-mud! Draw it mild, old timber-toes!

DEACON: Damn it all, sir, what—

CUTE: Oh! only think, now, what would people say to hear a deacon swearing like a trooper?

DEACON: Sir—I—you—this is too much, sir.

CUTE: Well, now, I calculate that's just about my opinion, so we'll have no more of it. Get out of this! start your boots, or by chowder! I'll pitch you from one end of the stairs to the other.

[*Enter* OPHELIA.]

OPHELIA: Hoity toity! What's the meaning of all these loud words?

CUTE: [*Together.*] Well, you see, Aunt—

DEACON: Miss Ophelia, I beg—

CUTE: Now, look here, you just hush your yap! How can I fix up matters if you keep jabbering?

OPHELIA: Silence! for shame, Mr. Cute. Is that the way you speak to the deacon?

CUTE: Darn the deacon!

OPHELIA: Deacon Perry, what is all this?

DEACON: Madam, a few words will explain everything. Hearing from this person that he was your nephew, I ventured to tell him that I cherished hopes of making you my wife, where upon he flew into a violent passion, and ordered me out of the house.

OPHELIA: Does this house belong to you or me, Mr. Cute?

CUTE: Well, to you, I reckon.

OPHELIA: Then how dare you give orders in it?

CUTE: Well, I calculated that you wouldn't care about marrying old half century there.

OPHELIA: That's enough; I will marry him; and as for you, [*Points.*] get out.

CUTE: Get out?

OPHELIA: Yes; the sooner the better.

CUTE: Darned if I don't serve him out first though.

[*Music.* CUTE *makes a dash at* DEACON, *who gets behind* OPHE-
LIA. TOPSY *enters, with a broom and beats* CUTE *around stage.*
OPHELIA *faints in* DEACON'S *arms.* CUTE *falls, and* TOPSY *butts
him kneeling over him. Quick drop.*]

ACT VI, SCENE I

[*Dark landscape. An old, roofless shed.* TOM *is discovered in shed,
lying on some old cotton bagging.* CASSY *kneels by his side, holding a cup to his lips.*]

CASSY: Drink all ye want. I knew how it would be. It isn't the first time
I've been out in the night, carrying water to such as you.

TOM: [*Returning cup.*] Thank you, missis.

CASSY: Don't call me missis. I'm a miserable slave like yourself—a lower
one than you can ever be! It's no use, my poor fellow, this you've
been trying to do. You were a brave fellow. You had the right
on your side; but it's all in vain for you to struggle. You are in
the Devil's hands; he is the strongest, and you must give up.

TOM: Oh! how can I give up?

CASSY: You see *you* don't know anything about it; I do. Here you are,
on a lone plantation, ten miles from any other, in the swamps;
not a white person here who could testify, if you were burned
alive. There's no law here that can do you, or any of us, the
least good; and this man! there's no earthly thing that he is not
bad enough to do. I could make one's hair rise, and their teeth
chatter, if I should only tell what I've seen and been knowing
to here; and it's no use resisting! Did I *want* to live with him?
Wasn't I a woman delicately bred? and he!—Father in Heaven!
what was he and is he? And yet I've lived with him these five
years, and cursed every moment of my life, night and day.

TOM: Oh heaven! have you quite forgot us poor critters?

CASSY: And what are these miserable low dogs you work with, that
you should suffer on their account? Every one of them would
turn against you the first time they get a chance. They are all

of them as low and cruel to each other as they can be; there's no use in your suffering to keep from hurting them?

TOM: What made 'em cruel? If I give out I shall get used to it and grow, little by little, just like 'em. No, no, Missis, I've lost everything, wife, and children, and home, and a kind master, and he would have set me free if he'd only lived a day longer—I've lost everything in *this* world, and now I can't lose heaven, too: no I can't get to be wicked besides all.

CASSY: But it can't be that He will lay sin to our account; he won't charge it to us when we are forced to it; he'll charge it to them that drove us to it. Can I do anything more for you? Shall I give you some more water?

TOM: Oh missis! I wish you'd go to Him who can give you living waters!

CASSY: Go to him! Where is he? Who is he?

TOM: Our Heavenly Father!

CASSY: I used to see the picture of him, over the altar, when I was a girl but *he isn't here!* there's nothing here but sin, and long, long despair! There, there, don't talk any more, my poor fellow. Try to sleep, if you can. I must hasten back, lest my absence be noted. Think of me when I am gone, Uncle Tom, and pray, pray for me.

[*Music. Exit* CASSY. TOM *sinks back to sleep.*]

SCENE II

[*Street in New Orleans. Enter* GEORGE SHELBY.]

GEORGE: At length my mission of mercy is nearly finished, I have reached my journey's end. I have now but to find the house of Mr. St. Clare, re-purchase old Uncle Tom, and convey him back to his wife and children, in old Kentucky. Some one approaches; he may, perhaps, be able to give me the information I require. I will accost him. [*Enter* MARKS.] Pray, sir, can you tell me where Mr. St. Clare dwells?

MARKS: Where I don't think you'll be in a hurry to seek him.

GEORGE: And where is that?

MARKS: In the grave!

GEORGE: Stay, sir! you may be able to give me some information concerning Mr. St. Clare.

MARKS: I beg pardon, sir, I am a lawyer; I can't afford to *give* anything.

GEORGE: But you would have no objections to selling it?

MARKS: Not the slightest.

GEORGE: What do you value it at?

MARKS: Well, say five dollars, that's reasonable.

GEORGE: There they are. [*Gives money.*] Now answer me to the best of your ability. Has the death of St. Clare caused his slaves to be sold?

MARKS: It has.

GEORGE: How were they sold?

MARKS: At auction—they went dirt cheap.

GEORGE: How were they bought—all in one lot?

MARKS: No, they went to different bidders.

GEORGE: Was you present at the sale?

MARKS: I was.

GEORGE: Do you remember seeing a negro among them called Tom?

MARKS: What, Uncle Tom?

GEORGE: The same—who bought him?

MARKS: A Mr. Legree.

GEORGE: Where is his plantation?

MARKS: Up in Louisiana, on the Red River; but a man never could find it, unless he had been there before.

GEORGE: Who could I get to direct me there?

MARKS: Well, stranger, I don't know of any one just at present 'cept myself, could find it for you; it's such an out-of-the-way sort of hole; and if you are a mind to come down handsomely, why, I'll do it.

GEORGE: The reward shall be ample.

MARKS: Enough said, stranger; let's take the steamboat at once. [*Exeunt.*]

SCENE III

[*A Rough Chamber.*]

[*Enter* LEGREE. *Sits.*]

LEGREE: Plague on that Sambo, to kick up this yer row between Tom and the new hands. [CASSY *steals on and stands behind him.*] The fellow won't be fit to work for a week now, right in the press of the season.

CASSY: Yes, just like you.

LEGREE: Hah! you she-devil! you've come back, have you? [*Rises.*]

CASSY: Yes, I have; come to have my own way, too.

LEGREE: You lie, you jade! I'll be up to my word. Either behave yourself or stay down in the quarters and fare and work with the rest.

CASSY: I'd rather, ten thousand times, live in the dirtiest hole at the quarters, than be under your hoof!

LEGREE: But you are under my hoof, for all that, that's one comfort; so sit down here and listen to reason. [*Grasps her wrist.*]

CASSY: Simon Legree, take care! [LEGREE *lets go his hold.*] You're afraid of me, Simon, and you've reason to be; for I've got the Devil in me!

LEGREE: I believe to my soul you have. After all, Cassy, why can't you be friends with me, as you used to?

CASSY: [*Bitterly.*] Used to!

LEGREE: I wish, Cassy, you'd behave yourself decently.

CASSY: *You* talk about behaving decently! and what have you been doing? You haven't even sense enough to keep from spoiling one of your best hands, right in the most pressing season, just for your devilish temper.

LEGREE: I was a fool, it's fact, to let any such brangle come up. Now when Tom set up his will he had to be broke in.

CASSY: You'll never break *him* in.

LEGREE: Won't I? I'd like to know if I won't? He'd be the first nigger that ever come it round me! I'll break every bone in his body but he shall give up. [*Enter* SAMBO, *with a paper in his hand, stands bowing.*] What's that, you dog?

SAMBO: It's a witch thing, mas'r.

LEGREE: A what?

SAMBO: Something that niggers gits from witches. Keep 'em from feeling when they's flogged. He had it tied round his neck with a black string. [LEGREE *takes the paper and opens it. A silver dollar drops on the stage, and a long curl of light hair twines around his finger.*]

LEGREE: Damnation. [*Stamping and writhing, as if the hair burned him.*] Where did this come from? Take it off! burn it up! [*Throws the curl away.*] What did you bring it to me for?

SAMBO: [*Trembling.*] I beg pardon, mas'r; I thought you would like to see um.

LEGREE: Don't you bring me any more of your devilish things. [*Shakes his fist at* SAMBO *who runs off.* LEGREE *kicks the dollar after him.*] Blast it! Where did he get that? If it didn't look just like—whoo! I thought I'd forgot that. Curse me if I think there's any such thing as forgetting anything, anyhow.

CASSY: What is the matter with you, Legree? What is there in a simple curl of fair hair to appall a man like you—you who are familiar with every form of cruelty.

LEGREE: Cassy, to-night the past has been recalled to me—the past that I have so long and vainly striven to forget.

CASSY: Has aught on this earth power to move a soul like thine?

LEGREE: Yes, for hard and reprobate as I now seem, there has been a time when I have been rocked on the bosom of a mother, cradled with prayers and pious hymns, my now seared brow bedewed with the waters of holy baptism.

CASSY: [*Aside.*] What sweet memories of childhood can thus soften down that heart of iron?

LEGREE: In early childhood a fair-haired woman has led me, at the sound of Sabbath bells, to worship and to pray. Born of a hard-tempered sire, on whom that gentle woman had wasted a world of unvalued love, I followed in the steps of my father. Boisterous, unruly and tyrannical, I despised all her counsel, and would have none of her reproof, and, at an early age, broke from her to seek my fortunes on the sea. I never came home but once after that; and then my mother, with the yearning of a heart that must love something, and had nothing else to love, clung to me, and sought with passionate prayers and entreaties to win me from a life of sin.

CASSY: That was your day of grace, Legree; then good angels called you, and mercy held you by the hand.

LEGREE: My heart inly relented; there was a conflict, but sin got the victory, and I set all the force of my rough nature against the conviction of my conscience. I drank and swore, was wilder and more brutal than ever. And one night, when my mother, in the last agony of her despair, knelt at my feet, I spurned her from me, threw her senseless on the floor, and with brutal curses fled to my ship.

CASSY: Then the fiend took thee for his own.

LEGREE: The next I heard of my mother was one night while I was carousing among drunken companions. A letter was put in my hands. I opened it, and a lock of long, curling hair fell from it, and twined about my fingers, even as that lock twined but now. The letter told me that my mother was dead, and that dying she blest and forgave me! [*Buries his face in his hands.*]

CASSY: Why did you not even then renounce your evil ways?

LEGREE: There is a dread, unhallowed necromancy of evil, that turns things sweetest and holiest to phantoms of horror and afright. That pale, loving mother,—her dying prayers, her forgiving love,—wrought in my demoniac heart of sin only as a damning sentence, bringing with it a fearful looking for of judgment and fiery indignation.

CASSY: And yet you would not strive to avert the doom that threatened you.

LEGREE: I burned the lock of hair and I burned the letter; and when I saw them hissing and crackling in the flame, inly shuddered as I thought of everlasting fires! I tried to drink and revel, and swear away the memory; but often in the deep night, whose solemn stillness arraigns the soul in forced communion with itself, I have seen that pale mother rising by my bed-side, and felt the soft twining of that hair around my fingers, 'till the cold sweat would roll down my face, and I would spring from my bed in horror—horror! [*Falls in chair—After a pause.*] What the devil ails me? Large drops of sweat stand on my forehead, and my heart beats heavy and thick with fear. I thought I saw something white rising and glimmering in the gloom before me, and it seemed to bear my mother's face! I know one thing; I'll let that fellow Tom alone, after this. What did I want with his cussed paper? I believe I am bewitched sure enough! I've been shivering and sweating ever since! Where did he get that hair? It couldn't have been that! I *burn'd* that up, I know I did! It would be a joke if hair could rise from the dead! I'll have Sambo and Quimbo up here to sing and dance one of their dances, and keep off these horrid notions. Here, Sambo! Quimbo! [*Exit.*]

CASSY: Yes, Legree, that golden tress was charmed; each hair had in it a spell of terror and remorse for thee, and was used by a mightier power to bind thy cruel hands from inflicting uttermost evil on the helpless! [*Exit.*]

SCENE IV

[*Street.*]

[*Enter* MARKS *meeting* CUTE, *who enters dressed in an old faded uniform.*]

MARKS: By the land, stranger, but it strikes me that I've seen you somewhere before.

CUTE: By chowder! do you know now, that's just what I was a going to say?

MARKS: Isn't your name Cute?

CUTE: You're right, I calculate. Yours is Marks, I reckon.

MARKS: Just so.

CUTE: Well, I swow, I'm glad to see you. [*They shake hands.*] How's your wholesome?

MARKS: Hearty as ever. Well, who would have thought of ever seeing you again. Why, I thought you was in Vermont?

CUTE: Well, so I was. You see I went there after that rich relation of mine—but the speculation didn't turn out well.

MARKS: How so?

CUTE: Why, you see, she took a shine to an old fellow—Deacon Abraham Perry—and married him.

MARKS: Oh, that rather put your nose out of joint in that quarter.

CUTE: Busted me right up, I tell you. The Deacon did the handsome thing though, he said if I would leave the neighborhood and go out South again, he'd stand the damage. I calculate I didn't give him much time to change his mind. And so, you see, here I am again.

MARKS: What are you doing in that soldier rig?

CUTE: Oh, this is my sign.

MARKS: Your sign?

CUTE: Yes; you see, I'm engaged just at present in an all-fired good speculation, I'm a Fillibusterow.

MARKS: A what?

CUTE: A Fillubusterow! Don't you know what that is? It's Spanish for Cuban Volunteer; and means a chap that goes the whole perker for glory and all that ere sort of thing.

MARKS: Oh! you've joined the order of the Lone Star!

CUTE: You've hit it. You see I bought this uniform at a second hand clothing store, I puts it on and goes to a benevolent individual and I says to him,—appealing to his feelings,—I'm one of the fellows that went to Cuba and got massacred by the bloody Spaniards. I'm in a destitute condition—give me a trifle to pay my passage back, so I can whop the tyrannical cusses and avenge my brave fellow soger what got slewed there.

MARKS: How pathetic!

CUTE: I tell you it works up the feelings of benevolent individuals dreadfully. It draws tears from their eyes and money from their pockets. By chowder! one old chap gave me a hundred dollars to help on the cause.

MARKS: I admire a genius like yours.

CUTE: But I say, what are you up to?

MARKS: I am the traveling companion of a young gentleman by the name of Shelby, who is going to the plantation of a Mr. Legree of the Red River, to buy an old darkey who used to belong to his father.

CUTE: Legree—Legree? Well, now, I calculate I've heard that ere name afore.

MARKS: Do you remember that man who drew a bowie knife on you in New Orleans?

CUTE: By chowder! I remember the circumstance just as well as if it was yesterday; but I can't say that I recollect much about the man, for you see I was in something of a hurry about that time and didn't stop to take a good look at him.

MARKS: Well, that man was this same Mr. Legree.

CUTE: Do you know, now, I should like to pay that critter off!

MARKS: Then I'll give you an opportunity.

CUTE: Chowder! how will you do that?

MARKS: Do you remember the gentleman that interfered between you and Legree?

CUTE: Yes—well?

MARKS: He received the blow that was intended for you, and died from the effects of it. So, you see, Legree is a murderer, and we are only witnesses of the deed. His life is in our hands.

CUTE: Let's have him right up and make him dance on nothing to the tune of Yandee Doodle!

MARKS: Stop a bit. Don't you see a chance for a profitable speculation?

CUTE: A speculation! Fire away, don't be bashful, I'm the man for a speculation.

MARKS: I have made a deposition to the Governor of the state on all the particulars of that affair at Orleans.

CUTE: What did you do that for?

MARKS: To get a warrant for his arrest.

CUTE: Oh! and have you got it?

MARKS: Yes; here it is. [*Takes out paper.*]

CUTE: Well, now, I don't see how you are going to make anything by that bit of paper?

MARKS: But I do. I shall say to Legree, I have got a warrant against you for murder; my friend, Mr. Cute, and myself are the only witnesses who can appear against you. Give us a thousand dollars, and we will tear the warrant and be silent.

CUTE: Then Mr. Legree forks over a thousand dollars, and your friend Cute pockets five hundred of it, is that the calculation?

MARKS: If you will join me in the undertaking.

CUTE: I'll do it, by chowder!

MARKS: Your hand to bind the bargain.

CUTE: I'll stick by you thro' thick and thin.

MARKS: Enough said.

CUTE: Then shake. [*They shake hands.*]

MARKS: But I say, Cute, he may be contrary and show fight.

CUTE: Never mind, we've got the law on our side, and we're bound to stir him up. If he don't come down handsomely we'll present him with a neck-tie made of hemp!

MARKS: I declare you're getting spunky.

CUTE: Well, I reckon, I am. Let's go and have something to drink. Tell you what, Marks, if we don't get *him,* we'll have his hide, by chowder!

[*Exeunt, arm in arm.*]

SCENE V

[*Rough Chamber.*]

[*Enter* LEGREE, *followed by* SAMBO.]

LEGREE: Go and send Cassy to me.

SAMBO: Yes, mas'r. [*Exit.*]

LEGREE: Curse the woman! she's got a temper worse than the devil; I shall do her an injury one of these days, if she isn't careful. [*Re-enter* SAMBO, *frightened.*] What's the matter with you, you black scoundrel?

SAMBO: S'help me, mas'r, she isn't dere.

LEGREE: I suppose she's about the house somewhere?

SAMBO: No, she isn't, mas'r; I's been all over de house and I can't find nothing of her nor Emmeline.

LEGREE: Bolted, by the Lord! Call out the dogs! saddle my horse. Stop! Are you sure they really have gone?

SAMBO: Yes, mas'r; I's been in every room 'cept the haunted garret and dey wouldn't go dere.

LEGREE: I have it! Now, Sambo, you jest go and walk that Tom up here, right away! [*Exit* SAMBO.] The old cuss is at the bottom of this yer whole matter; and I'll have it out of his infernal black hide, or I'll know the reason why! I *hate* him—I *hate* him! And isn't he *mine?* Can't I do what I like with him? Who's to hinder, I wonder? [TOM *is dragged on by* SAMBO *and* QUIMBO, LEGREE *grimly confronting* TOM.] Well, Tom, do you know I've made up my mind to *kill* you?

TOM: It's very likely, Mas'r.

LEGREE: *I—have—done—just—that—thing,* Tom, unless you'll tell me what do you know about these yer gals? [TOM *is silent.*] D'ye hear? Speak!

TOM: I han't got anything to tell, mas'r.

LEGREE: Do you dare to tell me, you old black rascal, you don't know? Speak! Do you know anything?

TOM: I know, mas'r; but I can't tell anything. *I can die!*

LEGREE: Hark ye, Tom! ye think, 'cause I have let you off before, I don't mean what I say; but, this time, I have made *up my mind,* and counted the cost. You've always stood it out agin me; now, I'll *conquer ye or kill ye!* one or t'other. I'll count every drop of blood there is in you, and take 'em, one by one, 'till ye give up!

TOM: Mas'r, if you was sick, or in trouble, or dying, and I could save you, I'd *give* you my heart's blood; and, if taking every drop of blood in this poor old body would save your precious soul, I'd give 'em freely. Do the worst you can, my troubles will be over soon; but if you don't repent yours won't never end.

[LEGREE *strikes* TOM *down with the butt of his whip.*]

LEGREE: How do you like that?

SAMBO: He's most gone, mas'r!

TOM: [*Rises feebly on his hands.*] There an't no more you can do. I forgive you with all my soul. [*Sinks back, and is carried off by* SAMBO *and* QUIMBO.]

LEGREE: I believe he's done for finally. Well, his mouth is shut up at last—that's one comfort. [*Enter* GEORGE SHELBY, MARKS *and* CUTE.] Strangers! Well what do you want?

GEORGE: I understand that you bought in New Orleans a negro named Tom?

LEGREE: Yes, I did buy such a fellow, and a devil of a bargain I had of it, too! I believe he's trying to die, but I don't know as he'll make it out.

GEORGE: Where is he? Let me see him?

SAMBO: Dere he is. [*Points to* TOM.]

LEGREE: How dare you speak? [*Drives* SAMBO *and* QUIMBO *off.* GEORGE *exits.*]

CUTE: Now's the time to nab him.

MARKS: How are you, Mr. Legree?

LEGREE: What the devil brought you here?

MARKS: This little bit of paper. I arrest you for the murder of Mr. St. Clare. What do you say to that?

LEGREE: This is my answer! [*Makes a blow at* MARKS, *who dodges, and* CUTE *receives the blow—he cries out and runs off,* MARKS *fires at* LEGREE, *and follows* CUTE.] I am hit!—the game's up! [*Falls dead.* QUIMBO *and* SAMBO *return and carry him off laughing.*]

[*Enter* GEORGE SHELBY, *supporting* TOM. *Music. They advance to front and* TOM *falls.*]

GEORGE: Oh! dear Uncle Tom! do wake—do speak once more! look up! Here's Master George—your own little Master George. Don't you know me?

TOM: [*Opening his eyes and speaking in a feeble tone.*] Mas'r George! Bless de Lord! it's all I wanted! They hav'n't forgot me! It warms my soul; it does my old heart good! Now I shall die content!

GEORGE: You shan't die! you mustn't die, nor think of it. I have come to buy you, and take you home.

TOM: Oh, Mas'r George, you're too late. The Lord has bought me, and is going to take me home.

GEORGE: Oh! don't die. It will kill me—it will break my heart to think what you have suffered, poor, poor fellow!

TOM: Don't call me, poor fellow! I *have* been poor fellow; but that's all past and gone now. I'm right in the door, going into glory! Oh, Mas'r George! *Heaven has come!* I've got the victory, the Lord has given it to me! Glory be to His name! [*Dies.*]

[*Solemn music.* GEORGE *covers* UNCLE TOM *with his cloak, and kneels over him. Clouds work on and conceal them, and then work off.*]

SCENE VII

[*Gorgeous clouds, tinted with sunlight.* EVA, *robed in white, is discovered on the back of a milk-white dove, with expanded wings, as if just soaring upward. Her hands are extended in benediction over* ST. CLARE *and* UNCLE TOM *who are kneeling and gazing up to her. Expressive music. Slow curtain.*]

End

The Christian Slave

Introduction

Harriet Beecher Stowe was deeply troubled by dramatizations of her blockbuster anti-slavery novel *Uncle Tom's Cabin* (1852). Works like George Aiken's version often not only changed the events of the novel, but also its message. As such, "Tom shows" joined a parade of opportunistic copycat novels, pro-slavery "answers," and memorabilia that often reduced the novel to minstrelsy. Where the novel's clear emphasis was on the subjects of slavery and abolition, dramatizations emphasized spectacle; theater-goers were likely to come away amazed, but certainly *not* radicalized. That such productions flaunted America's lack of strong copyright laws probably upset her even more; she—and the abolitionist causes she supported—saw no money from such productions. Stowe's puritanical dislike of the sinful theater initially stopped her from dramatizing the novel herself—even though the most famous abolitionist singing and stage group of the day, the Hutchinson Family Singers, asked her to do so. But by 1855, she clearly felt obligated to join the dramatic fray.

Stowe's biography sheds further light on her response to "Tom shows" and her final decision to dramatize her novel. Born June 14,

1811 in Litchfield, Connecticut, she was the daughter of prominent New England clergyman Lyman Beecher, a fairly conservative theologian and a lukewarm abolitionist. These roots shaped a generation full of contradictions: Stowe's sister Catherine chastised the radical abolitionist Grimke sisters for their public speech, but did so in a public written exchange, and Stowe's brother Henry Ward Beecher depicted himself—and was often treated—as the nation's moral center, even though he was a party to the century's most famous adultery scandal. Similarly, when Harriet Beecher married Reverend Calvin Stowe in 1836, most only saw the potential for a life as a minister's wife—raising children, helping support church activities, perhaps teaching or writing occasionally. Instead, from what she later claimed was a vision from God, she created a novel that sold like no novel before. The amazing success of *Uncle Tom's Cabin* made her one of the most famous women in the nation and then the world: different factions of the abolitionist movement courted her, the American and British aristocracy sought her out, and slaveholders both demonized and parodied her. But even though this fame allowed her to fashion a successful career as a writer, she remained hesitant about becoming a "public" woman for much of her life.

While hesitant about becoming a public presence, Stowe felt obligated to defend and build from her novel, given that it had quickly become a focal point in the debate over slavery. She released *The Key to Uncle Tom's Cabin* the year after the novel was published. This massive compilation of accounts of various incidents involving enslaved people and slave owners—as well as reviews of the novel—served as a proof-text designed to quiet critics who questioned the veracity of *Uncle Tom's Cabin*. But, if anything, the *Key* only intensified the debate, as did the growing number of "Tom shows."

Enter Mary Webb. Supposedly the daughter of a fugitive slave and a wealthy Spanish master, Webb was born in about 1828 and grew up in Massachusetts. She later moved to Philadelphia, where she met and married Frank Johnson Webb, who would later write one of the first novels by an African American, *The Garies and Their Friends* (1857). The Webbs worked in the clothing industry and socialized on the fringes of Philadelphia's Black elite. When their business failed, Webb, who had always been fascinated by poetry and drama, took lessons in elocution and offered a well-received pair of dramatic readings in Philadelphia in April 1855. Abolitionist attendees—Lucretia Mott among them—seem to have helped Webb connect with the movement, and she gave readings in both Boston and Worcester the next month. Billed as "the Black Siddons," after popular British actress Sarah Siddons, she read excerpts from William Shakespeare, Richard Brinsley Sheridan, and John Greenleaf Whittier, among others. Webb's Massachusetts readings—and the connections to other abolitionists like Thomas Wentworth Higginson that the readings offered—brought her to Stowe's attention, and the author, now an internationally known celebrity, seems to have become Webb's patron. Circumstantial evidence suggests that Stowe provided financial support for both lodging and further voice training, and she wrote *The Christian Slave*, her *only* dramatization of *Uncle Tom's Cabin*, "expressly" for Webb. Stowe's name in and of itself was a valuable commodity, and being attached to Stowe guaranteed that Webb would be noticed by the press and the public.

Still, there seems to have been more of an exchange than the term "patron" suggests. Webb gave Stowe a new voice in the debates over slavery and race. Her dignified carriage and dress—as well as her accomplished speech—distanced her from minstrel stereotypes, and her politics and background placed her clearly in the anti-slavery camp. Many nineteenth-century moralists associated women's appearances on the public stage with promiscuity; some critics have noted that this ironically gave some Black women—already stereotyped as more promiscuous by racist whites—a bit of agency in public speech. Given this, Webb's race and her non-theatrical approach to reading might have lessened Stowe's objections to theatrical performance. (Webb read from behind a lectern, had no elaborate sets or costumes, and emphasized Christian virtue.) The premiere reading of *The Christian Slave* also provided an opportunity to circulate the play in a cheap paperback edition, and so to move Stowe's dramatization of her novel into the land of family/amateur theatricals and reading as closet drama.

In essence, Webb provided Stowe with a potentially powerful answer to minstrelsy's theft of *Uncle Tom's Cabin*.

While, overall, the partnership met with decidedly mixed results, the first public reading of *The Christian Slave* was an unqualified success. Given at Boston's Tremont Temple as part of a lecture series that included anti-slavery luminaries like Wendell Phillips, Webb's reading attracted a large audience which counted poet Henry Wadsworth Longfellow and abolitionist William Cooper Nell as members and which gave "marked applause" at several moments during the reading. This success propelled Webb into a tour of the North—with performances in Worcester, Plymouth, Rochester, Buffalo, and Cleveland, among other cites. Still, few of the readings garnered either the massive audience or the level of praise of the Tremont Temple Reading. By the end of the tour, Webb had begun to supplement *The Christian Slave*—sometimes trimming Stowe's drama significantly—with new material, including author-sanctioned readings from Longfellow's *Hiawatha* (1855). Stowe, too, had moved on to other projects—especially her new anti-slavery novel *Dred, a Tale of the Dismal Swamp* (1856).

Still, Stowe aided the Webbs in setting up a mid-1856 trip to England, where *Uncle Tom's Cabin* had similarly suffered from appropriation by a popular consumer culture based more and more around minstrelsy. There, Webb returned to *The Christian Slave*. Her British premiere, held at the London home of the Duchess of Sutherland, was widely covered by the press and once again lauded, and she effectively used her work to secure friendships with several abolitionist English nobles. Their financial security arguably gave Webb's husband time to write his novel, which was prefaced by abolitionist Lord Brougham and Stowe. Probably to Stowe's chagrin, by the time her sister Mary Beecher Perkins visited London in 1857, it was the Webbs who provided Perkins with an entrée into British society—rather than the other way around.

Webb's worsening health, though, forced her from the podium and, eventually, from England to Jamaica, where the Webbs' noble friends found a post for Frank Webb. When she died on June 17,

1859, *The Christian Slave* was already being forgotten. After *Dred*, Stowe moved away from her anti-slavery focus and more deeply into New England regionalism; she did not even bother to have the play included in the various sets of her collected works issued in the decades before her death on July 1, 1896.

The Christian Slave, then, is probably best understood as a play of a specific historical moment. As an excerpted version of her novel—rather than an adaptation with new language—it presents what Stowe thought of as key moments in the book. Its three acts cover, respectively, Tom's time with the financially strapped paternalistic Shelbys, his time with the kind but morally lazy St. Clare, and his time with the demonic Legree. As such, it would certainly be possible to argue that, if one were to read an abridged version of the novel, *The Christian Slave* is the only such abridgement created and sanctioned by the author.

Still, because the excerpts are drawn from a *much* longer novel (the first edition of *The Christian Slave* was only 67 pages, as opposed to the 600-plus pages in the early editions of the novel) the reader's—and listener's—experience is in some ways notably different. Whether Stowe intended to reshape the experience of readers and listeners as compared to that of the novel is more open to debate. Nonetheless, white characters are de-emphasized, as are male characters; Eliza's husband George Harris, for example, never appears in *The Christian Slave*). It is certainly plausible that the move to highlight the Black women from *Uncle Tom's Cabin* was a conscious gesture by Stowe toward Webb's race and gender. This shift most radically changes the last thing we see. In the play's final act, the radical female slave Cassy is present in eight of the fourteen scenes and has the longest soliloquy—which details the destruction of both her birth and adult families by slavery in fiery language that promises God's judgment upon slaveholders.

Further, readers and listeners arguably come away seeing Cassy as the play's representative mother because of the significant cutting of white mothers from the text and because Eliza is essentially absent after the first act. They also might come away with a fuller sense of

African American agency and power, as the play becomes more about the Black characters themselves than what the white characters do with and to those Black characters (there is, for example, no George Harris, and so there is no colonizationist ending, which many Black readers found deeply troubling).

A Note on the Text

The text presented here is reproduced from the first edition of *The Christian Slave*, the inexpensive paperback published in Boston by Phillips, Sampson, and Company, in late 1855 and sold at Webb's Tremont Temple Reading. An 1856 British edition (London: Sampson, Low, Son, and Company) is substantially the same, except for an introduction by Mary Webb's husband Frank, which is available in Werner Sollors's edition of Frank Webb's works.

For Further Reading

Clark, Susan F. "Solo Black Performance before the Civil War: Mrs. Stowe, Mrs. Webb, and 'The Christian Slave.'" *New Theatre Quarterly* 13 (November 1997): 339–348.

Crockett, Rosemary. "Frank J. Webb: The Shift to Color Discrimination." *The Black Columbiad.* Eds. Werner Sollers and Maria Diedrich. Cambridge: Harvard University Press, 1994. 112–122

Gardner, Eric. " 'A Nobler End': Mary Webb and the Victorian Plat-form." *Nineteenth-Century Prose* 29.1 (Spring 2002): 103–116.

———. "Stowe Takes the Stage: Harriet Beecher Stowe's *The Chris-tian Slave." Legacy, A Journal of American Women Writers* 15.1 (Spring 1998): 78–84.

———. "Mary Webb." *American National Biography Online.* April 2003 Update. Available at <http://www.anb.org/articles/18/18-03725.html>.

Hedrick, Joan. *Harriet Beecher Stowe: A Life.* New York: Oxford University Press, 1995.

Lapsansky, Phillip. "Afro-Americana: Frank J. Webb and His Friends." *Annual Report of the Library Company of Philadelphia for the Year 1990* (1991): 27–43.

Railton, Stephen, ed. *Uncle Tom's Cabin and American Culture.* Avail-able at http://jefferson.village.virginia.edu/utc/.

Webb, Frank J. *Frank J. Webb: Fiction, Essays, and Poetry.* Ed. Werner Sollors. Toby Press, 2005.

The Christian Slave

Dramatized by Harriet Beecher Stowe
Expressly for the Readings of
MRS. MARY E. WEBB

ACT I, SCENE I

[*Uncle Tom's Cabin. A table with cups, saucers, &c.;* AUNT CHLOE *cooking at the fire;* UNCLE TOM *and* GEO. SHELBY *at a table, with slate between them;* MOSE *and* PETE *playing with baby in the corner.*]

GEO. SHELBY: Ha! ha! ha! Uncle Tom! Why, how funny!—brought up the tail of your *g* wrong side out—makes a *q*, don't you see?

UNCLE TOM: La sakes! now, does it?

GEO. S.: Why yes. Look here now, [*writing rapidly*] that's *g*, and that's *q*—that's *g*—that's *q*. See now?

AUNT CHLOE: How easy white folks al'ays does things! The way he can write now! and read, too! and then to come out here evenings and read his lessons to us—it's mighty interestin'!

GEO. S.: But, Aunt Chloe, I'm getting mighty hungry. Is n't that cake in the skillet almost done?

AUNT CHLOE: Mose done, Mas'r George; brownin' beautiful—a real lovely brown. Ah! let me alone for dat. Missis let Sally try to make some cake, t' other day, jes to *larn* her, she said. "O, go way, Missis," said I; "it really hurts my feelin's, now, to see good vittles spilt dat ar way! Cake ris all to one side—no shape at all; no more than my shoe; go way!" Here you, Mose and Pete, get out de way, you niggers! Get away, Polly, honey,—mammy'll give her baby some fin, by-and-by. Now, Mas'r George, you jest take off dem books, and set down now with my old man, and I'll take up de sausages, and have de first griddle-full of cakes on your plates in less dan no time.

GEO. S.: They wanted me to come to supper in the house, but I knew what was what too well for that, Aunt Chloe.

AUNT C. So you did—so you did, honey; you know'd your old aunty'd keep the best for you. O, let you alone for dat—go way!

GEO. S.: Now for the cake.

AUNT C.: La bless you! Mas'r George, you would n't be for cuttin' it wid dat ar great heavy knife? Smash all down—spile all de pretty rise of it. Here, I've got a thin old knife I keeps sharp a purpose. Dar now, see!—comes apart light as a feather. Now eat away; you won't get anything to beat dat ar.

GEO. S.: Tom Lincoln says that their Jinny is a better cook than you.

AUNT C.: Dem Lincons an't much count no way; I mean, set along side our folks. They's 'pectable folks enough in a plain way; but as to gettin' up anything in style, they don't begin to have a notion on't. Set Mas'r Lincon, now, alongside Mas'r Shelby. Good Lor! and Missis Lincon—can she kinder sweep it into a room like my missis,—so kinder splendid, yer know? O, go way! don't tell me nothin' of dem Lincons!

GEO. S.: Well, though, I've heard you say that Jinny way a pretty fair cook.

AUNT C.: So I did. I may say dat. Good, plain, common cookin', Jinny'll do; make a good pone o' bread—bile her taters *far*,—her corn cakes is n't extra, not extra, now, Jinny's corn cakes is n't; but then they's far. But, Lor, come to de higher branches, and what can she do? Why, she makes pies—sartin she does; but what kinder crust? Can she make your real flecky paste, as melts in your mouth and lies all up like a puff? Now, I went over thar when Miss Mary was gwine to be married, and Jinny she jest showed me de weddin' pies. Jinny and I is good friends, ye know. I never said nothin'; but go 'long, Mas'r George! Why, I shouldn't sleep a wink for a week if I had a batch of pies like dem ar. Why, dey wan't no 'count 't all.

GEO. S.: I suppose Jinny thought they were ever so nice.

AUNT C.: Thought so!—did n't she! Thar she was, showing 'em as innocent—ye see, it's jest here, Jinny *don't know*. Lor, the family an't nothing! She can't be spected to know! 'Ta'nt no fault o' hern. Ah, Mas'r George, you doesn't know half yer privileges in yer family and bringin' up! [*Sighs and rolls her eyes.*]

GEO. S.: I'm sure, Aunt Chloe, I understand all my pie-and-pudding privileges. Ask Tom Lincoln if I don't crow over him every time I meet him.

AUNT C.: [*Sitting back in her chair.*] Ya! ha! ha! And so ye telled Tom, did ye? Ha! ha! ha! O Lor—what young mas'r will be up to! Ha! ha! ha! Ye crowed over Tom! Ho! ho! ho! Lor, Mas'r George, if ye wouldn't make a hornbug laugh.

GEO. S.: Yes, I says to him, "Tom, you ought to see some of Aunt Chloe's pies; they're the right sort," says I.

AUNT C.: Pity, now, Tom couldn't. Ye oughter jest ax him here to dinner some o' these times, Mas'r George; it would look quite pretty of ye. Ye know, Mas'r George, ye oughtenter fur to feel 'bove nobody on 'count yer privileges, 'cause all our privileges is gi'n to us; we ought al'ays to 'member dat ar.

GEO. S.: Well, I mean to ask Tom here, some day next week; and you do your prettiest, Aunt Chloe, and we'll make him stare. Won't we make him eat so he won't get over it for a fortnight?

AUNT C.: Yes, yes—sartin; you'll see. Lor! to think of some of our dinners! Yer mind dat ar great chicken pie I made when we guv de dinner to General Knox? I and Missis, we come pretty near quarrellin' about dat ar crust. What does get into ladies sometimes, I don't know; but sometimes, when a body has de heaviest kind o' 'sponsibility on 'em, as ye may say, and is all kinder "*seris*" and taken up, dey takes dat ar time to be hangin' round and kinder interferin'! Now, Missis, she wanted me to do dis way, and she wanted me to do dat way; and finally I got kinder sarcy, and, says I, "Now, Missis, do jist look at dem beautiful white hands o' yourn, with long fingers, and all a sparklin' with rings, like my white lilies when de dew's on 'em; and look at my great black stumpin' hands. Now, don't ye think dat de Lord must have meant *me* to make de pie-crust, and you to stay in de parlor?" Dar! I was jist so sarcy, Mas'r George.

GEO. S. And what did mother say?

AUNT C.: Say?—why, she kinder larfed in her eyes—dem great hand-some eyes o' hern; and says she, "Well, Aunt Chloe, I think you are about in the right on 't," says she; and she went off in de parlor. She oughter cracked me over de head for bein' so sarcy; but dar's whar 't is—I can't do nothin' with ladies in de kitchen!

GEO. S.: Well, you made out well with that dinner—I remember everybody said so.

AUNT C.: Didn't I? And wan't I behind de dinin'-room door dat bery day? and didn't I see de Gineral pass his plate three times for some more dat bery pie? and, says he, "You must have an uncommon cook, Mrs. Shelby." Lor! I was jest fit fur ter split. And de Gineral, he knows what cookin' is. Bery nice man, de Gineral! He comes of one of de bery *fustest* families in Ole Virginny! He knows what's what, now, as well as I do—de Gineral. Ye see, there's *pints* in all pies, Mas'r George; but tan't everybody knows what they is, or fur to be. But the Gineral, he knows; I knew by his 'marks he made. Yes, he knows what de pints is!

GEO. S.: [*Throwing pieces of cake to the children.*] Here you Mose, Pete—you want some, don't you? Come, Aunt Chloe, bake them some cakes.

AUNT C.: [*Feeding baby, while Mose and Pete roll on the floor and pull baby's toes.*] O, go long, will ye? [*Kicking them.*] Can't ye be decent when white folks comes to see ye? Stop dat ar, now, will ye? Better mind yerselves, or I'll take ye down a button-hole lower, when Mas'r George is gone!

UNCLE TOM: La, now! they are so full of tickle all the while, they can't behave theirselves.

AUNT C.: Get along wid ye! ye'll all stick together. Go long to de spring and wash yerselves. Mas'r George! did ye ever see such aggravatin' young uns? Wall, now, I hopes you's done. Here, now, you Mose and Pete—ye got to go to bed, mighty sudden, I tell ye. Cause we's gwine to have meetin' here.

MOSE AND PETE: O, mother, we don't wanter. We wants to sit up to meetin'—meetin's is so curis. We likes 'em.

GEO. S.: [*Pushing the trundle-bed.*] La! Aunt Chloe, let 'em sit up.

AUNT C.: Well, mebbe 't will do 'em some good. What we's to do for cheers, now *I* declare I don't know.

MOSE: Old Uncle Peter sung both de legs out of dat oldest cheer, last week.

AUNT C.: You go long! I'll boun' you pulled 'em out; some o' your shines.

MOSE: Well, it'll stand, if it only keeps jam up agin de wall!

PETE: Den Uncle Peter mus' n't sit in it, 'cause he al'ays hitches when he gets a singing. He hitched pretty nigh cross de room t'udder night.

MOSE: Good Lor! get him in it den; and then he'd begin, "Come, saints and sinners, hear me tell," and then down he'll go. [*Mimicking.*]

AUNT C.: Come, now, be decent, can't ye? An't yer shamed yerself? Well, ole man, you'll have to tote in them ar bar'ls yerself.

MOSE: [*Aside to* PETE.] Mother's bar'ls is like dat ar widder's Mas'r George was reading 'bout in de good book—dey never fails.

PETE: [*Aside to* MOSE.] I'm sure one on 'em caved in last week, and let 'em all down in de middle of de singin'; dat ar was failin', warn't it?

AUNT C.: Mas'r George is such a beautiful reader, now, I know he'll stay to read for us; 'pears like 't will be so much more interestin'.

SCENE II

[*A Boudoir. Evening.* MR. *and* MRS. SHELBY.]

MRS. SHELBY: [*Arranging her ringlets at the mirror.*] By the by, Arthur, who was that low-bred fellow that you lugged in to our dinner-table to-day?

MR. SHELBY: [*Lounging on an ottoman, with newspaper.*] Haley is his name.

MRS. SHELBY: Haley! Who is he, and what may be his business here, pray?

MR. SHELBY: Well, he's a man that I transacted some business with last time I was at Natchez.

MRS. SHELBY: And he presumed on it to make himself quite at home, and call and dine here, eh?

MR. SHELBY: Why, I invited him; I had some accounts with him.

MRS. SHELBY: Is he a negro-trader?

MR. SHELBY: Why, my dear, what put that into your head?

MRS. SHELBY: Nothing—only Eliza came in here, after dinner, in a great worry, crying and taking on, and said you were talking with a trader, and that she heard him make an offer for her boy—the ridiculous little goose!

MR. SHELBY: She did, eh? It will have to come out. As well now as ever. [*Aside.*]

MRS. SHELBY: I told Eliza that she was a little fool for her pains, and that you never had anything to do with that sort of persons. Of course, I knew you never meant to sell any of our people—least of all, to such a fellow.

MR. SHELBY: Well, Emily, so I have always felt and said; but the fact is, my business lies so that I cannot get on without. I shall have to sell some of my hands.

MRS. SHELBY: To that creature? Impossible! Mr. Shelby, you cannot be serious.

MR. SHELBY: I am sorry to say that I am. I've agreed to sell Tom.

MRS. SHELBY: What! our Tom? that good, faithful creature! been your faithful servant from a boy! O, Mr. Shelby! and you have promised him his freedom, too—you and I have spoken to him a hundred times of it. Well, I can believe anything now; I can believe *now* that you could sell little Harry, poor Eliza's only child!

MR. SHELBY: Well, since you must know all, it is so. I have agreed to sell Tom and Harry both; and I don't know why I am to be rated as if I were a monster for doing what every one does every day.

MRS. SHELBY: But why, of all others, chose these? Why sell them of all on the place, if you must sell at all?

MR. SHELBY: Because they will bring the highest sum of any—that's why. I could chose another, if you say so. The fellow made me a high bid on Eliza, if that would suit you any better.

MRS. SHELBY: The wretch!

MR. SHELBY: Well, I didn't listen to it a moment, out of regard to your feelings, I wouldn't; so give me some credit.

MRS. SHELBY: My dear, forgive me. I have been hasty. I was surprised, and entirely unprepared for this; but surely you will allow me to intercede for these poor creatures. Tom is a noble-hearted, faithful fellow, if he is black. I do believe, Mr. Shelby, that if he were put to it, he would lay down his life for you.

MR. SHELBY: I know it—I dare say; but what's the use of all this? I can't help myself.

MRS. SHELBY: Why not make a pecuniary sacrifice? I'm willing to bear my part of the inconvenience. O, Mr. Shelby, I have tried—tried most faithfully, as a Christian woman should—to do my duty to these poor, simple, dependent creatures. I have cared for them, instructed them, watched over them, and know all their little cares and joys, for years; and how can I ever hold up my head again among them, if, for the sake of a little paltry gain, we sell such a faithful, excellent, confiding creature as poor Tom? I have taught them the duties of the family, of parent and child, and husband and wife; and how can I bear to have this open acknowledgment that we care for no tie, no duty, no relation? I have talked with Eliza about her boy—her duty to him as a Christian mother, to watch over him, pray for him, and bring him up in a Christian way; I have told her that one soul is worth more than all the money in the world; and how will she believe me when she sees us turn round and sell her child? sell him, perhaps, to certain ruin of body and soul!

MR. SHELBY: I'm sorry you feel so about it, Emily—indeed, I am; and I respect your feelings, too, though I don't pretend to share them to their full extent; but I tell you now, solemnly, it's of no use—I can't help myself. I didn't mean to tell you this Emily; but, in plain words, there is no choice between selling these two and selling everything. Either they must go, or *all* must. Haley has come into possession of a mortgage, which, if I don't clear off with him directly, will take everything before it. I've raked, and scraped, and borrowed, and all but begged, and the price of these two was needed to make up the balance, and I had to give them up. Haley fancied the child; he agreed to settle the matter that way, and no other. I was in his power, and *had* to do it. If you feel so to have them sold, would it be any better to have *all* sold?

MRS. SHELBY: This is God's curse on slavery!—a bitter, bitter, most accursed thing!—a curse to the master, a curse to the slave! I was a fool to think I could make anything good out of such a deadly evil. It is a sin to hold a slave under laws like ours. I always felt it was—I always thought so when I was a girl—I thought so still more after I joined the church; but I thought I could gild it over. I thought, by kindness, and care, and instruction, I could make the condition of mine better than freedom—fool that I was!

MR. SHELBY: Why, wife, you are getting to be an Abolitionist, quite.

MRS. SHELBY: Abolitionist! If they knew all I know about slavery they *might* talk. We don't need them to tell us. You know I never thought slavery was right—never felt willing to own slaves.

MR. SHELBY: Well, therein you differ from many wise and pious men. You remember Mr. B's sermon the other Sunday?

MRS. SHELBY: I don't want to hear such sermons. I never wish to hear Mr. B. in our church again. Ministers can't help the evil, perhaps,—can't cure it, any more than we can,—but defend it!—it always went against my common sense. And I think you didn't think much of the sermon, either.

MR. SHELBY: Well, I must say these ministers sometimes carry matters further than we poor sinners would exactly dare to do. We men of the world must wink pretty hard at various things, and get used to a deal that is n't the exact thing. But we don't quite fancy, when women and ministers come out broad and square, and go beyond us in matters of either modesty or morals, that's a fact. But now, my dear, I trust you see the necessity of the thing, and you see that I have done the very best that circumstances would allow.

MRS. SHELBY: [*Agitatedly.*] O yes, yes! I haven't any jewelry of any amount; but would not this watch do something? It was an expensive one when it was bought. If I could only at least save Eliza's child, I would sacrifice anything I have.

MR. SHELBY: I'm sorry, very sorry, Emily,—I'm sorry this takes hold of you so; but it will do no good. The fact is, Emily, the thing's done; the bills of sale are already signed, and in Haley's hands; and you must be thankful it is no worse. That man has had it in his power to ruin us all, and now he is fairly off. If you knew the man as I do you'd think that we had had a narrow escape.

MRS. SHELBY: Is he so hard, then?

MR. SHELBY: Why, not a cruel man, exactly, but a man of leather, a man alive to nothing but trade and profit; cool, and unhesitating, and unrelenting as death and the grave. He'd sell his own mother at a good percentage, not wishing the old woman any harm either.

MRS. SHELBY: And this wretch owns that good, faithful Tom and Eliza's child?

MR. SHELBY: Well, my dear, the fact is, that this goes rather hard with me; it's a thing I hate to think of. Haley wants to drive matters, and take possession to-morrow. I'm going to get out my horse bright and early, and be off. I can't see Tom, that's a fact; and you had better arrange a drive somewhere, and carry Eliza off. Let the thing be done when she is out of sight.

MRS. SHELBY: No, no; I'll be in no sense accomplice or help in this cruel business. I'll go and see poor old Tom—God help him!—in his distress! They shall see, at any rate, that their mistress can feel for and with them. As to Eliza, I dare not think about it. The Lord forgive us! What have we done that this cruel necessity should come on us?

SCENE III

[*Uncle Tom's Cabin. Midnight.* UNCLE TOM *and* AUNT CHLOE—*knocking without.*]

AUNT CHLOE: Good Lor! What's that? My sakes alive, if it an't Lizy! Get on yore clothes, ole man, quick! There's old Bruno, too, a-pawin' round—what on airth! I'm gwine to open the door.

[*Enter* ELIZA.]

ELIZA: I'm running away, Uncle Tom and Aunt Chloe—carrying off my child. Master's sold him.

UNCLE TOM and AUNT CHLOE: Sole him?

ELIZA: Yes, sold him! I crept into the closet by mistress' door to-night, and I heard master tell missis that he had sold my Harry and you, Uncle Tom, both to a trader, and that he was going off this morning on his horse, and that the man was to take possession to-day.

AUNT CHLOE: The good Lord hab pity on us! O, it don't seem like's if it was true! What has he done that mas'r should sell *him*?

ELIZA: He hasn't done anything—it isn't for that. Master don't want to sell, and missis—she's always good—I heard her plead and beg for us; but he told her't was no use—that he was in this man's debt, and that this man had got the power over him, and that if he did n't pay him off clear, it would end in his having to sell the place and all the people, and move off. Yes, I heard him say there was no choice between selling these two and selling all, the man was driving him so hard. Master said he was sorry; but, O missis! you ought to have heard her talk! If she an't a Christian and an angel, there never was one. I'm a wicked girl to leave her so; but then I can't help it. She said herself one soul was worth more than the world; and this boy has a soul, and if I let him be carried off, who knows what'll become of it? It must be right; but if it an't right, the Lord forgive me, for I can't help doing it!

AUNT CHLOE: Well, ole man, why don't you go too? Will you wait to be toted down river, whar dey kill niggers wid hard work and

starving? I'd a heap rather fur to die than go dar, any day! Dere's
time for ye; be off with Lizy—you've got a pass to come and go
any time. Come, bustle up, and I'll get your things together.

UNCLE TOM: No, no; I an't going. Let Eliza go; it's her right. I wouldn't
be the one to say no. 'T an't in *natur* for her to stay; but you
heard what she said! If I must be sold, or all the people on the
place, and everything go to rack, why, let me be sold. I s'pose I
can b'ar it as well as any on 'em. [*Sobbing.*] Mas'r always found
me on the spot—he always will. I never have broke trust, nor
used my pass noways contrary to my word, and I never will.
It's better for me alone to go, than to break up the place and
sell all. Mas'r an't to blame, Chloe; and he'll take care of you
and the poor—[*Covers his face with his hands.*]

ELIZA: And now, I saw my husband only this afternoon, and I little
knew then what was to come. They have pushed him to the
very last standing place, and he told me to-day he was going
to run away. Do try, if you can, to get word to him. Tell him
how I went, and why I went; and tell him I'm going to try and
find Canada. You must give my love to him, and tell him, if
I never see him again [*turning away, and speaking agitatedly*],
tell him to be as good as he can, and try and meet me in the
kingdom of heaven. Call Bruno in there. Shut the door on
him, poor beast! He must n't go with me!

[*Exit.*]

SCENE IV

[*Lawn before the house.* BLACK SAM *solus.*]

SAM: It's an ill wind dat blow nowhar—dat ar a fact. Yes, it's an ill
wind blows nowhar. Now, dar, Tom's down—wal, course der's
room for some nigger to be up; and why not dis nigger?—dat's
de idee. Tom, a ridin' round de country—boots blacked—pass
in his pocket—all grand as Cuffee; but who he? Now, why
should n't Sam?—dat's what I want to know.

[*Enter* ANDY, *shouting.*]

ANDY: Halloo, Sam! O Sam! Mas'r wants you to cotch Bill and Jerry.

SAM: High! what's afoot now, young un?

ANDY: Why, you don't know, I s'pose, that Lizy's cut stick, and clared out, with her young un?

SAM: You teach your granny! knowed it a heap sight sooner than you did. Dis nigger ain't so green, now.

ANDY: Well, anyhow, mas'r wants Bill and Jerry geared right up; and you and I's to go with Mas'r Haley, to look arter her.

SAM: Good, now! dat's de time o' day! It's Sam dat's called for in dese yer times. He's de nigger. See if I don't cotch her, now; mas'r'll see what Sam can do!

ANDY: Ah! but Sam, you'd better think twice; for missis don't want her cotched, and she'll be in yer wool.

SAM: High! how you know dat ar?

ANDY: Heard her say so, my own self, dis blessed mornin', when I bring in mas'r's shaving water. She sent me to see why Lizy did n't come to dress her; and when I telled her she was off, she jest riz up, and ses she, "The Lord be praised!" And mas'r he seemed real mad, and ses he, "Wife, you talk like a fool!" But, Lor! she'll bring him to! I knows well enough how that'll be—it's allers best to stand missis' side the fence, now I tell yer.

SAM: [*Scratching his head.*] Der an't no sayin'—never—'bout no kind o' thing in *dis* yer world. Now, sartin I'd a said that missis would a scoured the varsal world after Lizy.

ANDY: So she would; but can't ye see through a ladder, ye black nigger? Missis don't want dis yer Mas'r Haley to get Lizy's boy, dat's de go.

SAM: High!

ANDY: And I'll tell ye what, Sam, ye'd better be makin' tracks for dem hosses—mighty sudden too; mas'r's in a grand hurry.

SAM: Andy, chile, you go cotch 'em—you's a mighty good boy, Andy—and bring 'em long quick.

MRS. SHELBY: [*Calling from the balcony.*] Sam! Sam!

SAM: Andy! don't ye hear, ye nigger? be off quick, and bring the critturs up, and I'll go and 'scuse us to missis—dat ar takes dis chile to do.

MRS. SHELBY: [*From the balcony.*] Sam! what have you been loitering so for?

SAM: Lord bless you, missis! hosses won't be cotched all in a minnit; they'd done clared out way down to the south pasture, and the Lord knows whar!

MRS. SHELBY: Sam, how often must I tell you not to say "Lord bless you," and "the Lord knows," and such things? It's wicked.

SAM: O, Lord bless my soul! I done forgot, missis! I won't say nothing of de sort no more.

MRS. SHELBY: Why, Sam, you just *have* said it again.

SAM: Did I? O Lord! I mean—I did n't go fur to say dar ar.

MRS. SHELBY: You must be *careful*, Sam.

SAM: Jest let me get my breath, missis, and I'll start fair. I'll be wery careful.

MRS. SHELBY: Well, Sam, you are to go with Mr. Haley, to show him the road, and help him. Be careful of the horses, Sam; you know Jerry was a little lame last week; *don't ride them too fast.*

SAM: Let dis chile alone for dat! Lord knows! High! did n't say dat! Yes, missis, I'll look out fur de hosses.

SCENE V

[*The lawn before the house.*]

[*Enter* SAM *and* ANDY *with the horses.*]

ANDY: Here dey is! [*Fastens them to a post.*]

SAM: Here, now, Andy—see dis? [*Holding up a beech-nut.*]

ANDY: Laws! what?

SAM: Look here! [*Slips it under the saddle.*] Soh!

ANDY: Why Sam!

SAM: An't I a hoss!—ku! ku!—[*Strokes the horse.*]—Skeery are ye? I'll fix ye—Ku! [*Poking Andy in the side.*] Now, Andy, chile, I's gwine to be 'structin' ye in yer duties. Ye see, by'm-bye, when dat ar grand gentleman comes to be gettin' up, I would n't be't all surprised if this yer critter should gib a fling. Ye know, Andy, critters will do sich things. Ku! ku!

ANDY: High ah!

SAM: Yes, you see, Andy, missis wants to make time,—dat ar's clar to der most or'nary 'bserver. I jis make a little for her. Now, ye see, get all dese yer hosses loose, caperin' permiscus round dis yer lot and down to de wood dar, and I spec mas'r won't be off in a hurry.

ANDY: Ku! ku! ku!

SAM: Yer see, Andy, if any such thing *should* happen as that Mas'r Haley's horse *should* begin to act contrary, and cut up, you and I jist let's go of our 'n to help him; and *we'll help him*—O yes!

[*Enter* HALEY, *booted and spurred, with large riding-whip.*]

HALEY: Well, boys, look alive now; we must lose no time.

SAM: Not a bit of him, mas'r.

[HALEY *mounts, and is instantly thrown. The horses run away.* SAM *and* ANDY *chasing, waving their hats and shouting, followed by all the negro children.* HALEY *retires to the parlor.*]

SCENE VI

[*The Stable-yard.*]

[*Enter* SAM *and* ANDY, *leading the horses, covered with foam.*]

SAM: [*Panting.*] Did yer see him, Andy?—*did* yer see him? O, Lor, if it war n't as good as a meetin', now, to see him a dancin' and kickin' and swarin' at us. Did n't I hear him? Swar away, ole fellow, ses I; will yer have yer hoss now, or wait till you cotch him? ses I. Lor, Andy, I think I can see him now.

SAM and ANDY: Ha ha ha! he he he! hi hi hi! ho ho ho!

SAM: Yer oughter seen how mad he looked, when I brought the

hoss up. Lor, he'd a killed me, if he durs' to; and there I was a standin' as innercent and as humble.

ANDY: Lor, I seed you; an't you an old hoss, Sam?

SAM: Rather 'spects I am. Did yer see missis upstars at the winder? I seed her laughin'.

ANDY: I'm sure, I was racin' so, I did n't see nothing.

SAM: Well, yer see, I's 'quired what yer may call a habit o' *bobservation*, Andy. It's a very 'portant habit, Andy, and I 'commend yer to be cultivatin' it, now yer young. Hist up that hind foot, Andy. Yer see, Andy, it's *bobservation* makes all de difference in niggers. Did n't I see which way the wind blew dis yer mornin'? Did n't I see what Missis wanted, though she never let on? Dat ar's bobservation, Andy. I 'spects it's what you may call a faculty. Faculties is different in different peoples, but cultivation of 'em goes a great way.

ANDY: I guess if I had n't helped yer bobservation dis mornin', yer would n't have see yet way so smart.

SAM: Andy, you's a promisin' child, der an't no manner o' doubt. I thinks lots of yer, Andy; and I don't feel no ways ashamed to take idees from you. We oughtenter overlook nobody, Andy, 'cause the smartest on us gets tripped up sometimes. And so, Andy, let's go up to the house now. I'll be boun' missis 'll give us an uncommon good bite dis yer time.

SCENE VII

[*The Road.*]

[*Enter* HALEY, SAM *and* ANDY, *mounted.*]

HALEY: Your master, I s'pose, don't keep no dogs?

SAM: Heaps on 'em; that's Bruno—he's a roarer! and, besides that, 'bout every nigger of us keeps a pup of some natur' or uther.

HALEY: Ho! But your master don't keep no dogs—I pretty much know he don't—for trackin' out niggers?

SAM: Our dogs all smells round considerable sharp. I 'spect the's the kind, though they ha' n't never had no practice. The's *far* dogs, though, at most anything, if you'd get 'em started. Here, Bruno! [*Whistling.*]

HALEY: Bruno be————!

SAM: Lor, Mas'r Haley, do n't see no use, cursin on 'em, nuther!

HALEY: [*Smothering his anger.*] Take the straight road to the river. I know the way of all of 'em—they make tracks for the underground.

SAM: Sartin, dat's de idee. Mas'r Haley hits de things right in de middle. Now, der's two roads to de river—de dirt road and der pike—which mas'r mean to take?

ANDY: Dat am fact.

SAM: 'Cause, I'd rather be 'clined to 'magine that Lizy'd take de dirt road, bein' it's the least travelled.

ANDY: I tink so too.

HALEY: [*Contemplatively.*] If yet warn't both on yer such cussed liars, now!

SAM: Course, mas'r can do as he'd ruther; go de straight road, if mas'r think best—it's all one to us. Now, when I study 'pon it, I think de straight road de best, *decidedly.*

HALEY: She would naturally go a lonesome way.

SAM: Dar an't no sayin'; gals is pecular. They never does nothin' ye thinks they will; mose gen'lly the contrar. Gals is nat'lly made contrary; and so, if you thinks they've gone one road, it is sartin you'd better go t'other, and then you'll be sure to find 'em. Now, my private 'pinion is, Lizy took der dirt road; so I think we'd better take de straight one.

HALEY: On the whole, I shall take the dirt road. How far is it?

SAM: A little piece ahead [*winking to Andy*]; but I've studded on de matter, and I'm quite clar we ought not to go dat ar way. I nebber been over it no way. It's despit lonesome, and we might lose our way—whar we'd come to, de Lord only knows.

HALEY: Nevertheless, I shall go that way.

SAM: Now I think on't, I think I hearn 'em tell dat ar road was all fenced up and down by der creek, and that; an't it, Andy?

ANDY: Dunno 'zackly. So I hearn tell.

SAM: Its despit rough and bad for Jerry's lame foot, mas'r.

HALEY: Now, I jest give yer warning, I know yer; yer won't get me
to turn off this yer road, with all yer fussin'—so you shet up!

SAM: Mas'r will go his own way!

[*Exeunt.*]

SCENE VIII

[*The Parlor.*]

[*Enter* SAM *and* ANDY *below, horseback.* MRS. SHELBY *from
the window.*]

MRS. SHELBY: Is that you, Sam? Where are they?

SAM: Mas'r Haley's a-restin' at the tavern; he's drefful fatigued, missis.

MRS. SHELBY: And Eliza, Sam?

SAM: Wal, she's clar 'cross Jordan. As a body may say, in the land o'
Canaan.

MRS. SHELBY: Why Sam, what *do* you mean?

SAM: Wal, missis, de Lord he persarves his own. Lizy's done gone over
the river into 'Hio, as 'markably as if the Lord took her over
in a charrit of fire and two hosses.

[*Enter* MR. SHELBY.]

MR. SHELBY: Come up here, Sam, and tell your mistress what she
wants. Come, come, Emily, you are cold are all in a shiver;
you allow yourself to feel too much.

MRS. SHELBY: Feel too much! Am I not a woman—a mother? Are
we not both responsible to God for this poor girl? My God,
lay not this sin to our charge!

MR. SHELBY: What sin, Emily? You see yourself that we have only
done what we were obliged to.

MRS. SHELBY: There's an awful feeling of guilt about it, though. I
can't reason it away.

[*Enter* SAM *from below.*]

MR. SHELBY: Now, Sam, tell us distinctly how the matter was. Where is Eliza, if you know?

SAM: Wal, mas'r, I saw her, with my own eyes, a crossin' on the floatin' ice. She crossed most 'markably; it wasn't no less nor a miracle; and I saw a man help her up the 'Hio side, and then she was lost in the dusk.

MR. SHELBY: Sam, I think this rather apocryphal—this miracle. Crossing on floating ice is n't so easily done.

SAM: Easy! couldn't nobody a done it, without de Lord. Why, now, 't was jist dis yer way. Mas'r Haley, and me, and Andy, we comes up to de little tavern by the river, and I rides a leetle ahead—(I's so zealous to be a cotchin' Lizy, that I couldn't hold in, no way)—and when I comes by the tavern winder, sure enough there she was, right in plain sight, and dey diggin' on behind. Wal, I loses off my hat, and sings out nuff to raise the dead. Course Lizy she hars, and she dodges back, when Mas'r Haley he goes past the door; and then, I tell ye, she clared out de side door; she went down de river bank; Mas'r Haley he seed her, and yelled out, and him, and me, and Andy, we took arter. Down she came to the river, and thar was the current running ten feet wide by the shore, and over t' other side ice a sawin' and a jiggling up and down, kinder as 't were a great island. We come right behind her, and I thought my soul he'd got her sure enough—when she gin sich a screech as I never hearn, and thar she was, clar over t' other side of the current, on the ice, and then on she went, a screechin' and a jumpin'—the ice went crack! c'wallop! chunk! and she a boundin' like a buck! Lord, the spring that ar gal's got in her an't common, I'm o' 'pinion.

MRS. SHELBY: God be praised, she isn't dead! But where is the poor child now?

SAM: De Lord will pervide. As I've been a sayin', dis yer 's a providence and no mistake, as missis has allers been a instructin' on us. Thar's allers instruments ris up to do de Lord's will. Now, if 't hadn't been for me to-day, she'd a been took a dozen times. Warn't it I started off de hosses, dis yer mornin', and kept 'em chasin' till nigh dinner time? And didn't I car Mas'r Haley night five miles out of de road, dis evening? or else he'd a come up with Lizy as easy as a dog arter a coon. These yer's all providences.

MR. SHELBY: They are the kind of providences that you'll have to be pretty sparing of, Master Sam. I allow no such practices with gentlemen on my place.

SAM: Mas'r quite right—quite; it was ugly on me, there's no disputin' that ar; and of course mas'r and missis wouldn't encourage no such works. I'm sensible of dat ar; but a poor nigger like me 's 'mazin' tempted to act ugly sometimes, when fellers will cut up such shines as dat ar Mas'r Haley; he an't no gen'l'man no way; anybody's been raised as I've been can't help a seein' dat ar.

MRS. SHELBY: Well, Sam, as you appear to have a proper sense of your errors, you may go now and tell Aunt Chloe she may get you some of that cold ham that was left of dinner to-day. You and Andy must be hungry.

SAM: Missis is a heap too good for us.

SCENE IX

[SAM *and* ANDY *at Table.* AUNT CHLOE *and all the negroes surrounding in admiration.*]

SAM: [*Flourishing a greasy bone.*] Yer see, fellow-countrymen, yer see, now, what dis yer chile's up ter, for fendin' yer al,—yes, all on yer. For him as tries to get one o' our people is as good as tryin' to get all; yer see the principle's de same—dat ar's clar. And any one o' these yer drivers that comes smelling round arter any our people, why, he's got *me* in his way; *I'm* the feller he's got to set in with—I'm the feller for yer all to come to, bredren—I'll stand up for yer rights—I'll fend 'em to the last breath!

ANDY: Why, but Sam, yer telled me, only this mornin' that you'd help this yer mas'r fur to cotch Lizy; seems to me yer talk don't hang together, mun.

SAM: I tell you now, Andy, don't yer be a talkin' 'bout what yer don't know nothin' on; boys like you, Andy, means well, but they can't be 'spected to collusitate the great principles of action. Dat ar was *conscience,* Andy; when I thought of gwine arter Lizy, I railly spected mas'r was sot dat way. When I found Missis was sot the contrar, dat ar was conscience *more yet*—cause fellers allers gets more by stickin' to missis' *side*—so yer see I 's persistent either way, and sticks up to conscience, and holds on to principles. Yes, *principles,* what's principles good for, if we isn't persistent, I wanter know? Thar, Andy, you may have dat ar bone—tan't picked quite clean. Dis yer matter 'bout persistence, feller-niggers, dis yer 'sistency 's a thing what an't seed into very clar, by most anybody. Now, yer see, when a feller stands up for a thing one day, and right de contrar de next, folks ses (and nat'rally enough dey ses), why he an't persistent—hand me dat ar bit o' corn-cake, Andy. But let's look inter it. I hope the gen'lmen and der fair sex will scuse my usin' an or'nary sort o' 'parison. Here! I'm a trying to get top o' der hay. Wal, I puts up my larder dis yer side; 'tan't no go; den, 'cause I don't try dere no more, but puts my larder right de contrar side, an't I persistent? I'm persistent in wanting to get up which ary side my larder is; don't you see, all on yer?

AUNT CHLOE: It's the only thing ye ever was persistent in, Lord knows. [*Aside.*]

SAM: Yes, indeed! Yes, my feller-citizens and ladies of de other sex in general, I has principles, I has—I'm proud fur to 'oon 'em—they 's perquisite to dese yer times, and ter *all* times. I has principles, and I sticks to 'em like forty—jest anything that I thinks is principle, I goes in to 't; I wouldn't mind if dey burnt me 'live, I'd walk right up to de stake, I would, and say, Here I comes to shed my last blood fur my principles, fur my country, fur de gen'l interests of society.

AUNT CHLOE: Well, one o' yer principles will have to be to get to bed some time to-night, and not to be a keepin' everybody up till mornin'; now everyone of you young uns that don't want to be cracked had better be scarse, might sudden.

SAM: Niggers! all on yer, I give yer my blessin': go to bed now, and be good boys.

SCENE X

[*Uncle Tom's Cabin.* UNCLE TOM *with Testament open.* CHILDREN *asleep in trundle-bed.*]

UNCLE TOM: It's the last time!

AUNT CHLOE: [*Weeping.*] S'pose we must be resigned; but, O Lord! how ken I? If I know'd anything whar you 's goin', or how they 'd sarve you! Missis says she'll try and 'deem ye in a year or two; but, Lor! nobody never comes up that goes down that! They kills 'em! I've hearn 'em tell how dey works 'em up on dem ar plantations.

UNCLE TOM: There 'll be the same God there, Chloe, that there is here.

AUNT CHLOE: Well, s'pose dere will; but de Lord lets drefful things happen, sometimes. I don't seem to get no comfort day way.

UNCLE TOM: I'm in the Lord's hands; nothin' can go no furder than he lets it; and thar's *one* thing I can thank him for. It's *me* that's sold and going down, and not you nur the chil'en. Here you're safe; what comes will come only on me; and the Lord, he'll help me—I know he will. [*A sob.*] Let's think on our marcies!

AUNT CHLOE: Marcies! don't see no marcy in 't! 'tan't right! tan't right it should be so! Mas'r never ought ter left it so that ye *could* be took for his debts. Ye've arnt him all he gets for ye, twice over. He owed ye yer freedom, and ought ter gin 't to yer years ago. Mebbe he can't help himself now, but I feel it's wrong. Nothing can't beat that ar out o' me. Sich a faithful crittur as ye 've been, and allers sot his business 'fore yer own every way, and reckoned on him more than yer own wife and chil'en! Them as sells heart's love and heart's blood, to get out thar scrapes, de Lord 'll be up to 'em!

UNCLE TOM: Chloe! now, if ye love me, ye won't talk so, when mebbe jest the last time we'll ever have together! And I'll tell ye, Chloe, it goes agin me to hear one word agin mas'r. Wan't he put in my arms a baby? It's natur I should think a heap of him. And he couldn't be 'spected to think so much of poor Tom. Mas'rs is used to havin' all these yer things done for 'em, and nat'lly they don't think so much on 't. They can't be 'spected to, no way. Set him 'longside of other mas'rs—who 's had the treatment and the livin' I have had? And he never would have let this yer come on me, if he could have seed it aforehand. I know he would n't.

AUNT CHLOE: Wal, any way, thar's wrong about it *somewhar*. I can't jest make out whar 't is, but thar's wrong somewhar, I'm *clar* o' that.

UNCLE TOM: Yer ought ter look up to the Lord above—he's above all—thar don't a sparrow fall without him.

AUNT CHLOE: It don't seem to comfort me, but I 'spect it ort fur ter. But dar's no use talkin'; I'll jes get up de corn-cake, and get ye one good breakfast, 'cause nobody knows when you'll get another.

[AUNT CHLOE *gets the breakfast, and the children dress themselves.*]

MOSE: Lor, Pete, ha' n't we got a buster of a breakfast!

AUNT CHLOE: [*Boxing his ears.*] Thar now! crowing over the last breakfast yer poor daddy's gwine to have to home.

UNCLE TOM: O, Chloe!

AUNT CHLOE: Wal, I can't help it! I's so tossed about it, it makes me act ugly. Thar! now I's done, I hope—now do eat something. This yer's my nicest chicken. Thar, boys, ye shall have some, poor critturs! Yer mammy's been cross to yer. [*The boys eat.*] Now, I must put up yer clothes. Jest like as not, he'll take 'em all away. I know thar ways—mean as dirt, they is! Wal, now, yer flannels for rhumatis is in this corner; so be careful, 'cause there won't nobody make ye no more. Then here's yer old shirts, and these yer is new ones. I toed off these yer stockings last night, and put de ball in 'em to mend with. But Lor! who 'll ever mend for ye? [*Sobbing.*] To think on 't! no crittur to do for ye, sick or well! I don't railly think I ought ter be good now! [*Baby crows.*] Ay, crow away, poor crittur! ye'll have to come to it, too! ye'll live to see yer husband sold, or mebbe be sold yerself; and these yer boys, they's to be sold, I s'pose, too, jest like as not, when dey gets good for somethin'; an't no use in niggers havin' nothin'!

PETE: That's missis a-comin' in!

AUNT CHLOE: She can't do no good; what's she coming for?

[*Enter* MRS. SHELBY.]

MRS. SHELBY: Tom, I come to——[*Bursts into tears, and sits down in a chair, sobbing.*]

AUNT CHLOE: Lor, now, missis, don't—don't. [*All weep.*]

MRS. SHELBY to UNCLE TOM: My good fellow, I can't give you anything to do you any good. If I give you money, it will only be taken from you. But I tell you solemnly, and before God, that I will keep trace of you, and bring you back as soon as I can command the money; and, till then, trust in God!

MOSE and PETE: Mas'r Haley 's coming!

[*Enter* HALEY, *kicking the door open.*]

HALEY: Come, ye nigger, yer ready? Servant, ma'm. [*To* MRS. SHELBY.]

[UNCLE TOM *and* AUNT C. *go out, followed by the rest. A crowd of negroes around.*]

FIRST SLAVE: [*Weeping, to* AUNT C.] Why, Chloe, you bar it better 'n we do!

AUNT CHLOE: I'se done *my* tears! I doesn't feel to cry 'fore day ar old limb, nohow!

HALEY: Get in!

[TOM *gets in, and* HALEY *fastens on shackles. Groans.*]

MRS. SHELBY: Mr. Haley, I assure you that precaution is entirely unnecessary.

HALEY: Don't know, ma'am; I've lost one five hundred dollars from this ere place, and I can't afford to run no more risks.

AUNT CHLOE: What else could she 'spect on him?

UNCLE TOM: I'm sorry that Mas'r George happened to be away.

[*Enter* GEORGE, *springing into wagon and clasping* UNCLE TOM *round the neck.*]

GEORGE: I declare it's real mean! I don't care what they say, any of 'em! It's a nasty, mean shame! If I was a man they should n't do it—they should not, *so!*

UNCLE TOM: O, Mas'r George! this does me good! I couldn't bar to go off without seein' ye! It does me real good, ye can't tell!

[GEORGE *spies the fetters.*]

GEORGE: What a shame! I'll knock that old fellow down—I will!

UNCLE TOM: No, you won't, Mas'r George; and you must not talk so loud. It won't help me any to anger him.

GEORGE: Well, I won't then, for your sake; but only to think of it—is n't it a shame? They never sent for me, nor sent me any word, and if it hadn't been for Tom Lincoln, I should n't have heard it. I tell you, I blew 'em up well, all of 'em, at home!

UNCLE TOM: That ar was n't right, I'm feared, Mas'r George.

GEORGE: Can't help it! I say it's a shame! Look here, Uncle Tom, *I've brought you my dollar!*

UNCLE TOM: O! I couldn't think o' takin' on 'it, Mas'r George, no ways in the world!

GEORGE: But you *shall* take it! Look here; I told Aunt Chloe I'd do it, and she advised me just to make a hole in it, and put a string through, so you could hang it round your neck, and keep it out of sight; else this mean scamp would take it away. I tell ye, Tom, I want to blow him up! it would do me good!

UNCLE TOM: No, don't, Mas'r George, for it won't do *me* any good.

GEORGE: Well, I won't, for your sake; but there, now, button your coat tight over it, and keep it, and remember, every time you see it, that I'll come down after you, and bring you back. Aunt Chloe and I have been talking about it. I told her not to fear, I'll see to it, and I'll tease father's life out, if he don't do it.

UNCLE TOM: O, Mas'r George, ye mustn't talk so 'bout yer father!

GEORGE: Lor, Uncle Tom, I don't mean anything bad.

UNCLE TOM: And now, Mas'r George, ye must be a good boy; 'member how many hearts is sot on ye. Al'ays keep close to yer mother. Don't be gettin' into any of them foolish ways boys has, of getting too big to mind their mothers. Tell ye what, Mas'r George, the Lord gives good many things twice over, but he don't give ye a mother but once. Ye'll never see sich another woman, Mas'r George, if ye live to be a hundred years old. So, now, you hold on to her, and grow up, and be a comfort to her, thar's my own good boy—you will now, won't ye?

GEORGE: Yes, I will, Uncle Tom!

UNCLE TOM: And be careful of yer speaking, Mas'r George. Young boys, when they comes to your age, is willful, sometimes—it's natur' they should be. But real gentlemen, such as I hopes you'll be, never lets fall no words that isn't 'spectful to thar parents. Ye an't 'fended, Mas'r George!

GEORGE: No, indeed, Uncle Tom; you always did give me good advice.

UNCLE TOM: I's older, ye knows, and I sees all that's bound up in you. O, Mas'r George, you has everything—l'arnin', privileges, readin', writin',—and you'll grow up to be a great, learned, good man, and all the people on the place, and your mother and father'll be so proud on ye! Be a good mas'r, like yer father; and be a Christian, like yer mother. 'Member yer Creator in the days o' yer youth, Mas'r George.

GEORGE: I'll be *real* good, Uncle Tom, I tell you. I'm going to be a *first-rater*; and don't you be discouraged. I'll have you back to the place, yet. As I told Aunt Chloe this morning, I'll build your house all over, and you shall have a room for a parlor, with a carpet on it, when I'm a man. O, you'll have good times yet!

[UNCLE TOM *is handcuffed and driven off.*]

ACT II, SCENE I

[*New Orleans. A Parlor in St. Clare's house.* MARIE *reclining on a lounge.*]

[*Enter* EVA, *flying to embrace her mother.*]

EVA: Mamma!

MARIE: That'll do! [*Languidly kissing her.*] Take care, child—don't you make my headache!

[*Enter* ST. CLARE; *he embraces* MARIE *and presents* MISS OPHELIA.]

ST. CLARE: Marie! this is our cousin Ophelia.

MARIE: I am happy to see you, cousin.

[*Enter* SERVANTS, *crowding—foremost the old nurse.* EVA *flies to her and hugs and kisses her.*]

EVA: O, Mammy! dear Mammy!

MISS OPHELIA: Well, you Southern children can do something that I couldn't.

ST. CLARE: What, now, pray?

OPHELIA: Well, I want to be kind to everybody, and I wouldn't have anything hurt; but as to kissing—

ST. CLARE: Niggers, that you 're not up to; eh?

OPHELIA: Yes, that 's it. How can she?

ST. CLARE: [*Laughing.*] O, that's the way with you, is it? [*Goes among the servants.*] Here, you all, Mammy, Sukey, Jinny, Polly—glad to see mas'r? Look out for the babies! [*Stumbling over one.*] If I step on anybody let 'em mention it. [*Sees* TOM, *and beckons.*] Here, Tom. See here, Marie, I've brought you a coachman, at last, to order. I tell you he's a regular hearse for blackness and sobriety, and will drive you like a funeral, if you want. Open your eyes, now, and look at him. Now, don't say I never think about you when I'm gone.

MAR: I know he'll get drunk.

ST. CLARE: No, he's warranted a pious and sober article.

MAR: Well, I hope he may turn out well; it's more than I expect, though.

ST. CLARE: 'Dolph, show Tom down stairs; and mind yourself; remember what I told you.

[*Exit* TOM *and* DOLPH.]

MAR: He's a perfect behemoth!

ST. CLARE: Come, now, Marie, be gracious, and say something pretty to a fellow.

MAR: You've been gone a fortnight beyond the time.

ST. CLARE: Well, you know I wrote you the reason.

MAR: Such a short, cold letter!

ST. CLARE: Dear me! the mail was just going, and it had to be that or nothing.

MAR: That's just the way always; always something to make your journeys long, and letters short.

ST. CLARE: See here, now; here's a present I got for you in New York.

MAR: A daguerreotype! What made you sit in such an awkward position?

ST. CLARE: Well, the position may be a matter of opinion; but what do you think of the likeness?

MAR: If you don't think anything of my opinion in one case, I suppose you wouldn't in another.

ST. CLARE: Hang the woman! [*Aside.*] Come, now, Marie, what do you think of the likeness? Don't be nonsensical!

MAR: It's very inconsiderate of you, St. Clare, to insist on my talking and looking at things. You know I've been lying all day with the sick-headache; and there's been such a tumult made, ever since you came, I'm half dead.

OPHELIA: You're subject to the sick-headache, ma'am?

MAR: Yes, I'm a perfect martyr to it.

OPHELIA: Juniper-berry tea is good for sick-headache; at least, Augustine, Deacon Abraham Perry's wife used to say so; and she was a great nurse.

ST. CLARE: I'll have the first juniper-berries that get ripe in our garden by the lake brought in for that especial purpose. And now [*Rings the bell. Enter* MAMMY], show this lady to her room. [*To* MARIE, *offering her his arm.*] Come, now—come—I've got something for you in here—come.

[*Exeunt* ST. CLARE *and* MARIE.]

SCENE II

[*A Parlor. A Breakfast Table.* MARIE, ST. CLARE, EVA, OPHELIA.]

ST. CLARE: And now, Marie, your golden days are dawning. Here is our practical, business-like New England cousin, who will take the whole budget of cares off your shoulders, and give you time to refresh yourself, and grow young and handsome. The ceremony of delivering the keys had better come off forthwith.

MARIE: I'm sure she's welcome. I think she'll find one thing, if she does, and that is, that it's we mistresses that are the slaves, down here.

ST. CLARE: O, certainly, she will discover that, and a world of wholesome truths beside, no doubt.

MAR: Talk about our keeping slaves, as if we did it for our *convenience*! I'm sure, if we consulted *that*, we might let them all go at once.

EVA: What do you keep them for, mamma?

MAR: I don't know, I'm sure, except for a plague; they are the plague of my life. I believe that more of my ill-health is caused by them than by any one thing; and ours, I know, are the very worst that ever anybody was plagued with.

ST. CLARE: O, come, Marie, you've got the blues this morning. You know 't isn't so. There's Mammy, the best creature living—what could you do without her?

MAR: Mammy is the best I ever knew; and yet Mammy, now, is selfish—dreadfully selfish; it's the fault of the whole race.

ST. CLARE: Selfishness *is* a dreadful fault.

MAR: Well, now, there's Mammy; I think it's selfish of her to sleep so sound at nights; she knows I need little attentions almost every hour, when my worst turns are on, and yet she's so hard to wake. I absolutely am worse, this very morning, for the efforts I had to make to wake her last night.

EVA: Hasn't she sat up with you a good many nights lately, mamma?

MAR: How should you know that? She's been complaining, I suppose.

EVA: She didn't complain; she only told me what bad night you'd had—so many in succession!

ST. CLARE: Why don't you let Jane or Rosa take her place a night or two and let her rest?

MAR: How can you propose it? St. Clare, you really are inconsiderate! So nervous as I am, the least breath disturbs me; and a strange hand about me would drive me absolutely frantic. If Mammy felt the interest in me she ought to, she 'd wake easier—of course she would. I've heard of people who had such devoted servants, but it never was *my* luck. Now, Mammy has a *sort* of goodness; she's smooth and respectful, but she's selfish at heart. Now, she never will be done fidgeting and worrying about that husband of hers. You see, when I was married and came to live here, of course I had to bring her with me, and her husband my father couldn't spare. He was a blacksmith, and, of course, very necessary; and I thought, and said at the time, that Mammy and he had better give each other up, as it wasn't likely to be convenient for them ever to live together again. I wish now I'd insisted on it, and married Mammy to somebody else; but I was foolish and indulgent, and didn't want to insist. I told Mammy at the time that she mustn't ever expect to see him more than once or twice in her life again, for the air of father's place doesn't agree with my health, and I can't go there; and I advised her to take up with somebody else; but no—she wouldn't. Mammy has a kind of obstinacy about her, in spots, that everybody don't see as I do.

OPHELIA: Has she children?

MAR: Yes; she has two.

OPHELIA: I suppose she feels the separation from them?

MAR: Well, of course, I couldn't bring them. They were little, dirty things—I couldn't have them about; and, besides, they took up too much of her time; but I believe that Mammy has always kept up a sort of sulkiness about this. She won't marry anybody else; and I do believe now, though she knows how necessary she is to me, and how feeble my health is, she would go back to her husband to-morrow, if she only could. I *do*, indeed; they are just so selfish, now, the best of them!

ST. CLARE: [*Dryly.*] It's distressing to reflect upon.

MAR: Now, Mammy has always been a pet with me. I wish some of your northern servants could look at her closets of dresses—silks and muslins, and one real linen cambric, she has hanging there. I've worked sometimes whole afternoons, trimming her caps, and getting her ready to go to a party. As to abuse, she don't know what it is. She never was whipped in her whole life. She has her strong coffee or her tea every day, with white sugar in it. It's abominable, to be sure; but St. Clare will have high life below stairs, and they, every one of them, live just as they please. The fact is, our servants are over-indulged. I suppose it is partly our fault that they are selfish, and act like spoiled children; but I've talked to St. Clare till I am tired.

ST. CLARE: And I, too.

[EVA *goes to her mother, and puts her arms round her neck.*]

MAR: Well, Eva, what now?

EVA: Mamma, couldn't I take care of you one night—just one? I know I shouldn't make you nervous, and I shouldn't sleep. I often lie awake nights, thinking—

MAR: O, nonsense, child—nonsense! You are such a strange child!

EVA: But may I, mamma? I think that Mammy isn't well. She told me her head ached all the time, lately.

MAR: O, that's just one of Mammy's fidgets! Mammy is just like all the rest of them—makes such a fuss about every little head-ache or finger-ache; it'll never do to encourage it—never! I'm principled about this matter;—[*To* MISS OPHELIA] you'll find the necessity of it. If you encourage servants in giving way to every little disagreeable feeling, and complaining of every little ailment, you'll have your hands full. I never complain myself; nobody knows what I endure. I feel it a duty to bear it quietly, and I do.

[MISS OPHELIA *looks amazed, and* ST. CLARE *breaks out laughing.*]

MAR: [*Putting her handkerchief to her eyes.*] St. Clare always laughs when I make the least allusion to my ill-health. I only hope the day won't come when he'll remember it.

ST. CLARE: Come, Eva, I'll take you down street with me.

[*Exit* ST. CLARE *and* EVA.]

MAR: Now, that's just like St. Clare! He never realizes, never can, and never will, what I suffer, and have, for years. If I was one of the complaining sort, or ever made any fuss about my ailments, there would be some reason for it. Men do get tired, naturally, of a complaining wife. But I've kept things to myself, and borne, and borne, till St. Clare has got in the way of thinking I can bear anything. But it's no use talking, cousin. Well, here are the keys of the linen closet, and I hope you'll never let Jane or Rosa get hold of 'em or touch 'em. And I hope you'll be very particular about the way they fold the pillow-cases; I believe I'm foolishly particular, but I really have had a nerv-ous headache for a week, from the way those girls fold pillow-cases, if they are not looked to. There's two or three kinds of sheeting—you'll observe them; I think it important to keep each kind by itself. And here are the keys of the store-room;

you'll find Dinah always will be running after them—I dare
say she has half the things out in the kitchen now. Dinah's a
first-rate cook, and so she rules with a rod of iron—she knows
her importance. She will insist on having everything she wants
in the kitchen, and calling every five minutes for *something*;
it tires me to death. But, then, what can one do? O!—there
are the keys of some trunks of clothing in the blue chamber;
they'll have to be hung out and aired, I suppose. Dear knows
what a state you'll find them in; my poor head has n't allowed
me to do anything these three months; and Rosa and Jane
have always insisted on making one excuse or another to go
to them. I shouldn't wonder if half the things had been worn
out. And as to marketing, and all that, you must ask St. Clare;
I'm sure I don't know how that's to be arranged. And now—O
dear me! how my head does ache!—but—well—I believe I've
told you everything; so that, when my next sick turn comes
on, you'll be able to go forward entirely without consulting
me; only about Eva—she requires watching.

OPHELIA: She seems to be a good child, very; I never saw a better
child.

MAR: Eva's peculiar. There are things about her so singular; she isn't
like me, not, a particle.

OPHELIA: [*Aside.*] I hope she is n't.

MAR: Eva always was disposed to be with servants; and I think that
well enough with some children. Now, I always played with
father's little negroes—it never did me any harm. But Eva,
somehow, always seems to put herself on an equality with
every creature that comes near her. It's a strange thing about
the child. I never have been able to break her of it. St. Clare,
I believe, encourages her in it. The fact is, St. Clare indulges
every creature under this roof but his own wife.

OPHELIA: [*Coughs.*] Hem! ahem!

MAR: Now, there's no way with servants, but to *put them down*, and
keep them down. It was always natural to me, from a child. Eva
is enough to spoil a whole house-full. What she will do when
she comes to keep house herself, I'm sure I don't know. I hold

to being *kind* to servants—I always am; but you must make 'em *know their place.* Eva never does; there's no getting into the child's head the first beginning of an idea what a servant's place is! You heard her offering to take care of me nights, to let Mammy sleep! That's just a specimen of the way the child would be doing all the time, if she was left to herself.

OPHELIA: Well, I suppose you think your servants are human creatures, and ought to have some rest when they are tired?

MAR: Certainly, of course I'm very particular in letting them have everything that comes convenient—anything that doesn't put one at all out of the way, you know. Mammy can make up her sleep some time or other; there's no difficulty about that. She's the sleepiest concern that ever I saw. Sewing, standing, or sitting, that creature will go to sleep, and sleep anywhere and everywhere. No danger but Mammy gets sleep enough. But this treating servants as if they were exotic flowers, or china vases, is really ridiculous. You see, Cousin Ophelia, I don't often speak of myself. It isn't my *habit*; 't isn't agreeable to me. In fact, I haven't strength to do it. But there are points where St. Clare and I differ. St. Clare never understood me—never appreciated me. I think it lies at the root of all my ill health. St. Clare means well, I am bound to believe; but men are constitutionally selfish and inconsiderate to woman. That, at least, is my impression.

OPHELIA: Where 's my knitting? O—here 't is. [*Knits energetically.*]

MAR: You see, I brought my own property and servants into the connection, when I married St. Clare, and I am legally entitled to manage them my own way. St. Clare had his fortune and his servants, and I'm well enough content he should manage them his way; but St. Clare will be interfering. He has wild, extravagant notions about things, particularly about the treatment of servants. He really does act as if he set his servants before me, and before himself, too; for he lets them make him all sorts of trouble, and never lifts a finger. Now, about some things, St. Clare is really frightful—he frightens me—good-natured as he looks, in general. Now, he has set down his foot that, come what will, there shall not be a blow struck in this house, except what he or I strike; and he does it in a way that I really dare not cross him. Well, you may see what that leads to; for St. Clare wouldn't raise his hand, if every one of them walked over him, and I—you see how cruel it would be to require me to make the exertion. Now, you know these servants are nothing but grown-up children.

OPHELIA: I don't know anything about it, and I thank the Lord that I don't!

MAR: Well, but you will have to know something, and know it to your cost, if you stay here. You don't know what a provoking, stupid, careless, unreasonable, childish, ungrateful set of wretches they are. You don't know, and you can't, the daily, hourly trials that beset a housekeeper from them, everywhere and every way. But it's no use to talk to St. Clare. He talks the strangest stuff. He says we have made them what they are, and ought to bear with them. He says their faults are all owing to us, and that it would be cruel to make the fault and punish it too. He says we should n't do any better, in their place; just as if one could reason from them to us, you know!

OPHELIA: Don't you believe that the Lord made them of one blood with us?

MAR: No, indeed, not I! A pretty story, truly! They are a degraded race.

OPHELIA: Don't you think they've got immortal souls?

MAR: [*Yawning.*] O, well, that, of course—nobody doubts that. But as to putting them on any sort of equality with us, you know, as if we could be compared, why, it's impossible! Now, St. Clare really has talked to me as if keeping Mammy from her husband was like keeping me from mine. There's no comparing in this way. Mammy couldn't have the feelings that I should. It's a different thing altogether—of course, it is; and yet St. Clare pretends not to see it. And just as if Mammy could love her little, dirty babies as I love Eva! Yet St. Clare once really and soberly tried to persuade me that it was my duty, with my weak health, and all I suffer, to let Mammy go back, and take somebody else in her place! That was a little too much even for *me* to bear. I don't often show my feelings, I make it a principle to endure everything in silence; it's a wife's hard lot, and I bear it. But I did break out, that time, so that he has never alluded to the subject since. But I know by his looks, and little things that he says, that he thinks so as much as ever; and it's so trying, so provoking!

OPHELIA: [*Rattling her needles.*] Hem! ahem!

MAR: So, you just see what you've got to manage. A household without any rule; where servants have it all their own way, do what they please, and have what they please, except so far as I, with my feeble health, have kept up government.

OPHELIA: And how's that?

MAR: Why, send them to the calaboose, or some of the other places, to be flogged. That's the only way. If I wasn't such a poor, feeble piece, I believe I should manage with twice the energy that St. Clare does.

OPHELIA: And how does St. Clare contrive to manage? You say he never strikes a blow.

MAR: Well, men have a more commanding way, you know; it is easier for them. Besides, if you ever looked full in his eye, it's peculiar—that eye—and if he speaks decidedly, there 's a kind of flash. I'm afraid of it, myself; and the servants know they must mind. I couldn't do as much by a regular storm and scolding as St. Clare can by one turn of his eye, if once he is in earnest. O, there's no trouble about St. Clare! that's the reason he's no more feeling for me. But you'll find, when you come to manage, that there's no getting along without severity—they are so bad, so deceitful, so lazy!

[*Enter* ST. CLARE.]

ST. CLARE: The old tune! What an awful account these wicked creatures will have to settle, at last, especially for being lazy! You see, cousin, it's wholly inexcusable in them, in the light of the example that Marie and I set them, this laziness.

MAR: Come, now, St. Clare, you are too bad.

ST. CLARE: Am I now? Why, I thought I was talking good, quite remarkably for me. I try to enforce your remarks, Marie, always.

MAR: You know you mean no such thing, St. Clare.

ST. CLARE: O, I must have been mistaken, then! Thank you, my dear, for setting me right.

MAR: You do really try to be provoking.

ST. CLARE: O, come, Marie, the day is growing warm, and I have just had a long quarrel with 'Dolph, which has fatigued me excessively; so, pray be agreeable, now, and let a fellow repose in the light of your smile.

MAR: What's the matter about 'Dolph? That fellow's impudence has been growing to a point that is perfectly intolerable to me. I only wish I had the undisputed management of him a while. I'd bring him down!

ST. CLARE: What you say, my dear, is marked with your usual acuteness and good sense. As to 'Dolph, the case is this: that he has so long been engaged in imitating my graces and perfections, that he has at last really mistaken himself for his master, and I have been obliged to give him a little insight into his mistake.

MAR: How?

ST. CLARE: Why, I was obliged to let him understand explicitly that I preferred to keep *some* of my clothes for my own personal wearing; also, I put his magnificence upon an allowance of cologne-water, and actually was so cruel as to restrict him to one dozen of my cambric handkerchiefs. 'Dolph was particularly huffy about it, and I had to talk to him like a father to bring him round.

MAR: O! St. Clare, when will you learn how to treat your servants? It's abominable, the way you indulge them!

ST. CLARE: Why, after all, what's the harm of the poor dog's wanting to be like his master? and if I haven't brought him up any better than to find his chief good in cologne and cambric handkerchiefs, why shouldn't I give them to him?

OPHELIA: And why haven't you brought him up better?

ST. CLARE: Too much trouble; laziness, cousin, laziness—which ruins more souls than you can shake a stick at. If it weren't for laziness, I should have been a perfect angel, myself. I'm inclined to think that laziness is what your old Dr. Botherem, up in Vermont, used to call "the essence of moral evil." It's an awful consideration, certainly.

OPHELIA: I think you slaveholders have an awful responsbility upon you. I wouldn't have it for a thousand worlds. You ought to educate your slaves, and treat them like reasonable creatures, like immortal creatures, that you've got to stand before the bar of God with. That's my mind.

ST. CLARE: O! come, come, what do you know about us? [*Goes to the piano, and plays and sings.*] Well, now, cousin, you've given us a good talk, and done your duty; on the whole, I think the better of you for it. I make no manner of doubt that you threw a very diamond of truth at me, though you see it hit me so directly in the face, that it wasn't exactly appreciated at first.

MAR: For my part, I don't see any use in such sort of talk. I'm sure, if anybody does more for servants than we do, I'd like to know who; and it don't do 'em a bit good—not a particle; they get worse and worse. As to talking to them, or anything like that, I'm sure I have talked till I was tired and hoarse, telling them their duty, and all that; and I'm sure they can go to church when they like, though they don't understand a word of the sermon, more than so many pigs; so it isn't of any great use for them to go, as I see; but they do go, and so they have every chance; but, as I said before, they are a degraded race, and always will be, and there isn't any help for them; you can't make anything of them, if you try. You see, Cousin Ophelia, I've tried, and you haven't; I was born and bred among them, and I know. [ST. CLARE *whistles a tune.*] St. Clare, I wish you wouldn't whistle; it makes my head worse.

ST. CLARE: I won't. Is there anything else you wouldn't wish me to do?

MAR: I wish you *would* have some kind of sympathy for my trials; you never have any feeling for me.

ST. CLARE: My dear accusing angel!

MAR: It's provoking to be talked to in that way.

ST. CLARE: Then how will you be talked to? I 'll talk to order—any way you'll mention, only to give satisfaction.

[*A laugh heard below in the court.*]

OPHELIA: What is it? [*Rising and coming to the window.*] As I live! if there an't Eva, sitting in Uncle Tom's lap! Eugh! there, she's hanging a wreath of roses round his neck!

EVA: [*Below, laughing.*] O, Tom, you look so funny!

OPHELIA: How can you let her?

ST. CLARE: Why not?

OPHELIA: Why, I don't know, it seems so dreadful!

ST. CLARE: You would think no harm in a child's caressing a large dog, even if he was black; but a creature that can think, and reason, and feel, and is immortal, you shudder at; confess it, cousin. I know the feeling among some of you northerners well enough. Not that there is a particle of virtue in our not having it; but custom with us does what Christianity ought to do—obliterates the feeling of personal prejudice. I have often noticed, in my travels north, how much stronger this was with you than with us. You loathe them as you would a snake or a toad, yet you are indignant at their wrongs. You would not have them abused; but you don't want to have anything to do with them yourselves. You would send them to Africa, out of your sight and smell, and then send a missionary or two to do up all the self-denial of elevating them compendiously. Isn't that it?

OPHELIA: Well, cousin, there may be some truth in this.

ST. CLARE: What would the poor and lowly do, without children? Your little child is your only true democrat. Tom, now, is a hero to Eva; his stories are wonders in her eyes, his songs and Methodist hymns are better than an opera, and the traps and little bits of trash in his pocket a mine of jewels, and he the most wonderful Tom that ever wore a black skin. This is one of the roses of Eden that the Lord has dropped down expressly for the poor and lowly, who get few enough of any other kind.

OPHELIA: It's strange, cousin; one might almost think you were a *professor,* to hear you talk.

ST. CLARE: A professor?

OPHELIA: Yes; a professor of religion.

ST. CLARE: Not at all; not a professor, as your town folks have it; and, what it worse, I'm afraid, not a *practiser* either.

OPHELIA: What makes you talk so, then?

ST. CLARE: Nothing is easier than talking. I believe Shakspeare makes somebody say, "I could sooner teach twenty what were good to be done, than be one of the twenty to follow my own teaching." Nothing like division of labor. My forte lies in talking, and yours, cousin, lies in doing.

SCENE III

[*Sabbath morning. The hall.*]

[*Enter* MARIE *and* MISS OPHELIA, *dressed for church.*]

MARIE: Where 's Eva?

OPHELIA: The child stopped on the stairs, to say something to Mammy.

[*Enter* EVA.]

MAR: Eva, what were you stopping for?

EVA: I was just stopping to give Mammy my vinaigrette, to take to church with her.

MAR: Eva! your gold vinaigrette to *Mammy*! When will you learn what's *proper*? Go right and take it back, this moment!

[*Enter* ST. CLARE.]

ST. CLARE: I say, Marie, let the child alone; she shall do as she pleases.

MAR: St. Clare, how will she ever get along in the world?

ST. CLARE: The Lord knows; but she'll get along in heaven better than you or I.

EVA: O papa! don't; it troubles mother.

OPHELIA: Well, cousin, are you ready to go to the meeting?

ST. CLARE: I'm not going, thank you.

MAR: I do wish St. Clare ever would go to church; but he hasn't a particle of religion about him. It really isn't respectable.

ST. CLARE: I know it. You ladies go to church to learn how to get along in the world, I suppose, and your piety sheds respectability on us. If I do go at all, I would go where Mammy goes; there's something to keep a fellow awake there, at least.

MAR: What! those shouting Methodists? Horrible!

ST. CLARE: Anything but the dead sea of your respectable churches, Marie. Positively, it's too much to ask of a man. Eva, do you like to go? Come, stay at home and play with me.

EVA: Thank you, papa, but I'd rather go to church.

ST. CLARE: Isn't it dreadful tiresome?

EVA: I think it is tiresome, some, and I am sleepy, too; but I try to keep awake.

ST. CLARE: What do you go for, then?

EVA: Why, you know, papa, cousin told me that God wants to have us; and he gives us everything, you know; and it isn't much to do it, if he wants us to. It isn't so very tiresome, after all.

ST. CLARE: You sweet little obliging soul! go along, that's a good girl; and pray for me.

EVA: Certainly, I always do.

[*Exeunt.*]

ST. CLARE: [*Solus.*] O Evangeline! rightly named; hath not God made thee an evangel to me?

SCENE IV

[*The Dinner Table.* ST. CLARE, MARIE, OPHELIA, EVA, SERVANTS.]

ST. CLARE: Well, ladies, and what was the bill of fare at church to-day?

MARIE: O, Dr. G—— preached a splendid sermon! It was just such a sermon as you ought to hear; it expressed all my views exactly.

ST. CLARE: How very improving! The subject must have been an extensive one.

MAR: Well, I mean all my views about society, and such things. The text was, "He hath made everything beautiful in its season;" and he showed how all the orders and distinctions in society came from God; and that it was so appropriate, you know, and beautiful, that some should be high and some low, and that some were born to rule and some to serve, and all that, you know; and he applied it so well to all this ridiculous fuss that is made about slavery, and he proved distinctly that the Bible was on our side, and supported all our institutions so convincingly, I only wish you'd heard him.

ST. CLARE: O, I didn't need it! I can learn what does me as much good as that from the *Picayune* any time, and smoke a cigar besides; which I can't do, you know, in a church.

OPHELIA: Why, don't you believe in these views?

ST. CLARE: Who—I? You know I'm such a graceless dog that these religious aspects of such subjects don't edify me much. If I was to say anything on this slavery matter, I would say out, fair and square, "We 're in for it; we've got 'em, and mean to keep 'em—it's for our convenience and our interest;" for that 's the long and short of it; that 's just the whole of what all this sanctified stuff amounts to, after all; and I think that will be intelligible to everybody everywhere.

MAR: I do think, Augustine, you are so irreverent! I think it's shocking to hear you talk.

ST. CLARE: Shocking! it's the truth. This religious talk on such matters, why don't they carry it a little further, and show the beauty, in its season, of a fellow's taking a glass too much, and sitting a little too late over his cards, and various providential arrangements of that sort, which are pretty frequent among us young men? We 'd like to hear that those are right and godly too.

OPHELIA: Well, do you think slavery right or wrong?

ST. CLARE: I'm not going to have any of your horrid New England directness, cousin. If I answer that question, I know you'll be at me with half a dozen others, each one harder than the last; and I'm not a-going to define my position. I am one of that sort that lives by throwing stones at other people's glass-houses; but I never mean to put up one for them to stone.

MAR: That's just the way he's always talking; you can't get any satisfaction out of him. I believe it's just because he don't like religion that he's always running out in this way he's been doing.

ST. CLARE: Religion! Religion! Is what you have been hearing at church, religion? Is that which can bend and turn, and descend and ascend, to fit every crooked phase of selfish, worldly society, religion? Is that religion which is less scrupulous, less generous, less just, less considerate for man, than even my own ungodly, worldly, blinded nature? No! When I look for a religion, I must look for something above me, and not something beneath.

OPHELIA: Then you don't believe that the Bible justifies slavery?

ST. CLARE: The Bible was my *mother's* book. By it she lived and died, and I would be very sorry to think it did. I'd as soon desire to have it proved that my mother could drink brandy, chew tobacco, and swear, by way of satisfying me that I did right in doing the same. It would n't make me at all more satisfied with these things in myself, and it would take from me the comfort of respecting her; and it really is a comfort, in this world, to have anything one can respect. In short, you see [*gayly*], all I want is that different things be kept in different boxes. The whole frame-work of society, both in Europe and America, is made up of various things which will not stand the scrutiny of any very ideal standard of morality. It's pretty generally understood that men don't aspire after the absolute right, but only to do about as well as the rest of the world. Now, when any one speaks up, like a man, and says slavery is necessary to us, we can't get along without it, we should be beggared if we give it up, and, of course, we mean to hold on to it—this is strong, clear, well-defined language; it has the respectability of truth to it; and, if we may judge by their practice, the majority of the world will bear us out in it. But when he begins to put on a long face, and snuffle, and quote Scripture, I incline to think he isn't much better than he should be.

MAR: You are very uncharitable.

ST. CLARE: Well, suppose that something should bring down the price of cotton once and forever, and make the whole slave property a drug in the market; don't you think we should soon have another version of the Scripture doctrine? What a flood of light would pour into the church, all at once, and how immediately it would be discovered that everything in the Bible and reason went the other way!

MAR: Well, at any rate, I'm thankful I'm born where slavery exists; and I believe it's right—indeed, I feel it must be; and, at any rate, I'm sure I couldn't get along without it.

[*Enter* EVA.]

ST. CLARE: [*To* EVA.] I say, what do you think, pussy?

EVA: What about, papa?

ST. CLARE: Why, which do you like the best; to live as they do at your uncle's, up in Vermont, or to have a house-full of servants, as we do?

EVA: O, of course, our way is the pleasantest!

ST. CLARE: Why so?

EVA: Why, it makes so many more round you to love, you know.

MAR: Now, that's just like Eva; just one of her odd speeches.

EVA: Is it an odd speech, papa?

ST. CLARE: Rather, as this world goes, pussy. But where has my little Eva been, all dinner-time?

EVA: O, I've been up in Tom's room, hearing him sing, and Aunt Dinah gave me my dinner.

ST. CLARE: Hearing Tom sing, eh?

EVA: O, yes! He sings such beautiful things about the New Jerusalem, and bright angels, and the land of Canaan.

ST. CLARE: I dare say; it's better than the opera, is n't it?

EVA: Yes; and he's going to teach them to me.

ST. CLARE: Singing-lessons, eh?—you *are* coming on.

EVA: Yes, he sings for me, and I read to him in my Bible; and he explains what it means, you know.

MAR: On my word, that is the latest joke of the season.

ST. CLARE: Tom isn't a bad hand, now, at explaining Scripture, I'll dare swear. Tom has a natural genius for religion. I wanted the horses out early, this morning, and I stole up to Tom's cubiculum there, over the stables, and there I heard him holding a meeting by himself; and, in fact, I haven't heard anything quite so savory as Tom's prayer this some time. He put in for me with a zeal that was quite apostolic.

MAR: Perhaps he guessed you were listening. I've heard of that trick before.

ST. CLARE: If he did, he wasn't very polite; for he gave the Lord his opinion of me pretty feely. Tom seemed to think there was decidedly room for improvement in me, and seemed very earnest that I should be converted.

OPHELIA: I hope you'll lay it to heart.

ST. CLARE: [*Gayly.*] I suppose you are much of the same opinion. Well, we shall see—shan't we, Eva?

SCENE V

[*The Kitchen.* DINAH (*smoking*). *Negro children playing about.*]

DINAH: 'Still there, ye young uns, 'sturbin' me, while I's takin' my smoke!

[*Enter* JANE *and* ROSA.]

ROSA: Well, such a time as there's been in the house to-day, I never saw! Such a rummagin' and frummagin' in bandboxes and closets!—everything dragged out! Hate these yer northen misses!

JANE: Laws! ye orter seen her to the sheet trunk! Wan't it as good as a play to see her turn 'em out!

BOB: [*From floor.*] Tell ye, ef she don't sail round the house, coat-tail standin' out ahind her! Bound if she don't clar every one on us off the verandys minnit we shows our faces!

DINAH: An't gwine to have her in *my* diggin's, sturbin' my idees! Never let Miss Marie interfere, and she sartin shan't, *her!* Allus telled Miss Marie the kitchen wan't no place for ladies; Miss Marie got sense—she know'd it; but these yer northen misses—Good Lor! who is she, anyhow?

ROSA: Why, she's Mas'r St. Clare's cousin.

DINAH: 'Lation, is she? Poor, too, an't she?—hearn tell they done their own work up thar. Anything I hate, it's these yer poor 'lations!

ROSA: Hush! here she comes!

[*Enter* MISS OPHELIA.]

OPHELIA: [*Advances and opens a drawer.*] What's this drawer for, Dinah?

DINAH: Handy for most anything, missis.

OPHELIA: [*Rummaging—draws out a table-cloth.*] What's this? A beautiful French damask table-cloth, all stained and bloody! Why, Dinah, you don't wrap up meat in your mistress' best damask table-cloths?

DINAH: O Lor, missis, no! the towels was all a missin'—so I jest did it. I laid out to wash that are—that's why I put it thar.

OPHELIA: [*Disgusted—still rummaging.*] Shiftless! What's here?—nutmeg-grater—Methodist hymn-book—knitting-work! Faugh!—filthy old pipe! Faugh! what a sight! Where do you keep your nutmegs, Dinah?

DINAH: Most anywhar, missis; there's some in that cracked tea-cup up there, and there's some over in that ar cuboard.

OPHELIA: Here are some in the grater.

DINAH: Laws, yes! I put 'em there this morning. I likes to keep my things handy. You, Bob! what are you stopping for? You'll cotch it! Be still thar!

[*Striking at him with a stick.*]

OPHELIA: What's this?

[*Holding up a saucer.*]

313

DINAH: Laws, it's my har *grease*; I put it thar to have it handy.

OPHELIA: Do you use your mistress' best saucers for that?

DINAH: Law! it was cause I was driv, and in sich a hurry; I was gwine to change it this very day.

OPHELIA: Here are two damask table-napkins.

DINAH: Them table-napkins I put thar to get 'em washed out, some day.

OPHELIA: Don't you have some place here on purpose for things to be washed?

DINAH: Well, Mas'r St. Clare got dat ar chest, he said, for dat; but I likes to mix up biscuit and hev my things on it some days, and then it an't handy a liftin' up the lid.

OPHELIA: Why don't you mix your biscuits on the pastry-table, there?

DINAH: Law, missis, it get sot so full of dishes, and one thing and another, der an't no room, noways—

OPHELIA: But you should *wash* your dishes, and clear them away.

DINAH: [*Enraged.*] Wash my dishes! What does ladies know 'bout work, I want to know? When 'd mas'r ever get his dinner if I was to spend all my time a washin' and a puttin' up dishes? Miss Marie never told me so, nohow.

OPHELIA: Well, here are these onions.

DINAH: Laws, yes! thar *is* whar I put 'em, now. I couldn't 'member. Them's particular onions I was a savin' for dis yer very stew. I'd forgot they was in dar ar old flannel. [MISS OPHELIA *lifts a paper of herbs.*] I wish missis wouldn't touch dem ar. I likes to keep my things whar I knows what to go to 'em.

OPHELIA: But you don't want these holes in the papers.

DINAH: Them's handy for siftin' on't out.

OPHELIA: But you see it spills all over the drawer.

DINAH: Laws, yes! if missis will go a tumblin' things all up so, it will. Missis has spilt lots dat ar way. If missis only will go up stars till my clarin'-up time comes, I'll have everything right; but I can't do nothin' when ladies is round, a henderin'. You, Sam, don't you gib the baby dat ar sugar-bowl! I'll crack ye over, if ye don't mind!

OPHELIA: I'm going through the kitchen, and going to put everything in order *once*, Dinah; and then I'll expect you to *keep* it so.

DINAH: Lor, now! Miss 'Phelia, dat ar an't no way for ladies to do. I never did see ladies doin' no sich; my old missis nor Miss Marie never did, and I don't see no kinder need on't.

[*Enter* ST. CLARE.]

OPHELIA: There is no such thing as getting anything like system in this family!

ST. CLARE: To be sure there isn't.

OPHELIA: Such shiftless management, such waste, such confusion, I never saw!

ST. CLARE: I dare say you didn't.

OPHELIA: You would not take it so coolly if you were a house-keeper.

ST. CLARE: My dear cousin, you may as well understand, once for all, that we masters are divided into two classes, oppressors and oppressed. We who are good-natured and hate severity make up our minds to a good deal of inconvenience. If we *will* *keep* a shambling, loose, untaught set in the community, for our convenience, why, we must take the consequence. Some rare cases I have seen, of persons, who, by a peculiar tact, can produce order and system without severity; but I'm not one of them, and so I made up my mind, long ago, to let things go just as they do. I will not have the poor devils thrashed and cut to pieces, and they know it; and, of course, they know the staff is in their own hands.

OPHELIA: But to have no time, no place, no order—all going on in this shiftless way!

ST. CLARE: My dear Vermont, you natives up by the North Pole set an extravagant value on time! What on earth is the use of time to a fellow who has twice as much of it as he knows what to do with? As to order and system, where there is nothing to be done but to lounge on the sofa and read, an hour sooner or later in breakfast or dinner is n't of much account. Now, there's Dinah gets you a capital dinner—soup, ragout, roast fowl, dessert, ice-creams and all—and she creates it all out of Chaos and old Night out here in this kitchen. I think it really sublime, the way she manages. But, Heaven bless us! if we were to come out here, and view all the smoking and squatting about, and hurryscurryation of the preparatory process, we should never eat more. My good cousin, absolve yourself from that! It's more than a Catholic penance, and does no more good. You'll only lose your own temper, and utterly confound Dinah. Let her go her own way.

OPHELIA: But, Augustine, you don't know how I found things.

ST. CLARE: Don't I? Don't I know that the rolling-pin is under her bed, and the nutmeg-grater in her pocket with her tobacco—that there are sixty-five different sugar-bowls, one in every hole in the house—that she washes dishes with a dinner-napkin one day, and with the fragment of an old petticoat the next? But the upshot is, she gets up glorious dinners, makes superb coffee; and you must judge her, as warriors and statesmen are judged, *by her success.*

OPHELIA: But the waste—the expense!

ST. CLARE: O, well! lock everything you can, and keep the key. Give out by driblets, and never inquire for odds and ends—it isn't best.

OPHELIA: That troubles me, Augustine. I can't help feeling as if these servants were not *strictly honest.* Are you sure they can be relied on?

ST. CLARE: [*Laughing.*] O, cousin, that's too good! *Honest!*—as if that's a thing to be expected! Honest!—why, of course they arn't. Why should they be? What upon earth is to make them so?

OPHELIA: Why don't you instruct?

ST. CLARE: Instruct! O, fiddlestick! What instructing do you think I should do? I look like it! As to Marie, she has spirit enough, to be sure, to kill off a whole plantation, if I'd let her manage; but she would n't get the cheatery out of them.

OPHELIA: Are there no honest ones?

ST. CLARE: Well, now and then one, whom nature makes so impracticably simple, truthful and faithful, that the worst possible influence can't destroy it. But, you see, from the mother's breast the colored child feels and sees that there are none but underhand ways open to it. It can get along no other way with its parents, its mistress, its young master and missie play-fellows. Cunning and deception become necessary, inevitable habits. It isn't fair to expect anything else of him. He ought not to be punished for it. As to honesty, the slave is kept in that dependent, semi-childish state, that there is no making him realize the rights of property, or feel that his master's goods are not his own, if he can get them. For my part, I don't see how they *can* be honest. Such a fellow as Tom here is, is a moral miracle!

OPHELIA: And what becomes of their souls?

ST. CLARE: That isn't my affair, as I know of. I am only dealing in facts of the present life. The fact is, that the whole race are pretty generally understood to be turned over to the devil, for our benefit, in this world, however it may turn out in another!

OPHELIA: This is perfectly horrible! You ought to be ashamed of yourselves!

ST. CLARE: I don't know as I am. We are in pretty good company, for all that, as people in the broad road generally are.

SCENE VI

[*New Orleans. A Parlor in St. Clare's House.*]

[*Enter* ST. CLARE *and* TOPSY.]

ST. CLARE: Come down here, cousin; I've something to show you.

[*Enter* MISS OPHELIA, *sewing in hand.*]

OPHELIA: What is it?

ST. CLARE: I've made a purchase for your department—see here.

OPHELIA: Augustine, what in the world did you bring that thing here for?

ST. CLARE: For you to educate, to be sure, and train in the way she should go. I thought she was rather a funny specimen in the

Jim Crow line. Here, Topsy, this is your new mistress. I'm going to give you up to her; see, how, that you behave yourself.

TOPSY: Yes, mas'r.

ST. CLARE: You're going to be good, Topsy, you understand.

TOPSY: O, yes, mas'r!

OPHELIA: Now, Augustine, what upon earth is this for? Your house is so full of these little plagues, now, that a body can't set their feet down without treading on 'em. I get up in the morning, and find one asleep behind the door, and see one black head poking out from under the table, one lying on the door-mat; and they are mopping, and mowing, and grinning between all the railings, and tumbling over the kitchen floor! What on earth did you want to bring this one for?

ST. CLARE: For you to educate—didn't I tell you? You're always preaching about educating. I thought I would make you a present of a fresh-caught specimen, and let you try your hand on her, and bring her up in the way she should go.

OPHELIA: *I* don't want her, I am sure; I have more to do with 'em now than I want to.

ST. CLARE: That's you Christians, all over! You'll get up a society, and get some poor missionary to spend all his days among just such heathen. But let me see one of you that would take one into your house with you, and take the labor of their conversion on yourselves! No; when it comes to that, they are dirty and disagreeable, and it's too much care, and so on.

OPHELIA: Augustine, you know I didn't think of it in that light. Well, it might be a real missionary work. But I really didn't see the need of buying this one—there are enough now, in your house, to take all my time and skill.

ST. CLARE: Well, then, Cousin, I ought to beg your pardon for my good-for-nothing speeches. You are so good, after all, that there's no sense in them. Why, the fact is, this concern belonged to a couple of drunken creatures that keep a low restaurant that I have to pass by every day, and I was tired of hearing her screaming, and them beating and swearing at her. She looked bright and funny, too, as if something might be made of her;

so I bought her, and I'll give her to you. Try, now, and give her a good orthodox New England bringing up, and see what it'll make of her. You know I haven't any gift that way; but I'd like you to try.

OPHELIA: Well, I'll do what I can. Come here, Topsy. How old are you?

TOPSY: Dunno, missis.

OPHELIA: Don't know how old you are? Didn't anybody ever tell you? Who was your mother?

TOPSY: Never had none!

OPHELIA: Never had any mother? What do you mean? Where was you born?

TOPSY: Never was born!

OPHELIA: You mustn't answer me in that way, child; I'm not playing with you. Tell me where you were born, and who your father and mother were.

TOPSY: Never was born; never had no father nor mother, nor nothin'! I was raised by a speculator, with lots of others. Old Aunt Sue used to take car of us.

[*Enter* JANE, DINAH, *and* ROSA.]

JANE: Laws, missis, there's heaps of 'em! Speculators buys 'em up cheap, when they's little, and gets 'em raised for market.

OPHELIA: How long have you lived with your master and mistress?

TOPSY: Dunno, missis.

OPHELIA: Is it a year, or more, or less?

TOPSY: Dunno, missis.

JANE: Laws, missis, those low negroes, they can't tell; they don't know anything about time; they don't know what a year is; they don't know their own ages.

OPHELIA: Have you ever heard anything about God, Topsy?

TOPSY: [*Grins.*]

OPHELIA: Do you know who made you?

TOPSY: Nobody, as I knows on. I 'spect I grow'd. Don't think nobody never made me.

OPHELIA: Do you know how to sew?

TOPSY: No, missis.

OPHELIA: What can you do? What did you do for your master and mistress?

TOPSY: Fetch water, and wash the dishes, and rub knives, and wait on folks.

OPHELIA: Were they good to you?

TOPSY: 'Spect they was.

DINAH: [*Lifting up both hands.*] Good Lor, what a limb! What on 'arth Mas'r St. Care want to bring on dese yer low nigger young 'uns here for? Wont have her round under my feet, I know.

OPHELIA: Well, go to your work, all of you. [*Exeunt* JANE, DINAH, *and* ROSA.] Come, Topsy, to my room.

[*Exeunt.*]

SCENE VII

[*A Bed-room.* MISS OPHELIA *and* TOPSY.]

OPHELIA: Now, Topsy, I'm going to show you just how my bed is to be made. I am very particular about my bed. You must learn exactly how to do it.

TOPSY: Yes, ma'am.

OPHELIA: Now, Topsy, look here; this is the hem of the sheet—this is the right side of the sheet, and this is the wrong; will you remember?

TOPSY: Yes, ma'am.

OPHELIA: Well, now, the under sheet you must bring over the bolster—so—and tuck it clear down under the mattress nice and smooth—so; do you see?

TOPSY: Yes, ma'am.

OPHELIA: But the upper sheet must be brought down in this way, and tucked under firm and smooth at the foot—so—the narrow hem at the foot.

TOPSY: Yes, ma'am. [*Adroitly snatching a pair of gloves and a ribbon, and hiding them in her sleeve.*]

OPHELIA: Now, Topsy, let's see *you* do this.

[*As* TOPSY *goes to make the bed, the ribbon hangs out of her sleeve.*]

OPHELIA: [*Seizing it.*] What's this? You naughty, wicked child—you've been stealing this!

TOPSY: Laws! why, that ar's Miss Feely's ribbon, an't it? How could it a got in my sleeve?

OPHELIA: Topsy, you naughty girl, don't you tell me a lie; you stole that ribbon!

TOPSY: Missis, I declar for 't, I didn't; never seed it till dis yer blessed minnit!

OPHELIA: Topsy, don't you know it's wicked to tell lies?

TOPSY: I never tells no lies, Miss Feely; it's jist the truth I've been a tellin' now, and an't nothin' else.

OPHELIA: Topsy, I shall have to whip you, if you tell lies so.

TOPSY: Laws, missis, if you's to whip all day, couldn't say no other way. I never seed dat ar—it must a got caught in my sleeve. Miss Feely must have left it on the bed, and it got caught in the clothes, and so got in my sleeve.

OPHELIA: [*Shaking her.*] Don't you tell me that again! [*The gloves fall out.*] There, you! will you tell me now you didn't steal the ribbon?

TOPSY: Laws, missis, I did steal dem ar gloves—but I never did take dat ar ribbon, in the world, never!

OPHELIA: Now, Topsy! If you'll confess all about it, I won't whip you this time.

TOPSY: Well, den, missis, I did take de ribbon and de gloves both, I did so.

OPHELIA: Well, now, tell me. I know you must have taken other things since you have been in the house, for I let you run about all day yesterday. Now, tell me if you took anything, and I shan't whip you.

TOPSY: Laws, missis! I took Miss Eva's red thing she wars on her neck.

OPHELIA: You did, you naughty child! Well, what else?

TOPSY: I took Rosa's yer-rings—dem red ones.

OPHELIA: Go bring them to me this minute, both of 'em.

TOPSY: Laws, missis, I can't—they's burnt up!

OPHELIA: Burnt up? what a story! Go get 'em, or I'll whip you!

TOPSY: [*Crying and groaning.*] I can't missis, I can't no how! Dey's burnt up—dey is.

OPHELIA: What did you burn 'em up for?

TOPSY: 'Cause I 's wicked—I is. I's mighty wicked, any how. I can't help it, no how.

[*Enter* EVA, *with the coral necklace on her neck.*]

OPHELIA: Why, Eva, where did you get your necklace?

EVA: Get it? Why, I've had it on all day.

OPHELIA: Did you have it on yesterday?

EVA: Yes; and what is funny, aunty, I had it on all night. I forgot to take it off when I went to bed.

[*Enter* ROSA, *with a basket of newly-ironed linen poised on her head, and the coral ear-drops shaking in her ears.*]

OPHELIA: [*In despair.*] I'm sure I can't tell anything to do with such a child! What in the world did you tell me you took those things for, Topsy?

TOPSY: Why, missis said I must 'fess; and I couldn't think of nothin' else to 'fess.

OPHELIA: But, of course, I didn't want you to confess things you didn't do; that's telling a lie, just as much as the other.

TOPSY: Laws, now, is it? Why, how curus!

ROSA: La, there an't any such thing as the truth in that limb! If I was Mas'r St. Clare, I'd whip her till the blood run, I would! I'd let her catch it!

EVA: No, no, Rosa! you mustn't talk so, Rosa. I can't bear to hear it.

ROSA: La, sakes! Miss Eva, you's so good, you don't know nothing how to get along with niggers. There's no way but cut 'em well up, I tell ye.

EVA: Rosa, hush! Don't say another word of that sort.

ROSA: Miss Eva has got the St. Clare blood in her, that's plain. She can speak for all the world just like her papa.

[*Exit* ROSA.]

OPHELIA: Well, I don't know anything what I shall do with you, Topsy.

TOPSY: Laws, missis, you must whip me! Ole missis always whipped me. I s'pects's good for me.

OPHELIA: Why Topsy, I don't want to whip you. You can do well if you've a mind to. What's the reason you won't?

TOPSY: Why, missis, I's so used to whippin'.

OPHELIA: Well, I shall shut you in this closet, to think of your ways a while.

EVA: [*Goes up to* TOPSY.] Poor Topsy, why need you steal? You're going to be taken good care of now. I'm sure I'd rather give you anything of mine than have you steal it.

TOPSY: Ha! ha! dat ar's curus! Well, I's gwine in de closet—mebbe I'll come out better. [*Goes in.*]

[*Exeunt* EVA *and* MISS OPHELIA.]

SCENE VIII

[*A Veranda.* ST. CLARE *lounging on a sofa.* MISS OPHELIA *sewing.*]

OPHELIA: Topsy!

TOPSY: Hear me!

OPHELIA: Let me see if you can say your catechism; and if you can you may go and play. Did all mankind fall in Adam's first transgression?

TOPSY: [*Repeating very rapidly.*] Covenant being made with Adam not only for hisself but for his posterity, all mankind 'scending from him by ordinar transgression, sinned wid him, and fell in him, in that fust generation.

OPHELIA: Stop! stop!! stop!!! Topsy. Why, how are you saying it?

ST. CLARE: Why, what's the odds? I don't see but that it makes as good sense one way as the other.

OPHELIA: St. Clare! now—how can I teach this child if you will take so? And now you're laughing!

ST. CLARE: I'm done. Proceed. Topsy! you careless hussy, mind yourself! Be sure you get everything in right end first. Now for it!

OPHELIA: Into what state did the fall bring all mankind?

TOPSY: Fall brought all mankind into a state of sin and misery. Please ma'am——?

OPHELIA: What, Topsy?

TOPSY: Dar 'ar state Kintuck? De Lor' knows dey has sin and misery 'nough dar!

OPHELIA: Hush, hush, Topsy!

ST. CLARE: No personal reflections, Topsy!

TOPSY: Please, missis, can't I go play? Dar ar 'bout the generations was so curus! Never kin get it right nohow!

ST. CLARE: O, yes, coz, let her go. I want you to go up stairs and look at a new carpet I've been buying for Eva's room. There, Tops, there's some candy for you. Next time get the words straight.

[*Exeunt* ST. CLARE *and* OPHELIA.]

[*Enter* JAKE, AMANDA, *and other negro children.*]

TOPSY: Dar now, ye niggers! I'se gittin' eddecated, I is; 'cause I b'longs to Miss Feely. I larns catechize every day, and you por trash don't. Laws, you's runnin' wild all the while! What doos you know? Doos you know you's all sinners? Wal, you is, everybody is. White folks is sinners, too—Miss Feely says so; but I 'spects niggers is the biggest ones; but, lor! ye an't any on ye up to me. I's so awful wicked there can't nobody do nothin' with me. I used to keep old missis a swarin' at me half de time. I 'spects I's the wickedest crittur in the world.

JAKE: Ah! Den ye'll go to torment one dese days, anyhow. Ye won't be quite so crank then.

TOPSY: No I shan't—I's bound to go to heaven, I is.

AMANDA: No ye won't neither!

TOPSY: Shall too! Miss Feely's bound to go thar, and they'll have to let me come too; cors she's so curus they won't nobody else know how to wait on her dar! Come, now, be still touching that thing of mine, or I'll crack ye over!

[*Exit* JAKE, *running with* TOPSY'*s thimble.* TOPSY *follows, with all the rest, in pursuit.*]

SCENE IX

[*An Arbor, looking out on Lake Ponchartrain.* UNCLE TOM *and* EVA.]

EVA: O, Uncle Tom, I'm going to read you some such beautiful places!—now, *this*: "Behold, a throne was set in heaven, and one sat on the throne; and he that sat was to look upon like a jasper and a sardine stone; and there was a rainbow round about the throne, in sight like unto an emerald. And round about the throne were four-and-twenty seats; and upon the seats I saw four-and-twenty elders sitting clothed in white raiment, and they had on their heads crowns of gold." Only think of it! [*She turns to another place.*] And, now, *this*: "And I saw, as it were, a sea of glass, mingled with fire, and them that had gotten the victory over the beast stand on the sea of glass, having the harps of God, and they sing the song of Moses, the servant of God, and the song of the Lamb; saying, Great and marvellous are thy works, Lord God Almighty, just and true are thy ways, thou King of saints." [*Pointing to the lake.*] There 'tis, Uncle Tom! see! there 'tis—a sea of glass mingled with fire!

UNCLE TOM: What, Miss Eva?

EVA: Don't you see—there, that water? There's a "sea of glass mingled with fire."

UNCLE TOM: True enough, Miss Eva. [*Sings.*]

"*O, had I the wings of the morning,*
I'd fly away to Canaan's shore!
Bright angels should convey me home,
To the new Jerusalem."

EVA: Where do you suppose new Jerusalem is, Uncle Tom?

UNCLE TOM: O, up in the clouds, Miss Eva!

EVA: Then, I think I see it! Look in those clouds! they look like great gates of pearl; and you can see way, way beyond them—far, far off—it's all gold. Tom, sing about "spirits bright!"

UNCLE TOM: [*Sings.*]
"*O, what hath Jesus bought for me!*
Before my wondering eyes
Rivers of pure delight I see,
And streams of Paradise.

"*I see a band of spirits bright,*
That taste the glories there;
They all are robed in spotless white,
And conquering palms they bear."

EVA: Uncle Tom, I've seen *them*! They come to me sometimes in my sleep, those spirits. [*Sings.*]
"*They are all robed in spotless white,*
And conquering palms they bear."
Uncle Tom, I'm going there.

UNCLE TOM: Where, Miss Eva?

EVA: [*Rising and pointing up.*] I'm going *there*, to the spirits bright, Tom; *I'm going before long.*

OPHELIA: [*Calling from a distance.*] Eva! Eva! child—come in; the dew is falling! you must not be out there!

SCENE X

[*A Veranda.* ST. CLARE *and* MARIE *reclining on lounges.*]

MARIE: I say, Augustine, I must send to the city after my old doctor Posey; I'm sure I've got the complaint of the heart.

ST. CLARE: Well; why need you send for him? The doctor that attends Eva seems skilful.

MAR: I would not trust him in a critical case; and I think I may say mine is becoming so! I've been thinking of it these two or three nights past; I have such distressing pains, and such strange feelings.

ST. CLARE: O, Marie, you are blue! I don't believe it's heart complaint.

MAR: I dare say *you* don't; I was prepared to expect *that*. You can be alarmed enough, if Eva coughs, or has the least thing the matter with her; but you never think of me.

ST. CLARE: If it's particularly agreeable to you to have heart disease, why, I'll try and maintain you have it. I didn't know it was.

MAR: Well, I only hope you won't be sorry for this when it's too late! But, believe it or not, my distress about Eva, and the exertions I have made with that dear child, have developed what I have long suspected.

ST. CLARE: O, here comes cousin from her excursion. [*Enter* MISS OPHELIA *and* EVA.] Well, coz, what success in the religious line? Did you find a preacher?

OPHELIA: Wait till I put my bonnet and shawl away. [*Exit.*]

ST. CLARE: Here, Eva, you come to me.

EVA: [*Climbs into her father's lap.*]

OPHELIA: [*Within.*] What's this! You wicked little hussy, you! Come out here! Come out this very minute!

ST. CLARE: What new witchcraft has Tops been brewing?

[*Enter* MISS OPHELIA, *dragging* TOPSY.]

OPHELIA: Come out here, now. I *will* tell your master!

ST. CLARE: What's the row, pray?

OPHELIA: The fact is, I cannot be plagued with this child any longer! It's past all bearing; flesh and blood cannot endure it! Here I locked her up, and gave her a hymn to study; and what does she do, but spy out where I put my key, and has gone to my bureau, and got a bonnet-trimming, and cut it all to pieces to make dolls' jackets! I never saw anything like it, in my life!

327

MAR: I told you, cousin, that you'd find out that these creatures can't be brought up without severity. If I had *my* way, now, I'd send that child out, and have her thoroughly whipped; I'd have her whipped till she couldn't stand!

ST. CLARE: I don't doubt it. Tell me of the lovely rule of woman! I never saw above a dozen women that wouldn't half kill a horse, or a servant, either, if they had their own way with them, let alone a man!

MAR: There is no use in this shilly-shally way of yours, St. Clare! Cousin is a woman of sense, and she sees it now, as plainly as I do.

OPHELIA: I wouldn't have the child treated so, for the world; but I am sure, Augustine, I don't know what to do. I've taught and taught; I've talked till I'm tired; I've whipped her; I've punished her in every way I can think of, and she's just what she was at first.

ST. CLARE: Come here, Tops, you monkey! [TOPSY *comes.*] What makes you behave so?

TOPSY: 'Spects it's my wicked heart; Miss Feely says so!

ST. CLARE: Don't you see how much Miss Ophelia has done for you? She says she has done everything she can think of.

TOPSY: Lor, yes, mas'r! ole missis used to say so, too. She whipped me a heap harder, and used to pull my har, and knock my head agin the door; but it didn't do me no good; I 'spects, if they 's to pull every spear o' har out o' my head, it wouldn't do no good, neither—I's so wicked! Laws! I's nothin but a nigger, no ways!

OPHELIA: Well, I shall have to give her up; I can't have that trouble any longer.

ST. CLARE: Well, I'd just like to ask one question.

OPHELIA: What is it?

ST. CLARE: Why, if your Gospel is not strong enough to save one heathen child, that you can have at home here all to yourself, what's the use of sending one or two poor missionaries off with it among thousands of just such? I suppose this child is about a fair sample of what thousands of your heathen are.

EVA: [*Beckons to* TOPSY, *who follows her to the end of the veranda.*]

ST. CLARE: What's Eva about now? I mean to see.

EVA: What does make you so bad, Topsy? Why don't you try and be good? Don't you love *anybody*, Topsy?

TOPSY: Dunno nothing 'bout love; I loves candy and sich, that's all.

EVA: But you love your father and mother?

TOPSY: Never had none, ye know. I telled ye that, Miss Eva.

EVA: O, I know; but hadn't you any brother or sister, or aunt, or—

TOPSY: No, none on 'em; never had nothing nor nobody.

EVA: But, Topsy, if you'd only try to be good, you might—

TOPSY: Couldn't never be nothin' but a nigger if I was ever so good. If I could be skinned, and come white, I'd try then.

EVA: But people can love you, if you are black, Topsy. Miss Ophelia would love you if you were good.

TOPSY: [*Laughs.*]

EVA: Don't you think so?

TOPSY: No; she can't bar me, 'cause I'm a nigger! she'd's soon have a toad touch her. There can't nobody love niggers, and niggers can't do nothin'. *I* don't care! [*Whistles.*]

EVA: O, Topsy, poor child, *I* love you! I love you, because you haven't had any father, or mother, or friends; because you've been a poor, abused child! I love you, and I want you to be good. I am very unwell, Topsy, and I think I shan't live a great while, and it really grieves me, to have you be so naughty. I wish you would try to be good, for my sake; it's only a little while I shall be with you.

TOPSY: [*Weeps.*]

EVA: Poor Topsy! don't you know that Jesus loves all alike? He is just as willing to love you, as me. He loves you just as I do, only more, because he is better. He will help you to be good; and you can go to heaven at last, and be an angel forever, just as much as if you were white. Only think of it, Topsy, *you* can be one of those spirits bright Uncle Tom sings about!

TOPSY: O, dear Miss Eva! dear Miss Eva! I will try! I will try! I never did care nothin' about it before.

[*Exeunt.*]

SCENE XI

[EVA *lying in bed.* MISS OPHELIA *looks out of the door, and sees* UNCLE TOM *lying.*]

OPHELIA: Uncle Tom, what alive! have you taken to sleeping everywhere, and anywhere, like a dog? I thought you were one of the orderly sort, and liked to sleep in your bed, in a decent way.

UNCLE TOM: I do, Miss Feely; but now——[*Pauses.*]

OPHELIA: Well, what now?

UNCLE TOM: We mustn't speak loud; Mas'r St. Clare won't hear on't; but, Miss Feely, you know there must be somebody watchin' for the Bridegroom.

OPHELIA: What do you mean, Tom?

UNCLE TOM: You know it says in Scripture, "At midnight there was a great cry made, Behold, the Bridegroom cometh!" That's what I'm 'spectin' now, every night, Miss Feely; and I couldn't sleep out o' hearin', no ways.

OPHELIA: Why, Uncle Tom, what makes you think so?

UNCLE TOM: Miss Eva, she talks to me. The Lord, he sends his messenger in the soul. I must be thar, Miss Feely; for when that ar blessed child goes into the kingdom, they'll open the door so wide, we'll all get a look in at the glory, Miss Feely.

OPHELIA: Uncle Tom, did Miss Eva say she felt more unwell than usual to-night?

UNCLE TOM: No; but she told me this morning she was coming nearer; that's them that tells it to the child, Miss Feely. It's the angels; "it's the trumpet-sound afore the break o' day."

OPHELIA: Well, Tom, perhaps you had better lie down here by the door, so as to be ready if I should call you.

UNCLE TOM: Yes, ma'am.

OPHELIA: [*Closes the door and arranges the chamber. Takes the light and walks toward the bed, and examines the countenance of* EVA.] Ah!

indeed! [*Sets down the lamp and feels of her pulse.*] Is it possible? [*Goes to the door.*] Tom!

UNCLE TOM: [*Without.*] What, missis?

OPHELIA: Go and bring the doctor here, directly; don't lose a minute! [*Crosses the chamber and raps.*] Augustine! Augustine!

ST. CLARE: [*Opening.*] What, cousin? Anything the matter?

OPHELIA: Just look at Eva! feel of her hands!

ST. CLARE: [*Bending over* EVA.] O, my God!

[*Enter* MARIE.]

MAR: Augustine—Cousin—What? Why?

ST. CLARE: Hush! she's dying!

[SERVANTS *flocking into the room.*]

OMNES: O, Miss Eva! O, Miss Eva!

ST. CLARE: Hush! Eva! Eva! O, if she would only speak once more! Eva! darling!

OPHELIA: There! her eyes are opening!

ST. CLARE: Do you know me, Eva?

EVA: Dear papa! [*Throws her arms around his neck, then drops them and struggles, as in a spasm.*]

ST. CLARE: O, God! O, God! this is dreadful! [*Wrings* TOM's *hand.*] O, Tom, my boy, it's killing me!

UNCLE TOM: Lord, have mercy!

ST. CLARE: O, pray that it may be over!

UNCLE TOM: O, bless the Lord, it *is* over—there, look! look at her!

OPHELIA: O, what a look!

SERVANTS: [*All.*] O, those eyes! What does she see?

ST. CLARE: Eva!

OPHELIA: She doesn't hear you!

ST. CLARE: O, Eva! Tell us. What is it?

EVA: [*Gasping.*] O! [*Looks at her father.*] Love! [*Raises her hands.*] Joy! joy!

ST. CLARE: She's gone!

[*Falls on the bed. Curtain drops.*]

SCENE XII

[*A Parlor.* ST. CLARE, MISS OPHELIA. TOM *on a bench near the window, reading.*]

OPHELIA: Augustine, have you ever made any provision for your servants, in case of your death?

ST. CLARE: No!

OPHELIA: Then all your indulgence to them may prove a great cruelty by and by.

ST. CLARE: Well, I mean to make a provision by and by.

OPHELIA: When?

ST. CLARE: One of these days!

OPHELIA: What if you should die first?

ST. CLARE: Cousin, what's the matter? Do you think I show symptoms of yellow fever or cholera, that you are making post mortem arrangements with such zeal?

OPHELIA: "In the midst of life we are in death!"

ST. CLARE: [*Laying aside the paper, and rising.*] DEATH! Strange that there should be such a word, and such a thing, and we ever forget it; that one should be living, warm and beautiful, full of hopes, desires, and wants, one day, and the next be gone, utterly gone, and forever! [*To* TOM.] Want me to read to you, Tom?

UNCLE TOM: If mas'r pleases; mas'r makes it so much plainer.

ST. CLARE: [*Reads.*] "When the Son of Man shall come in his glory, and all his holy angels with him, then shall he sit upon the throne of his glory; and before him shall be gathered all nations: and he shall separate them one from another, as a shepherd divideth his sheep from the goats." [ST. CLARE *reads on, in an animated voice, till he comes to the last of the verses.*] "Then shall the King say unto them on his left hand, Depart from me, ye cursed, into everlasting fire: for I was an hungered, and ye gave me no meat: I was thirsty, and ye gave me no drink: I was a stranger, and ye took me not in: naked, and ye clothed me not: I was sick, and in prison, and ye visited me not. Then shall they answer unto him, Lord, when saw we thee an hungered, or athirst, or a stranger, or naked, or sick, or in prison, and did not minister unto thee. Then shall he say unto them, Inasmuch as ye did it not to one of the least of these my bethren, ye did it not to me." [*Pauses. To* TOM.] Tom, these folks that get such hard measure seem to have been doing just what I have—living good, easy respectable lives; and not troubling themselves to inquire how many of their brethren were hungry, or athirst, or sick, or in prison. [*Goes to the piano and plays and sings.*]

"*Dies irae dies illa,*
Solvet saeclum in favilla,
Teste David cum sybilla."

[*Speaks.*]

What a sublime conception is that of the last judgment! A righting of all the wrongs of ages! A solving of all moral problems by an unanswerable wisdom! It is, indeed, a wonderful image.

OPHELIA: It is a fearful one to us.

ST. CLARE: It ought to be to me, I suppose. Now, that which I was reading to Tom strikes singularly. One should have expected some terrible enormities charged to those who are excluded from heaven, as the reason; but, no,—they are condemned for *not* doing positive good, as if that included every possible harm.

OPHELIA: Perhaps it is impossible for a person who does no good not to do harm.

ST. CLARE: And what, what shall be said of one whose own heart, whose education, and the wants of society, have called in vain to some noble purpose; who has floated on, a dreamy, neutral spectator of the struggles, agonies, and wrongs of man, when he should be been a worker?

OPHELIA: I should say that he ought to repent, and begin now.

ST. CLARE: Always practical and to the point! You never leave me any time for general reflections, cousin; you always bring me short up against the actual present; you have a kind of eternal *now*, always in your mind.

OPHELIA: *Now* is all the time I have anything to do with.

ST. CLARE: Dear little Eva—poor child! she had set her little simple soul on a good work for me. [*A pause.*] I don't know what makes me think of my mother so much to-night. I have a strange kind of feeling, as if she were near me. I keep thinking of things she used to say. Strange what brings these past things so vividly back to us, sometimes! [*Walks.*] I believe I'll go down the street, a few moments, and hear the news to-night. [*Exit.*]

SCENE XIII

[*A Court-Yard.* SERVANTS *running distractedly to and fro; some looking in at the windows where lights are seen moving.*]

UNCLE TOM: [*Comes out.*] He's gone!

VOICES: O, mas'r! O! O! O, Lord! Good Lord! Do hab pity! O Lord, hab mercy! O, Mas'r St. Clare! O, mas'r, mas'r, mas'r! he's dead! he's dead! he's dead!

ACT III, SCENE I

[CASSY *is discovered sitting at a table covered with letters and papers, looking at a miniature.*]

CASSY: I'm tired! I'm sick! I'm dead! Dead? yes, dead at heart! dead at the root, and yet I live; so they say at least. O, to think of it! to *think* of it! Why *don't* I die? [*She rises and paces the room, and sings.*]

"*Una beldad existe que mis ajos
Sampre la ven con majica delicia;
De dia sabe disipar enojos,
De noche ensuenos dulces inspirar.*

Hay une labio que el mio ha,

Y que untes otro labio no comprimida,
Turo hareemo felez oj emaneeido,
Mi labio lo comprime y otro no.

Hay une seno todo el es'propio mio,
Do mi cabesa enferma reclino,
Und bosa que nie si yo nio,
Ojos que lloron euando lloro no."

Ah! that was his song! O, dear, why can't I ever forget it! My children too! O, Henry! O, Eliza! [*She sits down, and covers her face. A carriage heard approaching, she rises quickly.*]

What! back already! [*Looks out the window.*] There! another fly in the spider web! Handsome? O, yes! and what? Yes; some mother's darling. Hah! couldn't I kill him?

LEGREE: [*Opens the door, and pushes* EMMELINE *in.*] This way, little mistress!

CASSY: You wretch! another!

LEGREE: Shut your mouth!

CASSY: I shall shut my mouth; but your time is coming. I see it! I see it! Go on, go on! go as fast as you can! I see where it will end!

LEGREE: Hush, Cassy! be quiet; I mean no harm. You may take this girl up stairs. Come, be peaceable!

CASSY: [*To* EMMELINE.] You have come to the gates of Hell! Come with me. I'll show you the way.

[*Exit, drawing* EMMELINE *after her.*]

LEGREE: [*Solus.*] The creature scares me lately! Her eyes look so dreadful! I'll sell her, or get rid of her some way. Hang it, there's no joke in it!

SCENE II

[*Evening. Negro Quarters. Negroes in ragged clothes.* UNCLE TOM, MULATTO WOMAN, *and* SAMBO. QUIMBO, UNCLE TOM, *and* SAMBO, *walk along and look into houses.*]

UNCLE TOM: Which of these is mine?

SAMBO: Dunno. Turn in here, I 'spose; 'spect ders room for another dar. Right smart heap o' niggers to each on 'em. Sure I dunno what else to do with more. [*To the mulatto woman, throwing down a bag of corn.*] Ho! yer. What a cuss is yer name?

WOMAN: Lucy.

SAMBO: Wall, Lucy, yer my woman now; grind dis yer corn, and get my supper ready; d'ye har?

LUCY: I an't your woman, and I won't be! you go 'long!

SAMBO: I'll kick yo, then!

LUCY: Ye may kill me, if ye choose; the sooner the better! Wish't I was dead!

QUIMBO: I say, Sambo, you go to spilin' the hands I'll tell mas'r o' you.

SAMBO: And I'll tell him ye won't let the women come to the mills, yo old nigger! Yo jes keep to yo own row.

QUIMBO: [*To* UNCLE TOM, *throwing down a bag.*] Thar, yo nigger, grab! thar's yer corn; ye won't git no more dis yer week.

UNCLE TOM: [*To a woman at the mill.*] You're tired; let me grind.

WOMAN: Deed, I is dat!

[UNCLE TOM *grinds.*]

WOMAN: Wall, ye ground our meal, we'll fix yer cake for ye; 'spects ye an't much used to it.

[*Goes in.* UNCLE TOM *sits down by the fire to read the Bible. Women return and put the cakes at the fire.*]

1st WOMAN: [*To* UNCLE TOM.] What's dat ar?

UNCLE TOM: The Bible.

1st WOMAN: Good Lor! ha'n't seen none since I's in ole Kintuck!

UNCLE TOM: Was ye rais'd in Kintuck?

1st WOMAN: Yes, and well raised too. Never expected to come to dis yer.

SECOND WOMAN: [*Coming up.*] What dat ar, anyway?

1st WOMAN: Why, dat ar's the Bible.

2d WOMAN: Good Lor! what's dat?

1st WOMAN: Do tell! you never hearn of it? I used to har missis a readin' on't sometimes, in Kintuck; but, laws o' me! we don't har nothin' here but crackin' and swarin'.

2d WOMAN: Read a piece, anyways!

UNCLE TOM: [*Reads.*] "Come unto ME, all ye that labor and are heavy laden, and I will give you rest."

2d WOMAN: Them's good words enough; who says 'em?

UNCLE TOM: The Lord.

2d WOMAN: I jest wish I know'd whar to find Him; I would go. 'Pears like I never should get rested again. My flesh is fairly sore, and I tremble all over, every day, and Sambo's allers a jawin' a me, 'cause I doesn't pick faster; and nights it's most midnight 'fore I can get my supper; and then 'pears like I don't turn over and shut my eyes 'fore I hear de horn blow to get up and at it again in the mornin'. If I know'd whar de Lord was I'd tell Him.

UNCLE TOM: He's here; he's everywhere!

2d WOMAN: Lor! you an't gwine to make me believe dat ar! I know de Lord an't here; 't an't no use talking, though. I's jest gwine to camp down, and sleep while I ken.

UNCLE TOM: [*Solus.*] O Lord God! Where are thou? Verily thou art a God that hidest thyself, O God of Israel, the Saviour! [*Lies down to sleep.*]

MUSIC AND VOICE IN THE AIR: When thou passest through the waters, I will be with thee, and the rivers they shall not overflow thee; when thou walkest through the fire, thou shalt not be burned, neither shall the flame kindle upon thee; for I am the Lord thy God, the Holy One of Israel, thy Saviour.

SCENE III.

[The Cotton-House and Scales. LEGREE, QUIMBO *and* SAMBO.]

SAMBO: Dat ar Tom's gwine to make a powerful deal o' trouble; kept a puttin' into Lucy's basket. One o' these yer dat will get all der niggers to feelin' 'bused, if mas'r don't watch him!

LEGREE: Hey-day! The black cuss! He'll have to get a breakin' in, won't he, boys?

QUIMBO: Ay, ay! let Mas'r Legree alone for breakin' in! De debil heself couldn't beat mas'r at dat!

LEGREE: Wal, boys, the best way is to give him the flogging to do, till he gets over his notions. Break him in!

SAMBO: Lord, mas'r 'll have hard work to get dat out o' him!

LEGREE: It'll have to come out of him, though!

SAMBO: Now, dar's Lucy; de aggravatinest, ugliest wench on de place!

LEGREE: Take care, Sam! I shall begin to think what's the reason for your spite agin Lucy.

SAMBO: Well, mas'r knows she sot herself up agin mas'r, and wouldn't have me when he telled her to.

LEGREE: I'd a flogged her into't, only there's such a press of work it don't seem wuth a while to upset her jist now. She's slender; but these yer slender gals will bear half killin' to get their own way.

SAMBO: Wal, Lucy was reall aggravatin' and lazy, sulkin' round; wouldn't do nothin'—and Tom he tuck up for her.

LEGREE: He did, eh! Wal, then, Tom shall have the pleasure of flogging her. It'll be a good practice for him, and he won't put it on to the gals like you devils, neither.

SAMBO and QUIMBO: Ho, ho! haw! haw! haw!

SAMBO: Wal, but, mas'r, Tom and Misse Cassy, and dey among 'em, filled Lucy's basket. I ruther guess der weight's in it, mas'r!

LEGREE: *I do the weighing!* So Misse Cassy did her day's work.

SAMBO: She picks like de debil and all his angels!

LEGREE: She's got 'em all in her, I believe! O, here they come!

[*Enter* UNCLE TOM, *and women with baskets.*]

LEGREE: Come, on here! [*Weighs* TOM'*s basket.*] Soh! Ah! Well for you! [TOM *places* LUCY'*s basket on the scales.*] What, ye lazy beast! short again? Get away—ye'll catch it pretty soon!

LUCY: [*Groans.*] O Lor! O Lor! [*Sits.*]

CASSY: [*Brings her basket to the scales.*]

LEGREE: Well, my beauty! How d' ye like it?

CASSY: Beaucoup mieux que de vivre avec une bete telle comme vous.

[*Exit.*]

LEGREE: And now, come here, you Tom! You see, I telled ye I didn't buy ye jest for the common work; I mean to promote ye, and make a driver of ye; and to-night ye may jest as well begin to get yer hand in. Now, ye jest take this yer gal and flog her. Ye've seen enough on't to know how.

UNCLE TOM: I beg mas'r's pardon; hopes mas'r won't set me at that. It's what I an't used to; never did; and can't do, no way possible.

LEGREE: Ye'll larn a pretty smart chance of things ye never did know, before I've done with ye! [*Thrashes* TOM *with cowhide.*] There, now! will ye tell me ye can't do it?

UNCLE TOM: Yes, mas'r! I'm willin' to work, night and day, and work while there's life and breath in me; but this yer thing I can't feel it right to do; and, mas'r, I *never* shall do it—*never!*

LUCY: O Lord!

SLAVES: O! O!

LEGREE: [*Foaming.*] What! ye blasted black beast! tell *me* ye don't think it *right* to do what I tell ye! What have any of you cussed cattle to do with thinking what's right? I'll put a stop to it! Why, what do ye think ye are? May be ye think ye 'r a gentleman, master Tom, to be a telling your master what's right, and what an't! So you pretend it's wrong to flog the gal.

UNCLE TOM: I think so, mas'r; the poor crittur's sick and feeble; 't would be downright cruel, and it's what I never will do, nor begin to.

339

LEGREE: Well, here's a pious dog, at last set down among us sinners! a saint, a gentleman, and no less, to talk to us sinners about our sins; powerful holy critter he must be! Here, you rascal! you make believe to be so pious—didn't you never hear, out of your Bible, "Servants obey your masters"? An't I your master? Didn't I pay down twelve hundred dollars, cash, for all there is inside yer old cussed black shell? An't yet mine, now, body and soul? Tell me!

UNCLE TOM: No, no, no! my soul an't yours, mas'r! You haven't bought it—you can't buy it! It has been bought and paid for by One that 's able to keep it. No matter, no matter, you can't harm me!

LEGREE: I can't! we'll see! we'll see! Here Sambo! Quimbo! give this dog such a breakin' in as he won't get over this month!

SCENE IV

[*An old Gin-house Garret.* UNCLE TOM *lying on the floor.*]

UNCLE TOM: O, good Lord, do look down! Give me the vict'ry! give me the vict'ry!

[*Enter* CASSY, *with lantern.*]

UNCLE TOM: Who's there? O, for mercy's sake, give me some water!

CASSY: Drink all you want. I knew how't would be! 'Tan't the first time I been out o' night carrying water to such as you.

UNCLE TOM: Thank ye, missis!

CASSY: Don't call me missis! I'm a miserable slave like you. A lower one that you can ever be! But let me see if I can't make you more comfortable. [*Places a pillow under his head.*] There, my poor fellow, there! that's the best I can do for you!

UNCLE TOM: Thank you, missis!

CASSY: [*Sitting.*] It's no use, my poor fellow; it's of no use, this you've been trying to do. You were a brave fellow; you had the right on your side; but it's all in vain, and out of the question, for you to struggle. You are in the devil's hands; he is the strongest, and you must give up.

UNCLE TOM: O, Lord! O, Lord! how can I give up?

CASSY: There's no use calling on the Lord; he never hears! There isn't any God, I believe; or, if there is, he's taken sides against us. All goes against us, heaven and earth. Everything is pushing us into hell. Why shouldn't we go? You see, *you* don't know anything about it; I do. I've been on this place five years, body and soul, under this man's foot, and I hate him as I do the devil! Here you are, on a lone plantation, ten miles from any other, in the swamps; not a white person here who could testify if you were burned alive; if you were scalded, cut into inch-pieces, set up for the dogs to tear, or hung up and whipped to death. There's no law here, of God or man, that can do you, or any one of us, the least good; and this man! there's no earthly thing that he's too good to do. I could make any one's hair rise, and their teeth chatter, if I should only tell what I've seen and been knowing to here; and it's no use resisting! Did I *want* to live with him? Wasn't I a woman delicately bred? And he! God in heaven! what was he, and is he? And yet I've lived with him these five years, and cursed every moment of my life, night and day! And now he's got a new one; a young thing, only fifteen; and she brought up, she says, piously! Her good mistress taught her to read the Bible, and she's brought her Bible here, to hell, with her!

UNCLE TOM: O, Jesus! Lord Jesus! have you quite forgot us poor critturs? Help, Lord, I perish!

CASSY: And what are these miserable low dogs you work with, that you should suffer on their account? Every one of them would turn against you the first time they got a chance. They are all of 'em as low and cruel to each other as they can be; and there's no use in your suffering to keep from hurting them.

UNCLE TOM: Poor critturs! what made 'em cruel? And if I give out, I shall get used to't, and grow, little by little, just like 'em! No, no, missis! I've lost everything; wife, and children, and home, and a kind mas'r; and he would have set me free, if he'd only lived a week longer. I've lost everything in *this* world, and it's clean gone forever; and now I *can't* lose heaven, too; no, I can't get to be wicked, besides all!

CASSY: But it can't be that the Lord will lay sin to our account; he won't charge it to us, when we're forced to it; he'll charge it to tham that drove us to it.

UNCLE TOM: Yes; but that won't keep us from growing wicked. If I get to be as hard-hearted as that ar' Sambo, and as wicked, it won't make much odds to me how I came so; it's the *bein' so*; that ar 's what I'm a dreadin'.

CASSY: O, God a' mercy! you speak the truth! O! O! O!

UNCLE TOM: Please missis, I saw 'em throw my coat in that ar' corner. In the pocket is my Bible; if missis would please get it for me. [CASSY *brings it.*] There's a place marked here, if missis 'll please to read it. I want to hear it.

CASSY: [*Reads.*] "And when they were come to the place which is called Calvary, there they crucified him, and the malefactors one on the right hand, and the other on the left. Then said Jesus, Father, forgive them, they know not what they do!" [*She throws down the book violently, and buries her face in her hands.*]

UNCLE TOM: [*Sobbing.*] If we could only keep up to that ar'! it seemed to come so natural to him, and we have to fight so hard for 't! O, Lord, help us! O, blessed Lord Jesus, do help us! Missis, I can see that somehow you're quite 'bove me in everything; but there's one thing missis might learn, even from poor Tom. Ye said the Lord took sides against us, because he lets us be 'bused and knocked round; but ye see what come on his own Son—the blessed Lord of Glory! Wa'n't he al'ays poor? and have we, any on us, yet come so low as he come? The Lord ha'n't forgot us; I'm sartin o' that ar'! If we suffer with him, we shall also reign, Scripture says; but if we deny him, he also will deny us. Didn't they all suffer; the Lord and all his? It tells how they were stoned and sawn asunder, and wandered about in sheepskins and goatskins, and was destitute, afflicted, tormented. Sufferin' an't no reason to make us think the Lord's turned agin us, but jest the contrary, if we only hold on to him, and does n't give up to sin.

CASSY: But why does he put us where we can't help but sin?

UNCLE TOM: I think we *can* help it.

CASSY: You'll see! What 'll you do? To-morrow they'll be at you again! I know 'em, I have seen all their doings; I can't bear to think of all they'll bring you to; and they'll make you give out at last!

UNCLE TOM: Lord Jesus! you *will* take care of my soul! O, Lord, do! don't let me give out!

CASSY: O, dear, I've heard all this crying and praying before; and yet they've been broken down and brought under. There's Emmeline, she's trying to hold on, and you're trying; but what use? You must give up, or be killed by inches!

UNCLE TOM: Well, then, I *will* die! Spin it out as long as they can, they can't help my dying some time! and, after that, they can't do no more. I'm clar! I'm set! I *know* the Lord'll help me, and bring me through.

CASSY: Maybe it's the way, but those that *have* given up, there's no hope for them—none! We live in filth and grow loathsome, till we loathe ourselves! And we long to die, and we don't dare to kill ourselves. No hope! no hope! no hope! This girl now, just as old as I was. You see me now; see what I am! Well, I was brought up in luxury: the first I remember is, the playing about, when I was a child, in splendid parlors; kept dressed up like a doll; company and visitors praising me. There was a garden opening from the saloon windows; and there I used to play hide-and-go-seek, under the orange-trees, with my brothers and sisters. I went to a convent, and there I learned music, French, and embroidery, and what not. When I was fourteen, I came out to my father's funeral. He died very suddenly, and when the property came to be settled, they found that there was scarcely enough to cover the debts; and when the creditors took an inventory of the property, I was set down in it. My mother was a slave-woman, and my father had always meant to set me free; but he had not done it, and so I was set down in the list. I'd always known who I was, but never thought much about it. Nobody ever expects that a strong, healthy man is a going to die. My father was a well man only four hours before he died; it was one of the first cholera cases in New Orleans. The day after the funeral, my father's wife took her children and went up to her father's plantation. I thought they treated me strangely, but didn't know why. There was a young lawyer whom they left to settle the business; and he came every day, and was about the house and spoke very politely to me. He brought with him, one day, a young man, the handsomest I had ever seen. I shall never forget that evening. I walked with him in the garden. I was lonesome and full of sorrow, and he was so kind and gentle to me; and he told me that he had seen me before I went to the convent; and that he had loved me a great while, and that he would be my friend and protector; in short, though he didn't tell me, he had paid two thousand dollars for me, and I was his property. I became his willingly, for I *loved* him. Loved!—O, how I *did* love that man! How I love him now, and always shall, while I breathe! He was so beautiful, so high, so noble! Everything that money could buy, he gave me; but I didn't set any value on all that; I only cared for him. I loved him better than my God and my own soul; and, if I tried, I couldn't do any other way from what he wanted me to do. I wanted only one thing—I did want him to *marry* me. I thought if he loved me, as he said he did, and if I was what he seemed to think I was, he would be willing to marry me and set me free. But he convinced me that it would be impossible; and he told me that, if we were only faithful to each other, it was marriage before God. If that is true, wasn't I that man's wife? Wasn't I faithful? For seven years, didn't I study every look and motion, and only life and breathe to please him? He had the yellow fever, and for twenty days and nights I watched with him, I alone; and gave him all his medicine, and did everything for him; and then he called me his good angel, and said I'd saved his life. We have two beautiful children. The first was a boy, and we called him Henry. He was the image of his father. He had such beautiful eyes, such a forehead, and his hair hung all in curls around it! And he had all his father's spirit, and his talent too. Little Elise, he said, looked like me. He used to tell me that I was the most beautiful woman in Louisiana, he was so proud of me and the children. O, those were happy days! I thought I was as happy as any one could be; but then there came evil times. He had a cousin come to New Orleans who was his particular friend; he thought all the world of him; but from the first time I saw him, I couldn't tell why, I dreaded him, for I felt sure he was going to bring misery on us. He got Henry to going out with him, and often would not come home nights till two or three o'clock. I did not dare to say a word; for Henry was so high-spirited I was afraid to. He got him to the gaming houses; and he was one of the sort that, when he once got a going there, there was no holding back. And then he introduced him to another lady, and I saw soon that his heart was gone from me. He never told me, but I saw it; I knew it day after day. I felt my heart breaking, but I could not say a word. Would you believe it? at last the wretch offered to buy me and the children of Henry, to clear off his gambling debts, which stood in the way of his marrying as he wished!—and *he sold us!* He told me one day that he had business in the country, and should be gone two or three weeks. He spoke kinder than usual, and said he should come back; but *it didn't deceive me*; I knew that the time had come; I was just like one turned into stone; I couldn't speak nor shed a tear. He kissed me and kissed the children a good many times, and went out. He saw him get on his horse, and I watched him till he was quite out of sight; and then I fell down and fainted. Then *he* came, the cursed wretch! he came to take possession. He told me that he had bought me and my children, and showed me the papers. I cursed him before God, and told him I'd die sooner than live with him. "Just as you please," said he; "but if you don't behave reasonably I'll sell both the children, where you shall never see them again." He told me that he always had meant to have me, from the

first time he saw me; and that he had drawn Henry on, and
got him in debt, on purpose to make him willing to sell me.
That he got him in love with another woman; and that I might
know, after all that, that he should not give up for a few airs
and tears, and things of that sort. I gave up, for my hands were
tied. He had my children; whenever I resisted his will anywhere,
he would talk about selling them, and he made me as submis-
sive as he desired. O, what a life it was! To live with my heart
breaking every day,—to keep on, on, on, loving, when it was
only misery; and to be bound, body and soul, to one I hated!
Yet I was afraid to refuse him anything. He was very hard to
the children. Elise was a timid little thing; but Henry was bold
and high-spirited like his father,—he had always been so
indulged. He was always scolding him, and I used to live in
daily fear. I tried to make the child respectful. I tried to keep
them apart. No use—none! He sold both those children. One
day, when I came home from riding, I looked all over the house,
and called,—and they were gone! He told me he had sold them;
he showed me the money,—the price of their blood! Then it
seemed as if all good had forsaken me. I raved and cursed,—
cursed God and man; and, for a while, I believe he really was
afraid of me. But he didn't give up so. He told me that my
children were sold, but whether I ever saw their faces again
depended on him; and that, if I wasn't quiet, they should smart
for it. Well, you can do anything with a woman when you've
got her children! He *made* me submit; he *made* me peaceable;
he flattered me with hopes that, perhaps, he would buy them
back; and so things went on a week or two. One day, I was
out walking, and passed by the calaboose; I saw a crowd about
the gate, and I heard a child's voice; and, suddenly, my Henry
broke away from two or three men, who were holding him,
and ran, screaming, and caught my dress. They came up to
him, swearing dreadfully. O, there was one man!—I shall never
forget that man's face! He told him that he wouldn't get away
so; that he had got to go in with him and get a lesson he'd
never forget. The poor child screamed, and looked in my face,

and held on to me so that, when they tore him off, they tore
the skirt of my dress half away; and they carried him in screaming "Mother! mother! mother!" I turned and ran; every step I
heard him scream. I got to the house, all out of breath, into
the parlor, and found Butler. I told him, and begged him to
go and interfere. He only laughed, and told me the boy had
got his desserts. He'd got to be broken in; the sooner the better. What did I expect? he asked.—Look here! Do you know
something in my head *snapped* then?—*snapped*, you know! It's
never come right since. I saw a great knife—I caught it—and
then all grew dark—and I didn't know any more not for days
and days. When I came to myself I was in a nice room, but
not mine. An old black woman tended me, and a doctor came
to see me; and there was a great deal of care taken of me. After
a while I found that he had gone away, and left me at this
house to be sold; and that's why they took such pains with me.
I didn't mean to get well, and hoped I shouldn't; but, in spite
of me, the fever went off, and I grew healthy, and finally got
up. Then they made me dress up, every day; and gentlemen
used to come in and stand and smoke their cigars, and look at
me, and ask questions, and debate my price. I was so gloomy
and silent, that none of them wanted me. They threatened to
whip me if I wasn't gayer, and didn't take some pains to make
myself agreeable. At length, one day, came a gentleman named
Stuart. He seemed to have some feeling for me; he saw that
something dreadful was on my heart, and he came to see me
alone a great many times, and finally persuaded me to tell him.
He bought me, at last, and promised to do all he could to find
and buy back my children. He went to the hotel where my
Henry was; they told him he had been sold to a planter up on
Pearl river; that was the last that I ever heard of him. Then he
found where my daughter was; an old woman was keeping her.
He offered an immense sum for her, but they would not sell
her. Butler found out that it was for me he wanted her, and
he sent me word that I should never have her. Captain Stuart
was very kind to me; he had a splendid plantation, and took

me to it. In the course of a year I had a son born. O, that child! how I loved it! How just like my poor Henry the little thing looked! But I had made up my mind—yes, I had—I would never again let a child live to grow up! So, when he was two weeks old, I took the little fellow in my arms, and I gave him laudanum. It didn't hurt him; it made him so quiet, and I held him close—close to my bosom, and he slept to death! And I'm not sorry now! That's one of the few things I'm glad of. Yes, yes; he's safe! They'll never sell *him*—they'll never whip *him*! No, no; nothing can hurt *him*! Ah! death is the best thing we can give our children. After a while the cholera came, and Captain Stuart died; everybody died that wanted to live, and I—I, though I went down to death's door—*I lived!* Then I was sold, and passed from hand to hand, till I grew faded and wrinkled, and I had a fever; and then this wretch bought me, and brought me here—and here I am! [CASSY *rises and walks about—stops suddenly.*] You tell me there's a God,—a God that looks down and sees all these things. May be it's so. The sisters used to tell me of a day of judgment when everything is coming to light. *Won't* there be vengeance then! They think it's nothing what we suffer—nothing what our children suffer! It's all a small matter; yet I've walked the streets when it seemed as if I had misery enough in my one heart to sink the city! I've wished the houses would fall on me, or the stones sink under me. Yes! and in the judgment-day I will stand up before God, a witness against those that have ruined me and my children, body and soul! When I was a girl I thought I was religious; I used to love God and prayer. Now I'm a lost soul, pursued by devils that torment me day and night. They keep pushing me on and on—and I'll do it, too, some of these days! I'll send him where he belongs—a short way, too—one of these nights, if they burn me alive for it! [*Sobs and struggles.*] Can I do anything more for you, my poor fellow? Shall I give you some more water?

UNCLE TOM: O, missis, I wish you would go to Him that can give living waters.

CASSY: Go to Him! Where is he? Who is he?

UNCLE TOM: Him you read of, the Lord Jesus!

CASSY: I used to see the picture of him over the altar; but he isn't here. No; he isn't here! There's nothing here but sin—and long—long—long despair! Don't talk, poor fellow! it's no use. Try to make yourself comfortable, and sleep if you can.

[*Exit* CASSY.]

SCENE V

[*Sitting-Room.*]

LEGREE: [*Drinking.*] Plague on that Sambo, to kick up his yer row between me and the new hands! The fellow won't be fit to work for a week now,—right in the press of the season.

CASSY: Yes; just like you.

LEGREE: Hah! you she-devil! you've come back, have you?

CASSY: Yes, I have; come to have my own way, too!

LEGREE: You lie, you jade! I'll be up to my word. Either behave yourself, or stay down to the quarters, and fare and work with the rest.

CASSY: I'd rather, ten thousand times, live in the dirtiest hole at the quarters, than be under your hoof!

LEGREE: But you *are* under my hoof, for all that; that's one comfort. So, sit down here on my knee, my dear, and hear to reason.

CASSY: Simon Legree, take care! You're afraid of me, Simon; and you've reason to be! But be careful, for I've got the devil in me!

LEGREE: Get out! I believe to my soul you have! After all, Cassy, why can't you be friends with me as you used to?

CASSY: Used to!

LEGREE: Come, Cassy, I wish you'd behave yourself decently.

CASSY: *You* talk about behaving decently! And what have you been doing? You, who have n't even sense enough to keep from spoiling one of your best hands, right in the most pressing season, just for your devilish temper!

349

LEGREE: I was a fool, it's a fact, to let any such brangle come up; but when the boy set up his will, he had to be broke in.

CASSY: I reckon you won't break *him* in!

LEGREE: Won't I? I'd like to know if I won't! He'll be the first nigger that ever came it round me! I'll break every bone in his body but he *shall* give up!

CASSY: No, he won't!

LEGREE: I'd like to know *why*, mistress.

CASSY: Because he's done right, and he knows it, and won't say he's doing wrong.

LEGREE: Who a cuss cares what he knows? The nigger shall say what I please, or——

CASSY: Or you'll lose your bet on the cotton crop by keeping him out of the field just at this very press.

LEGREE: But he *will* give up; of course he will. Don't I know what niggers is? He'll beg like a dog this morning.

CASSY: He won't, Simon; you don't know this kind. You may kill him by inches, you won't get the first word of confession out him.

LEGREE: We'll see. Where is he?

CASSY: In the waste-room of the gin house.

[*Exit* LEGREE.]

CASSY: [*Solus.*] Would it be a sin to kill such a wretch as that?

[*Enter* EMMELINE.]

EMMELINE: O, Cassy! is it you? I'm so glad you've come! I was afraid it was——O, you won't know what a horrid noise there has been, down stairs, all this evening!

CASSY: I ought to know; I've heard it often enough.

EMMELINE: O, Cassy! Do tell me,—couldn't we get away from this place? I don't care where,—into the swamp among the snakes,—anywhere! *Couldn't* we get *somewhere* away from here?

CASSY: Nowhere but into our graves!

EMMELINE: Did you ever try?

CASSY: I've seen enough of trying, and what comes of it?

EMMELINE: I'd be willing to live in the swamps, and gnaw the bark from trees. I an't afraid of snakes! I'd rather have one near me than him.

CASSY: There have been a good many here of your opinion; but you couldn't stay in the swamps. You'd be tracked by the dogs, and brought back, and then—then—

EMMELINE: What would he do?

CASSY: What *wouldn't* he do, you'd better ask! He's learned his trade well among the pirates in the West Indies. You wouldn't sleep much, if I should tell you things I've seen,—things that he tells of, sometimes, for good jokes. I've heard screams here that I haven't been able to get out of my head for weeks and weeks. There's a place way out down by the quarters, where you can see a black, blasted tree, and the ground all covered with black ashes. Ask any one what was done there, and see if they will dare to tell you.

EMMELINE: O, what do you mean?

CASSY: I won't tell you. I hate to think of it. And, I tell you, the Lord only knows what we may see to-morrow, if that poor fellow holds out as he's begun!

EMMELINE: Horrid! O, Cassy, do tell me what I shall do!

CASSY: What I've done. Do the best you can—do what you must, and make it up in hating and cursing!

EMMELINE: He wanted to make me drink some of his hateful brandy; and I hate it so—

CASSY: You'd better drink. I hated it too; and now I can't live without it. One must have something—things don't look so dreadful when you take that.

EMMELINE: Mother used to tell me never to touch any such thing.

CASSY: *Mother* told you! What use is it for mothers to say anything? You are all to be bought and paid for, and your souls belong to whoever gets you. That's the way it goes. I say, *drink* brandy; drink all you can, and it'll make things come easier!

EMMELINE: O, Cassy, do pity me!

CASSY: Pity you!—and don't I? Haven't I a daughter?—Lord knows where she is, and whose she is now,—going the way her mother went before her, I suppose, and that her children must go after her! There's no end to the curse—forever!

EMMELINE: I wish I'd never been born!

CASSY: That's an old wish with me. I've got used to wishing that. I'd die if I dared to!

EMMELINE: It would be wicked to kill one's self.

CASSY: I don't know why;—no wickeder than things we live and do day after day. But the sisters told me things, when I was in the convent, that make me afraid to die. If it would only be the end of us, why then—

LEGREE: [*Calling.*] Cassy!—I say!—Emmeline!

CASSY: There he is!—What now?

[*Exeunt.*]

SCENE VI

[*Moonlight.*]

UNCLE TOM: *Solus.* [*Sings.*]
  "*Way down upon the Swanee river,*
  Far, far away,
  Dere's whar my heart is turning, ever,
  Dere's whar the old folks stay.

  All the world am sad and dreary,
  Everywhere I roam;
  O, Chloe, how my heart grows weary,
  Thinkin' of ye all at home!"

[*A pause. Looks up. His face brightens. Sings.*]

  "*When I can read my title clear*
  To mansions in the skies,
  I bid farewell to every fear,
  And wipe my weeping eyes.

Should earth against my soul engage,
And hellish darts be hurled,
Then I can smile at Satan's rage,
And face a frowning world."

[*Enter* LEGREE, *unperceived.*]

"Let cares like a wild deluge come,
And storms of sorrow fall,
May I but safely reach my home,
My God, my heaven, my all!"

LEGREE: [*Aside.*] So, ho! he thinks so, does he! How I hate these cursed Methodist hymns! [*To* TOM, *aloud.*] Here, you nigger! how dare you be gettin' up this yer row, when you ought to be in bed? Shut yer old black gash, and get along in with you!

UNCLE TOM: Yes, Mas'r.

LEGREE: [*Beating him.*] There, you dog! see if you feel so comfortable after that!

[*Exit* TOM.]

SCENE VII

[*Night. Before Uncle Tom's Cottage.*]

[*Enter* CASSY. *She raps.* UNCLE TOM *opens the door.*]

CASSY: Come here, father Tom! come here; I've news for you!

UNCLE TOM: What, Misse Cassy?

CASSY: Tom, wouldn't you like your liberty?

UNCLE TOM: I shall have it, misse, in God's time.

CASSY: Ay, but you may have it to-night! Come on!

[UNCLE TOM *holds back.*]

CASSY: Come! Come along! He's asleep—sound. I put enough into

353

his brandy to keep him so. I wish I'd had more, I shouldn't have wanted you. But come, the back-door is unlocked: there is an axe there; I put it there—his room-door is open; I'll show you the way. I'd a done it myself, only my arms are so weak. Come along!

UNCLE TOM: Not for ten thousand worlds, misse!

CASSY: But think of all these poor creatures. We might set them all free, and go somewhere in the swamps, and find an island, and live by ourselves; I've heard of its being done. Any life is better than this.

UNCLE TOM: No, no! good never comes of wickedness. I'd sooner chop my right hand off!

CASSY: Then I shall do it.

UNCLE TOM: O, misse Cassy! for the dear Lord's sake that died for ye, don't sell your precious soul to the devil, that way! Nothing but evil will come of it. The Lord has n't called us to wrath. We must suffer, and wait his time.

CASSY: Wait! Haven't I waited?—waited till my head is dizzy and my heart sick? What has he made me suffer! What has he made hundreds of poor creatures suffer! Is n't he wringing the life-blood out of you? I'm called on! They call me! His time's come, and I'll have his heart's blood!

UNCLE TOM: No, no, no! No, ye poor, lost soul, that ye mustn't do! The dear, blessed Lord never shed no blood but his own, and that he poured out for us when we was enemies. Lord, help us to follow his steps, and love our enemies!

CASSY: Love! love such enemies! it isn't in flesh and blood.

UNCLE TOM: No, misse, it isn't; but *He* gives it to us, and that's the *victory*. When we can love and pray over all, and through all, the battle's past and the victory's come—glory be to God! Misse Casse, if you could only get away from here—if the thing was possible—I'd 'vise ye and Emmeline to do it; that is, if ye could go without blood-guiltiness—not otherwise.

CASSY: Would you try it with us, father Tom?

UNCLE TOM: No; time was when I would; but the Lord's given me a work among these yer poor souls, and I'll stay with 'em, and bear my cross with 'em till the end. It's different with you; it's a snare to you—it's more 'n you can stand, and you'd better go if you can.

CASSY: I know no way but through the grave! There's no beast or bird but can find a home somewhere; even the snakes and the alligators have their places to lie down and be quiet; but there's no place for us. Down in the darkest swamps the dogs will hunt us out, and find us. Everybody and everything is against us; even the very beasts side against us, and where shall we go?

UNCLE TOM: He that saved Daniel in the den of lions—that saved the children in the fiery furnace—He that walked on the sea, and bade the winds be still—He's alive yet; and I've faith to believe he can deliver you. Try it, and I will pray with all my might for you.

CASSY: Father Tom, I'll try it!

[*Exit* CASSY, UNCLE TOM.]

SCENE VIII

[*A Room. Evening.* CASSY *and* EMMELINE *sorting and arranging baggage.*]

CASSY: These will be large enough; now on with your bonnet, and let's start.

EMMELINE: Why, they can see us yet.

CASSY: I mean they shall. Don't you know they must have that chase after us, at any rate? See here, now, their way will be just this: We steal out of the back door, and run down by the Court House. Sambo or Quimbo will be sure to see us. They will give chase, and we will get into the swamp. Then I can't go any further till they go up and turn out the dogs; and while they are blundering around, and tumbling over each other, as they always do, you and I will just slip along to a creek, and run into the water, till we get back to the house; that will put the dogs all at fault; for scent won't lie in the water. Every one will run out of the house to look after us, and then we'll whip into the back door, and then to the garret, where I have got a nice bed made up in one of the great boxes. We must stay there a good while; for, I tell you, he will raise heaven and earth after us. He boasts that no one ever got away from him. He'll muster all the old overseers on the other plantations, and have a great hunt, and they'll go over every inch of ground in that swamp. We'll let him hunt at his leisure.

EMMELINE: But won't he come to the garret?

CASSY: Not he, indeed! He is too much afraid of that place.

EMMELINE: Cassy, how well you have planned it! Who would ever have thought that of you?

CASSY: [*Reaching her hand to* EMMELINE.] Come.

SCENE IX

[*A Wood.* EMMELINE *and* CASSY *stealing cautiously through the trees.*]

[*Enter* LEGREE *at a distance. Perceives them.*]

LEGREE: Hallo! you, there!

EMMELINE: [*Staggers and catches hold of* CASSY'S *arm.*] O, Cassy, I am going to faint!

CASSY: [*Holding up a dagger.*] If you do, I'll kill you! [*She seizes* EMMELINE *under the arm and holds her up, as they disappear.*]

LEGREE: [*Coming in sight, and looking after them.*] Anyhow, they have got into a trap now,—the baggages! They are safe enough! They shall sweat for it! [*Turns and runs in another direction.*] Hallo! there, Sambo! Quimbo!—all hands!—two runaways in the swamp!—five dollars to any nigger that catches them!—turn out the dogs!—turn out Tiger!—Fury and fire! Halloo! be alive!

[*Enter* SAMBO, QUIMBO, *and a crowd of negroes with torches. They run about distractedly, and shouting and whooping, some getting pine knots and some getting the dogs.*]

SAMBO: Mas'r, shall we shoot them? Can't catch 'em.

LEGREE: [*Giving him a rifle.*] Fire on Cass, if you like—time she is gone where she belongs! Don't fire on the girl! Now, be spry! Five dollars to him that gets them! Glass of spirits to you all, any way!

[*Exit all, shouting.*]

[*Enter* UNCLE TOM; *looks after them and raises his hands.*]

UNCLE TOM: Please, good Lord, do, do help 'em—help 'em—help 'em, good Lord!

SCENE X

[*A Room in the House. From the windows is seen the light of flambeaux, and the sound of dogs and shouting is heard.*]

[*Enter* CASSY *and* EMMELINE *out of breath.*]

CASSY: [*Walking to the window and looking out.*] See there, the hunt is begun! Hark, the dogs! Don't you hear? If we were there now, our chance wouldn't be worth a picayune!

EMMELINE: O, for pity's sake! Do let's hide ourselves! Quick! quick!

CASSY: There is no occasion for hurry. The hunt is the amusement for the evening. They are all out after it. Meanwhile [*she walks to a desk and unlocks it.*] I shall take something to pay our passage.

EMMELINE: O, don't let's to that!

CASSY: [*Taking out a roll of bills and counting them.*] Why not? Would you have us starve in the swamp, or have what will pay our way to the free states? Money can do anything, girl!

EMMELINE: But it's stealing!

CASSY: [*Laughs scornfully.*] Stealing, is it! They who steal body and soul need not talk to us! Let *him* talk about stealing! Every one of these bills is stolen—stolen from poor, starving, sweating creatures, that must go to the devil at last for his profit! But *come*, we may as well go up garret. I have got a stock of candles there, and some books to pass away the time. You may be sure they won't come there to inquire after us.

[*Exit.*]

SCENE XI

[*The Dining-room.*]

LEGREE: [*Solus.*] It's all that Tom, I know! Did n't I see the old wretch lifting up his old black hands, praying? I *hate* him! I HATE him! And isn't he *mine*? Is he not MINE? Can't I do what I like with him? Who is to hinder, I wonder? I'll try once more to-morrow. If I don't catch them—I'll see what I'll do!

SCENE XII

EMMELINE: What do you see?

CASSY: At it again this morning! There's that old Stokes on the run. He has come over—has he? And Bill Daken, with his dogs! Hear them swear! There he goes, giving brandy round among them—niggers and all! [*Listens.*] So I am to be shot down—am I? "Save the girl!" Do you hear that, Emmeline? Is n't he kind? [CASSY *rises suddenly, clasps her hands, and looks up.*] Almighty God, what *is* this for? What have we done more than all the rest of the world, that we are treated so? [*After a pause, she lays her hand on* EMMELINE'S *shoulder.*] If it wasn't for you, child, I *would* go out there, and I'd thank any one that *would* shoot me down; for what use will freedom be to me? Can it give me back my children, or make me what I used to be?

EMMELINE: Poor Cassy! don't feel so! [*She takes her hand.*]

CASSY: [*Draws it away.*] Don't—you get me to loving you; and I never mean to love anything again.

EMMELINE: You shouldn't feel so, Cassy. If the Lord gives us liberty perhaps he will give you back your daughter. At any rate, I'll be like a daughter to you. I know I'll never see my poor old mother again. I shall love you, Cassy, whether you love me or not.

CASSY: [*Sits down, and puts her arm around* EMMELINE.] O, Em, I have hungered for my children, and thirsted for them! My heart is broken in longing for them! Here, here all is desperate, all empty! If God would give me back my children, then I could pray.

EMMELINE: You must trust him, Cassy. He is our Father.

CASSY: His wrath is upon us. He is turned away in anger.

EMMELINE: No, Cassy, he will be good to us.

SCENE XIII

[*Sitting-room.* LEGREE *and* QUIMBO.]

LEGREE: Now, Quimbo, if you'll just wake up that Tom right away—the old cuss is at the bottom of the whole matter, and I'll have it out of his old black hide, or I'll know the reason why! [*Exit* QUIMBO.] What if I did pay a thousand dollars for him!—two thousand would not pay the plague he has made me! I've *got* him! the—

[*Enter* QUIMBO, *dragging along* TOM.]

QUIMBO: Ah! you'll cotch it now, I'll be bound! Mas'r's back's up high. No sneaking up now—tell you, you'll get it—no mistake! See how you look now, helping mas'r's niggers to run away—see what ye got!

A VOICE FROM ABOVE: "Fear not them that kill the body, and after that have no more that they can do."

LEGREE: [*Seizing* TOM *by the collar.*] Tom, do you know I have made up my mind to kill you?

TOM: I think it's quite likely, mas'r.

LEGREE: I have—done—just—that—thing, Tom, unless you'll tell me what you know about these here girls!

[TOM *remains silent, and looks on the floor.*]

LEGREE: [*Stamping.*] Do you hear?—speak!

TOM: I an't got nothing to tell, mas'r.

LEGREE: Do you dare to tell me, you old black Christian, that you don't know?

[TOM *remains silent.*]

LEGREE: [*Furiously.*] Speak! Do you know anything?

TOM: I know, mas'r, but I can't tell anything. *I can die.*

LEGREE: [*Comes up to* TOM, *and speaks close to his face.*] Look here, Tom! you think, because I have let you off other times, that I don't mean what I say. But I *do*! I have made up my mind and counted the cost. You always have stood it out against me; but this time I'll conquer you, or I'll kill you—one or t' other! I'll count every drop of blood that is in you, and take them one by one till you give up!

TOM: [*Looking up to his master.*] Mas'r, if you were sick, or in trouble, or dying, and I could save ye, I'd give ye my heart's blood; and, if taking every drop of blood in this poor old body would save your precious soul, I'd give 'em freely, as the Lord gave his for me. O! mas'r, don't bring this great sin on your soul! It will hurt you more than't will me! Do the worst you can, my troubles will be over soon; but, if ye don't repent, yours won't ever end!

[LEGREE *hesitates a moment, and then knocks* TOM *down.* SAMBO *and* QUIMBO *rush in.*]

SAMBO and QUIMBO: Shall we take him, mas'r?

LEGREE: Yes, take him. I'll go with you. We'll see what we'll see!

[*Exit.*]

SCENE XIV

[*A Hut.* UNCLE TOM *lying on straw, apparently dead.*]

[*Enter* GEORGE SHELBY. *Kneels down.*]

GEORGE: Is it possible! Is it possible! Uncle Tom, my poor old friend!

UNCLE TOM: [*Moving in his sleep.*]
"*Jesus can make a dying bed*
Feel soft as downy pillows are."

GEORGE: O! Uncle Tom, do wake! do speak once more! Look up! Here's Mas'r George—your own little Mas'r George! Don't you know me?

UNCLE TOM: [*In a feeble voice.*] Mas'r George! Mas'r George! Bless the Lord! it is—it is—it's all I wanted! They have n't forgot me! It warms my soul; it does my old heart good! Now I shall die content! Bless the Lord, O my soul!

GEORGE: You shan't die! you *mustn't* die, nor think of it! I've come to buy you, and take you home.

UNCLE TOM: O, Mas'r George, ye're too late! The Lord's bought me, and is going to take me home; and I long to go. Heaven is better than Kintuck.

GEORGE: O, don't die! It'll kill me! it'll break my heart to think what you've suffered—and lying in this old shed, here! Poor, poor fellow!

UNCLE TOM: Don't call me a poor fellow! [*Solemnly.*] I *have* been poor fellow; but that's all past and gone now. I'm right in the door, going into glory! O, Mas'r George! *Heaven has come!* I've got the victory! the Lord Jesus has given it to me! Glory be to his name! [*He pauses, and then takes* GEORGE's *hand.*] Ye mustn't, now, tell Chloe—poor soul!—how ye found me; 't would be so dreful to her. Only tell her ye found me going into glory; and that I couldn't stay for no one. And tell her the Lord stood by me everywhere, and al'ays, and made everything light and easy. And, O! the poor chil'en, and the baby—my old heart's been most broken for 'em, time and again. Tell 'em all to follow me—follow me! Give my love to mas'r, and dear good missis, and everybody in the place! Ye don't know. 'Pears like I love 'em all! I loves every creatur', everywar!—it's nothing *but* love! O, Mas'r George, what a thing 't is to be a Christian!

[LEGREE *looks in.*]

GEORGE: The old Satan! It's a comfort to think the devil will pay *him* for this some of these days!

UNCLE TOM: O, don't!—O, you mustn't! [*Grasping his hand.*] He's a poor mis'able critter. It's awful to think on't. O, if he only would repent, the Lord would forgive him now; but I'm feared he never will!

GEORGE: I hope he won't. I never want to see *him* in heaven!

UNCLE TOM: Hush, Mas'r George; it worries me! Don't feel so. He an't done me no real harm—only opened the gate of the kingdom for me—that's all! [*A pause.* UNCLE TOM *seems to faint. Draws several long sighs, raises his hand.*] Who—who—who—shall—separate—us from—the—the—*love of Christ?* LOVE! LOVE! LOVE OF CHRIST!

End

The Escape; or, A Leap for Freedom

Introduction

W illiam Wells Brown's play *The Escape* (1858) is a landmark in American literature for a number of reasons. The earliest extant play published in the U.S. by a Black American, it is an important response both to novelistic treatments of slavery like *Uncle Tom's Cabin* (1852) and to the phenomena surrounding "Tom shows," as well as to the broader world of minstrelsy. It also alerts us to the changing place of African Americans at the lectern and on the stage in the years just before the Civil War. Finally, it is, in itself, a rich play: though there are some cumbersome, melodramatic moments, there are also starkly humorous attacks on the hypocrisy of slaveholders.

Brown was easily one of the most important African Americans in the later phases of the abolitionist movement, though he never attained the stature of fellow fugitive slave Frederick Douglass. Born in Kentucky in about 1814 to an enslaved woman and a white man (thought to be the brother-in-law of his master), Brown was raised in the border city of St. Louis. Over the next two decades, he saw (and often suffered in) several different kinds of enslavement. His first master, a medical doctor, had the young Brown assist him, but his wife was troubled by Brown's light complexion—a reminder of the consistent potential for white male family members' infidelity and sexual violence. Brown was hired out to various taverns in St. Louis as well as to a tailor and to abolitionist martyr Elijah Lovejoy's printshop during Lovejoy's relatively brief residence in that city. Like many African Americans in St. Louis, he was also hired out to work a variety of jobs on the Mississippi river; easily the worst was with the slave-trader James Walker, with whom he made two trips to New Orleans, where he was forced to help Walker buy and sell other African Americans. Brown escaped from slavery on New Year's Day in 1834, added "Wells Brown" to his name (in honor of a Quaker who had helped him escape), and, though he was initially bound for Canada, settled in Buffalo, New York.

Brown was in close contact with members of the abolitionist movement (including groups that aided fugitive slaves) by the early 1840s, and by the late 1840s, he was becoming a popular figure on the abolitionist lecture circuit and had authored a slave narrative, the *Narrative of William W. Brown, a Fugitive Slave* (1847). But Brown was always at risk in the States; at one 1848 rally in Harwich, Massachusetts, he was beaten and almost killed at an open-air antislavery meeting. Still, he toured widely until leaving for England in July of 1849, where he hoped to gain further British support for the American abolitionist cause. When the Fugitive Slave Law was passed in 1850, Brown decided to stay in Britain, and he did not return to the U.S. until 1854, when friends secured his freedom. While in Britain, he gave literally hundreds of lectures, wrote for several British newspapers, and published both a travel book, *Three Years in Europe* (1852), and *Clotel; or, The President's Daughter; A Narrative of Slave Life in the United States* (1853). The latter was the first novel published by an African American and would be revised and republished in a number of forms during the next three decades.

When Brown returned to the United States, he also returned to the abolitionist lecture circuit, and, given his connections within the movement, it is very likely that he knew of Mary Webb's successful dramatic readings that featured Harriet Beecher Stowe's *The Christian Slave* (1855). Whether impelled directly by Webb's success or more generally by desires to respond to "Tom shows" and minstrelsy, or simply to enrich his repertoire—or a combination of these and other factors—Brown began to consider ways to incorporate drama into his lectures. In early 1856, he wrote a short play that is no longer extant and was never published, *Experience; or, How to Give a Northern Man a Backbone*. A satiric attack on Northern clergyman Nehemiah Adams, who had written an anti-Uncle Tom, pro-slavery report of his Southern travels, *A Southside View of Slavery* (1854), the play garnered notice throughout the abolitionist press. Like Webb's readings, though, it was not performed with a cast and sets; rather, Brown read all of the different characters' parts from the lectern. The success of *Experience* led to *The Escape* and reenergized Brown's already immensely successful lecturing career, which he continue for several years. Brown would extend his activist work through the Civil War (for which he helped recruit Black troops) and continue writing for much of his life—turning more and more to history, but also still revisiting his autobiography. He died on November 6, 1884, in Chelsea, Massachusetts.

As in much of Brown's work, there are certainly autobiographical echoes in *The Escape*—though some of them are surprising. The title "leap" dramatizes an event Brown was involved in in late 1836. The craven Dr. Gaines certainly echoes the profession and general philosophy of Brown's first master, and Mrs. Gaines, like Brown's master's wife, worries over the light-skinned slaves in her household. Both are expertly minced through Brown's sarcasm and, as the play continues, become the embodiment of the evils (both large and petty) inherent in the slave system. Dick Walker, the slavetrader, seems almost a direct reference to James Walker, the trader Brown was forced to work with, and most of the other white characters seem to be echoes or amalgams of figures Brown knew. Similarly, Brown notes that the well-spoken (if, at times, melodramatic) house slaves Glen and Melinda are based on real people; one wonders if Glen did not also have similarities with Brown himself.

The most curious character linked to Brown's own life, though, is the enslaved Cato, who, for some of the play, is a minstrel-show stereotype; indeed, scholar John Ernest has pointed out that Cato actually looks like a character in a particularly nasty minstrel piece from the 1850s, *The Quack Doctor*. But, like Brown, Cato serves as his master's assistant in the "practice of medicine," is—very much in the spirit of a "trickster" figure—quite smart, and is certainly savvy about his master's hypocrisy. Contemporary readers may find his revisions of minstrel song lyrics—which were sung to popular minstrel tunes—quite different in content and tenor from those included in this anthology and, more generally, from predominant theatrical depictions of carefree, happy slaves.

Given this richness—and the number of different characters and voices—Brown understandably told his contemporary Martin Delaney that he would rather give two lectures than one reading. Still, the positive response that Brown's audiences seem to have repeatedly given his dramatic readings certainly made them worthwhile for his immediate work for abolitionism. They were also a key step—not only in terms of authorship, but of a set of strategies for Black writers (and especially dramatists) to deal with minstrelsy—in setting up the work of the next generation of Black writers, most notably, fellow Bostonian Pauline Hopkins, who won an award named for Brown in the 1870s and whose play *Peculiar Sam* is included in this volume.

A Note on the Text

The text presented here is from the play's first edition, published by R.F. Wallcut of 21 Cornhill, Boston, in 1858. Brown's preface, which boldly notes that "the play, no doubt, abounds in defects, but as I was born in slavery, and never had a day's schooling in my life, I owe the public no apology for errors," is retained, as is a section of "Notices from the Press." The play's language remains understandable, with the usual caveats about dialect; most allusions are explained above.

For Further Reading

Brown, Josephine. *Biography of an American Bondsman, by His Daughter.* 1856. In *Two Biographies by African American Women,* ed. William L. Andrews. New York: Oxford University Press, 1991.

Brown, William Wells. *The Black Man, His Antecedents, His Genius, and His Achievements.* New York: Thomas Hamilton, 1863.

Clotel; or, The President's Daughter. London: Partridge and Oakey, 1853.

———. *My Southern Home; or, The South and Its People*. Boston: A.G. Brown, 1880.

———. *Narrative of William W. Brown, a Fugitive Slave*. Boston: American Anti-Slavery Society, 1847.

———. *Three Years in Europe; or, Places I Have Seen and People I Have Met*. London: Charles Gilpin, 1852.

Ernest, John. "Introduction." *The Escape; or, A Leap for Freedom* by William Wells Brown. Knoxville: University of Tennessee Press, 2001.

———. "The Reconstruction of Whiteness: William Wells Brown's *The Escape; or, A Leap for Freedom*." PMLA 113 (1998): 1108–1121.

Farrison, William Edward. *William Wells Brown: Author and Reformer*. Chicago: University of Chicago Press, 1969.

———. "*Phylon* Profile XVI: William Wells Brown." *Phylon* 9.1 (1948): 13–23.

Gilmore, Paul. " 'De Genewine Artekil': William Wells Brown, Blackface Minstrelsy, and Abolitionism." *American Literature* 69.4 (1997): 743–780.

The Escape; or, A Leap for Freedom

"Look on this picture, and on this."—HAMLET

Author's Preface

T his play was written for my own amusement, and not with the remotest thought that it would ever be seen by the public eye. I read it privately, however, to a circle of my friends, and through them was invited to read it before a Literary Society. Since then, the Drama has been given in various parts of the country. By the earnest solicitation of some in whose judgment I have the greatest confidence, I now present it in a printed form to the public. As I never aspired to be a dramatist, I ask no favor for it, and have little or no solicitude for its fate. If it is not readable, no word of mine can make it so; if it is, to ask favor for it would be needless.

The main features in the Drama are true. Glen and Melinda are actual characters, and still reside in Canada. Many of the incidents were drawn from my own experience of eighteen years at the South. The marriage ceremony, as performed in the second act, is still adhered to in many of the Southern States, especially in the farming districts.

The ignorance of the slave, as seen in the case of "Big Sally," is common wherever chattel slavery exists. The difficulties created in the domestic circle by the presence of beautiful slave women, as found in Dr. Gaines's family, is well understood by all who have ever visited the valley of the Mississippi.

The play, no doubt, abounds in defects, but as I was born in slavery, and never had a day's schooling in my life, I owe the public no apology for errors.

W.W.B.

CHARACTERS REPRESENTED

DR. GAINES,	*proprietor of the farm at Muddy Creek*
REV. JOHN PINCHEN,	*a clergyman*
DICK WALKER,	*a slave speculator*
MR. WILDMARSH,	*neighbor to Dr. Gaines*
MAJOR MOORE,	*a friend of Dr. Gaines*
MR. WHITE,	*a citizen of Massachusetts*
BILL JENNINGS,	*a slave speculator*
JACOB SCRAGG,	*overseer to Dr. Gaines*
MRS. GAINES,	*wife of Dr. Gaines*
MR. *and* MRS. NEAL, *and* DAUGHTER,	*Quakers, in Ohio*
THOMAS,	*Mr. Neal's hired man*
GLEN,	*slave of Mr. Hamilton, brother-in-law of Dr. Gaines*
CATO, SAM, SAMPEY, MELINDA, DOLLY, SUSAN, *and* BIG SALLY,	*slaves of* DR. GAINES
PETE, NED, *and* BILL,	*slaves.*
OFFICERS, LOUNGERS, BARKEEPER, &C.	

ACT I, SCENE I

[*A Sitting-Room.* MRS. GAINES, *looking at some drawings—* SAMPEY, *a white slave, stands behind the lady's chair.*]

[*Enter* DR. GAINES, R.]

DR. GAINES: Well, my dear, my practice is steadily increasing. I forgot to tell you that neighbor Wyman engaged me yesterday as his family physician; and I hope that the fever and ague, which is now taking hold of the people, will give me more patients. I see by the New Orleans papers that the yellow fever is raging there to a fearful extent. Men of my profession are reaping a harvest in that section this year. I would that we could have a touch of the yellow fever here, for I think I could invent a medicine that would cure it. But the yellow fever is a luxury that we medical men in this climate can't expect to enjoy, yet we may hope for the cholera.

MRS. GAINES: Yes, I would be glad to see it more sickly here, so that your business might prosper. But we are always unfortunate. Every body here seems to be in good health, and I am afraid that they'll keep so. However, we must hope for the best. We must trust in the Lord. Providence may possibly send some disease amongst us for our benefit.

[*Enter* CATO, R.]

CATO: Mr. Campbell is at de door, massa.

DR. GAINES: Ask him in, Cato.

[*Enter* MR. CAMPBELL, R.]

DR. GAINES: Good morning, Mr. Campbell. Be seated.

MR. CAMPBELL: Good morning, doctor. The same to you, Mrs. Gaines. Fine morning, this.

MRS. GAINES: Yes, sir; beautiful day.

MR. CAMPBELL: Well, doctor, I've come to engage you for my family physician. I am tired of Dr. Jones. I've lost another very valuable nigger under his treatment; and, as my old mother used to say, "change of pastures makes fat calves."

DR. GAINES: I shall be most happy to become your doctor. Of course, you want me to attend to your niggers, as well as to your family?

MR. CAMPBELL: Certainly, sir. I have twenty-three servants. What will you charge me by the year?

DR. GAINES: Of course, you'll do as my other patients do, send your servants to me when they are sick, if able to walk?

MR. CAMPBELL: Oh, yes; I always do that.

DR. GAINES: Then I suppose I'll have to lump it, and say $500 per annum.

MR. CAMPBELL: Well, then, we'll consider that matter settled; and as two of the boys are sick, I'll send them over. So I'll bid you good day, doctor. I would be glad if you would come over some time, and bring Mrs. Gaines with you.

DR. GAINES: Yes, I will; and shall be glad if you will pay us a visit, and bring with you Mrs. Campbell. Come over and spend the day.

MR. CAMPBELL: I will. Good morning, doctor.

[*Exit* MR. CAMPBELL, R.]

DR. GAINES: There, my dear, what do you think of that? Five hundred dollars more added to our income. That's patronage worth having! And I am glad to get all the negroes I can to doctor, for Cato is becoming very useful to me in the shop. He can bleed, pull teeth, and do almost any thing that the blacks require. He can put up medicine as well as any one. A valuable boy, Cato!

MRS. GAINES: But why did you ask Mr. Campbell to visit you, and to bring his wife? I am sure I could never consent to associate with her, for I understand that she was the daughter of a tanner. You must remember, my dear, that I was born with a silver spoon in my mouth. The blood of the Wyleys runs in my veins. I am surprised that you should ask him to visit you at all; you should have known better.

DR. GAINES: Oh, I did not mean for him to visit me. I only invited him for the sake of compliments, and I think he so understood it; for I should be far from wishing you to associate with Mrs. Campbell. I don't forget, my dear, the family you were raised in, nor do I overlook my own family. My father, you know, fought by the side of Washington, and I hope some day to have a handle to my own name. I am certain Providence intended me for something higher than a medical man. Ah! by-the-by, I had forgotten that I have a couple of patients to visit this morning. I must go at once.

[*Exit* DR. GAINES, R.]

[*Enter* HANNAH, L.]

MRS GAINES: Go, Hannah, and tell Dolly to kill a couple of fat pullets, and to put the biscuit to rise. I expect brother Pinchen here this afternoon, and I want every thing in order. Hannah, Hannah, tell Melinda to come here.

[*Exit* HANNAH, L.]

We mistresses do have a hard time in this world; I don't see why the Lord should have imposed such heavy duties on us poor mortals. Well, it can't last always. I long to leave this wicked world, and go home to glory.

[*Enter* MELINDA.]

I am to have company this afternoon, Melinda. I expect brother Pinchen here, and I want every thing in order. Go and get one of my new caps, with the lace border, and get out my scolloped-bottomed dimity petticoat, and when you go out, tell Hannah to clean the white-handled knives, and see that not a speck is on them; for I want every thing as it should be while brother Pinchen is here.

[*Exit* MRS. GAINES, L., HANNAH, R.]

SCENE II

[*Doctor's shop—Cato making pills*]

[*Enter* DR. GAINES, L.]

DR. GAINES: Well, Cato, have you made the batch of ointment that I ordered?

CATO: Yes, massa; I dun made de intment, an' now I is making the bread pills. De tater pills is up on the top shelf.

DR. GAINES: I am going out to see some patients. If any gentlemen call, tell them I shall be in this afternoon. If any servants come, you attend to them. I expect two of Mr. Campbell's boys over. You see to them. Feel their pulse, look at their tongues, bleed them, and give them each a dose of calomel. Tell them to drink no cold water, and to take nothing but water gruel.

CATO: Yes, massa; I'll tend to 'em.

[*Exit* DR. GAINES, L.]

CATO: I allers knowed I was a doctor, an' now de ole boss has put me at it, I muss change my coat. Ef any niggers comes in, I wants to look suspectable. Dis jacket don't suit a doctor; I'll change it. [*Exit* CATO—*immediately returning in a long coat.*] Ah! now I looks like a doctor. Now I can bleed, pull teef, or cut off a leg. Oh! well, well, ef I aint put de pill stuff an' de intment stuff togedder. By golly, dat ole cuss will be mad when he finds it out, won't he? Nebber mind, I'll make it up in pills, and when de flour is on dem, he won't know what's in 'em; an' I'll make some new intment. Ah! yonder comes Mr. Campbell's Pete an' Ned; dems de ones massa sed was comin'. I'll see ef I looks right. [*Goes to the looking-glass and views himself.*] I em some punkins, ain't I? [*Knock at the door.*] Come in.

[*Enter* PETE *and* NED, R.]

380

PETE: Whar is de doctor?

CATO: Here I is; don't you see me?

PETE: But whar is de ole boss?

CATO: Dat's none you business. I dun tole you dat I is de doctor, an dat's enuff.

NED: Oh! do tell us whar de doctor is. I is almos dead. Oh me! oh dear me! I is so sick. [*Horrible faces.*]

PETE: Yes, do tell us; we don't want to stan here foolin'.

CATO: I tells you again dat I is de doctor. I larn de trade under massa.

NED: Oh! well, den, give me somethin' to stop dis pain. Oh dear me! I shall die. [*He tries to vomit, but can't—ugly faces.*]

CATO: Let me feel your pulse. Now put out your tongue. You is berry sick. Ef you don't mine, you'll die. Come out in de shed, an' I'll bleed you. [*Exit all—re-enter.*]

CATO: Dar, now take dese pills, two in de mornin' and two at night, and ef you don't feel better, double de dose. Now, Mr. Pete, what's de matter wid you?

PETE: I is got de cole chills, an' has a fever in de night.

CATO: Come out, an' I'll bleed you. [*Exit all—re-enter.*] Now take dese pills, two in de mornin' and two at night, an' ef dey don't help you, double de dose. Ah! I like to forget to feel your pulse and look at your tongue. Put out your tongue. [*Feels his pulse.*] Yes, I tells by de feel ob your pulse dat I is gib you de right pills.

[*Enter* MR. PARKER'S BILL, L.]

CATO: What you come in dat door widout knockin' for?

BILL: My toof ache so, I didn't tink to knock. Oh, my toof! my toof! Whar is de doctor?

CATO: Here I is; don't you see me?

BILL: What! you de doctor, you brack cuss! You looks like a doctor! Oh, my toof! my toof! Whar is de doctor?

CATO: I tells you I is de doctor. Ef you don't believe me, ax dese men. I can pull your toof in a minnit.

BILL: Well, den, pull it out. Oh, my toof! how it aches! Oh, my toof! [*Cato gets the rusty turnkeys.*]

CATO: Now lay down on your back.

BILL: What for?

CATO: Dat's de way massa does.

BILL: Oh, my toof! Well, den, come on. [*Lies down,* CATO *gets astrad-dle of Bill's breast, puts the turnkeys on the wrong tooth, and pulls*— BILL *kicks, and cries out.*]—Oh, do stop! Oh! oh! oh! [CATO *pulls the wrong tooth*— BILL *jumps up.*]

CATO: Dar, now, I tole you I could pull your toof for you.

BILL: Oh, dear me! Oh, it aches yet! Oh me! Oh, Lor-e-massy! You dun pull de wrong toof. Drat your skin! ef I don't pay you for this, you brack cuss! [*They fight, and turn over table, chairs and bench*— PETE *and* NED *look on.*]

[*Enter* DR. GAINES, R.]

DR. GAINES: Why, dear me, what's the matter? What's all this about? I'll teach you a lesson, that I will. [*The doctor goes at them with his cane.*]

CATO: Oh, massa! he's to blame, sir. He's to blame, he struck me fuss.

BILL: No, sir; he's to blame; he pull de wrong toof. Oh, my toof! oh, my toof!

DR. GAINES: Let me see your tooth. Open your mouth. As I live, you've taken out the wrong tooth. I am amazed. I'll whip you for this; I'll whip you well. You're a pretty doctor. Now lie down, Bill, and let him take out the right tooth; and if he makes a mistake this time, I'll cowhide him well. Lie down, Bill. [BILL *lies down, and* CATO *pulls the tooth.*] There now, why didn't you do that in the first place?

CATO: He wouldn't hole still, sir.

BILL: He lies, sir. I did hole still.

DR. GAINES: Now go home, boys; go home.

[*Exit* PETE, NED *and* BILL, L.]

DR. GAINES: You've made a pretty muss of it, in my absence. Look at the table! Never mind, Cato; I'll whip you well for this conduct of yours to-day. Go to work now, and clear up the office. [*Exit* DR. GAINES, R.]

CATO: Confound dat nigger! I wish he was in Ginny. He bite my finger and scratch my face. But didn't I give it to him? Well, den, I reckon I did. [*He goes to the mirror, and discovers that his coat is torn—weeps.*] Oh, dear me! Oh, my coat—my coat is tore! Dat nigger has tore my coat. [*He gets angry, and rushes about the room frantic.*] Cuss dat nigger! Ef I could lay my hands on him, I'd tare him all to pieces,—dat I would. An' de ole boss hit me wid his cane after dat nigger tore my coat. By golly, I wants to fight somebody. Ef ole massa should come in now, I'd fight him. [*Rolls up his sleeves.*] Let 'em come now, ef dey dare—ole massa, or any body else; I'm ready for 'em.

[*Enter* DR. GAINES, R.]

DR. GAINES: What's all this noise here?

CATO: Nuffin', sir; only jess I is puttin' things to rights, as you tole me. I didn't hear any noise except de rats.

DR. GAINES: Make haste, and come in; I want you to go to town.

[*Exit* DR. GAINES, R.]

CATO: By golly, de ole boss like to cotch me dat time, didn't he? But wasn't I mad? When I is mad, nobody can do nuffin' wid me. But here's my coat, tore to pieces. Cuss dat nigger! [*Weeps.*] Oh, my coat! oh, my coat! I rudder he had broke my head den to tore my coat. Drat dat nigger! Ef he ever comes here agin, I'll pull out every toof he's got in his head—dat I will.

[*Exit,* R.]

SCENE III

[*A Room in the Quarters*]

[*Enter* GLEN, L.]

GLEN: How slowly the time passes away. I've been waiting here two hours, and Melinda has not yet come. What keeps her, I cannot tell. I waited long and late for her last night, and when she approached, I sprang to my feet, caught her in my arms, pressed her to my heart, and kissed away the tears from her moistened cheeks. She placed her trembling hand in mine, and said, "Glen, I am yours; I will never be the wife of another." I clasped her to my bosom, and called God to witness that I would ever regard her as my wife. Old Uncle Joseph joined us in holy wedlock by moonlight; that was the only marriage ceremony. I look upon the vow as ever binding on me, for I am sure that a just God will sanction our union in heaven. Still, this man, who claims Melinda as his property, is unwilling for me to marry the woman of my choice, because he wants her himself. But he shall not have her. What he will say when he finds that we are married, I cannot tell; but I am determined to protect my wife or die. Ah! here comes Melinda.

[*Enter* MELINDA, R.]

I am glad to see you, Melinda. I've been waiting long, and feared you would not come. Ah! in tears again?

MELINDA: Glen, you are always thinking I am in tears. But what did master say to-day?

GLEN: He again forbade our union.

MELINDA: Indeed! Can he be so cruel?

GLEN: Yes, he can be just so cruel.

MELINDA: Alas! alas! how unfeeling and heartless! But did you appeal to his generosity?

GLEN: Yes, I did; I used all the persuasive powers that I was master of, but to no purpose; he was inflexible. He even offered me a new suit of clothes, if I would give you up; and when I told

him that I could not, he said he would flog me to death if I
ever spoke to you again.

MELINDA: And what did you say to him?

GLEN: I answered, that, while I loved life better than death, even
life itself could not tempt me to consent to a separation that
would make life an unchanging curse. Oh, I would kill myself,
Melinda, if I thought that, for the sake of life, I could consent
to your degradation. No, Melinda, I can die, but shall never
live to see you the mistress of another man. But, my dear girl,
I have a secret to tell you, and no one must know it but you.
I will go out and see that no person is within hearing. I will
be back soon.

[*Exit* GLEN, L.]

MELINDA: It is often said that the darkest hour of the night precedes
the dawn. It is ever thus with the vicissitudes of human suffering. After the soul has reached the lowest depths of despair,
and can no deeper plunge amid its rolling, foetid shades, then
the reactionary forces of man's nature begin to operate, resolu-
tion takes the place of despondency, energy succeeds instead
of apathy, and an upward tendency is felt and exhibited. Men
then hope against power, and smile in defiance of despair. I
shall never forget when first I saw Glen. It is now more than a
year since he came here with his master, Mr. Hamilton. It was
a glorious moonlight night in autumn. The wide and fruitful
face of nature was silent and buried in repose. The tall trees
on the borders of Muddy Creek waved their leafy branches
in the breeze, which was wafted from afar, refreshing over hill
and vale, over the rippling water, and the waving corn and
wheat fields. The starry sky was studded over with a few light,
flitting clouds, while the moon, as if rejoicing to witness the
meeting of two hearts that should be cemented by the purest
love, sailed triumphantly along among the shifting vapors. Oh,
how happy I have been in my acquaintance with Glen! That he
loves me, I do well believe it; that I love him, it is most true.
Oh, how I would that those who think the slave incapable

of the finer feelings, could only see our hearts, and learn our thoughts,—thoughts that we dare not utter in the presence of our masters! But I fear that Glen will be separated from me, for there is nothing too base and mean for master to do, for the purpose of getting me entirely in his power. But, thanks to Heaven, he does not own Glen, and therefore cannot sell him. Yet he might purchase him from his brother-in-law, so as to send him out of the way. But here comes my husband.

[*Enter* GLEN, L.]

GLEN: I've been as far as the overseer's house, and all is quiet. Now, Melinda, as you are my wife, I will confide to you a secret. I've long been thinking of making my escape to Canada, and taking you with me. It is true that I don't belong to your master, but he might buy me from Hamilton, and then sell me out of the neighborhood.

MELINDA: But we could never succeed in the attempt to escape.

GLEN: We will make the trial, and show that we at least deserve success. There is a slave trader expected here next week, and DR. GAINES would sell you at once if he knew that we were married. We must get ready and start, and if we can pass the Ohio river, we'll be safe on the road to Canada.

[*Exit,* R.]

SCENE IV

[*Dining-Room.* REV. MR. PINCHEN *giving* MRS. GAINES *an account of his experience as a minister*—HANNAH *clearing away the breakfast table*—SAMPEY *standing behind* MRS. GAINES' *chair.*]

MRS. GAINES: Now, do give me more of your experience, brother Pinchen. It always does my soul good to hear religious experience. It draws me nearer and nearer to the Lord's side. I do love to hear good news from God's people.

MR PINCHEN: Well, sister Gaines, I've had great opportunities in my time to study the heart of man. I've attended a great many camp-meetings, revival meetings, protracted meetings, and death-bed scenes, and I am satisfied, sister Gaines, that the heart of man is full of sin, and desperately wicked. This is a wicked world, sister Gaines, a wicked world.

MRS. GAINES: Were you ever in Arkansas, brother Pinchen? I've been told that the people out there are very ungodly.

MR. PINCHEN: Oh, yes, sister Gaines. I once spent a year at Little Rock, and preached in all the towns round about there; and I found some hard cases out there, I can tell you. I was once spending a week in a district where there were a great many horse thieves, and one night, somebody stole my pony. Well, I knowed it was no use to make a fuss, so I told brother Tarbox to say nothing about it, and I'd get my horse by preaching God's everlasting gospel; for I had faith in the truth, and knowed that my Savior would not let me lose my pony. So the next Sunday I preached on horse-stealing, and told the brethren to come up in the evenin' with their hearts filled with the grace of God. So that night the house was crammed brim full with anxious souls, panting for the bread of life. Brother Bingham opened with prayer, and brother Tarbox followed, and I saw right off that we were gwine to have a blessed time. After I got 'em pretty well warmed up, I jumped on to one of the seats, stretched out my hands, and said, "I know who stole my pony; I've found out; and you are in here tryin' to make people believe that you've got religion; but you ain't got it. And if you don't take my horse back to brother Tarbox's pasture this very night, I'll tell your name right out in meetin' to-morrow night. Take my pony back, you vile and wretched sinner, and come up here and give your heart to God." So the next mornin', I went out to brother Tarbox's pasture, and sure enough, there was my bob-tail pony. Yes, sister Gaines, there he was, safe and sound. Ha, ha, ha.

MRS. GAINES: Oh, how interesting, and how fortunate for you to get your pony! And what power there is in the gospel! God's children are very lucky. Oh, it is so sweet to sit here and listen to such good news from God's people! You Hannah, what are you standing there listening for, and neglecting your work? Never mind, my lady, I'll whip you well when I am done here. Go at your work this moment, you lazy huzzy! Never mind, I'll whip you well. [*Aside.*] Come, do go on, brother Pinchen, with your godly conversation. It is so sweet! It draws me nearer and nearer to the Lord's side.

MR. PINCHEN: Well, sister Gaines, I've had some mighty queer dreams in my time, that I have. You see, one night I dreamed that I was dead and in heaven, and such a place I never saw before. As soon as I entered the gates of the celestial empire, I saw many old and familiar faces that I had seen before. The first person that I saw was good old Elder Pike, the preacher that first called my attention to religion. The next person I saw was Deacon Billings, my first wife's father, and then I saw a host of godly faces. Why, sister Gaines, you knowed Elder Goosbee, didn't you?

MRS. GAINES: Why, yes; did you see him there? He married me to my first husband.

MR. PINCHEN: Oh, yes, sister Gaines, I saw the old Elder, and he looked for all the world as if he had just come out of a revival meetin'.

MRS. GAINES: Did you see my first husband there, brother Pinchen?

MR. PINCHEN: No, sister Gaines, I didn't see brother Pepper there; but I've no doubt but that brother Pepper was there.

MRS. GAINES: Well, I don't know; I have my doubts. He was not the happiest man in the world. He was always borrowing trouble about something or another. Still, I saw some happy moments with Mr. Pepper. I was happy when I made his acquaintance, happy during our courtship, happy a while after our marriage, and happy when he died. [*Weeps.*]

HANNAH: Massa Pinchen, did you see my ole man Ben up dar in hebben?

MR. PINCHEN: No, Hannah; I didn't go amongst the niggers.

MRS. GAINES: No, of course brother Pinchen didn't go among the
blacks. What are you asking questions for? Never mind, my
lady, I'll whip you well when I'm done here. I'll skin you from
head to foot. [*Aside.*] Do go on with your heavenly conversation, brother Pinchen; it does my very soul good. This is
indeed a precious moment for me. I do love to hear of Christ
and Him crucified.

MR. PINCHEN: Well, sister Gaines, I promised sister Daniels that I'd
come over and see her this morning, and have a little season
of prayer with her, and I suppose I must go. I'll tell you more
of my religious experience when I return.

MRS. GAINES: If you must go, then I'll have to let you; but before you
do, I wish to get your advice upon a little matter that concerns
Hannah. Last week, Hannah stole a goose, killed it, cooked
it, and she and her man Sam had a fine time eating the goose;
and her master and I would never have known a word about
it, if it had not been for Cato, a faithful servant, who told his
master. And then, you see, Hannah had to be severely whipped
before she'd confess that she stole the goose. Next Sabbath is
sacrament day, and I want to know if you think that Hannah
is fit to go to the Lord's supper after stealing the goose.

MR. PINCHEN: Well, sister Gaines, that depends on circumstances. If
Hannah has confessed that she stole the goose, and has been
sufficiently whipped, and has begged her master's pardon,
and begged your pardon, and thinks she'll never do the like
again, why then I suppose she can go to the Lord's supper;
for "While the lamp holds out to burn, the vilest sinner may
return." But she must be sure that she has repented, and won't
steal any more.

MRS. GAINES: Now, Hannah, do you hear that? For my own part,
I don't think she's fit to go to the Lord's supper, for she had
no occasion to steal the goose. We give our niggers plenty of
good wholesome food. They have a full run to the meal tub,
meat once a fortnight, and all the sour milk about the place,

and I'm sure that's enough for any one. I do think that our niggers are the most ungrateful creatures in the world, that I do. They aggravate my life out of me.

HANNAH: I know, missis, dat I steal de goose, and massa whip me for it, and I confess it, and I is sorry for it. But, missis, I is gwine to de Lord's supper, next Sunday, kase I ain't agwine to turn my back on my bressed Lord an' Massa for no old tough goose, dat I ain't. [*Weeps.*]

MR. PINCHEN: Well, sister Gaines, I suppose I must go over and see sister Daniels; she'll be waiting for me.

[*Exit* MR. PINCHEN, M.D.]

MRS. GAINES: Now, Hannah, brother Pinchen is gone, do you get the cowhide and follow me to the cellar, and I'll whip you well for aggravating me as you have to-day. It seems as if I can never sit down to take a little comfort with the Lord, without you crossing me. The devil always puts it into your head to disturb me, just when I am trying to serve the Lord. I've no doubt but that I'll miss going to heaven on your account. But I'll whip you well before I leave this world, that I will. Get the cowhide and follow me to the cellar.

[*Exit* MRS. GAINES *and* HANNAH, R.]

ACT II, SCENE I

[*Parlor.* DR. GAINES *at a table, letters and papers before him.*]

[*Enter* SAMPEY, L.]

SAMPEY: Dar's a gemman at de doe, massa, dat wants to see you, seer.

DR. GAINES: Ask him to walk in, Sampey.

[*Exit* SAMPEY, L.]

[*Enter* WALKER.]

WALKER: Why, how do you do, Dr. Gaines? I em glad to see you, I'll swear.

DR. GAINES: How do you do, Mr. Walker? I did not expect to see you up here so soon. What has hurried you?

WALKER: Well, you see, doctor, I comes when I em not expected. The price of niggers is up, and I em gwine to take advantage of the times. Now, doctor, ef you've got any niggers that you wants to sell, I em your man. I am paying the highest price of any body in the market. I pay cash down, and no grumblin'.

DR. GAINES: I don't know that I want to sell any of my people now. Still, I've got to make up a little money next month, to pay in bank; and another thing, the doctors say that we are likely to have a touch of the cholera this summer, and if that's the case, I suppose I had better turn as many of my slaves into cash as I can.

WALKER: Yes, Doctor, that is very true. The cholera is death on slaves, and a thousand dollars in your pocket is a great deal better than a nigger in the field, with cholera at his heels. Why, who is that coming up the lane? It's Mr. Wildmarsh, as I live! Jest the very man I wants to see.

[*Enter* MR. WILDMARSH.]

Why, how do you do, Squire? I was jest a thinkin' about you.

WILDMARSH: How are you, Mr. Walker! and how are you, doctor? I am glad to see you both looking so well. You seem in remarkably good health, doctor?

DR. GAINES: Yes, Squire, I was never in the enjoyment of better health. I hope you left all well at Licking?

WILDMARSH: Yes, I thank you. And now, Mr. Walker, how goes times with you?

WALKER: Well, you see, Squire, I em in good spirits. The price of niggers is up in the market, and I am lookin' out for bargains; and I was jest intendin' to come over to Lickin' to see you, to see if you had any niggers to sell. But it seems as ef the Lord knowed that I wanted to see you, and directed your steps over here. Now, Squire, ef you've got any niggers you wants to sell, I em your man. I am payin' the highest cash price of any body in the market. Now's your time, Squire.

WILDMARSH: No, I don't think I want to sell any of my slaves now. I sold a very valuable gal to Mr. Haskins last week. I tell you, she was a smart one. I got eighteen hundred dollars for her.

WALKER: Why, Squire, how you do talk! Eighteen hundred dollars for one gal? She must have been a screamer to bring that price. What sort of a lookin' critter was she? I should like to have bought her.

WILDMARSH: She was a little of the smartest gal I've ever raised; that she was.

WALKER: Then she was your own raising, was she?

WILDMARSH: Oh, yes; she was raised on my place, and if I could have kept her three or four years longer, and taken her to the market myself, I am sure I could have sold her for three thousand dollars. But you see, Mr. Walker, my wife got a little jealous, and you know jealousy sets the women's heads a teetering, and so I had to sell the gal. She's got straight hair, blue eyes, prominent features, and is almost white. Haskins will make a spec, and no mistake.

WALKER: Why, Squire, was she that pretty little gal that I saw on your knee the day that your wife was gone, when I was at your place three years ago?

WILDMARSH: Yes, the same.

WALKER: Well, now, Squire, I thought that was your daughter; she looked mightily like you. She was your daughter, wasn't she? You need not be ashamed to own it to me, for I am mum upon such matters.

WILDMARSH: You know, Mr. Walker, that people will talk, and when they talk, they say a great deal; and people did talk, and many said the gal was my daughter; and you know we can't help people's talking. But here comes the Rev. Mr. Pinchen; I didn't know that he was in the neighborhood.

WALKER: It is Mr. Pinchen, as I live; jest the very man I wants to see.

[*Enter* MR. PINCHEN, R.]

Why, how do you do, Mr. Pinchen? What in the name of Jehu brings you down here to Muddy Creek? Any camp-meetins, revival meetins, death-bed scenes, or any thing else in your line going on down here? How is religion prosperin' now, Mr. Pinchen? I always like to hear about religion.

MR. PINCHEN: Well, Mr. Walker, the Lord's work is in good condition every where now. I tell you, Mr. Walker, I've been in the gospel ministry these thirteen years, and I am satisfied that the heart of man is full of sin and desperately wicked. This is a wicked world, Mr. Walker, a wicked world, and we ought all of us to have religion. Religion is a good thing to live by, and we all want it when we die. Yes, sir, when the great trumpet blows, we ought to be ready. And a man in your business of buying and selling slaves needs religion more than any body else, for it makes you treat your people as you should. Now, there is Mr. Haskins,—he is a slave-trader, like yourself. Well, I converted him. Before he got religion, he was one of the worst men to his niggers I ever saw; his heart was as hard as stone. But religion has made his heart as soft as a piece of cotton. Before I converted him, he would sell husbands from their wives, and seem to take delight in it; but now he won't sell a man from his wife, if he can get any one to buy both of them together. I tell you, sir, religion has done a wonderful work for him.

WALKER: I know, Mr. Pinchen, that I ought to have religion, and I feel that I am a great sinner; and whenever I get with good pious people like you and the doctor, and Mr. Wildmarsh, it always makes me feel that I am a desperate sinner. I feel it the more, because I've got a religious turn of mind. I know that I would be happier with religion, and the first spare time I get, I am going to try to get it. I'll go to a protracted meeting, and I won't stop till I get religion. Yes, I'll scuffle with the Lord till I gets forgiven. But it always makes me feel bad to talk about religion, so I'll change the subject. Now, doctor, what about them thar niggers you thought you could sell me?

DR. GAINES: I'll see my wife, Mr. Walker, and if she is willing to part with Hannah, I'll sell you Sam and his wife, Hannah. Ah! here comes my wife; I'll mention it.

[*Enter* MRS. GAINES, L.]

Ah! my dear, I am glad you've come. I was just telling Mr. Walker, that if you were willing to part with Hannah, I'd sell him Sam and Hannah.

MRS. GAINES: Now, Dr. Gaines, I am astonished and surprised that you should think of such a thing. You know what trouble I've had in training up Hannah for a house servant, and now that I've got her so that she knows my ways, you want to sell her. Hav n't you niggers enough on the plantation to sell, without selling the servants from under my very nose?

DR. GAINES: Oh, yes, my dear; but I can spare Sam, and I don't like to separate him from his wife; and I thought if you could let Hannah go, I'd sell them both. I don't like to separate husbands from their wives.

MRS. GAINES: Now, gentlemen, that's just the way with my husband. He thinks more about the welfare and comfort of his slaves, than he does of himself or his family. I am sure you need not feel so bad at the thought of separating Sam from Hannah. They've only been married eight months, and their attachment can't be very strong in that short time. Indeed, I shall be glad if you do sell Sam, for then I'll make Hannah *jump the broomstick* with Cato, and I'll have them both here under my eye. I never will again let one of my house servants marry a field hand—never! For when night comes on, the servants are off to the quarters, and I have to holler and holler enough to split my throat before I can make them hear. And another thing: I want you to sell Melinda. I don't intend to keep that mulatto wench about the house any longer.

DR. GAINES: My dear, I'll sell any servant from the place to suit you, except Melinda. I can't think of selling her—I can't think of it.

MRS. GAINES: I tell you that Melinda shall leave this house, or I'll go. There, now you have it. I've had my life tormented out of me by the presence of that yellow wench, and I'll stand it no longer. I know you love her more than you do me, and I'll—I'll—I'll write—write to my father. [*Weeps.*]

[*Exit* MRS. GAINES, L.]

WALKER: Why, doctor, your wife's a screamer, ain't she? Ha, ha, ha. Why, doctor, she's got a tongue of her own, ain't she? Why, doctor, it was only last week that I thought of getting a wife myself; but your wife has skeered the idea out of my head. Now, doctor, if you wants to sell the gal, I'll buy her. Husband and wife ought to be on good terms, and your wife won't feel well till the gal is gone. Now, I'll pay you all she's worth, if you wants to sell.

DR. GAINES: No, Mr. Walker; the girl my wife spoke of is not for sale. My wife does not mean what she says; she's only a little jealous. I'll get brother Pinchen to talk to her, and get her mind turned upon religious matters, and then she'll forget it. She's only a little jealous.

WALKER: I tell you what, doctor, ef you call that a little jealous, I'd like to know what's a heap. I tell you, it will take something more than religion to set your wife right. You had better sell me the gal; I'll pay you cash down, and no grumblin'.

DR. GAINES: The girl is not for sale, Mr. Walker; but if you want two good, able-bodied servants, I'll I sell you Sam and Big Sally. Sam is trustworthy, and Sally is worth her weight in gold for rough usage.

WALKER: Well, doctor, I'll go out and take a look at 'em, for I never buys slaves without examining them well, because they are sometimes injured by over-work or under-feedin'. I don't say that is the case with yours, for I don't believe it is; but as I sell on honor, I must buy on honor.

DR. GAINES: Walk out, sir, and you can examine them to your heart's content. Walk right out, sir.

SCENE II

[*View in front of the Great House. Examination of* SAM *and*
BIG SALLY.—DR. GAINES, WILDMARSH, MR. PINCHEN *and*
WALKER *present.*]

WALKER: Well, my boy, what's your name?

SAM: Sam, sir, is my name.

WALKER: How old are you, Sam?

SAM: Ef I live to see next corn plantin' time, I'll be 27, or 30, or 35,
or 40—I don't know which, sir.

WALKER: Ha, ha, ha. Well, doctor, this is rather a green boy. Well,
mer feller, are you sound?

SAM: Yes, sir, I spec I is.

WALKER: Open your mouth and let me see your teeth. I allers judge
a nigger's age by his teeth, same as I dose a hoss. Ah! pretty
good set of grinders. Have you got a good appetite?

SAM: Yes, sir.

WALKER: Can you eat your allowance?

SAM: Yes, sir, when I can get it.

WALKER: Get out on the floor and dance; I want to see if you are
supple.

SAM: I don't like to dance; I is got religion.

WALKER: Oh, ho! you've got religion, have you? That's so much the
better. I likes to deal in the gospel. I think he'll suit me. Now,
mer gal, what's your name?

SALLY: I is Big Sally, sir.

WALKER: How old are you, Sally?

SALLY: I don't know, sir; but I heard once dat I was born at sweet
pertater diggin' time.

WALKER: Ha, ha, ha. Don't know how old you are! Do you know
who made you?

SALLY: I hev heard who it was in de Bible dat made me, but I dun
forget de gentman's name.

WALKER: Ha, ha, ha. Well, doctor, this is the greenest lot of niggers
I've seen for some time. Well, what do you ask for them?

DR. GAINES: You may have Sam for \$1000, and Sally for \$900. They are worth all I ask for them. You know I never banter, Mr. Walker. There they are; you can take them at that price, or let them alone, just as you please.

WALKER: Well, doctor, I reckon I'll take 'em; but it's all they are worth. I'll put the handcuffs on 'em, and then I'll pay you. I likes to go accordin' to Scripter. Scripter says ef eatin' meat will offend your brother, you must quit it; and I say, ef leavin' your slaves without the handcuffs will make 'em run away, you must put the handcuffs on 'em. Now, Sam, don't you and Sally cry. I am of a tender heart, and it allers makes me feel bad to see people cryin'. Don't cry, and the first place I get to, I'll buy each of you a great big *ginger cake,*—that I will. Now, Mr. Pinchen, I wish you were going down the river. I'd like to have your company; for I allers likes the company of preachers.

MR PINCHEN: Well, Mr. Walker, I would be much pleased to go down the river with you, but it's too early for me. I expect to go to Natchez in four or five weeks, to attend a camp-meetin', and if you were going down then, I'd like it. What kind of niggers sells best in the Orleans market, Mr. Walker?

WALKER: Why, field hands. Did you think of goin' in the trade?

MR. PINCHEN: Oh, no; only it's a long ways down to Natchez, and I thought I'd just buy five or six niggers, and take 'em down and sell 'em to pay my travellin' expenses. I only want to clear my way.

SCENE III

[*Sitting-Room—Table and Rocking-Chair.*]

[*Enter* MRS. GAINES, R., *followed by* SAMPEY.]

MRS. GAINES: I do wish your master would come; I want supper. Run to the gate, Sampey, and see if he is coming.

[*Exit* SAMPEY, L.]

That man is enough to break my heart. The patience of an
angel could not stand it.

[*Enter* SAMPEY, L.]

SAMPEY: Yes, missis, master is coming.

[*Enter* DR. GAINES, L.]

[*The Doctor walks about with his hands under his coat, seeming
very much elated.*]

MRS. GAINES: Why, doctor, what is the matter?

DR. GAINES: My dear, don't call me *doctor.*

MRS. GAINES: What should I call you?

DR. GAINES: Call me Colonel, my dear—Colonel. I have been
 elected Colonel of the Militia, and I want you to call me by
 my right name. I always felt that Providence had designed me
 for something great, and He has just begun to shower His
 blessings upon me.

MRS. GAINES: Dear me, I could never get to calling you Colonel;
 I've called you Doctor for the last twenty years.

DR. GAINES: Now, Sarah, if you will call me Colonel, other people
 will, and I want you to set the example. Come, my darling, call
 me Colonel, and I'll give you any thing you wish for.

MRS. GAINES: Well, as I want a new gold watch and bracelets, I'll com-
 mence now. Come, Colonel, we'll go to supper. Ah! now for
 my new shawl. [*Aside.*] Mrs. Lemme was here to-day, Colonel,
 and she had on, Colonel, one of the prettiest shawls, Colonel,
 I think, Colonel, that I ever saw, Colonel, in my life, Colonel.
 And there is only one, Colonel, in Mr. Watson's store, Colonel;
 and that, Colonel, will do, Colonel, for a Colonel's wife.

DR. GAINES: Ah! my dear, you never looked so much the lady since
 I've known you. Go, my darling, get the watch, bracelets and
 shawl, and tell them to charge them to Colonel Gaines; and
 when you say "Colonel," always emphasize the word.

MRS. GAINES: Come, Colonel, let's go to supper.

DR. GAINES: My dear, you're a jewel,—you are!

[*Exit,* R. *Enter* CATO, L.]

CATO: Why, whar is massa and missis? I tought dey was here. Ah! by golly, yonder comes a mulatter gal. Yes, it's Mrs. Jones's Tapioca. I'll set up to dat gal, dat I will.

[*Enter* TAPIOCA, R.]

Good ebenin', Miss Tappy. How is your folks?

TAPIOCA: Pretty well, I tank you.

CATO: Miss Tappy, dis wanderin' heart of mine is yours. Come, take a seat! Please to squze my manners; love discommodes me. Take a seat. Now, Miss Tappy, I loves you; an ef you will jess marry me, I'll make you a happy husband, dat I will. Come, take me as I is.

TAPIOCA: But what will Big Jim say?

CATO: Big Jim! Why, let dat nigger go to Ginny. I want to know, now, if you is tinkin' about dat common nigger? Why, Miss Tappy, I is surstonished dat you should tink 'bout frowin' yousef away wid a common, ugly lookin' cuss like Big Jim, when you can get a fine lookin', suspectable man like me. Come, Miss Tappy, choose dis day who you have. Afore I go any furder, give me one kiss. Come, give me one kiss. Come, let me kiss you.

TAPIOCA: No you shan't—dare now! You shan't kiss me widout you is stronger den I is; and I know you is dat. [*He kisses her.*]

[*Enter* DR. GAINES, R., *and hides.*]

CATO: Did you know, Miss Tappy, dat I is de head doctor 'bout dis house? I beats de ole boss all to pieces.

TAPIOCA: I hev hearn dat you bleeds and pulls teef.

CATO: Yes, Miss Tappy; massa could not get along widout me, for massa was made a doctor by books; but I is a natral doctor. I was born a doctor, jess as Lorenzo Dow was born a preacher. So you see I can't be nuffin' but a doctor, while massa is a bunglin' ole cuss at de bissness.

DR. GAINES: [*In a low voice.*] Never mind; I'll teach you a lesson, that I will.

399

CATO: You see, Miss Tappy, I was gwine to say—Ah! but afore I forget, jess give me anudder kiss, jess to keep company wid de one dat you give me jess now,—dat's all. [*Kisses her.*] Now, Miss Tappy, duse you know de fuss time dat I seed you?

TAPIOCA: No, Mr. Cato, I don't.

CATO: Well, it was at de camp-meetin'. Oh, Miss Tappy, dat pretty red calliker dress you had on dat time did de work for me. It made my heart flutter—

DR. GAINES: [*Low voice.*] Yes, and I'll make your black hide flutter.

CATO: Didn't I hear some noise? By golly, dar is teves in dis house, and I'll drive 'em out. [*Takes a chair and runs at the Doctor, and knocks him down. The Doctor chases* CATO *round the table.*]

CATO: Oh, massa, I didn't know 'twas you!

DR. GAINES: You scoundrel! I'll whip you well. Stop! I tell you. [*Curtain falls.*]

ACT III, SCENE I

[*Sitting-Room.* MRS. GAINES, *seated in an arm chair, reading a letter.*]

[*Enter* HANNAH, L.]

MRS. GAINES: You need not tell me, Hannah, that you don't want another husband, I know better. Your master has sold Sam, and he's gone down the river, and you'll never see him again. So, go and put on your calico dress, and meet me in the kitchen. I intend for you to *jump the broomstick* with Cato. You need not tell me that you don't want another man. I know that there's no woman living that can be happy and satisfied without a husband.

HANNAH: Oh, missis, I don't want to jump de broomstick wid Cato. I don't love Cato; I can't love him.

MRS. GAINES: Shut up, this moment! What do you know about love? I didn't love your master when I married him, and people don't marry for love now. So go and put on your calico dress, and meet me in the kitchen.

[*Exit* HANNAH, L.]

I am glad that the Colonel has sold Sam; now I'll make Hannah marry Cato, and I have them both here under my eye. And I am also glad that the Colonel has parted with Melinda. Still, I'm afraid that he is trying to deceive me. He took the hussy away yesterday, and says he sold her to a trader; but I don't believe it. At any rate, if she's in the neighborhood, I'll find her, that I will. No man ever fools me.

[*Exit* MRS. GAINES, L.]

SCENE II

[*The Kitchen—slaves at work.*]

[*Enter* HANNAH, R.]

HANNAH: Oh, Cato, do go and tell missis dat you don't want to jump de broomstick wid me,—dat's a good man! Do, Cato; kase I nebber can love you. It was only las week dat massa sold my Sammy, and I don't want any udder man. Do go tell missis dat you don't want me.

CATO: No, Hannah, I ain't a gwine to tell missis no such thing, kase I dose want you, and I ain't a-gwine to tell a lie for you ner nobody else. Dar, now you's got it! I don't see why you need to make so much fuss. I is better lookin' den Sam; an' I is a house servant, an' Sam was only a fiel hand; so you ought to feel proud of a change. So go and do as missis tells you.

[*Exit* HANNAH, L.]

Hannah needn't try to get me to tell a lie; I ain't a-gwine to do it, kase I dose want her, an' I is bin wantin' her dis long time, an' soon as massa sold Sam, I knowed I would get her. By golly,

I is gwine to be a married man. Won't I be happy! Now, ef I could only jess run away from ole massa, an' get to Canada wid Hannah, den I'd show 'em who I was. Ah! dat reminds me of my song 'bout ole massa and Canada, an' I'll sing it fer yer. Dis is my moriginal hyme. It comed into my head one night when I was fass asleep under an apple tree, looking up at de moon. Now for my song:—

AIR—"*Dandy Jim.*"

Come all ye bondmen far and near,
Let's put a song in massa's ear,
It is a song for our poor race,
Who're whipped and trampled with disgrace.

[*Chorus.*]
My old massa tells me, Oh,
This is a land of freedom, Oh;
Let's look about and see if it's so,
Just as massa tells me, Oh.

He tells us of that glorious one,
I think his name was Washington,
How he did fight for liberty,
To save a threepence tax on tea. [*Chorus.*]

But now we look about and see
That we poor blacks are not so free;
We're whipped and thrashed about like fools,
And have no chance at common schools. [*Chorus.*]

They take our wives, insult and mock,
And sell our children on the block,
They choke us if we say a word,
And say that "niggers" shan't be heard. [*Chorus.*]

Our preachers, too, with whip and cord,

Command obedience in the Lord;
They say they learn it from the big book,
But for ourselves, we dare not look. [*Chorus.*]

There is a country far away,
I think they call it Canada,
And if we reach Victoria's shore,
They say that we are slaves no more.

Now haste, all bondmen, let us go,
And leave this *Christian* country, Oh;
Haste to the land of the British Queen,
Where whips for negroes are not seen.

Now, if we go, we must take the night,
And never let them come in sight;
The bloodhounds will be on our track,
And wo to us if they fetch us back.

Now haste all bondmen, let us go,
And leave this *Christian* country, Oh;
God help us to Victoria's shore,
Where we are free and slaves no more!

[*Enter* MRS. GAINES, L.]

MRS. GAINES: Ah! Cato, you're ready, are you? Where is Hannah?

CATO: Yes, missis; I is bin waitin' dis long time. Hannah has bin here
tryin' to swade me to tell you dat I don't want her; but I telled
her dat you sed I must jump de broomstick wid her, an' I is
gwine to mind you.

MRS. GAINES: That's right, Cato; servants should always mind their
masters and mistresses, without asking a question.

CATO: Yes, missis, I allers dose what you and massa tells me, an' axes
nobody.

[*Enter* HANNAH, R.]

MRS. GAINES: Ah! Hannah; come, we are waiting for you. Nothing can be done till you come.

HANNAH: Oh, missis, I don't want to jump de broomstick wid Cato; I can't love him.

MRS. GAINES: Shut up, this moment. Dolly, get the broom. Susan, you take hold of the other end. There, now hold it a little lower— there, a little higher. There, now, that'll do. Now Hannah, take hold of Cato's hand. Let Cato take hold of your hand.

HANNAH: Oh, missis, do spare me. I don't want to jump de broom-stick wid Cato.

MRS. GAINES: Get the cowhide, and follow me to the cellar, and I'll whip you well. I'll let you know how to disobey my orders. Get the cowhide, and follow me to the cellar.

[*Exit* MRS. GAINES *and* HANNAH, R.]

DOLLY: Oh, Cato, do go an' tell missis dat you don't want Hannah. Don't you hear how she's whippin' her in de cellar? Do go an' tell missis dat you don't want Hannah, and den she'll stop whippin' her.

CATO: No, Dolly, I ain't a-gwine to do no such a thing, kase ef I tell missis dat I don't want Hannah, den missis will whip me; an' I ain't a-gwine to be whipped fer you, ner Hannah, ner nobody else. No, I'll jump de broomstick wid every woman on de place, ef missis wants me to, before I'll be whipped.

DOLLY: Cato, ef I was in Hannah's place, I'd see you in de bottomless pit before I'd live wid you, you great big wall-eyed, empty-headed, knock-kneed fool. You're as mean as your devilish old missis.

CATO: Ef you do n't quit dat busin' me, Dolly, I'll tell missis as soon as she comes in, an' she'll whip you, you know she will.

[*Enter* MRS. GAINES *and* HANNAH, R.]

[MRS. G. *fans herself with her handkerchief, and appears fatigued.*]

MRS. GAINES: You ought to be ashamed of yourself, Hannah, to make me fatigue myself in this way, to make you do your duty. It's very naughty in you, Hannah. Now, Dolly, you and Susan get the broom, and get out in the middle of the room. There, hold it a little lower—a little higher; here, that'll do. Now, remember that this is a solemn occassion; you are going to jump into matrimony. Now, Cato, take hold of Hannah's hand. There, now, why couldn't you let Cato take hold of your hand before? Now get ready, and when I count three, do you jump. Eyes on the *broomstick!* All ready. One, two, three, and over you go. There, now you're husband and wife, and if you don't live happy together, it's your own fault; for I am sure there's nothing to hinder it. Now, Hannah, come up to the house, and I'll give you some whiskey, and you can make some apple toddy, and you and Cato can have a fine time.

[*Exit* MRS. GAINES *and* HANNAH, L.]

DOLLY: I tell you what, Susan, when I get married, I is gwine to have a preacher to marry me. I ain't a-gwine to jump de broomstick. Dat will do for fiel' hands, but house servants ought to be 'bove dat.

SUSAN: Well, chile, you can't speck any ting else from ole missis. She come from down in Carlina, from 'mong de poor white trash. She don't know any better. You can't speck nothin' more dan a jump from a frog. Missis says she is one of de akastocacy; but she ain't no more of an akastocacy dan I is. Missis says she was born wid a silver spoon in her mouf; ef she was; I wish it had a-choked her, dat's what I wish. Missis wanted to make Linda jump de broomstick wid Glen, but massa ain't a-gwine to let Linda jump de broomstick wid anybody. He's gwine to keep Linda fer heself.

DOLLY: You know massa took Linda 'way las' night, an' tell missis dat he has sold her and sent her down de river; but I don't b'lieve he has sold her at all. He went ober towards de poplar farm, an' I tink Linda is ober dar now. Ef she is dar, missis'll find it out, fer she tell'd massa las' night, dat ef Linda was in de neighborhood, she'd find her.

[*Exit* DOLLY *and* SUSAN.]

SCENE III

[*Sitting Room—Chairs and Table.*]

[*Enter* HANNAH, R.]

HANNAH: I don't keer what missis says; I don't like Cato, an' I won't live wid him. I always love my Sammy, an' I loves him now. [*Knock at the door—goes to the door.*]

[*Enter* MAJ. MOORE, M.D.]

Walk in, sir; take a seat. I'll call missis, sir; massa is gone away. [*Exit* HANNAH, R.]

MAJ. MOORE: So I am here at last, and the Colonel is not at home. I hope his wife is a good-looking woman. I rather like fine looking-women, especially when their husbands are from home. Well, I've studied human nature to some purpose. If you wish to get the good will of a man, don't praise his wife, and if you wish to gain the favor of a woman, praise her children, and swear that they are the picture of their father, whether they are or not. Ah! here comes the lady.

[*Enter* MRS. GAINES, R.]

MRS. GAINES: Good morning, sir!

MAJ. MOORE: Good morning, madam! I am Maj. Moore, of Jefferson. The Colonel and I had seats near each other in the last Legislature.

MRS. GAINES: Be seated, sir. I think I've heard the Colonel speak of you. He's away, now; but I expect him every moment. You're a stranger here, I presume?

MAJ. MOORE: Yes, madam, I am. I rather like the Colonel's situation here.

MRS. GAINES: It is thought to be a fine location.

[*Enter* SAMPEY, R.]

Hand me my fan, will you, Sampey? [*Sampey gets the fan and passes near the Major, who mistakes the boy for the Colonel's son. He reaches out his hand.*]

MAJ. MOORE: How do you do, bub? Madam, I should have known that this was the Colonel's son, if I had met him in California; for he looks so much like his papa.

MRS. GAINES: [*To the boy.*] Get out of here this minute. Go to the kitchen.

[*Exit* SAMPEY, R.]

That is one of the niggers, sir.

MAJ. MOORE: I beg your pardon, madam; I beg your pardon.

MRS. GAINES: No offence, sir; mistakes will be made. Ah! here comes the Colonel.

[*Enter* DR. GAINES, M.D.]

DR. GAINES: Bless my soul, how are you, Major? I'm exceedingly pleased to see you. Be seated, be seated Major.

MRS. GAINES: Please excuse me, gentlemen; I must go and look after dinner, for I've no doubt that the Major will have an appetite for dinner, by the time it is ready.

[*Exit* MRS. GAINES, R.]

MAJ. MOORE: Colonel, I'm afraid I've played the devil here to-day.

DR. GAINES: Why, what have you done?

MAJ. MOORE: You see, Colonel, I always make it a point, wherever I go, to praise the children, if there are any, and so to-day, seeing one of your little servants come in, and taking him to be your son, I spoke to your wife of the marked resemblance between you and the boy. I am afraid I've insulted madam.

DR. GAINES: Oh! don't let that trouble you. Ha, ha, ha. If you did call him my son, you didn't miss it much. Ha, ha, ha. Come, we'll take a walk, and talk over matters about old times.

[*Exit,* L.]

SCENE IV

[*Forest Scenery.*]

[*Enter* GLEN, L.]

GLEN: Oh, how I want to see Melinda! My heart pants and my soul is moved whenever I hear her voice. Human tongue cannot tell how my heart yearns toward her. Oh, God! thou who gavest me life, and implanted in my bosom the love of liberty, and gave me a heart to love, Oh, pity the poor outraged slave! Thou, who canst rend the veil of centuries, speak, Oh, speak, and put a stop to this persecution! What is death, compared to slavery? Oh, heavy curse, to have thoughts, reason, taste, judgment, conscience and passions like another man, and not have equal liberty to use them! Why was I born with a wish to be free, and still be a slave? Why should I call another man master? And my poor Melinda, she is taken away from me, and I dare not ask the tyrant where she is. It is childish to stand here weeping. Why should my eyes be filled with tears, when my brain is on fire? I will find my wife—I will; and wo to him who shall try to keep me from her!

SCENE V

[*Room in a Small Cottage on the Poplar Farm, Ten miles from Muddy Creek, and owned by Dr. Gaines.*]

[*Enter* MELINDA, R.]

MELINDA: Here I am, watched, and kept a prisoner in this place. Oh, I would that I could escape, and once more get with Glen. Poor Glen! He does not know where I am. Master took the opportunity, when Glen was in the city with his master, to bring me here to this lonely place, and fearing that mistress would know where I was, he brought me here at night. Oh, how I wish I could rush into the arms of sleep!—that sweet sleep, which visits all alike, descending, like the dews of heaven, upon the bond as well as the free. It would drive from my troubled brain the agonies of this terrible night.

[*Enter* DR. GAINES, L.]

DR. GAINES: Good evening, Melinda! Are you not glad to see me?

MELINDA: Sir, how can I be glad to see one who has made life a burden, and turned my sweetest moments into bitterness?

DR. GAINES: Come, Melinda, no more reproaches! You know that I love you, and I have told you, and I tell you again, that if you will give up all idea of having Glen for a husband, I will set you free, let you live in this cottage, and be your own mistress, and I'll dress you like a lady. Come, now, be reasonable!

MELINDA: Sir, I am your slave; you can do as you please with the avails of my labor, but you shall never tempt me to swerve from the path of virtue.

DR. GAINES: Now, Melinda, that black scoundrel Glen has been putting these notions into your head. I'll let you know that you are my property, and I'll do as I please with you. I'll teach you that there is no limit to my power.

MELINDA: Sir, let me warn you that if you compass my ruin, a woman's bitterest curse will be laid upon your head, with all the crushing, withering weight that my soul can impart to it; a curse that shall cling to you throughout the remainder of your wretched life; a curse that shall haunt you like a spectre in your dreams by night, and attend upon you by day; a curse, too, that shall embody itself in the ghastly form of the woman whose chastity you will have outraged. Command me to bury myself in yonder stream, and I will obey you. Bid me do any thing else, but I beseech you not to commit a double crime,—outrage a woman, and make her false to her husband.

DR. GAINES: You got a husband! Who is your husband, and when were you married?

MELINDA: Glen is my husband, and I've been married four weeks. Old Uncle Joseph married us one night by moonlight. I see you are angry; I pray you not to injure my husband.

DR. GAINES: Melinda, you shall never see Glen again. I have bought him from Hamilton, and I will return to Muddy Creek, and roast him at the stake. A black villain, to get into my way in that manner! Here I've come ten miles tonight to see you, and this is the way you receive me!

MELINDA: Oh, master, I beg you not to injure my husband! Kill me, but spare him! Do! do! he is my husband!

DR. GAINES: You shall never see that black imp again, so good night, my lady! When I come again, you'll give me a more cordial reception. Good night!

[*Exit* DR. GAINES, L.]

MELINDA: I shall go distracted. I cannot remain here and know that Glen is being tortured on my account. I must escape from this place,—I must,—I must!

[*Enter* CATO, R.]

CATO: No, you ain't a-gwine to 'scape, nudder. Massa tells me to keep dese eyes on you, an' I is gwine to do it.

MELINDA: Oh, Cato, do let me get away! I beg you, do!

CATO: No; I tells you massa telled me to keep you safe; an' ef I let you go, massa will whip me. [*Exit* CATO, L.]

[*Enter* MRS. GAINES, R.]

MRS. GAINES: Ah, you trollop! here you are! Your master told me that he had sold you and sent you down the river, but I knew better; I knew it was a lie. And when he left home this evening, he said he was going to the city on business, and I knew that was a lie too, and determined to follow him, and see what he was up to. I rode all the way over here to-night. My side-saddle was lent out, and I had to ride ten miles bare-back, and I can scarcely walk; and your master has just left here. Now deny that, if you dare.

MELINDA: Madam, I will deny nothing which is true. Your husband has just gone from here, but God knows that I am innocent of any thing wrong with him.

MRS. GAINES: It's a lie! I know better. If you are innocent, what are you doing here, cooped up in this cottage by yourself? Tell me that!

MELINDA: God knows that I was brought here against my will, and I beg that you will take me away.

MRS. GAINES: Yes, Melinda, I will see that you are taken away, but it shall be after a fashion that you won't like. I know that your master loves you, and I intend to put a stop to it. Here, drink the contents of this vial,—drink it!

MELINDA: Oh, you will not take my life,—you will not!

MRS. GAINES: Drink the poison this moment!

MELINDA: I cannot drink it.

MRS. GAINES: I tell you to drink this poison at once. Drink it, or I will thrust this knife to your heart. The poison or the dagger, this instant! [*She draws a dagger;* MELINDA *retreats to the back of the room, and seizes a broom.*]

MELINDA: I will not drink the poison! [*They fight;* MELINDA *sweeps off* MRS. GAINES,—*cap, combs and curls. Curtain falls.*]

ACT IV, SCENE I

[*Interior of a Dungeon—Glen in chains.*]

GLEN: When I think of my unmerited sufferings, it almost drives me mad. I struck the doctor, and for that, I must remain here loaded with chains. But why did he strike me? He takes my wife from me, sends her off, and then comes and beats me over the head with his cane. I did right to strike him back again. I would I had killed him. Oh! there is a volcano pent up in the hearts of the slaves of these Southern States that will burst forth ere long. When that day comes, wo to those whom its unpitying fury may devour! I would be willing to die, if I could smite down with these chains every man who attempts to enslave his fellow-man.

[*Enter* SAMPEY, R.]

SAMPEY: Glen, I jess bin hear massa call de oberseer, and I spec somebody is gwine to be whipped. Anudder ting: I know whar massa took Linda to. He took her to de poplar farm, an' he went away las' night, an' missis she follow after massa, an' she ain't come back yet. I tell you, Glen, de debil will be to pay on dis place, but don't you tell any body dat I tole you.

[*Exit* SAMPEY, R.]

SCENE II

[*Parlor.* DR. GAINES, *alone.*]

DR. GAINES: Yes, I will have the black rascal well whipped, and then I'll sell him. It was most fortunate for me that Hamilton was willing to sell him to me.

[*Enter* MR. SCRAGG, L.]

I have sent for you, Mr. Scragg. I want you to take Glen out of the dungeon, take him into the tobacco house, fasten him down upon the stretcher, and give him five hundred lashes upon his bare back; and when you have whipped him, feel his pulse, and report to me how it stands, and if he can bear more, I'll have you give him an additional hundred or two, as the case may be.

SCRAGG: I tell you, doctor, that suits me to a charm. I've long wanted to whip that nigger. When your brother-in-law came here to board, and brought that boy with him, I felt bad to see a nigger dressed up in such fine clothes, and I wanted to whip him right off. I tell you, doctor, I had rather whip that nigger than go to heaven, any day,—that I had!

DR. GAINES: Go, Mr. Scragg, and do your duty. Don't spare the whip!

SCRAGG: I will, sir; I'll do it in order.

[*Exit* SCRAGG, L.]

DR. GAINES: Every thing works well now, and when I get Glen out of the way, I'll pay Melinda another visit, and she'll give me a different reception. But I wonder where my wife is? She left word that she was going to see her brother, but I am afraid that she has got on my track. That woman is the pest of my life. If there's any place in heaven for her, I'd be glad if the Lord would take her home, for I've had her too long already. But what noise is that? What can that be? What is the matter?

[*Enter* SCRAGG, L., *with face bloody.*]

SCRAGG: Oh, dear me! oh, my head! That nigger broke away from me, and struck me over the head with a stick. Oh, dear me! Oh!

DR. GAINES: Where is he, Mr. Scragg?

SCRAGG: Oh! sir, he jumped out of the window; he's gone. Oh! my head; he's cracked my skull. Oh, dear me, I'm kilt! Oh! oh! oh!

[*Enter* SLAVES, R.]

DR. GAINES: Go, Dolly, and wash Mr. Scragg's head with some whiskey, and bind it up. Go at once. And Bob, you run over to Mr. Hall, and tell him to come with his hounds; we must go after the rascal.

[*Exit all except the* DOCTOR, R.]

This will never do. When I catch the scoundrel, I'll make an example of him; I'll whip him to death. Ah! here comes my wife. I wonder what she comes now for? I must put on a sober face, for she looks angry.

[*Enter* MRS. GAINES, L.]

Ah! my dear, I am glad you 've come, I've been so lonesome without you. Oh! Sarah, I don't know what I should do if the Lord should take you home to heaven. I don't think that I should be able to live without you.

MRS. GAINES: Dr. Gaines, you ought to be ashamed to sit there and talk in that way. You know very well that if the Lord should call me home to glory to-night, you'd jump for joy. But you need not think that I am going to leave this world before you. No; with the help of the Lord, I'll stay here to foil you in your meanness. I've been on your track, and a dirty track it is, too. You ought to be ashamed of yourself. See what promises you made me before we were married; and this is the way you keep your word. When I married you, every body said that it was a pity that a woman of my sweet temper should be linked to such a man as you. [*She weeps and wrings her hands.*]

DR. GAINES: Come, my dear, don't make a fool of yourself. Come, let's go to supper, and a strong cup of tea will help your head.

MRS. GAINES: Tea help my head! tea won't help my head. You're a brute of a man; I always knew I was a fool for marrying you. There was Mr. Comstock, he wanted me, and he loved me, and he said I was an angel, so he did; and he loved me, and he was rich; and mother always said that he loved me more than you, for when he used to kiss me, he always squeezed my hand. You never did such a thing in your life. [*She weeps and wrings her hands.*]

DR. GAINES: Come, my dear, don't act so foolish.

MRS. GAINES: Yes; every thing I do is foolish. You're a brute of a man; I won't live with you any longer. I'll leave you—that I will. I'll go and see a lawyer, and get a divorce from you—so I will.

DR. GAINES: Well, Sarah, if you want a divorce, you had better engage Mr. Barker. He's the best lawyer in town; and if you want some money to facilitate the business, I'll draw a check for you.

MRS. GAINES: So you want me to get a divorce, do you? Well, I won't have a divorce; no, I'll never leave you, as long as the Lord spares me.

[*Exit* MRS. GAINES, R.]

SCENE III

[*Forest at Night—Large Tree.*]

[*Enter* MELINDA, L.]

MELINDA: This is indeed a dark night to be out and alone on this road. But I must find my husband, I must. Poor Glen! if he only knew that I was here, and could get to me, he would. What a curse slavery is. It separates husbands from their wives, and tears mothers from their helpless offspring, and blights all our hopes for this world. I must try to reach Muddy Creek before daylight, and seek out my husband. What's that I hear?—footsteps? I'll get behind this tree.

[*Enter* GLEN, R.]

GLEN: It is so dark, I'm afraid I've missed the road. Still, this must be the right way to the poplar farm. And if Bob told me the truth, when he said that Melinda was at the poplar farm, I will soon be with her; and if I once get her in my arms, it will be a strong man that shall take her from me. Aye, a dozen strong men shall not be able to wrest her from my arms. [MELINDA *rushes from behind the tree.*]

MELINDA: Oh, Glen! It is my husband,—it is!

GLEN: Melinda! Melinda! it is, it is. Oh God! I thank Thee for this manifestation of Thy kindness. Come, come, Melinda, we must go at once to Canada. I escaped from the overseer, whom Dr. Gaines sent to flog me. Yes, I struck him over the head with his own club, and I made the wine flow freely; yes, I pounded his old skillet well for him, and then jumped out of the window. It was a leap for freedom. Yes, Melinda, it was a leap for freedom. I've said "master" for the last time. I am free; I'm bound for Canada. Come, let's be off, at once, for the negro dogs will be put upon our track. Let us once get beyond the Ohio river, and all will be right. [*Exit* R.]

ACT V, SCENE I

[*Bar-Room in the American Hotel—Travellers Lounging in Chairs, and at the Bar.*]

[*Enter* BILL JENNINGS, R.]

BARKEEPER: Why, Jennings, how do you do?

JENNINGS: Say Mr. Jennings, if you please.

BARKEEPER: Well, Mr. Jennings, if that suits you better. How are times? We've been expecting you, for some days.

JENNINGS: Well, before I talk about the times, I want my horses put up, and want you to tell me where my niggers are to stay to-night. Sheds, stables, barns, and every thing else here, seems pretty full, if I am a judge.

BARKEEPER: Oh! I'll see to your plunder.

1st LOUNGER: I say, Barkeeper, make me a brandy cocktail, strong. Why, how do you do, Mr. Jennings?

JENNINGS: Pretty well, Mr. Peters. Cold evening, this.

1st LOUNGER: Yes, this is cold. I heard you speak of your niggers. Have you got a pretty large gang?

JENNINGS: No, only thirty-three. But they are the best that the country can afford. I shall clear a few dimes, this trip. I hear that the price is up.

[*Enter* MR. WHITE, R.]

WHITE: Can I be accommodated here to-night, landlord?

BARKEEPER: Yes, sir; we've bed for man and beast. Go, Dick, and take the gentleman's coat and hat. [*To the waiter.*] You're a stranger in these parts, I rec'on.

WHITE: Yes, I am a stranger here.

2ᵈ LOUNGER: Where mout you come from, ef it's a far question?

WHITE: I am from Massachusetts.

3ᵈ LOUNGER: I say cuss Massachusetts!

1ˢᵗ LOUNGER: I say so too. There is where the fanatics live; cussed traitors. The President ought to hang 'em all.

WHITE: I say, landlord, if this is the language that I am to hear, I would like to go into a private room.

BARKEEPER: We ain't got no private room empty.

1ˢᵗ LOUNGER: Maybe you're mad about what I said 'bout your State. Ef you is, I've only to say that this is a free country, and people talks what they please; an' ef you don't like it, you can better yourself.

WHITE: Sir, if this is a free country, why do you have slaves here? I saw a gang at the door, as I came in.

2ᵈ LOUNGER: He didn't mean that this was a free country for niggers. He meant that it's free for white people. And another thing, ef you get to talking 'bout freedom for niggers, you'll catch what you won't like, mister. It's right for niggers to be slaves.

WHITE: But I saw some white slaves.

1ˢᵗ LOUNGER: Well, they're white niggers.

WHITE: Well, sir, I am from a free State, and I thank God for it; for the worst act that a man can commit upon his fellow-man, is to make him a slave. Conceive of a mind, a living soul, with the germs of faculties which infinity cannot exhaust, as it first beams upon you in its glad morning of existence, quivering with life and joy, exulting in the glorious sense of its developing energies, beautiful, and brave, and generous, and joyous, and free,—the clear pure spirit bathed in the auroral light of its unconscious immortality,—and then follow it in its dark and dreary passage through slavery, until oppression stifles and kills, one by one, every inspiration and aspiration of its being, until it becomes a dead soul entombed in a living frame!

3ᵈ LOUNGER: Stop that; stop that, I say. That's treason to the country; that's downright rebellion.

BARKEEPER: Yes, it is. And another thing,—this is not a meeting-house.

1ˢᵗ LOUNGER: Yes, if you talk such stuff as that, you'll get a chunk of cold lead in you, that you will.

[*Enter* DR. GAINES *and* SCRAGG, *followed by* CATO, R.]

DR. GAINES: Gentlemen, I am in pursuit of two valuable slaves, and I will pay five hundred dollars for their arrest.

[*Exit* MR. WHITE, L.]

1ˢᵗ LOUNGER: I'll bet a picayune that your niggers have been stolen by that cussed feller from Massachusetts. Don't you see he's gone?

DR. GAINES: Where is the man? If I can lay my hands on him, he'll never steal another nigger. Where is the scoundrel?

1ˢᵗ LOUNGER: Let's go after the feller. I'll go with you. Come, foller me. [*Exit* ALL, L., *except* CATO *and the waiter.*]

CATO: Why don't you bring in massa's saddle-bags? What de debil you standin' dar for? You common country niggers do n't know nuffin', no how. Go an' get massa's saddle-bags, and bring 'em in.

[*Exit* SERVANT, R.]

By golly! ebry body's gone, an' de bar-keeper too. I'll tend de bar myself now; an' de fuss gemman I waits on will be dis gemman of color. [*Goes behind the counter, and drinks.*] Ah, dis is de stuff fer me; it makes my head swim; it makes me happy right off. I'll take a little more.

[*Enter* BARKEEPER, L.]

BARKEEPER: What are you doing behind that bar, you black cuss?

CATO: I is lookin' for massa's saddle-bags, sir. Is dey here?

BARKEEPER: But what were you drinking there?

CATO: Me drinkin'! Why, massa, you muss be mistaken. I ain't drink nuffin'.

BARKEEPER: You infernal whelp, to stand there and lie in that
way!

CATO: Oh, yes, seer, I did tase dat coffee in dat bottle; dat's all I
did.

[*Enter* MR. WHITE, L., *excited.*]

WHITE: I say, sir, is there no place of concealment in your house?
They are after me, and my life is in danger. Say, sir, can't you
hide me away?

BARKEEPER: Well, you ought to hold your tongue when you come
into our State.

WHITE: But, sir, the Constitution gives me the right to speak my
sentiments, at all times and in all places.

BARKEEPER: We don't care for Constitutions nor nothin' else. We
made the Constitution, and we'll break it. But you had better
hide away; they are coming, and they'll lynch you, that they
will. Come with me; I'll hide you in the cellar. Foller me.

[*Exit* BARKEEPER *and* WHITE, L.]

[*Enter the* MOB, R.]

DR. GAINES: If I can once lay my hands on that scoundrel, I'll blow
a hole through his head.

JENNINGS: Yes, I say so too; for no one knows whose niggers are safe,
now-a-days. I must look after my niggers. Who is that I see
in the distance? I believe it's that cussed Massachusetts feller.
Come, let's go after him.

[*Exit the* MOB, R.]

SCENE II

[*Forest at Night.*]

[*Enter* GLEN *and* MELINDA, R.]

419

MELINDA: I am so tired and hungry, that I cannot go further. It is so cloudy that we cannot see the North Star, and therefore cannot tell whether we are going to Canada, or further South. Let's sit down here.

GLEN: I know that we cannot see the North Star, Melinda, and I fear we've lost our way. But, see I the clouds are passing away, and it'll soon be clear. See! yonder is a star; yonder is another and another. Ah! yonder is the North Star, and we are safe!

> "Star of the North! though night winds drift
>   The fleecy drapery of the sky
>   Between thy lamp and me, I lift,
> Yea, lift with hope my sleepless eye,
>   To the blue heights wherein thou dwellest,
>   And of a land of freedom tellest.
>
> "Star of the North! while blazing day
>   Pours round me its full tide of light,
>   And hides thy pale but faithful ray,
> I, too, lie hid, and long for night:
>   For night: I dare not walk at noon,
>   Nor dare I trust the faithless moon—
>
> "Nor faithless man, whose burning lust
>   For gold hath riveted my chain,—
>   Nor other leader can I trust
> But thee, of even the starry train;
>   For all the host around thee burning,
>   Like faithless man, keep turning, turning.
>
> "I may not follow where they go:—
>   Star of the North! I look to thee
>   While on I press; for well I know,
> Thy light and truth shall set me free:—
>   Thy light, that no poor slave deceiveth;

Thy truth, that all my soul believeth.

"Thy beam is on the glassy breast
        Of the still spring, upon whose brink
        I lay my weary limbs to rest,
And bow my parching lips to drink.
        Guide of the friendless negro's way,
        I bless there for this quiet ray!

"In the dark top of southern pines
        I nestled, when the Driver's horn
        Called to the field, in lengthening lines,
My fellows, at the break of morn.
        And there I lay till thy sweet face
        Looked in upon "my hiding place."

"The tangled cane-brake, where I crept
        For shelter from the heat of noon,
        And where, while others toiled, I slept,
Till wakened by the rising moon,
        As its stalks felt the night wind free,
        Gave me to catch a glimpse of thee.

"Star of the North! in bright array
        The constellations round thee sweep,
        Each holding on its nightly way,
Rising, or sinking in the deep,
        And, as it hangs in mid heaven flaming,
        The homage of some nation claiming.

"*This* nation to the Eagle cowers;
        Fit ensign! she's a bird of spoil:—
        Like worships like! for each devours
The earnings of another's toil.
        I've felt her talons and her beak,

And now the gentler Lion seek.

"The Lion, at the Monarch's feet
    Crouches, and lays his mighty paw
    Into her lap!—an emblem meet
Of England's Queen, and English law:
    Queen, that hath made her Islands free!
    Law, that holds out its shield to me!

"Star of the North! upon that shield
    Thou shinest,—Oh, for ever shine!
    The negro, from the cotton field
Shall, then, beneath its orb recline,
    And feed the Lion, couched before it,
    Nor heed the Eagle, screaming o'er it!"

With the thoughts of servitude behind us, and the North
Star before us, we will go forward with cheerful hearts.
Come, Melinda, let's go on.

[*Exit*, L.]

SCENE III

[*A Street.*]

[*Enter* MR. WHITE, R.]

WHITE: I am glad to be once more in a free State. If I am caught
again south of Mason and Dixon's line, I'll give them leave
to lynch me. I came near losing my life. This is the way our
constitutional rights are trampled upon. But what care these
men about Constitutions, or any thing else that does not suit
them? But I must hasten on.

[*Exit*, L.]

[*Enter* CATO, *in disguise,* R.]

CATO: I wonder ef dis is me? By golly, I is free as a frog. But maybe I is mistaken; maybe dis ain't me. Cato, is dis you? Yes, seer. Well, now it is me, an' I em a free man. But, stop! I muss change my name, kase ole massa might foller me, and somebody might tell him dat dey seed Cato; so I'll change my name, and den he won't know me ef he sees me. Now, what shall I call myself? I'm now in a suspectable part of de country, an' I muss have a suspectable name. Ah! I'll call myself Alexander Washington Napoleon Pompey Cæsar. Dar, now, dat's a good long, suspectable name and every body will suspect me. Let me see; I wonder ef I can't make up a song on my escape? I'll try.

AIR—*"Dearest Mae."*
Now, freemen, listen to my song, a story I'll relate,
It happened in de valley of de ole Kentucky State:
Dey marched me out into de fiel', at every break of day,
And work me dar till late sunset, widout a cent of pay.

[*Chorus.*]—Dey work me all de day,
Widout a bit of pay,
And thought, because dey fed me well,
I would not run away.

Massa gave me his ole coat, an' thought I'd happy be,
But I had my eye on de North Star, an' thought of liberty;
Ole massa lock de door, an' den he went to sleep,
I dress myself in his bess clothes, an' jump into de street.

[*Chorus.*]—Dey work me all de day,
Widout a bit of pay,
So I took my flight, in the middle of de night,
When de sun was gone away.

423

Sed I, dis chile's a freeman now, he'll be a slave no more;
I travell'd faster all dat night, dan I ever did before.
I came up to a farmer's house, jest at de break of day,
And saw a white man standin' dar, sed he, "You are a runa-
way."

[*Chorus.*]—Dey work me all de day, *&c.*

I tole him I had left de whip, an' bayin' of de hound,
To find a place where man is man, ef sich dar can be found;
Dat I had heard, in Canada, dat all mankind are free,
An' dat I was going dar in search of liberty.

[*Chorus.*]—Dey work me all de day, *&c.*

I've not committed any crime, why should I run away?
Oh! shame upon your laws, dat drive me off to Canada.
You loudly boast of liberty, an' say your State is free,
But ef I tarry in your midst, will you protect me?

[*Chorus.*]—Dey work me all de day, *&c.*

[*Exit,* L.]

SCENE IV

[*Dining-Room—Table Spread.*]

[MRS. NEAL *and* CHARLOTTE.]

MRS. NEAL: Thee may put the tea to draw, Charlotte. Thy father will
be in soon, and we must have breakfast.

[*Enter* MR. NEAL, L.]

I think, Simeon, it is time those people were called. Thee knows that they may be pursued, and we ought not to detain them long here.

MR. NEAL: Yes, Ruth, thou art right. Go, Charlotte, and knock on their chamber door, and tell them that breakfast is ready.

[*Exit* CHARLOTTE, R.]

MRS. NEAL: Poor creatures! I hope they'll reach Canada in safety. They seem to be worthy persons.

[*Enter* CHARLOTTE, R.]

CHARLOTTE: I've called them, mother, and they'll soon be down. I'll put the breakfast on the table.

[*Enter* NEIGHBOR JONES, L.]

MR. NEAL: Good morning, James. Thee has heard, I presume, that we have two very interesting persons in the house?

JONES: Yes, I heard that you had two fugitives by the Underground road, last night; and I've come over to fight for them, if any persons come to take them back.

[*Enter* THOMAS, R.]

MR. NEAL: Go, Thomas, and harness up the horses and put them to the covered wagon, and be ready to take these people on, as soon as they get their breakfast. Go, Thomas, and hurry thyself.

[*Exit* THOMAS, R.]

And so thee wants to fight, this morning, James?

JONES: Yes; as you belongs to a society that don't believe in fighting, and I does believe in that sort of thing, I thought I'd come and relieve you of that work, if there is any to be done.

[*Enter* GLEN *and* MELINDA, R.]

MR. NEAL: Good morning, friends. I hope thee rested well, last night.

425

MRS. NEAL: Yes, I hope thee had a good night's rest.

GLEN: I thank you, madam, we did.

MR. NEAL: I'll introduce thee to our neighbor, James Jones. He's a staunch friend of thy people.

JONES: I am glad to see you. I've come over to render assistance, if any is needed.

MRS. NEAL: Come, friends, take seats at the table. Thee'll take seats there. [*To* GLEN *and* MELINDA.] [*All take seats at the table.*] Does thee take sugar and milk in thy tea?

MELINDA: I thank you, we do.

JONES: I'll look at your *Tribune*, Uncle Simeon, while you're eating.

MR. NEAL: Thee'll find it on the table.

MRS. NEAL: I presume thee's anxious to get to thy journey's end?

GLEN: Yes, madam, we are. I am told that we are not safe in any of the free States.

MR. NEAL: I am sorry to tell thee, that that is too true. Thee will not be safe until thee gets on British soil. I wonder what keeps Thomas; he should have been here with the team.

[*Enter* THOMAS, L.]

THOMAS: All's ready; and I've written the prettiest song that was ever sung. I call it "The Underground Railroad."

MR. NEAL: Thomas, thee can eat thy breakfast far better than thee can write a song, as thee calls it. Thee must hurry thyself, when I send thee for the horses, Thomas. Here lately, thee takes thy time.

THOMAS: Well, you see I've been writing poetry; that's the reason I've been so long. If you wish it, I'll sing it to you.

JONES: Do let us hear the song.

MRS. NEAL: Yes, if Thomas has written a ditty, do let us hear it.

MR. NEAL: Well, Thomas, if thee has a ditty, thee may recite it to us.

THOMAS: Well, I'll give it to you. Remember that I call it "The Underground Railroad."

Air—"Wait for the Wagon."

Oh, where is the invention
Of this growing age,
Claiming the attention
Of statesman, priest, or sage,
 In the many railways
 Through the nation found,
 Equal to the Yankees'
 Railway under-ground?
[*Chorus.*]—No one hears the whistle,
 Or rolling of the cars,
 While negroes ride to freedom
 Beyond the stripes and stars.

On the Southern borders
Are the Railway stations,
Negroes get free orders
While on the plantations;
For all, of ev'ry color,
First-class ears are found,
While they ride to freedom
By Railway under-ground.

[*Chorus.*]—No one hears the whistle, *&c.*

Masters in the morning
Furiously rage,
Cursing the inventions
Of this knowing age;
Order out the bloodhounds,
Swear they'll bring them back,
Dogs return exhausted,
Cannot find the track.

[*Chorus.*]—No one hears the whistle, *&c.*

Travel is increasing,
Build a double track,
Cars and engines wanted,

They'll come, we have no lack.
Clear the track of loafers,
See that crowded car!
Thousands passing yearly,
Stock is more than par.

[*Chorus.*]—No one hears the whistle, &c.

JONES: Well done! That's a good song. I'd like to have a copy of them verses. [*Knock at the door.* CHARLOTTE *goes to the door, and returns.*]

[*Enter* CATO, L., *still in disguise.*]

MR. NEAL: Who is this we have? Another of the outcasts, I presume?

CATO: Yes, seer; I is gwine to Canada, an' I met a man, an' he tole me dat you would give me some wittals an' help me on de way. By golly! ef dar ain't Glen an' Melinda. Dey don't know me in dese fine clothes. [*Goes up to them.*] Ah, chillen! is one wid you. I golly, I is here too! [*They shake hands.*]

GLEN: Why, it is Cato, as I live!

MELINDA: Oh, Cato, I am so glad to see you! But how did you get here?

CATO: Ah, chile, I come wid ole massa to hunt you; an' you see I get tired huntin' you, an' I am now huntin' for Canada. I leff de ole boss in de bed at de hotel; an' you see I thought, afore I left massa, I'd jess change clothes wid him; so, you see, I is fixed up,—ha, ha, ha. Ah, chillen! I is gwine wid you.

MRS. NEAL: Come, sit thee down, and have some breakfast.

CATO: Tank you, madam, I'll do dat. [*Sits down and eats.*]

MR. NEAL: This is pleasant for thee to meet one of thy friends.

GLEN: Yes, sir, it is; I would be glad if we could meet more of them. I have a mother and sister still in slavery, and I would give worlds, if I possessed them, if by so doing I could release them from their bondage.

THOMAS: We are all ready, sir, and the wagon is waiting.

MRS. NEAL: Yes, thee had better start.

CATO: Ef any body tries to take me back to ole massa, I'll pull ebry toof out of dar heads, dat I will! As soon as I get to Canada, I'll set up a doctor shop, an' won't I be poplar? Den I rec'on I will. I'll pull teef fer all de people in Canada. Oh, how I wish I had Hannah wid me! It makes me feel bad when I tink I ain't a-gwine to see my wife no more. But, come, chillen, let's be makin' tracks. Dey say we is most to de British side.

MR. NEAL: Yes, a few miles further, and you'll be safe beyond the reach of the Fugitive-Slave Law.

CATO: Ah, dat's de talk fer dis chile.

[*Exit,* M.D.]

SCENE V

[*The Niagara River. A Ferry.*]

[FERRYMAN, *fastening his small boat.*]

FERRYMAN: [*Advancing, takes out his watch.*] I swan, if it ain't one o'clock. I thought it was dinner time. Now there's no one here, I'll go to dinner, and if any body comes, they can wait until I return. I'll go at once.

[*Exit,* L. *Enter* MR. WHITE, R., *with an umbrella.*]

WHITE: I wonder where that ferryman is? I want to cross to Canada. It seems a little showery, or else the mist from the Falls is growing thicker. [*Takes out his sketch-book and pencils,—sketches.*]

[*Enter* CANE PEDLAR, R.]

PEDLAR: Want a good cane to-day, sir? Here's one from Goat Island,—very good, sir,—straight and neat,—only one dollar. I've a wife and nine small children,—youngest is nursing, and the oldest only three years old. Here's a cane from Table Rock, sir. Please buy one! I've had no breakfast to-day. My wife's got the rheumatics, and the children's got the measles. Come, sir, do buy a cane! I've a lame shoulder, and can't work.

WHITE: Will you stop your confounded talk, and let me alone? Don't you see that I am sketching? You've spoiled a beautiful scene for me, with your nonsense.

[*Enter* 2ᵈ PEDLAR, R.]

2ᵈ PEDLAR: Want any bead bags, or money purses? These are all real Ingen bags, made by the Black Hawk Ingens. Here's a pretty bag, sir, only 75 cents. Here's a money purse, 50 cents. Please, sir, buy something! My wife's got the fever and ague, and the house is full of children, and they're all sick. Come, sir, do help a worthy man!

WHITE: Will you hold your tongue? You've spoiled some of the finest pictures in the world. Don't *you* see that I am sketching?

[*Exit* PEDLARS, R., *grumbling.*]

I am glad those fellows have gone; now I'll go a little further up the shore, and see if I can find another boat. I want to get over.

[*Exit,* L.]

[*Enter* DR. GAINES, SCRAGG, *and an* OFFICER.]

OFFICER: I don't think that your slaves have crossed yet, and my officers will watch the shore below here, while we stroll up the river. If I once get my hands on them, all the Abolitionists in the State shall not take them from me.

DR. GAINES: I hope they have not got over, for I would not lose them for two thousand dollars, especially the gal.

[*Enter* 1ˢᵗ PEDLAR.]

PEDLAR: Wish to get a good cane, sir? This stick was cut on the very spot where Sam Patch jumped over the falls. Only fifty cents.

I have a sick wife and thirteen children. Please buy a cane; I ain't had no dinner.

OFFICER: Get out of the way! Gentlemen, we'll go up the shore.

[*Exit,* L.]
[*Enter* CATO, R.]

CATO: I is loss fum de cumpny, but dis is de ferry, and I spec dey'll soon come. But didn't we have a good time las' night in Buffalo? Dem dar Buffalo gals make my heart flutter, dat dey did. But, tanks be to de Lord, I is got religion. I got it las' night in de meetin.' Before I got religion, I was a great sinner; I got drunk, an' took de name of de Lord in vain. But now I is a conwerted man; I is bound for hebben; I toats de witness in my bosom; I feel dat my name is rote in de book of life. But dem niggers in de Vine Street Church las' night shout an' make sich a fuss, dey give me de headache. But, tank de Lord, I is got religion, an' now I'll be a preacher, and den dey'll call me de Rev. Alexander Washinton Napoleon Pompey Cæsar. Now I'll preach and pull teef, bofe at de same time. Oh, how I wish I had Hannah wid me! Cuss ole massa, fer ef it warn't for him, I could have my wife wid me. Ef I hadn't religion, I'd say "Damn ole massa!" but as I is a religious man, an' belongs to de church, I won't say no sich a thing. But who is dat I see comin'? Oh, it's a whole heap of people. Good Lord! what is de matter?

[*Enter* GLEN *and* MELINDA, L., *followed by* OFFICERS.]

GLEN: Let them come; I am ready for them. He that lays hands on me or my wife shall feel the weight of this club.

MELINDA: Oh, Glen, let's die here, rather than again go into slavery.

OFFICER: I am the United States Marshal. I have a warrant from the Commissioner to take you, and bring you before him. I command assistance.

[*Enter* DR. GAINES, SCRAGG, *and* OFFICER, R.]

DR. GAINES: Here they are. Down with the villain! down with him! but don't hurt the gal!

[*Enter* MR. WHITE, R.]

WHITE: Why, bless me! these are the slaveholding fellows. I'll fight for freedom! [*Takes hold of his umbrella with both hands.—The fight commences, in which* GLEN, CATO, DR. GAINES, SCRAGG, WHITE, *and the* OFFICERS, *take part*—FERRYMAN *enters, and runs to his boat.*—DR. GAINES, SCRAGG *and the* OFFICERS *are knocked down,* GLEN, MELINDA *and* CATO *jump into the boat, and as it leaves the shore and floats away,* GLEN *and* CATO *wave their hats, and shout loudly for freedom.—Curtain falls.*]

The End

Opinions Of The Press

The following are but few of the favorable notices given of "*The Escape*," where it has been publicly read:

A novel Dramatic Reading took place last evening at Sansom Street Hall, by Wm. Wells Brown, the colored dramatic writer, which was highly entertaining, and gave the greatest satisfaction to an intelligent and appreciative audience. The Drama is instructive, as well as very laughable.
—*Philadelphia Evening Bulletin*

All who headed Mr. Brown's Drama were highly gratified. It is well executed, and was finely delivered.
—*Philadelphia Morning Times*

The Dramatic Reading of Mr. Wm. Wells Brown, last evening, was well attended, and gave the most unbounded satisfaction. Mr. Brown's Drama is, in itself, a masterly refutation of all apologies for slavery, and abounds in wit, satire, philosophy, argument and facts, all ingeniously interwoven into one of the most interesting dramatic compositions of modern times.

—*Auburn (N.Y.) Daily Advertiser*

Mr. Brown exhibits a dramatic talent possessed by few who have, under the best instructions, made themselves famous on the stage. He evinces a talent for tragic and comic representation, rarely combined. If you want a good laugh, go and hear him. If you want instruction or information upon the most interesting question of the day, go and hear him. You cannot fail to be pleased. So highly pleased were those who heard it in Auburn, that twenty-eight of the leading men of the city, over their own signatures, extended an invitation to him, through the *Daily Advertise,* to return and repeat the Drama. Among them we recognize the names of Hon. B.F. Hall, of the State Senate, and the Rev. Wm. Hosmer, editor of the *Northern Independent.* Such a compliment entitles Mr. Brown to crowded houses wherever he goes.

—*Seneca Falls Courier*

The Stars and Stripes;
A Melo-Drama

Introduction

Casual readers may initially link the anonymous short play *The Fugitives* (1841) and Lydia Maria Child's *The Stars and Stripes* (1858), and, indeed, there are some useful comparisons. Both appeared in abolitionist gift-books: *The Fugitives* in *The Star of Emancipation* and *Stars and Stripes* in *The Liberty Bell*. Both were likely written by New England women who were active in the early phases of the abolitionist movement; the authors may even have known each other, given Child's early ties to the Boston Female Anti-Slavery Society. Of course, both treat slave life, focus on slave characters, and have an escape as a central piece of their plot. But, in terms of biographical and publication contexts, as well as content and approach, the two texts are quite different—and in the differences we can see the ways in which "gift-book" drama and the place of women in the abolitionist movement changed in the years between the two plays.

The author of *The Stars and Stripes*, Lydia Maria Francis Child was one of the best-known white female abolitionists. Thanks to the recovery work of late-twentieth century critics, Child is also recognized as one of the most important women writers and editors of her time. Born February 11, 1802, to baker David Convers Francis and Susannah Rand, Child was educated locally and prepared to teach. After her mother's death in 1814 and a residence in Maine, she joined her brother Convers, a Harvard-educated Unitarian minister in Watertown, Massachusetts. She opened a school for young women, interacted with area intellectuals ranging from Margaret Fuller to Theodore Parker, and began writing actively.

Her 1824 novel *Hobomok*, published under a male pseudonym, is perhaps her most-taught work and features a fascinating representation of an interracial marriage between a white Puritan woman and a Native American. While the response to *Hobomok*'s subject matter was mixed, her next novel, a story of the roots of American revolutionary impulses called *The Rebels; or, Boston before the Revolution* (1825), marked her as an important literary voice—important enough that she was able to start her own periodical for children, the *Juvenile Miscellany*, in 1826. Though she married attorney and editor David Lee Child in 1828, she stopped neither her writing nor her growing work on social issues (ranging from fighting against the removal of Native Americans from ancestral lands to fighting for abolition)—and, indeed, David Child introduced her to William Lloyd Garrison. By the early 1830s, Lydia Child's writing was responsible for most of the family's income, and the success of her domestic manual *The Frugal Housewife* (1829) and children's texts like *The Girl's Own Book* (1831) had gained her both a level of fame and some economic security.

That security was shattered by the public response to Child's first extended print foray into abolitionism, her 1833 *An Appeal in Favor of That Class of Americans Called Africans*. An extended argument for immediate abolition and against colonization, this text also made anti-racist arguments that were rare among white abolitionists and so shaped a generation of anti-slavery thought. It also led to many families canceling subscriptions to the *Juvenile Miscellany*—forcing the magazine out of business—and damaged sales of her other works both in the North and the South. She eventually found some economic support through editing the *National Anti-Slavery Standard* from 1841 to 1843, but both she, and then her husband, who took over the editorship, left because of their commitment to non-violent resistance.

The next decade was difficult for Child. Marital problems caused constant stress and a separation, though the couple reconciled in 1852. Child wrote prodigiously—gaining some positive notice for her collections of journalism and short sketches, *Letters from New York* (1843–1845)—but never regained her literary position. Her decidedly mixed experiences in organizations devoted to social causes—the Boston Female Anti-Slavery Society and the American Anti-Slavery Society, for example—kept her from the kinds of organizing activities that some of her female colleagues were undertaking, but she remained a committed fighter for abolition in specific and human rights in general.

The eve of the Civil War—and the wake of her play *The Stars and Stripes*—saw perhaps some of her most important later contributions to the abolitionist movement. After attempting to attend the imprisoned John Brown as his nurse, she fell into a fiery exchange of letters with Virginia Governor Henry Wise and Margaretta Mason (wife of one of the authors of the Fugitive Slave Law), which was published and sold briskly. She also lent her name and aid to Harriet Jacobs in producing what is now recognized as one of the most important women's slave narratives, *Incidents in the Life of a Slave Girl* (1861). But emancipation and the Union victory in the Civil War did not stop Child's activism: she compiled and published a text designed to aid in educating newly freed slaves, *The Freedmen's Book* (1865), and wrote a fascinating, controversial novel of race, *A Romance of the Republic* (1867). Until her death on October 20, 1880, she remained a champion for African Americans, Native Americans, and women.

The Stars and Stripes has never been recognized as one of Child's major works—in part because her oeuvre is simply so large, and in part because it lacks the narrative continuity of, say, *Hobomok*. Still, it is a fascinating text both in the context of the drama surrounding slavery and as a record of some key elements of abolitionist thought. The play loosely follows the escape of three slaves from the plantation of Mr. Masters. At some moments, the play seems, frankly, staged—especially with the obviously named white characters like the foolish Mr. North (Masters's easily convinced pro-slavery colleague from New England), and Mr. Freeman, the play's main abolitionist. Some of the characters' more extended speeches are stilted, and the plotting is sometimes fairly expected. Still, Child is more careful in her delineation of Black characters than some of her predecessors, and, even though there are other minstrel-like characters, some characters are surprising in some ways—as is the ending, which goes far beyond anything promised in more conservative works like *The Fugitives* and Stowe's *Uncle Tom's Cabin*. The central themes of the violence (including the sexual violence) of the slave system are present, but Child also emphasizes the hypocrisy of the nation: the play begins on the Fourth of July, with a gathering of planters singing about how they will never be the "slaves" of Britain.

Perhaps just as interesting are the ways in which the *real* anti-slavery struggle is integrated into the play's fiction. Many of Child's readers, for example, would have recognized the characters William and Ellen as loose dramatizations of William and Ellen Craft, who escaped slavery by having the light-skinned Ellen pass as a sickly young planter and William, as "his" valet. Several other incidents known within the abolitionist community, as Child's closing footnote indicates, were also loosely dramatized in the course of the play, and several of the references noted below suggest that *The Stars and Stripes*, while certainly attempting to reach a more general audience, was designed perhaps first and foremost for the abolitionist community. In this, like its forebear *The Fugitives*, it may have been designed for either or both closet drama/novelistic reading or small amateur (family or social) theatricals. It certainly also, though, functioned in dialogue with the range of Tom-shows and with the drama of William Wells Brown, who Child knew.

A Note on the Text

The text reproduced here comes from the original publication of *The Stars and Stripes* in *The Liberty Bell* (Boston: National Anti-Slavery Bazaar, 1858, pp. 122–185). While its language—even the attempt at slave dialect—is generally comprehensible to modern readers, understanding a handful of references will enrich reading. All of the songs sung by the slaves are common minstrel tunes; other songs mentioned or sung would be fairly well-known to Child's original audience—including the brief bit from "The Star Spangled Banner." The "treatment" of Charles Sumner by Preston Brooks is a direct reminder of South Carolina Congressman Brooks's vicious 1856 attack on abolitionist Senator Sumner after an anti-slavery speech by Sumner; this "caning" left a bloodied and unconscious Sumner on the floor of the U.S. Senate in what became a tableaux for the violence of "gentlemen" slaveholders. The August 1 anti-slavery picnic that sets a scene late in the play was a tradition throughout the abolitionist community which began in the early 1840s—with the date chosen to commemorate British emancipation in the West Indies. Canada and, less so, Haiti, are held out as fugitives' goals—but not because of any colonizationist sentiment on Child's part; quite the contrary,

Child is blunt about these being fugitives' goals because of the Fugitive Slave Law, which her character Mr. Freeman is ashamed of—and has vowed to fight against. Finally, the play has some of the earlier literary references to the Underground Railroad, with which Child had some limited connections.

For Further Reading

Child, Lydia Maria. *Hobomok*. Ed. Carolyn L. Karcher. New Brunswick: Rutgers University Press, 1986.

————. *An Appeal in Favor of That Class of Americans Called Africans*. Ed. Carolyn Karcher. Amherst: University of Massachusetts Press, 1996.

————. *The Freedmen's Book*. New York: Arno Press, 1968.

————. *A Romance of the Republic*. Ed. Dana D. Nelson. Louisville: University of Kentucky Press, 1997.

Craft, William and Ellen Craft. *Running a Thousand Miles for Freedom*. Ed. Barbara McCaskill. Athens: University of Georgia Press, 1999.

Jacobs, Harriet. *Incidents in the Life of a Slave Girl*. Ed. Jean Fagan Yellin. Cambridge: Harvard University Press, 2000.

Karcher, Carolyn L. *The First Woman of the Republic: A Cultural Biography of Lydia Maria Child*. Durham: Duke University Press, 1998.

————. *A Lydia Maria Child Reader*. Durham: Duke University Press, 1997.

Meltzer, Milton, ed. *Lydia Maria Child, Selected Papers*. Amherst: University of Massachusetts Press, 1982.

The Stars and Stripes

SCENE I

[*A planter's house, with negro huts in the rear of it. The Fourth of July. On the open lawn, under the shadow of a group of trees, is a picnic table spread with fruit, flowers, decanters of wine, &c. Near by, is an arch made of evergreens, with the word "Liberty" interwoven with flowers. A group of Carolinians, at the table, are singing a verse of "Adams and Liberty." At the close of the verse, they rise, touch glasses, and swinging them triumphantly, sing, "Ne'er shall the sons of Columbia be slaves!"*

While they are singing, the American Flag is brought in by two NEGROES, *attended by a vulgar-looking overseer, somewhat intoxicated. On the top of the flag-staff is a Liberty Cap, which falls, accidentally, while they are attempting to plant the pole in the ground.* WILLIAM, *a genteel-looking light mulatto, the personal attendant of* MR. MASTERS, *picks it up, and, excited by the general exhilaration, he claps it on his head, with a smile. The overseer snatches it off, and gives him a box on the ear.*]

OVERSEER: Take *that*, you black rascal!

[WILLIAM *turns upon him quickly, half raises his hand in anger, then lowers it, and walks sullenly away.*]

OVERSEER: Strike *me*, will you? You'd better *try* striking a white man, and see what you'll *git* by it.

There, take another, you damned nig! [*He strikes him again. William's breast swells, and his eyes flash, but he remains motionless. A youth at the picnic table exclaims:*]

Served him right! Damn his impudence! That'll teach him to remember the difference between masters and niggers.

445

[*While this by-scene has been going on, the flag-staff has been firmly fixed in the ground, and the American Flag surmounted by the Liberty Cap, is floating in the breeze. The gentlemen wave their handkerchiefs toward it, hurra, and sing:*]

"'Tis the star-spangled banner! O long may it wave
O'er the land of the free, and the home of the brave!"

MR. MASTERS: A pleasant scene this, eh?

MR. NORTH: I never spent a happier Fourth of July; and I consider it a great piece of good luck that I happen to be in this beautiful part of the country, to witness such a celebration. How I pity the poor, oppressed people in Europe, who have no idea what liberty is!

MR. MASTERS: Their situation is, indeed, pitiable. If they happen to get any ideas of freedom, by visiting our happy country, and seeing the working of our free and equal institutions, they are obliged to conceal their thoughts when they get home; otherwise, they would soon be silenced by some king, emperor, or pope. The British tried that game with *us*; but they found it was no go. You like the South, do you, sir?

MR. NORTH: I consider it the best and most favored portion of the country, sir. But it's none too good for the true gentlemen and true democrats, that govern it. Here's none of the cursed aristocracy there is in Boston. I've traded round in New England these ten years, and no rich gentleman ever invited me to his house. Here, I find one man's as good as another.

MR. MASTERS: "And a damned sight better," as the Irishman said. By the way, that Irish patriot, Mitchell, is a fine, sensible fellow, and a first rate democrat.

MR. NORTH: So he is, sir. No sentimental twaddle about *him*. I am of his opinion. There's nothing I should like better than a well-stocked plantation, myself.

MR. MASTERS: [*Slapping him heartily on the shoulder.*] Perhaps you will have it some day. So you don't believe what the Abolitionists tell about us? Eh?

MR. NORTH: Don't I see for myself, that their stories are a cursed pack of lies? I am free to say that I never set eyes on a happier set of fellows than your slaves.

MR. MASTERS: We always call 'em *boys*, sir. We never say slaves. I feed my boys well, and clothe 'em well, as you see. They're so attached to me and their mistress, that we couldn't *whip* 'em away from us, if we *tried*. [*He beckons to his mulatto servant,* WILLIAM.] Hallo, Bill! I say, Bill, you don't want your freedom, do you, you dog?

WILLIAM: Oh, no, massa.

MR. MASTERS: You wouldn't thank me for it, if I'd give it to you. *Would* you?

WILLIAM: No, indeed, massa. I'd rather be a stray dog, than a free nigger.

MR. MASTERS: That's right, Bill! You may go. Mr. North, you can tell that to the bobolitionists, when you get back to Yankee-land. *You* are a competent witness; for you have seen with your own eyes, and heard with your own ears.

MR. NORTH: So I have, sir; and I shall be proud to bear my testimony in favor of your patriarchal institution.

MR. MASTERS: [*Slapping him on the shoulder.*] I see that you are a man of sense. But let us rejoin my guests; they are preparing to give a toast.

[*A guest at the picnic table rises and proposes a toast.*] Confusion to the Abolitionists! If we catch one of 'em here we'll give him a suit of tar and feathers, and ride him on a rail.

MR. NORTH: Serve him right, too. I should like to *help* you do it.

MR. MASTERS: You're a true patriot, sir. If we catch one of the canting crew here, he'll run a fair chance of being treated as our brave Brooks served that miserable traitor, Summer.

[*The tipsy overseer swings his glass, and sings:*]

We'll feather him,
And ride him on a rail,
Then black his ugly face,
And lock him up in jail.
If he speaks, we'll pull the trigger,

And shoot him dead as any nigger.

[*The young men join, noisily, in repeating the chorus:*]

If he speaks, we'll pull the trigger,
And shoot him dead as any nigger.

[MASTERS, *waving his hand to silence them, says:*]

One of our friends has composed a song for this occasion. Please give
the gentleman an opportunity to sing it.

THE FILLIBUSTERS' SONG

What nation can with us compare,
In brav'ry, skill, or worth?
    Was ever a people like to us,
Upon the wide, wide earth?

    [*Chorus.*] John Bull! you'd better not set bounds
    Unto our bold career!
A whipping they will surely get,
    That dare to interfere.

We'll take and keep whate'er we like,
    And ask no leave of man;
"For they should take who have the power,
    And they should keep who can."

[*Chorus.*] John Bull! you'd better not set bounds, &c.

We've set our foot on Mexico,
    And got her mines of gold,
And land enough for twenty States,
    Where niggers may be sold.

[*Chorus.*] John Bull! &c.

448

The isle of Cuba we will wrest
    From the weak hand of Spain;
On Hayti, too, we'll get strong hold,
    And rule the Central Main.

      [*Chorus.*] John Bull! &c.

And if it suits our sov'reign will
    T'annex the planet Mars,
What business need it be to *you*,
    How we increase our stars?

      [*Chorus.*] John Bull! &c.

'Tis plain that Fate marks us to be
    The masters of the world!
O'er Sandwich Isles, and far Niphon,
    Our flag shall be unfurled.

      [*Chorus.*] John Bull! &c.

MR. MASTERS: That's a capital song.
MR. NORTH: Brim full of patriotism. We *are* a wonderful nation,
    that's a fact.

    [*Guests of the table.*] Encore! Encore!

SCENE II

[*Cotton fields and negro huts two miles from the planter's house. Evening of the Fourth of July. Pine torches stuck in the trees. Slaves dancing about, half tipsy, singing:*]

Hurra fur Dependent Day!
Hurra! de nigger may play!

449

Ole hoe on de groun he lay,
Ole massa gib rum to day.
Drink, boys, drink! fur we no pay,
Hurra fur Dependent Day!

OLD NEGRO WOMAN: Stop dat ar! Jim's gwine to sing; and you all
know Jim's extr'ornary.

[JIM, *a merry-looking black lad, sings to the accompaniment of his banjo:*]

"Come, broders, let us leave
     Dis Buckra lan for Hayti;
And dar we be receive
     As gran as Lar-fay-i-tee.

"Dar we'll make a mighty show,
     In gran-hus, as you'll see;
I shall be all the go,
     And you like Gub'nor Shootsy.

"Dar no more barrow wheel;
     And dat's a mighty jerkus;
Dar no more 'bliged to steal,
     And den be sent to work-hus.

"We'll dance in great big hall,
     Will hole full half a million;
We'll dance togeder all
     What white man call cotillion.

"We'll lead our partners out,
     Forward two, and backy;
Cross hans, an wheel about,
     And den go home in hacky."

[JIM *receives great applause. The slaves exclaim,* Dat's fustest rate! *They jump about, laughing and singing:*]

Hurra for Dependent Day!

[JIM *waves his hand with an air of importance, and says:*]

Now, you niggers, b'have spectable! will yer? I'se done got
    ready a song, spressly fur dis 'casion.

[*He takes his banjo and sings:*]

I hear massa tell 'em so!
    All de folks born free in dis'ere country, O!
But when I 'ave ask if Jim born so,
    Den my massa tell me no.

Mighty queer some tings I know,
    If all folks born free in dis'ere country, O!
Dis nigger he know dat tings no go,
    Jus as massa tole 'em, O!

[*This performance is received with guffaws of laughter, and rep-
etitions of—*]

Dis nigger he know dat tings no go,
    Jus as massa tole 'em O!

[JIM *again waves his hand magisterially, and says:*]

Nuff of dat ar! I'se gwine to sing the great big song dat
white folks made spressly fur dis splendiferous day, when
Freedom was dispensed wid throughout dis ere land. Come,
broders and sisters, jine wid me!

[*They sing:*]

"Fur ne'er shall de sons of Columby be slaves."

[*White men rush in among them, brandishing whips:*]

Damn your impudence, you black rascals! What are you at? Off with you! Every nigger of you! If one of you is seen out again tonight, he'll be tied up and get thirty-nine, well laid on. Off with you!

[*The slaves disperse hastily.* JIM *hides himself with one of his companions. When the white men have gone, they step out on tiptoe, stealthily.* JIM *nudges his companion, gyrates his finger on his nose, and says with great gravity:*]

Sambo, jus touch de banjo, while I sing—
"Hail Columby! *happy* lan!"

SCENE III

[*Interior of one of the servants huts, in the rear of Mr. Masters's house. The mulatto,* WILLIAM, *sits leaning his head thoughtfully on his hand, while* ELLEN, *his wife, clears their frugal supper table. Being favorite personal attendants upon their master and mistress, they have caught the language of genteel white people, and are familiar with the music they have heard in the parlor. Ellen, who might pass for a white woman, has an air of refinement in her dress and motions; and as she glides about the humble little apartment, she now and then sings snatches of favorite operas. From time to time she glances uneasily at her husband, and at last playfully places her hand on his shoulder, while she sings:*]

My love is sad! my love is sad!
    What shall I do to please him?
Will he be glad, will he be glad
    To have his Ellen tease him?

[*Meeting with no response, she chants slowly, with a kind of mock solemnity:*]

Shall I sing to him of the cold, dim moon,
    Sailing through weeping clouds over a tomb?
Shall I sing *so?*

[*She stops to look up in his troubled face, then springs back, singing gaily and rapidly:*]

No, no, no, no,
　　　I wont sing so;
But like the summer morning,
　　　When streamlets flow,
Bright dew-drops glow,
　　　And birds salute the dawning.

Rich warble and gush!
　　　Quick twitter and trill!
The twirling notes rush
　　　Like drops from a mill.

With trem'lous flow,
　　　The tones shall go,
Like fountains, when they're filling;
　　　No thought of woe
The heart shall know,
　　　While I, like birds, am trilling.

Rich warble and gush!
　　　Quick twitter and trill!
The twirling notes rush
　　　Like drops from a mill.

[*While she sings, William's countenance gradually relaxes into a smile. He looks up with fond admiration, and says:*]

Really, Jim was in the right, when he said it was extror'nary what yer upter. I believe the music master never gave young missis a lesson, without learning it by heart at the very first hearing. And *she!* what a bungling piece of work she makes with a new tune, even when she has been practising a month! What a shame that *she* should have a grand piano, while *you* haven't even an accordion!

ELLEN: Never mind, Willie, dear! God has given me an ear and a voice; and *they* can't be *bought*, like a piano.

WILLIAM: [*With mournful earnestness.*] But they can be *sold*, Ellen! They can be *sold!* I tremble when I hear you sing so sweetly, for fear somebody will buy you for the sake of your ear and voice. If a large price was offered, do you suppose massa would hesitate to sell you? Not *he*! Wasn't my handsome sister sold to a New Orleans trader, in order to raise money to buy that cursed piano? I want to smash all the wires whenever I see it.

ELLEN: [*Caressingly.*] You are sad and cross tonight, Willie. I'm afraid you're like the rest, head-achy with drinking, yesterday, and tired out with hurraing for Independence.

WILLIAM: [*Contemptuously.*] Independence! What a mockery! I hurraed with the rest, for fear they would take notice if I did not, and make it a pretext to hang me, on the charge of plotting an insurrection. How I wanted to kick that fellow, that struck me for putting on the Liberty Cap for fun! I didn't think of it when I put on the Cap, but perhaps there was an omen in it. Thoughts have been very busy in my head since yesterday morning; and it isn't the *first* time that the Fourth of July has set me to thinking. I told you what a rage massa was in about a newspaper sent to him from Boston. He said some damned Abolitionist had done it. He tore it into fifty pieces, and ground them under the heel of his boot. I found some of the crumpled pieces among the bottles, under the picnic table. I hid them in my shoes, and I've been reading them, till I've learned them by heart. Here is a verse that I shall always think of whenever I see the flags flying on Independent day. [*He reads from a scrap of newspaper.*]

"Oppression should not linger
    Where starry banners wave;
The swelling about of Freedom
    Should echo for the slave."

ELLEN: O pray burn all those scraps of paper, Willie. If they should find out that you picked them up and saved them, it might cost you a dreadful flogging.

WILLIAM: [*Laughing.*] Why should he be afraid to have his slaves read Abolition papers? You know he says he couldn't *whip* 'em away from him, if he *tried*. How came massa and missis to take *free* Negroes with them, when they started for the North, this morning? Why are you and I to be sent to his brother's tomorrow, to stay till they come back? Of course, it is because they are so sure that they couldn't *whip* us away from 'em if they *tried*. Heaven knows there's been whipping enough on the plantation to drive 'em all off, if *whipping* would do it. Yet how coolly he tells the lie before our very faces, and calls upon us to confirm it, because he knows we dare not do otherwise. If the Yankees were half as 'cute as they're cracked up to be, I should think they would see through such shams. How *tired* I am of hearing him repeat to every visitor that he couldn't *whip* us away from him, if he *tried*.

ELLEN: And so am I, Willie. But there are things worse to bear than *that*. I have been afraid to tell you all my troubles, for fear you would do something rash, and then they would burn you alive, as they did poor Peggy's husband. But now massa has gone away, and you will have time to get cool before he comes back; and so I will tell you all. When I am at the big house, sewing for missis, as sure as she goes out to ride, he comes into my room and asks me to sing, and tells me how pretty I am. And—and—I know by his ways that he don't mean any good. He gave me this breast-pin, and I was afraid not to take it. You know why poor Peggy's husband was to be sent off to Georgia, and how he tried to poison massa, when he found it out. Now massa says if I make him angry, he will sell *you* to the traders.

WILLIAM: [*Clenching his fist.*] The old villain! and he knows all the while that you are his own daughter!

ELLEN: I told him *that*, but he paid no attention to it. My poor, poor mother! I suppose *she* was afraid, too; for I remember she always seemed so modest. Oh, it is a dreadful situation to be in! [*She bursts into tears.*]

WILLIAM: Don't cry, dear Ellen. It shall never be. *Never!*

ELLEN: Oh, how can we help it? We are slaves; and there is no law to protect us. Sometimes, I have thought I would tell missis all about it, and ask *her* to protect me. But I am afraid to do it, for fear they will sell *me* to Georgia traders, and keep you. I think missis begins to mistrust something; for she has been terribly cross to me lately. See how she burned my arm with hot sealing-wax, because I broke a tooth from her comb, when I was dressing her hair for their great ball, Independent night.

[WILLIAM *stoops to kiss the arm, and says, in a low tone:*]

There is but *one* way, dear Ellen. We know the North Star; we have often talked of following it; and we must start to-night, before massa's brother comes for us.

ELLEN: Oh, Willie, if I only had courage enough! There seems to be nothing else left for us to do. But how *can* we get away? The patrols are always about. There's a man, only a mile off, who keeps blood-hounds to track runaways, and massa's brother will certainly send for him when he finds we are gone.

WILLIAM: He supposes us to be such contented slaves, that he won't hurry to come for us. Meanwhile, we must escape. Very likely the dogs will be after us; but it is better to *die* by dogs, than live to be *treated* as dogs. Tonight is our only chance.

ELLEN: But they say there are such deadly snakes in the swamps.

WILLIAM: That is very true. Snakes may sting your *body*, but they will not sting into the *soul*, like the brutal overseer's lash; and that will be your portion, if you resist your master.

ELLEN: Oh, Willie! [*She sobs violently.*]

WILLIAM: Come, dear Ellen, if you love me, try to be courageous. I know where there is a suit of young massa's clothes, and I have no doubt they will fit you. You can pass for a white lad, and I will be your servant.

ELLEN: [*Smiling through her tears.*] I will tell them I couldn't *whip* you away from me, if I *tried*. Hark! What's that? Has there been anybody about, listening to what we have said?

WILLIAM: [*After a moment's silence.*] It's nobody but Jim. I thought it was his whistle. And now don't you hear him singing, "The Blue-Tailed Fly?" I wish I could be as thoughtless as that merry fellow.

ELLEN: You can't, Willie, because you know too much.

[JIM *enters, singing:*]

"Jim crack corn—don't care!
Ole massa's gone away."

[*He gives a bobbing bow to* ELLEN, *and says, with a knowing grin:*]

Who's gwine to dress missis har? [*He nudges* WILLIAM, *and adds, with a wink.*] I'se boun dey tink bobolitionists wud talk to yer, if dey tuk yer way to de North. 'Peers like he's skeery. What's he skeered bout? You tole him, hunder times, you'd ruther be a stray dog nur a free nigger. Couldn't *whip* dis ere nigger away. *Could* he, now? [*Puts his hands on his knees, and laughs aloud.*]

WILLIAM: Take care, Jim! Don't make so much noise! Those cursed patrols may be prowling about.

JIM: Sound asleep, I'se be boun for 'em. Tuckered out, and done up wid drinkin.

"Jim crack corn—don't care!
Ole massa's gone away".

ELLEN: I'm afraid some of the rum got into *your* head, Jim.

JIM: Dis 'ere nigger's sober's deacon. I'se gwine to Metodist meetin. I'se boun to git religion. Now you'se an extror'nary critter! Up to ebery ting, jus de same as white folks. You know how massa write de pass. Mebbe you'd write a pass fur Jim?

[ELLEN *looks inquiringly at her husband, who nods assent. While she is writing the pass,* JIM *begins to sing.*]

I hearn massa tell 'em so!
All de folks born free in dis 'ere country, O!

WILLIAM: Hush! hush! Jim. You will bring us all into trouble with your noisy fun. If you *must* be singing all the time, do sing

"Old Dan Tucker", or "The Blue-tailed Fly," or something of that sort. But, tell me, seriously, *is* there a Methodist meeting in the woods, tonight?

JIM: I call dat ar an extror'nary question, when a spectable nigger asks to hab a pass gin to him. Dar's a mighty big meetin tree miles off, in Middleton Woods.

[ELLEN *hands him his pass.*]

JIM: Tankee! Tankee! You've allers bin rale kine to dis 'ere nigger. Hope de Lord's got a blessin fur bofe on yer. Good bye.

ELLEN: Thoughtless as Jim seems, I reckon he's going further than Middleton Woods, tonight. Did you notice how he bid us good bye?

WILLIAM: I had my own thought, as soon as he asked for a pass. If he wasn't so noisy, I should like to have him go with us. But it is safest to keep our own counsel, and go alone. I will go and bring young massa's clothes, and you must be thinking how to pass for a white young gentleman, if anybody speaks to us. Our greatest danger is in this county, where so many people know massa, and have seen me with him. But if you can only keep up your courage, Ellen, I trust the Lord will help us to arrive safe in Canada.

SCENE IV

[*A swampy island in the midst of a dense forest, the trees profusely hung with Virginia moss. Twilight is settling into evening, when* WILLIAM *and* ELLEN *creep stealthily toward the borders of the wood. They both look travel-worn and weary.*]

ELLEN: [*in a low voice.*] How awfully lonesome was the spot where we have been hiding all the day! I expected every minute to be stung by a rattlesnake, or a cotton-mouth. How tired we must have been, to drop asleep in such a place!

WILLIAM: It was out of the way of white men, Ellen; and we have more cause to dread *them*, than we have to dread the snakes.

ELLEN: I know it! I know it! Father of mercies! I seem to hear those blood-hounds yelping now. How close they came upon us! If we had crossed that brook a minute later, they would'nt have lost the track, and we should have been torn to pieces. I tremble all over, when I think of it.

WILLIAM: I'm afraid they got upon the track of some other poor fugitive, and so let *us* escape. I was sure I heard a scream.

ELLEN: Oh, Willie, *shall* we ever get to Canada?

WILLIAM: He who knoweth all things, alone can tell. We must put our trust in Him?

ELLEN: Before we start on our night-journey, let us kneel and ask his blessing.

THE FUGITIVES' PRAYER

Father of all! To Thee we bend;
    On Thee alone can we depend;
Guiltless of wrong, yet shunning light,
    Bewildered trav'lers of the night,
When others to their rest have gone,
    We wander through the world alone.
Thou, who created all,
    Oh, hear our anxious call,
And guide us right,
    Through the dark night.
Weary, and worn, and full of fear,
    We travel through the forests drear;
Fierce wolves may seek us for their prey,
    And cruel men, more fierce than they.
Help us to put our trust in Thee!
    Our efforts bless, and make us free!
On earth we have no friend,
    Oh, guide us to the end,
From ev'ry snare,
    Hear thou our prayer!

[*They rise and prepare for their journey. Suddenly a light gleams over the foliage, on one side of the forest.* ELLEN *grasps her husband's arm, and points to the light, saying, in low tones:*]

Now Heaven help us! There are men coming with torches.

WILLIAM: Creep into the bushes, and lie flat on your face.

[*Through the deep stillness voices are heard singing.*]

Trust in Him who blessed the poor!
    O, glory, hallelujah!
He's a friend forever sure!
    O, glory, hallelujah!
Broders, sisters, why do ye mourn?
    Sing glory, hallelujah!
He's got no massa whar he's gone!
    O, glory, hallelujah!

ELLEN: Oh, Willie, don't it seem as if God sent that hymn as an answer to our prayer?

WILLIAM: It does, indeed; and I joyfully accept the omen from my poor brothers in misfortune. They are slaves, secretly holding a meeting in the woods. Some of them have died lately, I suppose; and this is the way they give vent to their feelings. How wild and solemn it sounds, here among the trees, in the starlight.

ELLEN: We have been so lonely, all day, that the sound of friendly human voices is pleasant. Let us wait awhile, and listen.

WILLIAM: Poor fellows! Some of them might be tempted to betray us, in hopes of getting a silver bit, or a red handkerchief. Perhaps, too, there may be patrols lurking round to watch the meeting, and some of them might know me. It's not safe to stay here. So keep fast hold of me, and creep along through the darkest of the shadows.

[*They disappear, while the unseen chorus are repeating:*]

He's got no massa whar he's gone!
O, glory, hallelujah!

SCENE V

[*Past midnight. The moon shining on a broad river. No houses in sight.*]

[WILLIAM *and* ELLEN *creep out from a quantity of boards and barrels, piled up near the river.*]

ELLEN: It seemed frightful to be alone in the woods with wolves and snakes. But I'm more afraid here in the open country. [*She clings to him, and speaks low.*] When I pressed your arm a little while ago, didn't you think you heard something breathing near us?

WILLIAM: Yes, I did, and it brought my heart up into my throat. But I suppose it must have been some sleeping cat or pig. Try to keep up your courage a little longer. There is the Ohio! the river we have so *longed* to see! If we can only get across it, we shall be in the free States, at last. So far, we have got along very well, thanks to your white face, and passing yourself for a slaveholder. If we hadn't been so unlucky as to meet that acquaintance of massa's down at the tavern yonder, we needn't be skulking now. But he looked hard at me, and you were a little confused when you answered his questions. Perhaps he suspected something wrong, and perhaps he didn't. But it is safest for us to keep out of the way of the traveled roads. That nigger we overheard talking about taking some barrels across the river, said he was going to take them from such a place as this. We must try to get a passage with him. Your clothes are so worn and dusty, that you can hardly pass for the son of a rich slaveholder; but you may be taken for a poor white, emigrating with his only nigger. We have a little money left, and that may induce him to take us. The worst of it is, if he suspects us, he may inform against us, when he gets back to Kentucky, in hopes of getting more money. But we must run the risk.

ELLEN: When will the day dawn? This night seems as long as ten nights. That same moon is shining on our old home, Willie. On the tree, where we used to sit and sing, on Sundays, after

meeting. I loved that Southern land, where we were born,
and where all our friends live. If our situation hadn't been
so dreadful, I never *could* have left it to seek a home among
strangers.

WILLIAM: I, too, was thinking what a pleasant home Carolina might
be, if there was no Slavery there. But I long to breathe free air,
if it be the coldest blasts of a Canada winter.

[ELLEN *leans on her husband's shoulder, gazing pensively at the
moon. After looking furtively round, to see whether any one is
stirring, they sing, in a low voice.*]

O, moonlight, deep and tender,
    You shone thus silv'ry bright;
Or veiled in misty splendor,
    Where first we saw the light.

Those scenes of youth have vanished,
    We return to them no more;
For we are aliens, banished
    From our own native shore.

O, river, brightly glancing,
    How beautiful to see!
Beneath the moonbeams dancing,
    So joyfully and free!

And yet to *us* how dreary!
    Who see it through our tears;
So lonely, sad, and weary,
    And trembling with our fears.

O, river, gently flowing,
    Bear us in safety o'er!
The friendly moonlight showing
    Our way to Freedom's shore.

462

[*While they are singing, a black face peeps out from between the boards, and watches them curiously for a minute, and is then lighted up with a broad smile. The head is withdrawn behind the boards, and presently, when all is still, a voice is heard singing:*]

"Jim crack corn—don't care!
　　Ole massa's gone away!"

[WILLIAM *and* ELLEN *start, and look behind them.*]

WILLIAM: I could almost swear that was Jim's voice.

ELLEN: You know *all* the slaves sing that. It can't be that Jim is here. How my heart beats! What if we should be betrayed!

[*The voice behind the boards sings:*]

I hearn massa tell 'em so!
　　All de folks born free in des ere country, O!

WILLIAM: It is Jim! [*He sings in response:*]
"Ne'er shall the sons of Columbia be slaves."

[*The voice behind the boards answers:*]

Dis nigger he know dat tings no go,
　　Jus as massa tole 'em, O!

[JIM *jumps out, grasps their hands, and capers about.*]

JIM: Peers like you've done clared out, too. Dis 'ere nigger sorter spected so. I say, Bill! massa couldn't *whip* us away, *could* he? *Tried* hard nuff, didn't he? Wouldn't *take* our freedom, if massa *guv* it to us, *would* we? [*He sings:*]
Dis nigger he know dat tings no go,
　　Jus as massa tole 'em, O!

WILLIAM: It does me good to hear your merry voice again, Jim; but I think you had better keep more quiet till we get into Canada.

JIM: Skeered, ar ye? Who's feared? Not dis ere nigger. Cause, ye see, he knows what he's bout. You member my brudder Dick, dat was sole to Kentuck? Dick all'ers was quick as rat-trap. Extror'nary smart nigger! Dick's massa hires him out, to tote lumber down dis ere riber. Dick's got an arrant cross de riber, and he's gwine to tote dis ere nigger in a bar'l. Dars bar'ls nuff to tote us all. Dick wouldn't *take* his freedom, if his massa *guv* it to him; an't green nuff fur *dat*. But dis ere nigger sorter spects to see Dick in Canada. [*He bursts out singing:*]

"And dar we be receive
    As gran as Lar-fay-I-tee!:
ELLEN: But even if we succeed in crossing the river, we are not sure of reaching Canada. They say our masters have made a law, obliging people in the free States to catch runaway slaves, and send them back.
WILLIAM: [*Bitterly.*] And they *call* themselves *free* States! But they say that slaves have friends in Ohio, who help 'em on toward Canada, by some kind of underground railroad. I wish I knew how to find them.
JIM: You go away! You knows a heap, Bill. Dar an't no manner o'doubt o'dat ar. But dis ere nigger an't jus woke up, nudder. Dick tole all bout dem ere cars. Dick knows a man in Hi-o, dat'll put us aboard. If massa's car come rattlin arter us, *Ki!*—dey'll jus put on de steam like house a fire! and way we go!

[*He puffs like a steam engine, imitates the car-whistle, and ends by singing:*]

"Clar de track, ole Dan Tucker!"
ELLEN: [*Uneasily.*] When *will* your brother come? Every minute seems an hour.

[*From a boat on the river, a bell is heard to ring three times, followed by a voice, singing:*]

"Heigho! de boatmen row!"

[*They all run toward the river, and soon after, receding voices are heard singing:*]

"Heigho! de boatmen row!
Floatin down the riber Ohi-o!"

SCENE VI

[*Fields near Detroit. A company of men and women assembled to celebrate the first of August. Picnic tables are spread under an evergreen arch, with the word, "Emancipation," formed of dahlias. All the women wear veils, that* ELLEN, *who is among them, need not be easily recognized, in case of an emergency.* WILLIAM *has a neat new dress, and wears a brown wig.*]

MR. FREEMAN: [*Shaking hands with* ELLEN.] You are welcome here; and you may rest assured that you are among kind friends. I hear you have a voice like a bob-o'-link. Won't you give us a song, on this pleasant occasion?

ELLEN: I would most gladly, sir. But is it quite safe? I'm told the law compels you to give up fugitives.

MR. FREEMAN: I blush to acknowledge that we *are* disgraced by such a law; but we contrive many ways to evade it. You are more safe here, than you would be in a city. This is not a public meeting. It is a picnic for Abolitionists only. No Southerner will be likely to intrude upon us. Is your master at the North?

ELLEN: When he left home, he intended to travel North, sir.

MR. FREEMAN: What is his name?

ELLEN: Mr. Alfred Masters, of South Carolina.

MR. FREEMAN: I know of no such name at the hotels; and our friends keep pretty close watch. But, to make your mind perfectly easy, I will tell you a secret. In that ice-house, covered with straw, yonder, there are steps that lead to the underground railroad. You have heard of the underground railroad, perhaps?

ELLEN: [*Smiling.*] O, yes, sir. We *came* by that road.

MR. FREEMAN: I shall keep spies on the watch. If any strangers approach, I will begin to sing, "Get out of the way old Dan Tucker!" Then the women will run for ice, and you and your husband will run with them. There's *one* slave under the ice-house, already. He's so black, that it won't do for *him* to show his face here; but you and your husband are both so light, that you would attract no attention. As for *you*, no one unacquainted with your history would believe that you were not a white woman.

ELLEN: I wish it were possible to cross over to Canada soon, sir.

MR. FREEMAN: I deem it imprudent to attempt it just now. There are some Southerners at the hotel, in search of runaway slaves; and it is possible you might be recognized by some acquaintance of your master's. We will try to have you conveyed over to-morrow morning, before people are stirring. Meanwhile, I wish you would help us to celebrate the emancipation of your enslaved brethren in the British West Indies.

ELLEN: I will try, sir; but I am afraid my voice will tremble; for I am *very* anxious. I will call William, and we will sing together two verses, that a lady taught us last night. She said they were written by an Abolitionist, in Boston.

[ELLEN *sings:*]

"Oh, sunny South, the pride of lands,
Whose joyous spring as Eden blooms,
Whose rivers sweep o'er golden sands,
Whose harvests feed a million looms;
Why looks an anxious world on thee,
In sorrow for thy destiny?"

[WILLIAM *sings in response:*]

"It is, that when the joyous sea
Bore from West Indian Isles the song
Of earth's most glorious jubilee,
Of right, triumphant over wrong,—
Midst a world's welcome, thou alone
Answered the tidings with a groan."

MR. FREEMAN: [*To* ELLEN.] You *are* a bob-o'-link! We must hear your voices again, by-and-by. But now let us all join in a chorus, in honor of our mother country.

[*All the guests unite in singing:*]

"Blow ye the trumpet abroad o'er the sea!
    Brittania hath triumphed, the negro is free!"

[*The women begin to unpack bread, cakes, &c., from the baskets. While they are thus occupied,* MR. FREEMAN *sings:*]

"Get out of the way, Old Dan Tucker!"

[*The women exclaim:*]

O, we forgot the ice. Make haste and bring some ice!

[*Many of them run towards the ice-house;* WILLIAM *and* ELLEN *with them. While others arrange the tables, two strangers enter.*]

NORTH: [*Bowing to* MR. FREEMAN.] Allow me to introduce my friend, Mr. Masters, from South Carolina. He never attended an Abolition meeting, and he was curious to see one.

MASTERS: Not so much to *see* one, as to listen to the *arguments* that may be brought forward. I am a sincere seeker after light; and, perhaps you will be able to convince me.

MR. FREEMAN: This is not one of our public meetings for discussing the subject, sir; but you are welcome to the best we have to offer, either for mind or body. Doubtless, we *might* produce two or three arguments that would make some impression on you. But the ladies are preparing the refreshment tables. They can offer you some delicious fruit, refreshingly cool, for we have an ice-house near by.

[*The Abolitionists glance at each other with a significant smile; and one says aside to another:*]

Its contents wouldn't be very likely to cool *him!*

MASTERS: I thank you; but I came here for argument, rather than refreshments. I hear you are great reasoners; but I hope to convince you that you are laboring under a mistake on this subject. I assure you our servants at the South are a very happy set of people. This gentleman, from Connecticut, can vouch for what I say.

NORTH: Yes, sir, I can; and I am most happy to do it. I *know* something about it. I've *been* at the South; so, *I* am a competent witness. And I'm free to say, I never saw a happier set of fellows than the niggers there. The poor in England have reason to envy their condition.

MR. FREEMAN: Why don't you go as a missionary to England? They wouldn't mob you, as *we* did George Thompson; and if you have half *his* eloquence, perhaps you might persuade the English people to petition their government for leave to *become* slaves. Such petitions would doubtless find some advocates; for there is a class there, as well as here, who consider Slavery the most suitable condition for the poor.

MASTERS: You are pleased to be facetious, sir. But I do assure you, that my slaves have not the least *desire* to be free. I have an uncommonly intelligent slave, named William. He is so attached to me, that when I *offered* him his freedom, he would'nt *take* it. *Would* he, Mr. North?

NORTH: No. He told me, himself, that he'd rather be a stray dog than a free nigger.

MASTERS: William is not peculiar in that respect. They all have the greatest contempt for free niggers. I'm a very kind master; *all* my slaves are so contented with their situation that I couldn't *whip* 'em away, if I *tried. Could* I, Mr. North?

NORTH: No, indeed! They know too well on which side their bread is buttered.

[*A voice, not far off, sings:*]

Dis nigger he know *dat tings* no go,
  Jus as massa tole 'em, O!

MASTERS: [*Looking round.*] Who was that?

MR. FREEMAN: Ethiopian melodies are very popular here. Boys are always whistling or singing them. Some lad appears to have put new words to "Dandy Jim."

MASTERS: [*Smiling.*] It was an excellent imitation. It almost made me feel as if I were on the plantation, hearing my own boys singing merrily, at their work. They're a happy set, sir.

[*One of the Abolitionists aside to another.*]

Some of them are his *own* boys, in more senses than *one*, I reckon.

[*Meanwhile a man enters and hands* MR. MASTERS *a letter. He glances over it, and takes up his hat hastily.*]

MR. FREEMAN: You're not *going*, sir? We have made arrangements to have a *debate* with you, by-and-by. You said you wished to hear our arguments.

MASTERS: I must decline that pleasure, for the present, sir. I am summoned away on unexpected business.

[*He touches his hat, takes* MR. NORTH *by the arm, and turns away.* MR. FREEMAN *turns away in the opposite direction, and joins a knot of the Abolitionists, all of whom are keeping an eye on* MR. MASTERS *and* MR. NORTH, *as they stand talking together.*]

MASTERS: Would you *believe* it? That rascal, Bill, has taken advantage of my absence, to run away! He and his wife Nelly have been seen near Ohio. The ungrateful wench! When I was willing to do so *much* for her!

NORTH: Is it possible? Now I *am* surprised! What ingratitude!

MASTERS: The fact is, sir, the niggers are a singular race. They have several diseases, peculiar to themselves. The one which prevails most generally, is called by our doctors, drapetomania; and the only way I can account for this strange affair, is by supposing that Bill and Nelly had an attack of that disease.

NORTH: Pray what sort of disease may that be, sir?

MASTERS: Doctors like to show their learning, you know; so they made a word from Greek. It means a mania for *running away.*

When niggers appear unusually sulky and dissatisfied, it's a sign that the disease is coming on; and preventive remedies ought to be applied immediately. The learned Dr. Cartwright, of Louisiana University, has written a celebrated book about nigger diseases. He advises that the whip should be freely applied when the first symptoms of drapetomania appear. He calls it "whipping the devil out of 'em." But the fact is, I never perceived any symptoms of it in Bill. He always seemed healthy. It is a very *singular* disease, that drapetomania! There's no telling who may be seized by it. Some of the planters think it is becoming epidemic.

NORTH: It *is* singular, indeed, sir. Perhaps it's part of the curse that the Lord pronounced upon Canaan.

MASTERS: I've heard that idea suggested by our divines. The niggers *are* a cursed race, if ever there *was* one; that's a fact.

NORTH: How lucky it is for *them*, that they have kind masters to take care of them!

MASTERS: You know what good care I took of Bill; the ungrateful dog! Who would have thought of *his* being seized with drape-tomania? But what's to be done? Do you know anything about that infernal underground railroad, they tell of?

NORTH: I dare say the police may know something about it, sir.

MASTERS: If I could only *see* Bill and Nelly, and *reason* a little with 'em, I dare say they would be persuaded that they have done very wrong. When the disease of drapetomania begins to subside, they soon get tired enough of being free niggers, and would gladly go back, if they were not afraid of punishment.

NORTH: That drapetomania is a very strange disease. I never heard of anybody's having it in New England. It *must* be a part of the curse upon Canaan.

MASTERS: Come! let us make inquiries of the police. [*They go out.* MR. FREEMAN *says to the picnic guests:*] Some of you go and caution that merry black Jim, not to be singing any *more* scraps of songs till he gets into Canada. We've come to a narrow pass on the precipice, *now*. There can be no doubt what news that *letter* contained. I heard the word, police. How on earth shall we contrive to get them safely away from their hiding-place, and smuggle them over to Victoria's dominions?

ONE OF THE GUESTS: I see how it can be done. There's a store of ready-made coffins near by, and the man who sells them is an Abolitionist. The colored minister, Mr. Dickson, died yesterday, and we can get his family to help us. William and Ellen must be stained black, and go among the mourners. Jim, who *can't* be stained any blacker, must be carried in the coffin. They can all be locked up in a tomb; a place which the police will not think of searching. In the darkness of the night we can bring 'em near the ferry. The police will, doubtless, be on the watch during all the hours that the boat runs; but you know the ferryman is willing enough to oblige us, if he can do it without being found out. We must be scattered here and there, round the ferry, in numbers sufficient to divert the enemy's forces, if they take it into their heads to be stirring too early.

MR. FREEMAN: I believe it is the best plan that is left for us; but it's a risky business for all of us. That rogue, Jim, must be cautioned not to sing out from the coffin.

SCENE VII

[*Road near Detroit. On one side of the road* MR. FREEMAN *is passing slowly with a few Abolitionists. On the other side of the road are* POLICE OFFICERS, *with brass stars on their coats, and brass bands on their hats, with the word, Police. They pass back and forth, as if on sentinel duty. Rowdy-looking* TRUCKMEN, *with shirt sleeves rolled up, are armed with clubs and whips, as if ready for a mob. The sound of funeral music is heard approaching. A coffin is borne across the stage, followed by colored men and women, and a band of music. After it has passed,* MR. FREEMAN *stops in front of a Police Officer, and says to one of his* ABOLITION *companions:*]

Whose funeral was that? It is not *common* to have a *band* out on such occasions.

471

ABOLITIONIST: I presume it is done in honor of Mr. Dickson, the colored minister. I heard he was to be buried to-day, and I noticed his family among the mourners.

[*A* TRUCKMAN *says, in a loud voice, to the* POLICE OFFICER:] Damned set of amalgamationists! No doubt they're hob-nob with all the *fust* niggers.

[POLICE OFFICER *speaks apart to his companions:*] They must be *expected* on this road, or the *Abolitionists* would not linger about here so.

[*When* MR. FREEMAN *re-appears, talking with a friend, the* POLICE OFFICER *says gruffly to him:*]

What are you loitering about *here* for, sir?

MR. FREEMAN: I will imitate the Yankees, who, they say, answer one question by asking another. Pray what are *you* loitering about here for?

POLICE OFFICER: We're watching for two run-away niggers.

MR. FREEMAN: Only *two*, sir? *Many* pass through this place to Canada.

A TRUCKMAN: Yes, and it's all owing to the *cussed* jugglery of you bobolitionists and your friends, the niggers.

MR. FREEMAN: I am happy to hear that we are so useful.

POLICE OFFICER: But you won't catch a weasel asleep *this* time. Mr. Masters, of South Carolina, a very polite gentleman, and a very kind master, has lost two valuable servants. We've got on the track of 'em, and we're determined to catch 'em for him. We've got the *law* on *our* side.

MR. FREEMAN: As I have no wish to earn blood-money by turning slave-hunter for *any* of our Southern *masters*, the information does not particularly interest *me*.

[*Several of the* ABOLITIONISTS, *who have been looking on the* POLICE *and the rowdies with disgust, break out singing:*]

"No slave-hunt in *our* borders!
    No pirates on *our* strand!
No fetters in the *free* States!

No slave upon *our* land!"

[*The* TRUCKMEN *double their fists, and shake their whips. The* POLICE OFFICER *gets angry, and exclaims:*] I tell you what, you'd better go about your business, if you know what is good for yourselves.

MR. FREEMAN: I trust we are at liberty to *choose* our business. Our Southern masters are *kind* masters. They have left us a *few* privileges. I believe citizens of the free States are not *yet* forbidden by United States law to walk in their own streets; or even to *talk* together in the street, when they think proper. But why so angry, *gentlemen*? Is it not a *manly* employment? Is it not fitting business for *you*, sir, who bear the illustrious name of John Adams? And for *you*, sir, who are accustomed to boast, at political meetings, that you are a true *democrat*, dyed in the wool? I see you *are* ashamed, notwithstanding all the *brass* you have about you.

[*Some slink away; some shake their fists. One of the* POLICE *says:*] Damn your impudence! If you don't hold your tongue, I'll arrest you for disturbing the peace.

[*The* ABOLITIONISTS *laugh, and go off singing:*]

Bring garlands for the free and brave!
Bold hunters of the flying slave!

SCENE VIII

[*Early morning. The Ferry, at Detroit; half a mile across to the Canada shore.* MR. FREEMAN *appears, and after looking all round carefully, knocks three times at a door, near the water. The* FERRYMAN *opens the door.*]

MR. FREEMAN: The passengers you agreed to take are here. Please lose no time.

[FERRYMAN *hastens to the boat;* WILLIAM, ELLEN, *and* JIM *jump in. The fastenings are loosened. The boat is an oar's length*

473

from the shore, when MR. MASTERS *and* MR. NORTH *come running, out of breath, followed by ten or twelve* ABOLITION-ISTS. MR. MASTERS *points his pistol at the* FERRYMAN, *and calls out:*]

Put back that boat! Those are *my* slaves. Put back that boat, or I'll blow your brains out! Hell! There's Jim, too! Where the devil's the police! Call the police, Mr. North! Put back that boat!

[*For an instant, the* FERRYMAN *holds his oars suspended in hesitation.* WILLIAM, *in an agony of anxiety, springs upon him, and exclaims:*]

I'll strangle you, if you do.

FERRYMAN: If I *must* die, I'll die doing my *duty.*

[*He pushes off. Some one behind* MR. MASTERS *knocks the pistol from his hand. The* FERRYMAN *and* WILLIAM *row with all their might. The* ABOLITIONISTS *swing their hats, and hurra. The* POLICE *come in time to see the boat half way across. An American vessel is on the stocks near by, with the name of Henry Clay, floating on its banner. The workmen on board catch the contagion of the scene. They wave their caps, and hurra. The noise attracts people on the Canada side. They see a negro in the boat, and guessing the rest, they hurra. In the intervals, Jim's voice comes across the water.*]

"Don't care! *Ole* massa's gone away!"

[*From shore to shore:*] Hurra! Hurra! Hurra!

MR. FREEMAN TO MR. MASTERS: Couldn't *whip* 'em away from you; *could* you, sir?

FREEMAN TO THE POLICE OFFICER: Didn't catch a weasel asleep *this* time, did we?

[*From shore to shore:*] Hurra! Hurra! Hurra!

MR. NORTH WALKING AWAY WITH MR. MASTERS, SAYS: What a very remarkable case of drapetomania!

[*From shore to shore:*] Hurra! Hurra! Hurra!
[*On the Canada side, they strike up—*] "God save the Queen!"

[*On the other side, the* ABOLITIONISTS *respond:*]

"Blow ye the trumpet aloud o'er the sea!
    Freedom hath triumphed! The slaves are now free!"

N.B. *The scene here described did really occur at Detroit, some years ago, while a vessel, named the Henry Clay, was on the stocks; and the Ferryman made the exclamation here attributed to him.*

The Octoroon; or,
Life in Louisiana

Introduction

While modern readers may not be familiar with the title term of Dion Boucicault's 1859 play, his audience would have been. In the nineteenth and early twentieth centuries, white Americans, obsessed with race and sometimes fascinated with so-called "race science," wanted to mark the amount of Black ancestry in individuals. The generic term "mulatto" was used for individuals with mixed Black and white ancestry—though other ethnic groups like Native Americans might also play a part in that ancestry—and was often tied as much to color as to any specific genealogy. A quadroon supposedly had three white grandparents and one Black grandparent (thus, "quad") and theoretically had very light skin color. An octoroon was supposedly even lighter—perhaps light enough to "pass" for white—and supposedly had one-eighth Black ancestry (one Black great-grandparent).

Such designations had some legal significance: while, as is commonly known, slavery was based on maternal descent (that is, the child followed the condition of the mother), legalized segregation and the incredibly restrictive "Black codes" that limited free Black rights had no such gendering. But these designations also had significant rhetorical power: pro-slavery activists, for example, argued that prominent African American freedom fighters like Frederick Douglass and William Wells Brown gained whatever oratorical and mental powers they possessed from their "white blood" and that they could not be taken as representing the masses of African Americans.

But the figure of the enslaved person of mixed descent was rhetorically important to abolitionists for another reason: it marked the immorality of the slave system, which gave power to slaveholders to commit acts of sexual violence on their slaves. Thus, the figure of the "tragic mulatta"—the feminine noun reflects the fact that women were generally seen in this role—was already fairly commonplace in anti-slavery literature by 1859 and would be seen throughout the nineteenth century.

Boucicault's title "tragic mulatta" character consistently walks a line between these various approaches. Her situation is a clear argument (certainly abolitionist) about the tragedies caused by slavery, but the people around her—kind Southerners (including a slaveholding hero) as well as evil Northerners (especially a slaveholder who has, like Stowe's Simon Legree, come from New England)—argue in terms common to pro-slavery answers to abolitionism. And, of course, both Boucicault and his characters seem to fully believe that the title character's "white blood" accounts for all of her good qualities.

That the play effectively strides between anti-slavery and pro-slavery audiences is a testament to the skill—and perhaps the character—of the playwright. Dion Boucicault was one of the most successful antebellum playwrights both in the U.S. and in his native Great Britain. While he thrived on controversy, he seems not to have had deep political convictions about slavery and race. Born in Dublin in late 1820 to Anne Boursiquot, the sister of playwright George Darly, Boucicault was rumored to have been the illegitimate son of Dr. Dion Larder (who would later become his guardian)—though some biographers suggest that he may have been the legitimate son of Anne and Samuel Smith Boursiquot. Though he studied engineering at the University of London, he was already acting and writing plays by the time he was eighteen. His first major success, *The Willow Copes*, was an adaptation of a French play that he learned of while traveling in France in the early 1840s; this and other work led to an engagement with noted actor Charles Kean's company beginning in 1851. While this partnership led to successful stagings of, among other plays, Boucicault's popular *The Corsican Brothers* (1852; also an adaptation from the French), it also led to an affair with Kean's ward, actress Agnes Robertson. After quarreling with Kean, Boucicault and Robertson eloped and moved to New York, where they quickly became active in the American theater.

Almost immediately popular in the States, Boucicault had success prior to *The Octoroon* with *The Poor of New York* (1857), which, like *The Octoroon*, grafted sentimental melodrama onto stories that highlighted the socio-economic conditions of marginal groups. But it was easily *The Octoroon*, which starred Agnes Boucicault in the title role, that cinched Boucicault's American reputation. The hit of the 1859–1860 holiday season, it eventually became almost as popular across the North as Aiken's version of *Uncle Tom's Cabin*; the hanging of abolitionist martyr John Brown a mere three days before its opening certainly aided its success.

While some thought the subject matter and the play's central tragedy leaned toward abolitionism, most serious abolitionists—and even some pro-South New Yorkers—saw the play as a money-maker designed to capitalize on the controversy over slavery, especially given the play's sensational ending and its positive treatment of Southerners. Indeed, Boucicault was quick to distance himself from anti-slavery sentiments—even going so far as to write very public letters disavowing any belief in abolition. Boucicault's desire to please audiences first can be seen even more fully in what happened to the play when Boucicault returned to England the next year: he first composed a new fifth act that apparently spoke to British anti-slavery sentiments and was loaded with even more sensation (unfortunately, this version is no longer extant), and he finally collapsed the fourth and fifth acts into one, and radically changed the play's ending yet again.

In Britain, Boucicault restaged several of his plays—often revising them as he had *The Octoroon* (*The Poor of New York* became for a time *The Poor of Liverpool*, for example) and wrote some new work before returning to New York. By the 1870s, his plays were guaranteed money-makers, but he was also noted for his love of luxury. Even his success in theaters did not keep him consistently solvent. His marriage also grew complicated, and Boucicault left his wife in 1885, taking the much-younger actress Louise Thorndyke to Austria to bigamously marry her. He worked in journalism and taught briefly on their return to New York, but died on September 18, 1890.

Though much of his later work was well-received, Boucicault remains best known—at least in the U.S.—for *The Octoroon*, a play that combined not only a stunning integration of the topicality of slavery, but also a recognition of the ways in which Tomitudes had taken Stowe's obviously anti-slavery approach and rewritten it into something much more palatable to a racist, mass audience—and done so quite profitably.

A Note on the Text

The text included here follows the initial American version, which is recognized by bibliographers, as the title page indicates, as the "printed not published" edition and tentatively dates to early 1860.

However, in the interest of aiding readers who want a fuller sense of the life of the play, the fourth act from the final British version (the collapsed and revised version of the original British fourth and fifth acts, as published in the Samuel French edition) is included following the initial full text. The first three acts of the British version are almost identical to the American version.

For Further Reading

Degen, John A. "How to End *The Octoroon.*" *Educational Theatre Journal* 27 (1975): 170–178.
Fawkes, Richard. *Dion Boucicault: A Biography.* London: Quartet Books, 1979.

Hogan, Robert. *Dion Boucicault*. New York: Twayne, 1969.

Kaplan, Sidney. "*The Octoroon*: Early History of the Drama of Miscegenation." *Journal of Negro History 20* (1951): 547–557.

Parkin, Andrew, ed. *Selected Plays of Dion Boucicault*. Washington; The Catholic University of America Press, 1987.

Roach, Joseph R. "Slave Spectacles and Tragic Octoroons: A Cultural Genealogy of Antebellum Performance." *Theatre Survey 33* (1992): 167–187.

The Octoroon

The Scene is laid in the Delta of the Mississippi River, on the Plantation of Terrebonne. Time—the Present Day.

CHARACTERS

GEORGE PEYTON	*Mrs. Peyton's Nephew, educated in Europe, and just returned home*
JACOB M'CLOSKY	*formerly Overseer of Terrebonne, but now Owner of one half of the Estate*
SALEM SCUDDER	*a Yankee from Massachusetts, now Overseer of Terrebonne, great on improvements and inventions, once a Photographic Operator, and been a little of everything generally*
PETE	*an "Ole Uncle", once the late Judge's body servant, but now "too ole to work, sa"*
SUNNYSIDE	*a Planter, Neighbour, and Old Friend of the Peytons*
LAFOUCHE	*a Rich Planter*
PAUL	*a Yellow Boy, a favourite of the late Judge's, and so allowed to do much as he likes*
RATTS	*Captain of the Magnolia Steamer*
COLONEL POINDEXTER	*an Auctioneer and Slave Salesman*
JULES THIBODEAUX	*a Young Creole Planter*
CAILLOU	*an Overseer*

487

JACKSON	*a Planter*
CLAIBORNE	*the Auctioneer's Clerk*
SOLON	*a Slave*
WAH-NO-TEE	*an Indian Chief of the Lepan Tribe*
MRS. PEYTON	*of Terrebonne Plantation, in the Attakapas, Widow of the late Judge Peyton*
ZOE	*an Octoroon Girl, free, the Natural Child of the late Judge by a Quadroon Slave*
DORA SUNNYSIDE	*only Daughter and Heiress to Sunnyside, a Southern Belle*
GRACE	*a Yellow Girl, a Slave*
DIDO	*the Cook, a Slave*
MRS. CLAIBORNE	
MINNIE	*a Quadroon Slave*
PLANTERS, SLAVES, DECK HANDS, ETC.	

COSTUMES

GEORGE PEYTON—LIGHT TRAVELLING SUIT

JACOB—DARK COAT, LIGHT WAISTCOAT, BROWN TROUSERS

SCUDDER—LIGHT PLANTATION SUIT

PETE AND NEGROES—CANVAS TROUSERS, SHOES, STRIPED CALICO SHIRTS

SUNNYSIDE—PLANTER'S NANKEEN SUIT, BROAD-BRIMMED STRAW HAT.

RATTS—(CAPTAIN OF A STEAMER). BLACK COAT, WAISTCOAT, AND TROUSERS

PLANTERS—VARIOUS CHARACTERISTIC SUITS

INDIAN—DEER-SKIN TROUSERS AND BODY, BLANKET, MOCCASINS, INDIAN KNOT AND FEATHERS FOR THE HAIR

MRS. PEYTON—BLACK SILK DRESS

ZOE—WHITE MUSLIN DRESS

DORA—FASHIONABLE MORNING DRESS, HAT AND FEATHER

FEMALE SLAVES—STRIPED SKIRTS AND CALICO JACKETS, SOME
                                     WITH KERCHIEFS ROUND THE
                                     HEAD

ACT I

[*A View of the Plantation Terrebonne, in Louisiana—a branch of the Mississippi is seen winding through the Estate—a low built but extensive Planter's Dwelling, surrounded with a verandah, and raised a few feet from the ground, occupies the* L. *side—a table and chairs,* R.C. GRACE *discovered sitting at breakfast-table with* CHILDREN.]

[*Enter* SOLON *from house,* L.]

SOLON: Yah! you bomn'blefry—git out—a gen'lman can't pass for you.

GRACE: [*Seizing a fly whisk.*] Hee! ha—git out! [*Drives* CHILDREN *away—in escaping they tumble against and trip up* SOLON, *who falls with tray—the* CHILDREN *steal the bananas and rolls that fall about.*]

[*Enter* PETE, R.U.E. (*he is lame*)—*he carries a mop and pail.*]

PETE: Hey! laws a massey! why clar out? drop dat banana! I'll murder dis yer crowd. [*He chases* CHILDREN *about—they leap over railing at back.*]

[*Exit* SOLON, R.U.E.]

Dem little niggers is a judgment upon dis generation.

[*Enter* GEORGE, *from house,* L.]

GEORGE: What's the matter, Pete?

PETE: It's dem black trash, Mas'r George; dis ere property wants claring—dem's getting too numerous round; when I gets time, I'll kill some on 'em, sure!

GEORGE: They don't seem to be scared by the threat.

PETE: Top, you varmin! top till I get enough of you in one place!

GEORGE: Were they all born on this estate?

PETE: Guess they nebber was born—dem tings! what dem?—get away! Born here—dem darkies? What on Terrebonne! Don't believe it, Mas'r George, dem black tings never was born at all; dey swarmed one mornin' on a sassafras tree in the swamp—I cotched 'em, dey aint no count. Don't b'lieve dey'll turn out niggers when dere growed—dey'll come out sunthin else.

GRACE: Yes, Mas'r George, dey was born here; and old Pete is fonder on 'em, dan he is of his fiddle on a Sunday.

PETE: What? dem things—dem?—get away [*makes blow at the* CHIL-DREN.] Born here! dem darkies! What, on Terrebonne? Don't b'lieve it, Mas'r George—no. One morning they swarmed on a sassafras tree in de swamp, and I cotched 'em all in a sieve—dat's how dey come on top of dis yearth—git out, you—ya, ya! [*laughs.*]

[*Exit* GRACE, R.U.E.]

[*Enter* MRS. PEYTON, *from house.*]

MRS. P.: So, Pete, you are spoiling those children as usual?

PETE: Dat's right, missus! gib it to ole Pete! he's allers in for it. Git away dere! Ya! if dey aint all lighted like coons on dat snake fence, just out of shot. Look dar! Ya! ya! Dem debils. Ya!

MRS. P.: Pete! do you hear?

PETE: Git down dar! I'm arter you!

[*Hobbles off,* R.U.E.]

MRS. P.: You are out early this morning, George.

GEORGE: I was up before daylight. We got the horses saddled, and galloped down the shell road over the Piney Path; then coasting the Bayou Lake, we crossed the long swamps, by Paul's Path, and so came home again.

MRS. P.: [*Laughing.*] You seem already familiar with the names of every spot on the estate.

[*Enter* PETE—*arranges breakfast, &c.*]

GEORGE: Just one month ago I quitted Paris. I left that syren city as I would have left a beloved woman.

MRS. P.: No wonder! I dare say you left at least a dozen beloved women there, at the same time.

GEORGE: I feel that I departed amid universal and sincere regret. I left my loves and my creditors equally inconsolable.

MRS. P.: George, you are incorrigible. Ah! you remind me so much of your uncle the judge.

GEORGE: Bless his dear old handwriting, it's all I ever saw of him. For ten years his letters came every quarter-day with a remittance, and a word of advice in his formal cavalier style; and then a joke in the postscript that upset the dignity of the foregoing. Aunt, when he died, two years ago, I read over those letters of his, and if I didn't cry like a baby—

MRS. P.: No, George; say you wept like a man. And so you really kept those foolish letters?

GEORGE: Yes; I kept the letters, and squandered the money.

MRS. P.: [*embracing him.*] Ah! why were you not my son—you are so like my dear husband.

[*Enter* SALEM SCUDDER, R.]

SCUD: Ain't he! Yes—when I saw him and Miss Zoe galloping through the green sugar crop, and doing ten dollars' worth of damage at every stride, says I, how like his old uncle he do make the dirt fly.

GEORGE: Oh, aunt! what a bright, gay creature she is!

SCUD: What, Zoe! Guess that you didn't leave anything female in Europe that can lift an eyelash beside that gal. When she goes along, she just leaves a streak of love behind her. It's a good drink to see her come into the cotton-fields—the niggers get fresh on the sight of her. If she ain't worth her weight in sunshine you may take one of my fingers off, and choose which you like.

MRS. P.: She need not keep us waiting breakfast, though. Pete, tell Miss Zoe that we are waiting.

PETE: Yes, missus. Why, Minnie, why don't you run when you hear, you lazy crittur? [MINNIE *runs off.*] Dat's de laziest nigger on dis yere property. [*sits down*] Don't do nuffin.

MRS. P.: My dear George, you are left in your uncle's will heir to this estate.

GEORGE: Subject to your life interest and an annuity to Zoe, is it not so?

MRS. P.: I fear that the property is so involved that the strictest economy will scarcely recover it. My dear husband never kept any accounts, and we scarcely know in what condition the estate really is.

SCUD: Yes, we do, ma'am; it's in a darned bad condition. Ten years ago the Judge took as overseer a bit of Connecticut hardware called M'Closky. The Judge didn't understand accounts—the overseer did. For a year or two all went fine. The Judge drew money like Bourbon whiskey from a barrel, and never turned off the tap. But out it flew, free for everybody or anybody, to beg, borrow, or steal. So it went, till one day the Judge found the tap wouldn't run. He looked in to see what stopped it, and pulled out a big mortgage. "Sign that," says the overseer; "it's only a formality." "All right," says the Judge, and away went a thousand acres; so at the end of eight years, Jacob M'Closky, Esquire, finds himself proprietor of the richest half of Terrebonne—

GEORGE: But the other half is free.

SCUD: No, it ain't, because, just then, what does the Judge do but hire another overseer—a Yankee—a Yankee named Salem Scudder.

MRS. P.: Oh, no, it was—

SCUD: Hold on, now! I'm going to straighten this account clear out. What was this here Scudder? Well, he lived in New York by sittin' with his heels up in front of French's Hotel, and inventin'—

GEORGE: Inventing what?

SCUD: Improvements—anything, from a staylace to a fire-engine. Well, he cut that for the photographing line. He and his apparatus arrived here, took the Judge's likeness and his fancy, who made him overseer right off. Well, sir, what does this Scudder do but introduces his inventions and improvements on this estate. His new cotton gins broke down, the steam sugar-mills burst up, until he finished off with his folly what Mr. M'Closky with his knavery began.

MRS. P.: Oh, Salem! how can you say so? Haven't you worked like a horse?

SCUD: No, ma'am, I worked like an ass—an honest one, and that's all. Now, Mr. George, between the two overseers, you and that good old lady have come to the ground; that is the state of things, just as near as I can fix it.

[ZOE *sings without,* L.]

GEORGE: 'Tis Zoe.

SCUD: Oh! I have not spoiled that anyhow. I can't introduce any darned improvement there. Ain't that a cure for old age; it kinder lifts the heart up, don't it?

MRS. P.: Poor child! what will become of her when I am gone? If you haven't spoiled her, I fear I have. She has had the education of a lady.

GEORGE: I have remarked that she is treated by the neighbours with a kind of familiar condescension that annoyed me.

SCUD: Don't you know that she is the natural daughter of the Judge, your uncle, and that old lady thar just adored anything her husband cared for; and this girl, that another woman would a hated, she loves as if she'd been her own child.

GEORGE: Aunt, I am prouder and happier to be your nephew and heir to the ruins of Terrebonne, than I would have been to have had half Louisiana without you.

[*Enter* ZOE, *from house,* L.]

ZOE: Am I late? Ah! Mr. Scudder, good morning.

SCUD: Thank'ye. I'm from fair to middlin', like a bamboo cane, much the same all the year round.

ZOE: No: like a sugar cane—so dry outside, one would never think there was so much sweetness within.

SCUD: Look here; I can't stand that gal! if I stop here, I shall hug her right off. [*sees* PETE, *who has set his pail down* L.C. *up stage, and goes to sleep on it.*] If that old nigger ain't asleep, I'm blamed. Hillo! [*kicks pail from under* PETE, *and lets him down.*]

[*Exit,* L.U.E.]

PETE: Hi! Debbel's in the pail! Whar's breakfass?

[*Enter* SOLON *and* DIDO *with coffee-pot, dishes, &c.,* R.U.E.]

DIDO: Bless'ee, Missey Zoe, here it be. Dere's a dish of penpans—jess taste, Mas'r George—and here's fried bananas; smell 'em, do, sa glosh.

PETE: Hole yer tongue, Dido. Whar's de coffee? [*pours out.*] If it don't stain de cup, your wicked ole life's in danger sure! dat right! black as nigger; clar as ice. You may drink dat, Mas'r George. [*looks off.*] Yah! here's Mas'r Sunnyside, and Missey Dora, jis drov up. Some of you niggers, run and hole de hosses; and take dis, Dido. [*gives her coffee-pot to hold, and hobbles off, followed by* SOLON *and* DIDO, R.U.E.]

[*Enter* SUNNYSIDE *and* DORA, R.U.E.]

SUNNY: Good day, ma'am. [*Shakes hands with* GEORGE.] I see we are just in time for breakfast. [*sits,* R.]

DORA: Oh, none for me; I never eat. [*sits,* R.C.]

GEORGE: [*Aside.*] They do not notice Zoe. [*aloud.*] You don't see Zoe, Mr. Sunnyside.

SUNNY: Ah! Zoe, girl; are you there!

DORA: Take my shawl, Zoe. [ZOE *helps her.*] What a good creature she is.

SUNNY: I dare say, now, that in Europe you have never met any lady more beautiful in person, or more polished in manners, than that girl.

GEORGE: Your are right, sir; though I shrank from expressing that opinion in her presence, so bluntly.

SUNNY: Why so?

GEORGE: It may be considered offensive.

SUNNY: [*astonished.*] What? I say, Zoe, do you hear that?

DORA: Mr. Peyton is joking.

MRS. P.: [L.C.] My nephew is not yet acquainted with our customs in Louisiana, but he will soon understand.

GEORGE: Never, aunt! I shall never understand how to wound the feelings of any lady; and if that is the custom here, I shall never acquire it.

DORA: Zoe, my dear, what does he mean?

ZOE: I don't know.

GEORGE: Excuse me, I'll light a cigar. [*goes up.*]

DORA: [*aside to* ZOE.] Isn't he sweet? Oh, dear Zoe, is he in love with anybody?

ZOE: How can I tell?

DORA: Ask him. I want to know; don't say I told you to enquire, but find out—Minnie, fan me, it is so nice—and his clothes are French, ain't they?

ZOE: I think so: shall I ask him that too?

DORA: No, dear. I wish he would make love to me. When he speaks to one he does it so easy, so gentle, it isn't bar-room style—love lined with drinks—sighs tinged with tobacco—and they say all the women in Paris were in love with him—which I feel *I* shall be—stop fanning me—what nice boots he wears.

SUNNY: [*to* MRS. PEYTON.] Yes, ma'am, I hold a mortgage over Terrebonne, mine's a ninth, and pretty near covers all the property, except the slaves. I believe Mr. M'Closky has a bill of sale on them. Oh! here he is.

[*Enter* M'CLOSKY R.U.E.]

SUNNY: Good morning, Mr. M'Closky.

M'CLOSKY: Good morning, Mr. Sunnyside, Miss Dora, your servant.

DORA: [*seated,* R.C.] Fan me, Minnie. [*aside*] I don't like that man.

M'CLOSKY: [*aside,* C.] Insolent as usual. [*aloud.*] You begged me to call this morning. I hope I'm not intruding.

MRS. P.: My nephew, Mr. Peyton.

M'CLOSKY: Oh, how d'ye do, sir? [*offers hand,* GEORGE *bows coldly,*

R.C., *aside.*] A puppy, if he brings any of his European airs here we'll fix him. [*aloud*] Zoe, tell Pete to give my mare a feed, will ye?

GEORGE: [*angrily*] Sir.

M'CLOSKY: Hillo, did I tread on ye.

MRS. P.: What is the matter with George?

ZOE: [*takes fan from Minnie*] Go, Minnie, tell Pete, run!

[*Exit* MINNIE, R.]

MRS. P.: Grace, attend to Mr. M'Closky.

M'CLOSKY: A julep, gal, that's my breakfast, and a bit of cheese.

GEORGE: [*aside to* MRS. PETYTON] How can you ask that vulgar ruffian to your table?

MRS. P.: Hospitality in Europe is a courtesy; here it is an obligation. We tender food to a stranger not because he is a gentleman, but because he is hungry.

GEORGE: Aunt, I will take my rifle down to the Atchafalaya. Paul has promised me a bear and a deer or two. I see my little Nimrod yonder, with his Indian companion. Excuse me, ladies. Ho! Paul! [*enters house*]

PAUL: [*outside*] I'ss, Mas'r George.

[*Enter* PAUL, R.U.E., *with* INDIAN, *who goes up.*]

SUNNY: It's a shame to allow that young cub to run over the swamps and woods, hunting and fishing his life away instead of hoeing cane.

MRS. P.: The child was a favourite of the Judge, who encouraged his gambols. I couldn't bear to see him put to work.

GEORGE: [*returning with rifle*] Come, Paul, are you ready?

PAUL: I'ss, Mas'r George. Oh, golly! ain't dat a pooty gun.

M'CLOSKY: See here, you imps; if I catch you and your red-skin yonder, gunning in my swamps, I'll give you rats, mind—them vagabonds when the game's about shoot my pigs.

[*Exit* GEORGE *into house.*]

PAUL: You gib me ratten, Mas'r Clostry, but I guess you take a berry long stick to Wahnotee; ugh, he make bacon of you.

M'CLOSKY: Make bacon of me, you young whelp. Do you mean that I'm a pig?—hold on a bit. [*seizes whip and holds* PAUL]

ZOE: Oh, sir! don't pray don't.

M'CLOSKY: [*slowly lowering his whip*] Darn you, red skin, I'll pay you off some day, both of ye. [*returns to table and drinks*]

SUNNY: That Indian is a nuisance. Why don't he return to his nation out west.

M'CLOSKY: He's too fond of thieving and whiskey.

ZOE: No; Wahnotee is a gentle, honest creature, and remains here because he loves that boy with the tenderness of a woman. When Paul was taken down with the swamp fever the Indian sat outside the hut, and neither ate, slept, or spoke for five days, till the child could recognise and call him to his bedside. He who can love so well is honest—don't speak ill of poor Wahnotee.

MRS. P.: Wahnotee, will you go back to your people?

WAHNOTEEE: Sleugh.

PAUL: He don't understand; he speaks a mash up of Indian, French, and Mexican. Wahnotee Patira na sepau assa wigiran.

WAHNOTEE: Weal Omenee.

PAUL: Says he'll go if I'll go with him. He calls me Omenee, the pigeon, and Miss Zoe is Ninemoosha, the sweetheart.

WAHNOTEE: [*pointing to* ZOE] Ninemoosha.

ZOE: No, Wahnotee, we can't spare Paul.

PAUL: If Omenee remain Wahnotee will die in Terrebonne.

[*During the dialogue* WAHNOTEE *has taken* GEORGE's *gun.*]

[*Enter* GEORGE, L.]

GEORGE: Now I'm ready. [GEORGE *tries to regain his gun;* WAHNOTEE *refuses to give it up.* PAUL *quietly takes it from him, and remonstrates with him.*]

DORA: Zoe, he's going; I want him to stay and make love to me—that's what I came for to-day.

MRS. P.: George, I can't spare Paul for an hour or two; he must run over to the landing, the steamer from New Orleans passed up the river last night, and if there's a mail they have thrown it ashore.

SUNNY: I saw the mail bags lying in the shed this morning.

MRS. P.: I expect an important letter from Liverpool; away with you, Paul, bring the mail-bags here.

PAUL: I'm 'most afraid to take Wahnotee to the shed, there's rum there.

WAHNOTEE: Rum!

PAUL: Come, then, but if I catch you drinkin', oh, laws a-mussey, you'll get snakes! I'll gib it you! now mind.

[*Exit with* INDIAN, R.U.E.]

GEORGE: Come, Miss Dora, let me offer you my arm.

DORA: Mr. George, I am afraid, if all we hear is true, you have led a dreadful life in Europe.

GEORGE: That's a challenge to begin a description of my feminine adventures.

DORA: You have been in love, then?

GEORGE: Two hundred and forty-nine times! let me relate you the worst cases.

DORA: No! no!

GEORGE: I'll put the naughty parts in French.

DORA: I won't hear a word! Oh, you horrible man! go on.

[*Exit* GEORGE *and* DORA *to house.*]

M'CLOSKY: Now, ma'am, I'd like a little business, if agreeable. I bring you news: your banker, old La Fouche, of New Orleans, is dead; the executors are winding up his affairs, and have foreclosed on all overdue mortgages, so Terrebonne is for sale; Here's the *Picayune* [*producing paper*] with the advertisement.

ZOE: Terrebonne for sale!

MRS. P.: Terrebonne for sale, and you, sir, will doubtless become its purchaser.

M'CLOSKY: Well, ma'am, I spose there's no law agin my bidding for it.

The more bidders, the better for you. You'll take care, I guess, it don't go too cheap.

MRS. P.: Oh, sir, I don't value the place for its price, but for the many happy days I've spent here: that landscape, flat and uninteresting though it may be, is full of charm for me; those poor people, born around me, growing up about my heart, have bounded my view of life; and now to lose that homely scene, lose their black ungainly faces, oh, sir, perhaps you should be as old as I am, to feel as I do, when my past life is torn away from me.

M'CLOSKY: I'd be darned glad if somebody would tear my past life away from *me*. Sorry I can't help you, but the fact is, you're in such an all-fixed mess that you couldn't be pulled out without a derrick.

MRS. P.: Yes, there is a hope left yet, and I cling to it. The house of Mason Brothers, of Liverpool, failed some twenty years ago in my husband's debt.

M'CLOSKY: They owed him over 50,000 dollars.

MRS. P.: I cannot find the entry in my husband's accounts; but you, Mr. M'Closky, can doubtless detect it. Zoe, bring here the Judge's old desk, it is in the library. [*Exit* ZOE *to house.*]

M'CLOSKY: You don't expect to recover any of this old debt, do you?

MRS. P.: Yes, the firm has recovered itself, and I received a notice two months ago that some settlement might be anticipated.

SUNNY: Why, with principal and interest this debt has been more than doubled in twenty years.

MRS. P.: But it may be years yet before it will be paid off, if ever.

SUNNY: If there's a chance of it, there's not a planter round here, who wouldn't lend you the whole cash, to keep your name and blood amongst us. Come, cheer up, old friend.

MRS. P.: Ah! Sunnyside, how good you are—so like my poor Peyton.

[*Exit* MRS. PEYTON *and* SUNNYSIDE *to house.*]

M'CLOSKY: Curse their old families—they cut me—a bilious, conceited, thin lot of dried up aristocracy. I hate 'em. Just because my grandfather wasn't some broken-down Virginia-transplant, or a stingy old Creole—I ain't fit to sit down with the same meat with them—it makes my blood so hot I feel my heart hiss. I'll sweep these Peytons from this section of the country. Their presence keeps alive the reproach against me, that I ruined them; yet, if this money should come. Bah! There's no chance of it. Then, if they go they'll take Zoe—she'll follow them. Darn that girl; she makes me quiver when I think of her; she's took me for all I'm worth.

[*Enter* ZOE *from house,* L., *with the desk.*]

Oh, here! do you know what the annuity the old Judge left you is worth to-day? not a picayune.

ZOE: It's surely worth the love that dictated it; here are the papers and accounts. [*putting it on the table,* R.C.]

M'CLOSKY: Stop, Zoe; come here! how would you like to rule the house of the richest planter on Atchapalaga—eh? or say the word, and I'll buy this old barrack, and you shall be mistress of Terrebonne.

ZOE: Oh, sir, do not speak so to me!

M'CLOSKY: Why not? look here, these Peytons are bust, cut 'em; I am rich, jine me; I'll set you up grand, and we'll give these first families here our dust, until you'll see their white skins shrivel up with hate and rage; what d'ye say?

ZOE: Let me pass! Oh, pray, let me go!

M'CLOSKY: What, you won't, won't ye? If young George Peyton was to make you the same offer, you'd jump at it, pretty darned quick, I guess. Come, Zoe, don't be a fool, I'd marry you if I could, but you know I can't so just say what you want. Here, then, I'll put back these Peytons in Terrebonne, and they shall know you done it; yes, they'll have you to thank for saving them from ruin.

ZOE: Do you think they would live here on such terms?

M'CLOSKY: Why not? We'll hire out our slaves and live on their wages.

ZOE: But I'm not a slave.

M'CLOSKY: No; if you were I'd buy you, if you cost all I'm worth.

ZOE: Let me pass!

M'CLOSKY: Stop.

[*Enter* SCUDDER, R.]

SCUD: Let her pass!

M'CLOSKY: Eh?

SCUD: Let her pass! [*takes out his knife*]

[*Exit* ZOE *to house.*]

M'CLOSKY: Is that you, Mr. Overseer? [*Examines paper.*]

SCUD: Yes, I'm here, somewhere interferin'.

M'CLOSKY: [*sitting* R.C.] A pretty mess you've got this estate in—

SCUD: Yes—me and Co.—we done it; but, as you were senior partner in the concern, I reckon you got the big lick.

M'CLOSKY: What d'ye mean?

SCUD: Let me proceed by illustration. [*sits,* R.] Look thar! [*points with his knife off,* R.] D'ye see that tree?—it's called a live oak, and is a native here; beside it grows a creeper; year after year that creeper twines its long arms round and round the tree—sucking the earth dry all about its roots—living on its life—over-running its branches, until at last the live oak withers and dies out. Do you know what the niggers round here, call that sight? They call it the Yankee hugging the Creole. [*sits.*]

M'CLOSKY: Mr. Scudder, I've listened to a great many of your insinuations, and now I'd like to come to an understanding what they mean—if you want a quarrel—

SCUD: No, I'm the skurriest crittur at a fight you ever see; my legs have been too well brought up to stand and see my body abused; I take good care of myself, I can tell you.

M'CLOSKY: Because I heard that you had traduced my character.

SCUD: Traduced! Whoever said so, lied. I always said you were the darndest thief that ever escaped a white jail to misrepresent the North to the South.

M'CLOSKY: [*raises hand to back of his neck*] What!

SCUD: Take your hand down—take it down. [M'CLOSKY *lowers his hand*] Whenever I gets into company like yours, I always start with the advantage on my side.

M'CLOSKY: What d'ye mean?

SCUD: I mean that before you could draw that bowie-knife, you wear down your back, I'd cut you into shingles. Keep quiet, and let's talk sense. You wanted to come to an understanding, and I'm coming thar as quick as I can. Now, Jacob M'Closky, you despise me because you think I'm a fool; I despise you because I know you to be a knave. Between us we've ruined these Peytons; you fired the Judge and I finished off the widow. Now, I feel bad about my share in the business. I'd give half the balance of my life to wipe out my part of the work. Many a night I've laid awake and thought how to pull them through, till I've cried like a child over the sum I couldn't do; and you know how darned hard 'tis to make a Yankee cry.

M'CLOSKY: Well what's that to me?

SCUD: Hold on, Jacob, I'm coming to that; I tell ye, I'm such a fool—I can't bear the feeling, it keeps at me like a skin complaint, and if this family is sold up—

M'CLOSKY: What then?

SCUD: [*rising*] I'd cut my throat—or yours—yours I'd prefer.

M'CLOSKY: Would you now? why don't you do it?

SCUD: 'Cos I's skeered to try! I never killed a man in my life—and civilization is so strong in me I guess I couldn't do it—I'd like to though!

M'CLOSKY: And all for the sake of that old woman and that young puppy—eh? no other cause to hate—to envy me—to be jealous of me—eh?

SCUD: Jealous! what for?

M'CLOSKY: Ask the colour in your face; d'ye think I can't read you, like a book? With your New England hypocrisy, you would persuade yourself it was this family alone you cared for; it ain't—you know it ain't—'tis the "Octoroon;" and you love her as I do, and you hate me because I'm your rival—that's where the tears come from, Salem Scudder, if you ever shed any—that's where the shoe pinches.

SCUD: Wal, I do like the gal; she's a—

M'CLOSKY: She's in love with young Peyton; it made me curse—whar it made you cry, as it does now; I see the tears on your cheeks now.

SCUD: Look at 'em, Jacob, for they are honest water from the well of truth. I ain't ashamed of it—I do love the gal; but I ain't jealous of you, because I believe the only sincere feeling about you is your love for Zoe, and it does your heart good to have her image thar; but I believe you put it thar to spile. By fair means I don't think you can get her, and don't you try foul with her, 'cause if you do, Jacob, civilization be darned. I'm on you like a painter, and when I'm drawed out I'm pizin.

[*Exit* SCUDDER *to house*, L.]

M'CLOSKY: Fair or foul, I'll have her—take that home with you! [*opens desk*] What's here—judgments? yes, plenty of 'em; bill of costs; account with Citizen's Bank—what's this? "Judgment 40,000, 'Thibodeaux against Peyton,'": surely that is the judgment under which this estate is now advertised for sale—[*takes up paper and examines it*] yes, "Thibodeaux against Peyton, 1838." Hold on! whew! this is worth taking to; In this desk the Judge used to keep one paper I want—this should be it. [*reads*] "The free papers of my daughter, Zoe, registered February 4th, 1841." Why, Judge, wasn't you lawyer enough to know that while a judgment stood against you, it was a lien on your slaves? Zoe is your child by a quadroon slave, and you didn't free her; blood! if this is so, she's mine! this old Liverpool debt—that may cross me—if it only arrive too late—if it don't come by this mail—Hold on! this letter the old lady expects—that's it; let me only head off that letter, and Terrebonne will be sold before they can recover it. That boy and the Indian have gone down to the landing for the post-bags, they'll idle on the way as usual; my mare will take me across the swamp, and before they can reach the shed, I'll have purified them bags—ne'er a letter shall shew this mail. Ha, ha! [*calls*] Pete, you old turkey-buzzard, saddle my mare. Then, if I sink every dollar I'm worth in her purchase, I'll own that Octoroon. [*stands with his hand extended towards the house, and tableau*]

End of the First Act

ACT II

[*The Wharf—goods, boxes, and bales scattered about—a camera on stand.* R. SCUDDER, R. DORA, L., GEORGE *and* PAUL *discovered;* DORA *being photographed by* SCUDDER, *who is arranging photographic apparatus,* GEORGE *and* PAUL *looking on at back.*]

SCUD: Just turn your face a leetle this way—fix your—let's see—look here.

DORA: So?

SCUD: That's right. [*puts his head under the darkening apron*] It's such a long time since I did this sort of thing, and this old machine has got so dirty and stiff. I'm afraid it won't operate. That's about right. Now don't stir.

PAUL: Ugh! she look as though she war gwine to have a tooth drawed!

SCUD: I've got four plates ready, in case we miss the first shot. One of them is prepared with a self-developing liquid, that I've invented. I hope it will turn out better than most of my notions. Now fix yourself. Are you ready?

DORA: Ready!

SCUD: Fire!—one, two, three. [SCUDDER *takes out watch*]

PAUL: Now it's cooking, laws mussey, I feel it all inside, as if it was a lottery.

SCUD: So! [*throws down apron*] That's enough. [*withdraws slide, turns and sees* PAUL] What! what are you doing there, you young varmint! Ain't you took them bags to the house yet?

PAUL: Now, it ain't no use trying to get mad, Mas'r Scudder. I'm gwine! I only come back to find Wahnotee; whar is dat I'gnant Ingiun?

SCUD: You'll find him scenting round the rum store, hitched up by the nose.

[*Exit into room,* R.]

PAUL: [*calling at door*] Say, Mas'r Scudder, take me in dat telescope?

SCUD: [*inside room*] Get out, you cub! clar out!

PAUL: You got four ob dem dishes ready. Gosh, wouldn't I like to hav myself took! What's de charge, Mas'r Scudder? [*runs off, R.U.E.*]

[*Enter* SCUDDER, *from room,* R.]

SCUD: Job had none of them critters on his plantation, else he'd never ha'stood through so many chapters. Well, that has come out clear, ain't it? [*shews plate.*]

DORA: Oh, beautiful! Look, Mr. Peyton.

GEORGE: [*looking*] Yes, very fine!

SCUD: The apparatus can't mistake. When I traveled round with this machine, the homely folks used to sing out, "Hillo, mister, this ain't like me!" "Ma'am," says I, "the apparatus can't mistake." "But, mister, that ain't my nose." "Ma'am, your nose drawed it. The machine can't err—you may mistake your phiz, but the apparatus don't." "But, sir, it ain't agreeable." "No, ma'am, the truth seldom is."

[*Enter* PETE, L.U.E., *puffing.*]

PETE: Mas'r Scudder! Mas'r Scudder!

SCUD: Hillo! what are you blowing about like a steamboat with one wheel for?

PETE: *You* blow, Massa Scudder when I tole you; dere's a man from Noo Aleens just arriv' at de house, and he's stuck up two papers on de gates, "For sale—dis yer property," and a heap of oder tings—and he seen missus, and arter he shewn some papers she burst out crying—I yelled; den de corious of little niggers dey set up, den de hull plantation children—de live stock reared up and created a purpiration of lamentation as did de ole heart good to har.

DORA: What's the matter?

SCUD: He's come.

PETE: Dass it—I saw'm!

SCUD: The sheriff from New Orleans has taken possession—Terrebonne is in the hands of the law.

[*Enter* ZOE, L.U.E.]

ZOE: Oh, Mr. Scudder! Dora! Mr. Peyton! come home—there are strangers in the house.

DORA: Stay, Mr. Peyton; Zoe, a word! [*leads her forward—aside*] Zoe, the more I see of George Peyton the better I like him; but he is too modest—that is a very impertinent virtue in a man.

ZOE: I'm no judge, dear.

DORA: Of course not, you little fool, no one ever made love to you, and you can't understand, I mean that George knows I am an heiress; my fortune would release this estate from debt.

ZOE: Oh, I see!

DORA: If he would only propose to marry me I would accept him, but he don't know that, and he will go on fooling in his slow European way until it is too late.

ZOE: What's to be done?

DORA: You tell him.

ZOE: What? that he isn't to go on fooling in his slow—

DORA: No, you goose! twit him on his silence and abstraction—I'm sure it's plain enough, for he has not spoken two words to me all day; then joke round the subject, and at last speak out.

SCUD: Pete, as you came here did you pass Paul and the Indian with the letter bags?

PETE: No, sar; but dem vagabonds neber take de'specable straight road, dey goes by de swamp. [*Exit up path*, L.U.E.]

SCUD: Come, sir!

DORA: [*to* ZOE] Now's your time. [*aloud*] Mr. Scudder, take us with you—Mr. Peyton is so slow, there's no getting him on.

[*Exit* DORA *and* SCUDDER, L.U.E.]

ZOE: They are gone! [*glancing at* GEORGE] Poor fellow, he has lost all.

GEORGE: Poor child! how sad she looks now she has no resource.

ZOE: How shall I ask him to stay?

GEORGE: Zoe, will you remain here? I wish to speak to you.

ZOE: [*aside*] Well that saves trouble.

GEORGE: By our ruin, you lose all.

ZOE: Oh, I'm nothing; think of yourself.

GEORGE: I can think of nothing but the image that remains face to face with me: so beautiful, so simple so confiding—that I dare not express the feelings that have grown up so rapidly in my heart.

ZOE: [*aside*] He means Dora.

GEORGE: If I dared to speak!

ZOE: That's just what you must do, and do it at once, or it will be too late.

GEORGE: Has my love been divined?

ZOE: It has been more than suspected.

GEORGE: Zoe, listen to me then—I shall see this estate pass from me without a sigh, for it possesses no charm for me; the wealth I covet is the love of those around me—eyes that are rich in fond looks—lips that breathe endearing words; the only estate I value is the heart of one true woman, and the slaves I'd have, are her thoughts.

ZOE: George, George, your words take away my breath!

GEORGE: Work, Zoe, is the salt that gives savour to life;

ZOE: Dora said you were slow—if she could hear you now—

GEORGE: Zoe, you are young; your mirror must have told you that you are beautiful.—Is your heart free?

ZOE: Free? of course it is!

GEORGE: We have known each other but a few days, but to me those days have been worth all the rest of my life. Zoe, you have suspected the feeling that now commands an utterance—you have seen that I love you.

ZOE: Me! you love *me*?

GEORGE: As my wife—the sharer of my hopes, my ambitions, and my sorrows; under the shelter of your love I could watch the storms of fortune pass unheeded by.

ZOE: *My* love! *My* love? George you know not what you say. *I* the sharer of your sorrows—your wife. Do you know what I am?

GEORGE: Your birth—I know it. Has not my dear aunt forgotten it—she who had the most right to remember it. You are illegitimate, but love knows no prejudice.

ZOE: [*aside*] Alas! he does not know, he does not know! and will despise me, spurn me, loathe me, when he learns who, what, he has so loved. [*aloud*] George, oh! forgive me! Yes, I love you—I did not know until your words shewed me what has been in my heart, each of them awoke a new sense, and now I know how unhappy—how very unhappy I am.

GEORGE: Zoe, what have I said to wound you?

ZOE: Nothing; but you must learn what I thought you already knew. George, you cannot marry me, the laws forbid it!

GEORGE: Forbid it?

ZOE: There is a gulf between us, as wide as your love—as deep as my despair; but, oh tell me, say you will pity me! that you will pity me! that you will not throw me from you like a poisoned thing!

GEORGE: Zoe, explain yourself—your language fills me with shapeless fears.

ZOE: And what shall I say? I—my mother was—no, no—not her! Why should I refer the blame to her? George, do you see that hand you hold, look at these fingers, do you see the nails are of a blueish tinge?

GEORGE: Yes, near the quick there is a faint blue mark.

ZOE: Look in my eyes; is not the same colour in the white?

GEORGE: It is their beauty.

ZOE: Could you see the roots of my hair you would see the same dark fatal mark. Do you know what that is?

GEORGE: No.

ZOE: That—that is the ineffaceable curse of Cain. Of the blood that feeds my heart, one drop in eight is black—bright red as the rest may be, that one drop poisons all the flood; those seven bright drops give me love like yours, hope like yours—ambition like yours—life hung with passions like dew-drops on the morning flowers; but the one black drop gives me despair for I'm an unclean thing—forbidden by the laws—I'm an Octoroon!

GEORGE: Zoe, I love you none the less, this knowledge brings no revolt to my heart, and I can overcome the obstacle.

ZOE: But *I* cannot.

GEORGE: We can leave this country and go far away where none can know.

ZOE: And our mother, she, who from infancy treated me with such fondness, she who, as you said, had most reason to spurn me, can she forget what I am? Will she gladly see you wedded to the child of her husband's slave? No! she would revolt from it as all but you would, and if I consented to hear the cries of my heart, if I did not crush out my infant love, what would she say to the poor girl on whom she had bestowed so much? No, no!

GEORGE: Zoe, must we immolate our lives on her prejudice?

ZOE: Yes, for I'd rather be black than ungrateful! Ah, George, our race has at least one virtue—it knows how to suffer!

GEORGE: Each word you utter makes my love sink deeper into my heart.

ZOE: And I remained here to induce you to offer that heart to Dora!

GEORGE: If you bid me do so I will obey you—

ZOE: No, no! if you cannot be mine, oh, let me not blush when I think of you.

GEORGE: Dearest Zoe!

[*Exit* GEORGE *and* ZOE, L.U.E.]

[*As they exit* M'CLOSKY *rises from behind rock,* R., *and looks after them.*]

M'CLOSKY: She loves him! I felt it—and how she can love! [*advances*] That one black drop of blood burns in her veins and lights up her heart like a foggy sun. Oh, how I lapped up her words like a thirsty bloodhound! I'll have her, if it costs me my life! Yonder the boy still lurks with those mail bags, the devil still keeps him here to tempt me, darn his yellow skin—I arrived just too late, he had grabbed the prize as I came up. Hillo! he's coming this way, fighting with his Ingiun. [*conceals himself*]

[*Enter* PAUL *wrestling with* WAHNOTEE, R.3.E.]

PAUL: It ain't no use now, you got to gib it up!

WAHNOTEE: Ugh!

PAUL: It won't do! you got dat bottle of rum hid under your blanket—gib it up now, you—Yar! [*wrenches it from him*] You nasty, lying Injiun! It no use you putting on airs, I ain't gwine to sit up wid you all night and you drunk. Hillo! war's the crowd gone? And dar's de 'paratus—oh gosh! if I could take a likeness ob dis child! Uh-uh, let's have a peep. [*looks through camera*] Oh golly! yar, you Wahnotee! you stan' dar, I see you. Ta demine usti. [*goes* R. *and looks at* WAHNOTEE, L., *through the camera,* WAHNOTEE *springs back with an expression of alarm*]

WAHNOTEE: No tue Wahnotee.

PAUL: Ha, ha! he tinks it's a gun; you ign'ant Injiun, it can't hurt you! Stop, here's dem dishes—plates—dat's what he call 'em, all fix, I see Mas'r Scudder do it often—tink I can take likeness—stay dere, Wahnoteee.

WAHNOTEE: No, carabine tue.

PAUL: I must operate and take my own likeness too—how debbel I do dat? Can't be ober dar an'here too—I ain't twins. Ugh! ach! 'Top, you look, you Wahnotee, you see dis rag, eh? Well, when I say go, den lift dis rag like dis, see! den run to dat pine tree up dar, [*points*, L.U.E.] and back agin, and den pull down de rag so, d'ye see?

WAHNOTEE: Hugh!

PAUL: Den you hab glass ob rum.

WAHNOTEE: Rum!

PAUL: Dat wakes him up. Coute Wahnotee in omenee dit, go Wahnotee, poina la fa, comb a pine tree, la revieut sala, la fa.

WAHNOTEE: Firewater!

PAUL: Yes, den a glass ob firewater, now den. [*throws mail bags down and sits on them*, L.C.] Pret, now den, go. [WAHNOTEE *raises apron and runs off*, L.U.E., PAUL *sits for his picture*—M'CLOSKY *appears from* R.U.E.]

M'CLOSKY: Where are they? Ah, yonder goes the Indian!

PAUL: De time he gone just 'bout enough to cook dat dish plate.

M'CLOSKY: Yonder is the boy—now is my time! What's he doing; is he asleep? [*advances*] He is sitting on my prize! darn his carcase! I'll clear him off there—he'll never know what stunned him. [*takes Indian's tomahawk and steals to* PAUL]

PAUL: Dam dat Injun! is dat him creeping dar? I daren't move fear to spile myself. [M'CLOSKY *strikes him on the head, he falls dead*]

M'CLOSKY: Hooraw! the bags are mine—now for it! [*opens mail-bags*] What's here? Sunnyside, Pointdexter, Jackson, Peyton; here it is—the Liverpool post-mark sure enough! [*opens letter—reads*] "Madam, we are instructed by the firm of Mason and Co. to inform you that a dividend of forty per cent is payable on the 1st proximo, this amount in consideration of position, they send herewith, and you will find enclosed by draft to your order on the Bank of Louisiana, which please acknowledge—the balance will be paid in full, with interest, in three, six, and nine months—your drafts on Mason Brothers at those dates will be accepted by La Palisse and Compagnie, N.O., so that you may command immediate use of the whole amount at once if required. Yours, &c., James Brown." What a find! this infernal letter would have saved all. [*during the reading of letter he remains nearly motionless under the focus of camera*] But now

I guess it will arrive too late—these darned U.S. mails are to blame. The Injun! he must not see me.

[*Exit rapidly,* L.]

[WAHNOTEE *runs on, pulls down apron—sees* PAUL *lying on ground—speaks to him—thinks he is shamming sleep—gesticulates and jabbers—goes to him—moves him with feet, then kneels down to rouse him—to his horror finds him dead—expresses great grief—raises his eyes—they fall upon the camera—rises with savage growl, seizes tomahawk and smashes camera to pieces, then goes to* PAUL—*expresses grief, sorrow, and fondness, and takes him in his arm to carry him away—Tableau.*]

End of the Second Act

ACT III

[*A Room in* MRS. PEYTON'S *house; entrances* R.U.E. *and* L.U.E. *an Auction Bill stuck up* L.—*chairs* C. *and tables* R. *and* L. SOLON *and* GRACE *discovered.*]

PETE: [*outside,* R.U.E.] Dis way—dis way.

[*Enter* PETE, POINTDEXTER, JACKSON, LAFOUCHE, *and* CAILLON, R.U.E.]

PETE: Dis way, genl'men; now Solon—Grace—dey's hot and tirsty—sanagree, brandy, rum.
JACKSON: Well, what d'ye say, Lafouche—d'ye smile?

[*Enter* THIBODEAUX *and* SUNNYSIDE, R.U.E.]

THIBO: I hope we don't intrude on the family.
PETE: You see dat hole in dar, sar. [R.U.E.] I was raised on dis yar plantation—neber see no door in it—always open, sar, for stranger to walk in.

SUNNY: And for substance to walk out.

[*Enter* RATTS, R.U.E.]

RATTS: Fine southern style that, eh!

LAFOUCHE: [*reading bill*] "A fine well-built old family mansion, replete with every comfort."

RATTS: There's one name on the list of slaves scratched, I see.

LAFOUCHE: Yes; No. 49, Paul, a quadroon boy, aged thirteen.

SUNNY: He's missing.

POINT: Run away, I suppose.

PETE: [*indignantly*] No, sar; nigger nebber cut stick on Terrebonne; dat boy's dead, sure.

RATTS: What, Picayune Paul, as we called him, that used to come aboard my boat?—poor little darkey, I hope not; many a picayune he picked up for his dance and nigger songs, and he supplied our table with fish and game from the Bayous.

PETE: Nebber supply no more, sar—nebber dance again. Massa Ratts, you hard him sing about de place where de good niggers go, de last time?

RATTS: Well!

PETE: Well, he gone dar hisself; why, I tink so—cause we missed Paul for some days, but nebber tout nothin, till one night dat Inginn Wahnotee suddenly stood right dare mongst us—was in his war paint, and mighty cold and grave—he sit down by de fire. "Whar's Paul?" I say—he smoke and smoke, but nebber look out ob de fire; well knowing dem critters, I wait a long time—den he say, "Wahnotee, great chief;" den I say nothing—smoke anoder time—last, rising to go, he turn round at door, and say berry low—oh, like a woman's voice, he say, "Omenee Pangeuk,"—dat is, Paul is dead—nebber see him since.

RATTS: That red-skin killed him.

SUNNY: So we believe; and so mad are the folks around, that if they catch the red-skin they'll lynch him sure.

RATTS: Lynch him! Darn his copper carcass, I've got a set of Irish deck-hands aboard that just loved that child; and after I tell them this, let them get a sight of the red-skin, I believe they would eat him, tomahawk and all. Poor little Paul!

THIBO: What was he worth?

RATTS: Well, near on 500 dollars.

PETE: [*scandalized*] What, sar! You p'tend to be sorry for Paul, and prize him like dat—500 dollars! [*to* THIBODEAUX.] Tousand dollars, Massa Thibodeaux.

[*Enter* SCUDDER, L.U.E.]

SCUD: Gentlemen, the sale takes place at three. Good morning, Colonel. It's near that now, and there's still the sugar-houses to be inspected. Good day, Mr. Thibodeaux—shall we drive down that way? Mr. Lafouche, why, how do you do, sir? you're looking well.

LAFOUCHE: Sorry I can't return the compliment.

RATTS: Salem's looking a kinder hollowed out.

SCUD: What, Mr. Ratts, are you going to invest in swamps.

RATTS: No; I want a nigger.

SCUD: Hush.

PETE: [R.] Eh! wass dat?

SCUD: Mr. Sunnyside, I can't do this job of shewin' round the folks; my stomach goes agin it. I want Pete here a minute.

SUNNY: I'll accompany them certainly.

SCUD: [*eagerly*] Will ye? Thank ye; thank ye.

SUNNY: We must excuse Scudder, friends. I'll see you round the estate.

[*Enter* GEORGE *and* MRS. PEYTON, L.U.E.]

LAFOUCHE: Good morning, Mrs. Peyton. [*all salute*]

SUNNY: This way, gentlemen,

RATTS: [*aside to* SUNNYSIDE] I say, I'd like to say summit soft to the old woman; perhaps it wouldn't go well, would it?

THIBO: No; leave it alone.

RATTS: Darn it, when I see a woman in trouble, I feel like selling the skin off my back.

[*Exit* THIBODEAUX, SUNNYSIDE, RATTS, POINTDEXTER, GRACE, JACKSON, LAFOUCHE, CAILLOU, SOLON, R.U.E.]

SCUD: [*aside to* PETE] Go outside there; listen to what you hear, then go down to the quarters and tell the boys, for I can't do it. Oh, get out.

PETE: He said, I want a nigger; laws, mussey! what am going to cum ob us! [*Exit slowly, as if concealing himself,* R.U.E.]

GEORGE: [C.] My dear aunt, why do you not move from this painful scene; go with Dora to Sunnyside.

MRS. P.: [R.] No, George, your uncle said to me with his dying breath, "Nellie, never leave Terrebonne," and I never *will* leave it, till the law compels me.

SCUD: [L.] Mr. George—I'm going to say somethin' that has been chokin' me for some time. I know you'll excuse it—thar's Miss Dora—that girl's in love with you; yes, sir, her eyes are startin' out of her head with it; now her fortune would redeem a good part of this estate.

MRS. P.: Why, George, I never suspected this!

GEORGE: I did, aunt, I confess, but—

MRS. P.: And you hesitated, from motives of delicacy?

SCUD: No, ma'am, here's the plan of it; Mr. George is in love with Zoe.

GEORGE: Scudder!

MRS. P.: George!

SCUD: Hold on now! things have got so jammed in on top of us, we ain't got time to put kid gloves on to handle them. He loves Zoe, and has found out that she loves him. [*sighing*] Well, that's all right; but as he can't marry her, and as Miss Dora would jump at him—

MRS. P.: Why didn't you mention this before?

SCUD: Why, because *I* love Zoe too, and I couldn't take that young feller from her, and she jist living on the sight of him, as I saw her do, and they so happy in spite of this yer misery around them, and they reproachin' themselves with not feeling as they ought. I've seen it I tell you and darn it ma'am, can't you see that's what's been a hollowing me out so—I beg your pardon.

MRS. P.: Oh, George—my son, let me call you—I do not speak for my own sake, nor for the loss of the estate, but for the poor people here; they will be sold, divided, and taken away—they have been born here. Heaven has denied me children, so all the strings of my heart have grown around and amongst them, like the fibres and roots of an old tree in its native earth. Oh, let all go, but save them! with them around us, if we have not wealth, we shall at least have the home that they alone can make—

GEORGE: My dear mother—Mr. Scudder—you teach me what I ought to do; if Miss Sunnyside will accept me as I am, Terrebonne shall be saved, I will sell myself, but the slaves shall be protected.

MRS. P.: *Sell* yourself, George! is not Dora worth any man's—

SCUD: Don't say that, ma'am; don't say that to a man that loves another gal; he's going to do a heroic act, don't spile it.

MRS. P.: But Zoe is only an Octoroon.

SCUD: She's won this race agin the white anyhow; it's too late now to start her pedigree.

[*Enter* DORA, L.U.E.]

SCUD: [*seeing* DORA] Come, Mrs. Peyton, take my arm; hush! here's the other one; she's a little too thoroughbred—too much of the greyhound, but the heart's there, I believe.

[*Exit* SCUDDER *and* MRS. PEYTON, R.U.E.]

DORA: Poor Mrs. Peyton.

GEORGE: Miss Sunnyside, permit me a word, a feeling of delicacy has suspended upon my lips an avowal, which—

DORA: [*aside*] Oh dear, has he suddenly come to his senses?

[*Enter* ZOE, L.U.E., *she stops at back.*]

GEORGE: In a word—I have seen and admired you!

DORA: [*aside*] He has a strange way of shewing it—European, I suppose.

GEORGE: If you would pardon the abruptness of the question, I would like to ask you—Do you think the sincere devotion of my life to make yours happy, would succeed?

DORA: [*aside*] Well, he has the oddest way of making love.

GEORGE: You are silent?

DORA: Mr. Peyton, I presume you have hesitated to make this avowal, because you feared in the present condition of affairs here, your object might be misconstrued; and that your attention was rather to my fortune than myself. [*pause*] Why don't he speak?—I mean, you feared I might not give you credit for sincere and pure feelings?—Well, you wrong me. I don't think you capable of anything else than—

GEORGE: No, I hesitated, because an attachment I had formed before I had the pleasure of seeing you, had not altogether died out.

DORA: [*smiling*] Some of those sirens of Paris, I presume [*pause*] I shall endeavour not to be jealous of the past; perhaps I have no right to be. [*pause*] But now that vagrant love is—eh? faded—is it not? Why don't you speak, sir?

GEORGE: Because, Miss Sunnyside, I have not learned to lie.

DORA: Good gracious—who wants you to?

GEORGE: I do, but I can't do it; no, the love I speak of is not such as you suppose,—it is a passion that has grown up here, since I arrived; but it is a hopeless, mad, wild feeling, that must perish.

DORA: Here! since you arrived! Impossible; you have seen no one; whom can you mean?

ZOE: [*advancing,* C.] Me.

GEORGE: [L.] Zoe!

DORA: [R.] You!

ZOE: Forgive him, Dora, for he knew no better until I told him. Dora, you are right; he is incapable of any but sincere and pure feelings—so are you. He loves me—what of that? you know you can't be jealous of a poor creature like me. If he caught the fever, were stung by a snake, or possessed of any other poisonous or unclean thing, you could pity, tend, love him through it, and for your gentle care he would love you in return. Well, is he not thus afflicted now? I am his love—he loves an Octoroon.

GEORGE: Oh, Zoe, you break my heart!

DORA: At college they said I was a fool—I must be. At New Orleans they said, "She's pretty, very pretty, but no brains." I'm afraid they must be right; I can't understand a word of all this.

ZOE: Dear Dora, try to understand it with your heart. You love George, you love him dearly, I know it, and you deserve to be loved by him; he will love you—he must—his love for me will pass away—it shall; you heard him say it was hopeless. Oh, forgive him and me!

DORA: [*weeping*] Oh, why did he speak to me at all, then? You've made me cry, then, and I hate you both!

[*Exit*, L., *through room.*]

[*Enter* MRS. PEYTON *and* SCUDDER, M'CLOSKY *and* POINTDEXTER, R.]

M'CLOSKY: [C.] I'm sorry to intrude, but the business I came upon will excuse me.

MRS. PEY: Here is my nephew, sir.

ZOE: Perhaps I had better go.

M'CLOSKY: Wal, as it consarns you, perhaps you better had.

SCUD: Consarns Zoe?

M'CLOSKY: I don't know, she may as well hear the hull of it. Go on, Colonel—Colonel Pointdexter, ma'am—the mortgagee, auctioneer, and general agent.

POINT: [R.C.] Pardon, me, madam, but do you know these papers? [*hands papers to* MRS. PEYTON]

MRS. PEY: [*takes them*] Yes, sir, they were the free-papers of the girl Zoe; but they were in my husband's secretary, how came they in your possession?

M'CLOSKY: I—I found them.

GEORGE: And you purloined them?

POINT: The list of your slaves is incomplete—it wants one.

SCUD: The boy Paul—we know it.

POINT: No, sir, you have omitted the Octoroon girl, Zoe.

MRS. PEY: Zoe!

ZOE: Me!

POINT: At the time the judge executed those free-papers to his infant slave, a judgment stood recorded against him; while that was on record he had no right to make away with his property. That judgment still exists—under it and others this estate is sold to-day. Those free-papers ain't worth the sand that's on 'em.

MRS. PEY: Zoe, a slave! It is impossible!

POINT: It is certain, Madam; the Judge was negligent, and, doubtless, forgot this small formality.

SCUD: But the creditors will not claim the gal?

M'CLOSKY: Excuse me; one of the principal mortgagees has made the demand.

[*Exit* M'CLOSKY *and* POINTDEXTER, R.U.E.]

SCUD: Hold on yere, George Peyton, you sit down there, you're trembling so, you'll fall down directly—this blow has staggered me some.

MRS. PEY: Oh, Zoe, my child! don't think too hardly of your poor father.

ZOE: I shall do so if you weep—see, I'm calm.

SCUD: Calm as a tombstone, and with about as much life—I see it in your face.

GEORGE: It cannot be! It shall not be!

SCUD: Hold your tongue—it must; be calm—darn the things, the proceeds of this sale won't cover the debts of the estate; consarn those Liverpool English fellers, why couldn't they send something by the last mail? Even a letter, promising something—such is the feeling round amongst the planters—darn me if I couldn't raise thirty thousand on the envelope alone, and ten thousand more on the post-mark.

GEORGE: Zoe, they shall not take you from us while I live.

SCUD: Don't be a fool; they'd kill you, and then take her, just as soon as—stop, Old Sunnyside, he'll buy her! that'll save her.

ZOE: No, it won't; we have confessed to Dora that we love each other. How can she then ask her father to free me?

SCUD: What in thunder made you do that?

ZOE: Because it was the truth, and I had rather be a slave with a free soul than remain free with a slavish, deceitful heart. My father gives me freedom—at least he thought so—may heaven bless him for the thought, bless him for the happiness he spread around my life. You say the proceeds of the sale will not cover his debts—let me be sold then, that I may free his name—I give him back the liberty he bestowed upon me, for I can never repay him the love he bore his poor Octoroon child, on whose breast his last sigh was drawn, into whose eyes he looked with the last gaze of affection.

MRS. PEY: Oh! my husband! I thank heaven you have not lived to see this day.

ZOE: George, leave me! I would be alone a little while.

GEORGE: Zoe! [*turns away overpowered*]

ZOE: Do not weep, George—dear George, you now see what a miserable thing I am.

GEORGE: Zoe!

SCUDDER: I wish they could sell *me*! I brought half this ruin on this family, with my all-fired improvements; I deserve to be a nigger this day—I feel like one, inside.

[*Exit* SCUDDER, L.U.E.]

ZOE: Go now, George—leave me—take her with you.

[*Exit* MRS. PEYTON *and* GEORGE, L.U.E.]

A slave! a slave! Is this a dream—for my brain reels with the blow? He said so. What! then I shall be sold!—sold! and my master—oh! [*falls on her knees with her face in her hands*] no—no master but one. George—George—hush—they come!

522

save me! no, [*looks off,* R.] 'tis Pete and the servants—they come this way. [*Enters inner room,* R.U.E.]

[*Enter* PETE, GRACE, MINNIE, SOLON, DIDO, *and all* NIGGERS, R.U.E.]

PETE: Cum yer now—stand round, cause I've got to talk to you darkies—keep dem children quiet—don't make no noise, de missus up dar har us.

SOLON: Go on, Pete.

PETE: Genl'men, my coloured frens and ladies, dar's mighty bad news gone round. Dis yer prop'ty to be sold—old Terrebonne—whar we all been raised, is gwine—dey's gwine to tak it away—can't stop here no how.

OMNES: Oo!—Oo!

PETE: Hold quiet, you trash o'niggers! tink anybody wants you to cry? Who's you to set up screeching?—be quiet! But dis ain't all. Now, my culled brethren, gird up your lines, and listen—hold on yer bret—it's a comin—we taught dat de niggers would belong to de ole missus, and if she lost Terrebonne, we must live dere allers and we would hire out, and bring our wages to ole Missus Peyton.

OMNES: Ya! ya! Well—

PETE: Hush! I tell ye, taint so—we can't do it—we've got to be sold—

OMNES: Sold!

PETE: Will you hush? she will hear you. Yes! I listen dar jess now—dar was ole lady cryin—Massa George—ah! you seen dem big tears in his eyes. Oh, Massa Scudder, he didn't cry zackly, both ob his eye and cheek look like de bad Bayou in law season—so dry dat I cry for him. [*raising his voice*] Den say de missus, "Taint for de land I keer, but for dem poor niggars—dey'll be sold—dat wot stagger me." "No," say Massa George, "I'd rather sell myself fuss; but they shan't suffer nohow—I see 'em dam fuss."

OMNES: Oh, bless um! Bless Mas'r George.

PETE: Hole yer tongues. Yes, for you, for me, for dem little ones, dem folks cried. Now den, if Grace dere wid her chilr'n were all sold, she'll begin streetchin' like a cat. She didn't mind how kind old Judge was to her; and Solon, too, he'll holler, and break de ole lady's heart.

GRACE: No, Pete; no, I won't. I'll bear it.

PETE: I don't tink you will any more, but dis here will, cause de family spile Dido, dey has. She nebber was worth much 'a dat nigger.

DIDO: How dar you say dat? you black nigger, you. I fetch as much as any odder cook in Louisiana.

PETE: What's de use of your takin' it kind, and comfortin' de missus heart, if Minnie dere, and Louise, and Marie, and Julia, is to spile it?

MINNIE: We won't, Pete; we won't.

PETE: [*to the men*] Dar, do ye hear dat, ye mis'able darkeys; dem gals is worth a boat load of kinder men, dem is. Cum, for de pride of de family, let every darkey look his best for de Judge's sake—dat ole man so good to us, and dat ole woman—so dem strangers from New Orleans shall say, dem's happy darkies, dem's a fine set of niggars; every one say when he's sold, "Lor' bless dis yer family I'm gwine out of and send me as good a home."

OMNES: We'll do it, Pete; we'll do it.

PETE: Hush! hark! I tell ye dar's somebody in dar. Who is it?

GRACE: It's Missy Zoe. See! see!

PETE: Come along; she har what we say, and she's cryin' fore us. None o'ye ig'rant niggers could cry for yerselves like dat. Come here quite; now quite.

[*Exit* PETE *and all the* NEGROES, *slowly*, R.U.E.]

[*Enter* ZOE (*supposed to have overheard the last scene*), L.U.E.]

ZOE: Oh! must I learn from these poor wretches how much I owe, and how I ought to pay the debt? Have I slept upon the benefits I received, and never saw, never felt, never knew that I was forgetful and ungrateful? Oh, my father! my dear, dear father! forgive your poor child; you made her life too happy, and now these tears will flow; let me hide them till I teach my heart. Oh, my—my heart!

[*Exit with a low wailing suffocating cry,* L.U.E.]

[*Enter* M'CLOSKY, LAFOUCHE, JACKSON, SUNNYSIDE, *and* POINTDEXTER, R.U.E.]

POINT: [*looking at watch*] Come, the hour is past. I think we may begin business. Where is Mr. Scudder?

JACKSON: I want to get to Ophelensis to-night.

[*Enter* DORA, R.]

DORA: Father, come here.

SUNNY: Why, Dora, what's the matter? your eyes are red.

DORA: Are they? thank you. I don't care, they were blue this morning, but it don't signify now.

SUNNY: My darling! who has been teasing you?

DORA: Never mind. I want you to buy Terrebonne.

SUNNY: Buy Terrebonne! What for?

DORA: No matter—buy it!

SUNNY: It will cost me all I'm worth—this is folly, Dora.

DORA: Is my plantation at Comptableau worth this?

SUNNY: Nearly—perhaps.

DORA: Sell it, then, and buy this.

SUNNY: Are you mad, my love?

DORA: Do you want *me* to stop here and *bid* for it?

SUNNY: Good gracious! no.

DORA: Then I'll do it, if you don't.

SUNNY: I will! I will! But for heaven's sake go—here comes the crowd.

[*Exit* DORA, L.U.E.]

What on earth does that child mean or want?

[*Enter* SCUDDER, GEORGE, RATTS, CAILLOU, PETE, GRACE,

MINNIE, *and all the* NEGROES. *A large table is in the* C. *at back.* POINTDEXTER *mounts the table with his hammer—his* CLERK *sits at his feet. The* NEGRO *mounts the table from behind* C. *The* COMPANY *sit.*]

POINT: Now, gentleman, we shall proceed to business. It ain't necessary for me to dilate, describe, or enumerate; Terrebonne is known to you as one of the richest bits of sile in Louisiana, and its condition reflects credit on them as had to keep it. I'll trouble you for that piece of baccy, Judge—thank you—so, gentlemen, as life is short, we'll start right off. The first lot on here is the estate in block, with its sugar-houses, stock machines, implements, good dwelling-houses and furniture; if there is no bid for the estate and stuff we'll sell it in smaller lots. Come, Mr. Thibodeaux, a man has a chance once in his life—here's yours.

THIB: Go on. What's the reserve bid?

POINT: The first mortgagee bids forty thousand dollars.

THIB: Forty-five thousand.

SUNNY: Fifty thousand.

POINT: When you have done joking, gentlemen, you'll say one hundred and twenty thousand, it carried that easy on mortgage.

LAFOUCHE: [R.] Then why don't you buy it yourself, Colonel.

POINT: I'm waiting on your fifty thousand bid.

CAILLOU: Eighty thousand.

POINT: Don't be afraid, it ain't going for that, Judge.

SUNNY: [L.] Ninety thousand.

POINT: We're getting on.

THIB: One hundred—

POINT: One hundred thousand bid for this mag—

CAILLOU: One hundred and ten thousand—

POINT: Good again—one hundred and—

SUNNY: Twenty.

POINT: And twenty thousand bid. Squire Sunnyside is going to sell this at fifty thousand advance to-morrow [*looks round*]—Where's that man from Mobile that wanted to give one hundred and eighty thousand?

THIB: I guess he ain't left home yet, Colonel.

POINT: I shall knock it down to the squire—going—gone—for one hunderd and twenty thousand dollars. [*raises hammer*] Judge, you can raise the hull on mortgage—going for half its value. [*knocks*] Squire Sunnyside, you've got a pretty bit o'land, squire. Hillo darkey, hand me a smash dar.

SUNNY: I got more than I can work now.

POINT: Then buy the hands along with the property. Now, gentlemen, I'm proud to submit to you the finest lot of field hands and house servants that were ever offered for competition, they speak for themselves, and do credit to their owners. [*reads*] "No. 1, Solon, a guess boy and good waiter."

PETE: [R.C.] That's my son—buy him, Mass'r Ratts, he's sure to sarve you well.

POINT: Hold your tongue!

RATTS: [L.] Let the old darkey alone—800 for that boy.

CAILLOU: Nine.

RATTS: A thousand.

SOLON: Thank you, massa Ratts, I die for you, sar; hold up for me, sar.

RATTS: Look here, the boy knows and likes me, Judge; let him come my way.

CAILLOU: Go on—I'm dumb.

POINT: One thousand bid. [*knocks*] He's yours, Captain Ratts, Magnolia steamer. [SOLON *goes down and stands behind* RATTS]

POINT: No. 2, the yellow girl Grace, with two children, Saul aged 4, and Victoria 5. [*they get on table*]

SCUD: That's Solon's wife and children, Judge.

GRACE: [*to* RATTS] Buy me, massa Ratts, do buy me, sar.

RATTS: What in thunder should I do with you and those devils on board my boat?

GRACE: Wash, sar—cook, sar—anything.

RATTS: Eight hundred agin then—I'll go it.

JACKSON: Nine.

RATTS: I'm broke, Solon—I can't stop the Judge.

THIB: What's the matter, Ratts? I'll lend you all you want. Go it if you're a mind to.

RATTS: Eleven.

JACKSON: Twelve.

SUNNY: Oh, oh!

SCUD: [*to* JACKSON] Judge, my friend. The Judge is a little deaf. Hello! [*speaking in his ear trumpet*] This gal and them children belong to that boy Solon there. You're bidding to separate them, Judge.

JACKSON: The devil I am! [*rises*] I'll take back my bid, Colonel.

POINT: All right, Judge, I thought there was a mistake. I must keep you, Captain, to the eleven hundred.

RATTS: Go it.

POINT: Eleven hundred—going—going—sold!

POINT: No. 3, Pete, a house servant.

PETE: Dat's me—yer, I'm comin'—stand around dar. [*tumbles upon the table*]

POINT: Aged seventy-two.

PETE: What's dat? a mistake, sar—forty six.

POINT: Lame.

PETE: But don't mount to nuffin—kin work cannel. Come Judge! pick up—now's your time, sar.

JACKSON: One hundred dollars.

PETE: What, sar? me! for me—look ye here! [*dances*]

GEORGE: Five hundred.

PETE: Massa George—ah no, sar—don't buy me—keep your money for some udder dat is to be sold. I ain't no count, sar.

POINT: Five hundred bid—it's a good price. [*knocks*] He's yours, Mr. George Peyton. [PETE *goes down*] No. 4, the Octoroon girl, Zoe.

[*Enter* ZOE, L.U.E., *very pale, and stands on table.*—M'CLOSKY *hitherto has taken no interest in the sale, now turns his chair.*]

SUNNY: [*rising*] Gentlemen, we are all acquainted with the circumstances of this girl's position, and I feel sure that no one here will oppose the family who desires to redeem the child of our esteemed and noble friend, the late Judge Peyton.

OMNES: Hear! bravo! hear!

POINT: While the proceeds of this sale promises to realize less than the debts upon it, it is my duty to prevent any collusion for the depreciation of the property.

RATTS: Darn ye! you're a man as well as an auctioneer ain't ye?

POINT: What is offered for this slave?

SUNNY: One thousand dollars.

M'CLOSKY: Two thousand.

SUNNY: Three thousand.

M'CLOSKY: Five thousand.

GEORGE: [R.] Demon!

SUNNY: I bid seven thousand, which is the last dollar this family possesses.

M'CLOSKY: Eight.

THIBO: Nine.

OMNES: Bravo!

M'CLOSKY: Ten. It's no use, Squire.

SCUD: Jacob M'Closky, you shan't have the girl. Now take care what you do. Twelve thousand.

M'CLOSKY: Shan't I! Fifteen thousand. Beat that any of ye.

POINT: Fifteen thousand bid for the Octoroon.

[*Enter* DORA, L.U.E.]

DORA: Twenty thousand.

OMNES: Bravo!

M'CLOSKY: Twenty-five thousand.

OMNES: [*Groan.*] Oh! oh!

GEORGE: [L.] Yelping hound—take that [*rushes on* M'CLOSKY— M'CLOSKY *draws his knife*]

SCUDDER: [*Darts between them.*] Hold on, George Peyton—stand back. This is your own house; we are under your uncle's roof; recollect yourself. And, strangers, ain't we forgittin' there's a lady present. [*the knives disappear*] If we can't behave like Christians, let's try and act like gentlemen. Go on, Colonel.

LAFOU: He didn't ought to bid against a lady.

M'CLOSKY: Oh, that's it, is it? then I'd like to hire a lady to go to auction and buy my hands.

POINT: Gentlemen, I believe none of us have two feelings about the conduct of that man; but he has the law on his side—we may regret, but we must respect it. Mr. M'Closky has bid twenty-five thousand dollars for the Octoroon. Is there any other bid? For the first time, twenty-five thousand—last time! [*brings hammer down*] To Jacob M'Closky, the Octoroon girl Zoe, twenty-five thousand dollars. [*tableau*]

End of Third Act

ACT IV

[*The Wharf. The Steamer "Magnolia", alongside,* L., *a bluff rock,* R.U.E. RATTS *discovered, superintending the loading of ship.*]

[*Enter* LAFOUCHE AND JACKSON, L.]

JACKSON: How long before we start, captain?

RATTS: Just as soon as we put this cotton on board.

[*Enter* PETE, *with lantern, and* SCUDDER, *with note book,* R.]

SCUD: One hundred and forty-nine bales. Can you take any more?

RATTS: Not a bale. I've got engaged eight hundred bales at the next landing, and one hundred hogsheads of sugar at Patten's Slide—that'll take my guards under—hurry up thar.

VOICE. [*outside*] Wood's aboard.

RATTS: All aboard then.

[*Enter* M'CLOSKY, R.]

SCUD: Sign that receipt, captain, and save me going up to the clerk.

M'CLOSKY: See here—there's a small freight of turpentine in the fore hold there, and one of the barrels leaks; a spark from your engines might set the ship on fire, and you'd go with it.

RATTS: You be darned! Go and try it, if you've a mind to.

LAFOUCHE: Captain, you've loaded up here until the boat is sunk so deep in the mud she won't float.

RATTS: [*Calls off.*] Wood up thar, you Pollo—hang on to the safety valve—guess she'll crawl off on her paddles. [*shouts heard,* R.]

JACKSON: What's the matter?

[*Enter* SOLON, R.]

SOLON: We got him!

SCUD: Who?

SOLON: The Injiun!

SCUD: Wahnotee? Where is he? d'ye call running away from a fellow catching him?

RATTS: Here he comes.

OMNES: Where? Where?

[*Enter* WAHNOTEE, R.; *they are all about to rush on him.*]

SCUD: Hold on! stan' round thar! no violence—the critter don't know what we mean.

JACKSON: Let him answer for the boy, then.

M'CLOSKY: Down with him—lynch him.

OMNES: Lynch him!

[*Exit* LAFOUCHE, R.]

SCUD: Stand back, I say! I'll nip the first that lays a finger on him. Pete, speak to the red-skin.

PETE: Whar's Paul, Wahnotee? What's come ob de child?

WAHNOTEE: Paul wunce—Paul pangeuk.

PETE: Pangeuk—dead.

WAHNOTEE: Mort!

M'CLOSKY: And you killed him? [*they approach again*]

SCUD: Hold on!

PETE: Um, Paul reste?

WAHNOTEE: Hugh vieu. [*goes* L.] Paul rest ci!

SCUD: Here, stay! [*examines the ground*] The earth has been stirred here lately.

WAHNOTEE: Weenee Paul. [*points down, and shows by pantomime how he buried* PAUL]

SCUD: The Injiun means that he buried him there! Stop! here's a bit of leather; [*draws out mail-bags.*] the mail-bags that were lost! [*sees tomahawk in* Wahnotee's *belt—draws it out and examines it.*] Look! here are marks of blood—look thar, red-skin, what's that?

WAHNOTEE: Paul! [*makes sign that* PAUL *was killed by a blow on the head*]

M'CLOSKY: He confesses it; the Indian got drunk, quarreled with him, and killed him.

[*Re-enter* LAFOUCHE, R., *with smashed apparatus.*]

LAFOUCHE: Here are evidences of the crime; his rum bottle half emptied—this photographic apparatus smashed—and there are marks of blood and footsteps around the shed.

M'CLOSKY: What more d'ye want—ain't that proof enough? Lynch him.

OMNES: Lynch him! Lynch him!

SCUD: Stan' back, boys! He's an Injiun—fair play.

JACKSON: Try him, then—try him on the spot of his crime.

OMNES: Try him! Try him!

LAFOUCHE: Don't let him escape!

RATTS: I'll see to that. [*draws revolver*] If he stirs, I'll put a bullet through his skull, mighty quick.

M'CLOSKY: Come, form a court then, choose a jury—we'll fix this varmin.

[*Enter* THIBODEAUX *and* CAILLOU, L.]

THIBO: What's the matter?

LAFOUCHE: We've caught this murdering Injiun, and are going to try him. [WAHNOTEE *sits L., rolled in blanket*]

PETE: Poor little Paul—poor little nigger!

SCUD: This business goes agin me, Ratts—t'ain't right.

LAFOUCHE: We're ready; the jury's impaneled—go ahead—who'll be accuser?

RATTS: M'Closky.

M'CLOSKY: Me?

RATTS: Yes; you was the first to hail Judge Lynch.

M'CLOSKY: [R.] Well what's the use of argument whar guilt sticks out so plain; the boy and Injiun were alone when last seen.

SCUD: [L.C.] Who says that?

M'CLOSKY: Everybody—that is, I heard so.

SCUD: Say what you know—not what you heard.

M'CLOSKY: I know then that the boy was killed with that toma-hawk—the red-skin owns it—the signs of violence are all round the shed—this apparatus smashed—ain't it plain that in a drunken fit he slew the boy, and when sober concealed the body yonder?

OMNES: That's it—that's it.

RATTS: Who defends the Injiun?

SCUD: I will; for it is agin my natur' to b'lieve him guilty; and if he be, this ain't the place, nor you the authority to try him. How are we sure the boy is dead at all? There are no witnesses but a rum bottle and an old machine. Is it on such evidence you'd hang a human being?

RATTS: His own confession.

SCUD: I appeal against your usurped authority. This lynch law is a wild and lawless proceeding. Here's a pictur' for a civilized com-munity to afford: yonder, a poor, ignorant savage, and round him a circle of hearts, white with revenge and hate, thirsting for his blood; you call yourselves judges—you ain't—you're a jury of executioners. It is such scenes as these that bring disgrace upon our Western life.

M'CLOSKY: Evidence! Evidence! Give us evidence. We've had talk enough; now for proof.

OMNES: Yes, yes! Proof, proof.

SCUD: Where am I to get it? The proof is here, in my heart.

PETE: [*who has been looking about the camera.*] Top, sar! Top a bit! O, laws-a-mussey, see dis, here's a pictur' I found stickin' in that yar telescope machine, sar! look sar!

SCUD: A photographic plate. [PETE *holds lantern up*] What's this, eh? two forms! The child—'tis he! dead—and above him—Ah! ah! Jacob M'Closky, 'twas you murdered that boy!

M'CLOSKY: Me?

SCUD: You! You slew him with that tomahawk; and as you stood over his body with the letter in your hand, you thought that no witness saw the deed, that no eye was on you—but there was, Jacob M'Closky, there was. The eye of the Eternal was on you—the blessed sun in heaven, that, looking down, struck upon this plate the image of the deed. Here you are, in the very attitude of your crime!

M'CLOSKY: 'Tis false!

SCUD: 'Tis true! the apparatus can't lie. Look there, jurymen. [*shows plate to jury.*] Look there. O, you wanted evidence—you called for proof—heaven has answered and convicted you.

M'CLOSKY: What court of law would receive such evidence?

[*going*]

RATTS: Stop; *this* would—you called it yourself; you wanted to make us murder that Injiun, and since we've got our hands in for justice, we'll try it on *you*. What say ye? shall we have one law for the red-skin and another for the white?

OMNES: Try him! Try him!

RATTS: Who'll be accuser?

SCUD: I will! Fellow-citizens, you are convened and assembled here under a higher power than the law. What's the law? When the ship's abroad on the ocean, when the army is before the enemy, where in thunder's the law? It is in the hearts of brave men, who can tell right from wrong, and from whom justice can't be bought. So it is here, in the wilds of the west, where our hatred of crime is measured by the speed of our executions—where necessity is law! I say, then, air you honest men? air you true? Put your hands on your naked breasts, and let every man as don't feel a real American heart there, bustin' up with freedom, truth, and right, let that man step out—that's the oath I put to ye—and then say, darn ye, go it!

OMNES: Go on. Go on.

SCUD: No! I won't go on; that man's down. I won't strike him, even with words. Jacob, your accuser is that picter of the crime—let that speak—defend yourself.

M'CLOSKY: [*draws knife*] I will, quicker than lightning.

RATTS: Seize him, then! [*they rush on* M'CLOSKY, *and disarm him*] He can fight though he's a painter, claws all over.

SCUD: Stop! Search him, we may find more evidence.

M'CLOSKY: Would you rob me first, and murder me afterwards?

RATTS: [*searching him*] That's his programme—here's a pocket-book.

SCUD: [*opens it*] What's here? Letters! Hello! To "Mrs. Peyton, Terrebonne, Louisiana, United States." Liverpool post-mark. Ho! I've got hold of the tail of a rat—come out. [*reads*] What's this? A draft for eighty-five thousand dollars, and credit on Palisse and Co., of New Orleans, for the balance. Hi! the rat's out. You killed the boy to steal this letter from the mail-bags—you stole this letter, that the money should not arrive in time to save the Octoroon; had it done so, the lien on the estate would have ceased, and Zoe be free.

OMNES: Lynch him!—lynch him!—down with him!

SCUD: Silence in the court—stand back, let the gentlemen of the jury retire, consult, and return their verdict.

RATTS: I'm responsible for the crittur—go on.

PETE: [*to* WAHNOTEE] See Injiun; look dar [*shows him plate*], see dat innocent; look, dar's de murderer of poor Paul.

WAHNOTEE: Ugh! [*examines plate*]

PETE: Ya! as he? Closky tue Paul—kill de child with your tomahawk dar, 'twasn't you, no—ole Pete allus say so. Poor Injiun lub our little Paul. [WAHNOTEE *rises and looks at* M'CLOSKY—*he is in his war paint and fully armed*]

SCUD: What say ye, gentlemen? Is the prisoner guilty, or is he not guilty?

OMNES: Guilty!

SCUD: And what is to be his punishment?

OMNES: Death! [*All advance.*]

WAHNOTEE: [*Crosses to* M'CLOSKY.] Ugh!

SCUD: No, Injiun; we deal out justice here, not revenge. 'Tain't you he has injured, 'tis the white man, whose laws he has offended.

RATTS: Away with him—put him down the aft hatch, till we rig his funeral.

M'CLOSKY: Fifty against one! O! If I had you one by one, alone in the swamp, I'd rip ye all. [*He is borne off in boat, struggling.*]

SCUD: Now then to business.

PETE: [*Re-enters from boat.*] O, law, sir, dat debil Closky, he tore hisself from de gen'lam, knock me down, take my light, and trows it on de turpentine barrels, and de shed's all afire! [*Fire seen,* R.]

JACKSON: [*Re-entering.*] We are catching fire forward: quick, cut free from the shore.

RATTS: All hands aboard there—cut the starn ropes—give her headway!

ALL: Ay, ay! [*Cry of "fire" heard—Engine bells heard—steam whistle noise.*]

RATTS: Cut all away for'ard—overboard with every bale afire.

[*The Steamer moves off—fire kept up—*M'CLOSKY *re-enters,* R., *swimming on.*]

M'CLOSKY: Ha! have I fixed ye? Burn! burn! that's right. You thought you had cornered me, did ye? As I swam down, I thought I heard something in the water, as if pursuing me—one of them darned alligators, I suppose—they swarm hereabout—may they crunch every limb of ye! [*Exit,* L.]

[WAHNOTEE *swims on—finds trail—follows him. The Steamer floats on at back, burning. Tableaux. Curtain*]

End of Fourth Act

ACT V, SCENE I

[*Negroes' Quarters in 1.*]

[*Enter* ZOE, L.I.E.]

ZOE: It wants an hour yet to daylight—here is Pete's hut—[*Knocks.*] He sleeps—no; I see a light.

DIDO: [*Enters from hut*, R.F.] Who dat?

ZOE: Hush, aunty! 'Tis I—Zoe.

DIDO: Missey Zoe! Why you out in de swamp dis time ob night you catch de fever sure—you is all wet.

ZOE: Where's Pete?

DIDO: He gone down to de landing last night wid Mas'r Scudder: note come back since—kint make it out.

ZOE: Aunty, there is sickness up at the house: I have been up all night beside one who suffers, and I remembered that when I had the fever you gave me a drink, a bitter drink that made me sleep—do you remember it?

DIDO: Didn't I? Dem doctors ain't no 'count; dey don't know nuffin.

ZOE: No; but you, aunty, you are wise—you know every plant, don't you, and what it is good for?

DIDO: Dat you drink is fust rate for red fever. Is de folks head bad?

ZOE: Very bad, aunty; and the heart aches worse, so they can get no rest.

DIDO: Hold on a bit, I get you de bottle. [*Exit*, L.R.]

ZOE: In a few hours that man, my master, will come for me: he has paid my price, and he only consented to let me remain here this one night, because Mrs. Peyton promised to give me up to him to-day.

DIDO: [*Re-enters with phial.*] Here 'tis—now you give one timble-full—dat's nuff.

ZOE: All there is there would kill one, wouldn't it?

DIDO: Guess it kill a dozen—nebber try.

ZOE: It's not a painful death, aunty, is it? You told me it produced a long, long sleep.

537

DIDO: Why you tremble so? Why you speak so wild? What you's gwine to do, missey?

ZOE: Give me the drink.

DIDO: No. Who dat sick at de house?

ZOE: Give it to me.

DIDO: No. You want to hurt yourself. O, Miss Zoe, why you ask ole Dido for dis pizen?

ZOE: Listen to me. I love one who is here, and he loves me—George. I sat outside his door all night—I heard his sighs—his agony—torn from him by my coming fate; and he said, "I'd rather see her dead than his!"

DIDO: Dead!

ZOE: He said so—then I rose up, and stole from the house, and ran down to the bayou; but its cold, black, silent stream terrified me—drowning must be so horrible a death. I could not do it. Then, as I knelt there, weeping for courage, a snake rattled beside me. I shrunk from it and fled. Death was there beside me, and I dared not take it. O! I'm afraid to die; yet I am more afraid to live.

DIDO: Die!

ZOE: So I came here to you; to you, my own dear nurse; to you, who so often hushed me to sleep when I was a child; who dried my eyes and put your little Zoe to rest. Ah! give me the rest that no master but One can disturb—the sleep from which I shall awake free! You can protect me from that man—do let me die without pain. [*Music.*]

DIDO: No, no—life is good for young ting like you.

ZOE: O! good, good nurse: you will, you will.

DIDO: No—g'way.

ZOE: Then I shall never leave Terrebonne—the drink, nurse; the drink; that I may never leave my home—my dear, dear home. You will not give me to that man? Your own Zoe, that loves you, aunty, so much, so much.—[*Gets phial.*] Ah! I have it.

DIDO: No, missey. O! no—don't.

ZOE: Hush! [*Runs off,* L.I.E.]

DIDO: Here, Solon, Minnie, Grace.

[*They enter.*]

ALL: Was de matter?

DIDO: Miss Zoe got de pizen. [*Exit,* L.]

ALL: O! O!

[*Exeunt,* L.]

SCENE II

[*Cane-brake Bayou.—Bank,* C.*—Triangle Fire,* R.C.*—Canoe,* C.*—M'Closky discovered asleep.*]

M'CLOSKY: Burn, burn! blaze away! How the flames crack. I'm not guilty; would ye murder me? Cut, cut the rope—I choke—choke!—Ah! [*Wakes.*] Hello! where am I? Why, I was dreaming—curse it! I can never sleep now without dreaming. Hush! I thought I heard the sound of a paddle in the water. All night, as I fled through the cane-brake, I heard footsteps behind me. I lost them in the cedar swamp—again they haunted my path down the bayou, moving as I moved, resting when I rested—hush! there again!—no; it was only the wind over the canes. The sun is rising. I must launch my dug-out, and put for the bay, and in a few hours I shall be safe from pursuit on board of one of the coasting schooners that run from Galveston to Matagorda. In a little time this darned business will blow over, and I can show again. Hark! there's that noise again! If it was the ghost of that murdered boy haunting me! Well—I didn't mean to kill him, did I? Well, then, what has my all-cowardly heart got to skeer me so for? [*Music.*]

[*Gets in canoe and rows off,* L.*—*WAHNOTEE *paddles canoe on* R.*—gets out and finds trail—paddles off after him,* L.]

SCENE III

[*Cedar Swamp.*]

[*Enter* SCUDDER *and* PETE, L.I.E.]

SCUD: Come on, Pete, we shan't reach the house before mid-day.

PETE: Nebber mind, sa, we bring good news—it won't spile for de keeping.

SCUD: Ten miles we've had to walk, because some blamed varmin onhitched our dug-out. I left it last night all safe.

PETE: P'r'aps it floated away itself.

SCUD: No; the hitching line was cut with a knife.

PETE: Say, Mas'r Scudder, s'pose we go in round by de quarters and raise de darkies, den dey cum long wid us, and we 'proach dat ole house like Gin'ral Jackson when he took London out dar.

SCUD: Hello, Pete, I never heard of that affair.

PETE: I tell you, sa—hush!

SCUD: What? [*Music.*]

PETE: Was dat?—a cry out dar in de swamp—dar agin!

SCUD: So it is. Something forcing its way through the under-growth—it comes this way—it's either a bear or a runaway nigger. [*Draws pistol*—M'CLOSKY *rushes on, and falls at* SCUDDER's *feet.*]

SCUD: Stand off—what are ye?

PETE: Mas'r Clusky.

M'CLOSKY: Save me—save me! I can go no farther. I heard voices.

SCUD: Who's after you?

M'CLOSKY: I don't know, but I feel it's death! In some form, human, or wild beast, or ghost, it has tracked me through the night. I fled; it followed; Hark! there it comes—it comes—don't you hear a footstep on the dry leaves?

SCUD: Your crime has driven you mad.

M'CLOSKY: D'ye hear it—nearer—nearer—ah! [WAHNOTEE *rushes on, and at* M'CLOSKY, L.H.]

SCUD: The Injiun! by thunder.

PETE: You're a dead man, Mas'r Clusky—you got to b'lieve dat.

M'CLOSKY: No—no. If I must die, give me up to the law; but save me from the tomahawk. You are a white man; you'll not leave one of your own blood to be butchered by the red-skin?

SCUD: Hold on now, Jacob! we've got to figure on that—let us look straight at one thing. Here we are on the selvage of civilization. It ain't our side, I believe, rightly; but Nature has said that where the white man sets his foot, the red man and the black man shall up sticks and stand around. But what do we pay for that possession? In cash? No—in kind—that is, in protection, forbearance, gentleness, in all them goods that show the critters the difference between the Christian and the savage. Now, what have you done to show them the distinction? for, darn me, if I can find out.

M'CLOSKY: For what I have done, let me be tried.

SCUD: You have been tried—honestly tried and convicted. Providence has chosen your executioner. I shan't interfere.

PETE: O, no; Mas'r Scudder, don't leave Mas'r Closky like dat—don't sa—'tain't what good Christian should do.

SCUD: D'ye hear that, Jacob? This old nigger, the grandfather of the boy you murdered, speaks for you—don't that go through you? D'ye feel it? Go on, Pete, you've waked up the Christian here, and the old hoss responds. [*Throws bowie-knife to* M'CLOSKY.] Take that, and defend yourself.

[*Exit* SCUDDER *and* PETE, R.I.E—WAHNOTEE *faces him.*— *Fight*—*buss.*—M'CLOSKY *runs off,* L.I.E.—WAHNOTEE *follows him.*—*Screams outside.*]

SCENE IV

[*Parlor at Terrebonne.*]

[*Enter* ZOE, C. (*Music*).]

ZOE: My home, my home! I must see you no more. Those little flowers can live, but I cannot. To-morrow they'll bloom the same—all will be here as now, and I shall be cold. O! my life; my happy life. Why has it been so bright?

[*Enter* MRS. PEYTON *and* DORA, C.]

DORA: Zoe, where have you been?

MRS. P.: We felt quite uneasy about you.

ZOE: I've been to the negro quarters. I suppose I shall go before long, and I wished to visit all the places, once again, to see the poor people.

MRS. P.: Zoe, dear, I'm glad to see you more calm this morning.

DORA: But how pale she looks, and she trembles so.

ZOE: Do I? [*Enter* GEORGE, C.] Ah! he is here.

DORA: George, here she is?

ZOE: I have come to say good-by, sir; two hard words—so hard, they might break many a heart; mightn't they?

GEORGE: O, Zoe! can you smile at this moment?

ZOE: You see how easily I have become reconciled to my fate—so it will be with you. You will not forget poor Zoe! but her image will pass away like a little cloud that obscured your happiness a while—you will love each other; you are both too good not to join your hearts. Brightness will return amongst you. Dora, I once made you weep; those were the only tears I caused any body. Will you forgive me?

DORA: Forgive you—[*Kisses her.*]

ZOE: I feel you do, George.

GEORGE: Zoe, you are pale. Zoe!—she faints!

ZOE: No, a weakness, that's all—a little water. [DORA *gets water.*] I have a restorative here—will you pour it in a glass? [DORA *attempts to take it.*] No; not you—George. [GEORGE *pours contents of phial in glass.*] Now, give it to me. George, dear George, do you love me?

GEORGE: Do you doubt it, Zoe?

ZOE: No! [*Drinks.*]

DORA: Zoe, if all I possess would buy your freedom, I would gladly give it.

ZOE: I am free! I had but one Master on earth, and he has given me my freedom!

DORA: Alas! but the deed that freed you was not lawful.

ZOE: Not lawful—no—but I am going to where there is no law— where there is only justice.

GEORGE: Zoe, you are suffering—your lips are white—your cheeks are flushed.

ZOE: I must be going—it is late. Farewell, Dora. [*Retires.*]

PETE: [*Outside*, R.] Whar's Missus—whar's Mas'r George?

GEORGE: They come.

[*Enter* SCUDDER.]

SCUD: Stand around and let me pass—room thar! I feel so big with joy, creation ain't wide enough to hold me. Mrs. Peyton, George Peyton, Terrebonne is yours. It was that rascal M'Closky—but he got rats, I swow—he killed the boy, Paul, to rob this letter from the mail-bags—the letter from Liverpool you know—he sot fire to the shed—that was how the steamboat got burned up.

MRS. P.: What d'ye mean?

SCUD: Read—read that. [*Gives letter.*]

GEORGE: Explain yourself.

[*Enter* SUNNYSIDE.]

SUNNY: Is it true?

SCUD: Every word of it, Squire. Here, you tell it, since you know it. If I was to try, I'd bust.

MRS. P.: Read, George. Terrebonne is yours.

[*Enter* PETE, DIDO, SOLON, MINNIE, *and* GRACE.]

PETE: Whar is she—whar is Miss Zoe?

SCUD: What's the matter?

PETE: Don't ax me. Whar's de gal? I say.

SCUD: Here she is—Zoe!—water—she faints.

PETE: No—no. 'Tain't no faint—she's a dying, sa: she got pison from old Dido here, this mornin'.

GEORGE: Zoe.

SCUD: Zoe! is this true?—no, it ain't—darn it, say it ain't. Look here, you're free, you know nary a master to hurt you now: you will stop here as long as you're a mind to, only don't look so.

DORA: Her eyes have changed color.

PETE: Dat's what her soul's gwine to do. It's going up dar, whar dere's no line atween folks.

GEORGE: She revives.

ZOE: [*On sofa*, c.] George—where—where—

GEORGE: O, Zoe! what have you done?

ZOE: Last night I overheard you weeping in your room, and you said, "I'd rather see her dead than so!"

GEORGE: Have I then prompted you to this?

ZOE: No; but I loved you so, I could not bear my fate; and then I stood between your heart and hers. When I am dead she will not be jealous of your love for me, no laws will stand between us. Lift me; so—[GEORGE *raises her head.*]—let me look at you, that your face may be the last I see of the world. O! George, you may, without a blush, confess your love for the Octoroon! [*Dies.*—GEORGE *lowers her head gently.*—*Kneels.*—*Others form picture.*]

[*Darken front of house and stage.*]

[*Light fires.*—*Draw flats and discover* PAUL's *grave.*—M'CLOSKY *dead on it*—WANHOTEE *standing triumphantly over him. Slow Curtain.*]

An alternative ending to The Octoroon: *The British Act IV.*

ACT IV

[*The Wharf. The Steamer, "Magnolia" alongside, L.; a bluff rock,* R.U.E. RATTS *discovered, superintending the loading of ship.*]

[*Enter* LAFOUCHE I JACKSON, L.]

JACKSON: How long before we start, captain?

RATTS: Just as soon as we put this cotton on board.

[*Enter Pete, with lantern, and* SCUDDER, *with note book,* R.]

SCUD.: One hundred and forty-nine bales. Can you take any more?

RATTS: Not a bale. I've got engaged eight hundred bales at the next landing, and one hundred hogsheads of sugar at Patten's Slide—that'll take my guards under—hurry up thar.

VOICE: [*outside*] Wood's aboard.

RATTS: All aboard then.

[*Enter* M'CLOSKY, R.]

SCUD.: Sign that receipt, captain, and save me going up to the clerk.

M'CLOSKY: See here—there's a small freight of turpentine in the fore-hold there, and one of the barrels leaks; a spark from your engines might set the ship on fire, and you'd go with it.

RATTS: You be darned! go and try it if you've a mind to.

LAFOUCHE: Captain, you've loaded up here until the boat is sunk so deep in the mud she won't float.

RATTS: [*calls off*] Wood up thar, you Pollo—hang on to the safety valve—guess she'll crawl off on her paddles. [*shouts heard,* R.]

JACKSON: What's the matter?

545

[*Enter* SOLON, R.]

SOLON: We got him!

SCUD.: Who?

SOLON: The Inginn!

SCUD.: Wahnotee? where is he? d'ye call running away from a fellow catching him?

RATTS: Here he come.

OMNES: Where? where?

[*Enter* WAHNOTEE, R., *they are all about to rush on him.*]

SCUD.: Hold on! stan' round thar! no violence—the critter don't know what we mean.

JACKSON. Let him answer for the boy then.

M'CLOSKY: Down with him—lynch him.

OMNES: Lynch him! [*Exit* LAFOUCHE, R.]

SCUD.: Stan' back I say! I'll nip the first that lays a finger on him. Pete, speak to the red skin.

PETE: Whar's Paul, Wahnotee? what's come ob de child?

WAHNOTEE: Paul wunce—Paul pangeuk.

PETE: Pangeuk—dead.

WAHNOTEE: Mort!

M'CLOSKY: And you killed him? [*they approach again*]

SCUD.: Hold on!

PETE: Um, Paul reste?

WAHNOTEE: Hugh vieu [*goes* L.] Paul reste ci!

SCUD.: Here, stay! [*examines the ground*] the earth has been stirred here lately.

WAHNOTEE: Weenee Paul. [*points down and shews by pantomime how he buried Paul*]

SCUD.: The Injinn means that he buried him there. Stop! here's a bit of leather; [*draws out mail-bags*] the mail bags that were lost! [*sees tomahawk in* WAHNOTEE'S *belt—draws it out and examines it*] Look! here are marks of blood—look thar, red-skin, what's that?

546

WAHNOTEE: Paul! [*makes sign that* PAUL *was killed by a blow on the head*]

M'CLOSKY: He confesses it; the Indian got drunk, quarrelled with him, and killed him.

[*Re-enter* LAFOUCHE, R., *with smashed apparatus.*]

LAFOUCHE: Here are evidences of the crime; this rum bottle half emptied—the photagraphic apparatus smashed—and there are marks of blood and footsteps around the shed.

M'CLOSKY: What more d'ye want—aint that proof enough? Lynch him!

OMNES: Lynch him! Lynch him!

SCUD.: Stan' back, boys! he's an Inginn—fair play.

JACKSON: Try him then—try him on the spot of his crime.

OMNES: Try him! try him!

LAFOUCHE: Don't let him escape!

RATTS: I'll see to that. [*draws revolver*] If he stirs, I'll put a bullet through his skull, mighty quick.

M'CLOSKY: Come—form a court then, choose a jury—we'll fix this varmin.

[*Enter* THIBODEAUS *and* CAILLON, L.]

TIBO.: What's the matter?

LAFOUCHE: We've caught this murdering Inginn, and are going to try him. [WAHNOTEE *sits* L., *rolled in blanket*]

PETE: Poor little Paul—poor little nigger!

SCUD.: This business goes agin me, Ratts—'taint right.

LAFOUCHE: We're ready; the jury's empannelled—go ahead —who'll be accuser?

RATTS: M'Closky.

M'CLOSKY: Me!

RATTS: Yes; you was the first to hail Judge Lynch.

M'CLOSKY: [R.] Well, what's the use of argument, whar guilt sticks out so plain; the boy and Inginn were alone when last seen.

SCUD.: [L.C.] Who says that?

M'CLOSKY: Everybody—that is, I heard so.

SCUD.: Say what you know—not what you heard.

M'CLOSKY: I know then that the boy was killed with that toma-hawk—the red-skin owns it—the signs of violence are all round the shed—this apparatus smashed—ain't it plain that in a drunken fit he slew the boy, and when sober concealed the boy yonder?

OMNES: That's it—that's it.

RATTS: Who defend's the Indian?

SCUD.: I will; for it is agin my natur' to b'lieve him guilty; and if he be, this ain't the place, nor you the authority to try him. How are we sure the boy is dead at all? There are no witnesses but a rum bottle and an old machine. Is it on such evidence you'd hang a human being?

RATTS: His own confession.

SCUD.: I appeal against your usurped authority; this Lynch law is a wild and lawless proceeding. Here's a picture for a civilized community to afford; yonder, a poor ignorant savage, and round him a circle of hearts, white with revenge and hate, thirsting for his blood; you call yourselves judges—you ain't—you're a jury of executioners. It is such scenes as these that bring disgrace upon our Western life.

M'CLOSKY: Evidence! Evidence! give us evidence, we've had talk enough; now for proof.

OMNES: Yes, yes! Proof, proof.

SCUD.: Where am I to get it? the proof is here, in my heart!

PETE: [*who has been looking about the camera*] Top sar! top a bit! Oh, laws-a-mussey, see dis, here's a pictur I found sticking in that yar telescope machine, sar! look sar!

SCUD.: A photographic plate. [PETE *holds lantern up*] What's this, eh? two forms! the child—'tis he! dead—and above him—Ah, ah! Jacob M'Closky—'twas you murdered that boy!

M'CLOSKY: Me?

SCUD.: You! You slew him with that tomahawk, and as you stood over his body with the letter in your hand, you thought that no witness saw the deed, that no eye was on you but there was, Jacob M'Closky, there was—the eye of the Eternal was on you—the blessed sun in heaven, that looking down struck upon this plate the image of the deed. Here you are, in the very attitude of your crime!

M'CLOSKY: 'Tis false!

SCUDDER: 'Tis true! the apparatus can't lie. Look there jurymen, [*shews plate to* JURY] look there. Oh, you wanted evidence—you called for proof—heaven has answered and convicted you.

M'CLOSKY: What court of law would receive such evidence? [*going*]

RATTS: Stop, *this* would—you called it yourself, you wanted to make us murder that Inginn, and since we've got our hands in for justice, we'll try it on you. What say ye? shall we have one law for the red skin, and another for the white?

OMNES: Try him! try him.

RATTS: Who'll be accuser?

SCUDDER: I will! Fellow citizens, you are convened and assembled here under a higher power than the law. What's the law? when the ship's abroad on the ocean—when the army is before the enemy—where in thunder's the law? it is in the hearts of brave men who can tell right from wrong, and from whom justice can't be bought. So it is here, in the Wilds of the West, where our hatred of crime is measured by the speed of our executions—where necessity is law! I say, then, air you honest men? air you true? put your hands on your naked breasts, and let every man as don't feel a real American heart there, bustin' up with freedom, truth, and rights, let that man step out—that's the oath I put to ye—and then say darn ye, go it!

OMNES: Go on—Go on.

SCUDDER: No! I won't go on, that man's down, I won't strike him even with words. Jacob, your accuser is that picter of the crime—let that speak—defend yourself.

M'CLOSKY: [*draws knife*] I will, quicker than lightening.

RATTS: Seize him then! [*they rush on* M'CLOSKY *and disarm him*] He can fight though he's a painter, claws all over.

SCUDDER: Stop! Search him, we may find more evidence.

M'CLOSKY: Would you rob me first, and murder me afterwards?

RATTS: [*searching him*] That's his programme—here's a pocket book.

SCUDDER: [*opens it*] What's here? Letters? Hello! to "Mrs. Peyton, Terrebonne, Louisiana, United States." Liverpool post mark. Ho! I've got hold of the tail of a rat—come out [*reads*] What's this?—a draft for 85,000 dollars and credit on Palisse and Co., of New Orleans, for the balance. Hi! the rat's out—you killed the boy to steal this letter from the mail bags—you stole this lettter that the money should not arrive in time to save the Octoroon; had it done so, the lien on the estate would have ceased, and Zoe be free.

OMNES: Lynch him!—lynch him!—down with him!

SCUDDER: Silence in the court—stand back, let the gentlemen of the jury retire, consult, and return their verdict.

RATTS: I'm responsible for the crittur—go on.

PETE: [*to* WAHNOTEE] See Inginn, look dar, [*shews him plate*] see dat innocent, look, dares the murderer of poor Paul.

WAHNOTEE: Ugh! [*examines plate*]

PETE: Ya! as he? Closky tue Paul—kill de child with your tomahawk dar, 'twasn't you, no—ole Pete allus say so. Poor Inginn lub our little Paul.

[WAHNOTEE *rises and looks at* M'CLOSKY—*he is in his war paint and fully armed*]

SCUD.: What say ye, gentlemen? Is the prisoner guilty, or he not guilty?

OMNES: Guilty!

SCUD.: And what is to be his punishment?

OMNES: Death! [*all advance*]

WAHNOTEE: [*crosses to* M'CLOSKY] Ugh!

SCUD.: The Inginn, by thunder!

PETE: [*to* M'CLOSKY] You're a dead man, mas'r; you've got to b'lieve dat.

M'CLOSKY: No! If I must die, give me up to the laws, but save me from the tomahawk of the savage; you are a white man, you'll not leave one of your own blood to be butchered by the scalping knife of the redskin.

SCUD.: Hold on now, Jacob, we've got to figure that out, let us look straight at the thing. Here we are on the confines of civilization; it ain't our sile, I believe, rightly; Nature has said that were the white man sets his foot the red man and the black man shall up sticks and stan' round. Now, what do we pay for that possession? In cash? No—in-kind—that is, in protection and forbearance, in gentleness, and in all them goods that show the critturs the difference between the Christian and the Savage. Now what have you done to shew'em the distinction? for darn me if I can find out.

M'CLOSKY: For what I've done let me be tried.

SCUD.: Oh, you have been fairly and honestly tried, and convicted: Providence has chosen your executioner—I shan't interfere.

PETE: Oh! sar! hi, Mas'r Scudder, don't leave Mas'r 'Closky like dat—don't, sar—tain't what a good Christian would do.

SCUD.: D'ye hear that, Jacob?—this old nigger, the grandfather of the boy you murdered, speaks for you—don't that go through ye—d'ye feel it? Go on, Pete, you've woke up the Christian here, and the old hoss responds.

WAHNOTEE: [*placing his hand on* M'CLOSKY'S *head*] Wahnotee!

SCUD.: No, Inginn, we deal justice here, not revenge; taint you he has injured, 'tis the white man, whose laws he has offended.

RATTS: Away with him! put him down the hatch till we rig his funeral.

M'CLOSKY: Fifty against one! put him down the hatch till we rig his funeral.

M'CLOSKY: Fifty against one! Oh! if you were alone—if I had ye one by one in the swamp, I'd rip ye all.

PETE: [*lighting him off,* R.] Dis way, Mas'r 'Closky, take care, sar.

[*Exit with* M'CLOSKY *and* JACKSON *to steamer.*]

LAFOUCHE: Off with him quick—here come the ladies.

[*Enter* MRS. CLAIRBORNE, R. *1* E.]

MRS. CLAIR.: Shall we soon start, Captain?

RATTS: Yes, ma'am; we've only got a—take my hand ma'am, to steady you—a little account to square, and we're off.

MRS. CLAIR.: A fog is rising.

RATTS: Swamp mist; soon clear off. [*hands her to steamer*]

MRS. CLAIR.: Good night.

RATTS: Good night, ma'am—good night.

SCUD: Now to business.

[PETE *appears on deck.*]

PETE: OH! law, sar. Dat debbel, 'Closky—he tore hisself from de gentleman—knock me down—take away my light, and throwed it on de turpentine barrels—de ship's on fire!

[*all hurry off to ship—alarm bell rings—loud shouts; a hatch in the deck is opened—a glare of red—and* M'CLOSKY *emerges from the aperture; he is without his coat, and carries a bowie knife; he rushes down—* WAHNOTEE *alone is watching him from* R.U.E.]

M'CLOSKY: Ha, ha, ha! I've given them something to remember how they treated Jacob M'Closky. Made my way from one end of the vessel to the other, and now the road to escape is clear before me—and thus to secure it! [*he goes to* R.C., *and is met by* WAHNOTEE, *who silently confronts him*]

WAHNOTEE: Paul.

M'CLOSKY: Devils!—you here!—stand clear!

WAHNOTEE: Paul.

M'CLOSKY: You won't!—die, fool! [*thrusts at him—* WAHNOTEE, *with his tomahawk, strikes the knife out of his hand;* M'CLOSKY *starts back;* WAHNOTEE *throws off his blanket, and strikes at* M'CLOSKY *several times, who avoids him; at last he catches his arm, and struggles for the tomahawk, which falls; a violent struggle and fight take place, ending with the triumph of* WAHNOTEE, *who drags* M'CLOSKY *along the ground, takes up the knife and stabs him repeatedly;* GEORGE *enters, bearing* ZOE *in his arms—all the Characters rush on—noise increasing—the steam vessel blows up—grand Tableau, and curtain.*]

Later Minstrel Material

Introduction

While minstrelsy remained immensely popular after the Civil War, the character of that popularity changed significantly. Major theaters and performers shifted toward vaudeville; many audiences—especially in larger cities—followed. Thus, while there were well over a hundred professional minstrel troupes at the beginning of the Civil War, there were only a handful at the turn into the twentieth century.

But minstrelsy survived and thrived outside of the organized theater: a group of publishers—e.g., Happy Hours in the 1870s, Ames in the 1880s and 1890s—worked to mass-produce one-act scripts/ afterpieces, minstrel jokebooks, and songsters designed for amateurs. Often, they simply recycled material from older minstrel shows; they also, though, funded the creation of new material specifically for these purposes. They succeeded mightily. While it grew more and more difficult to find a physical theater that featured a full-length minstrel show of the type offered by Christy's, for example, in the 1850s, it became much easier to find a county fair that featured minstrel performers, a white men's—or even women's—club that offered minstrel material at a social event, or a group of white college students putting on a minstrel show. In this way, minstrelsy perhaps touched more of the nation than it had through just theaters.

The general approach of minstrel material did not change a great deal—as least in terms of its central base of surrounding whatever topical material was included with stereotypical African American characters. Robert Toll traces a shift in tenor in minstrelsy, though, beginning just after the *Emancipation Proclamation* (1863), that made these stereotypical representations even more vituperative. Toll suggests that, while early Civil War minstrel shows were heavily nationalistic and patriotic (and so supportive of the Union cause), the shift in the Union's emphasis toward anti-slavery—and especially the entry of African Americans into the Union army—led some minstrels toward even nastier attacks on abolitionists and African Americans. The "Black soldier" even became a regular character—a new version of Jim Crow and Zip Coon marked by his army uniform. After the War, the features of the Reconstruction—including the Freedmen's Bureau and African American legislators—provided fertile material for an updated racism. Radical Republicans—the architects of Reconstruction—were also frequent targets. (In the one-act play included here—*The Colored Senators*—both James Blaine and David Davis are impersonated by Zip Coon-style characters.)

It is no wonder that this chapter in the history of minstrelsy saw the South move fully into a "Jim Crow" system. The play on words here is intentional: the naming of this approach to race relations drew directly from the minstrel character popularized by "Daddy Rice" in the antebellum era; like Rice's character, Southern law and much of white American popular culture grew to assume that African Americans were lazy, shiftless, and foolish. As part of a larger campaign by the South to recoup a positive sense of the history of slavery—embodied in everything from the growing activism of various organizations of Confederate veterans to novels like Thomas Dixon's *The Klansmen* (1902), which heroicized the Ku Klux Klan and demonized African Americans—this widespread stereotyping had devastating effects on the progress of post-slavery cross-racial interaction.

Still, another development marked this period of minstrelsy— and it both demonstrates the complexity of the post-Civil War world and the new ways in which racism marked that world. While a handful of early Black performers—perhaps most notably dancer William Henry "Master Juba" Lane and musician Frank Johnson, but also a few non-minstrel acts like elocutionist Mary Webb and singer Elizabeth Taylor Greenfield, as well as a scattering of Black minstrel companies in the 1850s—had taken the stage, it was after the Civil War that notable Black companies began touring. Brooker and Clayton's Georgia Minstrels, who advertised themselves as a "Pure Negro Troupe," were perhaps the most famous of these early Reconstruction groups, but by the 1870s, there were several touring troupes. Many did not use burnt cork (the choice of white minstrels) to further "black" their faces, but most elements of the basic minstrel show (described in the "Introduction to Early Minstrel Material" earlier in this volume) stayed fairly intact. Sam Lucas, who began performing in the late 1860s, became perhaps the most famous of the Black minstrels—and created a career that ran four decades and included being the first African American to play Uncle Tom on the stage. Throughout the period, Black minstrels performed not only for white audiences, but also for Black ones—though the Black press and activists continued to frown on minstrelsy.

The existence of African Americans doing minstrelsy has troubled contemporary historians and critics almost as much as it troubled Black political and social activists of the time; this, in part, explains why they have received much less notice and discussion than the famous singing groups from historically Black colleges that toured the nation during the same period (like the Fisk University Jubilee Singers). On the one hand, Black minstrels were clearly engaging in and perpetuating the same kinds of stereotypes that were used to deny African Americans a whole slate of equal rights and treatment. Indeed, some white audiences undoubtedly walked away from performances thinking that the stereotypes were, simply, reality.

And yet Black minstrelsy provided one of the few outlets to talented African American performers of the time. Though diva Sissieretta Jones, for example, had sung for heads of state both in the United States and abroad, she was, quite simply, unable to find bookings at American opera houses and many theaters. Her troupe, which included some elements of minstrelsy in their performances—as well as Jones singing a rich range of popular and classical music—toured widely and with some success for several years. Minstrelsy would also lead to the early work of Will Marion Cook, James Bland, and W.C. Handy, important early Black musicians and composers. And for many less famous performers, it was, simply, the only way to make a living in the performing arts. Further, these early troupes worked cannily to create functional businesses in the white-dominated theater world and the largely segregated American culture. As such, then, minstrelsy certainly contributed to the early phases of jazz and Black theater even as it shaped wickedly negative representations of race throughout the modern era.

The selections here embody several of these issues—and can usefully be read in dialogue with Pauline Hopkins's play *Peculiar Sam* (1879), which was originally written for Black minstrel Sam Lucas.

A Note on the Texts

The shorter pieces included here—three representative exchanges between "Mr. Bones" and the "Interlocutor" as well as a "stump speech" delivered solo—are drawn from Orville Augustus Roorbach's compilation of work by a wide range of unidentified authors, *Minstrel Gags and End Men's Handbook* (New York: Happy Hours, 1875). *Colored Senators, an Ethiopian Burlesque* by Bert Richards (Clyde, Ohio: A.D. Ames, 1887) is representative of the one-act afterpieces of the time. Richards authored a handful of such one-act plays, all published by Ames in the 1880s and early 1890s, but other biographical information on him remains unknown.

Like most minstrel texts, the dialect in these can, at times, make for rough reading, though reading aloud generally will aid comprehension. Most allusions are to Reconstruction-era phenomena. "Carpet bagger" is a negative Southern term for Northerners who came South (supposedly with carpet bags—the period's equivalent of suitcases—in hand) to make their fortunes and take advantage of the South's loss of power. The idea of a Black president naturally came to the fore with the election of the first Black congressmen during the period. Mr. Bones's hope to write his autobiography is a jibe not only at autobiographies by figures like Frederick Douglass, but more generally at a range of Black-authored texts during the period. The Native American references demonstrate the ways in which late minstrelsy expanded its racism to cover a range of minority groups; Asian immigrants were also especially popular targets in the later period. James Blaine (1830–1893) and David Davis (1815–1886) were two key Republican legislators of the period. Blaine voted to impeach President Andrew Johnson and advocated African American suffrage. Davis had been the campaign manager of Abraham Lincoln's 1860 presidential campaign before taking a seat on the U.S. Supreme Court and then leaving it to serve in the U.S. Senate.

For Further Reading

Bean, Annemarie, James V. Hatch, and Brooks McNamara, eds. *Inside the Minstrel Mask: Readings in Nineteenth-Century Blackface Minstrelsy.* Hanover: Wesleyan University Press, 1996.

Booth, Michael R. *Theatre in Victorian America.* Cambridge: Cambridge University Press, 1991.

Elam, Harry J., Jr., and David Krasner, eds. *African American Performance and Theater History.* New York: Oxford University Press, 2001.

Engle, Ron and Tice L. Miller. *The American Stage: Social and Economic Issues from the Colonial Period to the Present.* Cambridge: Cambridge University Press, 1993.

Foner, Eric. *Reconstruction: America's Unfinished Revolution, 1863–1877.* New York: Harper and Row, 1988.

———. *Slavery and Freedom in Nineteenth Century America.* New York: Oxford University Press, 1994.

Hill, Errol G. and James V. Hatch. *A History of African American Theatre.* Cambridge: Cambridge University Press, 2003.

Levine, Lawrence. *Black Culture and Black Consciousness: Afro-American Folk Thought from Slavery to Freedom.* New York: Oxford University Press, 1977.

Levine, Lawrence. *Highbrow/Lowbrow: The Emergence of Cultural Hierarchy in America.* Cambridge: Harvard University Press, 1988.

Lott, Eric. *Love and Theft: Blackface Minstrelsy and the American Working Class.* New York: Oxford University Press, 1993.

Stuckey, Sterling. *Slave Culture: Nationalist Thought and the Foundations of Black America.* New York: Oxford University Press, 1987.

Toll, Robert C. *Blacking Up: The Minstrel Show in Nineteenth-Century America.* New York: Oxford University Press, 1974.

Bones Finds Himself Famous

INTERLOCUTOR: Can what I hear be true, Mr. Bones—that you are really going to write your own autobiography?

BONES: Yes—I's goin' to be autor of my own biography—Recollections of a Busy Life; busy as a fly in a tar barrel. Bought forty reams of paper, and a gallon of red ink, and a gross of steel pens.

INTERLOCUTOR: Of course there must have been some *steal* about it where you were concerned. And when your auto—what d'ya call it is finished, you, doubtless, intend to make an *auto da fe*—burn it up?

BONES: I'd hab to be pooty well *feed* to make me do dat. You know dere was a time when I stood high in de perfession.

INTERLOCUTOR: That's why they used to call you a *high old actor*, I suppose?

BONES: Yes—dat's it. I make my fust appearance in tragedy.

INTERLOCUTOR: Indeed! In what part, sir?

BONES: Why, in all de parts of de play, be sure. I carried a banner, too; and when I rounded de footlights, such a storm of 'plause busted out from de specletaters, golly! you'd tought de house was afire. "O, what legs!" yelled out one feller in de pit. "Walk up lively, young spindleshanks!" hollered out anudder. And den de nickles come rattlin' around me.

INTERLOCUTOR: They were only quizzing you, Mr. Bones. And at that eventful moment of your life, you were the counterpart of a boiling spring, because you was a *guy, sir* (geyser).

BONES: Only know dat I was *bilin' ober* wid indignation. But I paid dem back for it. Yes, I paid dem back. "Show me de feller dat said 'spindleshanks!' " said I, and wid dat I jump down into de pit and begin lammin' around me, regardless of expense. Phew! You ought to seen de buttons fly! Well, I tought dat would'a been de end ob me, den, but arterwards, as I was takin' a drink nex' do' wid de feller what I'd licked, de manager cum in, and says he, "you're my mutton," says he. "Any one dat can sling folks around in dat way can beat Forrist in Damon." "I know I'm some at dammin' and cussin'," says I; "ax dem galloots if I aint." Well, you wouldn't b'leeve it, but it um a fac'—de managem gib me an engagement right off and put me up for Damon. Well, sah, "de night dat was to undo me or to make me quite" had come round. Dey gave me a long night gownd from de wardrobe, and on I went, when, what you tink—a pooty gal comes up to me, and trows her arms around me, and brings two little chilluns and—and puts dem into my arms. But dat was too much for me. "Look a' here, says I; "you got de wrong man, nebber hadn't only one wife, and she's as black as de ace of spades. Go way!" Wid dat I tear myself away and make for de dressin' room, and when dey gits dis ole niggah to 'spose hisself in dat way agen, I guess dey'll know it. De papers said somefin next mornin' 'bout my *throwin' up* my engagement. Guess they couldn't have been so sick of it as I was.

INTERLOCUTOR: Now, gentlemen, let us hearken to a few notes from our mellifluous warbler:—

One pleasant morning I sallied forth
    My darling love to meet,
The glittering dew was on the leaves,
    The sun was shining sweet;
And as we stood within the glade,

From noise and strife quite free
Near by we used to tell our love
  Beneath the Greenwood Tree.

[*Chorus.*] Yes, indeed, I must confess on her depends my happiness;
Elvira is a darling, and truly so to me,
  And I'll ne'er regret the day we met beneath the
  Greenwood Tree.

Her name it was Elvira Jane—
  That name sounds sweet to me—
My wife I soon shall make this dear.
  If thus to me she'll be;
And as the moments pass along,
  Her heart to judge is free—
I've popped the question to my love,
  Beneath the Greenwood Tree.

[*Chorus.*] Elvira is a darling, &c.

Oh, she has promised to be mine.
  And the fond words she did say
That I shall take her to my heart,
  In one week from to-day;
Down in our little trysting place
  Our wedding is to be,
There where first we told our love
  Beneath the Greenwood Tree.

[*Chorus.*] Elvira is a darling. &c.

Brudder Bones as a Carpet-Bagger

INTERLOCUTOR: Eight o'clock and no Bones. I'm really afraid that young man has been getting himself into another of his scrapes, and we shall have to search the Morgue for him. O! here he comes. [*Enter Bones, with a carpet bag and umbrella.*]

BONES: [*Drops into his seat and fans himself with his hat.*] Phew!

INTERLOCUTOR: How now, Mr. Bones? You seem a little fatigued this evening.

BONES: Yes; I've been takin' a waxination up to de springs.

INTERLOCUTOR: I see; a political agent in disguise, with a satchel full of tracts, I'll warrant.

BONES: No, but I *made tracks* quite lively, dough, I tell you. De fellers called me a carpet bagger and race me off de boat, and I went, kase I's feared dey'd tost me in a blankit, but I fotch up at de hotel at last, and de gentlemanly clerk dat I tought was de proprietor, look at my dusty clothes, pucker up his nose as if he smell somefin' and says he, grinnin', "Fraid we aint got nuffin' good enuff. Will you hab a bed in de sky parlor?" And where you tink dey put me?

INTERLOCUTOR: I'm sure I can't tell, sir.

BONES: Fust dey lead me into a handsome 'partment on de fust flo', and jus' as I'd laid down on de sofy for a nap, a bell rings and off I rolls on de flo' and up I goes wid a jerk. Golly! I tought de house was comin' down, but instid of dat it was me dat was goin' up. "Stop dis dam concern!" I yells. Just den de ting stopped wid a bump and I was tumbled out on de toppermost floor like a sack of pertaters. I foun' my room, dough.

INTERLOCUTOR: You went up in the elevator.

BONES: I went up in anodder way 'fore I got troo—went *up de flume*. But I wusn't much elewated at de prospec'. Pooty bime-by de waiter come, dustin' around, and says he, "quarter dollar, sah." "Anything but such quarters as dese," says I, forkin' ober. "Goin' to de hop to-night? great time," says he, fluffin' at me wid his brush. "I don't know nuffin' 'bout your hops," says I, "but dere seems to be plenty of *skippers* about." "P'r'aps you prefer de *hoppera*," says he, grinnin'! By dat time he'd got me by de scruff ob de neck and was whalin' it into me wid his duster. "Le' go me!" says I; "I aint a bushel ob grain dat I want to be *thrashed*." "Quarter dollah," says he; and I gub it him, and he let go.

INTERLOCUTOR: You had what racing men would call a pretty *close brush*.

BONES: I know I went into de wash room and got a good scrub. Den dere come a noise as if all de animals in de menagerums had broke loose and was roarin' all togedderums. Dey said it was de gong, but jus' as I was startin' for a run, de waiter seize me by de scruff again, and anudder grab my boots, and a feller in a white apron frow me down in a char and empty a pint of pepper sass on my har, and dey all said, "a quarter, sah," I forked agin and bolted fo' de dinin' room. "What kind o' soup you got?" I ax. "Wormy celli, wid cat-sup," says de steward. "Wormy soup, cat soup—gid out wid your nonsense!" says I, and tumblin' ober my char backwards, I put fo' de balcomny. Den I go for de bar room for a smoke, but dey hadn't nuffin' but *Clay* cigars, and as I only smokes tobacco, I goes out on de balcomny agin and listen to de music.

INTERLOCUTOR: What kind of music, sir?

BONES: *Chin* music, wid wariations on de old jawbone. Bime-by it got to be bed time and I rusht up stars and bounced into bed. Somebody was dere already, but I tought it was all right till she put her arms aroun' me and hug me, and call me "lovey," and if it wusn't a female woman, dash my wig! But she got hold of my wool and gib one yell. "Arrah, Paddy, Paddy!" says she, "here's Barnum's What-Is-It's got in wid me!" And de waiter—dat was her husband—come wid a light. An' he grab me by de neck agen and gib me a kick an' land me in de entry, and jus' as I was 'spectin' to be shot, he says, smilin':—"One quarter, sah," and I gub it him and broke fo' my own room, and drest, and I went off and forgot to pay my bill.

INTERLOCUTOR: That will do for the present, and we'll now listen to the rejuvenated Mario:—

I have missed you, Mollie darling, from the spot we know
so well,
> Where I kessed you Mollie darling, long ago a sweet
> farewell;
Smiles of thine no more may greet me, while your voice I
never hear,
> Will you come again to greet me? for I miss you,
> Mollie dear.

[*Chorus.*] Yes, I've missed you, Mollie darling,
More than words of mine can tell,
> Since I kissed you, Mollie darling,
Long ago a sweet farewell.

> I have missed you, Mollie darling, missed the sunlight
> of your smile,
And the kisses, Mollie darling, that you gave me by the stile;
> I have listened in the gloaming for your footsteps
> drawing near,
Waiting vainly for your coming, for I miss you, Mollie dear.

[*Chorus.*] Yes, I've missed you, &c.

Presidency on the Brain

Feller Citizens!!—Correspondin' to your unanimous call, I shall not be de undertaker to an address you, and confine myself to de points and confluence to which I am annihilated. Feller citizens! dis is a day to be lookin' up, like a bobtailed hen on a ricketty henroost. Somefin' has bust!

Whar is we? I am here, and am goin' to stand here till I take root, if you'll only shout aloud and cast your vote for your humble servant. Jee-ru-se-lem is to pay, and we aint got no pitch.

Our patriotic canal boat ob creation has unshipped her rudder, de captin's broke his neck, and de cook has gone to de vasty deep in search ob diamonds. Our wigwams are torn to pieces and scattered like a shirt on a brushy fence. Are sich things going to be did? I ask in de name ob de shaggy-headed eagle, are such tings going to be conflumniated? I repeat to you in de name ob de peacock ob liberty dat's flyin' over de cap cloud summits ob de Rockygany mountains, are we goin' to be extraneously bigoted in dis fashion? Oh, answer me, as Shakspeal says: "Do not let me blush in ignorance."

Feller Citizens and Colleagues! you have called upon me to acknowledge de inwitation as a nominee for me to de candydate to de Presidence ob dese Uncle Sam's domitory at de White House

573

situated in dis our glorious Unicorn; and I tink if I am elected by you, it'll be "bully for me!"

And now, feller constituents, if yer elect me to be Presidens, de fust ting I'll do is to 'bolish all de toll gates and ebery man dat has to work fur a libin' shall hab instead ob a dollar a day, eight York shillin's. And jest as sartin as I'm 'lected, I'll pave the streets wid pancakes, and all de gutters shall run wid milk and sugar.

I'll pull down de taxes, I will—yes, sir—won't I—you'll see. And den ebery ting'il be cheaper.

I'll now git down from de high hoss dat I am on, and make room for some oder lunk-head, hopin' to see you all at de polls on 'lection day, whar you'll find a fresh watter million cub. I wish you a werry good ebenin'.

Bones on de War Path

INTERLOCUTOR: So, Brother Bones, you've been distinguishing yourself once more, I understand?

BONES: [*who is tricked out in war paint and feathers, with a ring in his nose*] Yes, I's been on de war paf agin. Got adopted into a tribe o'real Indjuns, and made a chief of.

INTERLOCUTOR: Then you've had plenty of fighting to do, I suppose?

BONES: Well, no. Dat's de *old kind ob Indjuns.* We don't do tings dat way, nowadays. Our tribe's got an engagement—took to de stage, you know.

INTERLOCUTOR: Taken to the stage? Then, I suppose, you go upon the principle that "all the world's a stage, and all the men and women merely players?"

BONES: Yes; you know de poet says: "Dis world am but a *fleeting show.*" You see, goin' cross de plains t'odder day in one ob Pull'em's palace coaches, we wus captured by de tribe ob Whan-a-bang-ers, and run off to de happy hunting grounds, whar dey tied us to de stake and put preparations on foot to *make steaks* of us. Dey wus just on de pint of lightin' de fire, when a happy idea struck me. "Dis all humbug," says I: "What you make by it? All de odder fellows is abandonin' de peraras fo' de freeayter and makin' money by it. Suppose we organize a company, and I'll be de managerum for you?"

INTERLOCUTOR: And *did* you organize?

BONES: Oh, yes, we did; formed ourselves into a company and hired de members ob de Nebraska Legislature, wid de Gub'ner to jine in wid us, and stuck up a lot o' bills and started out a lively opposition.

INTERLOCUTOR: I hope you didn't get "stuck up" yourselves, while you were about it.

BONES: Oh, no—no. Come near gittin' "stuck" at de fust place we come across, dough—stuck for our board bills. Well, we hired a house for de 'casion, an' started in. De play was Wild Buffalum ob de Wilderness, or de Scalp Eaters ob de Perarum. De Gub'ner he was de great chief Hunkey Punkey, I wus de odder todder great chief, Wankey Pankey, and de rest ob us personate de remainder ob de hi-yus, de hunters and de buffalum eaters and all dat.

INTERLOCUTOR: And did you take any money by the experiment?

BONES: Well, I can't say as we did, e'zactly; but we took a good many scalps, and as dey'm worth a hundred dollars apiece on de reservation, we tought we'd made a good ting ob it at dat. When I come on as Wankey Pankey, de house rose at us, and one old bald-headed cuss in de pit draw'd his six-shooter and sot on de back ob his seat, waitin' for de time to come to sail in. Dere was, fust dere wus a chorus, like de sons ob de wilderness always sings, you know, when dey goes out for scalps; and den a real train ob emigrants dey comes on and sets to work to cook deir hash, and dey busts out into a choris too—
O, we's all hunky fellers,
    Yes, we's all hunky fellers,
And we's all hunky fellers,
    And we's bound to go troo!

INTERLOCUTOR: The enterprise *went through*, I suppose, if *you* didn't.

BONES: Yes; went troo us all like a dose ob salts. When de she-roine she come onto de stage (she wus de real daughter ob ole Spotted Tail—one ob de real chiefs, you know), dere wus a wild yell arose amongst de real Indjuns, and dey went for her in a body, dey did; and den de pale-face sheroine, de sunflower ob de Peraras, *she* come on, and dey went for *her*; and den de ole feller wid de six-shooter and de rest ob dem, dey went for her, and charged onto de real Indjuns, ob de peraras, and de real Indjuns ob de peraras *dey* charged back, and sich a hullabaloo you nebber did see! And de Gub'ner he was de fust to git scalped, and I wus de next, and de leader ob de orchestrum he lost his wool, too, and pretty presently de wool wus flyin' round so lively you'd tought you wus in a barber's shop for certain. When I 'come away, de 'fair was 'bout settled, and de officers ob de house dey wus gadderin' up a half a dozen tons or so ob scalp locks and fedders and tings, and puttin' dem up in bales fo' de market. Nebber see such a time sense I wus born—no, nebber!

INTERLOCUTOR: I suppose you thought the greatest scalp-lock of all was when the manager locked the door on you and put you out of the building?

BONES: Can't say. All I know is, de only ting *raised* by de spec' wus a lot ob hair, and ob dat dere wus so much dat de price went down to nuffin'; and dat's de whole story.

INTERLOCUTOR: And that's quite sufficient.

The Colored Senators

An Ethiopian Burlesque, in one scene
by Bert Richards

CAST OF CHARACTERS

WINK ELLIS	*a tramp*
DYNAMITE ED	*a fellow sufferer*
GEO. WASHINGTON BROWN	*hotel keeper*

[*Costumes: Modern. Time: Twenty Minutes. Scene: Office at Brown's Hotel.*]

[*Enter* ELLIS, *right, and* ED, *left, at same time. They see each other, and each taking the other to be the Landlord, they speak together.*]

ELLIS AND ED: Am you the, [*pause*] am, [*pause*] am you—

ELLIS: What am de matter wid you, nigger—can't you let a 'spectable gemmen ax yer a question?

ED: Well, what's de matter wid you, you wizen-faced tar barrel? You mus' be one of dem dar new fangled machines wid wires to 'em, what am doin' all de talk n' dar is done in de world.

ELLIS: Close dat fly trap, nigger. I's gwine to do business wid you.

ED: Now you is talkin' sense. I's been waitin' yere long time now to do business wid you. Am you de landlord?

ELLIS: No. Ain't you de landlord?

ED: Go way from here, an' don't be tryin' no smart tricks on dis child or I's gwine to slap you so hard you am liable ter spit ink, yes indeed I am.

ELLIS: Look out dar, nigger, don't you cuss me, I's a tough nigger, I is.

ED: I swar to goodness I thought you was de ramrod.

ELLIS: But I ain't.

ED: Who am you den?

ELLIS: I's a summer tourist, I is. Doctor 'vised me to trable for my health dis summer. I's got a very bad dose ob de hay fever, I has; yes indeed. All us millyumnaries am liable to hab it. But ain't yer de ramrod ob dis yer 'stablishment?

ED: No I ain't de ramrod. I's a fellow sufferer like yourself. My name am Dynamite Ed, Col. Dynamite Ed.

ELLIS: Put her dar. [*extending hand*] Shake. I used to be a colonel once myself, yes indeed; [*they shake hands*] but I's got higher up de ladder now, I has. I's a general now, sure enough—Gen'l Wink Ellis.

ED: Well, Gen'l Wink, as we bofe wants de ramrod jes' you go an' see if he is up stairs an' I'll go to look 'round de front yard an' see if he am out dar.

ELLIS: All right, colonel. [*exit door at back*]

ED: Gosh, but ain't I struck it rich. If I don't have part of dat nigger's millyums den my name ain't Dynamite Ed. I's gwine for dat nigger's pockets in about free seconds, just like this. [*turns his own pockets inside out—*ELLIS *heard singing outside*]
He is a little picaninny,
    From Old Virginia;
Goodness how he grows.
He's gwan ter wish he was a picaninny or sumfin' else after I pick his pockets. Howsomever he is coming back, so I guess I'll meander. [*exit, right*]

[ELLIS *enters; door in back.*]

ELLIS: Don't seem ter be any ramrod 'round dis yer 'stablishment. I wonder where dat nigger, Col. Ed, has done gone to; guess he'd wish he had been home hoeing pertatoes instead of foolin' 'round Gen'l Wink Ellis 'fore he gets fru wid me. I's gwine to rob dat nigger, I is; an' den I fink dis chile gwine ter git a square meal. [*knock heard, right*] Come in. [*knocking continues*] Come in.

ED: [*Sticking head in at entrance and continuing to knock.*] Can't yer wait till I gets fru knocking. [*Enters right and goes over to* ELLIS.]

ELLIS: Did yer find de gov'ner?

ED: No. Did you?

ELLIS: No, but I left word for him ter come down soon as he gits time.

ED: [*aside*] Gosh, but dis nigger am gittin' mighty hungry—pretty loose 'round de belt, too. [*feels waist—aloud*] Well, Gen'l Wink, I guess we might as well sit down here and wait fer the gov'ner. [*aside*] Now I'll git dat nigger's money. [*starts towards bench at back*]

ELLIS: [*aside*] Things is coming my way now fer sure. I's got him now sure 'nuff. [*goes back and they sit together on bench facing audience*] Say, Col. Ed, how am de crops down in your section of the country dis season? [*puts hand in* ED'*s pocket and turns it inside out.*]

ED: Well, de crops am a good bit better nor they wou'd be if dey— [*turns one of Ellis's pockets out*]—was somewhat worse den dey might be, [ELLIS *turns another of Ed's pockets*] if de was considerable better nor dey am. [ED *turns another of Ellis's pockets*]

ELLIS: I suppose you ain't been gittin' much rain very lately, has yer? [*continues to go through pockets*]

ED: No, de rains am very prohibition like in scarcity, but de dews am so heavy dat dey am running de steamboats across de country now. [*pockets are all turned and found empty—both rise, with a look of disgust, and come down front,* ED, *right.*] [*aside*] Not a cent.

ELLIS: [*aside*] Not a cent.

ED: Look here, Gen'l Wink, I's 'clined to think you am no millyumnary, but jes' a common every day nigger tramp, so I is.

ELLIS: Yes, an' you, Col. Ed, you ain't got a cent neither. You don' hit de nail purty square on de head when you don' tole me you was a fellow sufferer. You is jes' a common nigger yourself. [*they discover their pockets are out and put them back at same time, casting angry glances at each other*]

ED: Look here, Gen'l Wink, if we both belong to der perfession les' quit dis yer foolin' an' skirmish for some perwishions, 'cause I's done gittin' mighty hungry myself, sure 'nuff.

ELLIS: Kerrect, Col. Ed. I done gota great scheme, never known to fail. Jes you sit down here an' I'll don' tole 'bout it. [*they sit on bench again with hands in pockets*]

ED: What's de matter wid dem pockets—ain't nuffin' in dar.

ELLIS: Oh, nuffin'. [*takes hands out*] What am de matter with yours? [ED *takes hands out*]

ED: But how 'bout dat scheme?

ELLIS: Well, we is two senators. You am David Davis and I am Jim Blaine. I'll 'splain eberythin' to de ramrod, an' we mus' order de best in de house, den you must offer to pay for it.

ED: Go long, nigger; how is I gwine to pay?

ELLIS: You jes' offer to pay, dat's all; den you see I'll want ter pay an' you'll want ter pay, an' den de gov'ner will jes' charge it in de bill to stop us from fightin'.

ED: All right, Wink, but you is startin' dis t'ing, an' you must offer to pay first.

ELLIS: All right, jes' you bring de gov'ner in an' I's gwin ter talk his arm off in jes' free minutes.

ED: [*rings bell and calls "ramrod"*] But how am we gwan ter pay de bill in de mornin'?

ELLIS: Well, I declar', you am de most ig'rant nigger ever I seed. You don't suppose we are gwine ter stay till mornin' do yer, you wizen-faced straight-haired coon? You see we are gwine to spread out our *white wings* and fly gently away in de silent *Waterbury* watches of de night.

ED: Whist! here comes de gov'ner.

[*Enter* BROWN, *right.*]

BROWN: Git out here you niggers, don't come pesterin' aroun' my 'stablishment. Git out, I say. [*reaches in hip pocket for revolver, but pulls out plug of tobacco*]

ELLIS: Skuse me, but am you de ramrod of dis 'stablishment?

BROWN: I am he, an' my name am Col. Geo. Washington Brown, Esq., who be you uns?

ELLIS: Colonel, allow me to introduce to you my ticklar friend, Senator David Davis. [*they shake hands*] And for fear that you may not recognize in me "The Plumed Knight," I will add that I am Senator Jim Blaine [*they shake hands—Brown turns back to audience, showing large card bearing the inscription, "I am something of a liar myself"*]

BROWN: Strikes me, gemmen, dat de late campaign had a very bad effect on your 'plexion.

ED: Well you see, Col. Brown, we has bin rusticating out in de country, an' am slightly sun burned, dat's all.

ELLIS: Yes, dat's all, an' as our private car won't be in until to-morrow

we will jes' stop wid you until den, an' we wants de very best
dere is in de house.

ED: Yes, de very best.

BROWN: All right; be seated, gemmen, I will order your dinner prepared immediately, but in the mean time wouldn't you like
some light refreshments here?

ELLIS: Yes, bring us up some champagne and some good Havana
cigars.

BROWN: All right, gemmen. [*exit, right.*]

ED: Gosh, but we has hit a snap, ain't we Wink?

ELLIS: Be careful dar, don't you call me Wink, 'cause I's Jim Blaine
now.

[*Enter* BROWN, *right, with service containing two glasses of water
and two cigars, which he places on table.*]

BROWN: Here, gemmen, am some wine, an' some ob de best cigars
in town.

ED: How much is it, colonel?

BROWN: Two dollars and a half.

ELLIS: Let me pay for them now.

ED: No. Let me pay. [*reaches in pocket*]

ELLIS: No, Senator Davis, I ordered dem an' I's gwine ter pay.

ED: But I say you shan't pay, Senator Blaine, I's gwine ter pay
myself.

BROWN: Never mind, gemmen, don't quarrel, 'bout a little thing like
dat, I'll jes' charge it in de bill, an' you can settle all together
in de mornin'. [*exit* BROWN, *right.*]

ED AND ELLIS: All right. [*they sit at table and light cigars*]

ED: Gosh, but ain't dis a soft snap.

ELLIS: Oh. I's a purty slick nigger, I is. [*drinks from glass*] Guess dis
am a new kind of champagne.

ED: So Jim Blaine, you can't tell de taste of dat kind of wine, cause
you ain't used to it. [*tastes water*] Dis am de boss wine.

BROWN: Shall I bring you somefin' more, gemmen?

[*Enter* BROWN, *right.*]

ED: Bring us some milk punch, an' let it be de bes' in de lan'. [*exit*
BROWN, *right*]

ELLIS: I feels like I owns de earth, don't you, Bruder Davis?

ED: Yes indeed.

[*Enter* BROWN, *right, with two glasses filled with flour, which
he puts on table.*]

BROWN: [*aside*] I'll fix dese here senator niggers.

ELLIS: Let me pay for dis now.

ED: No, let me, Brudder Blaine?

BROWN: Never mind, gemmen, I'll put it in de bill. [*exit, right*]

ED: [*takes up glass of flour*] Here's luck.

ELLIS: [*takes up glass*] Let her go dar. [*they try to drink and get flour
on their faces—sit back in their chairs and look at each other,
and fall asleep with cigars in their hands.* BROWN *enters and
takes cigars, leaving lighted candles instead, and exits right.* ED
*wakes up and tries to smoke candle, then puts candle on table,
wakes* ELLIS *who does same.*] Senator Davis, you yaller coon,
you stole my cigar.

ED: No, you took mine, Jim Blaine. [*they search each others' pockets
in vain.*]

ELLIS: We must have been "hoo dooed" some way, Davis; but let's
have some brandy, that's a sure pertection. [*rings*]

[BROWN *enters with big bottle.*]

ELLIS: Bring us some brandy.

BROWN: Here it is, gemmen. I knew you would want brandy, so I
brought it up when you rang. [*pours out of bottle into glasses,
they drink and fall asleep.* BROWN *brings tall dunce caps, which
he puts on their heads and sets tops on fire—exit. The Senators
wake up and put out fire, then are attacked with cramps in the
stomach—move around stage in agony, get bottle from table and
turn label to front, on which reads, "Rough on Rats." They run
off in agony. Curtain*]

Peculiar Sam; or, The Underground Railroad

Introduction

Pauline Hopkins's 1879 play *Peculiar Sam; or, The Underground Railroad* can be difficult for modern readers to reconcile with what they might expect from an African American author writing just after Reconstruction. On the one hand, it features a "peculiar" slave, Sam, who not only physically assaults a Black driver (slave "overseer" Jim), but also, with the help of the Underground Railroad, leads a party of escaping slaves toward Canada. Along the way, he outwits Jim (who hopes to capture the other slaves), steals his money, and holds him at gunpoint to ensure the success of the escape.

But this radical core is enveloped in minstrelsy: Jim wears immense false feet throughout the play, almost all of the characters' dialect leads to repeated malapropisms, characters frequently interrupt the play's action to sing and dance to minstrel songs, and slapstick humor rules several scenes. The play's relationship to the politics of African American equality Hopkins so eloquently fought for later in her life remains somewhat enigmatic. This perhaps explains why the play has received comparatively little critical attention—even as Hopkins's novels and journalistic writing have entered many American literature classrooms in the last decade. Still, Hopkins's biography and a sense of the American stage in the late 1870s help explain some of these seeming contradictions.

Born in the late 1850s—most scholars accept 1859 as the year, though it may well have been earlier—in Portland, Maine, Hopkins grew up in Boston. Several sources refer to her father as Northrup Hopkins and note that he was born in Virginia, but census records and performance materials for *Peculiar Sam* suggest either that her father also went by the name William A. Hopkins or that a William Hopkins was her step-father. Her mother, Sarah Allen Hopkins, was born in New Hampshire and was well-connected among free Blacks in the antebellum North: she was related to both the Paul family (which included powerhouse clergymen like Nathaniel and Thomas Paul, early activist Susan Paul, and, almost in Hopkins's own generation, activist and clubwoman Susan Paul Vashon) as well as to the early Black poet James Whitfield. From this very literate home, Hopkins excelled early at writing—winning a prize named for William Wells Brown from the Congregational Publishing Society of Boston for an essay on temperance.

Peculiar Sam, which went under several titles including *Slaves' Escape* and *The Great Moral Drama: Underground Railroad*, was not her first play; according to Eileen Southern, she copyrighted a work entitled *Aristocracy* in 1877. It was, though, her most success-ful. Nonetheless, by 1881, Hopkins had shifted most of her energies from writing to singing—and was somewhat successful; one Boston newspaper called her "Boston's Favorite Colored Soprano." Even here, though, opportunities were limited, and, in the early 1890s, she took courses in stenography, and this became her occupation for the rest of the decade.

When she returned to writing at the turn of the century, she quickly became a major voice in African American letters. The first issue of the *Colored American* magazine (May 1900) carried one of her short stories, and by the end of the decade, the magazine had featured three serialized novels and a half dozen more stories writ-ten by Hopkins. She also wrote a rich series of biographical pieces of nineteenth-century African Americans (ranging from Frederick Douglass to Sojourner Truth) for the magazine. The year 1900 also saw publication of her most celebrated novel, *Contending Forces*, in book form by the *Colored American*'s publisher, the Colored Co-operative Publishing Company. Popular among Black readers—and promoted especially by the Black women's club movement—the novel lapsed into obscurity later in the twentieth century, but is now recognized as a pioneering work. All of Hopkins's work argued forcefully for African American civil rights and often focused on the nexus of gender and race embodied in cross-racial relationships. Hopkins became the *Colored American*'s women's editor in 1901 and literary editor in 1903. In 1904 she undertook a large lecture tour—but, by the end of the year, ill health—and possibly differences with the editors—forced her to leave both it and her editorial position. The *Colored American* folded in 1909, and Hopkins wrote little after. She returned to stenography, never married, and worked for a range of employers before finally working at the Massachusetts Institute of Technology. She died on August 13, 1930, much of her work already forgotten.

In some ways, just as her novels were tied to the establishment of the *Colored American* and the Colored Co-operative Publishing Company, *Peculiar Sam* was the result of a confluence of events fairly rare for the late nineteenth century. In 1876, white author Joseph Bradford wrote a play about African American subjects, *Out of Bondage*, as a vehicle for the Hyers sisters—African American soprano Anna Madah Hyers and contralto Emma Louise Hyers. These pioneering Black singers toured the country, at times with Sam Lucas, one of the most famous African Americans to enter minstrelsy and the first African American to play Uncle Tom on the stage. *Out of Bondage* played in Boston, and, if Hopkins did not see the play, it is likely she heard of it. By early 1879, Hopkins was already working on her own play written for Lucas, *Peculiar Sam*.

The few scholars who have considered the play's history disagree on both the circumstances of its performance and its reception. Southern reports that Lucas was apparently initially pleased with—if a bit tardy in performing—the work and that the play toured the Northeast and northern Midwest with some success. Errol Hill, citing a 1909 piece by Lucas that wasn't published until 1916, argues that Lucas was simply helping Hopkins's work see the stage, that the play failed because audiences weren't ready for it, and that it was never tied to the Hyers sisters.

Regardless of which account is correct—and both have some merit—some areas are more clear. First, to sell such work, Hopkins obviously had to build her story around a great deal of music—especially popular minstrel songs like those the Hyers sisters sang regularly—and to the kinds of stereotypical humor that Lucas made his career on. Indeed, Eileen Southern notes that afterpieces for *Peculiar Sam* often included Lucas doing scenes from *Uncle Tom's Cabin*. Second, Hopkins—with her own troupe, Hopkins' Colored Troubadours, which included both her mother and William Hopkins—staged the show in a three-act version in Boston in the summer of 1880.

Given these circumstances, then, we might speculate that Hopkins—as Lucas, the Hyers sisters, and the other, rare Black popular entertainers like diva Sissieretta Jones did—made some ideological sacrifices so that she could participate in the white-dominated theater business, sacrifices she did not have to make for the *Colored American* two decades later. And, of course, Hopkins was quite young when the play was written.

Nonetheless, the play has suggestions of her much later and more radical work: for all of his minstrel antics, Sam is smart, savvy, and successful; the play treats a key set of issues in African American history and helped popularize remembrance of the Underground Railroad; and the characters end in positions quite different from their slave beginnings.

A Note on the Text

The text offered here is a transcription of the manuscript version of the play now housed in the Special Collections Library at Fisk University. Minor errors in Hopkins's handwritten copy have been corrected as they would have been for publication. A handful of additions are marked by double brackets. Readers interested in seeing a holograph of the manuscript will find Eileen Southern's *Nineteenth-Century American Musical Theater* especially enlightening. Southern's volume also usefully includes the songs referred to in the text—all of which were popular at the time and several of which were part of the late minstrel repertoire. Beyond these musical allusions, most of the text remains understandable, and the more difficult moments in the dialect are comprehensible if read aloud.

For Further Reading

Campbell, Jane. "Pauline Elizabeth Hopkins." *Dictionary of Literary*

Biography. Volume 50. Ed. Trudier Harris. Detroit: Gale, 1986. 182–189.

Hill, Errol. "The Hyers Sisters: Pioneers in Black Musical Comedy." *The American Stage: Social and Economic Issues from the Colonial Period to the Present*. Ed. Ron Engle and Tice L. Miller. Cambridge: Cambridge University Press, 1993. 115–130.

Hopkins, Pauline. *Contending Forces*. New York: Oxford University Press, 1988.

———. *The Magazine Novels of Pauline Hopkins*. New York: Oxford University Press, 1988.

Shockley, Ann Allen. "Pauline Elizabeth Hopkins: A Biographical Excursion into Obscurity." *Phylon 33* (1972): 22–26.

Southern, Eileen, ed. *Nineteenth-Century American Musical Theater*. New York: Taylor and Francis, 1994.

Tate, Claudia. "Pauline Hopkins: Our Literary Foremother." *Conjuring: Black Women, Fiction, and Literary Tradition*. Eds. Marjorie Pryse and Hortense J. Spillers. Bloomington: Indiana University Press, 1985.

Peculiar Sam; or The Underground Railroad

CHARACTERS

SAM, A PECULIAR FELLOW
JIM, OVERSEER (2nd TENOR)
CAESAR, STATION MASTER (BARITONE)
PETE, FRIEND TO SAM (TENOR)
POMP, FRIEND TO SAM (BASS)
VIRGINIA, THE PLANTATION NIGHTINGALE (SOPRANO)
JUNO, SISTER TO SAM (ALTO)
MAMMY, MOTHER TO SAM (SOPRANO 2nd)

COSTUMES

SAM   Act I: Gingham pants & shirt, old boots, dilapidated
            hat. 2nd dress: Very fair complexion, long curly
            black wig moustache to match, heavy boots, whip,
            &c. Act II: same as 2nd dress Act I, change to red
            flannel dressing gown and night cap. Scene II: Same.
            Change to old man's dress, white wig, &c. Act III:
            [[Same.]] Act IV: Full evening dress, ulster, fur cap,
            driving gloves.

JIM   Act I: Overeer's dress, whip, &c; *immense* false teeth.
            Act II, Scene I: Same. 2nd: same, covered with white
            sheet with eye holes. Scene 2: Same. Act III: Same.
            Act IV: Plaid pants and vest, high standing collar,
            swallow tail coat, roundabout jacket trimmed with
            brass buttons, overall. Tall hat, immense wig, cow-
            hide boots, immense feet.

CAESAR   Act II, Scene I: Red flannel dressing gown & night
            cap. 2nd: Same coat & hat. Scene 2: Same. Act III:

	Same. Act IV: Very white wig, common pants & vest, brick colored dressing gown with yellow cane &c.
PETE & POMP	Act I, II, and III: Field hand's dress. Act IV: Neat dark clothes, hats, overcoats.
VIRGINIA	Act I: Short calico dress, plain white collar, apron, sun hat. Act II and III: Same. Act IV: Handsome house dress of modest color.
JUNO	Act I: Short red calico, made sack fashion, tied round waist with string, red handkerchief tied under chin. Act II and III: Same. Act IV: Handsome short dress of blue, fancy pink apron.
MAMMY	Act I: Plain plaid house dress, yellow turban, immense bonnet in last part. Act II and III: Same. Act IV: Drab dress, short & plain, white neckerchief fastened at waist, long white apron, gay turban.

ACT I

[Interior of an old cabin. Entrance at back, usual furniture. Time, evening. Unseen chorus as curtain rises.]

[At close of chorus, enter SAM, *followed by* JIM, CAESAR, PETE, *and* POMP, *dressed as field hands.* POMP *with banjo.]*

SAM: Come on boys we'll hab a right smart time hyar, all to ourselves. Mammy and Juno is gone out an' de coast am clar.

PETE: I say Sam, show de boys dat new step you war takin' in de fiel' dis mornin'. *[To rest]* Clar, I neber seed a fellar use his feet as dat Sam kan.

[Laughter.]

SAM: I allers likes to be 'comidatin' to my frien's. Now Pomp you strike up suthin lively an' de res' ob you gemmens take a turn wid de music till you git kin' o' warmed up, an' soon as you's at de right pitch I'll wade in on de new step.

PETE: Jes' so sir.

*[*POMP *strikes up lively dance, each takes a turn.* SAM *beats time and grows more and more excited.]*

SAM: *[Unable to restrain himself longer.]* Take kar dar, de spirits a movin' in me, Ise comin'.

[Rest cease dancing, mark time until he drops, exhausted, into a seat.]

SAM: I tell you what gemmens, when I gits off on an ole Virginie, I feels jes like an onthoughtful horse, 'deed I does.

POMP: *[Rising]* I tell you boy you's a hi ole dancer, you doesn't kno' your own walloo. *[To rest]* Les all go down to uncle Eph's back-yard an' hearse dis new step. Clar, I jes tingles to get at it.

ALL: Dat's jes de ting.

[JIM, CAESAR, PETE, *and* POMP *move toward door.*]

SAM: I'll meet you dar, soon as I 'sposes ob some tickler bisness Ise got on han'.

[*Laughter.*]

PETE: 'Spec' boy you'd better look out for Jim; he's got young Marse mighty sweet, an' ole times am pas' since old Marse died. I doesn't like to say it, but Ise mighty 'fraid you's gwine to lose your gal.

SAM: [*answers* PETE *with solo*]
  One night as the moon was beamin'
      I lay fas' asleep a dreamin';
    That the sun was shinin' bright,
        In the middle of the night
    And the darkies had assembled to have a little fight.
        I woke an' the banjo was soundin'
    An' the bones through the air were boundin';
        How happy I did seem, I was married in a dream,
    In an ole Virginie mudscow floatin down stream.

[*Chorus, male quartette* (JIM, CAESAR, PETE, *and* POMP).]

SAM: Din I warn all de niggers not to love her,
      Ef they do it'll cause them to blubber;
        Now git out of my way an' member what I say,
    I'm gwine to marry her myself some very fine day.
ALL: Kiah! Kiah! Kiah!
PETE: I 'spec' you will Sam, 'spec' you will.

[*Exit* JIM, CAESAR, PETE, *and* POMP.]

SAM: Wonder whar all de folks is. [*Thoughtfully.*] 'Pears like to me suthin's wrong; I feel it inter my bones dat dars gwine to be a disjointin' hyar soon, an' when I gits dese 'pressions dey's neber wrong.

[*Enter* MAMMY, *excited.*]

MAMMY: [*Breathing hard*] For de Lor's sake boy do you kno' what dey's gone an' done up to de big house? Dey's gone an married dat dear chile, dat lamb ob a Jinny, to dat rascal ob an oberseer Jim.

SAM: [*Excited, grasps her arm*] Mammy, tell me agin! You don't mean it! Tell me dey haint done dat!

MAMMY: [*Astonished*] Hyar boy, lef' be my arm. You mean to scrunch me to a jelly? [*He drops her arm.*] Yes, deys bring dat gal up like a lady; she neber done nuthin' but jes wait on Marse fambly an' now ole Marser's dead dey's gone an' married her, their way to Jim an' de gal can't bar de sight ob him. It's de meanes' thing I eber seed.

SAM: [*Dejected*] An' dats' de way they treats dar slabes! An' den they tells how kin' dey is, an' how satisfied we is, an' all de time they treats us as if we hadn't got eny souls eny mo' den thar dogs an' horses. [*to* MAMMY] Mammy, when am dat time comin' dat you's tol me 'bout eber since I was knee high to a cricket, when am Moses gwine to lead us po' forsook niggers fro' de Red Sea? [*Covers face with arm, and turns away*]

MAMMY: [*Lays hand on his arm*] Poor boy! Poor Sammy! Chile, I didn't kno' you loved dat gal, but I might a knowed it, I might a knowed it. Don't yer gib up nor lose your spirits, for de Lord am comin' on his mighty chariot, drawn by his big white horse, an' de white folks hyar, am a gwine to tremble. Son Ise been waitin' dese twenty-five year, an' I aint guv up yet.

SAM: Yes Mammy, but Ise lubbed dat gal eber sense we made mud pies, down inter de holler, an' I used to steal milk fer her out ob de hog trof. [*Sorrowfully*] Po' Jinny, po' little gal [*Crosses to right, sings*]
Ah! Jinny is a simple chile,
　　Wif pretty shinin' curls,
An' white folks love her best, of all
　　The young mulatto girls;
Tell her to wait a little while,

Tell her in hope to wait,
For I will surely break the chain,
That binds her to the gate.

[*Chorus (mixed quartette, unseen).*]

SAM: Our old cabin stands upon the stream,
In old Mississippi state
And I must quickly hurry on
An' take po' Jinny from de gate.

Ole Marser's dead an' I am sold,
From Mississippi state;
But I can't leave her here alone,
To weep beside the gate;
I cannot tell her we must part,
Alas! Our cruel fate;
And so with patient eyes she'll watch
For me, beside the gate.

[*Chorus.*]

SAM: T'would be wrong for me to leave her 'lone,
In Mississippi state;
But cunning, it will break the chain
That binds her to the gate;
So I'll Marser's gol' an' silver get,
Pray heaven I'm not too late;
To set my darling Jinny free,
And take her from the gate.

[*Chorus.*]

SAM: If you should ever travel to the South.
To Mississippi state;
Don't fail to find this cabin out,
Where Jinny stood at the gate;
Tell her to wait a little while,

Tell her in hope to wait;
> For I am he, shall make her free,
An take her from the gate.

[*Chorus. At close, enter* VIRGINIA *and* JUNO *with bundle.*]

JUNO: Mammy, I jes toted Jinny down hyar, for you to use some salvation wif her; talk 'bout dat gal's bein' sof' and easy. She says she's gwine to run 'way tonight.

[SAM *takes* VIRGINIA *by one hand,* MAMMY *takes the other, Juno makes circuit around them up left, down right.*]

VIRGINIA: Yes, Mammy, and Sam, I have come to say good-bye, it's hard to leave the place where I was born, but it is better to do this, than to remain here, and become what they wish me to be. To fulfill this so-called marriage.

JUNO: Yes, Mammy, onlies thing they done in de worl' was, Marse he say, "Jim you want to marry Jinny?" Jim he say yes, course Jim say yes. Marse he say, "Jinny you want to marry Jim?" Jinny her say no, like to kno' what Jinny want of igernunt ole Jim. Marse say, "You man an' wife, an Lor' hab mussy on you soul." Dat no kin' ob weddin'.

SAM: Jinny, you isn't 'fraid to trust ol' peculiar Sam, I know, kase you see I'm allers willin' to die fer you. You needn't bid any on us good-bye, kase dis night I 'tends to tote you and Mammy and Juno 'way from hyar. Yas, an' I'll neber drop ye till Ise toted you safe inter Canidy.

MAMMY: [*Astonished*] Boy what you talkin' 'bout!

JUNO: Golly mighty jes hyar dat fellar.

SAM: Yas, we's all gwine to Canidy! Dars been suthin' a growin' an' a growin' inter me, an' it keep sayin', "Run 'way, run away, Sam. Be a man, be a free man." An' Mammy, ef it hadn't been fer you an' de gals I'd been gone long 'go. But Ise prepared myself, in kase ob a 'mergensy.

MAMMY: Look hyar boy, what has you been a doin'? I doesn't want you to bring no disrace onter me.

SAM: [*Looks carefully around*] See hyar.

> [*They gather around him* [[*as he*]] *produces slip of paper from his pocket.*]

SAM: Dat's a pass for us to go to camp meetin'. Now all ob you kno's dat dars a lot of fellars roun' hyar runnin' off slabes. Dey runs dem to Canidy, an' all 'long de road, de white 'litioners helps 'em deceitfully, an' dey calls dis, de underground railroad. Ef we kin get 'way from hyar inter te nex' state, we kin reach de fus' station ob de road, an' from dar, they'll take charge on us, an' hand us safe in Canidy.

JUNO: I kno's whar dat is, dar aint no slabe niggers dar, dey's all tooken care on by Mrs. Queen Victoria, she's de Presidunt ob Canidy.

MAMMY: You hish up gal, an' let your brudder talk. Day allers tol' me dat boy was pecoolar, but I neber 'spected it would revelop itself in dis way.

SAM: Dare a mullato fellar gwine to start a gang up river to-night, an' Ise gwine to be dat fellar, an' you's gwine to be de gang. Ef we kin 'complish dis we's all right, an' we'll say good-bye to the ole plantation.

JUNO: Sh! Dars somebody comin'. [*Runs quickly and seats herself on Virginia's bundle*]

> [*Enter* JIM *as overseer.*]

JIM: I 'spected I'd fin' you hyar Miss Airy but you's my wife now, an' you's got to do as I says. Dars dat hoe cake aint baked fer my supper, an' dars my ol' pants wants mendin', an' you's got it to do.

> [VIRGINIA *shrinks from him.* JIM *follows her.* SAM *follows him.*]

JIM: You's full o' airs, dat what you is, but I'll bring em out o' you, ef I has to tie you up an' gib you a dozen lashes. [*Seizes* VIRGINIA *by her arm,* SAM *seizes him by collar jerks him, then releases him.*]

SAM: [*Shudders with anger*] See hyar, Ise seed you swellin' roun' hyar consid'able, but when you talks 'bout struckin' Jinny, Ise got suthin' to say.

JIM: You's anoder sassy nigger. But you's fixed long wif de res' ob your 'culiar coons. Marse gwine to sell you all down Red riber to-morrer, den I reckon Miss Jinny will have herself. An meantime I don't want any ob your sass.

[*Women huddle together.*]

MAMMY: [*Rocking herself to and fro*] Ef old Marse had libed he'd neber 'low it. O Lor', O Lor'!

SAM: I jes wants you to answer one question, do you 'cider dat Jinny am your wife?

JIM: Yas sar, an' you's only mad kase she aint yourn. [*Cracks his whip at* SAM]

SAM: [*Leaps upon him, seizes whip*] You's a liar sar, dats what you is! You crack your whip at me! [*Flourishes whip around Jim, then takes it by butt end as if to strike him with it*] You say Jinny's your wife agin an' I'll mash you all up, you mean ol' yank nigger. [*Chases* JIM *around room with whip.* JIM *tries to take it from him.*]

JIM: Eff you strike me, Marse'll skun you.

SAM: [*Contemptuously.*] Marser's pet! [*Throws whip aside*] Come on, you, you lizard hearted coon, we'll hab a set-to, for Ise boun' to take your sass out on your hide. [*They spar with their fists. Two or three times Jim butts at* SAM, *but misses him,* SAM *passing over his head in careless manner. Make this set-to as comical as possible.*]

JIM: [*Glaring at him*] O, ef I only had you tied to the widder!

SAM: [*Edging up to* JIM] This thing is played out; as for havin' a common nigger talkin' 'bout tyin' me up, I isn't gwine to. I wouldn't be such a 'teriated coon as you is for all de Norf. I want you to know dat the ascendant ob sech a 'structible fambly as I is can lick a dozen sech cantankerferous niggers as you is. You can jes look out now Ise done foolin', Ise gwine to hurt you.

[*They stand and glare at each other.* JIM *is off guard, and* SAM *rushes at him head first, strikes him in the stomach,* JIM *staggers across room, doubles up.*]

JIM: [*Howls*] O, Ise gone dead, Ise gone dead.

[*Women rush at* SAM, *to hold him.*]

SAM: [*Rubs his head*] Jingo, dat nigger's stomick am made ob some kind ob cast of iron, I reckon.

MAMMY: O sonny, sonny, Marse'll kill us all.

[*Enter* POMP *and* PETE. PETE *with banjo.* JIM *rises, groaning, limps to door.*]

JIM: [*To* SAM] Neber min' my fine gemman, you'll be sol' down South, an' I'll take de res' ob it out o' Jinny. [*Exit* JIM *hurriedly, as* SAM *takes two long strides toward him.*]

PETE AND POMP: Why wha's de matter?

JUNO: Sam's been showin' de oberseer how 'culiar he is, dat's all.

VIRGINIA: O, let us leave as soon as possible, who can tell what may happen?

SAM: Dat's jes so Jinny. [*To* PETE *and* POMP.] Boys we's gwine to board de train to-night, am you ready?

PETE: Lord boy, Ise been ready for de las' year.

POMP: You kin bet on me, kase my trunk am packed. [*Holds up banjo*] An' I allers carries my walables wif me.

SAM: Well den I'll leave you hyar wif Mammy an' de girls while I goes to reconoyster, an' see ef de coas' am clar. [*Exit Sam.*]

[MAMMY *and* JUNO *pack up bundles.* JUNO *ties plaid handkerchief on her head.*]

VIRGINIA: While we are waiting for Sam let's sing again before we leave our old home. For though we leave it in darkness and sorrow, it is still our home.

[*She sings solo, others join in quartet. I should think "Home, Sweet Home" well sung by the soprano might be a decided hit. Reenter* SAM *at close, dressed as gentleman overseer.*]

JUNO: [*Not knowing him*] See hyar Marse, you's in de wrong place. De big house am up de road dar.

SAM: [*Flourising whip*] Why, don't you know me?

ALL: Am dat you Sam?

MAMMY: Why, honey, I hardly know'd my own chile.

JUNO: What a peccoliar fellar you is! Look jes like a gemman.

SAM: Am you ready? Now is our safest time.

> [*They pick up their bundles. Start for door, turn as they reach it and form tableau in door around* VIRGINIA *and* MAMMY.]

MAMMY: [*Weeping*] Good-bye ole home, de place whar my chillern war born, an' my ole man am buried. Ise ole now, I may neber see you 'gin, but my chillern's gwine, an' I'm boun' to go too. So Good-bye ole home.

[*Chorus. Curtain.*]

ACT II, SCENE I

[*Time, night. Front of an old hut in the woods; door lower right corner; window upper left corner. Entrances to stage right and left.*]

[*Enter* SAM, VIRGINIA, MAMMY, JUNO, PETE, *and* POMP *right. Sing several choruses.*]

CAESAR: [*Opens window as they finish*] Whar in de name ob de Lor' did all you stray coons drap down from? Ef you don't go 'way from hyar mislestin' 'spectible people, I'll set de dogs onter you, so you'd better git. [*Closes window.*]

SAM: [*Pounds at the door*] Ol' man, ol' man, open de do', it's de delegation from down de riber, don't be 'feard, it's only me, peculiar Sam.

CAESAR: [*Opens window slowly.*] Aint you gone yet? You needn't tell

me you's 'cular Sam, you's one ob dem tricksy m'latter fellars,
dat's what you is.

SAM: 'Deed it are me uncle, don't you 'member how I was to come
hyar by the the undergroun'—

CAESAR: [*Interrupts him*] You's bin 'tirely mistook, kase dar aint no
underhan' nuthin' hyar, done moved up Norf long 'go.

SAM: Now look hyar uncle dar aint no use bein' uppish, kase de black
clouds am risin'.

CAESAR: [*Astonished*] Wha', wha' dat you say? Finish dat now, say
de res' ob it.

JUNO: Say uncle, aint you got a 'possum leg in dar, Ise mos' starved?

MAMMY: You gal hish.

SAM: [*To* CAESAR] Uncle dar aint nuthin' in de worl' dat tastes so
sweet as a good ole ash cake.

CAESAR: [*Excited*] Dats de word! dats to word! ash cake am de word!!
How you tink I gwine to kno' you, comin hyar all dressed up
dat a way.

MAMMY: [*Peers at* CAESAR *from under her hand*] 'Pears like to me
Ise seed you befo'; aint you Caesar dat used to lib down on
de ol' 'Nolia plantation?

CAESAR: Who dat? In course Ise Caesar. [*Looks at her earnestly*] Why
Mammy, dat aint you am it? Jes wait til I comes down dar an'
takes a look at you. [*Disappears from window, reenters from door.*
MAMMY *and* CAESAR *laugh and shake hands heartily.*]

MAMMY: Why ol' man thought you war dead an' gone dese ten
year!

CAESAR: Why ol' 'ooman, Ise mighty glad to see you, you's lookin'
jes as han'som' as eny gal. [*Still shake hands*] Why whar's you
all gwine?

SAM: We're trablin' to Canidy. 'Deed uncle dey is gittin' so hi on des
plantations dat a fellar's got to run 'way ef he's got eny 'spectible feelin's 'tall.

CAESAR: Well children, Ise glad you's foun' de ol' man, an' hope
you'll 'scuse my 'section, but de slabe holders am layin' fer
de 'litioners an' I doesn't dar to breaf hard knowin' dat Ise in
charge ob one ob dese stations.

SAM: I tell you uncle Ise jes b'ginnin' te feel mysel', an' ef eny man puts his han' onter me to stop me dar's gwine te be trubble, kase Ise foo'ld long nuff. Ef you'll jes gib Mammy an' de gals a chance to take breaf an' den put us onto de nex station you'll 'lieve my min'; fer we's had a hard time, de white folks am arter us an' we's been almos' kotched, an' we haint got long to stay hyar.

[*Chorus.*]

CAESAR: [*At close*] Well son, you stay an' take keer ob de house, while I tote de folks to de care; den I'll come back fer you.

SAM: All right uncle, an' ef eny body cames, I reckon I can gib dem all de defamation dey wants. Now you jez han' ober dat dressum gown an' dat cap an' I'll reguise mysel' inter them. [*Places wig and moustache in his pocket, exchanges his coat and hat for* CAESAR'S]

CAESAR: [*Dons* SAM'S *hat and coat*] 'Member honey dat de black clouds is risin' an' ash cake am de words.

[*All, save* SAM, *exit left, singing.*]

SAM: [*Calls to* VIRGINIA] Don't git scared Jinny I'll meet you by me by. Now I reckon I'll make a reconoyster, an' den turn in an' take some sleep. [*Yawns, looks arounds carefully, yawns again. Disappears in hut.*]

[*Enter* JIM, *right.*]

JIM: I kno' dey mus' hab comed dis way, I'm mos' sho' dis am one ob dem stations. Wonder ef dat do' am fastened. [*Tries door, it does not yield, knocks, no answer*] Playin' 'possum. [*Knocks louder, no answer*] Wonder ef dar aint no one hyar sho' nuff. [*Knocks again*]

SAM: [*Faintly, as if half asleep.*] Who dar? Wha's de matter?

JIM: [*Still pounding*] Ol' man you'd better come down hyar, I wants to see you on a very reportant matter.

SAM: [*Appears at window with lighted candle, disguised voice.*] What you mean comin' hyar in sech a blunderous manner? Ef you don't go 'way fro' dat do', I'll, I'll, I'll spill suthin' on you, 'deed I will.

JIM: [*As* SAM *turns to go away*] See hyar uncle, you kno's me, you kno's oberseer Jim; Ise only come to ax you a few questions.

SAM: Well, what you want no how? Kase Ise a gemman ob bisness, I hires my time, I does.

JIM: I doesn't mean no defense uncle, but you sees some ob my nigs is runned away, an' I wants to kno' has you hyard ob dem eny whar?

SAM: [*In scolding voice*] What you doin' lettin' your slabes run 'way? What kin' oberseer is you losin' nigs, an' den runnin' all ober creation an' ebry whar else lookin' fer em. No I haint seed 'em, I jes haint.

JIM: See hyar uncle, dars a 'ward out for dem fellars, an' ef you'll gib me eny reformation, I'll 'zarve some o' it fer you.

SAM: Has you got eny idee whar dey is?

JIM: O yas, Marse gib me a hunded dollar; an' I foller de tail up from de plantation, an' jes as I get hyar I lose it. But I reckon de 'litioners am running dem off. But we'll kotch 'em sho. Has you seed enythig' on 'em?

SAM: Come to think ob it I did see some stray coons 'roun'. But Lor', my 'membance am so bad.

JIM: [*Excited*] You mus' 'member uncle, whar'd dey go, wha'd dey look like?

SAM: 'Clar, it are clean gone from me. My 'membance am so bad.

JIM: See hyar uncle, ef you'll tell me anythin' 'bout dem fellars, I'll gib you...[*Thoughtfully*] I'll gib you fifty cents.

SAM: Wha's fifty cents side ob a hunded dollars? No, I don't 'member nuthin'.

JIM: Ef you'll 'member anythin' 'bout dem pussons uncle, I'll gib you, yas I'll gib you dollar.

SAM: 'Pears like dar was a tall coon wif de crowd I seed, but I isn't sho.

JIM: Yas! Yas! Dem's em! Dem's em! An' a singin' gal, say dar war a singin' gal, an' I gib you...[*Pauses*] I'll gib you two whole dollars.

SAM: Lor' child 'taint no use axing on me, kase I jes don' kno' weafer I 'member dat tickler gal or not.

JIM: Ef you'll jes say she war dar, kase I know'd you seed her, I'll gib you free dollars, dat's all de change Ise got.

SAM: Lay de money onter de do' sill dar, den I'll see ef I can 'member any mo'! [JIM *lays money down*] I reckon de singin' gal war wif dem fellars, reckon you'll fin' her sho nuff, when you kotch 'em.

JIM: Whar'd dey go? Which way'd dey go?

SAM: Down de road a piece, dar's a empty house, an' I reckon deys done gone dar.

JIM: How'd you get at dat house?

SAM: Reckon you'd better take de railroad track on yer right an' de woods onto your lef' an' foller dat paf till you gits to a blasted juniper tree, an' when you git to dat tree you turn ober it, an' foller dat paf till you gits to de house. Ef you don't fin' it, you kin come back an' go 'roun' de tother way.

JIM: [*Ready to start*] How long's dey been gone?

SAM: 'Deed it might a bin a hour 'go, an' it might a bin fourteen hour 'go; an' den agin it might a bin longer, an' it mightent a bin so long, it war some whar 'roun' dar. My 'membance has 'clipses wery bad, but I reckun dat's about de time de whar hyar.

[SAM *disappears from window.*]

JIM: Dat fellar aint foolin' me eny, I hasn't got fer to go to fin' dem coons; I'll kotch him. [*Disappears right*]

[*Enter* SAM *from door.*]

SAM: [*Chuckles*] Hope dat fellar'll fin' dat house. [*laughs*] Don't blive dars any sech place on de face ob de earth. [*picks up money*] Dis money come in right smart, it'll be mighty handy up dar in Canidy. 'Clar I wishes I could git dat hunded dollars.

[*Enter* JIM, *right, as ghost, groans. Sam turns, startled, and stands shaking in terror.*]

SAM: Who, who'd you want to see sar? Kase dar aint nobody to home, I don't lib hyar mysel' Ise jes keepin' house till de fambly 'turns.

[*Ghost groans, extends right arm, moves slowly toward* SAM, *who retreats, followed by ghost, step for step.*]

SAM: O Marse debbil, jes 'low me to satisfy you dat I isn't de fellar you's lookin fer, 'deed I aint, he's done gone 'way five long year 'go. [*Ghost draws nearer*] I neber done nuthin' to nobody. I allers says my prayers ebery night, 'deed I does.

[*Ghost places his hand on* SAM. SAM *falls on his knees.*]

SAM: I'll 'fess, I'll 'fess. [*His eyes fall on ghost's feet.* SAM *rises to his feet with mouth open in astonishment. Aside*] I know dem feet! 'Course I kno's dem feet! [*Looks at them again*] Dem's de same pair o' feet. I know dey is, kase dem feet neber growed on no oder fellar but Jim, in de worl'. [*To ghost*] Playin' ghos' am you? Well reckon I'll make you de sickes' ghos' in 'Merica, 'fore I'm done wif you.

[*Ghost begins to recede slowly, followed by* SAM *step for step.*]

SAM: Did you fin' dat house Mr. Ghos'? Did ou git dat singin' gal, Mr. Ghos'? How's your Red riber gang Mr. Ghos'? Come on now, an' lis see how a corporal sperit can fight. I tends to knock de win' clean out o' you Mr. Ghos'.

[*Ghost turns to run.* SAM *grapples with him. Overcomes him and ties arms behind him.*]

SAM: Gwine to leab me war you? When you kno's how Mammy an' de gals will 'mire to see a ghos'. [*Helps* JIM *to his feet*] You's a pretty lookin' ghos', aint you? You's a disrace to de prefeshun. Now I wants you to hand out dat hunded dollar Marse guv you.

JIM: [*Feebly*] It's in my pants pocket.

[SAM *takes out pocket book, opens it, disclosing bills. Forgets ghost, sits down on stage floor, begins to count, chuckling to himself.*]

SAM: Dars a five, an' a ten, an' a one, an' a twenty…

[JIM *meantime steals along stage to entrance, right, stumbles in his dress, making noise.* SAM *stops counting, looks up, produces pistol, which he points at ghost.*]

SAM: Come back hyar sar, ef you moves dat karkass o' yourn de lengf of a 'possum's tail, I'll make a sho nuff ghos' ob you.

JIM: For de Lor's sake Sam don't shoot, Ise only playin' wif you.

SAM: [*Rising*] Well I isn't playin', an' ef you tries to git 'way I'll shoot you. 'Taint no harm to shoot ghosts, an' dis pistol got a piece ob silber in it, so you see Ise a peculiar fellar to play wif. Recken I'd better shoot you anyway, don't b'lieve anythin' else will 'bieve my feelin's.

JIM: See hyar Sam you wouldn't hurt an unabled fellar would you?

[*Enter* CAESAR, *left.*]

CAESAR: For de good Marser's sake boy, what is you doin', wha's dat you got?

SAM: Dis am a ghos' uncle, dat Ise captivated. He comed howlin' roun' hyar, tryin to do mischief, an' Ise been premisin' him to make a truly ghos' ob him.

CAESAR: [*Examines* JIM *curiously. To* SAM.] Ghos' hey! 'Pears like to me dat dis am oberseer Jim.

SAM: Dis am dat wery same ole snake.

CAESAR: Well chile, I reckon de ol' man'll hab to tot himself to Canidy 'long wif you. It's been gittin' woserer an' woserer, an' now dis fellar has foun' me out, de ol' man'll hab to go.

SAM: Den de sooner we's gone, de better. Ise glad you's gwine uncle. O', won't we be happy when we all "git on board."

[*Chorus, "Gospel Trail."*]

[CAESAR *disappears and returns with bundle, while* SAM *strikes up song and is answered by unseen chorus. They take* JIM *between them and exit, left.*]

ACT II, SCENE II

[*Scene 1 changes, disclosing interior of cavern, camp fire, table, three or four rude stools. Some of fugitives sitting, some stretched before fire.*]

MAMMY: Wonder whar dat boy ob mine are? I tell you chillern Ise clean tuckered out, trablin' to freedom.

JUNO: [*Sorrowfully*] Dar aint no use tryin' to be like white folks, we's jus made fer nuthin' but igerrant slabes, an' I jes b'lieve God don't want nuthin' to do wid us no how.

MAMMY: You Juno, hish, fer we's all His chillren, an He lubs us all.

JUNO: But Mammy dey say angels am all white. How's I gwine to be a angel Mammy? I jes don' 'lieve God wants eny brack angels, 'deed I don', less 'tis to tote things for Him.

MAMMY: Why chile, we's all to be washed in a powerful riber, an' arter that, we'll be all white.

JUNO: What Mammy, white as Marse and Misse?

MAMMY: Yes chile, jes as white as dem clouds Ise ofen showed you ridin' fro' God's blessed sky.

JUNO: Golly! Den I wants to be washed now, so's to be sho.

VIRGINIA: There Juno, don't plague Mammy any more but let's sing some of our old songs, and think we are back on the plantation.

[*Chorus, "Rise and Shine," Enter* SAM, JIM, *and* CAESAR *as they finish.*]

SAM: Hyar we is Mammy all back safe, an' we's brought you a kurosity in de shape ob a ghos'. [*Throws* JIM *on stool. All crowd around him.*]

MAMMY: Why honey, whar'd you git this fellar from?

JUNO: Am dat Jim? Lef me git at him!

VIRGINIA: O Sam! What made you bring him here?

SAM: Neber min' Jinny, he isn't gwine to tech you while Ise 'roun'. You see while I was waitin' for uncle to come back from totin' you, dis gemmun relieved himsel' to me in de shape ob a ghos' an

I captivated him; fus' I thought, as he 'joyed playin' ghos',
I'd sen' him whar he'd hab plenty ob dat kin' o' company;
but I took the secon' thought an' recluded to tote him
hyar, an' leave him to inflect on his pas', presunt, an' future
kreer. [*Produces pistol*] An' hyar's what I captivated him wif.

JUNO: Why Sam dats Marser's gun! Wha'd you git dat gun from?

SAM: Wha' you kno 'bout dis gun, who tol' you 'twas Marser's gun?

JUNO: Why I kno's all 'bout shootin' dat gun. I used to go up inter
Misse room, an' shoot dat ol' gun at de bedstead, an' Marse
he, he, Marse an' Misse wonder how dat bedstead kamed full
o' holes.

SAM: Well Juno, I want some liable pusson to 'gard dis gemman,
'spose you could take good care o' him.

JUNO: O, Sammy, please Sammy, jes lef me 'gard him, O, I take
rememse care ob him.

SAM: [*Gives her the pistol*] Hyar it are, an' ef he 'tempts to git off
dat stool, shoot him. [*thoughtfully*] Yas shoot him in de mos'
convenient place. [*To his mother*] Now Mammy jes git dem
bundles ready, kase we's got no time to tarry.

JUNO: [*Walks around* JIM, *and plays at shooting him.* JIM *rolls his eyes
in terror*] Ef you move one har, yas ef you wink, I'll shoot dem
feet clean off ob you. [*Keep this by-play through remainder of
this scene*]

SAM: [*To* CAESAR] Whar's dem 'rections?

CAESAR: Dey's right hyar son in de post office. [*Removes stone from
one side of cavern, takes out paper, gives it to* SAM] Dar honey, I
neber war no great at readin'; you see what dey says.

SAM: [*Reads slowly, sometimes stopping to spell*] Ef de party am large
[*Spells*] d-i, di, v-i, divide, yas dats it. Inter two parties. Come
one by s-e, se, c-r-e-t, secret road, an' one by public road, an'
when you gits on de oder shore you'll be tooken care on.

CAESAR: [*Admiring* SAM] Why boy yous eddicated, dat's wha' you is.
You doesn't kno' you're wally. Now 'cordin' to orders, you take
one lot en' I'll tote de tother wid de gal, kase she's de one dat
would make trouble for us. In de oder side ob dis cave, you'll
fin' a heap o' tings dat you'll kno' what to do wif.

SAM: All right uncle, be ready to start when I comes back. [*Exit, left.*]

[*Choruses, "Way Over in Jordan."*]

JUNO: [*Stops singing, points pistol at* JIM] I thought I hyard you wink. Kase ef I did ise gwine to shoot you right froo dem feet.

[*Reenter* SAM *dressed as old man.*]

MAMMY: [*Stares at him.*] Why boy, I hardly knowed you!

VIRGINIA: What should we do without Sam?

SAM: [*In disguised voice*] Ise po' ole uncle Ned, ladies an' gemmen, an' Ise trablin' to freedom, won't you lef de ole man go 'long wif you? [*Sings old man character songs, "Old Uncle Jake." At close they divide into two parties,* VIRGINIA *goes with* CAESAR *and* PETE; SAM *with* MAMMY, JUNO, *and* POMP. *They leave* JIM, *and exit, right and left, singing.*]

JUNO: Now min', Ise commin' back to see ef you wink, an' eff you do! [*Points pistol at his feet ominously, backs out.* JIM *moves himself, and begins to rise to his feet.* JUNO *returns*] I jes comed back to take a las' look at you, ef you dare to move or even breaf hard, I'll shoot de top ob dat ugly black head o' yourn clean off, 'deed I will.

MAMMY: [*Outside*] You Juno, you gal, come hyar, an' stop playin' yer tricks.

JUNO: You'd better min' kase one ob dese days, I'll drap on you, an' spile de beauty ob dem understanders o' yourn. [*Still threatening, she exits.*]

Curtain

ACT III

[*Time, night. Banks of a river. River at back. Entrances left and right. Trees and shrubbery along banks. Enter party led by* SAM.]

SAM: [*Looks around*] See hyar Mammy, I hope nuthin' aint happened to Jinny, kase when I was on de top ob dat las' hill we crossed 'pears like I seed a lot ob white folks comin'.

MAMMY: It's only through de blessin' ob de Lor', we haint been tooken long 'go. I dont' neber see wha's got inter Marser's dogs.

SAM: Mammy dar aint a dog widin' ten mile roun' Marser's place, dat aint so sick he kan't hol' his head up. 'Deed Mammy a chile could play wif 'em.

MAMMY: [*Holds up her hands in astonishment*] Wha! Wha' you been doin' to Marser's dogs? Why boy he'll kill us.

SAM: He will sho nuff Mammy ef he kotches us. Marse he hab plenty ob money an' I thought I'd done nuff to 'sarve some ob it, an' I jes helped mysel' to a pocket full. An' wif some ob it I bought de stuff wha' fixed dem dogs; 'deed I did, kase dis chile am no fool.

MAMMY: [*More surprised*] Been stealin' too. [*groans*] I neber 'spected dat ob you Sam.

SAM: No use Mammy, we mus' hab money, de 'litioners am good frien's to us, but money's ebery man's frien', an'll neber 'tray eben a po' forsook coon.

JUNO: [*Has been looking anxiously up the road*] Dey's comin Mammy! Here's Jinny Sam.

[*All rush right to look up road.* VIRGINIA *sings solo,* "Old Kentucky Home," *all join in chorus. At close enter* CAESAR, VIRGINIA, *and* PETE *throw down bundles, embrace.*]

CAESAR: Well my chillern, we's almos' froo de dark walley, le's sing one mo' hymn 'fo' we bids good-bye to de sunny Souf.

[*Choruses.*]

SAM: [*As they close picks up bundle*] Come on Mammy, come on Jinny, le's git on board de raf'. I tell you chillern I feels so happy I doesn't kno' mysel'. Jes feel dis air, it smells like freedom; jes see dese trees, dey look like freedom. [*Points across river*] an' look ober yonder chillern, look dar good, dat ar am ol' freedom himsel'. [*Gets happy, begins to sing*] "Dar's only one mo' riber to cross."

[*All join in song, shake hands, laugh and shout, exit, left. Singing grows fainter, but louder as raft shoots into sight, from left.* JIM *rushes panting on the stage, peers after raft. Tableau, music growing fainter. Curtain.*]

ACT IV

[*Six years after the war in Canada. Old fashioned kitchen, fireplace, in the home of the old folks. Fire in fireplace, left; old clock over it, table with cloth on it, at right, door at back, with window at the right of it, with closed inside blinds.* MAMMY *sits at table knitting,* CAESAR, *her husband now, sits before fire in armchair. Chairs, &c scattered around.*]

CAESAR: Ol' 'ooman it are a long time sense we an' de chillern lef' de ol' home, seems to me de Lor' has blessed us all. Hyars you an' me married, Jinny a singist, Juno a school marm; an' las' but not leas', dat boy, dat pecoolar Sam, eddicated an' gwine to de Nunited States Congress. I tell you ol' 'ooman de ways ob de Lor' am pas' findin' out.

MAMMY: Yas ol' man, an' hyar we is dis blessed Chrismas evenin', a settin' hyar like kings an' queens, waitin', fer dat blessed boy o' ours to come home to us. Tell you ol' man, it's 'mazin' how dat boy has 'scaped de gins an' sneers ob de worl', an' to-day am runnin' fer Congress dar in Cincinattie, it am 'mazin. D' ye s'pose he'll git it ol' man?

CAESAR: I don't spec' nothin' else, kase dat boy allers gits what he goes fer. But it's 'mos' time fer de train, wonder whar dem gals is.

[*Song by* VIRGINIA, *behind scenes, after style of* "Swanee River."]

MAMMY: [*At close*] Ol' man, Ise totable 'tented hyar till I hears dat dear chile sing dem ol' songs, in dat angel voice ob hers, an' den I feels so bad, kase dey carries me way bact to dem good ol' times dat'll neber return. De ol' plantation, an' Mistis an' ol' Marser, an' de dear little lily chillern; thar I kin seem to see de fiel's ob cotton, an' I kin seem to smell de orange blossoms dat growed on de trees down de carriage drive. [*wipes her eyes*] Ise been totable 'tented hyar, but Ise boun' to trabble back 'gin 'fo' I die.

CAESAR: [*Wiping his eyes*] An' ol' 'ooman, ef de ol' man dies firs', bury me at ol' Marser's feet, under de 'Nolia tree.

[*Clocks strikes seven. Enter* VIRGINIA *and* JUNO *right.*]

VIRGINIA: O, Mammy isn't it time for the train yet? It seems as if the hours would never pass [*Passes up right, throws open the blinds, disclosing moonlight on the snow. She stands looking out*]

JUNO: Virginia you're not the only anxious one. How I do long to see my dear old fellow, my own old Sam. I tell you Mammy I could dance. [*Places her hands in her apron pockets, and takes two or three steps of a jig*]

MAMMY: [*Interrupts her*] Quit dat, you Juno, quit dat. 'Deed I neber seed sech a crazy head as you has got.

CAESAR: Mammy do lef' dat gal 'lone, let her 'joy herself, fer I does like to see young people spirited.

JUNO: Of course you do Poppy. [*Hugs him with one arm around the neck*] And just to think, if Sam's elected you'll be poppy to a representative, and Mammy'll be mother to one, and I'll be sister to one. [*To* VIRGINIA] And what'll you be to him, Jinny?

VIRGINIA: Don't talk about that Juno; there can be nothing done until Jim is found. [*Turns to come down right from window*]

MAMMY: [*Listens.*] Shh! I thought I hyard sleigh bells!

[*All listen. Tableau. Sleigh bells outside.*]

SAM: [*Outside*] Whoa!

ALL: It's Sam! [*Rush to door. Enter* SAM, *all surround him, and advance to footlights followed by* PETE *and* POMP]

SAM: [*Throws off wraps,* JUNO *carries them off left, returns immediately.*] Yes, it is I, and I cannot tell you how happy I am to be at home once more.

PETE: Jes tell us one thing cap'n, 'fore you goes eny farther, is you 'lected?

VIRGINIA: Yes, Sam do relieve our anxiety.

SAM: I think you may safely congratulate me, on a successful election. My friends in Cincinati have stood by me nobly.

MAMMY: Praise de Lord! Chillern I hasn't nuthin' lef' to lib fer.

PETE: [*He and* POMP *shake hands with* SAM *in congratulation*] Ol' fellar Ise glad of it. Now I'll jes step out an' put up dat annimal, an' then return. [*Exits door*]

CAESAR: [*Goes up to* SAM] Lef' me look at you, I wants to see ef you's changed eny. [*Shakes his head solemnly*] No, you's all dar jes de same. [*To* MAMMY] Ol' 'ooman, I allers knowed dat boy neber growed dat high fer nuthin'.

[*Reenter* PETE. *Company seat themselves.*]

JUNO: If things don't stop happening I shall have to get someone to hold me. Virginia, imagine you and me at Washington leading the colored bong tongs. O my! [*Fans herself, laughter*]

SAM: [*To* VIRGINIA] Haven't you one word for me, Virginia?

VIRGINIA: Find Jim, and we will be happy.

SAM: Well, then sing for me. Surely you cannot refuse this request.

[*Solos, quartets, &c. "Virginia Rosebud."* MR. LUCAS [[SAM]] *introduces any of his songs that have not been sung elsewhere. At close loud knocking at door.*]

MAMMY: Wonder who dat is?

[*All rise.*]

SAM: [*Hurries to the door, opens it.* JIM *rushes past him into room*]

Whom do you wish to see sir? I think you have made a mistake.

CAESAR: [*aside*] 'Pears like I knows dat fellar.

JIM: [*Looks smilingly around*] Don't you know me? Well I don't reckon you do, bein's Ise changed so. There's my card. [*Gives immense card to* SAM.]

SAM: [*reads*] "Mr. James Peters, Esq., D.D., attorney at law, at the Massachusetts bar, and declined overseer of the Magnolia plantation."

[*All astonished,* VIRGINIA *shrinks behind* MAMMY.]

JIM: [*Bows profoundly*] Dat me. Declined overseer ob de 'Nolia plantation.

JUNO: Overseer Jim, as I live, turned monkey! [*Exits hurriedly left*]

SAM: If you have come here to create a disturbance, sir, I warn you to go out the way you came in, or I'll *throw* you out.

JUNO: [*Reenters on a run, left, with pistol; rushes at* JIM] Did you wink, did you dare to wink?

JIM: [*Frightened, stumbles over two or three chairs. Groans*] O Lord no! [*To company*] Don't let her shoot me, Ise oly called hyar to 'stantiate myself an' be frien's 'long wif you.

[JUNO *lays pistol aside, laughing.*]

SAM: Well sir, state your business, and be quick about it.

JIM: [*Goes toward* VIRGINIA *followed by* SAM] Virginie, you needn't be 'fraid on me, kase I isn't hyar to mislest you. Chile, I kno's dat warnt no weddin', de law wouldn't 'low it nohow. [*To all*] An' den you see, I has no free dislution ob mysel' at all, kase Ise got a truly wife, an' Ise got twins, a boy an' gal; one's nam'd Jinny an' de tother one Sam.

[*Laughter.*]

SAM: Mr. Peters I congratulate you, you have certainly made the most of your freedom.

JIM: [*Strutting up and down*] Fac'! An' you's all hyar. Mammy and

Caesar, an' the Virginie rose-bud, an' Juno, and Pete, and Pomp. [*Slaps* SAM *on arm*] An ol' Sam himself. [SAM *shrinks*] O, I know you feel big, but I can't forgit dem ol' times, an' what a chase I had after you, an' then jes missed of you.

MAMMY: Well tell us Jim, wha' ol' Marse done, when he foun' we was gone?

[*All gather around* JIM.]

JIM: Fus' place you see, I had to walk clean back home, kase dat pecoolar rascal thar, stole all my money. [*Laughter*] An' when I had done got back, Marse he nigh took all de skin off this po' ol' back o' mine; an' I declar, I wished I'd gone 'long wif you. Well arter that ol' Lincoln sent his sogers down dar, an' Marse he runned 'way an' seein' he didn't stop fo' his waluables, I propitiated 'em to my private uses. Then I started North, got as fer as Massatoosetts, found the eddicational devantages were wery perfectible, an' hyar I is, one ob de pillows ob de Massatoosetts bar.

SAM: Well Jim, I forgive you freely for all that's past, and here's my hand on it.

[JIM *shakes hands all around to* VIRGINIA.]

SAM: And now Virginia I await your answer, when shall our wedding take place?

MAMMY: Gals neber know nothin' 'bout sech things; an' seein's tomorror's Christmas, we'll celebrate it wif a weddin', whether Jinny's willin' or not. What d'yo say ol' man?

CAESAR: Dem's jes' my senimens ol' 'ooman, we'll hav' a weddin'.

[SAM *and* VIRGINIA *talk at one side.*]

JUNO: Somebody hold me, or I shall bust. I'm so full. [*To company*] Come on boys and girls, let's have an ol' Virginnie, it's the only safe exit for surplus steam.

CAESAR: [*Rising*] Dat's jes the thing, I feel mysel' growin' twenty-five years younger dis blessed minute, aint dat so ol' 'ooman?

MAMMY: Dat's jes so ol' man.

JUNO: But Lor', I forgot, we can't dance anything but high-toned dances, we must remember that there's the dignity of an M.C. to be upheld. But anyhow, you fellows move out the chairs and things, an' we'll have a quadrille.

[*Stage cleared. Lively music. Each one selects partner,* PETE *with* JUNO, JIM *with* POMP, SAM *as caller. Go through three or four figures lively,* JUNO, MAMMY, *and* CAESAR *begin to get happy. Suddenly* SAM *stops calling, rushes to footlights.*]

SAM: Ladies and gentlemen, I hope you will excuse me for laying aside the dignity of an elected M.C., and allow me to appear before you once more as peculiar Sam of the old underground railroad.

[*Plantation chorus,* SAM *dancing, remainder happy.* "*Golden Slippers.*" *Curtain.*]

Acknowledgments

The editor wishes to thank the library staffs at Saginaw Valley State University, Ball State University, the University of Illinois at Urbana-Champaign, and Fisk University for their kind assistance. Special thanks are due to the Special Collections Library at Fisk for encouraging the transcription and inclusion of Pauline Hopkins's play, *Peculiar Sam*. Several of my colleagues at Saginaw Valley State University (including Kenneth Jolly, Helen Raica-Klotz, Christopher Giroux, and Gina Mezzano) and beyond provided insightful commentary on the project's plans and execution, as did the staff at Toby Press, especially the press's publisher Matthew Miller, senior editor Deborah Meghnagi, and proofreaders Fern Allen and Allison Schiller. Pat Latty and Sharon Opheim helped with manucript preparation. My parents, both teachers, made me think deeply about what went on in any classroom—and the ways in which the world extended the classroom. My daughters, Abigail and Elisabeth, crawled and then walked over most of the Xerox copies of the plays, and my wife Jodie cheerfully helped me smooth the pages out.

About the Editor

Eric Gardner is an Associate Professor of English at Saginaw Valley State University, where he teaches courses in American literature and culture. A University of Illinois Ph.D., he first became interested in the drama of slavery while researching the career of African American elocutionist Mary Webb, for whom Harriet Beecher Stowe wrote *The Christian Slave*, included herein. Gardner's work on Webb led to articles in *Legacy* and *Nineteenth Century Prose* and to an essay on her husband Frank J. Webb in the *African American Review*.

The combination of literary analysis and historical research central to his work on the Webbs has led to diverse research on nineteenth-century African Americans, including pieces in the *American National Biography Online*, *African American Lives*, the *African American National Biography*, the *Encyclopedia of African American Literature*, and other reference sources. He recently discovered a chapbook-length fortune teller's manual and dream book, *The Complete Fortune Teller*, written c. 1824 about and perhaps by an African American woman from Boston named Chloe Russel; the text and his introduction appeared in the *New England Quarterly*—the same journal that published his first article, a study of the reception of Harriet Wilson's *Our Nig*.

He is currently at work on a book-length biography of Lucy Delaney, who wrote a narrative of her enslavement published in the early 1890s, *From the Darkness Cometh the Light*.